A PEOPLE AND A NATION

A PEOPLE AND A NATION

A History of the United States

Seventh Edition

Volume One: To 1877

Mary Beth Norton
Cornell University

David M. Katzman
University of Kansas

David W. Blight
Yale University

Howard P. Chudacoff
Brown University

Fredrik Logevall
University of California, Santa Barbara

Beth Bailey
University of New Mexico

Thomas G. Paterson
University of Connecticut

William M. Tuttle, Jr.
University of Kansas

Houghton Mifflin Company   Boston New York

Publisher: Charles Hartford
Editor-in-Chief: Jean Woy
Senior Sponsoring Editor: Sally Constable
Development Editor: Anne Hofstra Grogg
Editorial Assistant: Kisha Mitchell
Senior Project Editor: Bob Greiner
Editorial Assistant: Trinity Peacock-Broyles
Senior Production/Design Coordinator: Carol Merrigan
Senior Designer: Henry Rachlin
Senior Manufacturing Coordinator: Marie Barnes
Senior Marketing Manager: Sandra McGuire

Picture research by Pembroke Herbert and Sandi Rygiel, Picture Research Consultants & Archives.

Cover painting: *Mrs. Nancy Lawson* by William Matthew Prior, 1843. Courtesy of the Shelburne Museum, Shelburne, VT.

Printed in the U.S.A.

Library of Congress Catalog Number: 2003110158

ISBN: 0-618-39176-2

4 5 6 7 8 9-DOW-08 07 06 05

BRIEF CONTENTS

CONTENTS

SPECIAL FEATURES

Maps

Figures

Tables

Links to the World

Legacy for a People and a Nation

PREFACE

Some readers might think that a book entering its seventh edition would be little changed from the previous version. Nothing could be further from the truth. In this seventh edition, *A People and a Nation* has undergone major revisions, while still retaining the narrative strength and focus that characterized its earlier editions and made it so popular with students and teachers alike. In the years since the publication of the sixth edition, new documents have been uncovered, new interpretations advanced, and new themes (especially globalization) have come to the forefront of American historical scholarship. The authors—including two new members of our team—have worked diligently to incorporate those findings into this text.

Like other teachers and students, we are always re-creating our past, restructuring our memory, rediscovering the personalities and events that have influenced us, injured us, and bedeviled us. This book represents our continuing rediscovery of America's history—its diverse people and the nation they created and have nurtured. As this book demonstrates, there are many different Americans and many different memories. We have sought to present all of them, in both triumph and tragedy, in both division and unity.

About *A People and A Nation*

A People and a Nation, first published in 1982, was the first major textbook in the United States to fully integrate social and political history. Since the outset, the authors have been determined to tell the story of *all* the people of the United States. This book's hallmark has been its melding of social and political history, its movement beyond history's common focus on public figures and events to examine the daily life of America's people. All editions of the book have stressed the interaction of public policy and personal experience, the relationship between domestic concerns and foreign affairs, the various manifestations of popular culture, and the multiple origins of America and Americans. We have consistently built our narrative on a firm foundation in primary sources—on both well-known and obscure letters, diaries, public documents, oral histories, and artifacts of material culture. We have long challenged readers to think sabout the meaning of American history, not just to memorize facts. Both students and instructors have repeatedly told us how much they appreciate and enjoy our approach to the past.

As has been true since the first edition, each chapter opens with a dramatic vignette focusing on an individual or a group of people. These vignettes develop key questions, which then frame the chapters in succinct introductions and summaries. Numerous maps, tables, graphs, and charts provide readers with the necessary geographical and statistical context for observations in the text. Carefully selected illustrations—many of them unique to this book—offer readers visual insight into the topics under discussion, especially because the authors have written the captions. In this edition, as in all previous ones, we have sought to incorporate up-to-date scholarship, readability, a clear structure, critical thinking, and instructive illustrative material on every page.

What's New in This Edition

Planning for the seventh edition began at a two-day authors' meeting at the Houghton Mifflin headquarters in Boston. There we discussed the most recent scholarship in the field, the reviews of the sixth edition solicited from instructors, and the findings of our own continuing research. For this edition, we added two new colleagues, who experienced the intellectual exhilaration and rigor of such an authors' meeting for the first time. Beth Bailey, who has written acclaimed works on sexuality and popular culture in modern America, now writes the chapters and sections dealing with domestic matters after the 1920s. Fredrik Logevall, whose scholarship on the Vietnam War has won international recognition, now writes all the chapters and sections on foreign policy since the Civil War. These new authors have substantially reworked and reorganized the post-1945 chapters, in ways outlined below.

This seventh edition enhances the global perspective on American history that has characterized the book since its first edition. From the "Atlantic world" context of European colonies in North and South America to the discussion of international terrorism, the authors have incorporated the most recent globally oriented scholarship throughout the volume. We have worked to strengthen our treatment of the diversity of America's people by examining differences within the broad ethnic categories commonly employed and by paying greater attention to immigration, cultural and intellectual infusions from around the world, and America's growing religious diversity. At the same time, we have more fully integrated the discussion of such diversity into our narrative, so as not to artificially isolate any group from the mainstream. Treatments of environmental history and the history of technology have both been expanded. Finally, we have streamlined the useful chronologies that appear near the beginning of each chapter.

As always, the authors reexamined every sentence, interpretation, map, chart, illustration, and caption, refining the narrative, presenting new examples, and bringing to the text the latest findings of scholars in many areas of history, anthropology, sociology, and political science. More than a quarter of the chapter-opening vignettes are new, as is also true of the popular "Legacy" features introduced in the sixth edition.

To students who question the relevance of historical study, the legacies offer compelling and timely answers. Those brief essays, which follow the chapter summaries, explore the historical roots of contemporary topics. New subjects of legacies include the "self-made man" ideal, states' rights, reparations for slavery, Planned Parenthood, the Social Security system, the concern for human rights, and the Americans with Disabilities Act.

New "Links to the World"

In keeping with the emphasis on globalization in this edition, and building on the long-standing strength of this text in the history of American foreign relations, we have introduced a new feature in each chapter: "Links to the World." Examining both inward and outward ties between America (and Americans) and the rest of the world, the "Links" appear at appropriate places in each chapter to explore specific topics at considerable length. Tightly constructed essays detail the often little-known connections between developments here and abroad. The topics range broadly over economic, political, social, technological, medical, and cultural history, vividly demonstrating that the geographical region that is now the United States has never lived in isolation from other peoples and countries. Examples include the impact of American maize (corn) on the rest of the world, the introduction of coffee and tea into the American colonies, the discovery of gold in California, proposals to annex Cuba, baseball in Japan, Pan American Airways, the influenza pandemic of 1918, the 1936 Olympics, Barbie dolls, CNN, and the AIDS epidemic. Each "Link" highlights global interconnections with unusual and lively examples that will both intrigue and inform students.

Themes in This Book

Several themes and questions stand out in our continuing effort to integrate political, social, and cultural history. We study the many ways Americans have defined themselves—

gender, race, class, region, ethnicity, religion, sexual orientation—and the many subjects that have reflected their multidimensional experiences. We highlight the remarkably diverse everyday lives of the American people—in cities and on farms and ranches, in factories and in corporate headquarters, in neighborhoods and in legislatures, in love relationships and in hate groups, in recreation and in work, in the classroom and in military uniform, in secret national security conferences and in public foreign relations debates, in church and in voluntary associations, in polluted environments and in conservation areas. We pay particular attention to lifestyles, diet and dress, family life and structure, labor conditions, gender roles, migration and mobility, childbearing, and child rearing. We explore how Americans have entertained and informed themselves by discussing their music, sports, theater, print media, film, radio, television, graphic arts, and literature, in both "high" culture and popular culture. We study how technology has influenced Americans' lives, such as through the internal combustion engine and the computer.

Americans' personal lives have always interacted with the public realm of politics and government. To understand how Americans have sought to protect their different ways of life and to work out solutions to thorny problems, we emphasize their expectations of governments at the local, state, and federal levels; governments' role in providing answers; the lobbying of interest groups; the campaigns and outcomes of elections; and the hierarchy of power in any period. Because the United States has long been a major participant in world affairs, we explore America's participation in wars, interventions in other nations, empire-building, immigration patterns, images of foreign peoples, cross-national cultural ties, and international economic trends.

Section-by-Section Changes in This Edition

Mary Beth Norton, who had primary responsibility for Chapters 1 through 8 and served as coordinating author, expanded coverage of ancient North America (the Anasazi and Mississippians); Brazil, the Caribbean islands, and Nova Scotia; witchcraft, especially the 1692 Salem crisis; migration to the colonies from England, Ireland, and Germany; the trade in African and Indian slaves and the impact of that trade on African and Native American societies; the trans-Appalachian west in peace and war; and slavery and gradual emancipation after the Revolution. She also reorganized Chapter 3 to consolidate related materials on politics and the imperial context, and extensively revised and expanded Chapter 6 to reflect recent scholarship. There are new sections on the West during the revolutionary era and on the experiences of ordinary Americans in wartime, both in and out of the military.

David M. Katzman, with responsibility for Chapters 9 through 12, has continued (as in the sixth edition) to sharpen the chronological flow in these chapters. He has broadened the discussion of political culture and emerging partisanship in the young republic, reflecting the current rethinking of politics at that time. He has expanded coverage of religious life and the links between religion and social and political reform. The discussions of families, immigrant lives (especially the Irish), and African American identity, culture, and communities have all been completely revised. Throughout, there is greater attention paid to technology, global ties, and popular culture.

David W. Blight, who had primary responsibility for Chapters 13 through 16, enhanced the discussion of women and gender throughout these chapters. He also added material on the lives of freed people, before, during, and after the Civil War; the impact of the Fugitive Slave Law; the West in the Civil War and Reconstruction eras; and the home front during wartime. He revised the interpretation of the Denmark Vesey slave rebellion and increased coverage of the Underground Railroad, and of the role of the Mormons and westward expansion in the slavery crisis. In Chapter 15, he developed new sections on how the Civil War shaped the future of Indians in the far West, as well as the conflict's significance abroad, especially in England.

Howard P. Chudacoff, responsible for Chapters 17 through 21 and 24, has increased the coverage of technology throughout his chapters, adding discussions of farming technology, the machine tool industry, technological education in universities, birth control devices, and the automobile. He has included new material on the environment as well, expanding his discussion of such topics as water supply and sewage disposal, the unanticipated effects of national parks, and the conservation movement. Topics related to ethnicity—including anti-Chinese violence and exclusion laws, Mexican immigration, and holiday celebrations by ethnic groups—also receive increased attention. He has reconfigured portions of Chapters 18, 19, and 21 to clarify the narrative.

Fredrik Logevall, with primary responsibility for Chapters 22, 23, 26, and 28, worked to internationalize the treatment of America's foreign relations by giving greater attention to the perspectives of nations with which we interacted, and by examining the foreign policy aims of such leaders as Joseph Stalin, especially in Chapters 23 and 26. He significantly expanded the coverage of U.S. relations with the Middle East, showing the increasing importance of America's dealings with that region during the past four decades. He has also brought a sense of contingency to the narrative of American foreign relations, suggesting that matters might have turned out quite differently at various key junctures had policy-makers reached different decisions. He made major changes in Chapter 28 (formerly Chapter 29), creating greater thematic unity and incorporating much new scholarship on the Cold War and relations with China and the Soviet Union. Throughout, Logevall builds on the excellent foundation laid by Thomas G. Paterson, who wrote these and the post-1960 foreign-policy chapters in the previous six editions of this textbook, and who also served as the coordinating author for all six of those editions.

Beth Bailey, primarily responsible for Chapters 25, 27, and 29, integrated the experiences and actions of various groups into the main narrative while still focusing on the diversity of the American people in the modern era. In general, she enhanced coverage of the South and West (especially Latinos and Mexican immigrants in the Southwest) and added material on gender, sexuality, and popular culture. Throughout these chapters she placed Americans' fears about their nation's future in an international context. In Chapter 25, she strengthened the discussion of New Deal policies, showing how assumptions about race and gender structured these important social programs. Chapter 27 has a stronger chronological framework, as well as new treatments of culture and daily life during WWII, in combat and on the home front. Chapter 29 (formerly Chapter 28) has been extensively revised, assessing the myriad transformations of American society and culture in the 1950s, with particular attention to race, labor, masculinity, McCarthyism, and the impact of new federal policies. Bailey's work updates the domestic-policy chapters written superbly in the previous six editions by William M. Tuttle, Jr.

Post-1960 Chapters

Bailey and Logevall shared responsibility for the new Chapters 30 through 33. In these completely revamped chapters, domestic and foreign topics are discussed in tandem rather than separately, demonstrating the extensive linkages between them. The two authors collaborated closely to create a fresh and lively comprehensive, chronologically based narrative that places events in the United States in their appropriate international setting. The coverage of foreign relations includes increased attention to the Middle East and to the motivations of America's allies and opponents alike. The treatment of the Vietnam War now draws on Logevall's own scholarship, just as the discussion of recent popular culture and sexuality is based on Bailey's original research. Increased attention is given to the civil rights movement, the rise of second- and third-wave feminism, new patterns of immigration, and the growth of grassroots conservatism.

Teaching and Learning Aids

The supplements listed here accompany this Seventh Edition of *A People and a Nation*. They have been created with the diverse needs of today's students and instructors in mind, with extensive print and non-print resources available.

We are proud to announce the *History Companion*, your new primary source for history technology solutions. The *History Companion* has three components: the *Instructor Companion, the Student Study Companion,* and the *Student Research Companion*. Each of these components is described below: the *Instructor Companion* under instructor resources, and the *Student Research Companion* and *Student Study Companion* under student resources.

For the Instructor:
- *The Instructor Companion* is an easily searchable CD-ROM that makes hundreds of historical images and maps instantly accessible in PowerPoint format. Each image is accompanied by notes that place it in its proper historical context and tips for ways it can be presented in the classroom. With this edition of *A People and a Nation*, this CD also includes a wealth of additional resources, including testing, lecture, and course planning tools. A computerized test bank is included complete with search functions, which allows instructors to design tests thematically by entering keywords to bring up particular questions. An Instructor's Resource Guide is also included that can aid in encouraging classroom discussions or constructively enhance a class presentation. This CD is free to instructors with the adoption of this Houghton Mifflin textbook.

- A print **Test Bank,** prepared by George Warren of Central Piedmont Community College, also accompanies the text and contains many multiple choice, identification, geography, and essay questions for use in creating exams.

- In addition, a series of **PowerPoint** slides, created by Barney Rickman of Valdosta State University, are included to assist in instruction and discussion of key topics and material.

- The **Blackboard/WebCT Basic CD** provides instructors who want to offer all or part of their entire course online with much of the fundamental material for their course. From this base, instructors can customize the course to meet their needs.

- **The Houghton Mifflin U.S. History Transparency Set, Volumes I and II,** is a set of standard U.S. history transparencies, taken from illustrations and maps in the Houghton Mifflin survey texts. Includes 150 full-color maps.

- **BiblioBase for U.S. History** is a database of hundreds of primary source documents—including speeches, essays, travel accounts, government documents, and memoirs—covering U.S. history from the fifteenth century to the present. This comprehensive database enables you to create a customized course pack of primary sources to complement any U.S. history text. You can search for documents by period, region, approach, theme, and type and then view the documents in their entirety before choosing your course pack selections.

- The **Rand McNally Atlas of American History** is offered for packaging with the textbook. Please contact your sales representative for additional information.

For the Student:
The **Houghton Mifflin History Companion** for *A People and a Nation*, Seventh Edition, has two student components.

- The *Student Study Companion* is a free online study guide that contains ACE self-tests, flashcards, timelines, chronology exercises, graphic organizer exercises, map exercises, text feature exercises, web links, and Internet exercises. These study tools will help your students to be more successful.

- The *Student Research Companion* is a free Internet-based tool with 100 interactive maps and 500 primary sources. The primary sources include headnotes that provide pertinent background information, and both the maps and the primary sources include questions that students can answer and email to their instructors.

- **Study Guide Volumes I and II,** by George Warren, offers students learning objectives, vocabulary exercises, identification suggestions, skill-building activities, multiple choice questions, essay questions, and map exercises in two volumes.

- **American Ethnic Identities: Online Activities**
  By using examples throughout American history, these informative and lively activities will broaden

your understanding of the different ethnic groups that make up the United States.

Acknowledgments

The authors would like to thank the following persons for their assistance with the preparation of this edition: Shawn Alexander, David Anthony Tyeeme Clark, Mike Ezra, David Farber, Max Bailey/Farber, Steve Jacobson, Andrea Katzman, Eric Katzman, Julee Katzman, Theo Katzman, Ariela Katzman-Jacobson, Elieza Katzman-Jacobson, Iris Jane Katzman, Sharyn Brooks Katzman, Danyel Logevall, Chester Pach, Cheryl Ragar, Ann Schofield, Daniel Williams, and Norman Yetman.

At each stage of this revision, a sizable panel of historian reviewers read drafts of our chapters. Their suggestions, corrections, and pleas helped guide us through this momentous revision. We could not include all of their recommendations, but the book is better for our having heeded most of their advice. We heartily thank:

Marynita Anderson, *Nassau Community College*
Erica R. Armstrong, *University of Delaware*
Jim Barrett, *University of Illinois at Urbana-Champaign*
Virginia R. Boynton, *Western Illinois University*
Robert Cottrell, *California State University, Chico*
Bruce Dierenfield, *Canisius College*
Lisa Lindquist Dorr, *University of Alabama*
Latricia E. Gill-Brown, *Pensacola Junior College*
Melanie Gustafson, *University of Vermont*
Jorge Iber, *Texas Tech University*

Anthony E. Kaye, *Pennsylvania State University, University Park*
Carol A. Keller, *San Antonio College*
Kathleen Kennedy, *Western Washington University*
Anne Klejment, *University of St. Thomas*
Carolyn J. Lawes, *Old Dominion University*
Patrick K. Moore, *University of West Florida*
Jared Orsi, *Colorado State University*
Chester Pach, *Ohio University*
Marie Jenkins Schwartz, *University of Rhode Island*
Erik R. Seeman, *SUNY-Buffalo*
Sayuri G. Shimizu, *Michigan State University*
Manisha Sinha, *University of Massachusetts, Amherst*
Evelyn Sterne, *University of Rhode Island*
Benson Tong, *Wichita State University*
Michael M. Topp, *University of Texas, El Paso*

The authors once again thank the extraordinary Houghton Mifflin people who designed, edited, produced, and nourished this book. Their high standards and acute attention to both general structure and fine detail are cherished in the publishing industry. Many thanks, then, to Jean Woy, editor-in-chief; Sally Constable, sponsoring editor; Ann Hofstra Grogg, freelance development editor; Bob Greiner, senior project editor; Sandra McGuire, senior marketing manager; Henry Rachlin, senior designer; Carol Merrigan, senior production/design coordinator; Marie Barnes, senior manufacturing coordinator; Pembroke Herbert, photo researcher; Charlotte Miller, art editor; and Kisha Mitchell and Trinity Peacock-Broyles, editorial assistants.

THE AUTHORS

Mary Beth Norton

Born in Ann Arbor, Michigan, Mary Beth Norton received her B.A. from the University of Michigan (1964) and her Ph.D. from Harvard University (1969). She is the Mary Donlon Alger Professor of American History at Cornell University. Her dissertation won the Allan Nevins Prize. She has written *The British-Americans* (1972), *Liberty's Daughters* (1980, 1996), *Founding Mothers & Fathers* (1996), which was one of three finalists for the 1997 Pulitzer Prize in History, and *In the Devil's Snare* (2002), which was one of five finalists for the 2003 *LA Times* Book Prize in History and which won the English-Speaking Union's Ambassador Book Award in American Studies for 2003. She has coedited *Women of America* (with Carol Berkin, 1979), *To Toil The Livelong Day* (with Carol Groneman, 1987), and *Major Problems in American Women's History* (with Ruth Alexander, 2003). She was general editor of the *American Historical Association's Guide to Historical Literature* (1995). Her articles have appeared in such journals as the *American Historical Review, William and Mary Quarterly,* and *Journal of Women's History.* Mary Beth has served as president of the Berkshire Conference of Women Historians, as vice president for research of the American Historical Association, and as a presidential appointee to the National Council on the Humanities. She has received four honorary degrees and in 1999 was elected a fellow of the American Academy of Arts and Sciences. She has held fellowships from the National Endowment for the Humanities, the Guggenheim, Rockefeller, and Starr Foundations, and the Henry E. Huntington Library.

David M. Katzman

Born in New York City and a graduate of Queens College (B.A., 1963) and the University of Michigan (Ph.D., 1969), David M. Katzman is professor of American studies and courtesy professor of history and African American studies at the University of Kansas. He has written *Before the Ghetto* (1973) and *Seven Days a Week* (1978), which won the Philip Taft Labor History Prize. He has coedited *Plain Folk* (1982) and *Technical Knowledge in American Culture* (1996). He has also coauthored *Three Generations in Twentieth-Century America* (1982). David has been a visiting professor at University College, Dublin, Ireland, the University of Birmingham, England, Hong Kong University, and the University of Tokushima, Japan. He was recently a Fulbright lecturer at Kobe University, Japan. He has also directed National Endowment for the Humanities Summer Seminars for College Teachers. He has sat on the Board of Directors of the National Commission on Social Studies and is coeditor of *American Studies.* At the University of Kansas, he has directed the Honors Program and chaired the American Studies Program, and in 2002 he received the Ned Fleming Trust Award for Excellence in Teaching. The Guggenheim Foundation, National Endowment for the Humanities, Ford Foundation, and Rockefeller Foundation have supported his research.

David W. Blight

Born in Flint, Michigan, David W. Blight received his B.A. from Michigan State University (1971) and his Ph.D. from the University of Wisconsin (1985). He is now a professor of history at Yale University. For the first seven years of his career, David was a public high school teacher in Flint. He has written *Frederick Douglass's Civil War* (1989) and *Race and Reunion: The Civil War in American Memory, 1863–1915* (2000). His edited works include *When This Cruel War Is Over: The Civil War Letters of Charles Harvey Brewster* (1992), *Narrative of the Life of Frederick Douglass* (1993), W. E. B. Du Bois, *The Souls of Black Folk* (with Robert Gooding Williams, 1997), *Union and Emancipation* (with Brooks Simpson, 1997), and *Caleb Bingham, The Columbian Orator* (1997). David's essays have appeared in the *Journal of American History, Civil War History,* and Gabor Boritt, ed., *Why the Civil War Came* (1996), among others. In 1992-1993 he was senior Fulbright Professor in American Studies at the University of Munich, Germany. A consultant to several documentary films, David appeared in the 1998 PBS series, *Africans in America.* In 1999 he was elected to the Council of the American Historical Association. David also teaches summer seminars for secondary school teachers, as well as for park rangers and historians of the National Park Service. His book, *Race and Reunion: The Civil War in American Memory* (2000), received many honors in 2002, including The Bancroft Prize, Abraham Lincoln Prize, and the Frederick Douglass Prize. From the Organization of American Historians, he has received the Merle Curti Prize in Social History, the Merle Curti Prize in Intellectual History, the Ellis Hawley Prize in Political History, and the James Rawley Prize in Race Relations.

Howard P. Chudacoff

Howard P. Chudacoff, the George L. Littlefield Professor of American History at Brown University, was born in Omaha, Nebraska. He earned his A.B. (1965) and Ph.D. (1969) from the University of Chicago. He has written *Mobile Americans* (1972), *How Old Are You?* (1989), *The Age of the Bachelor* (1999), and *The Evolution of American Urban Society* (with Judith Smith, 2004). He has also coedited with Peter Baldwin *Major Problems in American Urban History* (2004). His articles have appeared in such journals as the *Journal of Family History*, *Reviews in American History*, and *Journal of American History*. At Brown University, Howard has cochaired the American Civilization Program, chaired the Department of History, and serves as Brown's faculty representative to the NCAA. He has also served on the board of directors of the Urban History Association. The National Endowment for the Humanities, Ford Foundation, and Rockefeller Foundation have given him awards to advance his scholarship.

Fredrik Logevall

A native of Stockholm, Sweden, Fredrik Logevall received his B.A. from Simon Fraser University (1986) and his Ph.D. from Yale University (1993). He is associate professor of history and codirector of the Center for Cold War Studies at the University of California at Santa Barbara. He is the author of *Choosing War: The Lost Chance for Peace and the Escalation of War in Vietnam* (1999), which won three prizes, including the Warren F. Kuehl Book Prize from the Society for Historians of American Foreign Relations (SHAFR). His other publications include *The Origins of the Vietnam War* (2001), *Terrorism and 9/11: A Reader* (2002), and, as coeditor, the *Encyclopedia of American Foreign Policy* (2002). In 2003 Fred was awarded the Stuart L. Bernath Lecture Prize from SHAFR, and he is a past recipient of the UCSB Academic Senate Distinguished Teaching Award. He is on the editorial advisory board of the Presidential Recordings Project at the Miller Center of Public Affairs at the University of Virginia, and of the journal *Diplomatic History*, and he is chair of the steering committee of the University of California's Institute for Global Conflict and Cooperation.

Beth Bailey

Born in Atlanta, Georgia, Beth Bailey received her B.A. from Northwestern University (1979) and her Ph.D. from the University of Chicago (1986). She is now a professor of American studies and Regents Lecturer at the University of New Mexico. Her research and teaching fields include American cultural history (nineteenth and twentieth centuries), popular culture, and gender and sexuality. She is the author of *From Front Porch to Back Seat: Courtship in 20th Century America* (1988), a historical analysis of conventions governing the courtship of heterosexual youth; *The First Strange Place: The Alchemy of Race and Sex in WWII Hawaii* (with David Farber, 1992), which analyzes cultural contact among Americans in wartime Hawaii; *Sex in the Heartland* (1999), a social and cultural history of the post-WWII "sexual revolution"; *The Columbia Companion to America in the 1960's* (with David Farber, 2001); and is co-editor of *A History of Our Time* (with William Chafe and Harvard Sitkoff, 6th ed., 2002). Beth has served as a consultant and/or on-screen expert for numerous television documentaries developed for PBS and the History Channel. She has received grants from the ACLS and NEH, was the Ann Whitney Olin scholar at Barnard College, Columbia University, from 1991 through 1994, where she was the director of the American Studies Program, and held a senior Fulbright lectureship in Indonesia in 1996. She teaches courses on sexuality and gender, war and American culture, research methods, and popular culture.

A PEOPLE AND A NATION

Prom Lupi

Portus Regalis, siue F.S. Helenæ

THREE OLD WORLDS CREATE A NEW 1492–1600

*a*s they neared the village called Cofitachequi on May 1, 1540, the band of Spanish explorers led by Hernán de Soto beheld a surprising scene. Villagers came to meet them, carrying their female chief, or *cacica,* "with much prestige on a litter covered in white (with thin linen)." The Lady of Cofitachequi, a Spanish chronicler recorded, was "young and of fine appearance." Speaking to Soto "with much grace and self-assurance," she welcomed the weary Spaniards to her domain in today's western South Carolina, giving de Soto a string of pearls from her neck. Her people offered gifts of "well tanned hides and blankets, all very good, and a large amount of jerked venison and dry wafers, and much and very good salt." Later, she gave the hungry men huge quantities of corn and, seeing that they especially valued pearls, suggested they take the ones they would find in nearby burial chambers.

The Spanish explorers had landed at Tampa Bay, Florida, about a year earlier. They would wander through what is now the southeastern United States for three more years, encountering many different peoples, whom they often treated with great cruelty. Always they futilely sought the greatest riches of all—gold and silver. The people of Cofitachequi told the Spaniards they might find these treasures in another ruler's domain, about twelve days' travel away. When de Soto left, he took the Lady with him as a captive. But the chronicler reported that she, "going one day with her slave women who were carrying her, stepped aside from the road and went into a wood saying that she had to attend to her necessities. Thus she deceived them and hid herself in the woods." Presumably, she then returned home.

Why had the Lady greeted de Soto's band so kindly? Perhaps she did not have enough men to resist the Spaniards. Her people had been devastated by an unknown "pestilence" two years earlier, the Spaniards learned, and they saw uninhabited settlements. Or possibly messengers had informed the Lady about de Soto's vicious treatment of villages he had previously encountered. Whatever her reasoning, the strategy worked: de Soto and his men moved on, and although they destroyed other villages and peoples, Cofitachequi survived to be recorded

◀ A 1591 print depicted what French adventurers saw in 1562 when they sailed into Port Royal River near today's Beaufort, South Carolina. From Theodor de Bry's *America,* the first book illustrating American scenes for a European audience. (John Carter Brown Library at Brown University)

CHRONOLOGY

12,000–10,000 B.C.E. • Paleo-Indians migrate from Asia to North America across the Beringia land bridge

7000 B.C.E. • Cultivation of food crops begins in America

c. 1000 B.C.E. • Olmec civilization appears

c. 300–600 C.E. • Height of influence of Teotihuacán

c. 600–900 C.E. • Classic Mayan civilization

1000 C.E. • Anasazi build settlements in modern states of Arizona and New Mexico

1001 • Norse establish settlement in "Vinland"

1050–1250 • Height of influence of Cahokia
• Prevalence of Mississippian culture in modern midwestern and southeastern United States

14th century • Aztec rise to power

1450s–80s • Portuguese explore and colonize islands in the Mediterranean Atlantic and São Tomé in Gulf of Guinea

1477 • Publication of Marco Polo's *Travels,* describing China

1492 • Columbus reaches Bahamas

1494 • Treaty of Tordesillas divides land claims between Spain and Portugal in Africa, India, and South America

1496 • Last Canary Island falls to Spain

1497 • Cabot reaches North America

1513 • Ponce de León explores Florida

1518–30 • Smallpox epidemic devastates Indian population of West Indies and Central and South America

1519 • Cortés invades Mexico

1521 • Tenochtitlán surrenders to Cortés; Aztec Empire falls to Spaniards

1524 • Verrazzano sails along Atlantic coast of United States

1534–35 • Cartier explores St. Lawrence River

1539–42 • De Soto explores southeastern United States

1540–42 • Coronado explores southwestern United States

1587–90 • Raleigh's Roanoke colony vanishes

1588 • Harriot publishes *A Briefe and True Report of the New Found Land of Virginia*

by Spanish, French, and finally English visitors in the course of the next 130 years.

For thousands of years before 1492, human societies in the Americas had developed in isolation from the rest of the world. The era that began in the Christian fifteenth century brought that long-standing isolation to an end. As Europeans sought treasure and trade, peoples from different cultures came into regular contact for the first time. All were profoundly changed. The brief encounter of de Soto and the Lady of Cofitachequi illustrates many elements of those contacts and changes: cruelty and kindness, greed and deception, trade and theft, surprise and sickness, captivity and enslavement. By the time de Soto and his men landed in Florida in 1539, the age of European expansion and colonization was already well under way. Over the next 350 years, Europeans would spread their influence across the globe. The history of the tiny colonies that would become the United States must be seen in this broad context of European exploration and exploitation.

The continents that European sailors reached in the late fifteenth century had their own histories, which the intruders largely ignored. The residents of the Americas were the world's most skillful plant breeders; they had developed vegetable crops more nutritious and productive than those grown in Europe, Asia, or Africa. They had invented systems of writing and mathematics and created calendars as accurate as those used on the other side of the Atlantic. In the Americas, as in Europe, states rose and fell as leaders succeeded or failed in expanding their political and economic power. But the arrival of Europeans immeasurably altered the Americans' struggles with one another.

After 1400, European nations not only warred on their own continent but also tried to acquire valuable colonies and trading posts elsewhere in the world. Initially interested primarily in Asia and Africa, Europeans eventually focused mostly on the Americas. Their contests for trade and conquest changed the course of history on four continents. Even as Europeans slowly achieved dominance, their fates were shaped by the strategies of Americans and Africans, such as that of the Lady of Cofitachequi. In the Americas of the fifteenth and sixteenth centuries, three old worlds came together to produce a new. ■

American Societies

uman beings originated on the continent of Africa, where humanlike remains about 3 million years old have been found in what is now Ethiopia. Over many millennia, the growing population slowly dispersed to the other continents. Because the climate was then far colder than it is now, much of the earth's water was concentrated in huge rivers of ice called glaciers. Sea levels were accordingly lower, and land masses covered a larger proportion of the earth's surface than they do today. Scholars have long believed that all the earliest inhabitants of the Americas crossed a land bridge known as Beringia (at the site of the Bering Strait) approximately 12,000 to 14,000 years ago. Yet striking new archaeological discoveries in both North and South America suggest that some parts of the Americas may have been settled much earlier, perhaps by seafarers crossing from northern Europe by island-hopping from Iceland to Greenland to Baffin Island, much as Norse explorers did many millennia later (see Map 1.1). When approximately 12,000 years ago the climate warmed and sea levels rose, Americans were separated from the peoples living on the connected continents of Asia, Africa, and Europe.

The first Americans are called Paleo-Indians. Nomadic hunters of game and gatherers of wild plants, they spread throughout North and South America, probably moving as bands composed of extended families. By about 11,500 years ago the Paleo-Indians were making fine stone projectile points, which they attached to wooden spears and used to kill and butcher bison (buffalo), woolly mammoths, and other large mammals then living in the Americas. But as the Ice Age ended and the human population increased, all the large American mammals except the bison disappeared. Scholars cannot agree whether overhunting or the change in climate caused their demise. In either case, deprived of their primary source of meat, the Paleo-Indians found new ways to survive.

ANCIENT AMERICA

By approximately 9,000 years ago, the residents of what is now central Mexico began to cultivate food crops, especially maize (corn), squash, beans, and peppers. In the Andes Mountains of South America, people started to grow potatoes. As knowledge of agricultural techniques improved and spread through the Americas, vegetables and maize proved a more reliable source of food than hunting and gathering. Except for those living in the harshest climates, most Americans started to adopt a more sedentary style of life so they could tend fields regularly. Some established permanent settlements; others moved several times a year among fixed sites. They became adept at clearing forests through the use of controlled burning. The fires not only created cultivable lands by killing trees and fertilizing the soil with ashes but also opened meadows that attracted deer and other wildlife. All the American cultures emphasized producing sufficient food to support themselves. Although they traded such items as shells, flint, salt, and copper, no society ever became dependent on another group for items vital to its survival.

Wherever agriculture dominated the economy, complex civilizations flourished. Such societies, assured of steady supplies of grains and vegetables, no longer had to devote all their energies to subsistence. Instead, they were able to accumulate wealth, produce ornamental objects, trade with other groups, and create elaborate rituals and ceremonies. In North America, the successful cultivation of nutritious crops such as maize, beans, and squash seems to have led to the growth and development of all the major civilizations: first the large city-states of Mesoamerica (modern Mexico and Guatemala), and then the urban clusters known collectively as the Mississippian culture and located in the present-day United States. Each of these societies, many historians and archaeologists now believe, reached its height of population and influence only after achieving success in agriculture. Each later declined and collapsed after reaching the limits of its food supply, with dire political and military consequences.

Archaeologists and historians still know little about the first major Mesoamerican civilization, that of the Olmecs, who about 3,000 years ago lived near the Gulf of Mexico in cities dominated by temple pyramids. Two societies that developed approximately 1,000 years later, those of the Mayas and of Teotihuacán, are better recorded. Teotihuacán, founded in the Valley of Mexico about 300 B.C.E. (Before the Common Era), eventually became one of the largest urban areas in the world, housing perhaps 100,000 people in the fifth century C.E. (Common Era). Teotihuacán's commercial network extended hundreds of miles in all directions; many peoples prized its obsidian (a green glass), used to make fine knives and mirrors. Pilgrims must also have traveled long distances to visit Teotihuacán's impressive pyramids and the great temple of Quetzalcoatl—the feathered serpent, primary god of central Mexico.

MESOAMERICAN CIVILIZATIONS

On the Yucatán Peninsula, in today's eastern Mexico, the Mayas built urban centers containing tall pyramids and temples. They studied astronomy and created the first writing system in the Americas. Their city-states, though, engaged in near-constant warfare with one another. Warfare and an inadequate food supply caused the collapse of the most powerful cities by 900 C.E., thus ending the classic era of Mayan civilization. By the time Spaniards arrived five hundred years later, only a few remnants of the once-mighty society remained.

Ancient native societies in what is now the United States learned to grow maize, squash, and beans from Mesoamericans, but the exact nature of the relationship of the various cultures is unknown. (No Mesoamerican artifacts have been found north of the Rio Grande, but some items resembling Mississippian objects have been excavated in northern Mexico.) The Hohokam, Mogollon, and Anasazi peoples of the modern states of Arizona and New Mexico subsisted by combining hunting and gathering with agriculture in an arid region of unpredictable rainfall. Hohokam villagers constructed extensive irrigation systems, but even so they occasionally had to relocate their settlements when water supplies failed. Between 900 and 1150 C.E. the Anasazi built fourteen "Great Houses" in Chaco Canyon, each a massive multistoried stone structure averaging two hundred rooms in size. The canyon, at the juncture of perhaps 400 miles of roads, served as a major regional trading and processing center for tur-

ANASAZI AND MISSISSIPPIANS

quoise, used then as now to create beautiful ornamental objects. Scholars have not determined why the Anasazi disappeared or where they went, but a major drought could well have forced them to move elsewhere.

At almost the same time, the unrelated Mississippian culture, which included the village of Cofitachequi, flourished in what is now the midwestern and southeastern United States. Relying largely on maize, squash, nuts, pumpkins, and venison for food, the Mississippians lived in substantial settlements. The largest of their urban centers was the City of the Sun (now called Cahokia), near modern St. Louis. Located on rich farmland close to the confluence of the Illinois, Missouri, and Mississippi Rivers, Cahokia, like Teotihuacán and Chaco Canyon, served as a focal point for both religion and trade. At its peak (in the eleventh and twelfth centuries C.E.), the City of the Sun covered more than 5 square miles and had a population of about twenty thousand—small by Mesoamerican standards but larger than any other northern community, and larger even than London in the same era.

Although the Cahokians never seem to have invented a writing system, these sun-worshippers developed an accurate calendar, evidenced by their creation of a woodhenge—a large circle of tall timber posts aligned with the solstices and the equinox. The city's main pyramid (one of 120 of varying sizes), today called Monks Mound, was at the time of its construction the third largest structure of any description in the Western Hemi-

■ Pueblo Bonito in Chaco Canyon in what is now the state of New Mexico. More than six hundred buildings were present on the well-defended site. The circular structures were kivas, used for food storage and for religious rituals.   (David Muench photography)

sphere; it remains the largest earthwork ever built anywhere in the Americas. It sat at the northern end of the Grand Plaza, surrounded by seventeen other mounds, some used for burials. Yet after 1250 C.E. the city was abandoned. Archaeologists believe that climate change and the degradation of the environment, caused by overpopulation and the destruction of nearby forests, brought about the city's collapse.

The Aztecs' histories tell of the long migration of their people (who called themselves Mexica) into the Valley of Mexico during the twelfth

AZTECS

century. The uninhabited ruins of Teotihuacán, which by then had been deserted for at least two hundred years, awed and mystified the migrants. Their chronicles record that their primary deity Huitzilopochtli—a war god represented by an eagle—directed them to establish their capital on an island where they saw an eagle eating a serpent, the symbol of Quetzalcoatl. That island city became Tenochtitlán, the center of a rigidly stratified society composed of hereditary classes of warriors, merchants, priests, common folk, and slaves.

The Aztecs conquered their neighbors, forcing them to pay tribute in textiles, gold, foodstuffs, and human beings who could be sacrificed to Huitzilopochtli. They also engaged in ritual combat, known as flowery wars, to obtain further sacrificial victims. The war god's taste for blood was not easily quenched. In the Aztec year Ten Rabbit (1502) at the coronation of Motecuhzoma II (the Spaniards could not pronounce his name correctly, so they called him Montezuma), five thousand people are thought to have been sacrificed by having their still-beating hearts torn from their bodies.

The Aztecs believed that they lived in the age of the Fifth Sun. Four times previously, they wrote, the earth and all the people who lived on it had been destroyed. They predicted that their own world would end in earthquakes and hunger. In the Aztec year Thirteen Flint, volcanoes erupted, sickness and hunger spread, wild beasts attacked children, and an eclipse of the sun darkened the sky. Did some priest wonder whether the Fifth Sun was approaching its end? In time, the Aztecs learned that Thirteen Flint was called, by Europeans, 1492.

North America in 1492

*O*ver the centuries, the Americans who lived north of Mexico adapted their once-similar ways of life to very different climates and terrains, thus creating the diverse cultures that the Europeans encountered when they first arrived (see Map 1.1). Scholars often refer to such cultures by language group (such as Algonquian or Iroquoian), since neighboring Indian nations commonly spoke related languages. Bands that lived in environments not well suited to agriculture—because of inadequate rainfall or poor soil, for example—followed a nomadic lifestyle similar to that of the Paleo-Indians. Within the area of the present-day United States, these groups included the Paiutes and Shoshones, who inhabited the Great Basin (now Nevada and Utah). Because of the difficulty of finding sufficient food for more than a few people, such hunter-gatherer bands were small, usually composed of one or more related families. The men hunted small animals, and women gathered seeds and berries. Where large game was more plentiful and food supplies therefore more certain, as in present-day central and western Canada and the Great Plains, bands of hunters were somewhat larger.

In more favorable environments, larger groups combined agriculture with gathering, hunting, and fishing. Those who lived near the seacoasts, like the Chinooks of present-day Washington and Oregon, consumed fish and shellfish in addition to growing crops and gathering seeds and berries. Residents of the interior (for example, the Arikaras of the Missouri River valley) hunted large animals while also cultivating maize, squash, and beans. The peoples of what is now eastern Canada and the northeastern United States also combined hunting and agriculture. They regularly used controlled fires both to open land for cultivation and to assist in hunting.

Societies that relied primarily on hunting large animals like deer and buffalo assigned that task to men,

SEXUAL DIVISION OF LABOR IN NORTH AMERICA

allotting food preparation and clothing production to women. Before such nomadic bands acquired horses from the Spaniards, women—occasionally assisted by dogs—also carried the family's belongings whenever the band relocated. Such a sexual division of labor was universal among hunting peoples, regardless of their location. Agricultural societies, by contrast, differed in their assignments of work to the sexes. The Pueblo peoples (descendants of the Anasazi), who lived in sixty or seventy autonomous villages and spoke five different languages, defined agricultural labor as men's work. In the east, large clusters of peoples speaking Algonquian, Iroquoian, and Muskogean languages allocated most agricultural chores to women, although men cleared the land. In all the farming societies, women gathered wild foods and prepared food for consumption or storage, while men were responsible for hunting.

Everywhere in North America, women cared for young children, while older youths learned adult skills

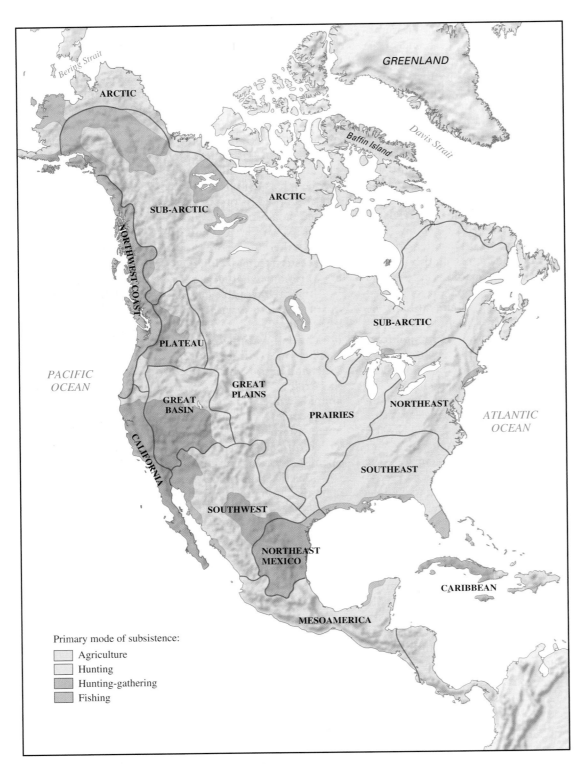

Map 1.1   **Native Cultures of North America**

The natives of the North American continent effectively used the resources of the regions in which they lived. As this map shows, coastal groups relied on fishing, residents of fertile areas engaged in agriculture, and other peoples employed hunting (often combined with gathering) as a primary mode of subsistence.

from the parent of the same sex. Young people usually chose their own marital partners, and in most societies couples could easily divorce if they no longer wished to live together. In contrast to the earlier Mississippian cultures, populations in these societies remained at a level sustainable by existing food supplies, largely because of low birth rates. Infants and toddlers were nursed until the age of two or even longer, and taboos prevented couples from having sexual intercourse during that period.

The southwestern and eastern agricultural peoples had similar social organizations. They lived in villages,

SOCIAL ORGANIZATION

sometimes with a thousand or more inhabitants. The Pueblos resided in multistory buildings constructed on terraces along the sides of cliffs or other easily defended sites. Northern Iroquois villages (in modern New York State) were composed of large, rectangular, bark-covered structures, or long houses; the name Haudenosaunee, which the Iroquois called themselves, means "People of the Long House." In the present-day southeastern United States, Muskogeans and southern Algonquians lived in large houses made of thatch. Most of the eastern villages were surrounded by wood palisades and ditches to aid in fending off attackers.

In all the agricultural societies, each dwelling housed an extended family defined matrilineally (through a female line of descent). Mothers, their married daughters, and their daughters' husbands and children all lived together. Matrilineal descent did not imply matriarchy, or the wielding of power by women, but rather served as a means of reckoning kinship. Extended families were linked into clans defined by matrilineal ties. The nomadic bands of the Great Plains, by contrast, were most often related patrilineally (through the male line). They lacked settled villages and defended themselves from attack primarily through their ability to move to safer locations when necessary.

The defensive design of eastern and western villages discloses the significance of warfare in pre-Columbian

WAR AND POLITICS

America. Long before Europeans arrived, residents of the continent fought one another for control of the best hunting and fishing territories, the most fertile agricultural lands, or the sources of essential items like salt (for preserving meat) and flint (for making knives and arrowheads). Bands of Americans protected by wooden armor battled while standing in ranks facing each other, the better to employ their clubs and throwing spears, which were effective only at close quarters. They began to shoot arrows from behind trees only when they confronted the more accurate and longer-range European guns, which also rendered their armor useless. People captured by the enemy in such wars were sometimes enslaved and dishonored by losing their previous names and identities, but slavery was never an important source of labor in pre-Columbian America.

American political structures varied considerably. Among Pueblo and Muskogean peoples, the village council, composed of ten to thirty men, was the highest political authority; no government structure connected the villages. Nomadic hunters also lacked formal links among separate bands. The Iroquois, by contrast, had an elaborate political hierarchy incorporating villages into nations and nations into a confederation; a council comprising representatives from each nation made crucial decisions of war and peace for the entire confederacy. In all the North American cultures, political power was divided between civil and war leaders, who wielded authority only so long as they retained the confidence of the people. Autocratic rule of the sort common in Europe (see page 13) was unusual in these political systems. Women more often assumed leadership roles among agricultural peoples, especially those in which females were the primary cultivators, than among nomadic hunters. Female sachems (rulers) led Algonquian villages in what is now Massachusetts, but women never became heads of Great Plains hunting bands. Iroquois women did not become chiefs, yet clan matrons exercised political power. The older women of each village chose its chief and could both start wars (by calling for the capture of prisoners to replace dead relatives) and stop them (by refusing to supply warriors with necessary foodstuffs).

Americans' religious beliefs varied even more than did their political systems, but all the peoples were poly-

RELIGION

theistic, worshiping a multitude of gods. Each group's most important beliefs and rituals were closely tied to its means of subsistence. The major deities of agricultural peoples like the Pueblos and Muskogeans were associated with cultivation, and their chief festivals centered on planting and harvest. The most important gods of hunters, such as those living on the Great Plains, were associated with animals, and their major festivals were related to hunting. A band's economy and women's role in it helped to determine women's potential as religious leaders. Women held the most prominent positions in those agricultural societies in which they were also the chief food producers, whereas in hunting societies men took the lead in religious as well as political affairs.

A wide variety of cultures, comprising more than 5 million people, thus inhabited mainland North America when Europeans arrived. The hierarchical kingdoms of

■ Jacques Le Moyne, an artist accompanying the French settlement in Florida in the 1560s (see page 35), produced some of the first European images of North American peoples. His depiction of native agricultural practices shows the sexual division of labor: men breaking up the ground with fish-bone hoes before women drop seeds into the holes. But Le Moyne's version of the scene cannot be accepted uncritically: unable to abandon a European view of proper farming methods, he erroneously drew plowed furrows in the soil. (John Carter Brown Library at Brown University)

Mesoamerica bore little resemblance to the nomadic hunting societies of the Great Plains or to the agricultural societies that dominated a significant share of the continent. The diverse inhabitants of North America spoke well over one thousand different languages. For obvious reasons, they did not consider themselves one people, nor did they—for the most part—think of uniting to repel the European invaders.

African Societies

Fifteenth-century Africa, like fifteenth-century America, housed a variety of cultures adapted to different terrains and climates (see Map 1.2). Many of these cultures were of great antiquity. In the north, along the Mediterranean Sea, lived the Berbers,

who were Muslims, or followers of the Islamic religion founded by the prophet Mohammed in the seventh century C.E. On the east coast of Africa, Muslim city-states engaged in extensive trade with India, the Moluccas (part of modern Indonesia), and China. In these ports, sustained contact and intermarriage among Arabs and Africans created the Swahili language and culture. Through the East African city-states passed waterborne commerce between the eastern Mediterranean and East Asia; the rest followed the long land route across Central Asia known as the Silk Road.

South of the Mediterranean coast in the African interior lie the great Saharan and Libyan Deserts, vast expanses of nearly waterless terrain crisscrossed by trade routes passing through oases. The introduction of the camel in the fifth century C.E. made long-distance travel possible, and as Islam expanded after the ninth century,

Map 1.2   Africa and Its Peoples, c. 1400

On the African continent resided many different peoples in a variety of ecological settings and political units. Even before Europeans began to explore Africa's coastlines, its northern regions were linked to the Mediterranean (and thus to Europe) by a network of trade routes.

commerce controlled by Muslim merchants helped to spread similar religious and cultural ideas throughout the region. Below the deserts, much of the continent is divided between tropical rain forests (along the coasts) and grassy plains (in the interior). People speaking a variety of languages and pursuing different subsistence strategies lived in a wide belt south of the deserts. South of the Gulf of Guinea, the grassy landscape came to be dominated by Bantu-speaking peoples, who left their homeland in modern Nigeria about two thousand years ago and slowly migrated south and east across the continent.

West Africa was a land of tropical forests and savanna grasslands where fishing, cattle herding, and agriculture had supported the inhabitants for at least ten thousand years before Europeans set foot there in the fifteenth century. The northern region of West Africa, or Upper Guinea, was heavily influenced by the Islamic culture of the Mediterranean. As early as the eleventh century C.E., many of the region's

WEST AFRICA (GUINEA)

inhabitants had become Muslims. Trade via camel caravans between Upper Guinea and the Muslim Mediterranean was sub-Saharan Africa's major connection to Europe and West Asia. In return for salt, dates, silk, and cotton cloth, Africans exchanged ivory, gold, and slaves with northern merchants.

Upper Guinea runs northeast-southwest from Cape Verde to Cape Palmas. The people of its northernmost region, the so-called Rice Coast (present-day Gambia, Senegal, and Guinea), fished and cultivated rice in coastal swamplands. The Grain Coast, the next region to the south, was thinly populated and not readily accessible from the sea because it had only one good harbor (modern Freetown, Sierra Leone). Its people concentrated on farming and raising livestock.

In the fifteenth century, most Africans in Lower Guinea were farmers who practiced traditional religions, not the precepts of Islam. Believing that spirits inhabited particular places, they invested those places with special significance. As did the agricultural peoples of the Americas, they developed rituals intended to ensure good harvests. Throughout the region, individual villages composed of kin groups were linked into hierarchical kingdoms. At the time of initial European contact, decentralized political and social authority characterized the region's polities.

The societies of West Africa, like those of the Americas, assigned different tasks to men and women. In general, the sexes shared agricultural duties. Men also hunted, managed livestock, and did most of the fishing. Women were responsible for childcare, food preparation, and cloth manufacture. Everywhere in West Africa women were the primary local traders. They managed the extensive local and regional networks through which goods were exchanged among the various families, villages, and small kingdoms.

COMPLEMENTARY GENDER ROLES

Despite their different economies and the rivalries among states, the peoples of Lower Guinea had similar social systems organized on the basis of what anthropologists have called the dual-sex principle. In Lower Guinea, each sex handled its own affairs: just as male political and religious leaders governed men, so females ruled women. In the Dahomean kingdom, for example, every male official had his female counterpart; in the thirty little Akan states on the Gold Coast, chiefs inherited their status through the female line, and each male chief had a female assistant who supervised other women. Many West African societies practiced polygyny (one man having several wives, each of whom lived separately with her children). Thus few adults lived permanently in marital households, but the dual-sex system

■ This decorative brass weight, created by the Asante peoples of Lower Guinea, was used for measuring gold dust. It depicts a family pounding fu-fu, a food made by mashing together plantains (a kind of banana), yams, and cassava. The paste was then shaped into balls to be eaten with soup. This weight, probably used in trading with Europeans, shows a scene combining foods of African origin (plantains and yams) with an import from the Americas (cassava), thus bringing the three continents together in ways both symbolic and real.
(Trustees of the British Museum. Photo by Michael Holford)

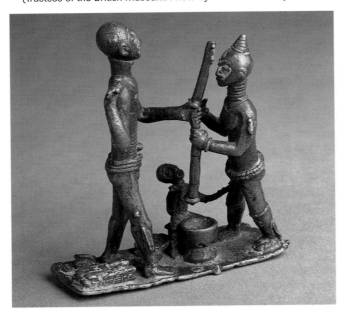

ensured that their actions were subject to scrutiny by members of their own sex.

Throughout Upper Guinea religious beliefs stressed complementary male and female roles. Both women and men served as heads of the cults and secret societies that directed the spiritual life of the villages. Young women were initiated into the Sandé cult, young men into Poro. Neither cult was allowed to reveal its secrets to the opposite sex. Although West African women (unlike some of their Native American contemporaries) rarely held formal power over men, female religious leaders did govern other members of their sex within the Sandé cult, enforcing conformity to accepted norms of behavior and overseeing their spiritual well-being.

West African law recognized both individual and communal land ownership, but men seeking to accumu-

SLAVERY IN GUINEA

late wealth needed access to labor—wives, children, or slaves—who could work the land. West Africans held in slavery on their own continent therefore composed essential elements of the economy. Africans could be enslaved for life as punishment for crimes, but more often such slaves were enemy captives or people who voluntarily enslaved themselves or their children in payment for debts. An African who possessed bondspeople had a right to the products of their labor, although the degree to which slaves were exploited varied greatly. Some slaves were held as chattel; others could engage in trade, retaining a portion of their profits; and still others achieved prominent political or military positions. All, however, found it difficult to overcome the social stigma of enslavement, and they could be traded or sold at the will of their owners.

West Africans, then, were agricultural peoples, skilled at tending livestock, hunting, fishing, and manufacturing cloth from plant fibers and animal skins. Both men and women were accustomed to working communally, alongside other members of their own sex or in family groups. They were also accustomed to a relatively egalitarian relationship between the sexes, especially within the context of religion. In the Americas, they entered societies that used their labor but had little respect for their cultural traditions.

European Societies

In the fifteenth century, Europeans, too, were agricultural peoples. The daily lives of Europe's rural people had changed little for several hundred years. Split into numerous small, warring countries, Europe was divided linguistically, politically, and economi-

cally, yet in social terms Europeans' lives were more similar than different. European societies were hierarchical: a few families wielded autocratic power over the majority of the people. English society in particular was organized as a series of interlocking hierarchies; that is, each person (except those at the very top or bottom) was superior to some, inferior to others. At the base of such hierarchies were people held in a variety of forms of bondage. Although Europeans were not subjected to perpetual slavery, Christian doctrine permitted the enslavement of "heathens" (non-Christians), and some Europeans' freedom was restricted by such conditions as serfdom, which tied them to the land if not to specific owners. In short, Europe's kingdoms resembled those of Africa or Mesoamerica but differed greatly from the more egalitarian societies found in America north of Mexico (see Map 1.3).

Most Europeans, like most Africans and Americans, lived in small villages. Only a few cities dotted the land-

SEXUAL DIVISION OF LABOR IN EUROPE

scape, most of them political capitals. European farmers, who were called peasants, owned or leased separate landholdings, but they worked the fields communally. Because fields had to lie fallow (unplanted) every second or third year to regain fertility, a family could not ensure itself a regular food supply unless the work and the crops were shared annually by all the villagers. Men did most of the fieldwork; women helped out chiefly at planting and harvest. In some areas men concentrated on herding livestock. Women's duties consisted primarily of childcare and household tasks, including preserving food, milking cows, and caring for poultry. If a woman's husband was a city artisan or storekeeper, she might assist him in business. Since Europeans kept domesticated animals (pigs, goats, sheep, and cattle) for meat, hunting had little economic importance in their cultures. Instead, hunting was primarily a sport for male aristocrats.

Unlike in African and American societies, in which women often played prominent roles in politics and religion, men dominated all areas of life in Europe. A few women—notably Queen Elizabeth I of England—achieved status or power by right of birth, but the vast majority were excluded from positions of political authority. Husbands and fathers likewise expected to control their families. European women generally held inferior social, economic, and political positions, yet within their own families they wielded power over children and servants.

Christianity was the dominant religion in Europe. In the West, authority rested in the Catholic Church, based in Rome and led by the pope, who directed a wholly

Map 1.3   Europe in 1490

The Europeans who ventured out into the Atlantic came from countries on the north-western edge of the continent, which was divided into numerous competing nations.

CHRISTIANITY — male clergy. The Catholic Church had an uneasy relationship with both secular rulers and the populace at large. Although European peoples were nominally Catholic, many adhered to local belief systems the church deemed heretical and proved unable to extinguish. Kings would ally themselves with the church when it suited their needs, but often acted independently. Yet even so the Christian nations of Europe from the twelfth century on publicly united in a goal of driving nonbelievers (especially Muslims) not only from their own do-

mains but also from the holy city of Jerusalem, which caused the series of wars known as the Crusades.

When the fifteenth century began, European nations were slowly recovering from the devastating epidemic of

EFFECTS OF PLAGUE AND WARFARE — plague known as the Black Death, which first struck them in 1346. The Black Death seems to have arrived in Europe from China, traveling with long-distance traders along the Silk Road to the eastern Mediterranean. The disease then recurred with particular severity in the 1360s and 1370s.

■ Daily life in early 16th-century Portugal, as illustrated in a manuscript prayer book. At top a prosperous family shares a meal being served by an African slave. Other scenes show male laborers clearing land and hunting birds (left) and chopping wood (right), while at bottom a woman plants seeds in a prepared bed and in the top background female servants work in the kitchen.   (Museu Nacional de Arte Antiga, Lisbon, Portugal)

Although no precise figures are available and the impact of the Black Death varied from region to region, the best estimate is that fully one-third of Europe's people died during those terrible years. A precipitous economic decline followed—in some regions more than half of the workers had died—as did severe social, political, and religious disruption because of the deaths of clergymen and other leading figures.

As plague ravaged the population, England and France waged the Hundred Years' War (1337–1453), initiated because the English monarchy claimed the French throne. The war interrupted overland trade routes through France connecting England and the Netherlands to the Italian city-states and thence to Central Asia. Merchants in the eastern Mediterranean found a new way of reaching their northern markets by forging a regular maritime link with the Netherlands that replaced the overland route. The use of a triangular, or lateen, sail (rather than the then-standard square rigging) improved the maneuverability of ships, enabling them to sail out of the Mediterranean and north around the European coast. Also of key importance was the perfection of navigational instruments like the astrolabe and the quadrant, which allowed oceangoing sailors to estimate their position (latitude) by measuring the relationship of the sun, moon, or certain stars to the horizon.

In the aftermath of the Hundred Years' War, European monarchs forcefully consolidated their previously diffuse political power and raised new revenues through increased taxation of an already hard-pressed peasantry. The long military struggle led to new pride in national identity, which eclipsed the prevailing regional and dynastic loyalties, and to heightened hostility to foreigners. In England, Henry VII in 1485 founded the Tudor dynasty and began uniting a previously divided land. In France, the successors of Charles VII unified the kingdom and levied new taxes. Most successful of all were Ferdinand of Aragón and Isabella of Castile, who married in 1469, founding a strongly Catholic Spain. In 1492 they defeated the Muslims, who had lived in Spain and Portugal for centuries, thereafter expelling all Jews and Muslims from their domain.

POLITICAL AND TECHNOLOGICAL CHANGE

The fifteenth century also brought technological change to Europe. Movable type and the printing press, invented in Germany in the 1450s, made information more accessible than ever before. Printing stimulated the Europeans' curiosity about fabled lands across the seas, lands they could now read about in books. The most important such work was Marco Polo's *Travels,* first published in 1477, which recounted a Venetian merchant's adventures in thirteenth-century China and, most intriguing, described that nation as bordered on the east by an ocean. Polo's account circulated widely among Europe's educated elites, first in manuscript and later in print. The book led many Europeans to believe that they could trade directly with China in oceangoing vessels instead of relying on the Silk Road or the route through East Africa. A transoceanic route, if it existed, would allow northern Europeans to circumvent the Muslim and Mediterranean merchants who hitherto had controlled their access to Asian goods.

Technological advances and the growing strength of newly powerful national rulers made possible the European explorations of the fifteenth and sixteenth centuries.

MOTIVES FOR EXPLORATION Each country craved easy access to African and Asian goods—spices like pepper, cloves, cinnamon, and nutmeg (to season the bland European diet), silk, dyes, perfumes, jewels, sugar, and gold. Avoiding Muslim and Venetian middlemen and acquiring such valuable products directly would improve a nation's income and its standing relative to other countries, in addition to supplying its wealthy leaders with coveted luxury items.

A concern for spreading Christianity around the world supplemented the economic motive. The linking of materialist and spiritual goals perhaps seems contradictory today, but fifteenth-century Europeans saw no necessary conflict between the two. Explorers and colonizers—especially Roman Catholics—honestly sought to convert "heathen" peoples to Christianity. At the same time they hoped to increase their nation's wealth by establishing direct trade with Africa, China, India, and the Moluccas (also known as the Spice Islands).

Early European Explorations

Before European mariners could discover new lands, they had to explore the oceans. To reach Asia, seafarers needed not just the maneuverable vessels and navigational aids increasingly used in the fourteenth century but also knowledge of the sea, its currents, and especially its winds. Wind would power their ships. But how did the winds run? Where would Atlantic breezes carry their square-rigged ships, which, even with the addition of a triangular sail, needed to run before the wind (that is, to have the wind directly behind the vessel)?

Europeans learned the answers to these questions in the region that has been called the Mediterranean Atlantic, the expanse of the Atlantic Ocean that is south and west of Spain and is bounded by the island groups of the Azores (on the west) and the Canaries (on the south), with the Madeiras in their midst (see Map 1.4). Europeans reached all three sets of islands during the fourteenth century—first the Canaries in the 1330s, then the Madeiras and the Azores. The Canaries proved a popular destination for mariners from Iberia, the peninsula that includes Spain and Portugal. Sailing to the Canaries from Europe was easy because strong winds known as the Northeast Trades blow southward along the Iberian and African coastlines. The voyage took about a week, and the volcanic peaks on the islands

SAILING IN THE MEDITERRANEAN ATLANTIC

made them difficult to miss even with navigational instruments that were less than precise.

The problem was getting back. The Iberian sailor attempting to return home faced a major obstacle: the very winds that had brought him so quickly to the Canaries now blew directly at him. Early travelers to the islands sometimes used galleys powered by oarsmen as well as by sails, but even oarsmen had a difficult time fighting the contrary winds and currents. Another alternative was similarly tedious: tacking back and forth to the east and west, attempting each time to make more headway north. The problem seemed intractable, and in earlier eras European sailors had been unable to solve it. When confronted with contrary winds, they simply waited for the wind to change. But for the most part, the Northeast Trades did not change. They blew steadily, shifting slightly with the seasons but never reversing course.

What could be done? Some unknown seafarer figured out the answer: sailing "around the wind." If a mariner could not sail against the trade winds, he had to sail as close as possible to the direction from which the wind was coming without being forced to tack. In the Mediterranean Atlantic, that meant pointing his vessel northwest into the open ocean, away from land, until— weeks later—he reached the winds that would carry him home, the so-called Westerlies. Those winds blow (we now know, though the mariners at first did not) northward along the coast of North America before heading east toward Europe.

This solution must at first have seemed to defy common sense, but it became the key to successful exploration of both the Atlantic and the Pacific Oceans. Once a sailor understood the winds and their allied currents, he no longer feared leaving Europe without being able to return. Faced with a contrary wind, all he had to do was sail around it until he found a wind to carry him in the proper direction. This strategy might seem to take him hundreds of miles out of the way, but in the long run it was safer and surer than attempting the monumental task of tacking against the wind.

During the fifteenth century, armed with knowledge of the winds and currents of the Mediterranean Atlantic, Iberian seamen regularly visited the three island groups, all of which they could reach in two weeks or less. The uninhabited Azores were soon settled by Portuguese migrants who raised wheat for sale in Europe and sold livestock to passing sailors. The Madeiras also had no native peoples, and by the 1450s Portuguese colonists were em-

ISLANDS OF THE MEDITERRANEAN ATLANTIC

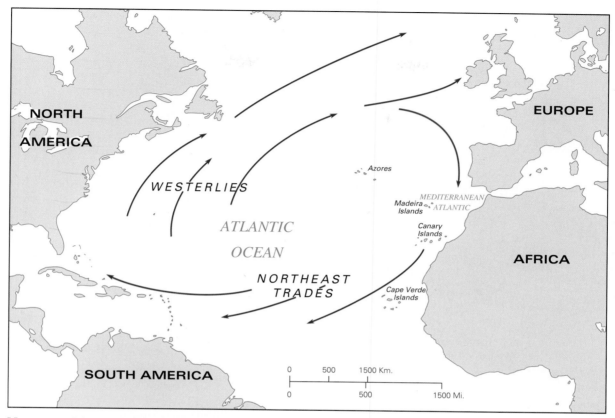

Map 1.4   Atlantic Winds and Islands

European mariners had to explore the oceans before they could find new lands.
The first realm they discovered was that of Atlantic winds and islands.

ploying slaves (probably Jews and Muslims brought from Iberia) to grow large quantities of sugar for export to the mainland. By the 1470s, Madeira had developed into a colonial plantation economy. For the first time in world history, a region had been settled explicitly to cultivate a valuable crop—sugar—to be sold elsewhere. Moreover, because the work involved in large-scale plantation agriculture was so backbreaking, only a supply of enslaved laborers (who could not opt to quit) could ensure the system's continued success.

The Canaries did have indigenous residents—the Guanche people, who began trading animal skins and dyes with their European visitors. In 1402 the French attacked one of the islands; thereafter, Portuguese and Spanish expeditions continued the sporadic assaults. The Guanches resisted vigorously, even though they were weakened by their susceptibility to alien European diseases. One by one the seven islands fell to Europeans,

who then carried off Guanches as slaves to the Madeiras or the Iberian Peninsula. Spain conquered the last island in 1496 and subsequently devoted the land to sugar plantations. Collectively, the Canaries and Madeira became known as the Wine Islands because much of their sugar production was directed to making sweet wines.

While some Europeans concentrated on exploiting the islands of the Mediterranean Atlantic, others used them as steppingstones to Africa. In 1415 Portugal seized control of Ceuta, a Muslim city in North Africa (see Map 1.2). Prince Henry the Navigator, son of King John I of Portugal, knew that vast wealth awaited the first European nation to tap the riches of Africa and Asia directly. Each year he dispatched ships southward along the African coast, attempting to discover an oceanic route to Asia. But not until after Prince Henry's death did

PORTUGUESE TRADING POSTS IN AFRICA

Nova Zemla

Strate de Naßauwe

Matflo Delgo

SAMVE TEN LANT

■ In the fifteenth and sixteenth centuries, caravels ventured into the open oceans, thereby changing the contours of the known world. This illustration from a manuscript account of William Barents's 1594 expedition into the Arctic Ocean shows the combination of square rigging and lateen sails that gave ships greater maneuverability and allowed them to navigate along unfamiliar coastlines far from their home ports.   (Bridgeman Art Library)

Bartholomew Dias round the southern tip of Africa (1488) and Vasco da Gama finally reach India (1498).

Long before that, Portugal reaped the benefits of its seafarers' voyages. Although West African states successfully resisted European penetration of the interior, they allowed the Portuguese to establish trading posts along their coasts. Charging the traders rent and levying duties on goods they imported, the African kingdoms set the terms of exchange and benefited considerably from their new, easier access to European manufactures. The Portuguese gained too, for they no longer had to rely on trans-Saharan camel caravans. Their vessels earned immense profits by swiftly transporting African gold, ivory, and slaves to Europe. By bargaining with African masters to purchase their slaves and then carrying those

bondspeople to Iberia, the Portuguese introduced black slavery into Europe.

An island off the African coast, previously uninhabited, proved critical to Portuguese success. São Tomé, located in the Gulf of Guinea (see Map 1.2), was colonized by the Portuguese in the 1480s. By that time Madeira had already reached the limit of its capacity to produce sugar. The soil of São Tomé proved ideal for raising that valuable crop, and plantation agriculture there expanded rapidly. Planters imported large numbers of slaves from the mainland to work in the cane fields, thus creating the first economy based primarily on the bondage of black Africans.

By the 1490s, even before Christopher Columbus set sail to the west, Europeans had learned three key lessons

LESSONS
OF EARLY
COLONIZATION

of colonization in the Mediterranean Atlantic. First, they had learned how to transplant their crops and livestock successfully to exotic locations. Second, they had discovered that the native peoples of those lands could be either conquered (like the Guanches) or exploited (like the Africans). Third, they had developed a viable model of plantation slavery and a system for supplying nearly unlimited quantities of such workers. The stage was set for a pivotal moment in world history.

The Voyages of Columbus, Cabot, and Their Successors

Christopher Columbus was well schooled in the lessons of the Mediterranean Atlantic. Born in 1451 in the Italian city-state of Genoa, Columbus, the largely self-educated son of a wool merchant, was by the 1490s an experienced sailor and mapmaker. Like many mariners of the day, he was drawn to Portugal and its islands, especially Madeira, where he commanded a merchant vessel. At least once he voyaged to the Portuguese outpost on the Gold Coast. There he acquired an obsession with gold, and there he came to understand the economic potential of the slave trade.

Like all accomplished seafarers, Columbus knew the world was round. (So, indeed, did most educated people: the idea that his contemporaries believed the world to be flat is a myth dating from the nineteenth century.) But he differed from other cartographers in his estimate of the earth's size: he thought that China lay only 3,000 miles from the southern European coast. Thus, he argued, it would be easier to reach Asia by sailing west than by making the difficult voyage around the southern tip of Africa. Experts scoffed at this crackpot notion, accurately predicting that the two continents lay 12,000 miles apart. When Columbus in 1484 asked the Portuguese authorities to back his plan to sail west to Asia, they rejected the proposal. After all, why should they adopt such a crazy scheme just as their efforts to round the Cape of Good Hope promised success?

Ferdinand and Isabella of Spain, jealous of Portugal's successes in Africa, were more receptive to Columbus's ideas. Urged on by some Spanish noblemen and a group of Italian merchants residing in Castile, the monarchs agreed to finance the risky voyage, in part because they hoped the profits would pay for a new expedition to conquer Muslim-held Jerusalem.

COLUMBUS'S
VOYAGE

And so, on August 3, 1492, in command of three ships—the *Pinta*, the *Niña*, and the *Santa Maria*—Columbus set sail from the Spanish port of Palos.

The first part of the journey must have been very familiar, for the ships steered down the Northeast Trades to the Canary Islands. There Columbus refitted his square-rigged ships, adding triangular sails to make them more maneuverable. On September 6, the ships weighed anchor and headed out into the unknown ocean.

Just over a month later, pushed by favorable trade winds, the vessels found land approximately where Columbus had predicted (see Map 1.5). On October 12, he and his men landed on an island in the Bahamas, which its inhabitants called Guanahaní but which he renamed San Salvador. (Because Columbus's description of his landfall can be variously interpreted, three different places—Samana Cay, Plana Cays, and Mayaguana Cay—are today proposed as the most likely locations for his landing site.) Later he went on to explore the islands now known as Cuba and Hispaniola, which their residents, the Taíno people, called Colba and Bohío. Because he thought he had reached the Indies, Columbus referred to the inhabitants of the region as Indians.

Three themes predominate in Columbus's log, the major source of information on this first encounter. First, he insistently asked the Taínos where he could find gold, pearls, and valuable spices. Each time, his informants replied (largely via signs) that such products could be obtained on other islands, on the mainland, or in cities in the interior. Eventually he came to mistrust such answers, noting, "I am beginning to believe . . . they will tell me anything I want to hear."

COLUMBUS'S
OBSERVATIONS

Second, Columbus wrote repeatedly of the strange and beautiful plants and animals. "Here the fishes are so unlike ours that it is amazing. . . . The colors are so bright that anyone would marvel," he noted, and again, "The song of the little birds might make a man wish never to leave here. I never tire from looking at such luxurious vegetation." Yet Columbus's interest was not only aesthetic. "I believe that there are many plants and trees here that could be worth a lot in Spain for use as dyes, spices, and medicines," he observed, adding that he was carrying home to Europe "a sample of everything I can," so that experts could examine them.

Third, Columbus also described the islands' human residents, and he seized some to take back to Spain. The Taínos were, he said, very handsome, gentle, and friendly, though they told him of fierce people who lived on other nearby islands and raided their villages. The

Map 1.5   European Explorations in America

In the century following Columbus's voyages, European adventurers explored the
coasts and parts of the interior of North and South America.

Caniba (today called Caribs), from whose name the word *cannibal* is derived, were reported to eat their captives, but today scholars disagree about whether the tales were true. Columbus believed the Taínos to be likely converts to Catholicism, remarking that "if devout religious persons knew the Indian language well, all these people would soon become Christians." But he had more in mind than conversion. The islanders "ought to make good and skilled servants," Columbus declared. It would be easy to "subject everyone and make them do what you wished."

Thus the records of the first encounter between Europeans and America and its residents revealed the themes that would be of enormous significance for centuries to come, motivating such later explorers as Hernán de Soto as well. Above all, Europeans wanted to extract profits from North and South America by exploiting their natural resources, including plants, animals, and peoples alike. Christopher

EUROPEANS AND "AMERICA"

Columbus made three more voyages to the west, exploring most of the major Caribbean islands and sailing along the coasts of Central and South America. Until the day he died in 1506 at the age of fifty-five, Columbus believed that he had reached Asia. Even before his death, others knew better. Because the Florentine Amerigo Vespucci, who explored the South American coast in 1499, was the first to publish the idea that a new continent had been discovered, Martin Waldseemüller in 1507 labeled the land "America," as is evident in his map (reproduced on page 21). By then, Spain, Portugal, and Pope Alexander VI had signed the Treaty of Tordesillas (1494), confirming Portugal's dominance in Africa—and later Brazil—in exchange for Spanish preeminence in the rest of the Americas.

Five hundred years before Columbus, about the year 1001, the Norseman Leif Ericsson and other Norse had sailed to North America across the Davis Strait, which separated their villages in Greenland from Baffin Island (located northeast of Hudson Bay; see Map 1.1) by just

■ This map, produced in 1489 by Henricus Marcellus, represents the world as Christopher Columbus knew it, for it incorporates information obtained after Bartholomew Dias, a Portuguese sailor, rounded the Cape of Good Hope at the southern tip of Africa in 1488. Marcellus did not try to estimate the extent of the ocean separating the west coast of Europe from the east coast of Asia.   (Trustees of the British Library)

■ In 1507 Martin Waldseemüller, a German mapmaker, was the first person to designate the newly discovered southern continent as "America." He named the continent after Amerigo Vespucci, the Italian explorer who realized that he had reached a "new world" rather than islands off the coast of Asia.   (John Carter Brown Library at Brown University)

NORSE AND OTHER NORTHERN VOYAGERS

200 nautical miles, settling at a site they named Vinland. Attacks by local residents forced them to depart hurriedly from Vinland after just a few years. In the 1960s, archaeologists determined that the Norse had established an outpost at what is now L'Anse aux Meadows, Newfoundland, but Vinland itself was probably located farther south.

Later Europeans did not know of the Norse explorers, but some historians argue that in the 1480s sailors may have located the rich fishing grounds off the coast of Newfoundland but kept the information to themselves so they alone could fish there. Whether or not fishermen crossed the entire width of the Atlantic, they thoroughly explored its northern reaches. In the same way the Portuguese traveled regularly in the Mediterranean Atlantic, fifteenth-century seafarers voyaged between the European continent, England, Ireland, and Iceland. The mariners who explored the region of North America that was to become the United States and Canada built on their knowledge.

The winds the northern sailors confronted posed problems on their outbound rather than homeward journeys. The same Westerlies that carried Columbus and other southern voyagers back to Europe blew in the faces of northerners looking west. But mariners soon learned that the strongest winds shifted southward during the winter and that, by departing from northern ports in the spring, they could make adequate headway if they steered northward to catch sporadic easterly breezes. Thus, whereas the first landfall of most sailors to the south was somewhere in the Caribbean, those taking the northern route usually reached America along the coast of what is now Maine or the Canadian maritime provinces.

The European generally credited with "discovering" North America is John Cabot. More precisely, Cabot brought to Europe the first formal knowledge of the northern coastline of the continent and claimed the land for England. Like Columbus, Cabot was a master mariner from the Italian city-state of Genoa. He is known to have been in Spain when Columbus returned from his first trip to America. Calculating that England—which traded with Asia only through a long series of middlemen stretching from Belgium to Venice to the Muslim world—would be eager to sponsor exploratory voyages, Cabot sought and won the support of King Henry VII. He set sail from Bristol in late May 1497 in the *Mathew,* reaching his destination on June 24. Scholars disagree about the location of his landfall (some say it was Cape Breton Island, others Newfoundland), but all recognize the importance of his month-long exploration of the coast. Having achieved his goal, Cabot rode the Westerlies back to England, arriving just fifteen days after he left North America.

JOHN CABOT'S EXPLORATIONS

The voyages of Columbus, Cabot, and their successors finally brought the Eastern and Western Hemispheres together. The Portuguese explorer Pedro Álvares Cabral reached Brazil in 1500; John Cabot's son Sebastian followed his father to North America in 1507; France financed Giovanni da Verrazzano in 1524 and Jacques Cartier in 1534; and in 1609 and 1610 Henry Hudson explored the North American coast for the Dutch West India Company (see Map 1.5). All these men were primarily searching for the legendary, nonexistent "Northwest Passage" through the Americas, hoping to find an easy route to the riches of Asia. Although they did not attempt to plant colonies in the Western Hemisphere, their discoveries interested European nations in exploring North and South America.

Spanish Exploration and Conquest

*O*nly in the areas that Spain explored and claimed did colonization begin immediately. On his second voyage in 1493, Columbus brought to Hispaniola seventeen ships loaded with twelve hundred men, seeds, plants, livestock, chickens, and dogs—along

■ Artifacts from L'Anse aux Meadows, Newfoundland, a site the Norse called Straumond. These inconspicuous items reveal a great deal to archaeologists investigating the Norse settlements in North America. The small circular object, a spindle whorl for use in spinning yarn, discloses women's presence at Straumond; the nut comes from a tree that grows only south of the St. Lawrence River, thus indicating the extent of Norse travel along the coast. (L'Anse aux Meadows, Canada)

with microbes, rats, and weeds. The settlement named Isabela (in the modern Dominican Republic) and its successors became the staging area for the Spanish invasion of America. On the islands of Cuba and Hispaniola the Europeans learned to adapt to the new environment, as did the horses, cattle, and hogs they imported. When the Spaniards moved on to explore the mainland, they rode island-bred horses and ate island-bred cattle and hogs.

At first, Spanish explorers fanned out around the Caribbean basin. In 1513 Juan Ponce de León reached Florida and Vasco Núñez de Balboa crossed the Isthmus of Panama to the Pacific Ocean. In the 1530s and 1540s, conquistadors traveled farther, exploring many regions claimed by the Spanish monarchs: Francisco Vásquez de Coronado journeyed through the southwestern portion of what is now the United States at approximately the same time as Hernán de Soto explored the southeast and encountered the Lady of Cofitachequi. Juan Rodríguez Cabrillo sailed along the California coast; and Francisco Pizarro, who ventured into western South America, acquired the richest silver mines in the world by conquering the Incas. But the most important conquistador was Hernán Cortés, who in 1521 seized control of the Aztec Empire.

Cortés, an adventurer who first arrived in the West Indies in 1504, embarked for the mainland in 1519 in search of wealthy cities rumored to exist there. As he moved his force inland from the Gulf of Mexico, local Mayas presented him with a gift of twenty young female

CORTÉS AND MALINCHE

slaves. One of them, Malinche (soon baptized as a Christian and renamed Doña Marina by the Spaniards), who had been sold into slavery by the Aztecs and raised by the Mayas, became Cortés's translator. Although some modern-day Mexicans regard her as a traitor, others question why she would owe loyalty to those who had enslaved her. No one at the time of the conquest made such a suggestion; instead, both Europeans and Indians accorded her great respect. Malinche bore Cortés a son, Martín—one of the first *mestizos,* or mixed-blood children—and eventually married one of his officers. When the Aztec capital Tenochtitlán fell to the Spaniards in 1521, Cortés and his men seized a fabulous treasure of gold and silver. Thus not long after Columbus's first voyage, the Spanish monarchs—who treated the American territories as their personal possessions—controlled the richest, most extensive empire Europe had known since ancient Rome.

Spain established the model of colonization that other countries later attempted to imitate, a model with three major elements. First, the Crown

SPANISH COLONIZATION

maintained tight control over the colonies, imposing a hierarchical government that allowed little autonomy to New World jurisdictions. That control included, for example, limiting the number of people permitted to emigrate to America and insisting that the colonies import all their manufactured goods from

■ An early illustration of a Carib lean-to shelter, with baskets, a pot, a loom (hanging at left), and a hammock—a novel place to sleep that fascinated European observers. The man at center has coated his skin with annatto, a plant extract that served as both insect repellent and sunscreen. (1996 MAPes MONDe Ltd.)

Spain. Roman Catholic priests ensured the colonists' conformity with orthodox religious views. Second, most of the colonists sent from Spain were male. They took Indian—and later African—women as their sexual partners, thereby creating the racially mixed population that characterizes much of Latin America to the present day.

Third, the colonies' wealth was based on the exploitation of both the native population and slaves imported from Africa. The Mesoamerican peoples, many of whom lived in urban areas, were accustomed to autocratic rule. Spaniards simply took over roles once assumed by native leaders, who had also exacted labor and tribute from their subjects. The *encomienda* system, which granted tribute from Indian villages to individual conquistadors as a reward for their services to the Crown, in effect legalized Indian slavery. Yet in 1542 a new code of laws reformed the system, forbidding Spaniards from enslaving Indians while still allowing them to collect money and goods from their tributary villages. In response, the conquerors, familiar with slavery in Spain, began to import Africans in order to increase the labor force under their direct control. They employed Indians and Africans primarily in gold and silver mines, on sugar plantations, and on huge horse, cattle, and sheep ranches. Yet African slavery was far more common in the Greater Antilles (the major Caribbean islands) than on the mainland.

GOLD, SILVER, AND SPAIN'S DECLINE

The New World's gold and silver, initially a boon, ultimately brought about the decline of Spain as a major power. The influx of unprecedented wealth led to rapid inflation, which (among other adverse effects) caused Spanish products to be overpriced in international markets and imported goods to become cheaper in Spain. The once-profitable Spanish textile-manufacturing industry collapsed, as did scores of other businesses. The seemingly endless income from American colonies emboldened successive Spanish monarchs to spend lavishly on wars against the Dutch and the English. Several times in the late sixteenth and early seventeenth centuries the monarchs repudiated the state debt, wreaking havoc on the nation's finances. When the South American gold and silver mines started to give out in the mid-seventeenth century, Spain's economy crumbled and the nation lost its international importance.

Spanish wealth derived from American suffering. The Spaniards deliberately leveled American cities, building cathedrals and monasteries on sites once occupied by Aztec, Incan, and Mayan temples. Some conquistadors sought to erase all vestiges of the great Indian cultures by burning the written records they found. With traditional ways of life in disarray, devastated by disease, and compelled to labor for their conquerors, many demoralized residents of Mesoamerica accepted the Christian religion brought to New Spain by friars of the Franciscan and Dominican orders.

The friars devoted their energies to persuading Mesoamerican people to move into new towns and to build Roman Catholic churches. In such towns, Indians were exposed to European customs and religious rituals designed to assimilate Catholic and pagan beliefs. Friars deliberately juxtaposed the cult of the Virgin Mary with that of the corn goddess, and the Indians adeptly melded aspects of their traditional world-view with Christianity, in a process called syncretism. Thousands of Indians residing in Spanish territory embraced Catholicism, at least partly because it was the religion of their new rulers and they were accustomed to obedience.

CHRISTIANITY IN NEW SPAIN

The Columbian Exchange

a broad mutual transfer of diseases, plants, and animals (called the Columbian Exchange by the historian Alfred Crosby; see Figure 1.1) resulted directly from the European voyages of the fifteenth and sixteenth centuries and from Spanish colonization. The Eastern and Western Hemispheres had evolved separately for thousands of years, developing widely different forms of life. Many large mammals like cattle and horses were native to the connected continents of Europe, Asia, and Africa, but the Americas contained no domesticated beasts larger than dogs and llamas. The vegetable crops of the Americas—particularly maize, beans, squash, cassava, and potatoes—were more nutritious and produced higher yields than those of Europe and Africa, such as wheat, millet, and rye. In time, native peoples learned to raise and consume European livestock, and Europeans and Africans became accustomed to planting and eating American crops. The diets of all three peoples were consequently vastly enriched. Partly as a result, the world's population doubled over the next three hundred years.

Diseases carried from Europe and Africa, though, had a devastating impact on the Americas. Indians fell victim to microbes that had long infested the other continents and had repeatedly killed hundreds of thousands but had also left survivors with some measure of immunity. The statistics are staggering. When Columbus landed on

SMALLPOX AND OTHER DISEASES

Maize

Maize, to Mesoamericans, was a gift from Quetzalcoatl, the plumed serpent god. Cherokees told of an old woman whose blood produced the prized stalks after her grandson buried her body in a cleared, sunny field. For the Abenakis, the crop began when a beautiful maiden ordered a youth to drag her by the hair through a burned-over field. The long hair of the Cherokee grandmother and the Abenaki maiden turned into silk, the flower on the stalks that Europeans called Indian corn.

Sacred to all the Indian peoples who grew it, maize was a cereal crop, a main part of their diet. They dried the kernels; ground into meal, maize was cooked as a mush or shaped into flat cakes and baked, the forerunners of modern tortillas. Indians also heated the dried kernels until they popped open, just as is done today. Although the European invaders of North and South America initially disdained maize, they soon learned that it could be cultivated in a wide variety of conditions—from sea level to twelve thousand feet, from regions with abundant rainfall to dry lands with as little as twelve inches of rain a year. Corn was also highly productive, yielding almost twice as many calories per acre as wheat. So Europeans, too, came to rely on corn, growing it not only in their American settlements but also in their homelands.

Maize cultivation spread to Asia and Africa. Today, China is second only to the United States in total corn production, and corn is more widely grown in Africa than any other crop. Still, the United States produces 45 percent of the world's corn—almost half of it in the three states of Illinois, Iowa, and Nebraska—and corn is the nation's single largest crop. More than half of American corn is consumed by livestock. Much of the rest is processed into syrup, which sweetens carbonated beverages and candies, or into ethanol, a gasoline additive that reduces both pollution and dependence on fossil fuels. Corn is an ingredient in light beer and toothpaste. It is used in the manufacture of tires, wallpaper, cat litter, and aspirin. Remarkably, of the ten thousand products in a modern American grocery store, about one-fourth rely to some extent on corn.

Today this crop bequeathed to the world by ancient American plant breeders provides one-fifth of all the calories consumed by the earth's peoples. The gift of Quetzalcoatl has linked the globe.

The earliest known European drawing of maize, the American plant that was to have such an extraordinary impact on the entire world. (Houghton Library, Harvard University)

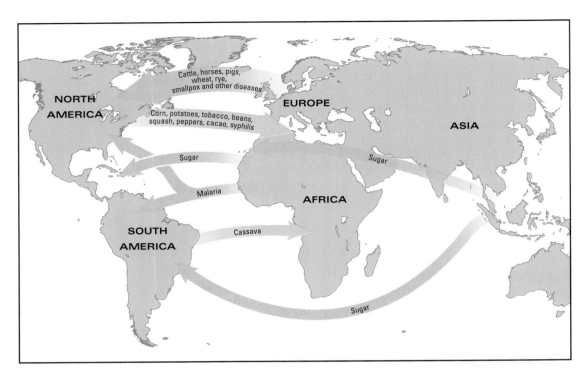

Figure 1.1   Major Items in the Columbian Exchange

As European adventurers traversed the world in the fifteenth and sixteenth centuries, they initiated the "Columbian Exchange" of plants, animals, and diseases. These events changed the lives of the peoples of the world forever, bringing new foods and new pestilence to both sides of the Atlantic.

■ A male effigy dating from 200–800 C.E., found in a burial site in Nayarit, Mexico. The lesions covering the figurine suggest that the person it represents is suffering from syphilis, which, untreated, produces these characteristic markings on the body in its later stages. Such evidence as this pre-Columbian effigy has now convinced most scholars that syphilis originated in the Americas—a hypothesis in dispute for many years.   (Private Collection)

Hispaniola in 1492, approximately half a million people resided there. Fifty years later, fewer than two thousand native inhabitants were still alive. Within thirty years of the first landfall at Guanahaní, not one Taíno survived in the Bahamas. Overall, historians estimate that the arrival of the alien microorganisms could have reduced the pre-contact American population by as much as 90 percent, especially because the epidemics continued to recur at twenty- to thirty-year intervals.

Although measles, typhus, influenza, malaria, and other illnesses severely afflicted the native peoples, the greatest killer was smallpox, spread primarily by direct human contact. A Spanish priest recorded the vivid words of an old Aztec man who survived the first small-pox epidemic in Tenochtitlán. That epidemic, which began on Hispaniola in December 1518, was carried to the mainland by Spaniards in the spring of 1520. The epidemic peaked about six months later, fatally weakening Tenochtitlán's defenders. "It spread over the people as great destruction," the elderly Aztec remembered. "Some it quite covered [with pustules] on all parts—their faces,

■ A Spanish map from 1519 showing the coast of Hispaniola, focusing on what is now the modern nation of Haiti. The decorative figures, shown with tools for hunting and cultivation, appear to be African slaves imported as laborers to replace the Indian population, already being rapidly depleted by disease and mistreatment.   (Bibliothèque Nationale)

their heads, their breasts. . . . There was great havoc. Very many died of it." Largely as a consequence, Tenochtitlán surrendered, and the Spaniards built Mexico City on its site.

Far to the north, where smaller American populations encountered only a few Europeans, disease also ravaged the countryside. A great epidemic, probably smallpox coupled with measles, swept through the villages along the coast north of Cape Cod from 1616 to 1618. Again the mortality rate may have been as high as 90 percent. An English traveler several years later commented that the people had "died on heapes, as they lay in their houses," and that bones and skulls covered the ruins of villages. Because of this dramatic depopulation of the area, just a few years later English colonists were able to establish settlements virtually unopposed.

The Americans, though, took a revenge of sorts. They gave the Europeans syphilis, a virulent venereal disease. The first recorded European case of the new ailment occurred in Barcelona, Spain, in 1493, shortly after Columbus's return from the Caribbean. Although less likely than smallpox to cause immediate death, syphilis was dangerous and debilitating. Carried by soldiers, sailors, and prostitutes, it spread quickly through Europe and Asia, reaching as far as China by 1505.

The exchange of three commodities had significant impacts on Europe and the Americas. Sugar, which was

SUGAR, HORSES, AND TOBACCO

first domesticated in the East Indies, was being grown on the islands of the Mediterranean Atlantic by 1450 (see page 17). The insatiable European demand for sugar, which after initially being regarded as a medicine became a desirable luxury foodstuff, led Columbus to take Canary Island sugar canes to Hispaniola on his 1493 voyage. By the 1520s, plantations in the Greater Antilles worked by African slaves regularly shipped cargoes of sugar to Spain. Half a century later, the Portuguese colony in Brazil (founded 1532) was producing sugar on an even larger scale for the European market, and after 1640 (see pages 40–41), sugar cultivation became the crucial component of English and French colonization in the Caribbean.

Horses, which like sugar were brought to America by Columbus in 1493, fell into the hands of North American Indians during the seventeenth century. Through trade and theft, horses spread among the peoples of the Great Plains, reaching most areas by 1750. Lakota, Comanches, and Crows, among others, came to use horses for transportation and hunting, calculated their wealth in the number of horses owned, and waged wars primarily from horseback. Women no longer had to carry the band's belongings on their backs. Some groups that previously had cultivated crops abandoned agriculture altogether. Because of the acquisition of horses, a mode of subsistence that had been based on hunting several different animals, in combination with gathering and agriculture, became one focused almost wholly on hunting buffalo.

In America, Europeans encountered tobacco, which at first they believed to have beneficial medicinal effects. Smoking and chewing the "Indian weed" became a fad in Europe after it was planted in Turkey in the sixteenth century. Despite the efforts of such skeptics as King James I of England, who in 1604 pronounced smoking "loathsome to the eye, hatefull to the Nose, harmfull to the brain, [and] dangerous to the Lungs," tobacco's popularity climbed. Its connection to lung cancer was discovered only in the twentieth century.

The European and African invasion of the Americas therefore had a significant biological component, for the invaders carried plants and animals with them. Some creatures, such as livestock, they brought deliberately. Others, including rats (which infested their ships), weeds, and diseases, arrived unexpectedly. And the same process occurred in reverse. When the Europeans returned home, they deliberately took back such crops as maize, potatoes, and tobacco, along with that unanticipated stowaway, syphilis.

Europeans in North America

Northern Europeans, denied access to the wealth of Mesoamerica by the Spanish and beaten to South America by the Portuguese, were initially more interested in exploiting North America's abundant natural resources than in the difficult task of establishing colonies on the mainland. John Cabot reported that fish were so plentiful along the North American coast that they could be caught merely by lowering baskets over the side of a vessel. Europeans rushed to take advantage of the abundance of fish, a product in great demand in their homelands as an inexpensive source of nourishment. By the 1570s, more than 350 ships, primarily from France and England, were capitalizing on the bounty of the Newfoundland Banks each year.

European fishermen soon learned that they could augment their profits by exchanging cloth and metal goods like pots and knives for the native trappers' beaver pelts, which Europeans used to make fashionable hats. At first the Europeans conducted their trading from ships sailing along the coast, but later they established permanent outposts on the mainland to centralize and control the traffic in furs. All were inhabited chiefly by male adventurers, whose major aim was to send as many pelts as possible home to Europe.

TRADE AMONG INDIANS AND EUROPEANS

The Europeans' demand for furs, especially beaver, was matched by the Indians' desire for European goods that could make their lives easier and establish their superiority over their neighbors. Some bands began to concentrate so completely on trapping for the European market that they abandoned their traditional economies. The Abenakis of Maine, for example, became partially dependent on food supplied by their neighbors to the south, the Massachusett tribe, because they devoted most of their energies to catching beaver to sell to French traders. The Massachusetts, in turn, intensified their production of foodstuffs, which they traded to the Abenakis in exchange for the European metal tools they preferred to their own handmade stone implements. The intensive trade in pelts also had serious ecological consequences. In some regions, beavers were completely wiped out. The disappearance of their dams led to soil erosion, especially when combined with the extensive clearing of forests by later European settlers.

Although their nation reaped handsome profits from fishing, English merchants and political leaders watched enviously as Spain's American possessions enriched Spain immeasurably. In the mid-sixteenth century,

CONTEST
BETWEEN SPAIN
AND ENGLAND

English "sea dogs" like John Hawkins and Sir Francis Drake began to raid Spanish treasure fleets sailing home from the West Indies. Their actions caused friction between the two countries and helped to foment a war that in 1588 culminated in the defeat of a huge invasion force—the Spanish Armada—off the English coast. As a part of the contest with Spain, English leaders started to think about planting colonies in the Western Hemisphere, thereby gaining better access to valuable trade goods and simultaneously preventing their enemy from dominating the Americas.

The first English colonial planners saw Spain's possessions as both a model and a challenge. They hoped to reproduce Spanish successes by dispatching to America men who would similarly exploit the native peoples for their own and their nation's benefit. In the mid-1570s, a group that included Sir Humphrey Gilbert and his younger half-brother Sir Walter Raleigh began to promote a scheme to establish outposts that could trade with the Indians and provide bases for attacks on New Spain. Approving the idea, Queen Elizabeth I authorized first Gilbert, then Raleigh, to colonize North America.

Gilbert failed to plant a colony in Newfoundland, dying in the attempt, and Raleigh was only briefly more

ROANOKE

successful. After two preliminary expeditions, in 1587 he sent 117 colonists to the territory he named Virginia, after Elizabeth, the "Virgin Queen." They established a settlement on Roanoke Island, in what is now North Carolina, but in 1590 a resupply ship—delayed in leaving England because of the Spanish Armada—could not find them. The colonists had vanished, leaving only the word Croatoan (the name of a nearby island) carved on a tree. Recent tree-ring studies have shown that the North Carolina coast experienced a severe drought between 1587 and 1589, which would have created a subsistence crisis for the settlers and which could well have led them to abandon the Roanoke site.

Thus England's first attempt to plant a permanent settlement on the North American coast failed, as had similar efforts by Portugal on Cape Breton Island (early 1520s) and France in northern Florida (mid-1560s). All three enterprises collapsed because of their inability to be self-sustaining in foodstuffs and the hostility of neighboring peoples. Spanish soldiers wiped out the French colony in 1565 (see page 35), and neither the Portuguese nor the English were able to maintain friendly relations with local Indians.

The explanation for such failings becomes clear in Thomas Harriot's *A Briefe and True Report of the New*

■ John White, an artist with Raleigh's 1585 expedition (and later the governor of the ill-fated 1587 colony), illustrated three different fishing techniques used by Carolina Indians: to the left, the construction of weirs and traps; in the background, spearfishing in shallow water; in the foreground, fishing from dugout canoes. The fish are accurately drawn and can be identified today.   (Trustees of the British Museum)

HARRIOT'S
BRIEFE AND
TRUE REPORT

Found Land of Virginia, published in 1588 to publicize Raleigh's colony. Harriot, a noted scientist who sailed with the second of the preliminary voyages to Roanoke, described the animals, plants, and people of the region for an English readership. His account revealed that although the explorers depended on nearby villagers for most of their food, they needlessly antagonized their neighbors by killing some of them for what Harriot himself admitted were unjustifiable reasons.

The scientist advised later colonizers to deal with the native peoples of America more humanely than his comrades had. But the content of his book suggested why that advice would rarely be followed. *A Briefe and True Report* examined the possibilities for economic development in America. Harriot stressed three points: the availability of commodities familiar to Europeans, like grapes, iron, copper, and fur-bearing animals; the potential profitability of exotic American products such as maize, cassava, and tobacco; and the relative ease of manipulating the native population to the Europeans' advantage. Should the Americans attempt to resist the English by force, Harriot asserted, the latter's advantages of disciplined soldiers and superior weaponry would quickly deliver victory.

Harriot's *Briefe and True Report* depicted for his English readers a bountiful land full of opportunities for quick profit. The people already residing there would, he thought, "in a short time be brought to civilitie" through conversion to Christianity, admiration for European superiority, or conquest—if they did not die from disease, the ravages of which he witnessed. Thomas Harriot understood the key elements of the story, but his prediction was far off the mark. European dominance of North America would be difficult to achieve. Indeed, some historians today argue that it never was fully achieved, in the sense Harriot and his compatriots intended, and that the societies that subsequently developed in North America owed as much to their native origins as to their immigrant ones.

Summary

*T*he process of initial contact between Europeans and Americans that ended with Thomas Harriot near the close of the sixteenth century began approximately 250 years earlier when Portuguese sailors first set out to explore the Mediterranean Atlantic and to settle on its islands. That region of the Atlantic so close to European and African shores nurtured the mariners who, like Christopher Columbus, ventured into previously unknown waters—those who sailed to India and Brazil as well as to the Caribbean and the North American coast. When Columbus first reached the Americas, he thought he had found Asia, his intended destination. Later explorers knew better but, except for the Spanish,

regarded the Americas primarily as a barrier that prevented them from reaching their long-sought goal of an oceanic route to the riches of China and the Moluccas. Ordinary European fishermen were the first to realize that the northern coasts had valuable products to offer: fish and furs, both much in demand in their homelands.

The wealth of the north could not compare to that of Mesoamerica. The Aztec Empire, heir to the trading networks of Teotihuacán as well as to the intellectual sophistication of the Mayas, dazzled the conquistadors with the magnificence of its buildings and its seemingly unlimited wealth. As an old man, Cortés's aide Bernal Díaz del Castillo recalled his first sight of Tenochtitlán, situated in the midst of Lake Texcoco: "We were amazed and said that it was like the enchantments . . . on account of the great towers and cues [temples] and buildings rising from the water, and all built of masonry." Some soldiers asked, he remembered, "whether the things that we saw were not a dream."

The Aztecs had predicted that their Fifth Sun would end in earthquakes and hunger. Hunger they surely experienced after Cortés's invasion; and, if there were no earthquakes, the great temples tumbled to the ground nevertheless, as the Spaniards used their stones (and Indian laborers) to construct cathedrals honoring their God and his son Jesus rather than Huitzilopochtli. The conquerors employed first American and later enslaved African workers to till the fields, mine the precious metals, and herd the livestock that earned immense profits for themselves and their mother country.

The initial impact of Europeans on the Americas proved devastating. Flourishing civilizations were, if not entirely destroyed, markedly altered in just a few short decades. The Europeans' diseases and livestock, along with a wide range of other imported animals and plants, irrevocably changed the American environment, affecting the lives of the Western Hemisphere's inhabitants. By the end of the sixteenth century, fewer people resided in North America than had lived there before Columbus's arrival, even taking into account the arrival of many Europeans and Africans. And the people who did live there—Indian, African, and European—resided in a world that was indeed new—a world engaged in the unprecedented process of combining foods, religions, economies, styles of life, and political systems that had developed separately for millennia. Understandably, conflict and dissension permeated that process.

LEGACY FOR A PEOPLE AND A NATION
Columbus Day

Each year, the United States celebrates the second Monday in October as a tribute to Christopher Columbus's landing in the Bahamas in 1492. When viewed in the context of other holidays that mark the birthdays of great Americans or key events in the nation's past, Columbus Day is an anomaly. After all, the Genoese mariner never set foot on North American soil.

The first known U.S. celebration of Columbus's voyage occurred in New York City on October 12, 1792, when a men's social club gave a dinner to mark its three hundredth anniversary. In the late 1860s, Italian American communities in New York City and San Francisco began to celebrate October 12, but not until the four hundredth anniversary in 1892 did a congressional resolution order a one-time national commemoration. Columbus Day was first observed as a national holiday in 1971, although a majority of the states already celebrated it (Colorado was the first, in 1907).

More than thirty years ago Congress proclaimed Columbus Day as a national holiday with little opposition, except from Americans of Scandinavian descent who would have preferred to honor the Norse explorers of 1001. Today, though, the annual observances can arouse strong emotions. The American Indian Movement (AIM), founded in 1968, has declared that "from an indigenous vantage point, Columbus' arrival was a disaster." Terming Columbus a "murderer," the AIM contends that he "deserves no recognition or accolades"—certainly not a holiday. At the same time, as immigration has increased the Latino presence in the United States, people of Hispanic descent have claimed Columbus as their own, insisting that his voyage was "a thoroughly Spanish event." In some cities—most notably New York—their celebrations rival those long organized by Italian Americans; in others, such as Miami, Hispanics control the official commemorations. Still other Latinos, especially those of Mexican descent living in Los Angeles, call October 12 Dia de la Raza and use it as an occasion to protest current U.S. immigration policy.

As ethnic diversity has increased in the nation, and as peoples of different origins have sought to claim a share of the American heritage, holidays have unsurprisingly become the occasion for heated contests. Each fall, the American people and nation therefore continue to confront the controversial legacy of Columbus's 1492 voyage.

The **history companion** *powered by Eduspace®*
Your primary source for interactive quizzes, exercises, and more to help you learn efficiently.
http://history.college.hmco.com/students

THE BAHAMA OR LUCAYO ISLES

OCE

FLORIDA
THE GULF OF FLORIDA

del Anclote
S.t Espirit
Carlos B.
Carlos
Muspa
Caico Marquet
Tortugas
Martiris

Amacuro R.
Pup S.t P.
OTchiagua
Matancas
C.Canaveral
Mimbres
Bahama Bank
Bahama I.
Lucaye I.
Aleblaster or Cigates I.
Guanahani or C. at I.
Triangulo
Vuma or Yxuma
Vumeta or Long I.
Samana S.
Mayaguana

B. of Honda
Cape S.t Anthony
Havana
CUBA ISLE
Contoy
I. Mugeres
Pinos I.
los Hermanas
B. Zagua
Jardins
la Trinite
S. Spirtu
Portillaicos
Cinega
de Pe
Old Bahama Streights

Mucaras
Verde I.
Inagua
Miraporos
Prta Prai
C. Mayze
Tortuga I.

Caicos
Abrochos, Here S.r W. Pelt
fisht for y.e Spanish Wra
Caico de Pla
Baiha
Mancenille
M.t Christo
Isabella ruind
P. Plata
C. Francois
B. y C. of Saman

Cosumel I.
Great Cayman
little Cayman
C Cruz
Seville
B. Baxains Baracoa
S. Iago
S.t Ann
Guanabel.
Caimites
Nichola
little Gouave
French
S. John
Mariana
Cotuq
DOMINGO
Spaniards
S.t Domingo
C. Engan

ita Sueño
of HONDURAS
Guanaja I.
C. Camaron
Viciosa
Santanilla
Misteriosa
P. Negrillo
I. JAMAICA
Carlile
Biroras
B.o Nuevo
Serranilla
Parcel
Morla
Mary Lage
C. Tiburon
C. Morant
Port Royal
Old harbour
C. Abacou
Vache I.
Altavela
Beata
Es.o
I. S.t Catherine
Saona I.
Mona
Roces

MOUNTAINS of Ocbia
George del Olancho
HONDURAS
NI
CARAGUA
Lake of Nicaragua
Vulcano of Bombraco
COSTARICA
Indians at War
VERAGUA
Pueblo Nuevo

C Gracios a Dios
Quinta Suenos
Serrana or I.s of Perls
Mesquitos
I.s of Perles
I. S.t Catharine or Providence
Roncador
Escudo de Veragua
PANAMA
Porto bel
Gulf of Darien

C.Coquibacoa
C.Vela
Rio de la Hacha
la Rancha
S. Martha
Maracaibo
Carthagena
Madre de Popa
Zenu
Teneriffe
los Reyes
Tamalamegue

PART
SOUTH A

EUROPEANS COLONIZE NORTH AMERICA 1600–1640

*C*aptain William Rudyerd seemed like the sort of man any Puritan colony in the Americas would prize, so when his older brother urged the planners of the new settlement to appoint him muster master general, they readily agreed. Rudyerd, a veteran of wars on the European continent, followed the new dissenting English faith, as did the planners and many of the settlers. In the first years of the colony, Rudyerd proved to be a vigorous soldier who worked hard to train the settlers to defend themselves from attack. But he also proved to be a vigorous defender of his own status, and his actions wreaked havoc in the fragile community. The captain beat to death a servant suffering from scurvy (Rudyerd thought the servant was merely lazy), and he also quarreled continually with other settlers, whom he believed failed to show the proper respect to a gentleman of noble birth.

One of Rudyerd's antagonists was the Reverend Lewis Morgan, with whom the captain argued about religious books and the conduct of church services. Rudyerd, traditional minded despite his Puritan beliefs, found Morgan's encouragement of congregational psalm singing scandalously radical. The disagreements quickly escalated into exchanges of insults. "Your foul mouthed answer deserves rather sharp retribution than any equal respect from A gentleman," the captain once haughtily told the clergyman; "I have given you too Much respect; which has begot so much incivility."

Similar conflicts occurred in all the Anglo-American settlements, as gentlemen accustomed to unquestioning deference from their inferiors learned to their dismay that in a colonial setting their inherited social standing could be challenged by upstarts of various descriptions. But in Rudyerd and Morgan's colony the disputes were especially dangerous, because the two lived on Providence Island, an isolated Puritan outpost off the coast of modern Nicaragua.

◀ This early eighteenth-century British map of the Caribbean and Central America vividly illustrates the precarious position of the seventeenth-century Providence Island settlers, on their tiny island surrounded by Spanish territory on the mainland to the east, south, and west, and the Spanish-dominated Greater Antilles to the north. (Colonial Williamsburg Foundation)

CHRONOLOGY

1533 • Henry VIII divorces Catherine of Aragón
• English Reformation begins

1558 • Elizabeth I becomes queen

1565 • Founding of St. Augustine (Florida), oldest permanent European settlement in present-day United States

1598 • Oñate conquers Pueblos in New Mexico for Spain

1603 • James I becomes king

1607 • Jamestown founded, first permanent English settlement in North America

1608 • Quebec founded by the French

1610 • Founding of Santa Fe, New Mexico

1611 • First Virginia tobacco crop

1614 • Fort Orange (Albany) founded by the Dutch

1619 • Virginia House of Burgesses established, first representative assembly in the English colonies

1620 • Plymouth colony founded, first permanent English settlement in New England

1622 • Powhatan Confederacy attacks Virginia

1624 • Dutch settle on Manhattan Island (New Amsterdam)
• English colonize St. Kitts, first island in Lesser Antilles to be settled by Europeans
• James I revokes Virginia Company's charter

1625 • Charles I becomes king

1630 • Massachusetts Bay colony founded

1634 • Maryland founded

1636 • Williams expelled from Massachusetts Bay, founds Providence, Rhode Island
• Connecticut founded

1637 • Pequot War in New England

1638 • Hutchinson expelled from Massachusetts Bay, goes to Rhode Island

c. 1640 • Sugar cultivation begins on Barbados

1642 • Montreal founded by the French

1646 • Treaty ends hostilities between Virginia and Powhatan Confederacy

Providence Island, founded by a company of Puritan adventurers in 1630—the same year as the Massachusetts Bay colony—sought to establish an English beachhead in the fertile tropics that could lead to successful colonization of the Central American mainland. Yet the outpost's perilous location amid Spanish settlements, its failure to establish a viable local economy, and, ultimately, its desperate attempts to stay afloat financially by serving as a base for English privateers caused its downfall. That decision led the Spaniards to conclude that the Puritans *had* to be removed. Twice, in 1635 and 1640, Providence Island fended off Spanish attacks. But in May 1641 a large Spanish fleet of seven ships carrying two thousand soldiers and sailors captured the island, and the English survivors scattered to other Caribbean settlements or returned to England.

By this time, though, Spain no longer predominated in the Americas. France, the Netherlands, and England all had permanent colonies in North America by the 1640s. The French and Dutch colonies, like the Spanish outposts, were settled largely by European men who interacted regularly with indigenous peoples, using their labor or seeking to convert them to Christianity. Like the conquistadors, French and Dutch merchants (on the mainland) and planters (in the Caribbean) hoped to make a quick profit and then perhaps return to their homelands. The English, as Thomas Harriot made clear in the 1580s, were just as interested in profiting from North America. But they pursued those profits in a different way.

In contrast to other Europeans, most of the English settlers—including those of the failed Providence Island colony—came to America intending to stay. Especially along the northeast Atlantic coast of the continent, in the area that came to be known as New England, they arrived in family groups, sometimes along with friends and relatives from neighboring villages back home. They recreated European society and family life to an extent not possible in the other colonies, where migrant men found their sexual partners within the Indian or African populations. Among the English colonies, those in the Chesapeake region and on the Caribbean islands most closely resembled colonies founded by other nations. Their economies, like those of Hispaniola or Brazil, soon came to be based on large-scale agricultural production for the international market by a labor force composed of bonded servants and slaves.

Wherever they settled, the English, like other Europeans, prospered only after they learned to adapt to the alien environment, something the Providence Islanders never achieved. The first permanent English colonies survived because nearby Indians assisted the newcomers. The settlers had to learn to grow unfamiliar American crops such as maize and tobacco. They also had to develop extensive trading relationships with native peoples and with colonies established by other European countries. Needing laborers for their fields, they first used English indentured servants, then later began to import African slaves, copying the example of the Spanish in the Atlantic and Caribbean islands, and the Portuguese in São Tomé and Brazil. Thus the early history of the region that became the United States and the English Caribbean is best understood not as an isolated story of English colonization but rather as a series of complex interactions among a variety of European, African, and American peoples and environments. ■

■ The women of Acoma pueblo have long been accomplished potters. Before the arrival of Europeans with iron utensils, residents of the pueblo stored food and water in pots like this. The unusual shape derived from its function: the low center of gravity allowed a woman to balance the pot easily on her head as she carried water from a cistern to the top of the mesa. (The Field Museum, #A109998c)

New Spain, New France, and New Netherland

Spaniards established the first permanent European settlement within the boundaries of the modern United States, but others initially attempted that feat. Twice in the 1560s groups of French Protestants (Huguenots) sought to escape persecution in their homeland by planting colonies on the south Atlantic coast. A passing ship rescued the starving survivors of the first, located in present-day South Carolina. The second, near modern Jacksonville, Florida, was destroyed in 1565 by a Spanish expedition under the command of Pedro Menéndez de Avilés. To ensure Spanish domination of the strategically important region (located near sea-lanes used by Spanish treasure ships bound for Europe), Menéndez set up a small fortified outpost, which he named St. Augustine—now the oldest continuously inhabited European settlement in the United States. Franciscan missionaries soon followed, but nearby Indians fiercely resisted the friars' efforts to Christianize them. Only after the native peoples were forcibly moved to mission towns did many assent to baptism. Even so, by the end of the sixteenth century a chain of Franciscan missions stretched westward across Florida and northward into the islands along the Atlantic coast.

More than thirty years passed after the founding of St. Augustine before conquistadors ventured anew into the present-day United States. In 1598, drawn northward by rumors of rich cities, Juan de Oñate, a Mexican-born adventurer, led a group of about five hundred soldiers and settlers to New Mexico. At first, the Pueblos greeted the newcomers cordially. When the Spaniards began to use torture, murder, and rape to extort food and clothing from the villagers, however, the residents of Acoma killed several soldiers. The invaders responded ferociously, killing more than eight hundred people and capturing the remainder. All the captives above the age of twelve were ordered enslaved for twenty years, and men older than twenty-five had one foot amputated. Not surprisingly, the other Pueblo villages surrendered.

Yet Oñate's bloody victory proved illusory, for New Mexico held little wealth. It also was too far from the Pacific coast to assist in protecting Spanish sea-lanes, which had been one of Oñate's aims (he, like others, initially believed the continent to be much narrower than it actually

NEW MEXICO

is). Many of the Spaniards returned to Mexico, and officials considered abandoning the isolated colony, which lay 800 miles north of the nearest Spanish settlement. Instead, in 1609, the authorities decided to maintain a small military outpost and a few Christian missions in the area, with the capital at Santa Fe (founded in 1610) (see Map 3.3). As in regions to the south, Spanish leaders were granted *encomiendas* guaranteeing them control over the labor of Pueblo villagers. But in the absence of mines or fertile agricultural lands, such grants yielded small profit.

On the Atlantic coast, the French turned their attention northward, to the area that Jacques Cartier had explored in the 1530s. Several times they

QUEBEC AND MONTREAL

tried to establish permanent bases along the Canadian coast but did not succeed until 1605, with the founding of Port Royal. Then in 1608 Samuel de Champlain set up a trading post at an interior site the local Iroquois had called Stadacona when Cartier spent the winter there seventy-five years earlier. Champlain renamed it Quebec. He had chosen well: Quebec was the most easily defended spot in the entire St. Lawrence River valley, a stronghold that controlled access to the heartland of the continent. In 1642 the French established a second post, Montreal, at the falls of the St. Lawrence (and thus at the end of navigation by oceangoing vessels), a place the Indians called Hochelaga.

Before the founding of these settlements, fishermen served as the major transporters of North American beaver pelts to France, but the new posts quickly took over control of the lucrative trade in furs (see Table 2.1). Only a few Europeans resided in New France; most were men, some of whom married Indian women. The colony's leaders gave land grants along the river to wealthy seigneurs (nobles), who then imported tenants to work their farms. A small number of Frenchmen brought their wives and took up agriculture; even so, more than twenty-five years after Quebec's founding, it had just sixty-four resident families, along with traders and soldiers. With respect to territory occupied and farmed, northern New France never grew much beyond the confines of the river valley between Quebec and Montreal (see Map 2.1). Thus it differed significantly from New Spain, where Europeans resided in widely scattered locations and Spanish men sometimes directly supervised Indian laborers.

Missionaries of the Society of Jesus (Jesuits), a Roman Catholic order dedicated to converting nonbelievers

JESUIT MISSIONS IN NEW FRANCE

to Christianity, also came to New France. First arriving in Quebec in 1625, the Jesuits, whom the Indians called Black Robes, tried to persuade indigenous peoples to live near French settlements and to adopt European agricultural methods. When that effort failed, the Jesuits concluded that they could introduce Catholicism to their new charges without insisting that they fundamentally alter their traditional ways of life. Accordingly, the Black Robes learned Indian languages and traveled to remote regions of the interior, where they lived in twos and threes among hundreds of potential converts.

TABLE 2.1			
The Founding of Permanent European Colonies in North America, 1565–1640			
Colony	**Founder(s)**	**Date**	**Basis of Economy**
Florida	Pedro Menéndez de Avilés	1565	Farming
New Mexico	Juan de Oñate	1598	Livestock
Virginia	Virginia Company	1607	Tobacco
New France	France	1608	Fur trading
New Netherland	Dutch West India Co.	1614	Fur trading
Plymouth	Separatists	1620	Farming, fishing
Maine	Sir Ferdinando Gorges	1622	Fishing
St. Kitts, Barbados, et al.	European immigrants	1624	Sugar
Massachusetts Bay	Massachusetts Bay Company	1630	Farming, fishing, fur trading
Maryland	Cecilius Calvert	1634	Tobacco
Rhode Island	Roger Williams	1636	Farming
Connecticut	Thomas Hooker	1636	Farming, fur trading
New Haven	Massachusetts migrants	1638	Farming
New Hampshire	Massachusetts migrants	1638	Farming, fishing

Map 2.1 **European Settlements and Indian Tribes in Eastern North America, 1650**

The few European settlements established in the east before 1650 were widely scattered, hugging the shores of the Atlantic Ocean and the banks of its major rivers. By contrast, America's native inhabitants controlled the vast interior expanse of the continent and Spaniards had begun to move into the West.

Using a variety of strategies, Jesuits sought to undermine the authority of village shamans (the traditional religious leaders) and to gain the confidence of leaders who could influence others. Trained in rhetoric, they won admirers by their eloquence. Immune to smallpox (for all had survived the disease already), they explained epidemics among the Indians as God's punishment for sin, their arguments aided by the ineffectiveness of the shamans' traditional remedies against the new pestilence. Drawing on European science, Jesuits predicted solar and lunar eclipses. Perhaps most important, they amazed the villagers by communicating with each other over long distances through marks on paper. The Indians' desire to learn how to harness the extraordinary power of literacy was one of the critical factors making them receptive to the missionaries' spiritual message.

Although the process took many years, the Jesuits slowly gained thousands of converts, some of whom moved to reserves set aside for Christian Indians. In those communities they followed Catholic teachings with fervor and piety. The converts replaced their own culture's traditional equal treatment of men and women with notions more congenial to the Europeans' insistence on male dominance and female subordination. Further, they altered their practice of allowing premarital sexual relationships and easy divorce because Catholic doctrine prohibited both customs.

Jesuit missionaries faced little competition from other Europeans for native peoples' souls, but French fur traders had to confront a direct challenge. In 1614, only five years after Henry Hudson explored the river that now bears his name, his sponsor, the Dutch West India Company, established an outpost (Fort Orange) on that river at the site of present-day Albany, New York. Like the French, the Dutch sought beaver pelts, and their presence so close to Quebec posed a threat to French domination of the region. The Netherlands, at the time the world's dominant commercial power, aimed primarily at trade rather than colonization. Thus New Netherland, like New France, remained small, largely confined to a river valley that offered easy access to its settlements. The colony's southern anchor was New Amsterdam, a town founded in 1624 on Manhattan Island, at the mouth of the Hudson River.

New Netherland

As the Dutch West India Company's colony in North America, New Netherland was an unimportant part of a vast commercial empire that included posts in Africa, Brazil, the West Indies, and modern-day Indonesia. Autocratic directors-general ruled the colony for the company; with no elected assembly, settlers felt little loyalty to their nominal leaders. Few migrants arrived. Even a company policy of 1629 offering a large land grant, or patroonship, to anyone who would bring fifty settlers to the province failed to attract takers. (Only one such tract—Rensselaerswyck, near Albany—was ever fully developed.) As late as the mid-1660s, New Netherland had only about five thousand inhabitants. Some were Swedes and Finns who resided in the former colony of New Sweden (founded in 1638 on the Delaware River; see Map 2.1), which was taken over by the Dutch in 1655.

The American Indian allies of New France and New Netherland clashed with each other in part because of fur-trade rivalries. In the 1640s, the Iroquois, who traded chiefly with the Dutch and lived in modern upstate New York, went to war against the Hurons, who traded primarily with the French and lived in present-day Ontario. The Iroquois wanted to become the major supplier of pelts to Europeans and to ensure the security of their hunting territories. They achieved both goals by using guns supplied by the Dutch to virtually exterminate the Hurons, whose population had already been decimated by a smallpox epidemic. The Iroquois thus established themselves as a major force in the region, one that Europeans could ignore only at their peril. And the European demand for beaver pelts had proved to have a disastrous effect on native communities and their interactions.

The Caribbean

In the Caribbean, France, the Netherlands, and England fought openly in the first half of the seventeenth century. The Spanish concentrated their colonization efforts on the Greater Antilles—Cuba, Hispaniola, Jamaica, and Puerto Rico. They left many smaller islands alone, partly because of resistance by their Carib inhabitants, partly because the mainland offered greater wealth for less effort. But the tiny islands attracted other European powers: they could provide bases from which to attack Spanish vessels loaded with American gold and silver, and they could serve as sources of valuable tropical products such as spices, dyes, and fruits.

England was the first northern European nation to establish a permanent foothold in the smaller West Indian islands (the Lesser Antilles). English people settled on St. Christopher (St. Kitts) in 1624, then later on other islands such as Barbados (1627) and Providence (1630). France was able to colonize Guadeloupe and Martinique only by defeating the Caribs, whereas the Dutch more easily gained control of tiny St. Eustatius (strategically located near St. Kitts). In addition to indigenous inhabitants, Europeans had to worry about conflicts with

Wampum

When Europeans first came to North America, they quickly learned that native peoples highly valued small cylindrical beads made from whelk and quahog shells, known collectively as wampum. The white and purple beads had been strung on fibers for centuries to make necklaces and ornamental belts, but with the Europeans' arrival wampum changed its character, becoming a currency widely employed by both groups.

The transformation of wampum occurred not only because the Indians prized it and would trade deerskins and beaver pelts to acquire the beads, but also because Dutch and English settlers lacked an equally handy medium of exchange. These settlers had limited access to coins and currency from their homelands, yet they needed to do business with each other and with their native neighbors. Wampum filled a key need, especially in the first decades of settlement.

Whelk (white) and quahog (purple) shells were found primarily along the shores of Long Island Sound. Narragansetts, Montauks, Niantics, and other local peoples had long gathered the shells during the summers; women then fashioned the beads during the long northeastern winters. The shells were hard and brittle, so shaping them into hollow beads was a time-consuming task involving considerable skill. But Europeans' metal tools, including fine drills, allowed a rapid increase in the quantity and quality of wampum. Some villages gave up their hunter-gatherer modes of subsistence and settled permanently in shell-rich areas where they focused almost exclusively on the manufacture of wampum. What had been a seasonal task for women became their year-round work.

Wampum played a key role in the early economy of both New Netherland and New England. Dutch settlers in Manhattan traded such manufactured goods as guns and kettles, axes, or knives with the wampum makers, then transported wampum up the Hudson River to Fort Orange, where they used it to purchase furs and skins from the Iroquois. In 1627, Isaac de Rasière, a Dutch trader, introduced wampum to the English colonists at Plymouth when he offered it in exchange for corn. Ten years later, the Massachusetts Bay colony made wampum legal tender for the payment of debts under 12 pennies, at a rate of six white beads or three purple beads (which were rarer) to 1 penny. Wampum beads could be traded in loose handfuls but more often were strung on thin cords in set amounts worth English equivalents ranging from 1 penny to 5 shillings (60 pennies) in white beads, or 2 pennies to 10 shillings (120 pennies) in purple beads. People trading larger sums measured in wampum always feared being short-changed. In 1660, one resident of New Netherland agreed to accept payment of a substantial debt in wampum only if his wife *personally* counted all the beads.

Wampum—originally with purely ornamental significance for its Indian makers—became an initial, indispensable link in the commerce between Europe and North America.

Before Europeans arrived in North America, wampum—requiring great skill to make—served primarily ceremonial purposes for native peoples, as in the "Four Huron Nations" wampum belt presented to Samuel de Champlain in 1611 to signify the alliance of France and the Hurons. But several decades later, after Dutch and English colonists came to rely on it as a medium of exchange and European tools made it easier to manufacture, wampum became far more utilitarian in design and appearance. (Left: American Museum of Natural History, photographed by Craig Chesek; right: Musee de L'Homme)

Spaniards and with one another. Like Providence Island, many colonies changed hands during the seventeenth century. For example, the English drove the Spanish out of Jamaica in 1655, and the French soon thereafter took over half of Hispaniola, creating the colony of St. Domingue (modern Haiti).

Why did other Europeans devote so much energy to gaining control of the small volcanic islands neglected by

SUGAR CULTIVATION

Spain? The primary answer to that question is sugar. Europeans loved sugar, which provided its users with both a sweet taste and a quick energy boost. Entering the European market in substantial quantities at approximately the same time as coffee and tea—the stimulating, addictive, and bitter Asian drinks improved by the addition of a sweetener—sugar quickly became a crucial element of the European diet.

Early in the 1640s, English residents of Barbados, who had already experimented unsuccessfully with growing tobacco, cotton, and indigo, discovered that the island's soil and climate were ideally suited for cultivat-

ing sugar cane. At the time, the world's supply of sugar came primarily from the Wine Islands, São Tomé, and especially Brazil, where numerous farmers, each with a few servants or slaves, grew much of the crop. Small Brazilian producers took their cane to central mills, where it was refined into brown and white sugars in the most technologically sophisticated enterprise of the day. To pay for processing, they turned a large proportion of their crop over to the mill owners, themselves wealthier planters who lacked the ability to coordinate the actions of the independent farmers. This production method was highly inefficient.

That changed in Barbados. Between 1630 and 1654 the Dutch took control of northeastern Brazil, where they learned Portuguese techniques for growing the canes and, more important, for processing the crop. Dutch merchants taught those skills to Barbadians, expecting to sell them African slaves and to transport barrels of sugar products to Europe. The results must have exceeded their wildest dreams. The Barbados sugar boom that began in the 1640s was both explosive and

■ In the 1660s, a French book illustrated the various phases of sugar processing for curious European readers. Teams of oxen (A) turned the mill, the rollers of which crushed the canes (C), producing the sap (D), which was collected in a vat (E), then boiled down into molasses (K). African slaves, with minimal supervision by a few Europeans (foreground), managed all phases of the process.   (Library Company of Philadelphia)

lucrative, as planters there increased the size of their landholdings, adopted large-scale gang labor by bondspeople, and built their own sugar mills that could operate with great efficiency. Planters, slave traders, and Dutch shipping interests alike earned immense profits from introducing economies of scale into the production of sugar.

As other Caribbean planters embraced sugar-cane cultivation, Barbadians' profit margins were reduced. Even so, sugar remained the most valuable American commodity for more than one hundred years. In the eighteenth century, sugar grown by large gangs of slaves in British Jamaica and French St. Domingue dominated the world market. Yet, in the long run, the future economic importance of the Europeans' American colonies lay on the mainland rather than in the Caribbean.

English Interest in Colonization

The failure of Raleigh's Roanoke colony ended English efforts to settle in North America for nearly two decades. When the English decided in 1606 to try once more, they again planned colonies that imitated the Spanish model. Yet greater success came when they abandoned that model and founded settlements very different from those of other European powers. Unlike Spain, France, or the Netherlands, England eventually sent large numbers of men and women to set up agriculturally based colonies on the mainland. Two major developments prompted approximately 200,000 ordinary English men and women to move to North America in the seventeenth century and led their government to encourage their emigration.

The onset of dramatic social and economic change stimulated many English folk to move to North America. *SOCIAL CHANGE IN ENGLAND* In the 150-year period after 1530, largely as a result of the introduction of nutritious American crops, England's population doubled. All those additional people needed food, clothing, and other goods. The competition for goods led to high inflation, coupled with a fall in real wages as the number of workers increased. In these new economic and demographic circumstances, some English people—especially those with sizable landholdings that could produce food and clothing fibers for the growing population—substantially improved their lot. Others, particularly landless laborers and those with very small amounts of land, fell into unremitting poverty. When landowners raised rents, took over common lands previously open to use by peasants, or decided to combine small holdings into large units,

they forced tenants off the land. Consequently, geographical as well as social mobility increased, and the population of the cities swelled. London, for example, more than tripled in size by 1650, when 375,000 residents lived in its crowded buildings.

Wealthy English people reacted with alarm to what they saw as the disappearance of traditional ways of life. Steady streams of the landless and homeless filled the streets and highways. Obsessed with the problem of maintaining order, officials came to believe that England was overcrowded. They concluded that colonies established in North America could siphon off England's "surplus population," thus easing social strains at home. For similar reasons, many English people decided that they could improve their circumstances by migrating from a small, land-scarce, apparently overpopulated island to a large, land-rich, apparently empty continent and its nearby islands. Among those attracted by prospects for emigration were such younger sons of gentlemen as William Rudyerd, who were excluded from inheriting land by wealthy families' practice of primogeniture, which reserved all real estate for the eldest son. Such economic considerations were rendered even more significant in light of the second development, a major change in English religious practice.

The sixteenth century witnessed a religious transformation that eventually led large numbers of English dissenters to leave their homeland. In *ENGLISH REFORMATION* 1533 Henry VIII, wanting a male heir and infatuated with Anne Boleyn, sought to annul his marriage to his Spanish-born queen, Catherine of Aragón, despite nearly twenty years of marriage and the birth of a daughter. When the pope refused to approve the annulment, Henry left the Roman Catholic Church. He founded the Church of England and—with Parliament's concurrence—proclaimed himself its head. In general, English people welcomed the schism, for many had little respect for the English Catholic Church. At first the reformed Church of England differed little from Catholicism in its practices, but under Henry's daughter Elizabeth I (child of his later marriage to Anne Boleyn), new currents of religious belief that had originated on the European continent early in the sixteenth century dramatically affected the English church.

These currents were the Protestant Reformation, led by Martin Luther, a German monk, and John Calvin, a French cleric and lawyer. Challenging the Catholic doctrine that priests were intermediaries between laypeople and God, Luther and Calvin insisted that people could interpret the Bible for themselves. That notion stimulated the spread of literacy: to understand and interpret

■ London in 1616, with London Bridge at center right. Overcrowding in the city led many observers to conclude that American colonization could remove "excess" population and provide new employment for poverty-stricken persons. The rapidly growing community of London merchants also sought to develop new sources of overseas profits.   (Trustees of the British Library)

the Bible, people had to learn how to read. Both Luther and Calvin rejected Catholic rituals, denying the need for an elaborate church hierarchy. They also asserted that faith in God was the key to salvation, rather than—as Catholic teaching had it—a combination of faith and good works. Calvin went further than Luther, stressing God's omnipotence and emphasizing the need for people to submit totally to God's will.

Elizabeth I tolerated diverse forms of Christianity as long as her subjects acknowledged her authority as head of the Church of England. During her long reign (1558–1603) Calvin's ideas gained influence within the English church, and some Catholics continued to practice their faith in private. By the late sixteenth century, many English Calvinists—those who came to be called Puritans because they wanted to purify the Church of England or Separatists because they wanted to leave it entirely—believed that the English Reformation had not gone far enough. Henry had simplified the church hierarchy; they wanted to abolish it altogether. Henry had subordinated the church to the interests of the state; they wanted a church free from political interference. And the

PURITANS AND SEPARATISTS

Church of England, like the Catholic Church, continued to include all English people in its membership. Puritans and Separatists preferred a more restricted definition; they wanted to confine church membership to persons they believed to be "saved"—those God had selected for salvation before birth.

Paradoxically, though, a key article of their faith insisted that people could not know for certain if they were "saved" because mere mortals could not comprehend or affect their predestination to heaven or hell. Thus pious Puritans and Separatists daily confronted serious dilemmas: If the saved (or "elect") could not be identified with certainty, how could proper churches be constituted? If one was predestined and could not alter one's fate, why should one attend church or do good works? Puritans and Separatists dealt with the first dilemma by admitting that their judgments as to eligibility for church membership only approximated God's unknowable decisions. And they resolved the second by reasoning that God gave the elect the ability to accept salvation and to lead a good life. Therefore, even though one could not earn a place in heaven by piety and good works, such practices could indicate one's place in the ranks of the saved.

TABLE 2.2

Tudor and Stuart Monarchs of England, 1509–1649

Monarch	Reign	Relation to Predecessor
Henry VIII	1509–1547	Son
Edward VI	1547–1553	Son
Mary I	1553–1558	Half-sister
Elizabeth I	1558–1603	Half-sister
James I	1603–1625	Cousin
Charles I	1625–1649	Son

Elizabeth I's Stuart successors, her cousin James I (1603–1625) and his son Charles I (1625–1649), exhibited less tolerance for Puritans and Separatists. As Scots, they also had little respect for the traditions of representative government that had developed in England under the Tudors and their predecessors (see Table 2.2). The wealthy landowners who sat in Parliament had grown accustomed to having considerable influence on government policies, especially taxation. But James I, taking a position later endorsed by his son, publicly declared his belief in the divine right of kings. The Stuarts insisted that a monarch's power came directly from God and that his subjects had a duty to obey him. They likened the king's absolute authority to a father's authority over his children.

THE STUART MONARCHS

Both James I and Charles I believed that their authority included the power to enforce religious conformity. Because Puritans and Separatists—and the remaining English Catholics—challenged many of the most important precepts of the English church, the Stuart monarchs authorized the removal of dissenting clergymen from their pulpits. In the 1620s and 1630s some English Puritans, Separatists, and Catholics decided to move to America, where they hoped to put their religious beliefs into practice unhindered by the Stuarts or the church hierarchy. Some fled hurriedly to avoid arrest and imprisonment.

In contrast to the migrations to New Spain and New France, which were largely funded by their governments, many of the dissenters and other English people who migrated to North America and the Caribbean were financed by joint-stock companies. Stock sales funded these forerunners of modern corporations, which had been developed decades earlier as a mechanism for pooling the resources of many small investors in trading voyages. They worked well for that purpose: no

JOINT-STOCK COMPANIES

one risked too much money, and investors usually received quick returns. But joint-stock companies turned out to be a poor way to finance colonies because the early settlements required enormous amounts of capital and, with rare exceptions, failed to return much immediate profit. Colonies founded by such companies consequently suffered from a chronic lack of capital and from constant tension between stockholders and colonists, who claimed they were not being adequately supported by the investors.

The Founding of Virginia

The initial impulse that led to England's first permanent colony in the Western Hemisphere came from a group of merchants and wealthy gentry. In 1606, envisioning the possibility of earning great profits by finding precious metals and opening new trade routes, the men established the Virginia Company and obtained a charter from King James I. A settlement they financed in present-day Maine soon collapsed, but a second enterprise was more successful.

In 1607 the company dispatched 104 men and boys to a region near Chesapeake Bay called Tsenacomoco by its native inhabitants. There they established the palisaded settlement called Jamestown on a swampy peninsula in a river they also named for their monarch. They quickly constructed small houses and a Church of England chapel. Ill equipped for survival in the unfamiliar environment, the colonists were afflicted by dissension and disease. Moreover, through sheer bad luck they arrived in the midst of a severe drought (now known to be the worst in the region for 1,700 years), which persisted until 1612. The lack of rainfall not only made it difficult to cultivate crops but also polluted their drinking water.

JAMESTOWN

By January 1608, only thirty-eight of the original colonists remained alive. Many of the first immigrants were gentlemen unaccustomed to working with their hands and soldiers who had fought against Spain in the Netherlands. They resisted hard labor, attempted to maintain traditional social hierarchies, and retained elaborate English dress and casual work habits despite their desperate circumstances. Such attitudes, combined with the effects of chronic malnutrition and epidemic disease, took a terrible toll. Only when Captain John Smith, one of the colony's lower-status founders, imposed military discipline on the still-resistant colonists in 1608 was Jamestown saved from collapse. But after Smith's departure the settlement experienced a severe "starving time" (the winter of 1609–1610), during which at least one colonist resorted to cannibalism. Although more settlers (including a few women and children) arrived in 1608 and 1609 and living conditions slowly improved, as late as 1624 only 1,300 of approximately 8,000 English immigrants to Virginia remained alive.

Jamestown owed its survival to the Indians of Tsenacomoco, a group of six Algonquian villages known as the Powhatan Confederacy (see Map 2.1).

POWHATAN CONFEDERACY A shrewd and powerful leader, Powhatan was aggressively consolidating his authority over some twenty-five smaller bands when the Europeans arrived. Fortunately for the colonists, Powhatan at first viewed them as potential allies. He found the English colony a reliable source of useful items such as knives and guns, which gave him a technological advantage over his Indian neighbors. In return, Powhatan's people traded their excess corn and other foodstuffs to the starving settlers. But the initially cordial relationship soon deteriorated. The Indians' crops failed during the drought, and they no longer had surpluses to exchange, though the English suspected duplicity. English colonists kidnapped Powhatan's daughter, Pocahontas, holding her as a hostage. In captivity, she agreed in 1614 to marry a colonist, John Rolfe, perhaps as a form of diplomatic alliance. She sailed with him to England, where she died in 1616 after bearing a son.

The Jamestown colony and the coastal Indians had an uneasy relationship. English and Algonquian peoples had much in common: deep religious beliefs, a lifestyle oriented around agriculture, clear political and social hierarchies, and sharply defined gender roles. Yet the English and the Powhatans themselves focused on their cultural differences, not their similarities. English men regarded Indian men as lazy because they did not cultivate crops and spent much of their time hunting (a sport, not work, in English eyes). Indian men thought English men effeminate because they did "women's work" of cultivation. In the same vein, the English believed that Algonquian women were oppressed because they did heavy field labor.

ALGONQUIAN AND ENGLISH CULTURAL DIFFERENCES

Other differences between the two cultures caused serious misunderstandings. Although both societies were hierarchical, the nature of the hierarchies differed considerably. Among East Coast Algonquians, political power and social status were not necessarily passed down through the male line. Members of the English gentry inherited their position from their fathers, and English political and military leaders tended to rule autocratically. By contrast, the authority of Algonquian leaders rested on consensus. Accustomed to the European concept of powerful kings, the English sought such figures in native villages. Often (for example, when negotiating treaties) they willfully overestimated the ability of chiefs to make independent decisions for their people.

Furthermore, Algonquians and English had very different notions of property ownership. Most Algonquian villages held their land communally. It could not be bought or sold absolutely, although certain rights to use the land (for example, for hunting or fishing) could be transferred. Many English people, in contrast, were accustomed to individual farms and to buying and selling land. The English also refused to accept the validity of Indians' claims to traditional hunting territories, insisting that only land intensively cultivated could be regarded as owned or occupied. As one colonist put it, "salvadge peoples" who "rambled" over a region without farming it could claim no "title or propertye" in the land. Ownership of such "unclaimed" property, the English believed, lay with the English monarchy, in whose name John Cabot had laid claim to North America in 1497.

Above all, the English settlers believed unwaveringly in the superiority of their civilization. Although in the early years of colonization they often anticipated living peacefully alongside Native Americans, they always assumed that they would dictate the terms of such coexistence. Like Thomas Harriot at Roanoke, they expected native peoples to adopt English customs and to convert to Christianity. They showed little respect for traditional Indian ways of life, especially when they believed their own interests were at stake. The Virginia colony's treatment of the Powhatan Confederacy in subsequent years clearly revealed that attitude.

The spread of tobacco cultivation upset the balance of power in early Virginia. In tobacco—the American crop previously introduced to Europe by the Spanish—the settlers and the Virginia Company found the salable commodity for which they had been searching. John Rolfe planted the first crop in 1611. Nine years later Virginians exported 40,000 pounds of cured leaves, and by the late 1620s shipments had jumped dramatically to 1.5 million pounds. The great tobacco boom had begun, fueled by high prices and substantial profits for planters as they responded to escalating demand from Europe and Africa. The price later fell almost as sharply as it had risen, fluctuating wildly from year to year in response to increasing supply and international competition. Nevertheless, tobacco made Virginia prosper, and the colony developed from a small outpost peopled exclusively by males into an agricultural settlement inhabited by both men and women.

TOBACCO CULTIVATION

■ A comparison of the portrait of Sir Walter Raleigh and his son (left), with that of an Algonquian Indian drawn by John White, from Raleigh's Roanoke expedition (right), shows a dramatic difference in standard dress styles that, for many, must have symbolized the apparent cultural gap between Europeans and Americans. Yet the fact that both men (and the young boy) were portrayed in similar stances, with "arms akimbo," demonstrated that all were high status individuals. In Europe, only aristocrats were represented in such an aggressive pose. ([Left] National Portrait Gallery, London; [right] Trustees of the British Museum)

Successful tobacco cultivation required abundant land, since the crop quickly drained soil of nutrients. Farmers soon learned that a field could produce only about three satisfactory crops before it had to lie fallow for several years to regain its fertility. Thus the once-small English settlements began to expand rapidly: eager applicants asked the Virginia Company for large land grants on both sides of the James River and its tributary streams. Lulled into a false sense of security by years of peace, Virginians established farms at some distance from one another along the riverbanks—a settlement pattern convenient for tobacco cultivation but dangerous for defense.

To attract more settlers to the colony, the Virginia Company in 1617 developed the "headright" system.

VIRGINIA COMPANY POLICIES Every new arrival paying his or her own way was promised a land grant of 50 acres; those who financed the passage of others received similar headrights for each person. To ordinary English farmers, many of whom owned little or no land, the headright system offered a powerful incentive to move to Virginia. To wealthy gentry, it promised even

more: the possibility of establishing vast agricultural enterprises worked by large numbers of laborers. Two years later, the company introduced a second reform, authorizing the landowning men of the major Virginia settlements to elect representatives to an assembly called the House of Burgesses. English landholders had long been accustomed to electing members of Parliament and controlling their own local governments; therefore, they expected the same privilege in the nation's colonies.

Opechancanough, Powhatan's brother and successor, watched the English colonists steadily encroaching on the confederacy's lands and attempting to convert its members to Christianity. Recognizing the danger his brother had overlooked, the war leader launched coordinated attacks all along the James River on March 22, 1622. By the end of the day, 347 colonists (about one-quarter of the total) lay dead, and only a timely warning from two Christian converts saved Jamestown itself from destruction.

INDIAN UPRISINGS

Virginia reeled from the blow but did not collapse. Reinforced by new shipments of men and arms from

England, the settlers attacked Opechancanough's villages. For some years an uneasy peace prevailed, but then in April 1644 Opechancanough tried one last time to repel the invaders. He failed, losing his life in the war that ensued. In 1646, survivors of the Powhatan Confederacy accepted a treaty formally subordinating them to English authority. Although they continued to live in the region, their alliance crumbled and their efforts to resist the spread of European settlement ended.

The 1622 Powhatan uprising that failed to destroy the colony succeeded in killing its parent. The Virginia Company never made any profits from the enterprise, for internal corruption and the heavy cost of supporting the settlers offset all its earnings. In 1624 James I revoked the charter, transforming Virginia into a royal colony ruled by officials he appointed. James continued the headright policy the company had adopted. Because he distrusted legislative bodies, though, James at first abolished the assembly. But Virginians protested so vigorously that by 1629 the House of Burgesses was functioning once again. Only two decades after the first permanent English settlement was planted in North America, the colonists successfully insisted on governing themselves at the local level. Thus the political structure of England's American possessions came to differ from that of New Spain, New France, and New Netherland, all of which were ruled autocratically.

Life in the Chesapeake

By the 1630s, tobacco was firmly established as the staple crop and chief source of revenue in Virginia. It quickly became just as important in the second English colony planted on Chesapeake Bay: Maryland, given by Charles I to George Calvert, first Lord Baltimore, as a personal possession (proprietorship), which was settled in 1634. (Because Virginia and Maryland both border Chesapeake Bay—see Map 2.1—they are often referred to collectively as "the Chesapeake.") Members of the Calvert family intended the colony to serve as a haven for their persecuted fellow Catholics. Cecilius Calvert, second Lord Baltimore, became the first colonizer to offer freedom of religion to all Christian settlers; he understood that protecting the Protestant majority could also ensure Catholics' rights. (The policy was codified in Maryland's Act of Religious Toleration in 1649.)

In everything but religion the two Chesapeake colonies resembled each other. In Maryland as in Virginia, tobacco planters spread out along the riverbanks, establishing isolated farms instead of towns. The region's deep, wide rivers offered dependable water transportation in an age of few and inadequate roads. Each farm or group of farms had its own wharf, where oceangoing vessels could take on or discharge cargo. Consequently, Virginia and Maryland had few towns, for their residents did not need commercial centers in order to buy and sell goods.

The planting, cultivation, and harvesting of tobacco were repetitive, time-consuming, and labor-intensive tasks. Clearing land for new fields, necessary every few years, demanded heavy labor, and undesirable shoots had to be regularly removed by hand from tobacco stalks. Above all else, then, successful Chesapeake farms required workers. But where and how could they be obtained? Nearby Indians, their numbers reduced by war and disease, could not supply these needs. Nor were enslaved Africans available: merchants could more easily and profitably sell slaves to Caribbean sugar planters. Thus only a few people of African descent, some of them free, initially trickled into the Chesapeake. By 1650 about three hundred blacks lived in Virginia—a tiny fraction of the population.

DEMAND FOR LABORERS

Chesapeake tobacco farmers thus looked primarily to England to supply their labor needs. Because of the headright system (which Maryland also adopted in 1640), a tobacco farmer anywhere in the Chesapeake could simultaneously obtain both land and labor by importing workers from England. Good management would make the process self-perpetuating: a farmer could use his profits to pay for the passage of more workers and thereby gain title to more land. Success could even bring movement into the ranks of the planter gentry that began to develop in the region.

Because men did the agricultural work in European societies, colonists assumed that field laborers should be men. Such male laborers, along with a few women, immigrated to America as indentured servants—that is, in return for their passage they contracted to work for periods ranging from four to seven years. Indentured servants accounted for 75 to 85 percent of the approximately 130,000 English immigrants to Virginia and Maryland during the seventeenth century. The rest tended to be young couples with one or two children.

Males between the ages of fifteen and twenty-four composed roughly three-quarters of the servants; only one immigrant in five or six was female. Most of these young men came from farming or laboring families, and many originated in regions of England experiencing severe social disruption. Some had already moved several times within England before relocating to America. Often they came from the middling ranks of society—what their contemporaries called the "common sort." Their youth indicated that most probably had not yet established themselves in their homeland.

For such people the Chesapeake appeared to offer good prospects. Servants who fulfilled the terms of their indentures earned "freedom dues" consisting of clothes, tools, livestock, casks of corn and tobacco, and sometimes even land. From a distance at least, America seemed to offer chances for advancement unavailable in England. Yet immigrants' lives were difficult. Servants typically worked six days a week, ten to fourteen hours a day, in a climate much warmer than England's. Their masters could discipline or sell them, and they faced severe penalties for running away. Even so, the laws did give them some protection. For example, their masters were supposed to supply them with sufficient food, clothing, and shelter, and they were not to be beaten excessively. Cruelly treated servants could turn to the courts for assistance, sometimes winning verdicts directing that they be transferred to more humane masters or released from their indentures.

CONDITIONS OF SERVITUDE

Servants and their owners alike contended with epidemic disease. Immigrants first had to survive the process the colonists called "seasoning," a bout with disease (probably malaria) that usually occurred during their first Chesapeake summer. They then often endured recurrences of malaria, along with dysentery, typhoid fever, and other illnesses. Consequently, about 40 percent of male servants did not survive long enough to become freedmen. Even young men of twenty-two who successfully weathered their seasoning could expect to live only another twenty years at best.

For those who survived the term of their indentures, though, the opportunities for advancement were real. Until the last decades of the seventeenth century, former servants often became independent farmers ("freeholders"), thereafter living a modest but comfortable existence. Some even assumed positions of political prominence such as justice of the peace or militia officer. But in the 1670s tobacco prices entered a fifty-year period of stagnation and decline. Simultaneously, good land grew increasingly scarce and expensive. In 1681 Maryland dropped its legal requirement that servants receive land as part of their freedom dues, forcing large numbers of freed servants to live for years as wage laborers or tenant farmers. By 1700 the Chesapeake was no longer the land of opportunity it once had been.

Life in the early Chesapeake was hard for everyone, regardless of sex or status. Farmers (and sometimes their wives) toiled in the fields alongside servants, laboriously clearing land, then planting and harvesting tobacco and corn. Because hogs could forage for themselves in the forests and needed little tending, Chesapeake households subsisted mainly on pork and corn, a filling diet but not sufficiently nutritious. Families supplemented this monotonous fare by eating fish, shellfish, and wildfowl, in addition to vegetables such as lettuce and peas, which they grew in small gardens. The near impossibility of preserving food for safe winter consumption magnified the health problems caused by epidemic disease. Salting, drying, and smoking, the only methods the colonists knew, did not always prevent spoilage.

STANDARD OF LIVING

Few households had many material possessions other than farm implements, bedding, and basic cooking and eating utensils. Chairs, tables, candles, and knives and forks were luxury items. Most people rose and went to bed with the sun, sat on crude benches or storage chests, and held plates or bowls in their hands while eating meat and vegetable stews with spoons. The ramshackle houses commonly had just one or two rooms. Colonists devoted their income to improving their farms, buying livestock, and purchasing more laborers instead of improving their standard of living. Rather than making items such as clothing and tools, tobacco-growing families imported necessary manufactured goods from England.

The predominance of males (see Figure 2.1), the incidence of servitude, and the high mortality rates combined to produce unusual patterns of family life. Female servants normally could not marry during their terms of indenture because masters did not want pregnancies to deprive them of workers. Many male ex-servants could not marry at all because of the scarcity of women; such men lived alone, in pairs, or as the third member of a household containing a married couple. In contrast, nearly every adult free woman in the Chesapeake married, and widows usually remarried within a few months of a husband's death. Yet because of high infant mortality and because almost all marriages were delayed by servitude or broken by death, Chesapeake women commonly reared only one to three healthy children, in contrast to English women, who normally had at least five.

CHESAPEAKE FAMILIES

Thus Chesapeake families were few, small, and short-lived. Youthful immigrants came to America as individuals free of familial control; they commonly died while their children were still young. In one Virginia county, for example, more than three-quarters of the children had lost at least one parent by the time they either married or reached age twenty-one. For the most part, then, Chesapeake men (unlike their English fathers) could not establish long-term control over their

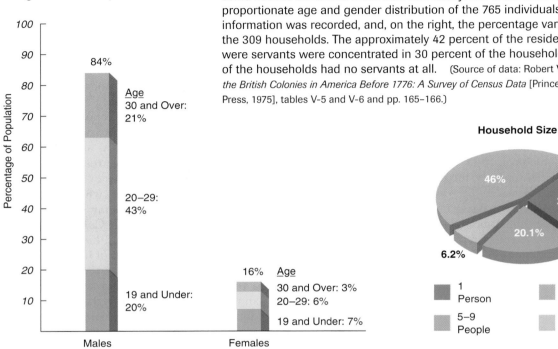

Figure 2.1 Population of Virginia, 1625

The only detailed census taken in the English mainland North American colonies during the seventeenth century was prepared in Virginia in 1625. It listed a total of 1,218 people, constituting 309 "households" and living in 278 dwellings—so some houses contained more than one family. The chart shows, on the left, the proportionate age and gender distribution of the 765 individuals for whom full information was recorded, and, on the right, the percentage variation in the sizes of the 309 households. The approximately 42 percent of the residents of the colony who were servants were concentrated in 30 percent of the households. Nearly 70 percent of the households had no servants at all. (Source of data: Robert V. Wells, *The Population of the British Colonies in America Before 1776: A Survey of Census Data* [Princeton: Princeton University Press, 1975], tables V-5 and V-6 and pp. 165–166.)

spouses or offspring. And the large number of orphaned children prompted a legal innovation: the establishment of orphans' courts to oversee the management of orphans' property and to ensure that such young people received the appropriate inheritance when they reached adulthood.

Because of the low rate of natural increase, throughout the seventeenth century immigrants composed a majority of the Chesapeake population, with important implications for regional political patterns. Most of the members of Virginia's House of Burgesses and Maryland's House of Delegates (established in 1635) were immigrants; they also dominated the governor's council, which simultaneously served as each colony's highest court, part of the legislature, and executive adviser to the governor. A cohesive, native-born ruling elite emerged only in the early eighteenth century.

CHESAPEAKE POLITICS

Representative institutions based on the consent of the governed usually function as a major source of political stability. In the seventeenth-century Chesapeake, most property-owning white males could vote, and such freeholders chose as their legislators the local elites who seemed to be the natural leaders of their respective areas. But because most such men were immigrants lacking strong ties to one another or to the colonies, the assemblies' existence did not create political stability. Unusual demographic patterns thus contributed to the region's contentious politics.

The Founding of New England

The economic motives that prompted English people to move to the Chesapeake and Caribbean colonies also drew men and women to New England (see Map 2.2). But because Puritans organized the New England colonies, and also because of environmental factors, the northern settlements turned out very differently from their counterparts to the south. The differences became apparent even as the would-be colonists left England.

Hoping to exert control over a migration that appeared disorderly (and which included dissenters seeking

CONTRASTING REGIONAL DEMOGRAPHIC PATTERNS

to flee the authority of the Church of England), royal bureaucrats in late 1634 ordered port officials in London to collect information on all travelers departing for the colonies. The resulting records for the year 1635 are a treasure trove for historians. They document the departure of 53 vessels in that year alone—20 to Virginia, 17 to New England, 8 to Barbados, 5 to St. Kitts, 2 to Bermuda, and 1 to Providence Island. On those ships sailed almost 5,000 people, with 2,000 departing for Virginia, about 1,200 for New England, and the rest for island destinations. Nearly three-fifths of all the passengers were between 15 and 24 years old, reflecting the predominance of young male servants among migrants to America.

But among those bound for New England, such youths constituted less than one-third of the total; nearly 40 percent were between ages 25 and 50, and another third were aged 14 and below. Whereas women made up just 14 percent of those going to Virginia, they composed almost 40 percent of the passengers to New England. Even from such composite figures, it is therefore evident that New Englanders often traveled in family groups. Moreover, they also brought more goods and livestock with them; ships bound for New England carried fewer passengers and considerably larger cargoes than those going elsewhere. Finally, the northern migrants also tended to travel with other people from the same regions: for example, aboard one vessel, more than half came from York; on another, nearly half came from Buckinghamshire. In short, although migrants to the Chesapeake and the islands most commonly left friends and families behind, those who moved to New England came in concert with their close associates. Their lives in North America accordingly must have been more comfortable and less lonely than that of their southern counterparts.

Among Chesapeake migrants, only the Catholics who moved to Maryland seem to have been motivated

CONTRASTING REGIONAL RELIGIOUS PATTERNS

by religious concerns. Yet religion inspired many, although certainly not all, of the people who colonized New England. Puritan congregations quickly became key institutions in colonial New England, whereas neither the Church of England nor Roman Catholicism had much impact on the settlers or the early development of the Chesapeake colonies. Catholic and Anglican bishops in England paid little attention to their coreligionists in America, and Chesapeake congregations languished in the absence of

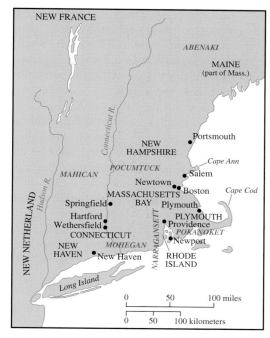

Map 2.2   New England Colonies, 1650

The most densely settled region of the mainland was New England, where English settlements and Indian villages existed side by side.

sufficient numbers of properly ordained clergymen. (For example, in 1665 an observer noted that only ten of the fifty Virginia parishes had resident clerics.) Not until the 1690s did the Church of England begin to take firmer root in Virginia; by then it had also replaced Catholicism as the established church in Maryland.

By contrast, religion constantly affected the lives of pious Puritans, who regularly reassessed the state of their souls. Many devoted themselves to self-examination and Bible study, and families prayed together each day under the guidance of the husband and father. Yet because even the most pious could never be certain that they were numbered among the elect, anxiety about their spiritual state troubled devout Puritans. That anxiety lent a special intensity to their religious beliefs and to their concern with proper behavior—their own and that of others.

Separatists who thought the Church of England too corrupt to be salvaged became the first to move to New

SEPARATISTS

England. In 1609 a Separatist congregation relocated to Leiden, in the Netherlands, where they found the freedom of worship denied them in Stuart England. But eventually the Netherlands worried them, for the nation that tolerated them also tolerated religions and behaviors they abhorred. Hoping to isolate themselves and their children from the corrupting influence of worldly temptations, these people, who came to be known as Pilgrims, received permission from the Virginia Company to colonize the northern part of its territory.

In September 1620, more than one hundred people, only thirty of them Separatists, set sail from England on the old and crowded *Mayflower*. Two months later they landed in America, but farther north than they had intended. Still, given the lateness of the season, they decided to stay where they were. Establishing their settlement on a fine harbor—the site of an Indian village wiped out by the epidemic of 1616–1618—the English people named it Plymouth.

Even before they landed, the Pilgrims had to surmount their first challenge—from the "strangers," or non-Separatists, who sailed with them to America. Because they landed outside the jurisdiction of the Virginia Company, some of the strangers questioned the authority of the colony's leaders. In response, the Mayflower Compact, signed in November 1620 on shipboard, established a "Civil Body Politic" as a temporary substitute for a charter. The male settlers elected a governor and initially made all decisions for the colony at town meetings. Later, after more towns had been founded and the population increased, Plymouth, like Virginia and Maryland, created an assembly to which the landowning male settlers elected representatives.

Mere survival also challenged the Pilgrims. Like the Jamestown settlers before them, they were poorly prepared to subsist in the new environment. Winter quickly descended, compounding their difficulties. Only half the *Mayflower*'s passengers lived to see the spring. But, again like the Virginians, the Pilgrims benefited from the political circumstances of nearby Indians.

INDIAN RELATIONS

The Pokanokets (a branch of the Wampanoags) controlled the area in which the Pilgrims settled. Their villages had suffered terrible losses in the recent epidemic, so to protect themselves from the powerful Narragansetts of the southern New England coast (who had been spared the ravages of the disease), the Pokanokets decided to ally themselves with the newcomers. In the spring of 1621, their leader, Massasoit, signed a treaty with the Pilgrims, and during the colony's first difficult years the Pokanokets supplied the English with essential

■ Some scholars now believe that this 1638 painting by the Dutch artist Adam Willaerts depicts the Plymouth colony about fifteen years after its founding. The shape of the harbor, the wooden gate, and the houses straggling up the hill all coincide with contemporary accounts of the settlement. No one believes that Willaerts himself visited Plymouth, but people returning from the colony to Holland, where the Pilgrims had lived for years before emigrating, could well have described Plymouth to him.   (© J. D. Bangs, Courtesy of Leiden American Pilgrim Museum, The Netherlands)

foodstuffs. The settlers were also assisted by Squanto, an Indian who, like Malinche, served as a conduit between native peoples and Europeans. Captured by fishermen in the early 1610s and taken to Europe, Squanto had learned to speak English. Upon returning to North America, he discovered that his village had been wiped out by the great epidemic. Squanto became the Pilgrims' interpreter and a major source of information about the unfamiliar environment.

Before the 1620s ended, a group of Puritan Congregationalists (who hoped to reform the Church of England from within) launched the colonial enterprise that would come to dominate New England and would absorb Plymouth in 1691. Charles I, who became king in 1625, was more hostile to Puritans than his father had been. Under his leadership, the Church of England attempted to suppress Puritan practices, driving clergymen from their pulpits and forcing congregations to hold clandestine meetings for worship. Some Congregationalist merchants, concerned about their long-term prospects in England, sent out a body of colonists to Cape Ann (north of Cape Cod) in 1628. The following year the merchants obtained a royal charter, constituting themselves as the Massachusetts Bay Company.

MASSACHUSETTS BAY COMPANY

The new joint-stock company quickly attracted the attention of Puritans of the "middling sort" who were becoming increasingly convinced that they no longer would be able to practice their religion freely in their homeland. They remained committed to the goal of reforming the Church of England but concluded that they should pursue that aim in America. In a dramatic move, the Congregationalist merchants boldly decided to transfer the Massachusetts Bay Company's headquarters to New England. The settlers would then be answerable to no one in the mother country and would be able to handle their affairs, secular and religious, as they pleased.

The most important recruit to the new venture was John Winthrop, a member of the lesser English gentry. In October 1629, the Massachusetts Bay Company elected Winthrop as its governor. (Until his death twenty years later, he served the colony continuously in one leadership post or another.) Winthrop organized the initial segment of the great Puritan migration to America. In 1630 more than one thousand English men and women moved to Massachusetts—most of them to Boston, which soon became the largest town in English North America. By 1643 nearly twenty thousand compatriots had followed them.

GOVERNOR JOHN WINTHROP

On board the *Arbella*, en route to New England in 1630, John Winthrop preached a sermon, "A Model of Christian Charity," laying out his expectations for the new colony. Above all, he stressed the communal nature of the endeavor on which he and his fellow settlers had embarked. God, he explained, "hath so disposed of the condition of mankind as in all times some must be rich, some poor, some high and eminent in power and dignity, others mean and in subjection." But differences in status did not imply differences in worth. On the contrary: God had planned the world so that "every man might have need of other, and from hence they might be all knit more nearly together in the bond of brotherly affection." In America, Winthrop asserted, "we shall be as a city upon a hill, the eyes of all people are upon us." If the Puritans failed to carry out their "special commission" from God, "the Lord will surely break out in wrath against us."

Winthrop's was a transcendent vision. He foresaw in Puritan America a true commonwealth, a community in which each person put the good of the whole ahead of his or her private concerns. Although, as in seventeenth-century England, that society would be characterized by social inequality and clear hierarchies of status and power, Winthrop hoped that its members would live according to the precepts of Christian love. Of course, such an ideal was beyond human reach. Early New England had its share of bitter quarrels and unchristian behavior. Remarkably, though, the ideal persisted well into the third and fourth generations of the immigrants' descendants.

The Puritans expressed their communal ideal chiefly in the doctrine of the covenant. They believed God had made a covenant—that is, an agreement or contract—with them when they were chosen for the special mission

■ An English beaver felt hat, made by combining American beaver fur with wool and other fibers. Men and women in England and on the European continent wore such fashionable items, thus creating the insatiable demand for pelts that fueled the fur trade for many years.
(The Pilgrim Society, Plymouth, Massachusetts)

COVENANT
IDEAL

to America. In turn they covenanted with one another, promising to work together toward their goals. The founders of churches, towns, and even colonies in Anglo-America often drafted formal documents setting forth the principles on which their institutions would be based. The Pilgrims' Mayflower Compact was a covenant; so too was the Fundamental Orders of Connecticut (1639), which laid down the basic law for the settlements established along the Connecticut River valley in 1636 and thereafter.

The leaders of Massachusetts Bay likewise transformed their original joint-stock company charter into the basis for a covenanted community based on mutual consent. Under strong and persistent pressure from landowning male settlers, they gradually changed the General Court—officially the company's small governing body—into a colonial legislature. They also granted the status of freeman, or voting member of the company, to all property-owning adult male church members. Like the Virginia men who won the reestablishment of the House of Burgesses after the king had abolished it, the male residents of Massachusetts insisted that their reluctant leaders allow them a greater voice in their government. Less than two decades after the first large group of Puritans arrived in Massachusetts Bay, the colony had a functioning system of self-government composed of a governor and a two-house legislature. The General Court also established a judicial system modeled on England's, although the laws they adopted differed from those of their homeland (see page 55).

NEW ENGLAND
TOWNS

The colony's method of distributing land helped to further the communal ideal. Unlike Virginia and Maryland, where individual applicants acquired headrights and sited their farms separately, in Massachusetts groups of men—often from the same region of England—applied together to the General Court for grants of land on which to establish towns (novel governance units that did not exist in England). The men receiving such a grant determined how the land would be distributed. Understandably, the grantees copied the villages whence they had come. First they laid out lots for houses and a church. Then they gave each family parcels of land scattered around the town center: a pasture here, a woodlot there, an arable field elsewhere. They reserved the best and largest plots for the most distinguished among them (including the minister). People who had been low on the social scale in England received much smaller and less desirable allotments. Still, every man and even a few single women obtained land, thus sharply differentiating these villages from their English counterparts.

Thus New England settlements initially tended to be more compact than those of the Chesapeake. Town centers developed quickly, evolving in three distinctly different ways. Some, chiefly isolated agricultural settlements in the interior, tried to sustain Winthrop's vision of harmonious community life based on diversified family farms. A second group, the coastal towns like Boston and Salem, became bustling seaports, serving as focal points for trade and places of entry for thousands of new immigrants. The third category, commercialized agricultural towns, grew up in the Connecticut River valley, where easy water transportation made it possible for farmers to sell surplus goods readily. In Springfield, Massachusetts, for example, the merchant-entrepreneur William Pynchon and his son John began as fur traders and ended as large landowners with thousands of acres. Even in New England, then, the entrepreneurial spirit characteristic of the Chesapeake found some room for expression.

INTERNAL
MIGRATION

When migrants began to move beyond the territorial limits of the Massachusetts Bay colony into Connecticut (1636), New Haven (1638), and New Hampshire (1638), the same pattern of land grants persisted. (Only Maine, with coastal regions thinly populated by fishermen and their families, deviated from the standard practice.) The migration to the Connecticut valley ended the Puritans' relative freedom from clashes with nearby Indians. The first English people in the valley moved there from Massachusetts Bay under the direction of their minister, Thomas Hooker. Although their new settlements were remote from other English towns, the wide river promised ready access to the ocean. The site had just one problem: it fell within the territory controlled by the powerful Pequots.

PEQUOT WAR

The Pequots' dominance stemmed from their role as primary middlemen in the trade between New England Indians and the Dutch in New Netherland. The arrival of English settlers signaled the end of the Pequots' power over such regional trading networks, for previously subordinate bands could now trade directly with Europeans. Clashes between Pequots and English colonists began even before the establishment of settlements in the Connecticut valley, but their founding tipped the balance toward war. The Pequots tried without success to enlist other Indians in resisting English expansion. After two English traders were killed (not by Pequots), the English raided a Pequot village. In return, the Pequots attacked the new town of Wethersfield in April 1637, killing nine and capturing two. To retaliate, a Massachusetts Bay expedition the following month attacked and burned the main Pequot town on the Mystic River. The Englishmen and their Narragansett allies slaughtered at least four hundred Pequots, mostly women and children, capturing and enslaving many of the survivors.

For the next thirty years, New England Indians accommodated themselves to the spread of European settlement. They traded with the newcomers and sometimes worked for them, but for the most part they resisted acculturation or incorporation into English society. Native Americans persisted in using traditional farming methods, which did not employ plows or fences, and women rather than men continued to be the chief cultivators. When Indian men learned "European" trades in order to survive, they chose those—like broom making, basket weaving, and shingle splitting—that most nearly accorded with their customary occupations and ensured both independence and income. The one European practice they adopted was keeping livestock, for domesticated animals provided excellent sources of meat once earlier hunting territories had been turned into English farms and wild game had consequently disappeared.

Although the official seal of the Massachusetts Bay colony showed an Indian crying "Come over and help us," most colonists showed little interest in converting the Algonquians to Christianity. Only a few Massachusetts clerics, most notably John Eliot, seriously undertook missionary activities. Eliot insisted that converts reside in towns, farm the land in English fashion, assume English names, wear European-style clothing and shoes, cut their hair, and stop observing a wide range of their own customs. Since Eliot demanded a total cultural transformation from his adherents—on the theory that Indians could not be properly Christianized unless they were also "civilized"—he understandably met with little success. At the peak of Eliot's efforts, only eleven hundred Indians (out of many thousands) lived in the fourteen "Praying Towns" he established, and just 10 percent of those town residents had been formally baptized.

JOHN ELIOT'S PRAYING TOWNS

The Jesuits' successful missions in New France contrasted sharply with the Puritans' failure to win many converts and the Franciscans' mixed results in New Mexico and Florida. Catholicism had several advantages, more fully exploited by Jesuits than Franciscans. The Catholic Church employed beautiful ceremonies, instructed converts that through good works they could help to earn their own

MISSIONARY ACTIVITIES COMPARED

■ Among John Eliot's principal converts to Christianity was a young Native American named Daniel Takawampbartis. Ordained as a minister, he served at the head of the Indian congregation at Natick, Massachusetts, a "Praying Town," until his death in 1716. Members of his congregation made this desk for him in about 1677, incorporating elements of English design (brass pulls), Native American motifs (incised lines), and uniquely American hooved feet. The top, a hinged box, is intended to hold a Bible. (The Morse Institute, Natick, Massachusetts. Photo by Mark Sexton of the Peabody Essex Museum, Salem)

salvation, and offered Indian women an inspiring role model—the Virgin Mary. In Montreal and Quebec but not in New Mexico, communities of nuns taught Indian women and children and ministered to their needs. Furthermore, the few French colonists on the St. Lawrence did not alienate potential converts by encroaching steadily on their lands (as did New Englanders) or by demanding labor tribute (as did New Mexicans). Perhaps most important, Jesuits recognized that Christian beliefs could be compatible with Native American culture. Unlike Puritans and Franciscans, Jesuits accepted converts who did not wholly adopt European styles of life.

What attracted Indians to these religious ideas? Conversion often alienated new Christians (both Catholic and Puritan) from their relatives and traditions—a likely outcome that must have caused many potential converts

In 1664 an eight-year-old girl, Elizabeth Eggington, became the subject of the earliest known dated New England painting. Her mother died shortly after her birth, perhaps because of childbirth complications; the girl's rich clothing, elaborate jewelry, and feather fan not only reveal her family's wealth but also suggest that she was much loved by her father, a merchant and ship captain. Unfortunately, Elizabeth died about the time this portrait was painted; perhaps it—like some other colonial portraits of young children—was actually painted after her death to memorialize her.   (Wadsworth Atheneum, Hartford. Gift of Mrs. Walter H. Clark. Endowed by her daughter, Mrs. Thomas L. Archibald)

to think twice about making such a commitment. But surely many hoped to use the Europeans' religion as a means of coping with the dramatic changes the intruders had wrought. The combination of disease, alcohol, new trading patterns, and loss of territory disrupted customary ways of life to an unprecedented extent. Shamans had little success in restoring traditional ways. Many Indians must have concluded that the Europeans' own ideas could provide the key to survival in the new circumstances.

John Winthrop's description of a great smallpox epidemic that swept through southern New England in the early 1630s reveals the relationship among smallpox, conversion to Christianity, and English land claims. "A great mortality among the Indians," he noted in his diary in 1633. "Divers of them, in their sickness, confessed that the Englishmen's God was a good God; and that if they recovered, they would serve him." But most did not recover: in January 1634 an English scout reported that smallpox had spread "as far as any Indian plantation was known to the west." By July, Winthrop observed that most of the Indians within a 300-mile radius of Boston had died of the disease. Therefore, he declared with satisfaction, "the Lord hath cleared our title to what we possess."

Life in New England

New England's colonizers adopted lifestyles that differed considerably from those of both their Indian neighbors and their counterparts in the Chesapeake. Algonquian bands usually moved four or five times each year to take full advantage of their environment. In spring, women planted the fields, but once crops were established, they did not need regular attention for several months. Villages then divided into small groups, women gathering wild foods and men hunting and fishing. The villagers returned to their fields for harvest, then separated again for fall hunting. Finally, the people wintered together in a sheltered spot before returning to the fields to start the cycle anew the following spring.

Unlike the mobile Algonquians, English people lived year-round in the same location. And unlike residents of the Chesapeake, New Englanders constructed sturdy dwellings intended to last. (Many still survive to this day.) They used the same fields again and again, believing it was less arduous to employ manure as fertilizer than to clear new fields every few years. Furthermore, they fenced their croplands to prevent them from being overrun by the cattle, sheep, and hogs that were their chief sources of meat. Animal crowding rather than human crowding caused New Englanders to spread out across the countryside; all their livestock constantly needed more pasturage.

Because Puritans commonly moved to America in family groups, the age range in early New England was wide; and because many more women *NEW ENGLAND* migrated to New England than to the *FAMILIES* tobacco colonies, the population could immediately begin to reproduce itself. Lacking such tropical diseases as malaria, New England was also much healthier than the Chesapeake. Once Puritan settlements had survived the difficult first few years and established self-sufficiency in foodstuffs, New England proved to be even healthier than the mother country. Adult male migrants to the Chesapeake lost about ten years from their English life expectancy of fifty to fifty-five years; their Massachusetts counterparts gained five or more years.

Consequently, while Chesapeake population patterns gave rise to families that were few in number, small in size, and transitory, the demographic characteristics of New England made families there numerous, large, and long-lived. In New England most men married; immigrant women married young (at age twenty, on the average); and marriages lasted longer and produced more children, who were more likely to live to maturity. If seventeenth-century Chesapeake women could expect to rear one to three healthy children, New England women could anticipate raising five to seven.

The nature of the population had other major implications for family life. New England in effect created grandparents, since in England people rarely lived long enough to know their children's children. And whereas early Chesapeake parents commonly died before their children married, New England parents exercised a good deal of control over their adult offspring. Young men could not marry without acreage to cultivate, and because of the communal land-grant system they had to depend on their fathers to give them that land. Daughters, too, needed a dowry of household goods supplied by their parents. Yet parents relied on their children's labor and often seemed reluctant to see them marry and start their own households. These needs at times led to conflict between the generations. On the whole, though, children seem to have obeyed their parents' wishes, for they had few alternatives.

Another important difference lay in the influence of religion on New Englanders' lives. Puritans controlled the governments of Massachusetts Bay, Plymouth, Connecticut, and the other early northern colonies. Congregationalism was the only officially recognized religion; except in Rhode Island, founded by dissenters from Massachusetts, members of other sects had no freedom of worship. Some non-Puritans voted in town meetings, but in Massachusetts Bay and New Haven, church membership was a prerequisite for voting in colony elections. All the early colonies taxed residents to build meetinghouses and pay ministers' salaries, but only in New England were provisions of criminal codes based on the Old Testament. Massachusetts's first bodies of law (1641 and 1648) incorporated regulations drawn from scriptures; New Haven, Plymouth, New Hampshire, and

IMPACT OF RELIGION

Connecticut later copied those codes. All colonists were required to attend religious services, whether or not they were church members, and people who expressed contempt for ministers or their preaching could be punished with fines or whippings.

The Puritan colonies attempted to enforce strict codes of moral conduct. Colonists there were frequently tried for drunkenness, card playing, even idleness. Couples who had sex during their engagement—as revealed by the birth of a baby less than nine months after their wedding—were fined and publicly humiliated. (Maryland, by contrast, did not penalize premarital pregnancy, only bastardy.) More harshly treated were men—and a handful of women—who engaged in behaviors that today would be called homosexual. (The term did not then exist, nor were some people thought to be more likely than others to perform such acts.) Several men who had consenting same-sex relationships were hanged, as were other men suspected of bestiality (sex with animals). Executions for such offenses were far more common in New England than in the Chesapeake, even though men in the two regions probably behaved similarly.

In New England, church and state were thus intertwined to a greater extent than in the Chesapeake. Puritans objected to secular interference in religious affairs but at the same time expected the church to influence the conduct of politics and the affairs of society. They also believed that the state was obliged to support and protect the one true church—theirs. As a result, although they came to America seeking freedom to worship as they pleased, they saw no contradiction in refusing to grant that freedom to others.

Roger Williams, a Separatist who immigrated to Massachusetts Bay in 1631, quickly ran afoul of that Puritan orthodoxy. He told his fellow settlers that the king of England had no right to grant them land already occupied by Indians, that church and state should be kept entirely separate, and that Puritans should not impose their religious beliefs on others. Because Puritan leaders placed a heavy emphasis on achieving consensus in both religion and politics, they could not long tolerate significant dissent. In October 1635, the Massachusetts General Court tried Williams for challenging the validity of the colony's charter and for maintaining that New England Congregationalists had not separated themselves, their churches, or their polity sufficiently from England's corrupt institutions and practices.

ROGER WILLIAMS

Convicted and banished, Williams journeyed in early 1636 to the head of Narragansett Bay, where he founded the town of Providence on land he obtained from the

Narragansetts and Wampanoags. Because Williams believed that government should not interfere with religion in any way, Providence and other towns in what became Rhode Island adopted a policy of tolerating all religions, including Judaism. Along with Maryland the tiny colony founded by Williams thus presaged the religious freedom that eventually became one of the hallmarks of the United States.

A dissenter who presented a more sustained challenge to Bay Colony leaders was Mistress Anne Marbury

ANNE HUTCHINSON

Hutchinson. (The title *Mistress* revealed her high status.) A skilled medical practitioner popular with the women of Boston, she greatly admired John Cotton, a minister who stressed the covenant of grace, or God's free gift of salvation to unworthy human beings. By contrast, most Massachusetts clerics emphasized the need for Puritans to engage in good works, study, and reflection in preparation for receiving God's grace. (In its most extreme form, such a doctrine could verge on the covenant of works, or the idea that people could earn their salvation.) After spreading her ideas for months in the context of gatherings at childbirths—when no men were present—Mistress Hutchinson began holding women's meetings in her home to discuss Cotton's sermons. She emphasized the covenant of grace more than did Cotton himself, and she even adopted the belief that the elect could be assured of salvation and communicate directly with God. Such ideas had an immense appeal for Puritans. Anne Hutchinson offered them certainty of salvation instead of a state of constant anxiety. Her approach also lessened the importance of the institutional church and its ministers.

Thus Hutchinson's ideas posed a dangerous threat to Puritan orthodoxy. So in November 1637, officials charged her with having maligned the colony's ministers by accusing them of preaching the covenant of works. For two days she defended herself cleverly, matching scriptural references and wits with John Winthrop himself. But then Anne Hutchinson triumphantly and boldly declared that God had spoken to her directly, explaining that he would curse the Puritans' descendants for generations if they harmed her. That assertion assured her banishment, for what member of the court could acknowledge the legitimacy of such a revelation? After she had also been excommunicated from the church, she and her family, along with some faithful followers, were exiled to Rhode Island in 1638. Several years later, after she moved to New Netherland, she and most of her children were killed by Indians.

The authorities in Massachusetts Bay perceived Anne Hutchinson as doubly dangerous to the existing order: she threatened not only religious orthodoxy but also traditional gender roles. Puritans believed in the equality before God of all souls, including those of women, but they considered actual women (as distinct from their spiritual selves) inferior to men. Christians had long followed Saint Paul's dictum that women should keep silent in church and submit to their husbands. Mistress Hutchinson did neither. The magistrates' comments during her trial reveal that they were almost as outraged by her "masculine" behavior as by her religious beliefs. Winthrop charged her with having set wife against husband, since so many of her followers were women. A minister at her church trial told her bluntly: "You have stept out of your place, you have rather bine a Husband than a Wife and a preacher than a Hearer; and a Magistrate than a Subject."

The New England authorities' reaction to Anne Hutchinson reveals the depth of their adherence to European gender-role concepts. To them, an orderly society required the submission of wives to husbands as well as the obedience of subjects to rulers and ordinary folk to gentry. English people intended to change many aspects of their lives by colonizing North America, but not the sexual division of labor, the assumption of male superiority, or the maintenance of social hierarchies.

Summary

B y the middle of the seventeenth century, Europeans had come to North America and the Caribbean to stay, a fact that signaled major changes for the peoples of both hemispheres. Europeans had indelibly altered not only their own lives but also those of native peoples. Europeans killed Indians with their weapons and diseases and had but limited success in converting them to Christian sects. Contacts with indigenous peoples taught Europeans to eat new foods, speak new languages, and recognize—however reluctantly—the persistence of other cultural patterns. The prosperity and even survival of many of the European colonies depended heavily on the cultivation of American crops (maize and tobacco) and an Asian crop (sugar), thus attesting to the importance of post-Columbian ecological change.

Political rivalries once confined to Europe spread around the globe, as England, Spain, Portugal, France, and the Netherlands vied for control of the peoples and resources of Asia, Africa, and the Americas. In America, Spaniards reaped the benefits of their South and Central American gold and silver mines, while French people earned their primary profits from Indian trade (in

Canada) and cultivating sugar (in the Caribbean). Sugar also enriched the Portuguese. The Dutch, by contrast, concentrated on commerce—trading in furs and sugar as well as carrying human cargoes of enslaved Africans to South America and the Caribbean.

Although the English colonies, too, at first sought to rely on trade, they quickly took another form altogether when so many English people of the "middling sort" decided to migrate to North America. To a greater extent than their European counterparts, the English transferred the society and politics of their homeland to a new environment. Their sheer numbers, coupled with their need for vast quantities of land on which to grow their crops and raise their livestock, inevitably brought them into conflict with their Indian neighbors. New England and the Chesapeake differed in the sex ratio and age range of their immigrant populations, in the nature of their developing economies, in their settlement patterns, and in the impact of religious beliefs on their settlers' lives. Yet they resembled each other in the conflicts their expansion engendered. In the years to come, both regions would become embroiled in increasingly fierce rivalries besetting the European powers. Those rivalries would continue to affect Americans of all races until after the mid-eighteenth century, when France and England fought the greatest war yet known, and the Anglo-American colonies won their independence.

LEGACY FOR A PEOPLE AND A NATION

The Foxwoods Casino and the Mashantucket Pequot Museum

In 1992 the Mashantucket Pequots opened the enormously successful Foxwoods Resort Casino on their small reservation in southeastern Connecticut. Just six years later, in August 1998, the Pequots proudly inaugurated a new museum (built with some of their substantial profits) presenting their people's story, meticulously researched by historians and archaeologists. Both developments surprised many Americans, who associated Indians only with territories west of the Mississippi and did not realize that American Indians still lived in New England. The existence of the Pequots was particularly startling, because histories had long recorded that the nation was destroyed in the Pequot War of 1637.

Survivors of the Mystic River massacre had regrouped in the Mashantucket swamps, building lives as farmers, laborers, and craftspeople. Some left the area, finding work on whaling vessels or eventually migrating to Wisconsin. But a few Pequots remained—the 1910 census, the source today for determining Pequot tribal membership, counted sixty-six residents of a reservation just 213 acres in size. By the 1970s, the residents had been reduced to two, and the state of Connecticut threatened to turn the reservation into a park. But an elder, Elizabeth George, persuaded several hundred people tracing descent from those listed in 1910 to return to live on the reservation. In 1983 the determined Pequots won formal federal recognition, and in turn that allowed them to build the profitable casino, a hotel, and several restaurants, and to begin purchasing more land.

Now the museum introduces the history of the Pequots and of eastern Algonquian peoples to hundreds of thousands of visitors each year. At its heart is a re-creation of a Pequot village as it would have looked shortly before Europeans first arrived on Connecticut's shores, complete with sounds and smells controlled by state-of-the-art computers. Exhibits detail the origins of the Pequot War, and a film narrates the tale of the massacre. Furthermore, excavations nearby continue to uncover new evidence about the overlooked history of these indomitable descendants of America's early residents.

The Pequots' success has helped to embolden other eastern Algonquian nations—for example, Wampanoags and Mashpees—to reassert publicly their long-suppressed Indian identities. The Pequot people's dedication to preserving their culture and reaffirming their history has created a remarkable legacy for the nation.

The **history Companion** powered by Eduspace®

Your primary source for interactive quizzes, exercises, and more to help you learn efficiently.
http://history.college.hmco.com/students

Why why should ye world be minding,
Heaven & World Finding thy Jarres
Then Farwell World: Farwell thy Warrs
thy Joys, thy Toies thy Wiles thy Wares
Truly Content: I am yet sorye,
The Eternall Drawes to him my hart
By Faith (which can my Force Subbert)
Crowne me (after grace) with Glory.

NORTH AMERICA IN THE ATLANTIC WORLD 1640–1720

*T*he *Seaflower*, Captain Thomas Smith, master, lay at anchor in Boston harbor in early September 1676, awaiting official documents signed by Governor John Leverett of Massachusetts and his Plymouth counterpart, Josiah Winslow. Like other mariners of the period, Smith expected to sell the cargo in his hold in the West Indies. But that cargo differed from most: it comprised human beings, nearly two hundred "heathen Malefactors—men, women, and Children."

The certificates from the governors, dated September 12, explained "To all People" the origins of Captain Smith's human cargo: "Philip an heathen Sachem . . . with others his wicked complices and abettors have treacherously and perfidiously rebelled against" these colonies. "By due and legall procedure" the captives on board the *Seaflower* were "Sentenced & condemned to perpetuall Servitude" as punishment for their "inhumane and barbarous crueltys murder, outrages and vilainies." The Pokanoket leader King Philip (called Metacom at birth and later renamed "Philip" by New Englanders) had been killed a month earlier in the war that bore his name. His captured wife and young son subsequently languished for months in a Boston jail; her fate is unknown, but the boy seems to have been sold into slavery, along with many shiploads of Philip's followers.

Only one prominent New Englander objected on moral grounds to the policy of selling the vanquished Algonquians into West Indian slavery. The Reverend John Eliot (see page 53) reminded the authorities that the Bay colony's charter called for the conversion of Indians, "not theire exstirpation." The colonists had a solemn duty, he contended, to "inlarge the kingdom of Jesus Christ"; "to sell them away for slaves, is to hinder the inlargement of his kingdom." If the Indians deserved to die, then "godly governors" should ensure that

◀ Captain Thomas Smith, a Boston mariner, painted this remarkable self-portrait in the late seventeenth century. It links his sailing career—illustrated in the background battle scene, which is thought to represent a combined Anglo-Dutch assault on a North African fort in 1670—with his pious Puritan faith. The skull under his hand serves to remind viewers of the brevity of life, which the poem underscores. "Why, why should I the World be minding?" the poet asks, looking forward to a future in which "The Eternall" would "Crowne me (after Grace) with Glory." (Worcester Art Museum, Worcester, Massachusetts, Museum purchase) they died "penitently," rather than depriving them of "all meanes of grace" by selling them as slaves. Not even Eliot, then, argued against enslavement itself, nor did he deny that the captured Algonquians deserved punishment. Rather, he believed that the chosen penalty would subvert God's plan for Massachusetts.

What the pious Captain Thomas Smith (whose self-portrait is reproduced on page 58) thought about his human cargo is unknown. The *Seaflower* arrived in Jamaica in November, and perhaps he disposed of some of the captives there. Eliot learned from a correspondent seven years later that a few enslaved Algonquians had ended up in Tangier (in modern Morocco) because so many countries had turned away the vessels carrying them. Some, it is now known, were carried to the tiny island of St. David's, part of Bermuda. Derided by other Bermudans as "Mohawks" (a generic term for "Indian" in the seventeenth century), they lived almost wholly isolated from other island residents until World War II. But they preserved in their oral histories the tale of New England Indian ancestry, and in the summer of 2002 were happily reunited with Wampanoags visiting from Massachusetts.

The tale of Thomas Smith and the *Seaflower*'s human cargo illustrates not only the English colonists' willingness to enslave "heathen" peoples and their increasingly contentious relationship with Native Americans, but also the participation of the mainland colonies in a growing international network. North America, like England itself, was becoming embedded in a worldwide matrix of trade and warfare. The web woven by oceangoing vessels—once composed of only a few strands spun by Columbus and his successors—now crisscrossed the globe, carrying European goods to America and Africa, West Indian sugar to New England and Europe, Africans to the Americas, and New England fish and wood products—and occasionally Indian slaves—to the Caribbean. Formerly tiny outposts, the North American colonies expanded their territorial claims and diversified their economies after the mid-seventeenth century.

Three developments shaped life in the mainland English colonies between 1640 and 1720: the expansion of slavery, especially in the southern coastal regions; changes in the colonies' political and economic relationships with England; and escalating conflicts with Indians and other European colonies in North America.

The explosive growth of the slave trade significantly altered the Anglo-American economy. Carrying human cargoes paid off handsomely, as many mariners and ship owners learned. Planters who could afford to buy slaves also reaped huge profits. At first primarily encompassing Indians and already enslaved Africans from the Caribbean, the trade soon came to focus on cargoes brought to the Americas directly from Africa. The arrival of large numbers of West African peoples dramatically reshaped colonial society and fueled the international trading system.

The burgeoning North American economy, invigorated by the arrival of so many laborers, attracted new attention from colonial administrators. Especially after the Stuarts had been restored to the throne in 1660 (having lost it for a time because of the English Civil War), London bureaucrats attempted to supervise the American settlements more effectively and to ensure that the mother country benefited from their economic growth. By the early eighteenth century, following three decades of upheaval, a new stability characterized colonial political institutions.

Neither English colonists nor London administrators could ignore other peoples living on the North American continent. As English settlements expanded, they came into violent conflict not only with powerful Indian nations but also with the Dutch, the Spanish, and especially the French. Moreover, all the European colonies confronted significant crises during the decade of the 1670s. By 1720, war—between Europeans and Indians, among Europeans, and among Indians allied with different colonial powers—had become an all-too-familiar feature of American life. No longer isolated from each other or from Europe, the people and products of the North American colonies had become integral to the world trading system and inextricably enmeshed in its conflicts. ■

The Growth of Anglo-American Settlements

etween 1642 and 1646 civil war between supporters of King Charles I and the Puritan-dominated Parliament engulfed the colonists' English homeland. Parliament triumphed, leading to the execution of the king in 1649 and interim rule by the parliamentary army's leader, Oliver Cromwell, during the so-called

TABLE 3.1		
Restored Stuart Monarchs of England, 1660–1714		
Monarch	**Reign**	**Relation to Predecessor**
Charles II	1660–1685	Son
James II	1685–1688	Brother
Mary	1688–1694	Daughter
William	1688–1702	Son-in-law
Anne	1702–1714	Sister, sister-in-law

Commonwealth period. But after Cromwell's death Parliament decided to restore the monarchy if Charles I's son and heir agreed to restrictions on his authority. Charles II did so, and the Stuarts were returned to the throne in 1660 (see Table 3.1). The new king subsequently rewarded nobles and others who had supported him during the Civil War with huge tracts of land on the North American mainland. The colonies thereby established made up six of the thirteen polities that eventually would form the American nation: New York, New Jersey, Pennsylvania (including Delaware), and North and South Carolina (see Map 3.1). Collectively, these became known as the Restoration colonies because they were created by the restored Stuart monarchy. All were proprietorships; in each of them, as in Maryland, one man or several men held title to the soil and controlled the government.

Charles's younger brother James, the duke of York, quickly benefited from his brother's generosity. In 1664,

NEW YORK acting as though the Dutch colony of New Netherland did not exist, Charles II gave James the region between the Connecticut and Delaware Rivers, including the Hudson valley and Long Island. James immediately organized an invasion fleet. In August James's warships anchored off Manhattan Island and demanded New Netherland's surrender. The colony complied without resistance. Although in 1672 the Netherlands briefly retook the colony during a later Anglo-Dutch war, the Dutch permanently ceded the province in 1674.

Thus James acquired a heterogeneous possession, which he renamed New York (see Table 3.2). In 1664 a significant minority of English people (mostly Puritan New Englanders who had moved to Long Island) already lived there, along with the Dutch and sizable numbers of Indians, Africans, Germans, French-speaking Walloons (from the southern part of modern Belgium), Scandinavians, and a smattering of other European peoples. The Dutch West India Company, the world's greatest

Map 3.1   The Anglo-American Colonies in the Early Eighteenth Century

By the early eighteenth century, the English colonies nominally dominated the Atlantic coastline of North America. But the colonies' formal boundary lines are deceiving because the western reaches of each colony were still largely unfamiliar to Europeans and because much of the land was still inhabited by Native Americans.

TABLE 3.2

The Founding of English Colonies in North America, 1664–1681

Colony	Founder(s)	Date	Basis of Economy
New York (formerly New Netherland)	James, duke of York	1664	Farming, fur trading
New Jersey	Sir George Carteret, John Lord Berkeley	1664	Farming
North Carolina	Carolina proprietors	1665	Tobacco, forest products
South Carolina	Carolina proprietors	1670	Rice, indigo
Pennsylvania (incl. Delaware)	William Penn	1681	Farming

slave-trading power at midcentury (see page 77), had actively imported slaves into the colony, intending some for resale in the Chesapeake. Many, though, remained in New Netherland as laborers; at the time of the English conquest, almost one-fifth of Manhattan's approximately fifteen hundred free and enslaved inhabitants were of African descent. Slaves then made up a higher proportion of New York's urban population than of the Chesapeake's rural people.

Recognizing the population's diversity, James's representatives moved cautiously in their efforts to establish English authority. The Duke's Laws, a legal code proclaimed in 1665, applied solely to the English settlements on Long Island, only later being extended to the rest of the colony. James's policies initially maintained Dutch forms of local government, confirmed Dutch land titles, and allowed Dutch residents to maintain customary legal practices. Each town was permitted to decide which church (Dutch Reformed, Congregational, or Church of England) to support with its tax revenues. Much to the dismay of English residents, the Duke's Laws made no provision for a representative assembly. Like other Stu-

arts, James distrusted legislative bodies, and not until 1683 did he agree to the colonists' requests for an elected legislature. Before then, an autocratic governor ruled New York.

The English takeover thus had little immediate effect on the colony. Its population grew slowly, barely reaching eighteen thousand by the time of the first English census in 1698. Until the second decade of the eighteenth century, New York City remained a commercial backwater within the orbit of Boston.

The English conquest brought so little change to New York primarily because the duke of York in 1664 regranted the land between the Hudson and Delaware Rivers—East and West Jersey—to his friends Sir George Carteret and John Lord Berkeley. That grant left the duke's own colony hemmed in between Connecticut to the east and the Jerseys to the west and south, depriving it of much fertile land and hindering its economic growth. He also failed to promote migration. Meanwhile, the Jersey proprietors acted rapidly to attract settlers, promising generous land grants, limited freedom of

NEW JERSEY

■ About 1650 a Dutch artist produced this copper engraving of New Amsterdam. Dominated by a prominent windmill, tall government buildings, and European-style row houses, the small community closely resembled towns in the Netherlands. Note the many contrasts to the view of Plymouth on page 50. (Museum of the City of New York. Gift of Dr. N. Sulzberber)

religion, and—without authorization from the Crown—a representative assembly. In response, large numbers of Puritan New Englanders migrated southward to the Jerseys, along with some Barbadians and Dutch New Yorkers. New Jersey grew quickly; in 1726, at the time of its first census as a united colony, it had 32,500 inhabitants, only 8,000 fewer than New York.

Within twenty years, Berkeley and Carteret sold their interests in the Jerseys to separate groups of investors. The purchasers of all of Carteret's share (West Jersey) and portions of Berkeley's (East Jersey) were members of the Society of Friends, also called Quakers. That new, small sect rejected earthly and religious hierarchies. Quakers believed that anyone could be saved by directly receiving God's "inner light" and that all people were equal in God's sight. With no formally trained clergy, Quakers allowed anyone, male or female, to speak in meetings or become a "public Friend" and travel to spread God's word. The Quaker message of radical egalitarianism was not welcome in the hierarchical society of seventeenth-century England or the colonies, and Quakers encountered persecution every-

where. Mary Dyer—who had followed Anne Hutchinson into exile—became a Quaker, returned to Boston as a missionary, and was hanged in 1660 (along with several men) for preaching Quaker doctrines.

The Quakers obtained their own colony in 1681, when Charles II granted the region between Maryland and New York to his close friend William Penn, a prominent member of the sect. Penn was then thirty-seven years old; he held the colony as a personal proprietorship, one that earned profits for his descendants until the American Revolution. Even so, Penn, like the Roman Catholic Calverts of Maryland before him, saw his province not merely as a source of revenue but also as a haven for persecuted coreligionists. Penn offered land to all comers on liberal terms, promised toleration of all religions (although only Christians were given the vote), guaranteed English liberties such as the right to bail and trial by jury, and pledged to establish a representative assembly. He also publicized the ready availability of land in Pennsylvania through widely distributed promotional tracts printed in German, French, and Dutch.

PENNSYLVANIA

■ William Penn, later the proprietor of Pennsylvania, as he looked during his youth in Ireland. In such pamphlets as the one shown here, Penn spread the word about his new colony to thousands of readers in England and its other colonial possessions. (Historical Society of Pennsylvania)

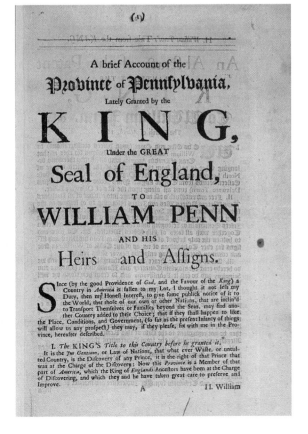

Penn's activities and the Quakers' attraction to his lands gave rise to a migration whose magnitude equaled the Puritan exodus to New England in the 1630s. By mid-1683, more than three thousand people—among them Welsh, Irish, Dutch, and Germans—had already moved to Pennsylvania, and within five years the population reached twelve thousand. (By contrast, it had taken Virginia more than thirty years to achieve a comparable population.) Philadelphia, carefully sited on the easily navigable Delaware River and planned to be the major city in the province, drew merchants and artisans from throughout the English-speaking world. From mainland and Caribbean colonies alike came Quakers seeking religious freedom; they brought with them years of experience on American soil and well-established trading connections. Pennsylvania's plentiful and fertile lands soon enabled its residents to begin exporting surplus flour and other foodstuffs to the West Indies. Practically overnight Philadelphia acquired more than two thousand citizens and started to challenge Boston's commercial dominance.

A pacifist with egalitarian principles, Penn attempted to treat native peoples fairly. He learned to speak the language of the Delawares (or Lenapes), from whom he purchased tracts of land to sell to European settlers. Penn also established strict regulations for trade and forbade the sale of alcohol to Indians. His policies attracted native peoples who moved to Pennsylvania near the end of the seventeenth century to escape repeated clashes with English colonists in Maryland, Virginia, and North Carolina. Most important were the Tuscaroras, whose experiences are described later in this chapter. Likewise, Shawnees and Miamis chose to move eastward from the Ohio valley. By a supreme irony, however, the same toleration that attracted Native Americans also brought non-Quaker Europeans who showed little respect for Indian claims to the soil. In effect, Penn's policy was so successful that it caused its own downfall. The Scots-Irish, Germans, and Swiss who settled in Pennsylvania in the first half of the eighteenth century clashed repeatedly over land with Indians who had also recently migrated to the colony.

CAROLINA   The southernmost proprietary colony, granted by Charles II in 1663, encompassed a huge tract stretching from the southern boundary of Virginia to Spanish Florida. The area had great strategic importance: a successful English settlement there would prevent Spaniards from pushing farther north. The fertile semitropical land also held forth the promise of producing exotic and valuable commodities such as figs, olives, wines, and silk. The proprietors named their new province Carolina in honor of Charles, whose Latin name was Carolus. The "Fundamental Constitutions of Carolina," which they asked the political philosopher John Locke to draft for them, set forth an elaborate plan for a colony governed by a hierarchy of landholding aristocrats and characterized by a carefully structured distribution of political and economic power.

But Carolina failed to follow the course the proprietors laid out. Instead, it quickly developed two distinct population centers, which in 1729 split into separate colonies. Virginia planters settled the Albemarle region that became North Carolina. They established a society much like their own, with an economy based on cultivating tobacco and exporting such forest products as pitch, tar, and timber. Because North Carolina lacked a satisfactory harbor, its planters relied on Virginia's ports and merchants to conduct their trade, and the colonies remained tightly linked. The other population center, which eventually formed the core of South Carolina, developed at Charles Town, founded in 1670 near the juncture of the Ashley and Cooper Rivers. Many of its early residents migrated from Barbados, which was already overcrowded. These sugar planters expected to reestablish plantation agriculture in their new homeland.

But the Carolinians soon learned that tropical plants (including sugar) would not grow successfully on the mainland, and so they instead began to raise corn and herds of cattle, which they sold to Caribbean planters hungry for foodstuffs. Like other colonists before them, they also depended on trade with nearby Indians to supply commodities they could sell elsewhere. In Carolina, those items were deerskins (almost as valuable as beaver pelts in Europe) and Indian slaves, which were shipped to the West Indies and the northern colonies. Nearby Indian nations hunted deer with increasing intensity and readily sold captured enemies to the English settlers. During the first decade of the eighteenth century, South Carolina exported an average of 54,000 skins annually, and overseas shipments later peaked at 160,000 a year. Before 1715, Carolinians additionally exported an estimated 30,000 to 50,000 Indian slaves.

THE CHESAPEAKE AND NEW ENGLAND   The English Civil War also affected the earlier English settlements, retarding their development. In the Chesapeake, struggles between supporters of the king and Parliament caused military clashes in Maryland and political upheavals in Virginia. But once the war ended and immigration resumed, the colonies expanded once again. Wealthy Chesapeake tobacco growers imported increasing numbers

■ Map from *A New Description of Carolina,* by John Ogilby, 1671 (with south at the top). Ogilby's tract, illustrated by a map drawn from information supplied by John Lederer, a German Indian trader, was intended to attract settlers to the new Carolina colony. He filled his text with information supplied by the Lords Proprietors, stressing the colony's pleasant climate, abundant resources, and friendly Native peoples, a message underscored by the peaceful scenes in the corner cartouches. (Colonial Williamsburg Foundation)

of English indentured servants to work on their farms, which had by then begun to develop into large plantations. Freed from concerns about Indian attack by the final defeat of the Powhatan Confederacy in 1646 they—especially recent immigrants—eagerly sought to enlarge their landholdings.

In New England, migration essentially ceased after the Civil War began in 1642. While Puritans were first challenging the king and then governing England as a commonwealth, they had little incentive to leave their homeland, and few migrated after the Restoration. Yet the Puritan colonies' population continued to grow dramatically because of natural increase. By the 1670s, New England's population had more than tripled to reach approximately seventy thousand. Such a rapid expansion placed great pressure on available land. Colonial settlement spread far into the interior of Massachusetts and Connecticut, and many members of the third and fourth

generations had to migrate—north to New Hampshire or Maine, south to New York or New Jersey, west beyond the Connecticut River—to find sufficient farmland for themselves and their children. Others abandoned agriculture and learned such skills as blacksmithing or carpentry to support themselves in the growing towns.

The people who remained behind in the small yet densely populated New England communities experienced a new phenomenon after approximately 1650: burgeoning witchcraft accusations and trials. The rural Chesapeake, urban Philadelphia or Charles Town, and newer settlements largely escaped such incidents, even though most seventeenth-century people believed that witches existed. These allies of the Devil were thought to harness invisible spirits for good or evil purposes. For example, a witch might engage in fortunetelling, prepare healing potions or charms, or harm others by causing the death

WITCHCRAFT

of a child or valuable animals. Yet only New England witnessed many trials of accused witches (about one hundred in all before 1690). Most, though not all, of the accused were middle-aged women who had angered their neighbors. Historians have accordingly concluded that the dynamics of daily interactions in the close-knit communities, where the same families lived nearby for decades, fostered longstanding quarrels that led some colonists to believe that others had diabolically caused certain misfortunes. Even so, only a few of the accused were convicted, and fewer still were executed, because judges and juries remained skeptical of such charges.

That New England courts thus halted questionable prosecutions suggests the maturity of colonial institutions.

COLONIAL POLITICAL STRUCTURES By the last quarter of the seventeenth century, almost all the Anglo-American colonies had well-established political and judicial structures. In New England, property-holding men or the legislature elected the governors; in other regions, the king or the proprietor appointed such leaders. A council, either elected or appointed, advised the governor on matters of policy and served as the upper house of the legislature. Each colony had a judiciary with local justices of the peace, county courts, and, usually, an appeals court composed of the councilors.

Local political institutions also developed. In New England, elected selectmen initially governed the towns, but by the end of the seventeenth century, town meetings—held at least annually and attended by most free adult male residents—handled matters of local concern. In the Chesapeake colonies and both of the Carolinas, appointed magistrates ran local governments. At first the same was true in Pennsylvania, but by the early eighteenth century elected county officials began to take over some government functions. And in New York, local elections were the rule even before the establishment of the colonial assembly in 1683.

A Decade of Imperial Crises: The 1670s

*a*s the Restoration colonies were extending the range of English settlement on the North American landscape, the first English colonies and French and Spanish settlements in North America faced new crises caused primarily by their changing relationships with America's indigenous peoples. Between 1670 and 1680, New England, Virginia, New France, and New Mexico experienced bitter conflicts as their inter-

ests collided with those of America's original inhabitants. All the early colonies changed irrevocably as a result.

In the mid-1670s, Louis de Buade de Frontenac, the governor-general of Canada, decided to expand New

NEW FRANCE AND THE IROQUOIS France's reach into the south and west, hoping to establish a trade route to Mexico and to gain direct control of the valuable fur trade on which the prosperity of the colony rested. Accordingly, he encouraged the explorations of Father Jacques Marquette, Louis Jolliet, and René-Robert Cavelier de La Salle in the Great Lakes and Mississippi valley regions. His goal, however, brought him into conflict

■ Contemporary engraving of John Verelst's 1710 portrait of the Mohawk chief known as Hendrick to Europeans (his Indian name was rendered as "Dyionoagon" or "Tee Yee Neen Ho Ga Row"). Hendrick and three other Iroquois leaders visited London in 1710, symbolically cementing the Covenant Chain negotiated in 1677. His primarily European dress and the wampum belt in his hand accentuate his identity as a cross-cultural diplomatic emissary. (John Carter Brown Library at Brown University)

with the powerful Iroquois Confederacy, composed of five Indian nations—the Mohawks, Oneidas, Onondagas, Cayugas, and Senecas. (In 1722 the Tuscaroras became the sixth.)

Under the terms of a unique defensive alliance forged early in the sixteenth century, a representative council made decisions of war and peace for the entire Iroquois Confederacy, although each nation still retained some autonomy and could not be forced to comply with a

Map 3.2   Louisiana, c. 1720

By 1720 French forts and settlements dotted the Mississippi River and its tributaries in the interior of North America. Two isolated Spanish outposts were situated near the Gulf of Mexico.   (Source: Adapted from *France in America*, by William J. Eccles. Copyright © 1972 by William J. Eccles. Reprinted by permission of HarperCollins Publishers, Inc.)

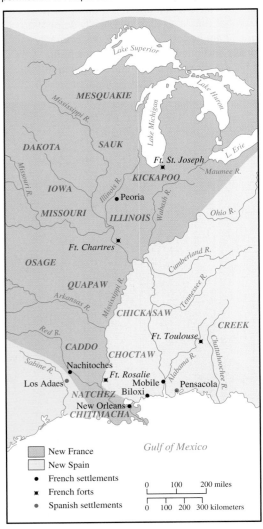

council directive against its will. Before the arrival of Europeans, the Iroquois waged wars primarily to acquire captives to replenish their population. Contact with foreign traders brought ravaging disease as early as 1633, intensifying the need for captives. Simultaneously, the Europeans' presence created an economic motive for warfare: the desire to dominate the fur trade and to gain unimpeded access to European goods. The war with the Hurons in the 1640s initiated a series of conflicts with other Indians known as the Beaver Wars, in which the Iroquois fought to achieve control of the lucrative peltry trade. Iroquois warriors did not themselves trap beaver; instead, they raided other villages in search of caches of pelts or attacked Indians from the interior as they carried furs to European outposts. Then the Iroquois traded that booty for European-made blankets, knives, guns, alcohol, and other desirable items.

In the mid-1670s, as Iroquois dominance grew, the French intervened, for an Iroquois triumph would have destroyed France's plans to trade directly with western Indians. Over the next twenty years the French launched repeated attacks on Iroquois villages. The English offered little assistance other than weapons to their trading partners, even though in 1677 New Yorkers and the Iroquois established a formal alliance known as the Covenant Chain. Its people and resources depleted by constant warfare, the confederacy in 1701 finally negotiated a neutrality treaty with France and other Indians. For the next half-century the Iroquois nations maintained their power through trade and skillful diplomacy rather than warfare.

The wars against the Iroquois initiated in the 1670s were crucial components of French Canada's plan to penetrate the heartland of North America. Unlike Spaniards, French adventurers did not attempt to subjugate the Indians they encountered. Nor, at first, did they even formally claim large territories for France. Still, when France decided to strengthen its presence near the Gulf of Mexico by founding New Orleans in 1718—to counter both westward thrusts of the English colonies and eastward moves of the Spanish—the Mississippi posts became the glue of empire. *Coureurs de bois* (literally, "forest runners") used the rivers and lakes of the American interior to travel regularly between Quebec and Louisiana, carrying French goods to outposts such as Michilimackinac (at the junction of Lakes Michigan and Huron), Kaskaskia (in present-day Illinois), and Fort Rosalie (Natchez), on the lower Mississippi River (see Map 3.2).

FRENCH EXPANSION

At most such sites lived a small military garrison and a priest, surrounded by powerful nations such as the Choctaws, Chickasaws, and Osages. Indians gained easy access to valuable trade goods by tolerating the minimal European presence, and France's primarily political and economic aims did not include systematic missionary work. The largest French settlements in the region, known collectively as *le pays de Illinois* ("the Illinois country"), never totaled much above three thousand in population. Located along the Mississippi south of modern St. Louis and north of Fort Chartres, the settlements produced wheat for export to New Orleans. In all the French outposts, the shortage of European women led to interracial unions between French men and Indian women and to the creation of mixed-race people known as *metís*.

In New Mexico, too, events of the 1670s led to a crisis with long-term consequences. Over the years under Spanish domination, the Pueblo peoples had added Christianity to their religious beliefs while still retaining traditional rituals, engaging in syncretic practices as had Mesoamericans. But as decades passed Franciscans adopted increasingly brutal and violent tactics in order to erase all traces of the native religion. Priests and secular colonists who held *encomiendas* also

POPÉ AND THE PUEBLO REVOLT

placed heavy labor demands on the population. In 1680 the Pueblos revolted under the leadership of Popé, a respected shaman, successfully driving the Spaniards out of New Mexico (see Map 3.3). Even though Spain managed to restore its authority by 1700, imperial officials had learned their lesson. Afterward, Spanish governors stressed cooperation with the Pueblos, no longer attempting to reduce them to bondage or to violate their cultural integrity. The Pueblo revolt constituted the most successful and longest-sustained Indian resistance movement in colonial North America.

When Spaniards expanded their territorial claims to the east and north, they followed the same strategy they adopted in New Mexico, establishing their presence through military outposts and Franciscan missions. The army maintained order among the subject Indians—to protect them from attack and ensure the availability of their labor—and guarded the boundaries of New Spain from possible incursions, especially by the French. The friars concentrated on conversions and allowed religious syncretism. By the late eighteenth century, Spain claimed a vast

SPAIN'S NORTH AMERICAN POSSESSIONS

Map 3.3

New Mexico, c. 1680
In 1680, the lone Spanish settlement at Santa Fe was surrounded and vastly outnumbered by the many Pueblo villages nearby.
(Source: Adapted from *Apache, Navaho, and Spaniard,* by Jack D. Forbes. Copyright © 1960 by the University of Oklahoma Press. Used by permission.)

Pueblo population c. 1680
■ 5,000
● 2,000–3,000
○ Less than 1,000
● Spanish settlement

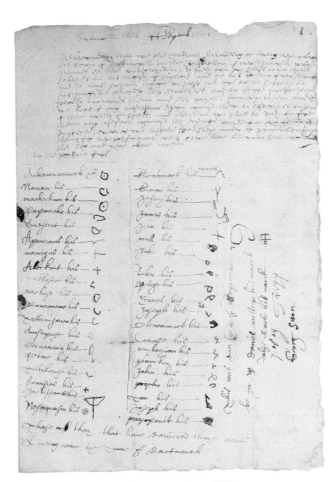

■ In September 1671 a large number of Wampanoags renewed their long-standing alliance with the Plymouth colony by signing this document. Yet less than four years later the peace collapsed as King Philip launched devastating attacks on settlements in southern New England.   (Boston Athenaeum)

territory that stretched from California (first colonized in 1769 to prevent Russian sea-otter trappers from taking over the region) through Texas (settled after 1700) to the Gulf Coast. Throughout that region, the Spanish presence consisted of a mixture of missions and forts dotting the countryside, sometimes at considerable distances from one another.

In the more densely settled English colonies, hostilities developed in the decade of the 1670s not over religion (as in New Mexico) or trade (as in New France) but rather over land. Put simply, the rapidly expanding Anglo-American population wanted more of it. In both New England and Virginia—though for different reasons—settlers began to encroach on territories that until then had remained in the hands of Native Americans.

By the early 1670s the growing settlements in southern New England surrounded Wampanoag ancestral lands on Narragansett Bay. The local

KING PHILIP'S WAR

chief, King Philip (son of Massasoit, who had welcomed the Pilgrims in 1621), was troubled by the loss of territory and concerned about the impact of European culture and Christianity on his people. Philip led his warriors in attacks on nearby communities in June 1675. Other Algonquian peoples, among them Nipmucks and Narragansetts, soon joined King Philip's forces. In the fall, the Indian nations jointly attacked settlements in the northern Connecticut River valley, and the war spread to Maine, too, when the Abenakis entered the conflict. In early 1676, the Indian allies devastated well-established villages and even attacked Plymouth and Providence; later that year, Abenaki assaults forced the abandonment of most settlements in Maine. Altogether, the alliance wholly or partially destroyed twenty-seven of ninety-two northern towns and attacked forty others, pushing the line of English settlement back toward the east and south.

The tide turned in the south in the summer of 1676. The Indian coalition ran short of food and ammunition, and colonists began to use Christian Indians as guides and scouts. On June 12, the Mohawks—ancient Iroquois enemies of New England Algonquians—devastated a major Wampanoag encampment while most of the warriors were away attacking an English town. After King Philip was killed that August, the southern alliance crumbled. Fighting, though, continued on the Maine frontier for another two years. There the English colonists never defeated the Abenakis; both sides, their resources depleted, simply agreed to end the conflict in 1678.

As the chapter-opening vignette reveals, many surviving Wampanoags, Nipmucks, Narragansetts, and Abenakis were captured and sold into slavery, and still more died of starvation and disease. New Englanders had broken the power of the southern coastal tribes. Thereafter the southern Indians lived in small clusters, subordinated to the colonists and often working as servants or sailors. Only on the isolated island of Martha's Vineyard did some Wampanoags preserve their cultural identity intact.

But the settlers paid a terrible price for their victory in King Philip's War: an estimated one-tenth of the able-bodied adult male population was killed or wounded. Proportional to population, it was the most costly conflict in American history. New Englanders did not fully rebuild abandoned interior towns for another three decades, and not until the American Revolution did the region's per capita income again reach pre-1675 levels.

Not coincidentally, conflict with Indians simultaneously wracked Virginia. In the early 1670s, land-hungry

BACON'S REBELLION

Virginians avidly eyed rich lands north of the York River reserved for Native peoples by early treaties. Using as a pretext the July 1675 killing of an English servant by some Doeg Indians, settlers attacked not only the Doegs but also the Susquehannocks, a powerful nation that had recently occupied the area. In retaliation, Susquehannock bands raided outlying farms early in 1676. Governor William Berkeley, the leader of an entrenched coterie of large landowners, resisted starting a major war to further the aims of disgruntled men who overtly challenged his hold on power. Dissatisfied colonists, including former indentured servants unable to establish their own tobacco farms, rallied behind the leadership of a recent immigrant, the wealthy Nathaniel Bacon, who like other new arrivals had found that all the desirable land in settled areas was already claimed by earlier residents.

Berkeley and Bacon soon clashed. After Bacon held members of the House of Burgesses hostage until they authorized him to attack the Indians, Berkeley declared Bacon and his men to be in rebellion. As the chaotic summer of 1676 wore on, Bacon alternately pursued Indians and battled the governor's supporters. In September Bacon marched on Jamestown itself, burning the capital to the ground. But when Bacon died of dysentery the following month, the rebellion began to collapse. Even so, the rebels had made their point, and a new treaty signed in 1677 opened much of the disputed territory to English settlement.

The war, a turning point in Virginia's relationship with nearby Indians, also marked a turning point in the colony's internal race relations. After Bacon's Rebellion, Virginia landowners for the first time began to purchase large numbers of imported African slaves. Historians disagree about whether they did so in part because they feared dealing with successive waves of the discontented ex-servants who had followed Bacon's lead. But regardless of their motives, in the last two decades of the seventeenth century Anglo-Americans in the Chesapeake irrevocably altered the racial composition of their labor force.

African Slavery on the Mainland

In the 1670s and 1680s, the prosperity of the Chesapeake rested on tobacco, and successful tobacco cultivation depended, as it always had, on an ample labor supply. But fewer and fewer English men and women proved willing to indenture themselves for long terms of service in Maryland and Virginia. Population pressures had eased in England, and the founding of the Restoration colonies meant that migrants could choose other American destinations. Furthermore, fluctuating tobacco prices in Europe and the growing scarcity of land made the Chesapeake less appealing to potential settlers. That posed a problem for wealthy Chesapeake tobacco

■ European traders hoped to avoid purchasing sick slaves who would carry diseases on board their vessels, thereby causing high mortality rates among other bondspeople and destroying the profitability of the voyages. Some mistakenly believed that by tasting the slaves' sweat they could determine their captives' health. An artist sketched just such a scene in 1725. (*Traite général du commerce de l'Amérique*, by Chambon. Bibliothèque Municipale, Nantes, France)

growers. Where could they obtain the workers they needed? They found the answer in the Caribbean sugar islands, where since the 1640s Dutch, French, English, and Spanish planters had eagerly purchased African slaves.

Slavery had been practiced in Europe (although not in England) for centuries. European Christians—both Catholics and Protestants—believed that enslaving heathen peoples, especially those of exotic origin, was justifiable in religious terms. Some argued, piously, that holding heathens in bondage would lead to their conversion. Others believed that any heathen taken prisoner in wartime could legitimately be enslaved. Consequently, when Portuguese mariners reached the sub-Saharan African coast and encountered non-Christian societies holding slaves (see page 18), they purchased bondspeople as one component of the exchange of many items, especially gold. Starting in the 1440s, Portugal imported large numbers of these slaves into the Iberian Peninsula and the Wine Islands; one historian has estimated that by 1500, enslaved Africans composed about one-tenth of the population of Lisbon and Seville, the chief cities of Portugal and Spain.

WHY AFRICAN SLAVERY?

Iberians then exported African slavery to their American possessions, New Spain and Brazil. Because the Catholic Church prevented the formal enslavement of Indians in those domains (see page 24) and free laborers saw no reason to work voluntarily in mines or on sugar plantations when they could earn better wages under easier conditions elsewhere, African bondspeople (who had no choice) became mainstays of the Caribbean and Brazilian economies. Sugar planters on English islands, who had the same problems of labor supply as did their French, Dutch, and Spanish counterparts, also purchased slaves.

Yet that slave system—well-established in the Caribbean by the mid-1650s—did not immediately take root in the English mainland colonies, largely because they were then well supplied with English laborers. Before the 1660s, the few residents of African descent on the mainland varied in status: some were free, some indentured, some enslaved. All came from a population that the historian Ira Berlin has termed Atlantic creoles. Often of mixed race, many came to the English colonies from elsewhere in the Americas. Already familiar with Europeans, the Atlantic creoles fitted easily into established niches in the many-faceted hierarchical social structures of the early colonies. Berlin has characterized all the early mainland colonies as "societies with slaves"—that is, societies in which some people were held in perpetual

ATLANTIC CREOLES IN SOCIETIES WITH SLAVES

bondage but that did not rely wholly on slave labor. He usefully contrasts such communities with "slave societies," or societies in which slavery served as the fundamental basis of the economy.

The many ambiguities of status in societies with slaves are evident in early laws in which Virginians and Marylanders revealed the initial difficulty of developing all-encompassing definitions of enslavement. Several Virginia statutes employed the term *Christian* to mean "free person"; when at least one slave therefore claimed freedom as a consequence of conversion to Christianity, the House of Burgesses legislated (in 1667) that "the blessed sacrament of baptism" would not liberate bondspeople from perpetual servitude. The two colonies did not concur on how slave status would be transmitted to the next generation: Virginia in 1662 linked the condition of children to that of their mother, whereas Maryland two years later tied it to the status of their father. And when in 1670 the House of Burgesses sought for the first time to define who was enslaveable and who was not, it declared that "all servants not being christians imported into this colony by shipping shalbe slaves for their lives," but similar servants that "shall come by land" would serve only for a term of years. The awkward phrases attempted to differentiate Africans from Indians; Virginians saw both groups as distinguishable from English people but expressed those distinctions in terms of religion and geography rather than race.

Yet just a few years later, Chesapeake legislators started to employ racial terminology. As increasing numbers of slaves arrived each year, first from the Caribbean and then directly from Africa, the majority of the enslaved population changed from acculturated creole to newly imported African. Virginia in 1682 altered its definition of who could be enslaved, declaring bluntly that "Negroes, Moors, Mollatoes or Indians" arriving "by sea or land" could all be held in bondage for life if their "parentage and native country are not christian." Most of the English colonies, even those without many bondspeople, adopted detailed codes to govern slaves' behavior. By 1700 African slavery was firmly established as the basis of the economy in the Chesapeake and South Carolina as well as in the Caribbean. Under Berlin's definition, those colonies had become "slave societies."

MAINLAND SLAVE SOCIETIES

English enslavers evidently had few moral qualms about these actions. Few at the time questioned the decision to hold Africans and their descendants—or captive Indians from New England or Carolina—in perpetual bondage. The convoluted and contradictory early attempts to define slave status and how it would descend to the next generation suggest, however, that seventeenth-century English colonists nevertheless initially lacked clear conceptual categories defining both "race" and "slave." They developed such categories and their meanings over time, through their experience with the institution of African and Indian slavery, originally adopted for economic reasons.

Between 1492 and 1770 more Africans than Europeans came to the Americas, the overwhelming majority of them as slaves. Most went to Brazil or the Caribbean: of at least 10 million enslaved people brought to the Americas during the existence of slavery, only about 260,000 were imported by 1775 into the region that became the United States. This massive trade in human beings is best understood within the context of the Atlantic trading system that developed during the middle years of the seventeenth century.

The Web of Empire and the Atlantic Slave Trade

*T*he elaborate Atlantic economic system is commonly called the triangular trade. In that context, the traffic in slaves from Africa to the Americas has become known as the middle passage because it constituted the middle leg of such a theoretical triangle. But both *triangular trade* and *middle passage* fail to convey the complexities of the commercial relationships that by the late seventeenth century linked the various elements of the Atlantic trading system in Europe, Africa, North and South America, and the Caribbean. People and products did not move across the ocean in easily diagrammed patterns. Instead, their movements created a complicated web of exchange that inextricably tied the peoples of the Atlantic world together (see Map 3.4).

The traffic in enslaved human beings served as the linchpin of the system. Although slavery had long been

ATLANTIC TRADING SYSTEM

practiced, the oceanic slave *trade* was entirely new. The expanding network of commerce between Europe and its colonies was fueled by the sale and transport of slaves, the exchange of commodities produced by slave labor, and the need to feed and clothe so many bound laborers. Yet the various elements had different relationships within the system and with the wider web of exchange. Chesapeake tobacco and Caribbean and Brazilian sugar were in great demand in Europe, so planters shipped their products directly to their home countries. The profits paid for both the African laborers who grew their crops and European manufactured goods. The African coastal rulers who ran the entrepôts

where European slavers acquired their human cargoes received their payment in European manufactures and East Indian textiles; they had little need for most American products. Europeans purchased slaves from Africa for resale in their colonies and acquired sugar and tobacco from America, in exchange dispatching their manufactures everywhere.

New England had the most complex relationship to the trading system. The region produced only one item

NEW ENGLAND AND THE CARIBBEAN

England wanted: tall trees to serve as masts for sailing vessels. To buy English manufactures, New Englanders therefore needed profits earned elsewhere—the Wine Islands and the Caribbean. Those islands lacked precisely the items that New England could produce in abundance: cheap food (primarily corn and salt fish) to feed the burgeoning slave population and wood for barrels to hold wine, sugar, and molasses. By the late 1640s, decades before the Chesapeake

■ By the middle of the eighteenth century, American tobacco had become closely associated with African slavery. An English woodcut advertising tobacco from the York River in Virginia accordingly depicted not a Chesapeake planter but rather an African, shown with a hoe in one hand and a pipe in the other. Usually, of course, slaves would not have smoked the high-quality tobacco produced for export, although they were allowed to cultivate small crops for their own use.   (Colonial Williamsburg Foundation)

York Tobacco LONDON

Map 3.4

Atlantic Trade Routes

By the late seventeenth century, an elaborate trade network linked the countries and colonies bordering the Atlantic Ocean. The most valuable commodities exchanged were enslaved people and the products of slave labor.

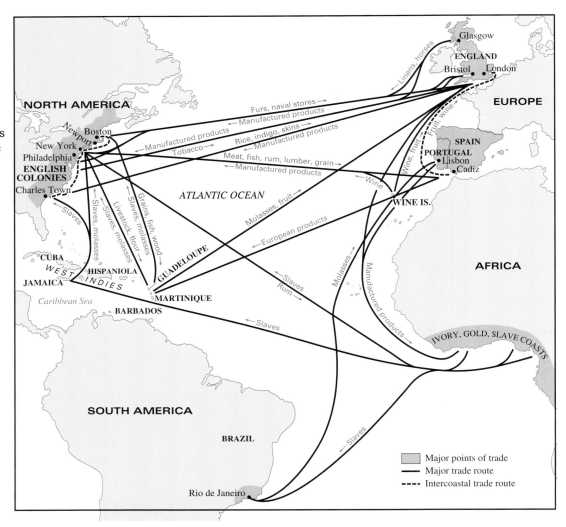

economy became dependent on *production* by slaves, New England's already rested on *consumption* by slaves and their owners. The sale of foodstuffs and wood products to Caribbean sugar planters provided New England farmers and merchants with a major source of income. After the founding of Pennsylvania, New York, and New Jersey, those colonies too participated in the lucrative West Indian trade.

Shopkeepers in the interior of New England and the middle colonies bartered with local farmers for grains, livestock, and barrel staves, then traded those items to merchants located in port towns. Such merchants dispatched ships to the Caribbean, where they sailed from island to island, exchanging their cargoes for molasses, sugar, fruit, spices, and slaves. The system's sole constant was uncertainty, due to the weather, rapid shifts in supply and demand in the small island markets, and the del-

icate system of credit on which the entire structure depended. Once they had a full load, the ships returned to Boston, Newport, New York, or Philadelphia to dispose of their cargoes, trading the items they did not use to other nearby colonies. Americans began to distill molasses into rum, a crucial aspect of the only part of the trade that could accurately be termed triangular. Rhode Islanders took rum to Africa and traded it for slaves, whom they carried to the West Indies to exchange for more molasses to produce still more rum.

Tying the system together was the voyage that brought Africans to the Americas, where they cultivated the profitable crops and—in the Caribbean—consumed foods produced in North America. That voyage, always traumatic, was sometimes fatal for the people who composed a ship's cargo. An average of 10 to 20 percent of the newly enslaved died en route. On unusually long or

International Piracy

The web of commerce across the Atlantic drove trade—and theft—to new levels. The last decades of the seventeenth century were the heyday of pirates, who, from bases in North America and the Caribbean, ranged the world. In New York and Charles Town, merchants asked few questions about the origins of valuable goods, and the solitary ocean voyages of merchant and slaving vessels were easy prey for resourceful marauders. The cargoes of precious metals, slaves, and luxury goods such as fine wines and silks made the return worth the risk.

As early as the sixteenth century, European kingdoms encouraged attacks on the commerce of rivals. Queen Elizabeth knighted Francis Drake for the treasure he stole from Spain. Though in wartime letters of marque could transform law-breaking pirates into legal privateers, authorized to prey on the enemy, the line between pirates and privateers was easily breached. Privateers could keep most of their booty, and the crews, with sailors of many nations, were loyal primarily to themselves.

The infamous Captain William Kidd (c. 1645–1701) was both pirate and privateer. Probably Scots by birth, he plundered in the Caribbean before settling in New York, where he married a rich widow and cultivated local politi-

cians. In 1696 he returned to sea with new privateering credentials, issued in London. With a crew recruited in England and New York, he sailed to the Indian Ocean, picking up other mariners along the way. Kidd encountered no vessels he could legally capture, and his crew—composed largely of pirates—became restive, so he resumed marauding. Over the next months Kidd and his men seized Dutch and Portuguese ships and eventually a freighter sailing from India to the Moluccas. In late 1698, they headed for the Americas with a booty of valuable textiles. But in Boston, Kidd was arrested for piracy and murder. The English and colonial governments, he discovered, were newly committed to stamping out piracy. Sent to London for trial, he was convicted and hanged in May 1701.

Captain Kidd's exploits were a product of his time and place. In the 1690s international crews of buccaneers sailed from the Americas to wherever in the world they thought they would find rich prizes. The rapidly developing web of international commerce that linked the Western Hemisphere to Africa, Asia, and Europe also spawned the legendary thieves who preyed on it.

The sorts of valuable, exotic items pictured here were among the cargoes pirates sought. Fine ceramics and textiles from Asia commanded high prices from American and European purchasers who did not concern themselves with the origins of these desirable consumer goods. (Left: V&A Images, The Victoria and Albert Museum, London; right: The Metropolitan Museum of Art, purchased by subscription, 1879)

disease-ridden voyages, mortality rates could be much higher. In addition, another 20 percent or so of slaves died either before the ships left Africa or shortly after their arrival in the Americas. Their European captors also died at high rates, chiefly through exposure to such diseases as yellow fever and malaria, which were endemic to Africa. Just 10 percent of the men sent to run the Royal African Company's forts in Lower Guinea

lived to return home to England, and one in every four or five European sailors died on slaving voyages. Once again, the exchange of diseases caused unanticipated death and destruction.

Most of the enslaved people carried to North America originated in West Africa. Some came from the Rice and Grain Coasts, especially the former, but even more had resided in the Gold and Slave Coasts and the Bight of

WEST AFRICA AND THE SLAVE TRADE

Biafra (modern Nigeria) and Angola (see Map 1.2). Certain coastal rulers—for instance, the Adja kings of the Slave Coast—served as middlemen, allowing the establishment of permanent slave-trading posts in their territories and supplying resident Europeans with slaves to fill ships that stopped regularly at coastal forts. Such rulers controlled European traders' access to slaves and simultaneously controlled inland peoples' access to desirable European goods such as cloth, alcohol, tobacco, and guns.

The slave trade had varying political and economic consequences for the nations of West Africa. The trade's centralizing tendencies helped to create such powerful eighteenth-century kingdoms as Dahomey and Asante (formed from the Akan States). Traffic in slaves thus destroyed smaller polities and disrupted traditional economic patterns, as goods once sent north toward the Mediterranean were redirected to the coast, and as local manufactures declined in the face of European competition. Further, the extent of nations' participation in the trade varied according to their involvement in warfare. Because prisoners of war constituted the bulk of the slaves shipped to the Americas, the most active traders were also the most successful in battle. Some nations even initiated conflicts specifically to acquire valuable captives.

The trade in human beings did not uniformly depopulate West Africa, a fertile and densely inhabited region. Instead, the slave trade affected African societies unevenly. For example, the growing state of Benin actively sold captive enemies to the Portuguese in the late fifteenth century; did not do so at the height of its power in the sixteenth and seventeenth centuries; and renewed the sale of prisoners in the eighteenth century when its waning power led to conflicts with neighboring states. Rulers in parts of Upper Guinea, especially modern Gambia and Senegal, largely resisted involvement with the trade; the

■ A Procession in Benin, 1668. A contemporary European engraving shows a royal procession leaving the city of Benin, capital of the prosperous West African kingdom. During the seventeenth century, the power of Benin's rulers scared off would-be challengers, and so the kingdom did not engage in frequent warfare. In the fifteenth and eighteenth centuries, by contrast, when the kingdom was weaker, it did capture and sell its enemies.   (Library of Congress)

few slave vessels that departed from that area were much more likely than others to experience onboard rebellions. Despite planters' preference for male slaves, women predominated in cargoes originating in the Bight of Biafra. And in such regions as the Gold Coast, the trade had a significant impact on the sex ratio of the remaining population. There a relative shortage of men increased work demands on women, encouraged polygyny, and opened new opportunities to women and their children.

This traffic in slaves chiefly benefited Europeans, despite its importance to some African kings. The European economy, previously oriented toward the Mediterranean and Asia, shifted its emphasis to the Atlantic. Whereas European merchants' profits had once come primarily from trade with North Africa, the eastern Mediterranean, and China, by the late seventeenth century commerce in slaves and the products of slave labor constituted the basis of the European economic system. The irony of Columbus's discoveries thus became complete: seeking the wealth of Asia, Columbus instead found the lands that—along with Africa—ultimately replaced Asia as the source of European prosperity.

EUROPEAN RIVALRIES AND THE SLAVE TRADE

European nations fought bitterly to control the slave trade. The Portuguese, who at first dominated the trade, were supplanted by the Dutch in the 1630s. The Dutch in turn lost out to the English, who controlled the trade through the Royal African Company, a joint-stock company chartered by Charles II in 1672. Holding a monopoly on all English trade with sub-Saharan Africa, the company built and maintained seventeen forts and trading posts, dispatched to West Africa hundreds of ships carrying English manufactured goods, and transported about 100,000 slaves to England's Caribbean colonies. It paid regular dividends averaging 10 percent yearly, and some of its agents made fortunes. Yet even before the company's monopoly expired in 1712, many individual English traders had illegally entered the market for slaves. By the early eighteenth century, such independent traders carried most of the Africans imported into the colonies, earning huge profits from successful voyages.

English officials seeking a new source of revenue after the disruptions of the Civil War decided to tap into the profits produced by the expanding Atlantic trading system. Chesapeake tobacco and Caribbean sugar had obvious value, but other colonial products also had considerable potential. Additional tax revenues could put England back on a sound financial footing, and English merchants wanted to ensure that they—not their Dutch rivals—reaped the benefits of trading with English colonies. Parliament and the restored Stuart monarchs accordingly began to draft laws designed to confine the proceeds of the English imperial web of trade primarily to the mother country.

Like other European nations, England based its commercial policy on a series of assumptions about the operations of the world's economic system. Collectively, these assumptions are usually called *mercantilism*, although neither the term itself nor a unified mercantilist theory was formulated until a century later. The theory viewed the economic world as a collection of national states, whose governments actively competed for shares of a finite amount of wealth. What one nation gained, another nation automatically lost. Each nation sought to become as economically self-sufficient as possible while maintaining a favorable balance of trade with other countries by exporting more than it imported. Colonies had an important role to play in such a scheme. They could supply the mother country with valuable raw materials to be consumed at home or sent abroad, and they could serve as a market for the mother country's manufactured goods.

MERCANTILISM

Parliament applied mercantilist thinking to the American colonies in laws known as the Navigation Acts. The major acts—passed between 1651 and 1673—established three main principles. First, only English or colonial merchants and ships could engage in trade in the colonies. Second, certain valuable American products could be sold only in the mother country or in other English colonies. At first, these "enumerated" goods included wool, sugar, tobacco, indigo, ginger, and dyes; later acts added rice, naval stores (masts, spars, pitch, tar, and turpentine), copper, and furs to the list. Third, all foreign goods destined for sale in the colonies had to be shipped by way of England, paying English import duties. Some years later, a new series of laws established a fourth principle: the colonies could not export items (such as wool clothing, hats, or iron) that competed with English products.

NAVIGATION ACTS

The Navigation Acts aimed at forcing American trade to center on England. The mother country would benefit from colonial imports and exports both. England had first claim on the most valuable colonial exports, and all foreign imports into the colonies had to pass through England first, enriching its customs revenues in the process. The laws adversely affected some colonies, like those in the Caribbean and the Chesapeake, because planters there could not seek new markets for their staple crops. In others, the impact was minimal or even positive. Builders and owners of ships benefited from the monopoly on American trade given to English and colonial merchants; the laws stimulated the creation of a lucrative

■ The harbor of Christiansted, St. Croix, in the Danish West Indies. Although this view was painted over one hundred years after the events discussed in this chapter, the town had not changed much in the interim. Scenes like this would have been very familiar to seventeenth- and eighteenth-century colonial mariners, for such ports existed all over the Caribbean. Anchored merchant vessels await the hogsheads of molasses being prepared for shipment at the wharf. (1996 MAPes MONDe Ltd.)

colonial shipbuilding industry, especially in New England. And the northern and middle colonies produced many unenumerated goods—for example, fish, flour, meat and livestock, and barrel staves. Such products could be traded directly to the French and Dutch Caribbean islands as long as they were carried in English or American ships.

The English authorities soon learned that writing mercantilist legislation was far easier than enforcing it. The many harbors of the American coast provided ready havens for smugglers, and colonial officials often looked the other way when illegally imported goods were offered for sale. In ports such as St. Eustatius in the Dutch West Indies, American merchants could easily dispose of enumerated goods and purchase foreign items on which duty had not been paid. Consequently, Parliament in 1696 enacted another Navigation Act. This law established in America a number of vice-admiralty courts, which operated without juries. In England such courts dealt only with cases involving piracy, vessels taken as wartime prizes, and the like. But since American juries had already demonstrated a tendency to favor local smugglers over customs officers (a colonial customs service was instituted in 1671), Parliament decided to remove Navigation Act cases from the regular colonial courts.

Enslavement of Africans and Indians

Following Bacon's Rebellion, so many Africans were imported into Virginia and Maryland so rapidly that as early as 1690 those colonies contained more slaves than English indentured servants. By 1710 people of African descent composed one-fifth of the region's population. Even so, and despite sizable continuing imports, a decade later American-born slaves already outnumbered their African-born counterparts in the Chesapeake, and the native-born proportion of the slave population continued to increase thereafter.

Slaves brought from Africa tended to be assigned to outlying parts of Chesapeake plantations (called quarters),

AFRICAN ENSLAVEMENT IN THE CHESAPEAKE

at least until they learned some English and the routines of tobacco cultivation. Those from Upper Guinea might have grown the crop in Africa; one historian has speculated that slaves from that region, whence tobacco was exported by the 1680s, could have offered expert advice to Chesapeake planters, who at the time were still experimenting with curing and processing techniques. Such Africans—the vast majority of them men—lived in quarters composed of ten to fifteen workers housed together in one or two buildings and supervised by an Anglo-American overseer. Each man was expected to cultivate about two acres of tobacco a year. Their lives must have been filled with toil and loneliness, for few spoke the same language and all were expected to work for their owners six days a week. On Sundays, planters allowed them a day off. Many used that time to cultivate their own gardens or to hunt or fish to supplement their meager diets. Only rarely could they form families because of the scarcity of women among newly imported Africans.

Slaves usually cost about two and a half times as much as indentured servants, but they repaid the greater investment with a lifetime of service, assuming they survived—which large numbers, weakened by the voyage and sickened by exposure to new diseases, did not. Many planters could not afford to purchase such expensive workers. Thus the transition from indentured to enslaved labor increased the social and economic distance between richer and poorer planters. Those with enough money could acquire slaves, accumulate greater wealth, and establish large plantations worked by tens, if not hundreds, of bondspeople, whereas the less affluent could not even buy indentured servants, whose price rose because of scarcity. As time passed, Anglo-American society in the Chesapeake became more and more stratified—that is, the gap between rich and poor steadily widened. The introduction of large numbers of Africans into the Chesapeake thus had a significant impact on the shape of Anglo-American society, in addition to reshaping the population as a whole.

Africans who had lived in the Caribbean came with their masters to South Carolina from Barbados in 1670, composing one-quarter to one-third of the early population. The Barbadian slaveowners quickly discovered that African-born slaves had a variety of skills well suited to the semitropical environment of South Carolina.

AFRICAN ENSLAVEMENT IN SOUTH CAROLINA

African-style dugout canoes became the chief means of transportation in the colony, which was crossed by rivers and included large islands just offshore. Fishing nets copied from African models proved more efficient than those of English origin. Baskets that enslaved laborers wove and gourds that they hollowed out came into general use as containers for food and drink. Africans' skill at killing crocodiles equipped them to handle alligators. And, finally, Africans adapted their traditional techniques of cattle herding for use in America. Since meat and hides numbered among the colony's chief exports in its earliest years, Africans contributed significantly to South Carolina's prosperity.

Not until after 1700 did South Carolinians begin to import slaves directly from Africa. Nevertheless, by 1710 African-born slaves already outnumbered those born in the Americas, and they constituted a majority of the slave population in South Carolina until about midcentury. The similarity of the South Carolinian and West African environments, coupled with the large proportion of Africans in the population, ensured that more aspects of West African culture survived in that colony than elsewhere on the North American mainland. Only in South Carolina did enslaved parents continue to give their children African names; only there did a dialect develop that combined English words with African terms. (Known as Gullah, it has survived to the present day in isolated areas.) African skills remained useful, so techniques lost in other regions when the migrant generation died were instead passed down to the migrants' children. And in South Carolina African women became the primary petty traders, dominating the markets of Charles Town as they did those of Guinea.

The importation of large numbers of Africans coincided with the successful introduction of rice in South

RICE AND INDIGO

Carolina. English people knew little about the techniques of growing and processing rice. Unsurprisingly, they failed at their first attempts to raise the crop, for which there was strong demand in Europe. But people from Africa's Rice Coast had spent their lives working with rice. Although the evidence is circumstantial, the Africans' expertise almost certainly assisted their English masters in cultivating the crop profitably. Slaves on rice plantations, which were far larger than Chesapeake tobacco quarters, were each expected to cultivate three to four acres of rice a year. To cut expenses, planters also expected slaves to grow part of their own food. A universally adopted task system of predefined work assignments provided that after bondspeople had finished their set "tasks" for the day, they could then rest or work in their own garden plots or on other projects. Experienced slaves could often complete their tasks by early afternoon; after that, as on Sundays, their masters had no legitimate claim on their time.

Developers of South Carolina's second cash crop also used the task system and drew on slaves' specialized skills. Indigo, the only source of blue dye for the growing English textile industry, was much prized. Eliza Lucas, a young woman managing her father's plantations, accordingly began to experiment with indigo cultivation during the early 1740s. Drawing on the knowledge of slaves and overseers from the Caribbean, she developed the planting and processing techniques later adopted throughout the colony. Indigo grew on high ground, and rice was planted in low-lying swamps; rice and indigo also had different growing seasons. Thus the two crops complemented each other. South Carolina indigo never matched the quality of that from the Caribbean, but indigo plantations flourished because the crop was so valuable that Parliament offered Carolinians a bounty on every pound exported to Great Britain.

Among the people held in slavery in both Carolinas were Indian captives who had been retained rather than

INDIAN ENSLAVEMENT IN NORTH AND SOUTH CAROLINA

exported, many of them Catholic converts captured in raids that destroyed nearby Spanish missions early in the eighteenth century. In 1708, enslaved Indians composed as much as 14 percent of the South Carolina population.

The widespread and lucrative traffic in Indian slaves significantly affected South Carolina's relationship with its indigenous neighbors. Native Americans knew they could always find a ready market for captive enemies in Charles Town, so they took that means of ridding themselves of real or potential rivals. Yet native groups soon learned that Carolinians could not be trusted. As settlers and traders shifted their priorities, first one set of former allies, then another, found themselves the enslaved rather than the enslavers.

At first the Carolinians themselves did not engage directly in conflicts with neighboring tribes. But in 1711 the Tuscaroras, an Iroquoian people, attacked a Swiss-German settlement at New Bern, North Carolina, which had expropriated their lands. South Carolinians and their Indian allies then combined to defeat the Tuscaroras in a bloody war. Afterward, more than a thousand Tuscaroras were enslaved, and the remnants of the group drifted northward, where they joined the Iroquois Confederacy.

Four years later, the Yamasees, who had helped to overcome the Tuscaroras, themselves turned on their

In 1726, William Smith, an employee of the Royal African Company, sketched this musician playing a traditional marimba-like instrument called a *balafo*. Later in the eighteenth century Virginians described slaves playing the same instrument, thus showing that African music came to North America with the enslaved multitudes. (Joseph Regenstein Library)

onetime English allies. In what seems to have been long-planned retaliation for multiple abuses by traders as well as threats to their own lands, the Yamasees enlisted the Creeks and other Muskogean peoples in coordinated attacks on outlying English settlements. In the spring and summer of 1715, English and African refugees by the hundreds streamed into Charles Town. The Creek-Yamasee offensive was eventually thwarted when reinforcements arrived from the north, colonists hastily armed their African slaves, and Cherokees joined the fight against the Creeks, their ancient foes. After the war, Carolinian involvement in the Indian slave trade essentially ceased, for all their native neighbors moved away for self-protection: Creeks migrated west, Yamasees went south, and other groups moved north. The abuses of the Carolina slave trade thus in effect caused its own destruction.

Indian or African slavery was not of great importance to Spain's North American territories, which had

SLAVES IN SPANISH AND FRENCH NORTH AMERICA

no plantations or cash crops. Moreover, as slavery took deeper root in South Carolina, Florida officials in 1693 offered freedom to fugitives who would convert to Catholicism. Hundreds of South Carolina runaways took advantage of the offer, although not all won their liberty. Many settled in a town founded for them near St. Augustine, Gracia Real de Santa Teresa de Mose, headed by a former slave and militia captain, Francisco Menéndez.

In early Louisiana, too, slaves—some Indians, some Atlantic creoles—at first composed only a tiny proportion of the residents. But a growing European population demanded that the French government supply them with slaves, and in 1719 officials finally acquiesced, dispatching more than six thousand Africans, mostly from Senegal, over the next decade. The residents failed to develop a successful plantation economy, although they experimented with both tobacco and indigo. They did succeed in angering the Natchez Indians, whose lands they had usurped. In 1729 the Natchez, assisted by newly arrived slaves, attacked northern reaches of the colony, killing more than 10 percent of its European people. The French struck back, slaughtering the Natchez and their enslaved allies, but throughout much of the century Louisiana remained a society with slaves rather than a slave society.

Atlantic creoles from the Caribbean and Indians from the Carolinas and Florida composed almost all the bondspeople in the northern mainland colonies. Yet the intricate involvement of northerners in the web of commerce surrounding the slave trade ensured that many people of African descent lived in America north of Virginia, and that "Spanish Indians" became an identifiable component of the New England population. Some bondspeople resided in urban areas, especially New York, which in 1700 had a larger black population than any other mainland city. Women tended to work as domestic servants, men as unskilled laborers. At the end of the seventeenth century, three-quarters of wealthy Philadelphia households included one or two slaves.

ENSLAVEMENT IN THE NORTH

Yet even in the North most bondspeople worked in the countryside, the majority at agricultural tasks. Dutch farmers in the Hudson Valley and northern New Jersey were especially likely to rely on enslaved Africans, as were the owners of large landholdings in the Narragansett region of Rhode Island. Some bondsmen toiled in new rural enterprises such as ironworks, working alongside hired laborers and indentured servants at forges and foundries. Although relatively few northern colonists owned slaves, those who did relied extensively on their labor. Therefore, even though slavery overall did not make a substantial contribution to the northern economy, certain individual slaveholders benefited greatly from the institution and had good reason to want to preserve it.

Imperial Reorganization and the Witchcraft Crisis

he crises of the 1670s in Virginia and New England focused the attention of reform-minded English officials on the mainland colonies. In the early 1680s, London administrators confronted a bewildering array of colonial governments. Massachusetts Bay (including Maine) functioned under its original charter. Neighboring Connecticut (having absorbed New Haven) and Rhode Island were granted charters by Charles II in 1662 and 1663, respectively, but Plymouth remained autonomous. Virginia, a royal colony, was joined in that status by New Hampshire in 1679 and New York in 1685 when its proprietor ascended the throne as James II. All the other mainland settlements were proprietorships.

By the 1670s, these colonial governments and their residents had become accustomed to a considerable degree of local political autonomy. The tradition of consent was especially firmly established in New England. Massachusetts, Plymouth, Connecticut, and Rhode Island operated essentially as independent entities, subject neither to the direct authority of the king nor to a proprietor. Everywhere in the English colonies, free adult men who owned more than a minimum amount of property (which varied from place to place) expected to have an influential voice in their governments, especially in decisions concerning taxation.

COLONIAL AUTONOMY CHALLENGED

After James II became king in 1685, such expectations clashed with those of the monarch. The new king and his successors sought to bring order to the apparently chaotic state of colonial administration by tightening the reins of government and by reducing the colonies' political autonomy. Simultaneously, officials used the Navigation Acts to reduce the colonies' economic autonomy. Administrators began to chip away at the privileges granted in colonial charters and to reclaim proprietorships for the Crown. Massachusetts (1691), New Jersey (1702), and the Carolinas (1729) all became royal colonies. The charters of Rhode Island, Connecticut, Maryland, and Pennsylvania were temporarily suspended but ultimately were restored to their original status.

The most drastic reordering of colonial administration targeted Puritan New England. Reports from America convinced English officials that New England was a hotbed of smuggling. Moreover, Puritans refused to allow freedom of religion to non-Congregationalists and

DOMINION OF NEW ENGLAND

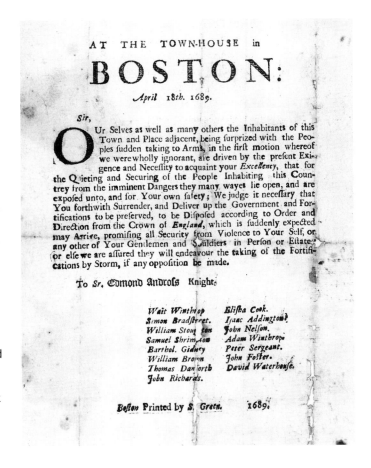

■ Sir Edmund Andros (1637–1714), the much-detested autocratic governor of the Dominion of New England, and a broadside issued at the height of the crisis caused by the Glorious Revolution, calling on Andros to surrender control of the government. The signers were the foremost leaders of the Massachusetts Bay colony, among them a son and grandson of John Winthrop. (Portrait: Massachusetts State Archives; Broadside: Massachusetts Historical Society)

insisted on maintaining laws incompatible with English practice. New England thus seemed an appropriate place to exert English authority with greater vigor. The charters of all the colonies from New Jersey to Maine were revoked, and a Dominion of New England established in 1686. (For the boundaries of the Dominion, see Map 3.1.) Sir Edmund Andros, the governor, had immense power: Parliament dissolved all the assemblies, and Andros needed only the consent of an appointed council to make laws and levy taxes.

New Englanders endured Andros's autocratic rule for more than two years. Then they learned that James

GLORIOUS REVOLUTION IN AMERICA

II's hold on power was crumbling. James had angered his subjects by levying taxes without parliamentary approval and by announcing his conversion to Catholicism. In April 1689, Boston's leaders jailed Andros and his associates. The following month they received definite news of the bloodless coup known as the Glorious Revolution, in which James was replaced on the throne in late 1688 by his daughter Mary and her husband, the Dutch prince

William of Orange. When Parliament offered the throne to the Protestants William and Mary, the Glorious Revolution affirmed the supremacy of both Parliament and Protestantism.

Thus the Bostonians quickly proclaimed their loyalty to William and Mary, writing to England for instructions about the form of government they should now adopt. Most of Massachusetts's political leaders hoped that the new monarchs would renew their original charter. In other colonies, too, the Glorious Revolution emboldened people for revolt. In Maryland the Protestant Association overturned the government of the Catholic proprietor, and in New York a militia officer of German origin, Jacob Leisler, assumed control of the government. Like New Englanders, the Maryland and New York rebels allied themselves with the supporters of William and Mary. They saw themselves as carrying out the colonial phase of the English revolt against Stuart absolutism.

But, like James II, William and Mary believed that England should exercise tighter control over its unruly American possessions. Consequently, only the Maryland rebellion received royal sanction, primarily because of its anti-Catholic thrust. In New York, Leisler was hanged for treason, and Massachusetts (including the formerly independent jurisdiction of Plymouth) became a royal colony with an appointed governor. The province retained its town meeting system of local government and continued to elect its council, but the new 1691 charter eliminated the traditional religious test for voting and office holding. A parish of the Church of England appeared in the heart of Boston. The "city upon a hill," as John Winthrop had envisioned it, had ended.

A war with the French and their Algonquian allies compounded New England's difficulties. King Louis XIV

KING WILLIAM'S WAR

of France allied himself with the deposed James II, and England declared war on France in 1689. (In Europe, this conflict was known as the War of the League of Augsburg, but the colonists called it King William's War.) Even before war broke out in Europe, Anglo-Americans and Abenakis clashed over the English settlements in Maine that had been reoccupied after the 1678 truce and were once again expanding (see page 70). Indian attacks wholly or partially destroyed a number of towns, including Schenectady, New York, and such Maine communities as Falmouth (now Portland), Salmon Falls (now Berwick), and York. Expeditions organized by the colonies against Montreal and Quebec in 1690 failed miserably, and throughout the rest of the conflict New England found itself on the defensive. Even the Peace of Ryswick (1697), which formally ended the war in Europe, failed to bring much respite from warfare to the northern frontiers. Maine could not be fully resettled for several decades because of the continuing conflict.

During the hostilities, New Englanders understandably feared a repetition of the devastation of King Philip's War. For eight months in 1692,

THE 1692 WITCHCRAFT CRISIS

witchcraft accusations spread like wildfire through the rural communities of Essex County, Massachusetts—precisely the area most threatened by the Indian attacks in southern Maine and New Hampshire. Earlier incidents in which personal disputes occasionally led to isolated witchcraft charges (see pages 66–67) bore little relationship to the witch fears that convulsed the region in 1692 while the war raged just to the north. Before the crisis ended, 14 women and 5 men were hanged, 1 man was pressed to death with heavy stones, 54 people confessed to being witches, and more than 140 people were jailed, some for many months.

The crisis began in late February when several young women in Salem Village (an outlying precinct of the bustling port of Salem) formally charged some older female neighbors with having tortured them in spectral

The Wonders of the Invisible World.

OBSERVATIONS

As well *Historical* as *Theological*, upon the NATURE, the NUMBER, and the OPERATIONS of the

DEVILS.

Accompany'd with,

I. Some Accounts of the Grievous Molestations, by DÆMONS and WITCHCRAFTS, which have lately annoy'd the Countrey; and the Trials of some eminent *Malefactors* Executed upon occasion thereof: with several Remarkable *Curiosities* therein occurring.

II. Some Counsils, Directing a due Improvement of the terrible things, lately done, by the Unusual & Amazing Range of EVIL SPIRITS, in Our Neighbourhood: & the methods to prevent the *Wrongs* which those *Evil Angels* may intend against all sorts of people among us; especially in Accusations of the Innocent.

III. Some Conjectures upon the great EVENTS, likely to befall, the WORLD in General, and NEW-ENGLAND in Particular; as also upon the Advances of the TIME, when we shall see BETTER DAYES.

IV. A short Narrative of a late Outrage committed by a knot of WITCHES in *Swedeland*, very much Resembling, and so far Explaining, *That* under which our parts of *America* have laboured!

V. THE DEVIL DISCOVERED: In a Brief Discourse upon those TEMPTATIONS, which are the more Ordinary *Devices* of the Wicked One.

By **Cotton Mather.**

Boston Printed by *Benj. Harris* for *Sam. Phillips.* 1693.

■ The Reverend Cotton Mather of Boston, twenty-nine years old in 1692 at the time of the Salem witchcraft crisis, rushed this book—*The Wonders of the Invisible World*—into print shortly after the trials ended. He tried to explain to his fellow New Englanders the "Grievous Molestations by Daemons and Witchcrafts which have lately annoy'd the Countrey" by providing both brief trial narratives and examples of similar recent occurrences elsewhere, most notably in Mohra, Sweden.   (Massachusetts Historical Society)

form. Soon other accusers and confessors chimed in, some of them female domestic servants who had been orphaned in the Indian attacks on Maine. One had lost her grandparents in King Philip's War and other relatives in King William's War. These young women, perhaps the most powerless people in a region apparently powerless to affect its fate, offered their fellow New Englanders a compelling explanation for the seemingly endless chain of troubles afflicting them: their province was under direct assault not only by the Indians but also by the Devil and his allied witches.

The so-called afflicted girls accused not just the older women commonly suspected of such offenses but also prominent men from the Maine frontier who had traded with or failed to defeat the Indians. The leader of the witch conspiracy, accusers and confessors alike declared, was the Reverend George Burroughs, a Harvard graduate who had ministered in both Maine and Salem Village and was suspected of bewitching the soldiers sent to combat the Abenakis. The colony's magistrates, who were also its political and military leaders, were all too willing to believe such accusations, because if the Devil had caused New England's current troubles, they personally bore no responsibility for the terrible losses on the frontier.

In October, the worst phase of the crisis ended when the governor dissolved the special court established to try the suspects. He and several prominent clergymen began to regard the girls' descriptions of spectral torturers as "the Devil's testimony"—and everyone knew the Devil could not be trusted to tell the truth. Most critics of the trials did not think the girls were faking, nor did they conclude that witches did not exist or that confessions were false. Rather, they questioned whether the guilt of the accused could be *legally* established by the evidence presented in court. Accordingly, during the final trials (ending in May 1693) in regular courts, almost all the defendants were acquitted, and the governor quickly reprieved the few found guilty.

In 1696, England took a major step in colonial administration by creating the fifteen-member Board of Trade and Plantations, which thereafter served as the chief organ of government concerned with the American colonies. Previously, no single body in London had that responsibility. The board gathered information, reviewed Crown appointments in America, scrutinized legislation passed by colonial assemblies, supervised trade policies, and advised successive ministries on colonial issues. Still, the Board of Trade did not have any direct powers of enforcement. It also shared jurisdiction over American affairs not only with the customs service and the navy but also with a member of the ministry. Although this reform improved the quality of colonial administration, supervision of the American provinces remained decentralized and haphazard.

New Imperial Measures

That surely made it easier for Massachusetts and the rest of the English colonies in America to accommodate themselves to the new imperial order. Most colonists resented alien officials who arrived in America determined to implement the policies of king and Parliament, but they adjusted to their demands and to the trade restrictions imposed by the Navigation Acts. They fought another of Europe's wars—the War of the Spanish Succession, called Queen Anne's War in the colonies—from 1702 to 1713, without enduring the stresses of the first, despite the heavy economic burdens the conflict imposed. Colonists who allied themselves with royal government received patronage in the form of offices and land grants and composed "court parties" that supported English officials. Others, who were either less fortunate in their friends or more principled in defense of colonial autonomy, made up the opposition, or "country" interest. By the end of the first quarter of the eighteenth century, most men in both groups had been born in America. They were members of elite families whose wealth derived in the South from staple-crop production and in the North from commerce.

Summary

The eighty years from 1640 to 1720 established the basic economic and political patterns that were to structure subsequent changes in mainland colonial society. In 1640 just two isolated centers of English population, New England and the Chesapeake, existed along the seaboard, along with the tiny Dutch colony of New Netherland. In 1720 nearly the entire east coast of North America was in English hands, and Indian control east of the Appalachian Mountains had largely been broken by the outcomes of King Philip's War, Bacon's Rebellion, the Carolina wars, and Queen Anne's War. To the west of the mountains, though, Iroquois power reigned supreme. What had been an immigrant population was now mostly American-born, except for the many African-born people in South Carolina; economies originally based on trade in fur and skins had become far more complex and more closely linked with the mother country; and a wide variety of political structures had been reshaped into a more uniform pattern. Yet at the same time the adoption of large-scale slavery in the Chesapeake and the Carolinas differentiated their societies from those of the colonies to the north. The production of tobacco, rice, and indigo for international markets distinguished the southern regional economies. They had become true slave societies, heavily reliant on a system of perpetual servitude, not societies with slaves, in which a few bondspeople mingled with larger numbers of indentured servants and laborers of other descriptions.

Even the economies of the northern colonies, though, rested on profits derived from the Atlantic trading system, the key element of which was traffic in enslaved humans, primarily Africans but also including Indians. New England sold corn, salt fish, and wood products to the West Indies, where slaves consumed the foodstuffs and whence planters shipped sugar and molasses in barrels made from staves crafted by northern farmers. Pennsylvania and New York too found in the Caribbean islands a ready market for their livestock, grains, and wheat flour. The rapid growth of enslavement drove all the English colonial economies in these years.

Meanwhile, from a small outpost in Santa Fe, New Mexico, and missions in Florida, the Spanish had expanded their influence throughout the Gulf Coast region and, by just after midcentury, as far north as California. The French had moved from a few settlements along the St. Lawrence to dominate the length of the Mississippi River and the entire Great Lakes region. Both groups of colonists lived near Indian nations and depended on the indigenous people's labor and goodwill. The Spanish could not fully control their Indian allies, and the French did not even try. The extensive Spanish and French presence to the south and west of the English settlements meant that future conflicts among the European powers in North America were nearly inevitable.

By 1720, the essential elements of the imperial administrative structure that would govern the English colonies until 1775 had been put firmly in place. The regional economic systems originating in the late seventeenth and early eighteenth centuries also continued to dominate North American life for another century—until after independence had been won. And Anglo-Americans had developed the commitment to autonomous local government that later would lead them into conflict with Parliament and the king.

LEGACY FOR A PEOPLE AND A NATION
Americans of African Descent

Before 1640, people of African descent composed only a tiny proportion of the population of the mainland North American colonies. After the 1670s, the rise of southern economies based largely on the enslavement of Africans, coupled with the widespread employment of enslaved Africans in northern colonies, dramatically altered the composition of the American population. By 1775, more than a quarter million Africans had been imported into the territory that later became the United States, constituting about 20 percent of the population at the time of the Revolution.

According to the 2000 census, 12.5 percent of the American people now claim descent from African ancestors. Because the legal importation of African slaves ended in 1808, and because the United States attracted relatively few voluntary migrants of African descent until late in the twentieth century, most of today's African Americans have colonial ancestors—a claim few Americans of European descent can make. Most European Americans are descended at least in part from the massive European migrations of the nineteenth and early twentieth centuries.

The modern African American population includes people with many different skin colors, reflecting the large number of interracial sexual relationships (both coerced and voluntary) that have developed during the long African residence in mainland North America. African Americans, both free and enslaved, have had children with both Europeans and Indians since the colonial period; more recently, they have intermarried with Asian immigrants. In large part the mingling of different peoples of color resulted from state miscegenation laws, which from the early years of the American republic until 1967—when they were struck down by the Supreme Court—forbade legal marriages between people of European descent and those of other races. That forced the non-European groups to seek partners only among themselves. And other state and federal laws then defined people with any appreciable African ancestry as "black."

Recently, increasing numbers of interracial unions have produced multiracial children. The 2000 census for the first time allowed Americans to define themselves simultaneously as members of more than one race. Opposition to this change came largely from leaders of the African American community, and on census forms people of African descent proved less willing to define themselves as multiracial than did people with other origins. The racial self-definition of this large component of the American people thus continues to be influenced by a legacy of discrimination.

The **history companion** *powered by Eduspace®*
Your primary source for interactive quizzes, exercises, and more to help you learn efficiently.
http://history.college.hmco.com/students

AMERICAN SOCIETY TRANSFORMED 1720–1770

*W*as I in that Country I would not Stay one day longer in it," Alexander McAllister told his cousin in late 1770. "If god Spers [spares] you in this Cuntrie but a few years you will blis the day you left." McAllister, who as a youth had moved to North Carolina with his parents, clearly did bless the day he had left the Scottish Highlands. In many letters to friends and family back in Argyleshire, McAllister elaborated on the attractions of his adopted home at Cross Creek (near modern Fayetteville, North Carolina). Anyone could easily grow corn, wheat, barley, rye, oats, potatoes, and tobacco; "in truth it is the Best poor mans Cuntry I Ever heard of and I have had the opertunity of hearing from South & north." Lest his Scots correspondents think he exaggerated, McAllister assured them that other immigrants too were doing well. They had harvested "plenty of Corn for them Selves and famile and seemes to be very well Satisfied." Underscoring his point, he insisted that "ther is non but what is in a good way."

One historian has estimated that Alexander McAllister's letters were central to a network of correspondents that brought about five thousand of his fellow countrymen to North America in the two decades after the mid-1750s. His connections in the Highlands recognized that he was a ready source of advice, encouragement, and accurate information for potential emigrants. When Scots arrived in North Carolina with letters of introduction from people McAllister knew, he helped them find land and supplies. Although he understood that, as he told one correspondent, "the best [land] is taken up many years ago," and that newcomers' first two or three years would be hard, he never altered his recommendations. People should "take currage" and move to North America, McAllister asserted; "it will be of Benefitt to ther riseing generation." Certainly McAllister himself thrived in his new homeland; by the late 1780s, having fathered numerous children by two wives, he owned forty slaves and more than 2,500 acres of land. He served as an elder of the Presbyterian church, as a

◄ A farmer, probably an immigrant like Alexander McAllister, plows his field outside the town of Salem, North Carolina, in this 1787 painting by Ludwig G. von Redeken. (Collection of the Wachovia Historical Society; Photograph courtesy of Old Salem, Inc.)

and the Scottish lowlands. The British colonies south of New England drew by far the largest number of new-comers. Their arrival not only swelled the population but also altered political balances and affected the religious climate by introducing new sects. Unwilling immigrants too (slaves and transported convicts) clustered primarily in the middle and southern colonies.

Several key themes marked colonial development in the mid-eighteenth century: not only population growth (through natural increase as well as immigration) and the new ethnic diversity, but also the increasing importance of colonial urban centers, the creation of a prosperous urban elite, rising levels of consumption for all social ranks, and the new significance of internal markets. In the French and British mainland colonies, exports continued to dominate the economy. Settlers along the Atlantic and Gulf of Mexico coasts were tied to an international commercial system that fluctuated wildly for reasons having little to do with the colonies but inescapable in their effects. Yet expanding local populations demanded greater quantities and types of goods, and Europe could not supply all those needs. Therefore, in English and French America, as well as in the northern portions of New Spain known as the Borderlands (where exports were never an important element of the economy), colonists came increasingly to depend on exploiting and consuming their own resources (see Map 5.2).

Intermarried networks of wealthy families developed in each of Europe's American possessions by the 1760s. These well-off, educated colonists participated in transatlantic intellectual life, such as the movement known as the Enlightenment, whereas many colonists of the "lesser sort" could neither read nor write. The elites lived in comfortable houses and enjoyed leisure-time activities. Most colonists, whether free or enslaved, worked with their hands daily from dawn to dark. Such divisions were most pronounced in British America, the largest and most prosperous settlements on the continent. By the last half of the century, the social and economic distance among different ranks of Anglo-Americans had widened noticeably. As such stratification increased, so did conflicts—political, economic, and even religious—among people of diverse origins and social ranks.

member of the colonial assembly, and as a state senator after independence was won. Although he was more successful than most migrants, his prosperity showed what some could achieve.

Alexander McAllister and other Highland Scots took part in a massive eighteenth-century migration of European and African peoples that by 1770 had changed the nature of the American population and the look of the American landscape. Ethnic diversity was especially pronounced in the small colonial cities, but the countryside too attracted settlers from many nations. Near McAllister's Cross Creek, for example, also resided large numbers of people from England, Germany, France, Wales,

In 1720 much of North America was still under Indian control. By 1770, in sharp contrast, settlements of Europeans and Africans ruled by Great Britain filled almost all of the region between the Appalachian Mountains and the Atlantic Ocean; and the British, following their victory over France in the Seven Years War (see pages 120–123), dominated the extensive system of rivers and lakes running through the heart of the continent. Spanish missions extended in a great arc from present-day northern California to the Gulf Coast. Such geographical, economic, and social changes transformed the character of Europe's North American possessions. ■

Population Growth and Ethnic Diversity

*D*ramatic population growth characterized the British mainland colonies in the eighteenth century. Only about 250,000 European and African Americans resided in the colonies in 1700. Thirty years later, that number had more than doubled, and by 1775 it had become 2.5 million. Such rapid expansion appears even more remarkable when it is compared with the modest changes that occurred in French and Spanish North America. At the end of the eighteenth century, Texas had only about 2,500 Spanish residents and California even fewer; the largest Spanish colony, New Mexico, included just 20,000 or so. The total European population of New France expanded from approximately 15,000 in 1700 to about 70,000 in the 1760s, but only along the St. Lawrence River between Quebec and Montreal and in New Orleans were there significant concentrations of French settlers.

Although migration accounted for a considerable share of the growth in Anglo America, most of the gain resulted from natural increase. Once the difficult early decades of settlement had passed and the sex ratio evened out in the South (after 1700), the American population doubled approximately every twenty-five years. Such a rate of growth, unparalleled in human history until very recent times, had a variety of causes, chief among them women's youthful age at the onset of childbearing (early twenties for European Americans, late teens for African Americans). Since married women became pregnant every two or three years, women normally bore five to ten children. Because the colonies, especially those north of Virginia, were relatively healthful places to live,

a large proportion of children who survived infancy reached maturity and began families of their own. Consequently, about half of the American population was under sixteen years old in 1775. (By contrast, only about one-quarter of the American population was under sixteen in 2000.)

Even though Spaniards first brought enslaved Africans to the Americas in the sixteenth century, the

INVOLUNTARY MIGRANTS FROM AFRICA

height of the slave trade occurred in the eighteenth century, when about two-thirds of all slaves were carried across the Atlantic. Rice, indigo, tobacco, and sugar plantations expanded rapidly, thus steadily increasing the demand for bonded laborers. Furthermore, in the slaveholding societies of South America and the Caribbean, a surplus of males over females and appallingly high mortality rates meant that only a large, continuing influx of slaves could maintain the work force at constant levels. South Carolina, where rice cultivation was difficult and unhealthful (chiefly because malaria-carrying mosquitoes bred in the rice swamps), and where planters preferred to purchase men, resembled such colonies because it too required an inflow of Africans to sustain as well as expand its labor force. But in the Chesapeake the number of bondspeople grew especially rapidly because the new imports were added to an enslaved population that after 1740 began to sustain itself through natural increase. The work routines involved in cultivating tobacco, coupled with a roughly equal sex ratio, reduced slave mortality and increased fertility.

The involuntary migrants came from many different ethnic groups and regions of Africa (see Map 4.1). Standard slave-trading practice, in which a vessel loaded an entire cargo at one port, meant that people from the same area (enemies as well as allies) tended to be taken to the Americas together. That tendency was heightened by planter partiality for slaves of particular ethnic groups. Virginians, for example, evidently preferred to purchase Igbos from the Bight of Biafra (modern Cameroon, Gabon, and southeastern Nigeria), whereas South Carolinians and Georgians selected Senegambians and people from West Central Africa (modern Congo and Angola). Louisiana planters first chose slaves from the Bight of Benin (modern Togo, Benin, and southwestern Nigeria) but later bought many from West Central Africa. Rice planters' desire to purchase Senegambians, who had cultivated rice in their homeland, is easily explained, but historians disagree about the reasons for the other preferences. (Some contend, for example, that Chesapeake planters did not care about the ethnicity of

Map 4.1 Major Origins and Destinations of Africans Enslaved in the Americas

As this schematic map shows, enslaved Africans were drawn from many regions of western Africa (with some coming from the interior of the continent) and were shipped to areas throughout the Americas.

■ In August 1753, the slave-trading firm of Austin & Laurens advertised the upcoming sale of slaves from the desirable locales of Angola and Gambia in Charleston's *South Carolina Gazette.*   (Library of Congress)

their slaves, taking Igbos only because Carolinians and Georgians explicitly rejected them and so made them available for sale elsewhere.)

Thousands, possibly tens of thousands, of these enslaved Africans were Muslims. Some were literate in Arabic, and several came from aristocratic families. The discovery of noble birth could lead to slaves being freed to return home. Job Ben Solomon, for example, arrived in Maryland in 1732. Himself a slave trader from Senegal, he had been captured by raiders while selling bondspeople in Gambia. A letter he wrote in Arabic so impressed his owners that he was liberated the next year. Abd al-Rahman, brought to Louisiana in 1788, was less fortunate. Known to his master as "Prince" because of his aristocratic origins, he was not freed until 1829, through the assistance of a European he had befriended in West Africa.

Despite the approximately 280,000 slaves brought to the mainland, American-born people of African descent soon numerically dominated the enslaved population because of high levels of natural increase. A planter who owned adult female slaves could watch the size of his labor force expand steadily—through the births of their children, by then designated as slaves in all the colonies—without making additional major purchases of workers. Not coincidentally, the first truly large Chesapeake plantations appeared in the 1740s. Even in South Carolina, where substantial imports continued, African-born slaves were outnumbered by American-born slaves as early as 1750. Some years later, the slaveholder Thomas Jefferson indicated that he fully understood the connections when he observed, "I consider a woman who brings a child every two years more profitable than the best man of the farm. What she produces is an addition to the capital, while his labors disappear in mere consumption."

In addition to the new group of Africans, about 585,000 Europeans moved to North America during the eighteenth century, most of them after 1730. Late in the seventeenth century, English officials decided to recruit German and French Protestants in order to prevent further large-scale emigration from England itself. Influenced by mercantilist thought, they had come to regard a large, industrious population at home as an asset rather than a liability. Thus they ordered the deportation to the colonies of "undesirables"—convicts and Jacobite rebels (supporters of the deposed Stuart monarchs)—but otherwise discouraged emigration. They offered foreign Protestants free lands and religious toleration, even financing the passage of some groups (for example, Germans sent to New York in the 1710s). After 1740 they relaxed citizenship (naturalization) requirements, insisting on only the payment of a small fee, seven years' colonial residence, evidence of adherence to Protestant beliefs, and an oath of allegiance to the king.

NEWCOMERS FROM EUROPE

The patterns evident in the chapter-opening vignette applied generally to all the voluntary eighteenth-century European migrants. Early arrivals wrote home, urging others to come; those contacts created chains of migration from particular regions. The most successful migrants came well prepared, having learned from their American correspondents that land and resources were abundant, especially in the inland areas known as the backcountry, but that they would need capital to take full advantage of the new opportunities. People who arrived penniless did less well. Thus, for instance, the poverty-stricken folk (generally of English or German origin) who emigrated as indentured servants often struggled to survive after their terms of service had been completed.

One of the largest groups of immigrants—nearly 150,000—came from Ireland or Scotland. About 66,000 Scots-Irish descendants of Presbyterian Scots

SCOTS-IRISH, GERMANS, AND SCOTS who had settled in the north of Ireland during the seventeenth century joined some 35,000 people who, like Alexander McAllister, came directly to America from Scotland (see Table 4.1). Another 43,000, both Protestants and Catholics, migrated from southern Ireland. High rents, poor harvests, and religious discrimination (in Ireland) combined to push people from lands their families had long occupied. Many of the Irish mi-

grants had supported themselves in Ireland by weaving linen cloth, but linen prices declined significantly in the late 1710s. Because the flax used in the weaving was imported from Pennsylvania and the less bulky cloth was largely exported back to the same place, vessels with plenty of room for passengers regularly sailed from Ireland to Pennsylvania. By the 1720s, the migration route was well established, fueled by positive reports of prospects for advancement in North America.

TABLE 4.1

Who Moved to America from England and Scotland in the Early 1770s, and Why?

	English Emigrants	Scottish Emigrants	Free American Population	
Destination				
13 British colonies	81.1%	92.7%	—	
Canada	12.1	4.2	—	Note: Between December 1773 and March 1776, the British government questioned individuals and families leaving ports in Scotland and England for the American colonies to learn who they were, where they were going, and why they were leaving. This table summarizes just a few of the findings of the official inquiries, which revealed a number of significant differences between the Scottish and English emigrants.
West Indies	6.8	3.1	—	
Age Distribution				
Under 21	26.8	45.3	56.8%	
21–25	37.1	19.9	9.7	
26–44	33.3	29.5	20.4	
45 and over	2.7	5.3	13.1	
Sex Distribution				
Male	83.8	59.9	—	
Female	16.2	40.1	—	
Unknown	4.2	13.5	—	
Traveling Alone or with Families				
In families	20.0	48.0	—	
Alone	80.0	52.0	—	
Known Occupation or Status				
Gentry	2.5	1.2	—	
Merchandising	5.2	5.2	—	
Agriculture	17.8	24.0	—	
Artisanry	54.2	37.7	—	
Laborer	20.3	31.9	—	
Why They Left				
Positive reasons (e.g., desire to better one's position)	90.0	36.0	—	
Negative reasons (e.g., poverty, unemployment)	10.0	64.0	—	

Source of data: Bernard Bailyn, *Voyagers to the West* (New York: Knopf, 1986), Tables 4.1, 5.2, 5.4, 5.7, 5.23, and 6.1.

Such immigrants usually landed in Philadelphia or New Castle, Delaware. They moved into the backcountry of western Pennsylvania along the Susquehanna River, where the colonial government created a county named Donegal for them. Later migrants moved farther west and south, to the backcountry of Maryland, Virginia, and the Carolinas. Frequently unable to afford any acreage, they lived illegally on land belonging to Indians, land speculators, or colonial governments. In the frontier setting, they gained a reputation for lawlessness, hard drinking, and ferocious fighting, both among themselves and with neighboring Indians.

Migrants from Germany and German-speaking areas of Switzerland numbered about 85,000, most of them emigrating from the Rhineland between 1730 and 1755. They too usually arrived in Philadelphia, becoming known locally as Pennsylvania Dutch (a corruption of *Deutsch*, as the Germans called themselves). Late in the century they and their descendants accounted for one-third of Pennsylvania's residents. More important, they—like other ethnic groups—tended to settle together, and so they composed up to half of the population of some counties. Many Germans moved west and then south into the backcountry of Maryland and Virginia. Others landed in Charles Town and settled in the southern interior. The Germans belonged to a wide variety of Protestant sects—primarily Lutheran, German Reformed, and Moravian—and therefore added to the already substantial religious diversity of Pennsylvania. So many Germans had arrived by 1751 that Benjamin Franklin, for one, feared they would "Germanize" Pennsylvania. They "will never adopt our Language or Customs," he predicted (inaccurately).

The most concentrated period of immigration to the colonies fell between 1760 and 1775. Tough economic times in Germany and the British Isles led many to decide to seek a better life in America; simultaneously, the slave trade burgeoned. In those fifteen years alone more than 220,000 persons arrived—nearly 10 percent of the entire population of British North America in 1775. Late-arriving free immigrants had little choice but to remain in the cities or move to the edges of settlement; land elsewhere was fully occupied (see Map 4.2). In the peripheries they became the tenants of, or bought property from, land speculators who had purchased giant tracts in the (usually vain) hope of making a fortune.

Because of these migration patterns and the concentration of slaveholding in the South, half the colonial population south of New England had non-English origins by 1775. Whether the migrants assimilated readily into Anglo-American culture depended on patterns of

In December 1729, probably in New York's Hudson Valley, an unknown artist portrayed J. M. Stolle, son of a Palatine immigrant who came to North America from Germany in 1709. The young man's fancy clothing and the column and balustrade in the background suggest that the artist wanted to convey an image of the family's economic success, though whether that image was accurate is unknown.   (National Gallery of Art, Washington, D.C. Gift of Edgar William and Bernice Chrysler Garbisch)

MAINTAINING ETHNIC AND RELIGIOUS IDENTITIES

settlement, the size of the group, and the strength of the migrants' ties to their common culture. For example, the Huguenots—French Protestants who fled religious persecution in their homeland after 1685—settled in tiny enclaves in American cities like Charles Town and New York. Unable to sustain either their language or their religious practices, they largely assimilated into the dominant culture within two generations. By contrast, the equally small group of colonial Jews maintained a distinct identity. Most were Sephardic, descended from persecuted Spanish and Portuguese Jews who had first fled to the Netherlands or its American colonies, then later migrated into English territory. In places like New York and Newport, Rhode Island, they established synagogues and worked actively to preserve their religion (for instance, by observing dietary

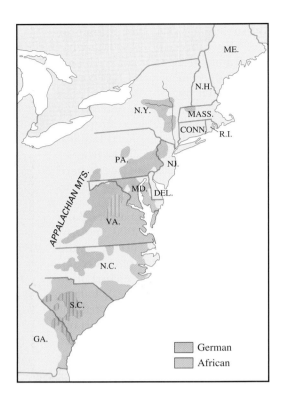

Map 4.2   Non-English Ethnic Groups in the British Colonies, c. 1775

Non-African immigrants arriving in the years after 1720 were pushed to the peripheries of settlement, as is shown by these maps. Scottish, Scots-Irish, French, and German newcomers had to move to the frontiers. The Dutch remained where they had originally settled in the seventeenth century. Africans were concentrated in coastal plantation regions.

laws and by trying to prevent their children from marrying Christians).

Members of the larger groups of migrants (Germans, Irish, and Scots) found it easier to sustain European ways. Some ethnic groups dominated certain localities. Near Frederick, Maryland, a visitor would have heard more German than English; in Anson and Cumberland Counties, North Carolina, the same visitor might have thought she was in Scotland. Where migrants from different countries settled in the same region, ethnic antagonisms often surfaced. One German clergyman in Pennsylvania, for example, explained his efforts to prevent German youths from marrying people of different ethnic origins by asserting that Scots-Irish migrants were "lazy, dissipated and poor" and that "it is very seldom that German and English blood is happily united in wedlock." Anglo-American elites fostered such antagonisms in order to maintain their political and economic power, and they frequently subverted the colonies' generous naturalization laws, thus depriving even long-resident immigrants of a voice in government.

The elites probably would have preferred to ignore the English colonies' growing racial and ethnic diversity, but ultimately they could not do so. When they moved toward revolution in the 1770s, they recognized that they needed the support of non-English Americans. Quite deliberately, they began to speak of "the rights of man," rather than "English liberties," when they sought recruits for their cause.

Economic Growth and Development

*T*he dramatic increase in the population of Anglo America served as one of the few sources of stability for the colonial economy, which was driven primarily by the vagaries of international markets. A comparison with French and Spanish America reveals significant differences. The population and economy of New Spain's northern Borderlands stagnated. The isolated settlements produced few items for export (notably,

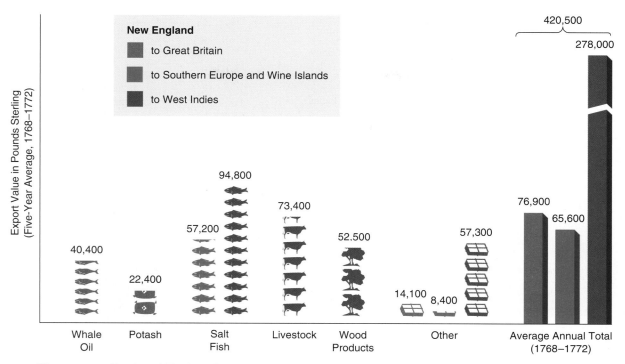

Figure 4.1   Regional Trading Patterns: New England

New England's major exports—salt fish, livestock, and wood products—were sold primarily in the West Indies.

(Source: James F. Shepherd and Gary M. Walton, *Shipping, Maritime Trade, and the Economic Development of Colonial North America* [Cambridge: Cambridge University Press, 1972]. Copyright 1972. Used by permission of Cambridge University Press.)

hides obtained from nearby Indians); residents more often exchanged goods illegally with their French and English neighbors than with Spanish Mexico or the Caribbean. French Canada exported large quantities of furs and fish, but monopolistic trade practices ensured that most of the profits ended up in the home country. The Louisiana colony required substantial government subsidies to survive, despite its active internal trade and some agricultural exports. Of France's American possessions, only the Caribbean islands flourished economically.

In British North America, by contrast, each year the rising population generated ever-greater demands for

OVERVIEW OF
THE ANGLO-
AMERICAN
ECONOMY

goods and services, leading to the development of small-scale colonial manufacturing and a complex network of internal trade. Roads, bridges, mills, and stores were built to serve the many new settlements. A lively coastal trade developed; by the late 1760s, more than half the vessels leaving Boston harbor sailed to other mainland colonies. Such ships not only collected goods for export and dis-

tributed imports but also sold items made in America. The colonies thus began to move away from their earlier pattern of dependence on European manufactured goods. For the first time, the American population generated sufficient demand to encourage manufacturing enterprises. Iron making became the largest indigenous industry; by 1775, Anglo America's iron production—most of it for domestic consumption—surpassed England's.

The major energizing, yet destabilizing, influence on the colonial economy nevertheless remained foreign trade. Colonial prosperity still depended heavily on overseas demand for American products like tobacco, rice, indigo, fish, and barrel staves. The sale of such items earned the colonists the credit they needed to purchase English and European imports. If demand for American exports slowed, the colonists' income dropped, as did their ability to buy imported goods. Merchants were particularly vulnerable to economic downswings, and bankruptcies were common.

Despite fluctuations, the American economy slowly grew during the eighteenth century. That growth, which resulted partly from higher earnings from exports, in

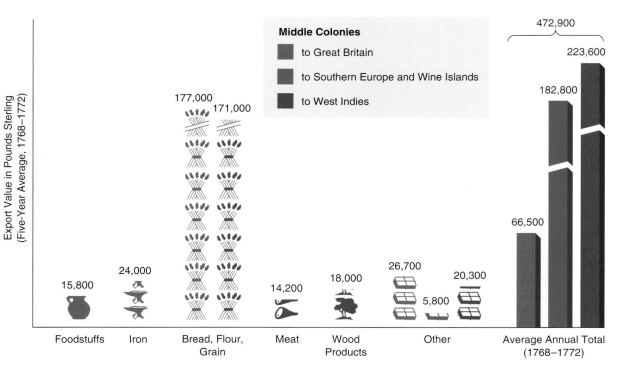

Figure 4.2   Regional Trading Patterns: Middle Colonies

The middle colonies' major trading partners were the West Indies, the Wine Islands, and southern Europe. Bread, flour, and grains were the region's most valuable exports.   (Source: James F. Shepherd and Gary M. Walton, *Shipping, Maritime Trade, and the Economic Development of Colonial North America* [Cambridge: Cambridge University Press, 1972]. Copyright 1972. Used by permission of Cambridge University Press.)

WEALTH AND POVERTY

turn produced better standards of living for all property-owning Americans. Early in the century, as the price of British manufactures fell in relation to Americans' incomes, households began to acquire amenities such as chairs and earthenware dishes. Diet also improved as trading networks brought access to more varied foodstuffs. After 1750, luxury items like silver plate could be found in the homes of the wealthy, and the "middling sort" started to purchase imported English ceramics and teapots. Even the poorest property owners had more and better household possessions. Thus the colonists became consumers, in the sense that for the first time they could make choices among a variety of products and also could afford to buy items not essential for subsistence.

Yet the benefits of economic growth were unevenly distributed: wealthy Americans improved their position relative to other colonists. The native-born elite families who dominated American political, economic, and social life by 1750 had begun the century with sufficient capital to take advantage of the changes caused by population growth. They were the urban merchants who

exported raw materials and imported luxury goods, the large landowners who rented small farms to immigrant tenants, the slave traders who supplied wealthy planters with their bondspeople, and the owners of rum distilleries. The rise of this group of moneyed families helped to make the social and economic structure of mid-eighteenth-century America more stratified than before.

New arrivals did not have the opportunities for advancement that had greeted their predecessors. Even so, few free settlers in rural areas (where about 95 percent of the colonists lived) appear to have been truly poor. But in the cities, families of urban laborers lived on the edge of destitution. In Philadelphia, for instance, a male laborer's average annual earnings fell short of the amount needed to supply his family with the bare necessities. Even in a good year, his wife or children had to do wage work; in a bad year, the family could be reduced to beggary. By the 1760s applicants for assistance overwhelmed public urban poor-relief systems, and some cities began to build workhouses or almshouses to shelter the growing number of poor people. Among them were recent immi-

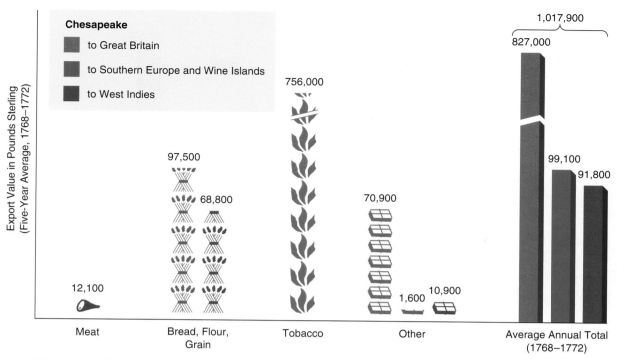

Figure 4.3 Regional Trading Patterns: The Chesapeake

Tobacco—legally exported only to Great Britain under the terms of the Navigation Acts—was the Chesapeake's dominant product. Grain made up an increasing proportion of the crops this region sold to other destinations.
(Source: James F. Shepherd and Gary M. Walton, *Shipping, Maritime Trade, and the Economic Development of Colonial North America* [Cambridge: Cambridge University Press, 1972]. Copyright 1972. Used by permission of Cambridge University Press.)

grants, the elderly and infirm, and widows, especially those with small children.

Within this overall picture, different regional patterns can be identified. New England, the middle colonies (Pennsylvania, New York, and New Jersey), the Chesapeake (including North Carolina), and the Lower South (South Carolina and Georgia) each had its own economic rhythm derived from the nature of its export trade.

In New England, three elements combined to influence economic development: the nature of the landscape, New England's leadership in shipping, and the impact of imperial wars. New England's poor soil failed to produce surpluses other than livestock, so wood products constituted important salable commodities. Farms were worked primarily by family members; the region had relatively few hired laborers. It also had the lowest average wealth per freeholder in the colonies. But New England had many wealthy merchants and professionals who profited substantially from trade with the Caribbean in items such as salt fish, livestock, and molasses (see Figure 4.1).

NEW ENGLAND AND KING GEORGE'S WAR

Boston, by the 1730s a major shipbuilding center, soon felt the impact when warfare between European powers resumed in 1739. British vessels clashed with Spanish ships in the Caribbean, sparking a conflict that became known in America as King George's War (Europeans called it the War of the Austrian Succession). The war initially energized Boston's economy, for ships—and sailors—were in great demand to serve as privateers. Wealthy merchants profited from contracts to supply military expeditions. But then New Englanders suffered major losses in Caribbean battles and forays against Canada. In 1745 a New England expedition captured the French fortress of Louisbourg (in modern Nova Scotia), which guarded the sea-lanes leading to New France. The expensive victory, though, led to heavy taxation of Massachusetts residents, and after the war unprecedented numbers of widows and children crowded Boston's relief rolls. The shipbuilding boom ended when the war did, the economy stagnated, and taxes remained high. Britain even returned Louisbourg to France in the Treaty of Aix-la-Chapelle (1748).

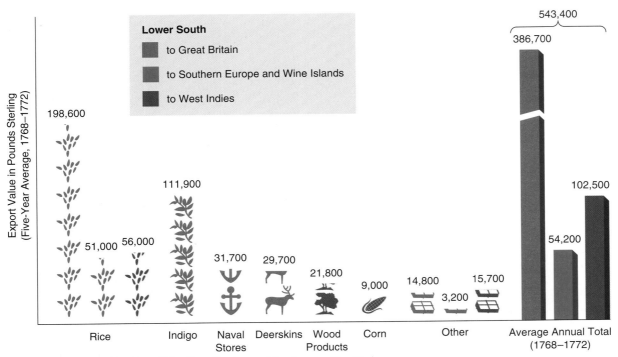

Figure 4.4　Regional Trading Patterns: The Lower South

Rice and indigo, sold primarily in the mother country, dominated the exports of the Lower South.

(Source: James F. Shepherd and Gary M. Walton, *Shipping, Maritime Trade, and the Economic Development of Colonial North America* [Cambridge: Cambridge University Press, 1972]. Copyright 1972. Used by permission of Cambridge University Press.)

King George's War and its aftermath affected the middle colonies and the Chesapeake more positively because of the greater fertility of the soil in those regions, where commercial farming prevailed. An average Pennsylvania farm family consumed only 40 percent of what it produced, selling the rest. New York and New Jersey both had many tenant farmers who leased acreage from large landowners, often paying their rent by sharing crops with their landlords. Prosperous landlords and farmers thus occupied an ideal position to profit from the wartime demand for grain and flour, especially in the Caribbean (see Figure 4.2). After the war a series of poor grain harvests in Europe caused flour prices to rise rapidly. Philadelphia and New York, which could draw on large fertile grain- and livestock-producing areas, took the lead in the foodstuffs trade.

MIDDLE COLONIES AND THE CHESAPEAKE

Increased European demand for grain had a significant impact on the Chesapeake as well. After 1745, when the price of grain began rising faster than that of tobacco, some Chesapeake planters began to convert tobacco fields to wheat and corn. By diversifying their crops, they could avoid dependency on one product for their income (see Figure 4.3). Tobacco still ruled the region and remained the largest single export from the mainland colonies. The value of tobacco exports was nearly double that of grain products, the next contender. Yet the conversion to grain cultivation brought about the first significant change in Chesapeake settlement patterns by encouraging the development of port towns (like Baltimore) to house the merchants who marketed the new products.

The Lower South too depended on staple crops and an enslaved labor force but had a distinctive pattern of economic growth. After Parliament in 1730 removed rice from the list of enumerated products (see page 77), South Carolinians could trade directly with continental Europe. Rice prices thereafter climbed steeply, doubling by the late 1730s (see Figure 4.4). But dependence on European sales had its drawbacks, as rice growers discovered when the outbreak of King George's War in 1739 disrupted trade with the continent. Rice prices plummeted,

LOWER SOUTH

and South Carolina entered a depression from which it did not emerge for a decade. Still, prosperity returned by the 1760s because of rapidly rising European demand for South Carolina's exports. Indeed, the Lower South experienced more rapid economic growth in that period than did the other colonial regions. Partly as a result, it had the highest average wealth per freeholder in mainland Anglo America by the time of the American Revolution.

Closely linked to South Carolina geographically, demographically, and economically was the newest

GEORGIA

settlement on the mainland, Georgia, chartered in 1732 as a haven for English debtors, who would be released from confinement if they agreed to relocate to the colony. Its founder, James Oglethorpe, envisioned Georgia as a garrison province peopled by sturdy farmers who would defend the southern flank of English settlement against Spanish Florida. Accordingly, its charter prohibited slavery. But Carolina rice planters successfully won the removal of the restriction in 1751. Thereafter, they essentially invaded Georgia, which—despite remaining politically independent and becoming a royal colony in 1752—developed into a rice-planting slave society resembling South Carolina.

King George's War initially helped New England and hurt the Lower South, but in the long run those effects were reversed. In the Chesapeake and the middle colonies, the war ushered in a long period of prosperity. These variations in economic experience highlight a crucial fact about the British mainland colonies: they did not compose a unified whole. Although linked economically into regions, they had few political or social ties beyond or even within those regions. Despite increasing coastal trade, the individual colonies' economic fortunes depended not on their neighbors in North America but rather on the shifting markets of Europe and the Caribbean. Had it not been for an unprecedented crisis in the British imperial system (discussed in Chapter 5), it is hard to see how they could have been persuaded to join in a common endeavor. Even with that impetus, they found unity difficult to maintain.

Colonial Cultures

a seventeenth-century resident of England's American possessions transported through time to 1750 would have been surprised not only by the denser and more diverse population but also by the new extremes of wealth and poverty visible in the growing cities. Native-born colonial elites sought to distinguish themselves from ordinary folk in a variety of ways as they consolidated their hold on the local economy and political power.

One historian has termed these processes "the refinement of America." Colonists who acquired wealth

GENTEEL
CULTURE

through trade, agriculture, or manufacturing spent their money ostentatiously, dressing fashionably, traveling in horse-drawn carriages driven by uniformed servants, and entertaining one another at lavish parties. Most notably, they built large houses containing rooms designed for such forms of socializing as dancing, cardplaying, or drinking tea. Sufficiently well-off to enjoy "leisure" time (a first for North America), they

■ Elizabeth Murray, the subject of this 1769 painting by John Singleton Copley, was the wife of James Smith, a wealthy rum distiller. Her fashionable dress and pose would seem to mark her as a lady of leisure, yet both before and during her marriage this Scottish immigrant ran a successful dry goods shop in Boston. She thus simultaneously catered to and participated in the new culture of consumption.   (Gift of Joseph W. R. Rogers and Mary C. Rogers. Museum of Fine Arts, Boston. Reproduced with permission. © Museum of Fine Arts, Boston)

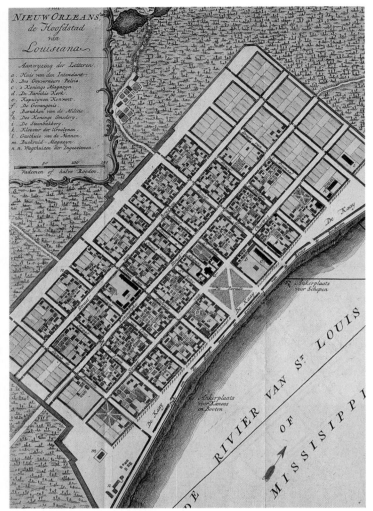

■ One of the very few institutions of higher learning open to females in eighteenth-century North America is clearly marked on this 1769 map from a Dutch atlas: the Ursuline convent in New Orleans. There young women studied religion and other subjects. As indicated in the label to the left, the convent is located at letter *k*, in the lower right corner of the map (which shows the area of the modern city known as the French Quarter).   (Private Collection)

ately constructed a genteel culture quite different from that of ordinary colonists.

Men from such families prided themselves not only on their possessions and on their positions in the colonial political, social, and economic hierarchy, but also on their level of education and their intellectual connections to Europe. Many had been tutored by private teachers hired by their families; some even attended college in Europe or America. (Harvard, the first colonial college, founded in 1636, was joined by William and Mary in 1693, Yale in 1701, and later by several others—for example, Princeton, established in 1747.) In the seventeenth century, only aspiring clergymen attended college, studying a curriculum focused heavily on ancient languages and theology. But by the mid-eighteenth century, colleges broadened their curricula to include mathematics, the natural sciences, law, and medicine. Accordingly, a minuscule number of young men from elite or upwardly mobile families enrolled in college to study for careers other than the ministry. American women were mostly excluded from advanced education, with the exception of some who joined nunneries in Canada or Louisiana, and who could engage in sustained study within convent walls.

The intellectual current known as the Enlightenment deeply affected the learned clergymen who headed colonial colleges and their students.

THE ENLIGHTENMENT Around 1650, some European thinkers began to analyze nature in order to determine the laws governing the universe. They employed experimentation and abstract reasoning to discover general principles behind phenomena such as the motions of planets and stars, the behavior of falling objects, and the characteristics of light and sound. Above all, Enlightenment philosophers emphasized acquiring knowledge through reason, taking particular delight in challenging previously unquestioned assumptions. John Locke's *Essay Concerning Human Understanding* (1690), for example, disputed the notion that human beings are born already imprinted with innate ideas. All knowledge, Locke asserted, derives from one's observations of the external world. Belief in witchcraft and astrology, among other similar phenomena, thus came under attack.

The Enlightenment had an enormous impact on educated, well-to-do people in Europe and America. It supplied them with a common vocabulary and a unified view of the world, one that insisted that the enlightened eighteenth century was better, and wiser, than all previous ages. It joined them in a common endeavor, the effort to make sense of God's orderly creation. Thus American

attended concerts and the theater, gambled at horseraces, and played billiards and other games. They also cultivated polite manners, adopting stylized forms of address and paying attention to "proper" ways of behaving. Although the effects of accumulated wealth were most pronounced in Anglo America, elite families in New Mexico, Louisiana, and Quebec as well set themselves off from the "lesser sort." Together these wealthy families delibernaturalists like John and William Bartram supplied European scientists with information about New World plants and animals so that they could be included in newly formulated universal classification systems. So, too, Americans interested in astronomy took part in an international effort to learn about the solar system by studying a rare occurrence, the transit of Venus across the face of the sun in 1769. A prime example of America's participation in the Enlightenment was Benjamin Franklin, who retired from a successful printing business in 1748 when he was just forty-two, thereafter devoting himself to scientific experimentation and public service. His *Experiments and Observations on Electricity* (1751) established the terminology and basic theory of electricity still used today.

The experimentation encouraged by the Enlightenment affected the lives of ordinary Americans most dramatically through advances in medicine—specifically, the control of smallpox. The Reverend Cotton Mather, the prominent Puritan cleric, learned from his African-born slave about the benefits of inoculation (deliberately infecting a person with a mild case of a disease) as a protection against smallpox. When Boston in 1720–1721 suffered a major smallpox epidemic, Mather urged the adoption of inoculation despite fierce opposition from the city's leading physician. Mortality rates eventually supported Mather—of those inoculated, just 3 percent died; of others, 15 percent. Although inoculation was not widely accepted until midcentury, science provided colonial Americans with a means of preventing the greatest killer disease of all.

Enlightenment rationalism affected politics as well as science. Locke's *Two Treatises of Government* (1691) and other works by French and Scottish philosophers challenged previous concepts of a divinely sanctioned, hierarchical political order originating in the power of fathers over families. Men created governments and so could alter them, Locke declared. A ruler who broke his contract with the people and failed to protect their rights could legitimately be ousted from power by peaceful—or even violent—means. Government should aim at the good of the people, Enlightenment theorists proclaimed. A proper political order could prevent the rise of tyrants; God's natural laws governed even the power of monarchs.

The world in which such ideas were discussed was that of the few, not the many. Most residents of North

ORAL CULTURES

America did not know how to read or write. Even those with basic literacy skills—a small proportion in French or Spanish America, about half of the people in British America—knew only the rudiments. Books were scarce and expensive, and ordinary folk rarely had occasion to write a letter. No colony required children to attend school; European American youngsters who learned to read usually did so in their own homes, taught by their parents or older siblings. A few months at a private "dame school" run by a literate local widow might complete their education by teaching them the basics of writing and simple arithmetic. Few Americans other than some Church of England missionaries in the South tried to instruct enslaved children. And only the most zealous Indian converts learned Europeans' literacy skills.

Thus the cultures of colonial North America were primarily oral, communal, and—at least through the first half of the eighteenth century—intensely local. In the absence of literacy, face-to-face conversation served as the major means of communication. Information tended to travel slowly and within relatively confined regions. Different locales developed divergent cultural traditions, and racial and ethnic variations heightened those differences. Public rituals served as the chief means through which the colonists forged their cultural identities.

Attendance at church was perhaps the most important such ritual. In Congregational (Puritan) churches,

RELIGIOUS AND CIVIC RITUALS

church leaders assigned seating to reflect standing in the community. In early New England, men and women sat on opposite sides of a central aisle, arranged in ranks according to age, wealth, and church membership. By the mid-eighteenth century, wealthy men and their wives sat in privately owned pews; their children, servants, and the less fortunate still sat in sex-segregated fashion at the rear or sides of the church. In eighteenth-century Virginia, seating in Church of England parishes also conformed to the local status hierarchy. Planter families purchased their own pews, and in some parishes landed gentlemen customarily strode into church as a group just before the service, deliberately drawing attention to their exalted position. In Quebec City, formal processions of men into the parish church celebrated Catholic feast days; each participant's rank determined his placement in the procession. By contrast, Quaker meetinghouses in Pennsylvania and elsewhere used an egalitarian but sex-segregated seating system. The varying rituals surrounding people's entrance into and seating in colonial churches thus symbolized their place in society and the values of the local community.

Communal culture also centered on the civic sphere. In New England, governments proclaimed official days of thanksgiving (for good harvests, victories in war, and so forth) and days of fasting and prayer (when the colony

■ Convicted criminals were publicly punished and shamed in front of their friends, relatives, and neighbors. A man might be put in the stocks for offenses such as contempt of authority, drunken and disorderly conduct, or theft. The intent was not simply to deter him from future misbehavior but to let his fate serve as a warning to all who saw his humiliating posture. (Library of Congress)

was experiencing difficulties such as droughts or epidemics). Everyone was expected to participate in the public rituals held in churches on such occasions. Monthly militia musters (known as training days) also brought the community together, since all able-bodied men between the ages of sixteen and sixty participated in the militia.

In the Chesapeake, important cultural rituals occurred on court and election days. When the county court met, men came from miles around to file suits, appear as witnesses, or serve as jurors. Attendance at court functioned as a method of civic education; from watching the proceedings men learned what behavior their neighbors expected of them. Elections served the same purpose, for property-holding men voted in public. An election official, often flanked by the candidates for the office in question, would call each man forward to declare his preference. The voter would then be thanked politely by the gentleman for whom he had cast his oral ballot. Traditionally, the candidates afterward treated their supporters to rum at nearby taverns.

Everywhere in colonial North America, the public punishment of criminals served not just to humiliate the offender but also to remind the community of proper behavioral standards. Public hangings and whippings, along with orders to sit in the stocks, expressed the community's outrage about crimes and restored harmony to its ranks. Judges often assigned penalties that shamed miscreants in especially appropriate ways. In San Antonio, Texas, for example, one cattle thief was sentenced to be led through the town's streets "with the entrails hanging from his neck"; and when a New Mexico man assaulted his father-in-law, he was directed not merely to pay medical expenses but also to kneel before him and to beg his forgiveness publicly. New Englanders reprieved after being convicted of capital offenses did not thereby escape public humiliation: frequently they were ordered to wear nooses around their necks for years as a constant reminder to themselves, their families, and their neighbors of their heinous violation of community norms.

The wide availability of consumer goods after the early years of the eighteenth century fostered new rituals centered on consumption, establishing novel links among the various residents of North America and creating what historians have termed "an empire of goods." First came the acquisition of desirable items. In the seventeenth century, settlers acquired necessities by bartering with neighbors or by ordering products from a home-country merchant. By the middle of the eighteenth century, specialized shops selling nonessentials had proliferated in cities such as New York, Philadelphia, and New Orleans. In 1770 Boston alone had more than five hundred stores, which offered consumers a vast selection of millinery, sewing supplies, tobacco, gloves, tableware, and the like. Even small and medium-size towns had one or two retail establishments. A colonist with money to spend would set aside time to "go shopping," a novel and pleasurable activity. The purchase of a desired object—for example, a ceramic bowl, a mirror, or a length of beautiful fabric—marked just the beginning of consumption rituals.

Consumers would then deploy their purchases in an appropriate manner: hanging the mirror prominently on

RITUALS OF CONSUMPTION

Exotic Beverages

As colonists became consumers, they developed a taste not only for tea (from China) but for coffee (from Arabia), chocolate (from Mesoamerica), and rum (distilled from sugar, which also sweetened the bitter taste of the other three). The demand for these once-exotic beverages in America and Europe helped reshape the world economy after the mid-seventeenth century. Indeed, one historian has estimated that approximately two-thirds of the people who migrated across the Atlantic before 1776 were involved in one way or another, primarily as slaves, in the production of tobacco, calico, and these four drinks for the world market. The exotic beverages had a profound impact, too, on custom and culture, as they moved swiftly from luxury to necessity.

Each beverage had its own pattern of consumption. Chocolate, brought to Spain from Mexico and enjoyed there for a century before spreading more widely throughout Europe, became the preferred drink of aristocrats, consumed hot at intimate gatherings in palaces and mansions. Coffee, by contrast, became the preeminent morning beverage of English and colonial businessmen, who praised its caffeine for keeping drinkers sober and focused. Coffee was served in new public coffeehouses, patronized only by men, where politics and business were the topics of conversation. The first coffeehouse opened in London in the late 1660s; Boston had several by the 1690s. By the mid-eighteenth century, though, tea had supplanted coffee as the preferred hot, caffeinated beverage in England and America. It was consumed in the afternoons, in private homes at tea tables presided over by women. Tea embodied genteel status and polite conversation. In contrast, rum was the drink of the masses. This inexpensive, potent distilled spirit, made possible by new technology and the increasing production of sugar, was devoured by free working people everywhere in the Atlantic world.

The American colonies played a vital role in the production, distribution, and consumption of each of these beverages. Chocolate, most obviously, originated in America, and cacao plantations in the South American tropics multiplied in size and number to meet the rising demand. Coffee and tea (particularly the latter) were as avidly consumed in the colonies as in England. And rum involved Americans in every phase of its production and consumption. The sugar grown on French and English Caribbean plantations was transported to the mainland in barrels and ships made from North American wood. There the syrup was turned into rum at 140 distilleries. The Americans themselves drank a substantial share of the distilleries' output—an estimated four gallons per person annually—but exported much of it to Africa. There the rum purchased more slaves to produce more sugar to make still more rum, and the cycle began again.

Thus new tastes and customs connected to four different beverages linked the colonies to the rest of the world and altered their economic and social development.

The frontispiece of Peter Muguet, *Tractatus De Poto Caphe, Chinesium The et de Chocolata,* 1685. Muguet's treatise visually linked the three hot, exotic beverages recently introduced to Europeans. The drinks are being consumed by representatives of the cultures in which they originated: a turbaned Turk (with coffeepot in the foreground), a Chinese man (with teapot on the table), and an Indian drinking from a hollowed, handled gourd (with a chocolate pot and ladle on the floor in front of him). (Library of Congress)

■ This trade card (advertisement) issued by a Philadelphia tobacco dealer in 1770 shows a convivial group of wealthy men at a tavern. Both the leisurely activity depicted here and the advertisement itself were signs of the new rituals of consumption. Merchants began to advertise only when their customers could choose among different ways of spending money. (Library Company of Philadelphia)

a wall of the house, displaying the bowl on a table or sideboard, turning the fabric into a special piece of clothing. Individual colonists took pleasure in owning lovely objects, but they also proudly displayed their acquisitions (and thus their wealth and good taste) publicly to kin and neighbors. A rich man might even hire a portraitist to paint his family using the objects and wearing the clothing, thereby creating a pictorial record that also would be displayed for admiration.

Tea drinking, a consumption ritual dominated and controlled by women, played an especially important role in Anglo America. From early in the eighteenth century, households with aspirations to genteel status sought to acquire the items necessary for the proper consumption of tea: not just pots and cups but also strainers, sugar tongs, bowls, and even special tables. Tea provided a focal point for socializing and, because of its cost, served as a crucial marker of status. Wealthy women regularly entertained their male and female friends at afternoon tea parties. A hot and mildly stimulating drink, tea also appeared healthful. Thus even poor households consumed tea, although they could not afford the fancy equipment used by their better-off neighbors. Some Mohawk Indians adopted the custom, much to the surprise of a traveler from Sweden, who observed them drinking tea in the late 1740s.

Other sorts of rituals allowed the disparate cultures of colonial North America to interact with one another. Particularly important rituals developed on what the

RITUALS ON THE "MIDDLE GROUND" historian Richard White has termed the "middle ground"—that is, the psychological and geographical space in which Indians and Europeans encountered each other. Most of those cultural encounters occurred in the context of trade or warfare.

When Europeans sought to trade with Indians, they encountered an indigenous system of exchange that stressed gift giving rather than formalized buying and selling. Although French and English traders complained constantly about the need to present Indians with gifts prior to negotiating with them for pelts and skins, successful bargaining required such a step. Over time, an appropriate ritual developed. A European trader arriving at a village would give gifts (cloth, rum, gunpowder, and other items) to Indian hunters. Eventually, those gifts would be reciprocated, and formal trading could then take place. To the detriment of Indian societies, rum became a crucial component of these intercultural trading rituals. Traders soon concluded that drunken Indians would sell their furs more cheaply; and some Indians refused to hunt or trade unless they first received rum. Alcohol abuse hastened the deterioration of villages already devastated by disease and dislocation.

Intercultural rituals also developed to deal with murders. Indians and Europeans both believed that murders required a compensatory act but differed in their notions of what that act should be. Europeans sought primarily to identify and punish the murderer. To Indians, such "eye for an eye" revenge was just one of many possible responses to murder. Compensation could also be accomplished by capturing another Indian or a colonist who could take the dead person's place, or by "covering the dead"—that is, by providing the family of the deceased with compensatory goods, a crucial strategy for maintaining peace on the frontiers. Eventually, the French and the Algonquians evolved an elaborate ritual for handling frontier murders that encompassed elements of both societies' traditions: murders were investigated and murderers identified, but by mutual agreement deaths were usually "covered" by trade goods rather than by blood revenge.

Colonial Families

Families (rather than individuals) constituted the basic units of colonial society; never-married adults were extremely rare. People living together as families, commonly under the direction of a marital pair, everywhere constituted the chief mechanisms for both production and consumption. Yet family forms and structures varied widely in the mainland colonies, and not all were headed by couples.

As Europeans consolidated their hold on North America during the first three-quarters of the eighteenth century, Native Americans had to

INDIAN FAMILIES

adapt to novel circumstances. Bands reduced in numbers by disease and warfare recombined into new units; for example, the group later known as the Catawbas emerged in the 1730s in the western Carolinas from the fragmentary remains of several earlier Indian nations, including the Yamasees. Likewise, European secular and religious authorities reshaped Indian family forms. Whereas many Indian societies had permitted easy divorce, English, French, and Spanish missionaries frowned on such practices; and those societies that had allowed polygynous marriages (including New England Algonquians) redefined such relationships, designating one wife as "legitimate" and others as "concubines."

Continued high mortality rates created Indian societies in which extended kin took on new importance, for when parents died, aunts, uncles, and other relatives—even occasionally nonkin—assumed child-rearing responsibilities. Furthermore, once Europeans established dominance in any region, Indians there could no longer pursue traditional modes of subsistence. That led to unusual family structures as well as to a variety of economic strategies. In New England, for instance, Algonquian husbands and wives often could not live together, for adults supported themselves by working separately (perhaps wives as domestic servants, husbands as sailors). And in New Mexico, detribalized Navajos, Pueblos, and Apaches employed as servants by Spanish settlers clustered in the small towns of the Borderlands. Known collectively as *genizaros,* they lost contact with Indian cultures, instead living on the fringes of Latino society.

Wherever the population contained relatively few European women, sexual liaisons (both inside and outside

MIXED-RACE FAMILIES

marriage) occurred among European men and Indian women. The resulting mixed-race population of *mestizos* and *métis* worked as a familial "middle ground" to ease other cultural interactions. In New France and the Anglo-American backcountry, such families frequently resided in Indian villages and were enmeshed in trading networks. Often, children of these unions became prominent leaders of Native American societies. (For example, Peter Chartier, son of a Shawnee mother and a French father, led a pro-French Shawnee band in western Pennsylvania in the 1740s.) By contrast, in the Spanish Borderlands the offspring of Europeans and *genizaros* were treated as degraded individuals. Largely denied the privilege of legal marriage, they bore generations of "illegitimate" children of various racial mixtures, giving rise in Latino society to a wide range of labels describing degrees of skin color with a precision unknown in English or French America.

Eighteenth-century Anglo-Americans used the word *family* to mean all the people who occupied one household

EUROPEAN AMERICAN FAMILIES

(including any resident servants or slaves). The many European migrants to North America had more stable family lives than did Indian and *mestizo* peoples. European men or their widows headed households considerably larger than American families today. In 1790 the average home in the United States contained 5.7 free people; few such households included extended kin like grandparents. Family members—bound by ties of blood or servitude—worked together to produce goods for consumption or sale. The head of the household represented it to the outside world, managing the finances and holding legal authority over the rest of the family—his wife, his children, and his servants or slaves.

In English, French, and Spanish America alike, the vast majority of European families supported themselves through agriculture, by cultivating crops and raising livestock. The scale and nature of the work varied: the production of indigo in Louisiana or tobacco in the

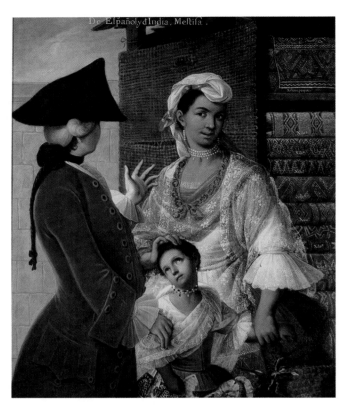

De Eſpañol y d India. Meſtiſa.

■ One of the few extant depictions of a mixed-race family in eighteenth-century North America, by the Mexican artist Miguel Cabrera, 1763. The Spanish father and Indian mother have produced a *mestiza* daughter. Families such as this would have been frequently seen in New Mexico as well.   (Private Collection)

Chesapeake required different sorts of labor from subsistence farming in New England or cattle ranching in New Mexico and Texas. Still, just as in the European, African, and Native American societies discussed in Chapter 1, household tasks were allocated by sex. The master, his sons, and his male servants or slaves performed one set of chores; the mistress, her daughters, and her female servants or slaves, a different set.

The mistress took responsibility for what Anglo-Americans called "indoor affairs." She and her female helpers prepared food, cleaned the house, did laundry, and often made clothing. Preparing food alone involved planting and cultivating a garden, harvesting and preserving vegetables, salting and smoking meat, drying apples and pressing cider, milking cows and making butter and cheese, not to mention cooking and baking. The head of the household and his male helpers, responsible for "outdoor affairs," also had heavy workloads. They planted and cultivated the fields, built fences, chopped wood for the fireplace, harvested and marketed crops, cared for livestock, and butchered cattle and hogs to provide the household with meat. So extensive was the work involved in maintaining a farm household that a married couple could not do it alone. If they had no children to help them, they turned to servants or slaves.

Most African American families lived as components of European American households—sometimes on plantations that masters perceived as one large family. More than 95 percent of colonial African Americans were held in perpetual bondage. Although many African Americans lived on farms with only one or two other slaves, others had the experience of living and working in a largely black setting. In South Carolina, a majority of the population was of African origin; in Georgia, about half; and in the Chesapeake, 40 percent. Portions of the Carolina low country were nearly 90 percent African American by 1790.

AFRICAN AMERICAN FAMILIES

The setting in which African Americans lived determined the shape of their families, yet wherever possible slaves established strong family structures in which youngsters carried relatives' names. In the North, the scarcity of other blacks often made it difficult for bondspeople to form stable households. In the Chesapeake, men and women who regarded themselves as married (slaves could not legally wed) frequently lived on different quarters or even on different plantations. Children generally resided with their mothers, seeing their fathers only on Sundays. Simultaneously, the natural increase of the population created wide American-born kinship networks among Chesapeake slaves. On large Carolina and Georgia rice plantations, enslaved couples not only usually lived together with their children but also accumulated property through working for themselves after they had completed their daily "tasks" (see pages 79–80). Some Georgia slaves sold their surplus produce at the market in Savannah, thereby earning money to buy nice clothing or such luxuries as tobacco or jewelry, but rarely enough to purchase themselves.

Because all the British colonies legally permitted slavery, bondspeople had few options for escaping servitude other than fleeing to Florida (see pages 80–81). Some recently arrived Africans stole boats to try to return home or ran off in groups to frontier regions to join the Indians or establish independent communities. Among American-born slaves, family ties strongly affected such decisions. South Carolina planters soon learned, as one wrote, that slaves "love their families

FORMS OF RESISTANCE

■ William L. Breton's watercolor of "The Old London Coffee House" in eighteenth-century Philadelphia shows a slave auction taking place on its porch. That such a scene could have occurred in front of such a prominent and popular meeting place serves as a reminder of the ubiquity of slavery in the colonies, north as well as south.   (Historical Society of Pennsylvania)

dearly and none runs away from the other," so many owners sought to keep families together for purely practical reasons. In the Chesapeake, where family members often lived separately, affectionate ties could by contrast cause slaves to run away, especially if a family member had been sold or moved to a distant quarter.

Although colonial slaves rarely rebelled collectively, they often resisted enslavement in other ways. Bondspeople uniformly rejected attempts by their owners to commandeer their labor on Sundays without compensation. Extended-kin groups protested excessive punishment of relatives and sought to live near each other. The links that developed among African American families who had lived on the same plantation for several generations served as insurance against the uncertainties of existence under slavery. If parents and children were separated by sale, other relatives could help with child rearing and similar tasks. Among African Americans, just as among Indians, the extended family thus served a more important function than it did among European Americans.

Most slave families managed to carve out a small measure of autonomy, especially in their working and spiritual lives and particularly in the Lower South. Enslaved Muslims often clung to their Islamic faith, a pattern especially evident in Louisiana and Georgia. Some

African Americans preserved traditional beliefs and others converted to Christianity (often retaining some African elements), finding comfort in the assurances of their new religion that all people would be free and equal in heaven. South Carolina and Georgia slaves jealously guarded their customary ability to control their own time after the completion of their "tasks." Even on Chesapeake tobacco plantations, slaves planted their own gardens, hunted, or fished to supplement the minimal diet their masters supplied. Late in the century, some Chesapeake planters with a surplus of laborers began to hire out slaves to others, often allowing the workers to keep a small part of their earnings. Such accumulated property could buy desired goods or serve as a legacy for children.

Just as African and European Americans resided together on plantations, so too they lived in unsegregated

LIFE IN THE CITIES   urban neighborhoods. (In 1760s Philadelphia one-fifth of the work force was enslaved, and by 1775 blacks composed nearly 15 percent of the population of New York City.) Such cities were nothing but medium-sized towns by today's standards. In 1750 the largest, Boston and Philadelphia, had just seventeen thousand and thirteen thousand inhabitants, respectively. Life in the cities nonetheless differed considerably from that on northern farms, southern plantations, or southwestern ranches. City dwellers everywhere purchased food and wood in the markets. Urban residents lived by the clock rather than the sun, and men's jobs frequently took them away from their households. City people also had much more contact with the world beyond their own homes than did their rural counterparts.

By the 1750s, most major cities had at least one weekly newspaper, and some had two or three. Anglo-American newspapers printed the latest "advices from London" (usually two to three months old) and news from other English colonies, as well as local reports. Newspapers were available at taverns, coffeehouses, and inns, so people who could not afford to buy them could catch up on the news. Even illiterates could do so, since literate customers often read the papers aloud. Contact with the outside world, however, had its drawbacks. Sailors sometimes brought deadly diseases into port. Boston, New York, Philadelphia, and New Orleans endured terrible epidemics of smallpox and yellow fever, which Europeans and Africans in the countryside largely escaped.

Politics: Stability and Crisis in British America

*E*arly in the eighteenth century, Anglo-American political life exhibited a new stability. Despite substantial migration from overseas, most residents of the mainland had been born in America. Men from genteel families dominated the political structures in each province, for voters (free male property holders) tended to defer to their well-educated "betters" on election days.

Throughout the Anglo-American colonies, political leaders sought to increase the powers of elected assemblies relative to the powers of the governors and other appointed officials. Assemblies began to claim privileges associated with the British House of Commons, such as the rights to initiate all tax legislation and to control the militia. The assemblies also developed effective ways of influencing British appointees, especially by threatening to withhold their salaries. In some colonies (Virginia and South Carolina, for example), elite members of the assemblies usually presented a united front to royal officials, but in others (such as New York), they fought among themselves long and bitterly. To win hotly contested elections, New York's genteel leaders began to appeal to "the people," competing openly for the votes

RISE OF THE ASSEMBLIES

of ordinary voters. Yet in 1733 that same New York government imprisoned a newspaper editor, John Peter Zenger, who had too vigorously criticized its actions. Defending Zenger against the charge of "seditious libel," his lawyer argued that the truth could not be defamatory, thus helping to establish a free-press principle now found in American law.

Much of the business of colonial assemblies would today be termed administrative; only on rare occasions did they formulate new policies or pass significant laws. Assemblymen saw themselves as acting defensively to prevent encroachments on the colonists' liberties—for example, by preventing governors from imposing oppressive taxes. By midcentury, they were comparing the structure of their governments to Britain's balanced polity, a combination of monarchy, aristocracy, and democracy that had been thought to produce a stable polity since the days of ancient Greece and Rome. Drawing rough analogies, political leaders equated their governors with the monarch, their councils with the aristocracy, and their assemblies with the House of Commons. All three were believed essential to good government, but Anglo-Americans did not regard them with the same degree of approval. They viewed governors and appointed councils as potential threats to customary colonial ways of life, since such people primarily represented Britain. Many colonists saw the assemblies, however, as the people's protectors. And in turn the assemblies regarded themselves as representatives of the people.

Yet such beliefs should not be equated with modern practice. The assemblies, firmly controlled by dominant families whose members were reelected year after year, rarely responded to the concerns of their poorer constituents. Although settlements continually expanded, assemblies failed to reapportion themselves to provide adequate representation for newer communities—a lack of action that led to serious grievances among frontier dwellers, especially those from non-English ethnic groups. The colonial ideal of the assembly as the defender of the people's liberties must therefore be distinguished from the colonial reality: the most dearly defended were the wealthy colonists, particularly the assembly members themselves.

At midcentury, the political structures that had stabilized in a period of relative calm confronted a series of crises. None affected all the mainland colonies, but no colony escaped wholly untouched. The crises of various descriptions—ethnic, racial, economic, regional—exposed the internal tensions building in the pluralistic American society, foreshadowing the greater disorder of the revolutionary era. Most important, they demon-

■ In 1713 the colony of Massachusetts constructed its impressive State House in Boston. Here met the assembly and the council. The solidity and imposing nature of the building must have symbolized for its users the increasing consolidation of power in the hands of the Massachusetts legislature. (The Bostonian Society)

strated that the political accommodations arrived at in the aftermath of the Glorious Revolution were no longer adequate to govern Britain's American empire. Once again, changes appeared necessary, and imminent.

One of the first and greatest crises occurred in South Carolina. Early one morning in September 1739, about twenty South Carolina slaves, most from Angola, gathered near the Stono River south of Charles Town. Seizing guns and ammunition from a store, they killed the storekeepers and some nearby planter families. Then, joined by other local slaves, they headed toward Florida in hopes of finding refuge at Gracia Real de Santa Teresa de Mose. By midday, however, the alarm had been sounded among slaveowners in the district. That afternoon a troop of militia attacked the fugitives, who then numbered about a hundred, killing some and dispersing the rest. More than a week later, most of the remaining conspirators were captured. The colony quickly executed those not killed on the spot, but for over two years rumors about escaped renegades haunted the colony.

STONO REBELLION

The Stono Rebellion shocked slaveholding South Carolinians as well as residents of other colonies. Throughout British America, laws governing the behavior of African Americans were stiffened. The most striking response came in New York City, which had suffered a slave revolt in 1712. There the news from the South, coupled with fears of Spain generated by the outbreak of King George's War, set off a reign of terror in the summer of 1741. Hysterical whites suspected a biracial gang of thieves and arsonists of conspiring to foment a slave uprising under the guidance of a white schoolteacher thought to be a priest in the pay of Spain. By summer's end, thirty-one blacks and four whites had been executed for participating in the alleged plot. The Stono Rebellion and the New York conspiracy not only exposed and confirmed Anglo-Americans' deepest fears about the dangers of slaveholding but also revealed the assemblies' inability to prevent serious internal disorder. Events of the next two decades confirmed that pattern.

NEW YORK CONSPIRACY

By midcentury most of the fertile land east of the Appalachians had been purchased or occupied. Consequently,

LAND RIOTS conflicts over land titles and conditions of landholding grew in number and frequency. In 1746, for example, some New Jersey farmers clashed violently with agents of the East Jersey proprietors. The proprietors claimed the farmers' land as theirs and demanded annual payments, called quit-rents, for the use of the property. Similar violence occurred in the 1760s in the region that later became Vermont. There, farmers holding land grants issued by New Hampshire battled with speculators claiming title to the area through grants from New York authorities.

The most serious land riots took place along the Hudson River in 1765–1766. Late in the seventeenth century, the governor of New York had granted huge tracts in the lower Hudson valley to prominent colonial families. The proprietors in turn divided these estates into small farms, which they rented chiefly to poor Dutch and German migrants who regarded tenancy as a step on the road to independent freeholder status. By the 1750s some proprietors earned large sums annually from quit-rents and other fees.

After 1740, though, increasing migration from New England brought conflict to the great New York estates. The New Englanders resisted the tenancy system. Many squatted on vacant portions of the manors, rejecting all attempts at eviction. In the mid-1760s the Philipse family sued New Englanders who had lived on Philipse land for two decades or more. New York courts upheld the Philipse claim, ordering squatters to make way for tenants with valid leases. Instead of complying, the farmers rebelled, terrorizing proprietors and loyal tenants, freeing their friends from jail, and on one occasion battling a county sheriff and his posse. The rebellion lasted nearly a year, ending only when British troops finally captured its leaders.

Violent conflicts of a different sort erupted just a few years later in the Carolinas. The Regulator movements of the late 1760s (South Carolina) and early 1770s (North Carolina) pitted backcountry farmers against wealthy eastern planters who controlled the provincial governments. Frontier dwellers, most of Scots-Irish origin, protested their lack of an adequate voice in colonial political affairs. South Carolinians for months policed the countryside in vigilante bands known as Regulators, complaining of lax and biased law enforcement. North Carolina Regulators, who primarily objected to heavy taxation, fought and lost a battle with eastern militiamen at Alamance in 1771. Regional, ethnic, and economic tensions thus combined to create these disturbances, which ultimately arose from frontier people's dissatisfaction with the Carolina governments.

REGULATORS IN THE CAROLINAS

A Crisis in Religion

*T*he most widespread crisis, though, was religious. From the mid-1730s through the 1760s, waves of religious revivalism—today known collectively as the First Great Awakening—swept over various colonies, primarily New England (1735–1745) and Virginia (1750s and 1760s). Orthodox Calvinists sought to combat Enlightenment rationalism, which denied innate human depravity. Simultaneously, the economic and political uncertainty accompanying King George's War made colonists receptive to evangelists' spiritual messages. Moreover, many recent immigrants and residents of the backcountry had no prior religious affiliation, thus presenting evangelists with many potential converts.

The Great Awakening began in New England, where descendants of the Puritan founding generation still composed the membership of Congregational churches. Whether in full or "halfway" communion—the latter, a category established in 1662 to ensure that people who had not experienced saving faith would still be subject to church discipline—such members were predominantly female. From the beginnings of the Awakening, though, men and women responded with equal fervor. During 1734 and 1735, the Reverend Jonathan Edwards, a noted preacher and theologian, noticed a remarkable reaction among the youthful members of his church in Northampton, Massachusetts, to a message based squarely on Calvinist principles. Individuals could attain salvation, Edwards contended, only through recognition of their own depraved natures and the need to surrender completely to God's will. Such surrender brought to Congregationalists of both sexes an intensely emotional release from sin, coming to be seen as a single identifiable moment of conversion.

The effects of such conversions remained isolated until 1739, when George Whitefield, a Church of England clergyman already celebrated for leading revivals in England, arrived in America. For fifteen months he toured the British colonies, preaching to large audiences from Georgia to New England and concentrating his efforts in the major cities: Boston, New York, Philadelphia, Charles Town, and Savannah. A gripping orator, Whitefield in effect generated the Great Awakening. The historian Harry Stout has termed him "the first

GEORGE WHITEFIELD

■ Reverend George Whitefield, the charismatic evangelist who sparked the First Great Awakening in the mainland British colonies, attracted harsh critics as well as avid admirers. Here an English cartoonist satirizes him as a money-grubbing charlatan who hoodwinks his gullible followers into believing that he is a "Pious Churchman" motivated by "Holy Zeal." Whitefield's crossed eyes, obvious in this image as in others, played a prominent role in contemporary depictions of him.　(Trustees of the British Museum)

trine and matters of faith. They disliked the emotional style of the revivalists, whose itinerancy also disrupted normal patterns of church attendance because it took churchgoers away from the services they usually attended. Particularly troublesome to the orthodox were the dozens of female exhorters who took to streets and pulpits, proclaiming their right (even duty) to expound God's word.

Opposition to the Awakening heightened rapidly, causing congregations to splinter. "Old Lights"—traditional clerics and their followers—engaged in bitter disputes with the "New Light" evangelicals. Already characterized by numerous sects, American Protestantism fragmented even further as the major denominations split into Old Light and New Light factions and as new evangelical sects—Methodists and Baptists—gained adherents. Paradoxically, the angry fights and the rapid rise in the number of distinct denominations eventually led to an American willingness to tolerate religious diversity. No single sect could make an unequivocal claim to orthodoxy, so they had to coexist if they were to exist at all.

IMPACT OF THE AWAKENING

Most significantly, the Awakening challenged traditional modes of thought, for the revivalists' message directly contested the colonial tradition of deference. Itinerant preachers, only a few of whom were ordained clergymen, claimed they understood the will of God better than did elite college-educated clerics. Moreover, they and their followers divided the world into two groups—the saved and the damned—without respect to gender, age, or status, the previously dominant social categories. The Awakening's emphasis on emotion rather than learning undermined the validity of received wisdom, and New Lights questioned not only religious but also social and political orthodoxy. For example, New Lights began to defend the rights of groups and individuals to dissent from a community consensus, thereby challenging one of the fundamental tenets of colonial political life. The egalitarian themes of the Awakening simultaneously attracted ordinary folk and repelled the elite.

Nowhere was this trend more evident than in Virginia, where tax money supported the established Church of England, and the plantation gentry and their ostentatious lifestyle dominated society. By the 1760s Baptists had gained a secure foothold in Virginia; inevitably, their beliefs and behavior clashed with the way most genteel families lived. They rejected as sinful the horseracing, gambling, and dancing that occupied much of the gentry's leisure time. They dressed plainly, in

VIRGINIA BAPTISTS

modern celebrity" because of his skillful self-promotion and clever manipulation of both his listeners and the newspapers. Everywhere he traveled, his fame preceded him. Thousands of free and enslaved folk turned out to listen—and to experience conversion. Whitefield's journey, the first such ever undertaken, created new interconnections among the previously distinct colonies.

Regular clerics initially welcomed Whitefield and the American-born itinerant evangelist preachers who quickly imitated him. Soon, however, many clergymen began to realize that although "revived" religion filled their churches, it ran counter to their own approach to doccontrast to the gentry's fashionable opulence. They addressed one another as "Brother" and "Sister" regardless of social status, and they elected the leaders of their congregations—more than ninety of them by 1776. Their monthly "great meetings," which attracted hundreds of people, introduced new public rituals that rivaled the weekly Anglican services.

Strikingly, almost all the Virginia Baptist congregations included both free and slave members. At the founding of the Dan River Baptist Church in 1760, for example, eleven of seventy-four members were African Americans, and some congregations had African American majorities. Church rules applied equally to all members; interracial sexual relationships, divorce, and adultery were forbidden to all. In addition, congregations forbade masters from breaking up slave couples through sale. Biracial committees investigated complaints about church members' misbehavior. Churches excommunicated slaves for stealing from their masters, but they also excommunicated masters for physically abusing their slaves. One such slaveowner so dismissed in 1772 experienced a true conversion. Penalized for "burning" one of his slaves, Charles Cook apologized to the congregation and became a preacher in a largely African American church. Other Baptists decided that owning slaves was "unrighteous" and freed their bondspeople; the immensely wealthy Robert Carter, for one, manumitted hundreds of slaves in the 1790s.

Summary

*T*he Great Awakening thus injected an egalitarian strain into Anglo-American life at midcentury. Although primarily a religious movement, the Awakening had important social and political consequences, calling into question habitual modes of behavior in the secular as well as the religious realm. In short, the Great Awakening helped to break Anglo-Americans' ties to their seventeenth-century origins. So, too, did the newcomers from Germany, Scotland, Ireland, and Africa, who brought their languages, customs, and religions to British North America. The European immigrants settled throughout the English colonies but were concentrated in the growing cities and in the backcountry. By contrast, enslaved migrants from Africa lived and worked primarily within 100 miles of the Atlantic coast. In many areas of the colonial South, 50 to 90 percent of the population was of African origin.

The economic life of all Europe's North American colonies proceeded simultaneously on two levels. On the

farms, plantations, and ranches on which most colonists resided, the daily, weekly, monthly, and yearly rounds of chores for men, women, and children alike dominated people's lives while providing the goods consumed by households and sold in the markets. Simultaneously, an intricate international trade network affected the economies of the British, French, and Spanish colonies. The bitter wars fought by European nations during the eighteenth century inevitably involved the colonists by creating new opportunities for overseas sales or by disrupting their traditional markets. The volatile colonial economy fluctuated for reasons beyond Americans' control. Those fortunate few who—through skill, control of essential resources, or luck—reaped the profits of international commerce made up the wealthy class of merchants and landowners who dominated colonial political and social life.

A century and a half after European peoples first settled in North America, the colonies mixed diverse European, American, and African traditions into a novel cultural blend that owed much to Europe but just as much, if not more, to North America itself. Europeans who interacted regularly with peoples of African and American origin—and with Europeans who came from nations other than their own—had to develop new identities and new methods of accommodating intercultural differences in addition to creating ties within their own potentially fragmenting communities. Yet at the same time the dominant colonists continued to identify themselves as French, Spanish, or British rather than as Americans. That did not change in Canada, Louisiana, or the Spanish Borderlands, but in the 1760s some Anglo-Americans began to realize that their interests did not necessarily coincide with those of Great Britain or its monarch. For the first time, they offered a direct challenge to British authority.

LEGACY FOR A PEOPLE AND A NATION
"Self-Made Men"

One of the most common American themes celebrates the "self-made man" (always someone explicitly *male*) of humble origins who gains wealth and/or prominence through his own extraordinary effort and talent. Most commonly, those cited as examples are such successful nineteenth-century businessmen as Andrew Carnegie (once a poor immigrant from Scotland) or John D. Rockefeller (born on a hardscrabble farm in a little town in upstate New York).

The initial exemplars of this tradition, though, lived in eighteenth-century America and the wider Atlantic world. Benjamin Franklin's *Autobiography* chronicled his method for achieving success as a printer after beginning life as the seventeenth child of a Boston candlemaker. From such humble origins Franklin became a wealthy, influential man active in science, politics, education, and diplomacy. Yet Franklin's tale is rivaled by that of a man apparently born a slave in South Carolina who subsequently worked for years as a sailor. He purchased his freedom, learned to read and write, held an important administrative post, married a wealthy young English woman, became an influential abolitionist, and eventually—like Franklin—published a popular autobiography. His first master called him Gustavus Vassa, the name he primarily used. But when publishing his *Interesting Narrative* in 1789, he called himself Olaudah Equiano.

In that *Narrative,* Equiano claimed to have been born in Africa in 1745, kidnapped at the age of eleven, and carried first to Barbados, then to Virginia, where he was purchased by the British naval officer who introduced him to a maritime life. For years scholars and students have relied on that account for its insights into the experience of the middle passage. But evidence recently uncovered by Vincent Carretta, while confirming the accuracy of much of Equiano's autobiography, shows that Equiano twice publicly identified his birthplace as Carolina and was three to five years younger than he claimed. Why would Equiano conceal his origins and alter his age? Carretta speculates that the *Narrative* gained part of its credibility from Equiano's African birth and that admitting his real age would have raised questions about the account of his early life by revealing his youth at the time of the reputed kidnapping.

Equiano, or Vassa, thus truly "made himself," just as Benjamin Franklin and many others have done. (Franklin tended to omit, rather than alter, inconvenient parts of his personal history—for example, his having fathered an illegitimate son.) Equiano used information undoubtedly gleaned from acquaintances who *had* experienced the middle passage to craft an accurate depiction of the horrors of the slave trade. In the process he became one of the first Americans to explicitly reinvent himself.

The **history companion** *powered by Eduspace®*

Your primary source for interactive quizzes, exercises, and more to help you learn efficiently.
http://history.college.hmco.com/students

SEVERING THE BONDS OF EMPIRE 1754–1774

The two men must have found the occasion remarkable. The artist customarily painted portraits of the wealthy and high born, not of artisans, even well-connected, affluent ones. The subject himself was an artist—a maker of beautiful silver and gold objects, an engraver of cartoons and townscapes. The political sympathies of the painter, John Singleton Copley, lay primarily with Boston's conservatives, whereas the sitter, Paul Revere, was a noted leader of resistance to British policies. Yet sometime in 1768 Revere commissioned Copley to paint his portrait, and the result (opposite page) is one of the greatest works of American art.

Copley was thirty, Revere thirty-four. Each man had learned his trade from a parent. Revere's father, Apollos, who had arrived in Boston as a teenage Huguenot refugee early in the century, was an accomplished gold- and silversmith; Paul served as his father's apprentice and took over the family business when Apollos died in 1754. Copley, whose Irish parents had immigrated to Boston in the 1730s, was taught to paint by his stepfather, Peter Pelham, an English artist. The two young tradesmen had undoubtedly known each other for years. In 1763 and thereafter, Copley hired Revere to make silver and gold frames for the miniature portraits that were among his earliest works.

But their finest collaboration was the painting reproduced here. Copley portrayed Revere surrounded by the tools of his trade and contemplating a teapot he was crafting. The silversmith wears a loose-fitting linen shirt and an open vest rather than the formal dress usually worn by colonial artists' subjects. Even so, Revere is not actually at work: his clothes are too clean, and the table is too polished to be a work surface. The silversmith's pose and apparel convey an impression of thoughtfulness, virtuous labor, and solidity. The teapot too carries a message, especially in the year 1768. Simultaneously a reflection of a craftsman's skills and a prominent emblem of the new "empire of goods" in British America, it resonated with symbolism because, as shall be seen later in this chapter,

◀ John Singleton Copley's portrait of Paul Revere is generally regarded as one of his masterpieces. Copley captured Revere's character as a hard-working, respectable artisan—a man unafraid of displaying his humble origins to the world. (Museum of Fine Arts, Boston. Gift of Joseph W., William B., and Edward H. R. Revere)

CHRONOLOGY

1754 • Albany Congress meets to try to forge colonial unity
• Fighting breaks out with Washington's defeat at Fort Necessity

1756 • Britain declares war on France; Seven Years War officially begins

1759 • British forces take Quebec

1760 • American phase of war ends with fall of Montreal to British troops
• George III becomes king

1763 • Treaty of Paris ends Seven Years War
• Pontiac's allies attack British forts in West
• Proclamation of 1763 attempts to close land west of Appalachians to English settlement

1764 • Sugar Act lays new duties on molasses, tightens customs regulations
• Currency Act outlaws paper money issued by the colonies

1765 • Stamp Act requires stamps on all printed materials in colonies
• Sons of Liberty formed

1766 • Stamp Act repealed
• Declaratory Act insists that Parliament can tax the colonies

1767 • Townshend Acts lay duties on trade within the empire, send new officials to America

1768–70 • Townshend duties resisted; boycotts and public demonstrations divide merchants and urban artisans

1770 • Lord North becomes prime minister
• Townshend duties repealed, except for tea tax
• Boston Massacre kills five colonial rioters

1772 • Boston Committee of Correspondence formed

1773 • Tea Act aids East India Company
• Boston Tea Party protests the Tea Act

1774 • Coercive Acts punish Boston and Massachusetts as a whole
• Quebec Act reforms government of Quebec
• First Continental Congress called

tea boycotts were an important component of colonial resistance to Great Britain. Both artist and subject, indeed, were to be active participants (though in very different ways) in the 1773 event known to history as the Boston Tea Party.

In retrospect, John Adams identified the years between 1760 and 1775 as the era of the true American Revolution. The Revolution, Adams declared, ended before the fighting started, for it was "in the Minds of the people," involving not the actual winning of independence but a fundamental shift of allegiance from Britain to America. Today, not all historians would concur with Adams that the shift he identified constituted the Revolution. But none would deny the importance of the events of those crucial years, which divided the American population along political lines and set the colonies on the road to independence.

The story of the 1760s and early 1770s describes an ever-widening split between Great Britain and Anglo America and among their respective supporters in the colonies. In the long history of British settlement in the Western Hemisphere, considerable tension had occasionally marred the relationship between individual provinces and the mother country. Still, that tension had rarely persisted for long, nor had it been widespread, except during the crisis following the Glorious Revolution in 1689. The primary divisions affecting the colonies had been internal rather than external. In the 1750s, however, a series of events began to draw the colonists' attention from domestic matters to their relations with Great Britain. It all started with the Seven Years War.

Britain's overwhelming victory in that war, confirmed by treaty in 1763, forever altered the balance of power in North America. France was ousted from the continent and Spain from Florida, events with major consequences for both the indigenous peoples of the interior and the residents of the British colonies. Indians could no longer play off European powers against one another and so lost one of their major diplomatic tools. Anglo-Americans no longer had to fear the French threat on their northern and western borders or the Spanish in the Southeast. The British colonies along the coast would never have dared to break with their mother country, some historians contend, had France still controlled the Mississippi River and the Great Lakes.

The British victory in 1763, then, dramatically affected all the residents of North America. That victory also had a significant impact on Great Britain, one that soon involved the colonies. Britain's massive war-related debt needed to be paid, and so Parliament for the first time imposed revenue-raising taxes on the colonies in addition to the customs duties that had long regulated trade. That decision exposed differences in the political thinking of Americans and Britons—differences that until then had been obscured by a shared political vocabulary.

During the 1760s and early 1770s a broad coalition of the residents of Anglo America, men and women alike, resisted new tax levies and attempts by British officials to tighten controls over provincial governments. The colonies' elected leaders became ever more suspicious of Britain's motives as the years passed. They laid aside old antagonisms to coordinate their responses to the new measures, and they slowly began to reorient their political thinking. As late as the summer of 1774, though, most were still seeking a solution within the framework of the empire; few harbored thoughts of independence. ■

Renewed Warfare Among Europeans and Indians

I n the mid-eighteenth century, the British colonies along the Atlantic seaboard were surrounded by hostile, or potentially hostile, neighbors: Indians everywhere, the Spanish in Florida and along the coast of the Gulf of Mexico, the French along the great inland system of rivers and lakes that stretched from the St. Lawrence to the Mississippi. The Spanish outposts posed little direct threat, for Spain's days as a major power had passed. The French were another matter. Their long chain of forts and settlements dominated the North American interior, facilitating trading partnerships and alliances with the Indians. In none of the three wars fought between 1689 and 1748 was England able to shake France's hold on the American frontier. Under the Peace of Utrecht, which ended Queen Anne's War in 1713, the English won control of such peripheral northern areas as Newfoundland, Hudson's Bay, and Acadia (Nova Scotia). But Britain made no territorial gains in King George's War (see Table 5.1 and Map 5.2).

During both Queen Anne's War and King George's War, the Iroquois Confederacy maintained the policy of neutrality it first developed in 1701.

IROQUOIS NEUTRALITY While British and French forces fought for nominal control of the North American continent, the confederacy skillfully manipulated the Europeans, refusing to commit warriors fully to either side despite being showered with

TABLE 5.1

The Colonial Wars, 1689–1763

American Name	European Name	Dates	Participants	American Sites	Dispute
King William's War	War of the League of Augsburg	1689–97	England, Holland versus France, Spain	New England, New York, Canada	French power
Queen Anne's War	War of Spanish Succession	1702–13	England, Holland, Austria versus France, Spain	Florida, New England	Throne of Spain
King George's War	War of Austrian Succession	1739–48	England, Holland, Austria versus France, Spain, Prussia	West Indies, New England, Canada	Throne of Austria
French and Indian War	Seven Years War	1756–63	England versus France, Spain	Ohio country, Canada	Possession of Ohio country

An eighteenth-century Iroquois warrior as depicted by a European artist. Such men of the Six Nations confederacy dominated the North American interior before the Seven Years War. Lines drawn on maps by colonizing powers and the incursions of traders made little impact on their power.   (Library of Congress, Rare Book and Special Collections Division)

previous patterns, that conflict spread from America to Europe, decisively resolving the contest for North America. Trouble began in the mid-1740s, when at two treaty conferences Iroquois negotiators, claiming to speak for Delawares and Shawnees, ceded large tracts of the subordinate tribes' land to English colonists. Disgruntled Delawares and Shawnees migrated west, and Virginia land speculators (soon organized as the Ohio Company) began pressing to develop the ceded territory, focusing first on the crucial area where the Allegheny and Monongahela Rivers join to form the Ohio (see Map 5.1).

Yet not only was that region claimed by Pennsylvania as well, it was also vital to the French, for the Ohio River offered direct access by water to French posts on the Mississippi. A permanent British presence in the Ohio country would challenge France's control of the western fur trade and threaten its prominence in the Mississippi valley. Thus in the early 1750s Pennsylvania fur traders, Ohio Company representatives, and the French military all jostled for position in the region. A devastating 1752 raid by the French and Indians on a trading outpost at the site of modern Cleveland rid the region of Pennsylvanians, but the Virginians posed a more serious challenge. Accordingly, in 1753 the French pushed southward from Lake Erie, building fortified outposts at strategic points.

In response to the French threat, delegates from seven northern and middle colonies gathered in Albany, New York, in June 1754. With the backing of London officials, they sought two goals: to persuade the Iroquois to abandon their traditional neutrality and to coordinate the defenses of the colonies. They succeeded in neither. The Iroquois listened politely to the colonists' arguments but saw no reason to change a policy that had served them well for half a century. And although the Albany Congress delegates adopted a Plan of Union (which would have established an elected intercolonial legislature with the power to tax), their provincial governments uniformly rejected the plan—primarily because those governments feared a loss of autonomy.

ALBANY CONGRESS

While the Albany Congress delegates deliberated, the war they sought to prepare for was already beginning. Governor Robert Dinwiddie of Virginia sent a small militia troop to build a palisade at the forks of the Ohio, then later dispatched reinforcements. When a substantial French force arrived at the forks, the first contingent of Virginia militia surrendered, peacefully abandoning the strategic site. The French then began to construct the larger and more elaborate Fort Duquesne. Upon learning of the confrontation, the inexperienced young officer who commanded the Virginia reinforcements pressed on—

gifts by both. The Iroquois continued a longstanding conflict with Cherokees and Catawbas in the South, thus giving their young warriors combat experience and allowing the replacement of population losses by acquiring new captives. They also cultivated peaceful relationships with Pennsylvania and Virginia, in part to obtain the colonists' imprimatur for their domination of the Shawnees and Delawares. And they forged friendly ties with Algonquians of the Great Lakes region, thereby thwarting potential assaults from those allies of the French and simultaneously making themselves indispensable middlemen for commerce and communication between the Atlantic coast and the West. Thus the Iroquois consolidated their control over the entire American interior north of Virginia and south of the Great Lakes.

But even the Iroquois could not prevent the region inhabited by the Shawnees and Delawares (now western Pennsylvania and eastern Ohio) from providing the spark that set off a major war. In a significant reversal of

Map 5.1   European Settlements and Indians, 1754

By 1754, Europeans had expanded the limits of the English colonies to the eastern slopes of the Appalachian Mountains. Few independent Indian nations still existed in the East, but beyond the mountains they controlled the countryside. Only a few widely scattered English and French forts maintained the Europeans' presence there.

ward instead of awaiting further instructions. He attacked a French detachment and then allowed himself to be trapped in his crudely built Fort Necessity at Great Meadows, Pennsylvania. After a day-long battle (on July 3, 1754), during which more than one-third of his men were killed or wounded, twenty-two-year-old George Washington surrendered. He and his men were allowed to return to Virginia.

Washington's grievous blunder helped ignite a war that eventually would encompass nearly the entire

SEVEN YEARS WAR

world. He also ensured that the Ohio Indians, angry with the Iroquois and trading partners of the French, would support France in that conflict. In July 1755, a few miles south of Fort Duquesne, a combined force of French and Indians ambushed British and colonial troops readying a renewed assault on the fort. In the devastating defeat, General Edward Braddock was killed

and his surviving soldiers were demoralized. The Pennsylvania frontier then bore the brunt of repeated attacks by Ohio Indians for two more years. After news of the debacle reached London, Britain—already poised for renewed conflict with old enemies—declared war on France in 1756, thus formally beginning the Seven Years War.

For three years one disaster followed another. British officers tried without much success to coerce the colonies into supplying men and materiel to the army. The war went so badly that Britain began to fear that France would try to retake Newfoundland and Nova Scotia. Afraid that the approximately twelve thousand French residents of Nova Scotia would abandon their pledges of neutrality, British commanders forced about seven thousand of them from their homeland—the first large-scale modern deportation. Ships crammed with Acadians sailed to each of the mainland colonies, where the dispirited exiles encountered hostility and discrimination as they

■ A 1769 Dutch atlas charted the successful British attack on Quebec ten years earlier. Ships of the British fleet fill the St. Lawrence River. Cannon on the southern shore bombard the fortified town (indicated by the lines across the river). And to the left of the city, on the Plains of Abraham, the string of small red blocks represents the British troops who had stealthily climbed the heights at night to confront Quebec's French defenders (the blue blocks). (Private Collection)

The First Worldwide War

Today we call two twentieth-century conflicts "world wars," but the first worldwide war predated them by more than a century. The contest began in the backwoods of southwestern Pennsylvania, in the spring of 1754, over a seemingly local quarrel—whether Britain or France would build a fort at the forks of the Ohio. That it eventually involved combatants around the world attests not only to the growing importance of European nations' overseas empires but also to the increasing centrality of North America in their struggles for dominance.

Previous wars among Europeans had taken place mostly in Europe, though overseas colonies occasionally got involved. But the contest at the forks of the Ohio helped to reinvigorate a conflict between Austria and Prussia that sent the nations of Europe scrambling for allies. Eventually England, Hanover, and Prussia lined up against France, Austria, and Russia, joined by Sweden, Saxony, and, later, Spain. The war in Europe would last seven years. In 1763 these nations signed a peace treaty that returned the continent to the status quo before the war, but elsewhere, in the rest of the world, Britain had decisively vanquished both France and Spain.

"Elsewhere" included a mind-boggling list of battles. In the Caribbean, Britain seized the French islands of Guade-loupe and Martinique and took Havana from Spain. In North America, the British recaptured the French fortress of Louisbourg and conquered the capital of New France, Quebec. In Africa, the British overwhelmed France's slave-trading posts in Senegambia. In India, British forces won control of Bengal by defeating both a local ruler and French soldiers stationed there. Three years later the British beat a French army at Pondicherry. So four months after France lost Canada, its influence in India was also extinguished. At the very end of the war, a British expedition took Manila in the Philippines from Spain. The commander there had not yet learned that his nation had declared war on Britain, so the assault caught him unawares.

Thus the war that started in the American backcountry revealed the steadily growing links between North America and the rest of the world. And the aftermath exposed an unexpected further link. Both winners and losers had to pay for this first worldwide war. Financial struggles in Britain and France, though separate, ultimately produced similar outcomes: revolutions abroad (for Britain, in America) and at home (for France).

In 1771 the artist Dominic Serres, the Elder, depicted British naval vessels attacking the French fortress at Chandernagore in India in 1757 (at left in background). Cannon fire from the warships was critical to the British victory, one of the keys to the conquest of India during the Seven Years War. (National Maritime Museum, London)

were dispersed into widely scattered communities. After 1763 the survivors relocated: some returned to Canada, others traveled to France or its West Indian islands, and many eventually settled in Louisiana, where they became known as Cajuns.

Led by William Pitt, the civilian official placed in charge of the war effort in 1757, Britain finally pursued a successful military strategy. Pitt agreed to reimburse the colonies for their wartime expenditures and placed recruitment in local hands, thereby gaining greater American support for the war. Colonial militiamen thereafter primarily served as support troops for the large numbers of red-coated regulars sent to North America from Britain. In July 1758, British forces recaptured the fortress at Louisbourg, winning control of the entrance to the St. Lawrence River and cutting the major French supply route. In the fall, the Ohio Indians accepted British peace overtures and the French abandoned Fort Duquesne. Then, in a stunning attack in September 1759, General James Wolfe's regulars defeated the French on the Plains of Abraham and took Quebec. Sens-

ing a British victory, the Iroquois abandoned their traditional neutrality, hoping to gain a postwar advantage by allying themselves with Britain. A year later the British captured Montreal, the last French stronghold on the continent, and the American phase of the war ended.

In the Treaty of Paris (1763), France ceded its major North American holdings to Britain. Spain, an ally of France toward the end of the war, gave Florida to the victors. France, meanwhile, ceded Louisiana west of the Mississippi to Spain, in partial compensation for its ally's losses elsewhere. The British thus gained control of the continent's fur trade. No longer would the English seacoast colonies have to worry about the threat to their existence posed by France's extensive North American territories (see Map 5.2).

The overwhelming British triumph stimulated some Americans to think expansively. People like the Philadelphia printer Benjamin Franklin, who had long touted the colonies' wealth and potential, predicted a glorious new future for British North America—a future that included not just geographical expansion but also economic de-

Map 5.2   European Claims in North America

The dramatic results of the British victory in the Seven Years (French and Indian) War are vividly demonstrated in these maps, which depict the abandonment of French claims to the mainland after the Treaty of Paris in 1763.

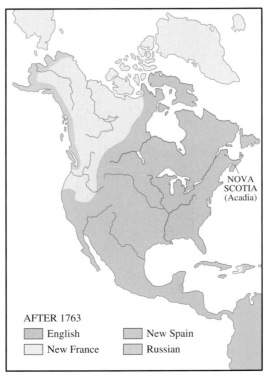

velopment and population growth. Such men were to lead the resistance to British measures in the years after 1763. They uniformly opposed any laws that would retard America's growth and persistently supported steps to increase Americans' control over their own destiny. Many of them also invested heavily in western land speculations.

1763: A Turning Point

*T*he great victory over France had an irreversible impact on North America, felt first by the indigenous peoples of the interior. With France excluded from the continent altogether and Spanish territory now confined to west of the Mississippi, the diplomatic strategy that had served the Indians well for so long was now obsolete. The consequences were immediate and devastating.

Even before the Treaty of Paris, southern Indians had to adjust to the new circumstances. After Britain gained the upper hand in the American war in 1758, Creeks and Cherokees lost their ability to force concessions by threatening to turn instead to France or Spain. In desperation, and in retaliation for British atrocities, Cherokees attacked the Carolina and Virginia frontiers in 1760. Though initially victorious, the Indians were defeated the following year by a force of British regulars and colonial militia. Late in 1761 the two sides concluded a treaty under which the Cherokees allowed the construction of British forts in their territories and opened a large tract of land to European settlement.

The fate of the Cherokees in the South portended events in the Ohio country. There, the Ottawas,

NEOLIN AND
PONTIAC

Chippewas, and Potawatomis reacted angrily when Great Britain, no longer facing French competition, raised the price of trade goods and ended traditional gift-giving practices. Settlers rapidly moved into the Monongahela and Susquehanna valleys. A shaman named Neolin (also known as the Delaware Prophet) urged Indians to oppose British incursion on their lands and European influence on their culture. For the first time since King Philip in 1675, an influential native leader called for the unity of all tribes in the face of an Anglo-American threat. Contending that Indian peoples were destroying themselves by becoming dependent on European goods (especially alcohol), Neolin advocated resistance, both peaceful and armed. If all Indians west of the mountains united to reject the invaders, Neolin declared, the Master of Life would replenish the depleted deer herds and once again look kindly upon his people.

■ Benjamin West, the first well-known American artist, engraved this picture of a prisoner exchange at the end of Pontiac's Uprising, with Colonel Henry Bouquet supervising the return of settlers abducted during the war. In the foreground, a child resists leaving the Indian parents he had grown to love. Many colonists were fascinated by the phenomenon West depicted—the reluctance of captives to abandon their adoptive Indian families.
(Ohio Historical Society)

Yet, ironically, Neolin's call for a return to native traditions itself revealed European origins; his reference to a single Master of Life showed the influence of a syncretic Christianity on his thinking.

Pontiac, the war chief of an Ottawa village near Detroit, became the leader of a movement based on Neolin's precepts. In the spring of 1763, Pontiac forged an unprecedented alliance among Hurons, Chippewas, Potawatomis, Delawares, Shawnees, and Mingoes (Pennsylvania Iroquois). Pontiac then laid siege to Fort Detroit while war parties attacked other British outposts in the Great Lakes. Detroit withstood the siege, but by late June all the other forts west of Niagara and north of Fort Pitt (formerly Fort Duquesne) had fallen to the alliance. Indians then raided the Virginia and

Pennsylvania frontiers at will throughout the summer, slaying at least two thousand settlers. Still, they failed to take the strongholds of Niagara, Fort Pitt, or Detroit. In early August, colonial militiamen soundly defeated a combined Indian force at Bushy Run, Pennsylvania. Conflict ceased when Pontiac broke off the siege of Detroit in late October. A treaty ending the war was finally negotiated three years later.

The uprising demonstrated that the huge territory Britain had acquired from France would be difficult to

PROCLAMATION OF 1763

govern. Officials in London had no experience managing such a vast area, particularly one inhabited by restive peoples—the remaining French settlers along the St. Lawrence and the many Indian communities. In October, the ministry issued the Proclamation of 1763, which designated the headwaters of rivers flowing into the Atlantic from the Appalachians as the temporary western boundary for colonial settlement (see Map 5.1). Its promulgators expected the proclamation to prevent clashes by forbidding colonists to move onto Indian lands until tribes had given up their territory by treaty. But it infuriated two distinct groups of colonists: those who had already squatted on lands west of the line (among them many recent Scots-Irish immigrants) and land-speculation companies from Pennsylvania and Virginia.

In the years after 1763, the latter groups (which included such men as George Washington, Thomas Jefferson, Patrick Henry, and Benjamin Franklin) lobbied vigorously to have their claims validated by colonial governments and London administrators. At a treaty conference at Fort Stanwix, New York, in 1768, they negotiated with Iroquois representatives to push the boundary line farther west and south, opening Kentucky to their speculations. The Iroquois, still claiming to speak for the Delawares and the Shawnees—who used Kentucky as their hunting grounds—agreed to the deal, which brought them valuable trade goods and did not affect their own territories. Yet even though the Virginia land companies eventually gained the support of the House of Burgesses for their claims, they never made any headway where it really mattered—in London—because administrators there realized that significant western expansion would require the expenditure of funds they did not have.

The hard-won victory in the Seven Years War had cost Britain millions of pounds and created an immense

GEORGE III

war debt. The problem of paying it, and of finding the money to defend the newly acquired territories, bedeviled King George III, who in 1760 suc-

ceeded his grandfather, George II. The twenty-two-year-old monarch, an intelligent, passionate man with a mediocre education, was unfortunately an erratic judge of character. During the crucial years between 1763 and 1770, when the rift with the colonies grew ever wider and a series of political crises beset England, the king replaced ministries with bewildering rapidity. Although determined to assert the power of the monarchy, George III was immature and unsure of himself. He often substituted stubbornness for cleverness, and he regarded adherence to the status quo as the hallmark of patriotism.

The man he selected as prime minister in 1763, George Grenville, believed that the American colonies should be more tightly administered than previously. Grenville confronted a financial crisis: England's burden of indebtedness had nearly doubled since 1754, from £73 million to £137 million. Annual expenditures before the war had amounted to no more than £8 million; now the yearly interest on the debt alone came to £5 million. Grenville's ministry had to find new sources of funds, and the British people themselves were already heavily taxed. Since the colonists had benefited greatly from wartime expenditures, Grenville concluded that Anglo-Americans should be asked to pay a larger share of the cost of running the empire.

Grenville did not question Great Britain's right to levy taxes on the colonies. Like all his countrymen, he

THEORIES OF REPRESENTATION

believed that the government's legitimacy derived ultimately from the consent of the people, but he defined consent differently from the colonists. Americans had come to believe that they could be represented only by men who lived nearby and for whom they or their property-holding neighbors actually voted; otherwise, they could not count on legislators to represent their interests properly. Grenville and his English contemporaries, however, believed that Parliament—king, lords, and commons acting together—by definition represented all British subjects, wherever they resided (even overseas) and whether or not they could vote.

Parliament saw itself as collectively representing the entire nation; the particular constituency that chose a member of the House of Commons had no special claim on that member's vote, nor did he have to live near his constituents. According to this theory of government, called *virtual representation*, the colonists were seen as virtually, if not actually, represented in Parliament. Thus their consent to acts of Parliament could be presumed. In the colonies, by contrast, members of the lower houses of the assemblies were viewed as specifically representing the regions that had elected them. Before Grenville proposed to tax the colonists, the two notions coexisted because no conflict exposed the central contradiction. But events of the 1760s revealed the incompatibility of the two definitions of representation.

The same events threw into sharp relief Americans' attitudes toward political power. The colonists had

REAL WHIGS

become accustomed to a central government that wielded limited authority over them, affecting their daily lives very little. Consequently, they believed that a good government was one that largely left them alone, a view in keeping with the theories of a group of British writers known as the Real Whigs. Drawing on a tradition of dissenting thought that reached back to John Locke and even to the English Civil War, the Real Whigs stressed the dangers inherent in a powerful government, particularly one headed by a monarch. Some of them even favored republicanism, which proposed to eliminate monarchs altogether and rest political power more directly on the people. Real Whigs warned the people to guard constantly against government's attempts to encroach on their liberty and seize their property. Political power was always to be feared, wrote John Trenchard and Thomas Gordon in their essay series *Cato's Letters* (originally published in London in 1720–1723 and reprinted many times thereafter in the colonies). Rulers would try to corrupt and oppress the people. Only perpetual vigilance could preserve the people's precious yet fragile liberty, which was closely tied to their right to private property.

Britain's attempts to tighten the reins of government and to raise revenues from the colonies in the 1760s and early 1770s convinced many Americans that the Real Whigs' reasoning applied to their circumstances, especially because of the link between liberty and property rights. Excessive and unjust taxation, they believed, could destroy their freedoms. They began to interpret British measures in light of the Real Whigs' warnings and to see oppressive designs behind the actions of Grenville and his successors. Historians disagree over the extent to which those perceptions were correct, but by 1775 a large number of colonists believed they were. In the mid-1760s, however, colonial leaders did not immediately accuse Grenville of conspiring to oppress them. They at first merely questioned the wisdom of the laws he proposed.

Parliament passed the first such measures, the Sugar and Currency Acts, in 1764. The Sugar Act (also known as the Revenue Act) revised existing customs regulations

SUGAR AND
CURRENCY ACTS

and laid new duties on some foreign imports into the colonies. Its most important provisions, strongly advocated in London by the influential planters of the British Caribbean, aimed at discouraging American rum distillers from smuggling French West Indian molasses, thereby increasing demand for sugar from British islands. It also established a vice-admiralty court at Halifax, Nova Scotia, to adjudicate violations of the law, along with other maritime offenses. Although the Sugar Act appeared to resemble the Navigation Acts, which the colonies had long accepted as legitimate, it broke with tradition in being explicitly designed to raise revenue, not to channel American trade through Britain. The Currency Act effectively outlawed most colonial issues of paper money, because British merchants had long complained that Americans were paying their debts in inflated local currencies. Americans could accumulate little sterling, since they imported more than they exported; thus the act seemed to the colonists to deprive them of a useful medium of exchange.

The Sugar and Currency Acts were imposed on an economy already in the midst of depression. A business boom accompanied the Seven Years War, but the brief spell of prosperity ended abruptly in 1760 when the war shifted overseas. Urban merchants could not sell all their imported goods to colonial customers alone, and without the military's demand for foodstuffs, American farmers found fewer buyers for their products. The bottom dropped out of the European tobacco market, threatening the livelihood of Chesapeake planters. Sailors were thrown out of work, and artisans found few customers. In such circumstances, the prospect of increased import duties and inadequate supplies of currency aroused merchants' hostility.

Individual American essayists and incensed colonial governments protested the new policies. But, lacking any precedent for a united campaign against acts of Parliament, Americans in 1764 took only hesitant and uncoordinated steps. Eight colonial legislatures sent separate petitions to Parliament requesting the Sugar Act's repeal. They argued that its commercial restrictions would hurt Britain as well as the colonies and that they had not consented to its passage. The protests had no effect. The law remained in force, and Grenville proceeded with another revenue plan.

The Stamp Act Crisis

*T*he Stamp Act (1765), Grenville's most important proposal, was modeled on a law that had been in effect in Britain for almost a century. It touched nearly every colonist by requiring tax stamps on most printed materials, but it placed the heaviest burden on merchants and other members of the colonial elite, who used printed matter more frequently than did ordinary folk. Anyone who purchased a newspaper or pamphlet, made a will, transferred land, bought dice or playing cards, applied for a liquor license, accepted a government appointment, or borrowed money would have to pay the tax. Never before had a revenue measure of such scope been proposed for the colonies. The act also required that tax stamps be purchased with sterling, which was scarce, and that violators be tried by vice-admiralty courts, in which judges alone rendered decisions. Americans feared the loss of their right to trial by a jury of their peers. Finally, such a law would break decisively with the colonial tradition of self-imposed taxation.

The most important colonial pamphlet protesting the Sugar Act and the proposed Stamp Act was *The*

■ In 1765 a clerk in the offices of British tax officials prepared this register to contain examples of the tax stamps intended for use in the American colonies. But because the law was never enforced and soon repealed, the register is largely empty, and the other volumes the clerk anticipated were never readied at all.   (The British Library Philatelic Section, Inland Revenue Archives)

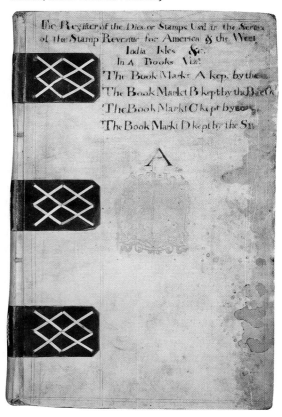

James Otis's Rights of the British Colonies

Rights of the British Colonies Asserted and Proved, by James Otis Jr., a brilliant young Massachusetts attorney. Otis starkly exposed the ideological dilemma that confounded the colonists for the next decade. How could they justify their opposition to certain acts of Parliament without questioning Parliament's authority over them? On the one hand, Otis asserted, Americans were "entitled to all the natural, essential, inherent, and inseparable rights" of Britons, including the right not to be taxed without their consent. "No man or body of men, not excepting the parliament . . . can take [those rights] away," he declared. On the other hand, Otis admitted that under the British system established after the Glorious Revolution, "the power of parliament is uncontrollable but by themselves, and we must obey. . . . Let the parliament lay what burthens they please on us, we must, it is our duty to submit and patiently bear them, till they will be pleased to relieve us."

Otis's first contention, drawing on colonial notions of representation, implied that Parliament could not constitutionally tax the colonies because Americans were not represented in its ranks. Yet his second point both acknowledged political reality and accepted the prevailing theory of British government: that Parliament was the sole, supreme authority in the empire. Even unconstitutional laws enacted by Parliament had to be obeyed until Parliament decided to repeal them.

According to orthodox British political theory, there could be no middle ground between absolute submission to Parliament and a frontal challenge to its authority. Otis tried to find such a middle ground by proposing colonial representation in Parliament, but his idea was never taken seriously on either side of the Atlantic. The British believed that colonists were already virtually represented in Parliament, and Anglo-Americans quickly realized that a handful of colonial delegates to London would simply be outvoted.

Otis published his pamphlet before the Stamp Act was passed. When Americans first learned of the act's adoption in the spring of 1765, they reacted indecisively. Few colonists—even appointed government officials—publicly favored the law. But colonial petitions had already failed to prevent its adoption, and further lobbying appeared futile. Perhaps Otis was correct: the only course open to Americans was to pay the stamp tax, reluctantly but loyally. Acting on that assumption, colonial agents in London sought the appointment of their American friends as stamp distributors so that the law would at least be enforced equitably.

Not all the colonists resigned themselves to paying the new tax. A twenty-nine-year-old lawyer serving his

PATRICK HENRY AND THE VIRGINIA STAMP ACT RESOLVES

first term in the Virginia House of Burgesses was appalled by his fellow legislators' unwillingness to oppose the Stamp Act. Patrick Henry later recalled that he was "young, inexperienced, unacquainted with the forms of the house and the members that composed it"—but he decided to act. "Alone, unadvised, and unassisted, on a blank leaf of an old law book," he wrote the Virginia Stamp Act Resolves.

Little in Henry's earlier life foreshadowed his success in the political arena he entered so dramatically. The son of a prosperous Scottish immigrant to western Virginia, Henry had little formal education. After marrying at eighteen, he failed at both farming and storekeeping before turning to the law as a means of supporting his wife and their six children. Henry lacked legal training, but his oratorical skills made him an effective advocate, first for his clients and later for his political beliefs. A prominent Virginia lawyer observed, "He is by far the most powerful speaker I ever heard. Every word he says not only engages, but commands the attention; and your passions are no longer your own when he addresses them."

Patrick Henry introduced his seven proposals near the end of the legislative session, when many burgesses had already departed for home. Henry's fiery speech led the Speaker of the House to accuse him of treason. (Henry denied the charge, contrary to the nineteenth-century myth that he exclaimed, "If this be treason, make the most of it!") The few burgesses remaining in Williamsburg adopted five of Henry's resolutions by a bare majority. Although they repealed the most radical of the five the next day, their action had far-reaching effects. Some colonial newspapers printed Henry's seven original resolutions as if they had been uniformly passed by the House, even though one was rescinded and two others were never debated or voted on at all.

The four propositions adopted by the burgesses repeated Otis's arguments, asserting that the colonists had never forfeited the rights of British subjects, among which was consent to taxation. The other three resolutions went much further. The one that was repealed claimed for the burgesses "the only exclusive right" to tax Virginians, and the final two (those never considered) asserted that residents of Virginia need not obey tax laws passed by other legislative bodies (namely Parliament), terming any opponent of that opinion "an Enemy to this his Majesty's Colony."

■ In 1795 the artist Lawrence Sully painted the only known life portrait of Patrick Henry. The old man's fierce gaze reflects the same intensity that marked his actions thirty years earlier, when he introduced the Virginia Stamp Act Resolves in the House of Burgesses. (Mead Art Museum, Amherst College. Bequest of Herbert L. Pratt, Class of 1985)

The burgesses' decision to accept only the first four of Henry's resolutions anticipated the position most

CONTINUING LOYALTY TO BRITAIN

Americans would adopt throughout the following decade. Though willing to contend for their rights, the colonists did not seek independence. They rather wanted some measure of self-government. Accordingly, they backed away from the assertions that they owed Parliament no obedience and that only their own assemblies could tax them. Indeed, declared the Maryland lawyer Daniel Dulany, whose *Considerations on the Propriety of Imposing Taxes on the British Colonies* was the most widely read pamphlet of 1765, "The colonies are dependent upon Great Britain, and the supreme authority vested in the king, lords, and commons, may justly be exercised to secure, or preserve their dependence." But, warned Dulany, a superior did not have the right "to seize the property of his inferior when he pleases"; there was a crucial distinction between a condition of "dependence and inferiority" and one of "absolute vassalage and slavery."

Over the next ten years, America's political leaders searched for a formula that would enable them to control their internal affairs, especially taxation, but remain under British rule. The chief difficulty lay in British officials' inability to compromise on the issue of parliamentary power. The notion that Parliament could exercise absolute authority over all colonial possessions inhered in the British theory of government. Even the harshest British critics of the ministries of the 1760s and 1770s questioned only the wisdom of specific policies, not the principles on which they rested. In effect, the Americans wanted British leaders to revise their fundamental understanding of the workings of their government. But that was simply too much to expect.

The ultimate effectiveness of Americans' opposition to the Stamp Act rested on more than ideological arguments over parliamentary power. The decisive and inventive actions of some colonists during the late summer and fall of 1765 gave the resistance its primary force.

In August the Loyal Nine, a Boston social club of printers, distillers, and other artisans, organized a demonstration

ANTI–STAMP ACT DEMONSTRATIONS

against the Stamp Act. Hoping to show that people of all ranks opposed the act, they approached the leaders of the city's rival laborers' associations, based in Boston's North End and South End neighborhoods. The two gangs, composed of unskilled workers and poor tradesmen, often battled each other, but the Loyal Nine convinced them to lay aside their differences to participate in the demonstration. All colonists, not just affluent ones, would have to pay the stamp taxes.

Early on August 14, the demonstrators hung an effigy of Andrew Oliver, the province's stamp distributor, from a tree on Boston Common. That night a large crowd led by a group of about fifty well-dressed tradesmen paraded the effigy around the city. The crowd tore down a small building they thought was intended as the stamp office, making a bonfire near Oliver's house with wood from the structure. Beheading the effigy, they added it to the flames. Demonstrators broke most of Oliver's windows and threw stones at officials who tried to disperse them. In the midst of the melee, the North End and South End leaders drank a toast to their successful union. The Loyal Nine achieved success when Oliver publicly promised not to fulfill the duties of his office. One Bostonian jubilantly wrote to a relative, "I believe people never was more Universally pleased not so much one could I hear say he was sorry, but a smile sat on almost every ones countinance."

But another crowd action twelve days later, aimed this time at Oliver's brother-in-law, Lieutenant Governor Thomas Hutchinson, drew no praise from Boston's respectable citizens. On the night of August 26, a mob reportedly led by the South End leader Ebenezer MacIntosh attacked the homes of several customs officers. The crowd then completely destroyed Hutchinson's elaborately furnished townhouse in one of Boston's most fashionable districts. The lieutenant governor reported that by the next morning "one of the best finished houses in the Province had nothing remaining but the bare walls and floors." His trees and garden were ruined, his valuable library was lost, and the mob "emptied the house of every thing whatsoever except a part of the kitchen furniture." But Hutchinson took some comfort in the fact that "the encouragers of the first mob never intended matters should go this length and the people in general express the utmost detestation of this unparalleled outrage." (A portrait of Hutchinson is on page 130.)

The differences between the two Boston mobs of August 1765 exposed divisions that would continue to

AMERICANS' DIVERGENT INTERESTS

characterize subsequent colonial protests. Few residents of the colonies sided with Great Britain during the 1760s, but various colonial groups had divergent goals. The skilled craftsmen who composed the Loyal Nine, and merchants, lawyers, and other members of the educated elite preferred orderly demonstrations confined to political issues. For the city's laborers, by contrast, economic grievances may have been paramount. Certainly, their "hellish Fury" as they wrecked Hutchinson's house suggests a resentment against his ostentatious display of wealth.

Colonists, like Britons, had a long tradition of crowd action in which disfranchised people took to the streets to redress deeply felt local grievances. But the Stamp Act controversy drew ordinary urban folk into the vortex of transatlantic politics for the first time. Matters that previously had been of concern only to the gentry or to members of colonial legislatures were now discussed on every street corner and in every tavern. Benjamin Franklin's daughter observed as much when she informed her father, then serving as a colonial agent in London, that "nothing else is talked of, the Dutch [Germans] talk of the stompt act the Negroes of the tamp, in short every body has something to say."

The entry of unskilled workers, slaves, and women into the realm of imperial politics both threatened and aided the elite men who wanted to mount effective opposition to British measures. On the one hand, crowd ac-

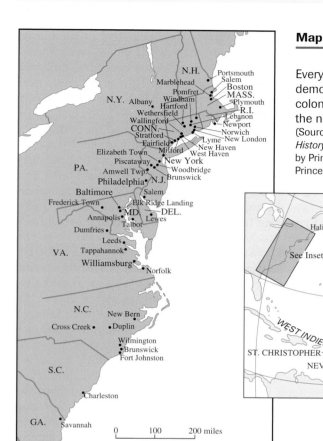

Map 5.3 Sites of Major Demonstrations Against the Stamp Act

Every place named on these maps was the site of a demonstration against the Stamp Act of 1765; British colonies outside the eventual United States joined in the nearly universal opposition to the hated measure. (Source: From Lester J. Cappon et al., eds., *Atlas of Early American History: The Revolutionary Era, 1760–1790.* Copyright © 1976 by Princeton University Press. Reprinted by permission of Princeton University Press.)

yers, and prosperous tradesmen like Paul Revere, the Sons of Liberty by early 1766 linked protest leaders from Charleston, South Carolina, to Portsmouth, New Hampshire. Not surprisingly, in light of the central role of taverns as settings for the exchange of news and opinions, a considerable number of members were tavern owners.

The Sons of Liberty could influence events but not control them. In Charleston in October 1765, an informally organized crowd shouting "Liberty Liberty and stamp'd paper" forced the resignation of the South Carolina stamp distributor. The victory celebration a few days later—the largest demonstration the city had ever known—featured a British flag with the word "Liberty" emblazoned on it. But the new Charleston chapter of the Sons of Liberty was horrified when in January 1766 local slaves paraded through the streets similarly crying "Liberty!" Freedom from slavery was not the sort of liberty elite slaveowners had in mind.

In Philadelphia, too, resistance leaders were dismayed when an angry mob threatened to attack Benjamin Franklin's house. The city's laborers believed Franklin to be partly responsible for the Stamp Act, since he had obtained the post of stamp distributor for a close friend. But Philadelphia's artisans—the backbone of the opposition movement there and elsewhere—were fiercely

tion could have a stunning impact. Anti–Stamp Act demonstrations occurred in cities and towns stretching from Halifax in the north to the Caribbean island of Antigua in the south (see Map 5.3). They were so successful that by November 1, when the law was scheduled to take effect, not one stamp distributor was willing to carry out his official duties. Thus the act could not be enforced. But on the other hand, wealthy men recognized that mobs composed of the formerly powerless—whose goals were not always identical to theirs (as the Boston experience showed)—could endanger their own dominance of the society. What would happen, they wondered, if the "hellish Fury" of the crowd turned against them?

They therefore attempted to channel resistance into acceptable forms by creating an intercolonial association, the Sons of Liberty. New Yorkers organized the first such group in early November, and branches *Sons of Liberty* spread rapidly through the coastal cities. Composed of merchants, law-

■ The haughty and powerful Thomas Hutchinson, lieutenant governor of Massachusetts, whose townhouse in Boston's North End was torn apart by a mob on August 26, 1765. (Massachusetts Historical Society)

loyal to Franklin, one of their own who had made good. They gathered to protect his home and family from the crowd. The house was saved, but the resulting split between the better-off tradesmen and the common laborers prevented the establishment of a successful workingmen's alliance like that of Boston.

During the fall and winter of 1765–1766, opposition to the Stamp Act proceeded on three separate fronts.

OPPOSITION AND REPEAL Colonial legislatures petitioned Parliament to repeal the hated law, and courts closed because they could not obtain the stamps now required for all legal documents. In October nine colonies sent delegates to a general congress, the first since the 1754 Albany Congress. The Stamp Act Congress met in New York to draft a unified but conservative statement of protest that stressed the law's adverse economic effects rather than its perceived violations of Americans' rights. At the same time, the Sons of Liberty held mass meetings, attempting to rally public support for the resistance movement. Finally, American merchants organized nonimportation associations to pressure British exporters. By the 1760s, one-quarter of all British exports went to the colonies,

and American merchants reasoned that London merchants whose sales suffered severely would lobby for repeal. Since times were bad and American merchants were finding few customers for imported goods anyway, a general moratorium on future purchases would also help to reduce their bloated inventories.

In March 1766, Parliament repealed the Stamp Act. The nonimportation agreements had had the anticipated effect, creating allies for the colonies among wealthy London merchants. But boycotts, formal protests, and crowd actions were less important in winning repeal than was the appointment of a new prime minister, chosen by George III for reasons unrelated to colonial politics. Lord Rockingham, who replaced Grenville in the summer of 1765, had opposed the Stamp Act, not because he believed Parliament lacked power to tax the colonies but because he thought the law unwise and divisive. Thus although Rockingham proposed repeal, he linked it to passage of a Declaratory Act, which asserted Parliament's authority to tax and legislate for Britain's American possessions "in all cases whatsoever."

News of the repeal arrived in Newport, Rhode Island, in May, and the Sons of Liberty quickly dispatched messengers to carry the welcome tidings throughout the colonies. They organized celebrations commemorating the glorious event, all of which stressed the Americans' unwavering loyalty to Great Britain. Their goal achieved, the Sons of Liberty dissolved. Few colonists saw the ominous implications of the Declaratory Act.

Resistance to the Townshend Acts

The colonists had accomplished their immediate aim, but the long-term prospects were unclear. In the summer of 1766, another change in the ministry in London revealed how fragile their victory had been. The new prime minister, William Pitt, had fostered cooperation between the colonies and Great Britain during the Seven Years War. Now, however, Pitt was ill much of the time, and another man, Charles Townshend, became the dominant force in the ministry. An ally of Grenville and a supporter of colonial taxation, Townshend decided to renew the attempt to obtain additional funds from Britain's American possessions (see Table 5.2).

The duties Townshend proposed in 1767 were to be levied on trade goods like paper, glass, and tea, and thus seemed to be nothing more than extensions of the existing Navigation Acts. But the Townshend duties differed from previous customs levies in two ways. First, they applied to items imported into the colonies from Britain, not from foreign countries. Thus they violated mercantilist theory (see page 77). Second, the revenues were designed to fund the salaries of some royal officials in the colonies. Those men, previously paid from local taxation, would therefore be freed from what had been a powerful weapon to ensure their cooperation, for assemblies would no longer be able to threaten to withhold their salaries, as had been done regularly in the past. Additionally, Townshend's scheme provided for establishing an American Board of Customs Commissioners and vice-admiralty courts at Boston, Philadelphia, and Charleston. Both moves angered merchants, whose profits would be threatened by more vigorous enforcement of the Navigation Acts.

JOHN DICKINSON'S FARMER'S LETTERS

In 1765, months had passed before the colonists protested the Stamp Act. The passage of the Townshend Acts, however, drew a quick response. One series of essays in particular, *Letters from a Farmer in Pennsylvania*, by the prominent lawyer John Dickinson, expressed a broad consensus. Eventually all but four colonial newspapers printed Dickinson's essays; in pamphlet form they went through seven American editions. Dickinson contended that Parliament could regulate colonial trade but could not exercise that power to raise revenue. By distinguishing between trade regulation and unacceptable commercial taxation, Dickinson avoided the sticky issue of consent and how it affected colonial subordination to Parliament. But his argument created a different, and equally knotty, problem. In effect it obligated the colonies to assess Parliament's motives in passing any law pertaining to trade before deciding whether to obey it. That was unworkable in the long run.

The Massachusetts assembly responded to the Townshend Acts by drafting a letter to circulate among the other colonial legislatures, calling for unity and suggesting a joint petition of protest. Not the letter itself but the ministry's reaction to it united the colonies. When Lord Hillsborough, recently named to the new post of secretary of state for America, learned of the circular letter, he ordered Governor Francis Bernard of Massachusetts to insist that the assembly recall it. He also directed other governors to prevent their assemblies from discussing the letter. Hillsborough's order gave colonial assemblies the incentive they needed to join forces to oppose this new threat to their prerogatives. In late 1768 the Massachusetts legislature met, debated, and resoundingly rejected recall by a vote of 92 to 17. Bernard immediately dissolved the assembly, and other governors followed suit when their legislatures debated the circular letter.

RITUALS OF RESISTANCE

The number of votes cast against recalling the circular letter—92—assumed ritual significance for the supporters of resistance. The figure 45 already had symbolic meaning because John Wilkes, a radical Londoner sympathetic to the American cause, had been jailed for libel in Britain for publishing an essay entitled *The North Briton*, No. 45. In Boston, Paul Revere made a punchbowl weighing 45 ounces that held 45 gills (half-cups) and was engraved with the names of opposition legislators; James Otis, John Adams, and others publicly drank 45 toasts from it. In Charleston the city's tradesmen decorated a tree with 45 lights and set off 45 rockets. Carrying 45 candles, they adjourned to a tavern, where 45 tables were set with 45 bowls of wine, 45 bowls of punch, and 92 glasses.

Such public rituals served important unifying and educational functions. Just as the pamphlets by Otis, Dulany, Dickinson, and others acquainted literate colonists with the issues raised by British actions, so public rituals taught illiterate Americans about the reasons for resistance and familiarized them with the terms of the argument. When Boston's revived Sons of Liberty invited hundreds of city residents to dine with them each August 14 to commemorate the first Stamp Act uprising, and the Charleston Sons of Liberty held their meetings in public, crowds gathered to watch and listen. Likewise, the public singing of songs supporting the American cause helped to spread the word. The participants in such events openly expressed their commitment to the cause of resistance and encouraged others to join them.

TABLE 5.2	
British Ministries and Their American Policies	
Head of Ministry	**Major Acts**
George Grenville	Sugar Act (1764)
	Currency Act (1764)
	Stamp Act (1765)
Lord Rockingham	Stamp Act repealed (1766)
	Declaratory Act (1766)
William Pitt/ Charles Townshend	Townshend Acts (1767)
Lord North	Townshend duties (except for the tea tax) repealed (1770)
	Coercive Acts (1774)
	Quebec Act (1774)

■ Paul Revere crafted a punchbowl to commemorate the 92 members of the Massachusetts Assembly who in 1768 voted against rescinding the circular letter. The bowl was also linked symbolically to John Wilkes by its size and weight, and through its use in rituals incorporating the number 45. (Courtesy, Museum of Fine Arts, Boston. Gift by Subscription and Francis Bartlett Fund. Reproduced with permission. © 1999 Museum of Fine Arts, Boston. All rights reserved.)

During the campaign against the Townshend duties, the Sons of Liberty and other American leaders made a deliberate effort to involve ordinary folk in the resistance movement. Most important, they urged colonists of all ranks and both sexes to sign agreements not to purchase or consume British products. The new consumerism that previously had linked colonists economically now linked them politically as well, supplying them with a ready method of displaying their allegiance. As "A Tradesman" wrote in a Philadelphia paper in 1770, it was essential "for the Good of the Whole, to strengthen the Hands of the Patriotic Majority, by agreeing not to purchase British Goods."

As the primary purchasers of textiles and household goods, women played a central role in the nonconsumption movement. In Boston more than three hundred matrons publicly promised not to buy or drink tea, "Sickness excepted." The women of Wilmington, North Carolina, burned their tea after walking through town in a solemn procession. Women throughout the colonies exchanged recipes for tea substitutes or drank coffee instead. The best known of the protests, the so-called Edenton Ladies Tea Party, actually had little to do with tea. It was a meeting of prominent North Carolina women who pledged formally to work for the public good and to support resistance to British measures.

DAUGHTERS OF LIBERTY

Women also encouraged home manufacturing. In many towns, young women calling themselves Daughters of Liberty met to spin in public in an effort to per-

suade other women to make homespun, thereby ending the colonies' dependence on British cloth. These symbolic displays of patriotism—publicized by newspapers and broadsides—served the same purpose as the male rituals involving the numbers 45 and 92. When young ladies from well-to-do families sat publicly at spinning wheels all day, eating only American food and drinking local herbal tea, and later listening to patriotic sermons, they were serving as political instructors. Many women took great satisfaction in their newfound role. When a New England satirist hinted that women discussed only "such triffling subjects as Dress, Scandal and Detraction" during their spinning bees, three Boston women replied angrily: "Inferior in abusive sarcasm, in personal invective, in low wit, we glory to be, but inferior in veracity, sincerity, love of virtue, of liberty and of our country, we would not willingly be to any."

But the colonists were by no means united in support of nonimportation and nonconsumption. If the Stamp Act protests had occasionally (as in Boston and Philadelphia) revealed a division between artisans and merchants on the one side and common laborers on the other, resistance to the Townshend Acts exposed new splits in American ranks. The most significant—which arose from a change in economic circumstances—divided urban artisans and merchants, allies in 1765.

DIVIDED OPINION OVER BOYCOTTS

The Stamp Act boycotts had helped to revive a depressed economy by creating a demand for local products and reducing merchants' inventories. But in 1768 and 1769, merchants were enjoying boom times and had no financial incentive to support a boycott. As a result, merchants signed the agreements only reluctantly, sometimes violating them secretly. In contrast, artisans supported nonimportation enthusiastically, recognizing that the absence of British goods would create a ready market for their own manufactures. Thus tradesmen formed the core of the crowds that coerced both importers and their customers by picketing stores, publicizing offenders' names, and sometimes destroying property.

Such tactics were effective: colonial imports from England dropped dramatically in 1769, especially in New York, New England, and Pennsylvania. But they also aroused heated opposition, creating a second major division among the colonists. Some Americans who supported resistance to British measures began to question the use of violence to force others to join the boycott. In addition, wealthier and more conservative colonists were frightened by the threat to private property inherent in the campaign. Political activism by ordinary colonists challenged the ruling elite's domination, just as its members had feared in 1765.

Disclosures that leading merchants had violated the nonimportation agreement caused dissension in the

Townshend Duties Repealed

ranks of the boycotters, so Americans were relieved when news arrived in April 1770 that the Townshend duties had been repealed, with the exception of the tea tax. A new prime minister, Lord North, persuaded Parliament that duties on trade within the empire were ill-advised. Although some colonial leaders argued that nonimportation should continue until the tea tax was repealed, merchants quickly resumed importing. The rest of the Townshend Acts remained in force, but repealing the duties made the other provisions (establishing vice-admiralty courts and the American Board of Customs Commissioners, and promising to pay officials' salaries from customs revenues at some future time) appear less objectionable.

Confrontations in Boston

*a*t first the new ministry in London did nothing to antagonize the colonists. Yet on the very day Lord North proposed repeal of the Townshend duties, a confrontation between civilians and soldiers in Boston led to the death of five Americans. The origins of the event that patriots called the Boston Massacre lay in repeated clashes between customs officers and the people

A 1769 Boston broadside commended the spinners, "Rich and Poor," who had "Compassion for their Country" and promoted "Frugality" during the Townshend Act crisis. The poet put into verse precisely the message the spinners intended to convey.   (Massachusetts Historical Society)

of Massachusetts. The decision to base the American Board of Customs Commissioners in Boston was the source of the problem.

Mobs targeted the customs commissioners from the day they arrived in November 1767. In June 1768 their seizure of the patriot leader John Hancock's sloop *Liberty* on suspicion of smuggling caused a riot in which prominent customs officers' property was destroyed. The riot in turn helped to convince the ministry in London that troops were needed to maintain order in the unruly port. The assignment of two regiments of regulars to their city confirmed Bostonians' worst fears; the redcoats constantly reminded city dwellers of the oppressive potential of British power. Guards on Boston Neck, the entrance to the city, checked all travelers and their goods. Redcoat patrols roamed the city day and night, questioning and sometimes harassing passersby. Military parades were held on Boston Common, accompanied by martial music and often the public whipping of deserters and other violators of army rules. Parents began to fear for the safety of their daughters, who were subjected to soldiers' coarse sexual insults. But the greatest potential for violence lay in the uneasy relationship between the soldiers and Boston laborers. Many redcoats sought employment in their off-duty hours, competing for unskilled jobs with the city's ordinary workingmen. Members of the two groups brawled repeatedly in taverns and on the streets.

Early on the evening of March 5, 1770, a crowd of laborers began throwing hard-packed snowballs at soldiers guarding the Customs House. Goaded

BOSTON MASSACRE — beyond endurance, the sentries acted against express orders and fired on the crowd, killing four and wounding eight, one of whom died a few days later. Resistance leaders idealized the dead rioters as martyrs for the cause of liberty, holding a solemn funeral and later commemorating March 5 annually with patriotic orations. Paul Revere's engraving of the massacre (based on a drawing by John Singleton Copley's half-brother Henry Pelham and reproduced on page 135) was part of the propaganda campaign.

Leading patriots wanted to ensure that the soldiers did not become martyrs as well. Despite the political benefits the patriots derived from the massacre, they probably did not approve the crowd action that provoked it. Ever since the destruction of Hutchinson's house in August 1765, men allied with the Sons of Liberty had supported orderly demonstrations and expressed distaste at such uncontrolled riots as the one that provoked the Boston Massacre. Thus when the soldiers were tried for the killings in November, John Adams and Josiah Quincy Jr., both unwavering patriots, acted as their defense attorneys. Almost all the accused were acquitted, and the two men convicted were released after being branded on the thumb. Undoubtedly the favorable outcome of the trials persuaded London officials not to retaliate against the city.

For more than two years after the Boston Massacre and the repeal of the Townshend duties, a superficial calm descended on the colonies. The

A BRITISH PLOT? — most outspoken colonial newspapers, such as the *Boston Gazette*, the *Penn-*

sylvania Journal, and the *South Carolina Gazette*, published essays drawing on Real Whig ideology and accusing Great Britain of deliberately scheming to oppress the colonies. After the Stamp Act's repeal, the patriots had praised Parliament; following repeal of the Townshend duties, they warned of impending tyranny. What had seemed to be an isolated mistake, a single ill-chosen stamp tax, now appeared to be part of a plot against American liberties. Essayists pointed to Parliament's persecution of the British radical John Wilkes, the stationing of troops in Boston, and the growing number of vice-admiralty courts as evidence of plans to enslave the colonists. Indeed, patriot writers played repeatedly on the word *enslavement*. Most free colonists had direct knowledge of slavery (either as slaveholders themselves or as neighbors of slaveowners), and the threat of enslavement by Britain must have hit them with peculiar force.

Still, no one yet advocated complete independence from the mother country. Although the patriots were becoming increasingly convinced that they should seek freedom from parliamentary authority, they continued to acknowledge their British identity and their allegiance to George III. They began, therefore, to envision a system that would enable them to be ruled by their own elected legislatures while remaining subordinate to the king. But any such scheme violated Britons' conception of the nature of their government, which posited that Parliament wielded sole, undivided sovereignty over the empire. Furthermore, in the British mind, Parliament encompassed the king as well as lords and commons, so separating the monarch from the legislature was impossible.

Then, in the fall of 1772, the North ministry began to implement the Townshend Act that provided for governors and judges to be paid directly from customs revenues. In early November, voters at a Boston town meeting established a Committee of Correspondence to publicize the decision by exchanging letters with other Massachusetts towns. Heading the committee was the man who had proposed its formation, Samuel Adams.

Fifty-one in 1772, Samuel Adams was thirteen years older than his distant cousin John and by a decade the senior of most other leaders of Ameri-

SAMUEL ADAMS AND COMMITTEES OF CORRESPONDENCE — can resistance. He had been a Boston tax collector, a member and clerk of the Massachusetts assembly, an ally of the Loyal Nine, and a member of the Sons of Liberty. Unswerving in his devotion to the American cause, Adams drew a sharp contrast between a corrupt, vice-ridden Britain and the colonies, peopled by simple, liberty-loving folk. An experienced

■ Shortly after the Boston Massacre, Paul Revere printed this illustration of the confrontation near the customs house on March 5, 1770. Offering visual support for the patriots' version of events, it showed the British soldiers firing on an unresisting crowd (instead of the aggressive mob described at the soldiers' trial) and—even worse—a gun firing from the building itself, which has been labeled "Butchers Hall." (Courtesy of the John Carter Brown Library at Brown University)

political organizer, Adams continually stressed the necessity of prudent collective action in speeches in the Boston town meeting. His Committee of Correspondence thus undertook the task of creating an informed consensus among all the residents of Massachusetts.

Such committees, which were eventually established throughout the colonies, represented the next logical step in the organization of American resistance. Until 1772, the protest movement was largely confined to the seacoast and primarily to major cities and towns (see Map 5.3). Adams realized that the time had come to widen the movement's geographic scope, to attempt to involve more colonists in the struggle. Accordingly, the Boston town meeting directed the Committee of Correspondence "to state the Rights of the Colonists and of this Province in particular," to list "the Infringements and Violations thereof that have been, or from time to time may be made," and to send copies to the other towns in the province. In return, Boston requested "a free communication of their Sentiments on this Subject."

The statement of colonial rights prepared by the Bostonians declared that Americans had absolute rights to life, liberty, and property. The idea that "a British house of commons, should have a right, at pleasure, to give and grant the property of the colonists" was "irreconcileable" with "the first principles of natural law and Justice . . . and of the British Constitution in particular." The list of grievances complained of taxation without representation, the presence of unnecessary troops and customs officers on American soil, the use of imperial revenues to pay colonial officials, the expanded jurisdiction of vice-admiralty courts, and even the nature of the instructions given to American governors by their superiors in London.

The entire document, which was printed as a pamphlet for distribution to the towns, exhibited none of the hesitation that had characterized colonial claims against Parliament in the 1760s. No longer were patriots—at least in Boston—preoccupied with defining the precise limits of parliamentary authority. No longer did they mention the necessity of obedience to Parliament. They were committed to a course that placed American rights first, loyalty to Great Britain a distant second.

The response of the Massachusetts towns to the committee's pamphlet must have caused Samuel Adams to rejoice. Some towns disagreed with Boston's assessment of the state of affairs, but most aligned themselves with the city. From Braintree came the assertion that "all civil officers are or ought to be Servants to the people and dependent upon them for their official Support, and every instance to the Contrary from the Governor downwards tends to crush and destroy civil liberty." The town of Holden declared that "the People of New England have never given the People of Britain any Right of Jurisdiction over us." The citizens of Petersham commented that resistance to tyranny was "the first and highest social Duty of this people." And Pownallborough warned, "Allegiance is a relative Term and like Kingdoms and commonwealths is local and has its bounds." Beliefs like these made the next crisis in Anglo-American affairs the final one.

Tea and Turmoil

The tea tax was the only Townshend duty still in effect by 1773. In the years after 1770, some Americans continued to boycott English tea, while others resumed drinking it either openly or in secret. As was explained in Chapter 4, tea figured prominently in both the colonists' diet and their social lives, so observing the boycott required them not only to forgo a favorite beverage but also to alter habitual forms of socializing. Tea thus retained an explosively symbolic character even though the boycott began to fall apart after 1770.

In May 1773, Parliament passed an act designed to save the East India Company from bankruptcy. The

TEA ACT

company, which held a monopoly on British trade with the East Indies, was critically important to the British economy (and to the financial well-being of many prominent British politicians who had invested in its stock). According to the Tea Act, legal tea would henceforth be sold in America only by the East India Company's designated agents, which would enable the company to avoid middlemen in both England and the colonies and to price its tea competitively with that offered by smugglers. The net result would be cheaper tea for American consumers. Resistance leaders, however, interpreted the new measure as a pernicious device to make them admit Parlia-

ment's right to tax them, for the less expensive tea would still be taxed under the Townshend law. Others saw the Tea Act as the first step in the establishment of an East India Company monopoly of all colonial trade. Residents of the four cities designated to receive the first shipments of tea accordingly prepared to respond to what they perceived as a new threat to their freedom.

In New York City, tea ships never arrived. In Philadelphia, Pennsylvania's governor persuaded the captain to sail back to Britain. In Charleston, the tea was unloaded and stored; some was destroyed, the rest sold in 1776 by the new state government. The only confrontation occurred in Boston, where both sides—the town meeting, joined by participants from nearby towns, and Governor Thomas Hutchinson, two of whose sons were tea agents—rejected compromise.

The first of three tea ships, the *Dartmouth,* entered Boston harbor on November 28. The customs laws

THE BOSTON TEA PARTY

required cargo to be landed and the appropriate duty paid by its owners within twenty days of a ship's arrival; otherwise, the cargo had to be seized by customs officers and sold at auction. After a series of mass meetings, Bostonians voted to post guards on the wharf to prevent the tea from being unloaded. Hutchinson refused to permit the vessels to leave the harbor. John Singleton Copley, whose father-in-law was a tea agent, tried to mediate the dispute.

On December 16, one day before the cargo would have been confiscated, more than five thousand people (nearly a third of the city's population) crowded into Old South Church. The meeting, chaired by Samuel Adams, made a final attempt to convince Hutchinson to send the tea back to England. But the governor remained adamant. In the early evening Adams reportedly announced "that he could think of nothing further to be done—that they had now done all they could for the Salvation of their Country." Cries then rang out from the back of the crowd: "Boston harbor a tea-pot tonight! The Mohawks are come!" Small groups pushed their way out of the meeting. Within a few minutes, about sixty men crudely disguised as Indians assembled at the wharf, boarded the three ships, and dumped the cargo into the harbor. By 9 P.M. their work was done: 342 chests of tea worth approximately £10,000 floated in splinters on the water.

Among the "Indians" were many representatives of Boston's artisans, including the silversmith Paul Revere. Five masons, eleven carpenters and builders, three leatherworkers, a blacksmith, two barbers, a coachmaker, a shoemaker, and twelve apprentices have been identified as participants. That their ranks also included

The planners of the Boston Tea Party met here, at the Green Dragon Tavern, sketched later by one of their number, the portrait painter John Johnson. (Courtesy, American Antiquarian Society)

GREEN DRAGON TAVERN

Where we met to Plan the Consignment of few Shiploads of Tea. Dec 16 1773

Jn Johnson + Water Street Boston Mass. 1773

four farmers from outside Boston, ten merchants, two doctors, a teacher, and a bookseller illustrated the widespread support for the resistance movement. The next day John Adams exulted in his diary that the Tea Party was "so bold, so daring, so firm, intrepid and inflexible" that "I cant but consider it as an Epocha in history."

The North administration reacted with considerably less enthusiasm when it learned of the Tea Party. In March 1774, Parliament adopted the first of four laws that became known as the Coercive, or Intolerable, Acts. It ordered the port of Boston closed until the tea was paid for, prohibiting all but coastal trade in food and firewood. Later in the spring, Parliament passed three other punitive measures. The Massachusetts Government Act altered the province's charter, substituting an appointed council for the elected one, increasing the governor's powers, and forbidding most town meetings. The Justice Act provided that a person accused of committing murder in the course of suppressing a riot or enforcing the laws could be tried outside the colony where the incident had occurred. Finally, the Quartering Act allowed military officers to commandeer privately owned buildings to house their troops. Thus the Coercive Acts punished not only Boston but also Massachusetts as a whole, alerting other colonies to the possibility

COERCIVE AND QUEBEC ACTS

that their residents, too, could be subject to retaliation if they opposed British authority.

After passing the last of the Coercive Acts, Parliament turned its attention to much-needed reforms in the government of Quebec. The Quebec Act thereby became linked with the Coercive Acts in the minds of the patriots. Intended to ease strains that had arisen since the British conquest of the formerly French colony, the Quebec Act granted greater religious freedom to Catholics—alarming Protestant colonists, who equated Roman Catholicism with religious and political despotism. It also reinstated French civil law, which had been replaced by British procedures in 1763, and it established an appointed council (rather than an elected legislature) as the governing body of the colony. Finally, in an attempt to provide northern Indians with some protection against Anglo-American settlement, the act annexed to Quebec the area east of the Mississippi River and north of the Ohio River. That region, parts of which were claimed by individual seacoast colonies, was thus removed from their jurisdiction—and the task of wealthy colonists who hoped to develop the Ohio Country became much more difficult.

Members of Parliament who voted for the punitive legislation believed that the acts would be obeyed and that at long last they had solved the problem posed by the troublesome Americans. But the patriots showed little inclination to bow to the wishes of Parliament. In their eyes, the Coercive Acts and the Quebec Act proved what they had feared since 1768: that Great Britain had embarked on a deliberate plan to oppress them. If the port of Boston could be closed, why not the ports of Philadelphia or New York? If the royal charter of Massachusetts could be changed, why not the charter of South Carolina? If certain people could be transferred to distant colonies for trial, why not any violator of any law? If troops could be forcibly quartered in private houses, did not that action pave the way for the occupation of all of America? If the Roman Catholic Church could receive favored status in Quebec, why not everywhere? It seemed as though the full dimensions of the plot against American rights and liberties had at last been revealed.

The Boston Committee of Correspondence urged all the colonies to join in an immediate boycott of British goods. But the other provinces hesitated to take such a drastic step. Rhode Island, Virginia, and Pennsylvania each suggested that another intercolonial congress be convened to consider an appropriate response, and in mid-June 1774 Massachusetts acquiesced. Few people wanted to take hasty action; even the most ardent patriots remained loyal to Britain and hoped for reconciliation with its leaders. Despite their objections to British policy, they continued to see themselves as part of the empire. Americans were approaching the brink of confrontation, but they had not committed themselves to an irrevocable break. So the colonies agreed to send delegates to Philadelphia in September to attend a Continental Congress.

Summary

*J*ust twenty years earlier, at the outbreak of the Seven Years War in the wilderness of western Pennsylvania, no one could have predicted that the future would bring such swift and dramatic change to Britain's mainland colonies. Yet that conflict—which simultaneously removed France from North America and created a huge war debt Britain had to find ways to pay—set in motion the process leading to the convening of the First Continental Congress.

In the years after the war ended in 1763, momentous changes occurred in the ways colonists thought about themselves and their allegiances. The number of colonists who defined themselves as political actors increased substantially. Once linked unquestioningly to Great Britain,

they began to develop a sense of their own identity as Americans, including a recognition of the cultural and social gulf that separated them from Britons. They started to realize that their concept of the political process differed from that held by people in the mother country. They also came to understand that their economic interests did not necessarily coincide with those of Great Britain. Colonial political leaders reached such conclusions only after a long train of events, some of them violent, altered their understanding of their relationship with the mother country. Parliamentary acts such as the Stamp Act and the Townshend Acts elicited colonial responses—both ideological and practical—that produced further responses from Britain. Tensions escalated until they climaxed in the Tea Party. From that point on, there was to be no turning back.

In the late summer of 1774, the Americans were committed to resistance but not to independence. Even so, they had started to sever the bonds of empire. During the next decade, they would forge the bonds of a new American nationality to replace those rejected Anglo-American ties.

LEGACY FOR A PEOPLE AND A NATION
The Census and Reapportionment

When in the prerevolutionary years American colonists argued that "they were not represented in" Parliament, they developed a definition of representation very different from the understanding traditionally accepted in Great Britain. There, numbers did not matter: the entire British population was seen as being "virtually" represented in Parliament, regardless of how many men had the vote or how many electors lived in each district. In eighteenth-century Britain, some districts had few or no voters, some had many, and some heavily populated areas could vote for no one, because Parliament had not been reapportioned for centuries.

Americans, by contrast, placed great emphasis on the importance of being represented in government by someone for whom they—or at least their better-off male neighbors—had actually voted. And that carried with it the related desire for election districts that were regularly reapportioned in accordance with the movements and increase of the population; otherwise the goal of actual representation could not be ensured. Article 1, Section 2, of the U.S. Constitution thus provides for an "actual enumeration" of the nation's residents every ten years so that "representatives . . . shall be apportioned among the several States . . . according to their respective numbers." Each decade, from 1790 to 2000, the government has tried to count the nation's residents accurately—although, according to historians and demographers, it has often failed to achieve that goal. Even Thomas Jefferson, who as secretary of state oversaw the first census in 1790, recognized that it undercounted the population and should be adjusted upward.

The 2000 census, the planning for which Congress debated heatedly, turned out to be the most accurate in recent decades. It also led to two Supreme Court decisions: one outlining appropriate techniques for conducting the mandated "actual enumeration" of the American population, and another rejecting Utah's challenge to the final count. (Utah, which has only one member of the House and hoped to obtain a second, charged that the Census Bureau had improperly awarded a seat to North Carolina.) In other years too—especially 1920, near the close of an era of dramatic demographic change—planning and conducting the census proved highly contentious. The commonly unacknowledged origin of such contests lies in Americans' prerevolutionary experience.

Every ten years, in short, the nation must still wrestle with an enduring legacy of the colonial period: the need to enumerate the American people and to alter the boundaries of electoral districts according to the results.

The **history companion** *powered by Eduspace®*

Your primary source for interactive quizzes, exercises, and more to help you learn efficiently.
http://history.college.hmco.com/students

a REVOLUTION, INDEED 1774–1783

*T*he Shawnee chief Blackfish named his new captive Sheltowee, or Big Turtle, and adopted him as his son. Blackfish's warriors had easily caught the lone hunter, who was returning with a slaughtered buffalo to an encampment of men making salt at the briny spring known as Blue Licks. The captive then persuaded his fellow frontiersmen to surrender to the Shawnees (allies of the British) without a fight. It was February 1778. The hunter was Daniel Boone, who less than three years earlier had moved his family from North Carolina to the western region of Virginia known as Kentucky. Both his contemporaries and some historians have wondered about Boone's allegiance during the American Revolution, for he moved to the frontier just as the war began. His encounter with the Shawnees in 1778, which can be interpreted in several ways, highlights many ambiguities of revolutionary-era loyalties.

The Shawnees were seeking captives to cover the death (see pages 104–105) of their chief Cornstalk, who had been killed several months earlier while a prisoner of American militiamen in the Ohio country. Of the twenty-six men taken at the spring, about half were adopted into Shawnee families; the others—less willing to conform to Indian ways—were dispatched as prisoners to the British fort at Detroit. Boone, who assured Blackfish that in the spring he would negotiate the surrender of the women and children remaining at his home settlement of Boonesborough, watched and waited, outwardly content with his new life. In June 1778 he escaped, hurrying home to warn the Kentuckians of impending attack.

When Blackfish's Shawnees and their British allies appeared outside the Boonesborough stockade in mid-September, Boone proved amenable to negotiations. Although the settlers adamantly refused to move back across the mountains, fragmentary evidence suggests that they agreed to swear allegiance to the British in order to avert a bloody battle. But the discussions dissolved into a melee and the Indians then futilely besieged the fort for a week before withdrawing.

◀ A statue of George III standing in the Bowling Green in New York City was one of the first casualties of the American Revolution, as colonists marked the adoption of the Declaration of Independence by pulling it down. Much of the metal was melted to make bullets, but in the twentieth century the head—largely intact—was unearthed in Connecticut. (Lafayette College Art Collection, Easton, Pennsylvania) twice deceived the Shawnees? Or had he rather made the survival of the fragile settlements his highest priority? Kentucky was a borderland—a region where British, Indians, and various groups of American settlers all vied for control. Boone and other residents of the Appalachian backcountry did not always face clear-cut choices as they struggled to establish themselves securely under such precarious circumstances.

Daniel Boone was not the only American of uncertain or shifting allegiance in the 1770s. As a civil war that affected much of North America east of the Mississippi River, the American Revolution uprooted thousands of families, disrupted the economy, reshaped society by forcing many colonists into permanent exile, led Americans to develop new conceptions of politics, and created a nation from thirteen separate colonies. Much more than a series of clashes between the British and patriot armies, it marked a significant turning point in Americans' collective history.

The struggle for independence required revolutionary leaders to accomplish three separate but closely related tasks. The first was political and ideological: transforming a consensus favoring loyal resistance into a coalition supporting independence. Pursuing a variety of measures (ranging from persuasion to coercion) to enlist all European Americans in the patriot cause, the colonies' elected leaders also tried to ensure the neutrality of Indians and slaves in the impending conflict.

The second task involved foreign relations. To win independence, patriot leaders knew they needed international recognition and aid, particularly from France. Thus they dispatched to Paris the most experienced American diplomat, Benjamin Franklin, who had served for years as a colonial agent in London. Franklin skillfully negotiated the Franco-American alliance of 1778, which was to prove crucial to winning independence.

Only the third task directly involved the British. George Washington, commander-in-chief of the American army, soon recognized that his primary goal should be not to win battles but to avoid losing them decisively. The outcome of any one battle was less important than ensuring that his army survived to fight another day. Consequently, the story of the Revolutionary War reveals British action and American reaction, British attacks and

With that threat gone, Boone was charged with treason and court-martialed by Kentucky militia. Although he was cleared, questions about the incident at Blue Licks and its aftermath haunted him for the rest of his life.

Where did Daniel Boone's loyalties lie? To the British? to the Americans? to other Kentuckians? His actions could be viewed in all three lights. Had he betrayed the settlers to Shawnees and sought to establish British authority in Kentucky? Had he—as he later claimed—

American defenses and withdrawals. The American war effort was aided by the failure of British military planners to analyze accurately the problem confronting them. Until it was too late, they treated the war against the colonists as they treated wars against other Europeans: they concentrated on winning battles and did not consider the difficulties of achieving their main goal, retaining the colonies' allegiance. In the end, the Americans' triumph owed more to their own endurance and to Britain's mistakes than to their military prowess. ■

Government by Congress and Committee

*W*hen the fifty-five delegates to the First Continental Congress convened in Philadelphia in September 1774, they knew that any measures they adopted were likely to enjoy widespread support. That summer, open meetings held throughout the colonies had endorsed the idea of another nonimportation pact. Participants in such meetings promised (in the words of the freeholders of Johnston County, North Carolina) to "strictly adhere to, and abide by, such Regulations and Restrictions as the Members of the said General Congress shall agree to and judge most convenient." Committees of correspondence publicized these meetings so effectively that Americans everywhere knew about them. Most of the congressional delegates were selected by extralegal provincial conventions whose members were chosen at local gatherings, since governors had forbidden regular assemblies to conduct formal elections. Thus the very act of designating delegates to attend the Congress involved Americans in open defiance of British authority.

The colonies' leading political figures—most of them lawyers, merchants, and planters representing every colony but Georgia—attended the Philadelphia Congress. The Massachusetts delegation included both Samuel Adams, the experienced organizer of Boston resistance, and his younger cousin John, an ambitious lawyer. Among others, New York sent John Jay, a talented young attorney. From Pennsylvania came the conservative Joseph Galloway and his long-time rival, John Dickinson. Virginia elected Richard Henry Lee and Patrick Henry, both noted for their patriotic zeal, as well as George Washington. Most of these men had never met, but in the weeks, months,

FIRST CONTINENTAL CONGRESS

and years that followed they became the chief architects of the new nation.

The congressmen faced three tasks when they convened at Carpenters Hall on September 5. The first two were explicit: defining American grievances and developing a plan for resistance. The third—articulating their constitutional relationship with Great Britain—was less clear-cut and proved troublesome. The most radical congressmen, like Lee of Virginia, argued that colonists owed allegiance only to George III and that Parliament was nothing more than a legislature for Britain, with no authority over the colonies. The conservatives—Joseph Galloway and his allies—proposed a formal plan of union that would have required Parliament and a new American legislature to consent jointly to all laws pertaining to the colonies. After heated debate, delegates narrowly rejected Galloway's proposal, but they were not prepared to embrace the radicals' position either.

Finally, they accepted a compromise position worked out by John Adams. The crucial clauses in the Congress's Declaration of Rights and Grievances declared that Americans would obey Parliament, but only because that action was in everyone's best interest, and asserted that colonists would resist all taxes in disguise, like the Townshend duties. Remarkably, such a position—which only a few years before would have been regarded as extreme—represented a compromise in the fall of 1774. The Americans had come a long way since their first hesitant protests against the Sugar Act ten years earlier.

With the constitutional issue resolved, the delegates readily agreed on the laws they wanted repealed (notably the Coercive Acts) and decided to implement an economic boycott while petitioning the king for relief. They adopted the Continental Association, which called for nonimportation of British goods (effective December 1, 1774), nonconsumption of British products (effective March 1, 1775), and nonexportation of American goods to Britain and the British West Indies (effective September 10, 1775).

CONTINENTAL ASSOCIATION

The provisions of the Association—far more comprehensive than any previous economic measure adopted by the colonies—were carefully designed to appeal to different groups and regions. For example, the inclusive language of the nonimportation agreement banned the traffic in slaves as well as manufactures, which accorded with a longstanding desire of the Virginia gentry to halt, or at least to slow, the arrival of enslaved Africans on their shores. (Leading Virginians believed that continuing slave importations had discouraged the immigration to their colony of free Europeans with useful skills.) The

The CON GRESS or The NECESSARY POLITICIAN

■ In 1775 a British cartoonist demonstrated his contempt for the pronouncements of the Continental Congress by setting his satire in a privy, or "necessary house," and showing a politician who has used a torn congressional resolution as toilet paper. The person at right is poring over a political pamphlet while portraits of John Wilkes and a man who has been tarred and feathered decorate the walls.   (Library of Congress)

delay of the nonconsumption agreement until three months after nonimportation took effect would allow northern urban merchants to sell items they had acquired legally before December 1. And both the novel tactic of nonexportation and its postponement for nearly a year served other interests. In 1773 small farmers in Virginia had already vowed to stop exporting tobacco to raise prices in a then-glutted market. The next year, they enthusiastically welcomed an Association that accomplished the same end, while permitting them to profit from higher prices for their 1774 crop, which had to be dried and cured before shipment. The delay of the nonexportation agreement also benefited the northern exporters of wood products and foodstuffs to the Caribbean, giving them a final season of sales before the embargo began.

To enforce the Continental Association, Congress recommended the election of committees of observation and inspection in every American local-

COMMITTEES OF OBSERVATION

ity. By specifying that committee members be chosen by all men qualified to vote for members of the lower houses of colonial legislatures, Congress guaranteed the committees a broad popular base. In some places the com-

mitteemen were former local officeholders; in other towns they were men who had never before held office. Everywhere, these committeemen—perhaps seven to eight thousand in the colonies as a whole—became the local leaders of American resistance.

Such committees were officially charged only with overseeing implementation of the boycott, but in the course of the next six months they became de facto governments. They examined merchants' records and published the names of those who continued to import British goods. They promoted home manufactures, encouraging Americans to adopt simple modes of dress and behavior to symbolize their commitment to liberty and virtuous conduct. Since expensive leisure-time activities were believed to reflect vice and corruption, Congress urged Americans to forgo dancing, gambling, horseracing, cockfighting, and other forms of "extravagance and dissipation." Some committees extracted apologies from people caught gambling, partying, or racing. Thus private activities acquired public significance.

The committees gradually extended their authority over many aspects of American life. They attempted to identify opponents of American resistance, developing elaborate spy networks, circulating copies of the Continental Association for signatures, and investigating reports of questionable remarks and activities. Suspected dissenters were urged to support the colonial cause publicly; if they refused, the committees had them watched, restricted their movements, or tried to force them to leave the area. People engaging in casual political exchanges with friends one day could find themselves charged with "treasonable conversation" the next. One Massachusetts man, for example, was called before his local committee for maligning the Congress as "a Pack or Parcell of Fools" that was "as tyrannical as Lord North and ought to be opposed & resisted." When he refused to recant, the committee put him under surveillance.

While the committees of observation were expanding their power during the winter and early spring of

PROVINCIAL CONVENTIONS

1775, the regular colonial governments were collapsing. Only a few legislatures continued to meet without encountering patriot challenges to their authority. In most colonies, popularly elected provincial conventions took over the task of running the government, sometimes entirely replacing the legislatures and at other times holding concurrent sessions. In late 1774 and early 1775, these conventions approved the Continental Association, elected delegates to the Second Continental Congress (scheduled for May), organized militia units, and gathered arms and ammunition. Unable to stem the tide of resistance, the British-appointed governors and councils watched helplessly as their authority crumbled.

Royal officials suffered humiliation after humiliation. Courts were prevented from holding sessions; taxes were paid to the conventions' agents rather than to provincial tax collectors; sheriffs' powers were challenged; and militiamen would muster only when committees ordered. In short, during the six months preceding the battles at Lexington and Concord, independence was being won at the local level, but without formal acknowledgment and for the most part without bloodshed. Not many Americans fully realized what was happening. The vast majority still proclaimed their loyalty to Great Britain, denying that they sought to leave the empire.

Contest in the Backcountry

hile the committees of observation were consolidating their authority in the East, some colonists were heading west. Ignoring the Proclamation of 1763, pronouncements by colonial governors, and the threat of Indian attacks alike, land-hungry folk—many of them recent immigrants from Ireland and soldiers who demobilized in North America after the Seven Years War—swarmed onto lands along the Ohio River and its tributaries after the mid-1760s. Sometimes they purchased property from opportunists with grants of dubious origin; often, they simply surveyed and claimed land, squatting on it in hopes that their titles would eventually be honored. Britain's 1771 decision to abandon (and raze) Fort Pitt removed the final restraints on settlement in the region, for the withdrawal rendered the Proclamation of 1763 wholly unenforceable. By late 1775, thousands of new homesteads dotted the landscape of the backcountry from western Pennsylvania south through Virginia and eastern Kentucky into western North Carolina.

Few of the backcountry folk saw the region's native peoples in a positive light. (Rare exceptions were the

DISTRUST AND WARFARE

Moravian missionaries who settled with their Indian converts in three small frontier communities in the upper Ohio valley.) The frontier dwellers had little interest in the small-scale trade that had once helped to sustain an uneasy peace in the region; they only wanted land on which to grow crops and pasture their livestock. They interpreted Pontiac's uprising as a sign that no Indian—regardless of religion or tribal affiliation—could be trusted. That adamant and widely held opinion, first publicly exhibited when a group of fifty Scots-Irish men

from Paxton Township, Pennsylvania, massacred twenty peaceful Christian Conestoga Indians in two separate incidents in December 1763, reflected the thinking of many frontier dwellers.

In 1774 Virginia, headed by a new governor, Lord Dunmore, moved vigorously to assert its title to the rapidly developing backcountry. During the spring and early summer, tensions mounted as Virginians surveyed land in Kentucky, on the south side of the Ohio River—territory still claimed by the Shawnees, who rejected the Fort Stanwix treaty of 1768 (see page 124). "Lord Dunmore's war" consisted of one large-scale confrontation between Virginia militia and some Shawnee warriors. Neither side won a clear-cut victory, but in the immediate aftermath thousands of settlers—including Daniel Boone and his associates—flooded across the mountains.

When the Revolutionary War began just as large numbers of people were migrating into Kentucky, the loyalties of all Indians and settlers in the backcountry remained, like Boone's, fluid and uncertain. They were more or less at war with each other, but which side should either take in the imperial struggle? The answer might well depend on which could better serve their interests. Understanding that, the Continental Congress moved to reoccupy the site of Fort Pitt and to establish other garrisons in the Ohio country. Relying on such protection, as many as twenty thousand settlers poured into Kentucky by 1780. Yet frontier affiliations were not clear: the growing town of Pittsburgh, for example, harbored many active loyalists.

The native peoples' grievances against the European American newcomers predisposed many toward an alliance

INDIANS' CHOICES

with Great Britain. Yet some chiefs urged caution: after all, the British abandonment of Fort Pitt (and them) suggested that Britain lacked the will and ability to protect them in the future. Furthermore, Britain hesitated to make full and immediate use of its potential native allies. Officials on the scene recognized that neither the Indians' style of fighting nor their war aims necessarily coincided with British goals and methods. Accordingly, they at first sought from Indians only a promise of neutrality.

Recognizing that their standing with native peoples was poor, the patriots also sought the Indians' neutrality. In 1775 the Second Continental Congress sent a general message to Indian communities describing the war as "a family quarrel between us and Old England" and requesting that they "not join on either side" since "you Indians are not concerned in it." A group of Cherokees led by Chief Dragging Canoe nevertheless decided to

■ An eighteenth-century watercolor, by an unknown artist, showing the village and fort at Detroit. Once a French stronghold, it had been taken over by the British after the Seven Years War. American forces tried but failed to capture the fort during the Revolutionary War. (William L. Clements Library)

take advantage of the "family quarrel" to regain some land. In the summer of 1776, they attacked settlements along the western borders of the Carolinas and Virginia. But a militia campaign destroyed many Cherokee towns, along with crops and supplies. Dragging Canoe and his die-hard followers fled to the west, establishing new villages; the rest of the Cherokees agreed to a treaty that ceded still more of their land.

Bands of Shawnees and Cherokees continued to attack frontier settlements in the backcountry throughout the war, but dissent in their own ranks crippled their efforts. The British victory over France had destroyed the Indian nations' most effective means of maintaining their independence: playing European powers off against one another. Successful strategies were difficult to envision under these new circumstances, and Indian leaders could no longer concur on a unified course of action. Communities split asunder as older and younger men, or civil and war leaders, disagreed vehemently over what policy to adopt. Only a few communities (among them the Stockbridge Indians of New England and the Oneidas in New York) unwaveringly supported the American revolt; most other native villages either tried to remain neutral or hesitatingly aligned themselves with the British. And the settlers

INDIANS DURING THE REVOLUTION

fought back: in 1778 and early 1779 a frontier militia force under George Rogers Clark captured British posts in modern Illinois (Kaskaskia) and Indiana (Vincennes), but the Anglo-Americans could never mount an effective attack against the redcoats' major stronghold at Detroit.

Warfare between settlers and Indian bands persisted in the backcountry long after fighting between the patriot and redcoat armies had ceased. Indeed, the Revolutionary War itself essentially constituted a brief chapter in the ongoing struggle for control of the region west of the Appalachians that began in 1763 and continued into the next century.

Choosing Sides

In 1765, protests against the Stamp Act had won the support of most colonists in the Caribbean and Nova Scotia as well as in the future United States. Demonstrations occurred in Halifax (the major Nova Scotian port, founded 1748) as well as in Boston, New York, and Charleston. Although provisions of the 1764 Sugar Act benefited Britain's Caribbean possessions, the Stamp Act levied higher duties on them than on the mainland colonies; the residents of St. Christopher and Nevis in particular joined mainlanders in demonstrating against the law (see Map 5.3). When the act went into effect, though, islanders loyally paid the stamp duties until repeal. And eventually a significant number of colonists in North America and the West Indies began to question both the aims and the tactics of the resistance movement. Doubts arose with particular urgency in Nova Scotia and the Caribbean.

Both the northern mainland and southern island colonies depended heavily on Great Britain militarily and

NOVA SCOTIA AND THE CARIBBEAN

economically. Despite the overwhelming British victory in the Seven Years War, they believed themselves vulnerable to French counterattack and were eager to have regular troops and naval vessels stationed within their borders. Additionally, sugar planters—on some islands outnumbered by their bondspeople 25 to 1—feared the potential for slave revolts in the absence of British troops. Neither region had a large population of European descent, nor were local political structures very strong. Fewer people lived in Halifax in 1775 than in the late 1750s, and the sugar islands had only a few resident planters to provide leadership, because successful men headed to England to buy great manors, leaving supervision of their property to hired managers.

Both Nova Scotians and West Indians had major economic reasons for ultimately choosing to support the mother country. In the mid-1770s the northerners finally broke into the Caribbean market with their cargoes of dried and salted fish. They also began to reduce New England's domination of the northern coastal trade, and once the shooting started they benefited greatly from Britain's retaliatory measures against the rebels' commerce. British sugar producers relied for their profits primarily on their monopoly of trade within the empire, for more efficient French planters were able to sell their sugar for one-third less. Further, the West Indian planters' effective lobbyists in London won the islands' exclusion from some provisions of the Townshend Acts. Accordingly, they could well have concluded that their interests could be adequately protected within the empire. Neither islanders nor Nova Scotians had reason to believe that they would be better off independent.

Many residents of the thirteen colonies—especially members of the groups that dominated colonial society

PATRIOTS

numerically or politically—reached different conclusions, choosing to support resistance, then independence. Active revolutionaries accounted for about two-fifths of the European American population. Among them were small and middling farmers, members of dominant Protestant sects (both Old and New Lights), Chesapeake gentry,

merchants dealing mainly in American commodities, city artisans, elected officeholders, and people of English descent. Wives usually but not always adopted their husbands' political beliefs. Although all these patriots supported the Revolution, they pursued divergent goals within the broader coalition, as they had in the 1760s. Some sought limited political reform, others extensive political change, and still others social and economic reforms. (The ways in which their concerns interacted are discussed in Chapter 7.)

Some colonists, though, found that they could not in good conscience endorse independence. Like their more radical counterparts, most objected to parliamentary policies, but they preferred the remedy of imperial constitutional reform. The events of the crucial year between the passage of the Coercive Acts and the outbreak of fighting in Massachusetts crystallized their thinking. Their objections to violent protest, their desire to uphold legally constituted government, and their fears of anarchy combined to make them sensitive to the dangers of resistance.

About one-fifth of the European American population remained loyal to Great Britain, firmly rejecting

LOYALISTS

independence. Most loyalists had long opposed the men who became patriot leaders, though for varying reasons. British-appointed government officials; Anglican clergy everywhere and lay Anglicans in the North, where their denomination was in the minority; tenant farmers, particularly those whose landlords sided with the patriots; members of persecuted religious sects; many of the back-country southerners who had rebelled against eastern rule in the late 1760s and early 1770s; and non-English ethnic minorities, especially Scots: all these groups feared the power wielded by those who controlled the colonial assemblies and who had shown little concern for their welfare in the past. Joined by merchants whose trade depended on imperial connections and by former officers and enlisted men from the British army who had settled in America after 1763, they formed a loyalist core that remained true to a self-conception that revolutionaries proved willing to abandon.

During the war, loyalists congregated in cities held by the British army. When those posts were evacuated at war's end, loyalists scattered to different parts of the British Empire—Britain, the Bahamas, and especially Canada. In the provinces of Nova Scotia, New Brunswick, and Ontario they re-created their lives as colonists, laying the foundations of British Canada. All told, perhaps as many as 100,000 Americans preferred exile to life in a nation independent of British rule.

Between the patriots and the loyalists, there remained in the middle perhaps two-fifths of the European

NEUTRALS   American population. Some who tried to avoid taking sides were sincere pacifists, such as Quakers. Others opportunistically shifted their allegiance to whatever side happened to be winning currently. Still others simply wanted to be left alone; they cared little about politics and usually obeyed whoever was in power. Such colonists also resisted British and Americans alike when the demands on them seemed too heavy—when taxes became too high, or when calls for militia service came too often. Their attitude might best be summed up as "a plague on both your houses." Such people made up an especially large proportion of the population in the backcountry (including Boone's Kentucky), where Scots-Irish settlers had little love for either the patriot gentry or the English authorities.

To patriots, apathy or neutrality was as heinous as loyalism: those who were not for them were surely against them. By the winter of 1775–1776, the Second Continental Congress was recommending that all "disaffected" persons be disarmed and arrested. State legislatures passed laws prescribing severe penalties for suspected loyalists or neutrals. Many began to require all voters (or, in some cases, all free adult men) to take oaths of allegiance; the penalty for refusal was usually banishment to England or extra taxes. After 1777 many states confiscated the property of banished persons, using the proceeds for the war effort.

The patriots' policies helped to ensure that their scattered and persecuted opponents could not band together to threaten the revolutionary cause. But loyalists and neutrals were not the patriots' only worry, for revolutionaries could not assume that their slaves would support them.

SLAVERY AND REVOLUTIONARY FERVOR

In New England, with few resident bondspeople, revolutionary fervor was widespread, and free African Americans enlisted in local patriot militias. The middle colonies, where slaves constituted a small but substantial proportion of the population, were more divided but still largely revolutionary. In Virginia and Maryland, where free people constituted a slender majority, the potential for slave revolts raised occasional but not disabling fears. By contrast, South Carolina and Georgia, where slaves composed more than half of the population, were noticeably less enthusiastic about resistance to Britain. Georgia sent no delegates to the First Continental Congress and reminded its representatives at the second one to consider its circumstances, "with our blacks and tories [loyalists] within us," when voting on the question of independence. On the mainland as well as in the Caribbean islands, therefore, colonists feared the potential enemy in their midst.

Bondspeople faced a dilemma during the Revolution. Above all, their goal was *personal* independence. But how best could they escape from slavery? Should they fight with or against their masters? African Americans made different decisions, but to most slaves, supporting the British appeared more promising. In late 1774 and early 1775, groups of slaves began to offer to assist the British army in return for freedom. Some bondspeople futilely petitioned General Thomas Gage, the commander-in-chief of British forces in Boston, promising to fight for the redcoats if he would liberate them. The most serious incident occurred in 1775 in Charleston, where Thomas Jeremiah, a free black harbor pilot, was brutally executed after being convicted of attempting to foment a slave revolt.

SLAVES' DILEMMA

The slaveowners' worst fears were realized in November 1775, when Virginia's royal governor, Lord Dunmore, offered to free any slaves and indentured servants who would leave their patriot masters to join the British forces. Dunmore hoped to use African Americans in his fight against the revolutionaries and to disrupt the economy by depriving planters of their labor force. But only about one thousand African Americans initially rallied to the British standard, and many of them perished in a smallpox epidemic. Even so, Dunmore's proclamation led Congress in January 1776 to modify an earlier policy that had prohibited the enlistment of African Americans in the regular American army.

Although slaves did not pose a serious threat to the revolutionary cause in its early years, the patriots turned rumors of slave uprisings to their own advantage. In South Carolina, resistance leaders argued that unity under the Continental Association would protect masters from their slaves at a time when royal government was unable to muster adequate defense forces. Undoubtedly many wavering Carolinians were drawn into the revolutionary camp by fear that an overt division among the colony's free people would encourage rebellion by the bondspeople.

Patriots could never completely ignore the threats posed by loyalists, neutrals, slaves, and Indians as well, but only rarely did fear of these groups seriously hamper the revolutionary movement. Occasionally backcountry militiamen refused to turn out for duty on the seacoast because they feared Indians would attack at home in their absence. Sometimes southern troops refused to serve in the North because they (and their political leaders) were unwilling to leave their regions unprotected against a slave insurrection. But the practical impossibility of a large-scale slave revolt, coupled with dissension

New Nations

The American Revolution not only created the United States but led directly to the formation of three other nations: English-dominated Canada, Sierra Leone, and Australia.

In northern North America before the Revolution, only Nova Scotia had a sizable number of English-speaking settlers. Those people, largely New Englanders, had been recruited after 1758 to repopulate the region forcibly taken from the exiled Acadians. During and after the Revolution, however, many loyalist families, especially those from the northern and middle colonies, moved to the region that is now Canada, which remained under British rule. The provinces of New Brunswick and Upper Canada (later Ontario) were established to accommodate them, and some exiles settled in Quebec as well. In just a few years, the loyalist refugees transformed the sparsely populated former French colony, laying the foundation of the modern bilingual (but majority English-speaking) Canadian nation.

Sierra Leone, too, was founded by colonial exiles—African Americans who had fled to the British army during the war, many of whom ended up in London. Seeing the refugees' poverty, a group of charitable merchants—calling themselves the Committee to Aid the Black Poor—developed a plan to resettle the African Americans elsewhere. After the refugees refused to be sent to the Bahamas, fearing that in the West Indies they would be reenslaved, they concurred in a scheme to return them to the land of their ancestors. In early 1787, vessels carrying about four hundred settlers reached Sierra Leone in West Africa, where representatives of the Black Poor Committee acquired land from local rulers. The first years of the new colony were difficult, and many of the newcomers died of disease and deprivation. But in 1792 they were joined by several thousand other loyalist African Americans who had originally moved to Nova Scotia. The influx ensured the colony's survival; it remained a part of the British Empire until achieving its independence in 1961.

While the Sierra Leone migrants were preparing to sail from London in late 1786, the first prison ships were simultaneously being readied for Australia. At the Paris peace negotiations in 1782, American diplomats adamantly rejected British suggestions that the United States continue to serve as a dumping ground for convicts, as had been true throughout the eighteenth century. Britain thus needed another destination for the convicts sentenced in its courts to transportation for crimes such as theft, assault, and manslaughter. It decided to send them halfway round the world, to the continent Captain James Cook had explored and claimed in 1770. Britain continued to dispatch convicts to some parts of Australia until 1868, but, long before then, voluntary migrants had also begun to arrive. The modern nation was created from a federation of separate colonial governments on January 1, 1901.

Thus the founding event in the history of the United States links the nation to the formation of its northern neighbor and to new nations in West Africa and the Asian Pacific.

An early view of the settlement of black loyalists in West Africa, the foundation of the modern nation of Sierra Leone. (Miriam and Ira D. Wallach Division of Art, Prints and Photographs, The New York Public Library. Astor, Lenox, and Tilden)

Thomas Rowlandson, an English artist, sketched the boatloads of male and female convicts as they were being ferried to the ships that would take them to their new lives in the prison colony of Australia. Note the gibbet on the shore with two hanging bodies—symbolizing the fate these people were escaping. (National Library of Australia) in Indian communities and the patriots' successful campaign to disarm and neutralize loyalists, ensured that the revolutionaries would by and large remain firmly in control of the countryside as they fought for independence.

War and Independence

*O*n January 27, 1775, Lord Dartmouth, secretary of state for America, addressed a fateful letter to General Thomas Gage in Boston, urging him to take a decisive step. Opposition could not be "very formidable," Dartmouth wrote, and even if it were, "it will surely be better that the Conflict should be brought on, upon such ground, than in a riper state of Rebellion."

After Gage received Dartmouth's letter on April 14, he sent an expedition to confiscate colonial military supplies stockpiled at Concord. Bostonians dispatched two messengers, William Dawes and Paul Revere (later joined by Dr. Samuel Prescott), to rouse the countryside. So when the British vanguard of several hundred men approached Lexington at dawn on April 19, they found a ragtag group of seventy militiamen—about half of the adult male population of the town—mustered on the common. The Americans' commander ordered his men to withdraw, realizing they could not halt the redcoats' advance. But as they began to disperse, a shot rang out; the British soldiers then fired several volleys. When they stopped, eight Americans lay dead and another ten had been wounded. The British moved on to Concord, 5 miles away.

BATTLES OF LEXINGTON AND CONCORD

There the contingents of militia were larger, Concord residents having been joined by groups of men from nearby towns. An exchange of gunfire at the North Bridge spilled the first British blood of the Revolution: three men were killed and nine wounded. Thousands of militiamen then fired from houses and from behind trees and bushes at the British forces as they retreated to Boston. By the end of the day, the redcoats had suffered 272 casualties, including 70 deaths. Only the arrival of reinforcements and the American militia's lack of coordination prevented much heavier British losses. The patriots suffered just 93 casualties.

By the evening of April 20, perhaps as many as twenty thousand American militiamen had gathered around Boston, summoned by local committees that spread the alarm across the countryside. Many did not stay long (they were needed at home for spring planting), but those who remained dug in along

FIRST YEAR OF WAR

siege lines encircling the city. For nearly a year the two armies sat and stared at each other across those lines. The redcoats attacked their besiegers only once, on June 17, when they drove the Americans from trenches atop Breed's Hill in Charlestown. In that misnamed Battle of Bunker Hill, the British incurred their greatest losses of the entire war: over 800 wounded and 228 killed. The Americans, though forced to abandon their position, lost less than half that number.

During the same eleven-month period, patriots captured Fort Ticonderoga, a British fort on Lake Champlain, acquiring much-needed cannon. Trying to bring Canada into the war on the American side, they also mounted a northern campaign that ended in disaster at Quebec in early 1776 after their troops were ravaged by smallpox. But the chief significance of the war's first year lay in the long lull in fighting between the main armies at Boston. The delay gave both sides a chance to regroup, organize, and plan their strategies.

Lord North and his new American secretary, Lord George Germain, made three central assumptions about the war they faced. First, they concluded that patriot forces could not withstand the assaults of trained British regulars. They and their generals were convinced that the 1776 campaign would be the first and last of the war. Accordingly, they dispatched to America the largest force Great Britain had ever assembled anywhere: 370 transport ships carrying 32,000 troops and tons of supplies, accompanied by 73 naval vessels and 13,000 sailors. Such an extraordinary effort, they thought, would ensure a quick victory. Among the troops were thousands of German mercenaries (many from the state of Hesse); eighteenth-century armies were often composed of such professional soldiers who hired out to the highest bidder.

BRITISH STRATEGY

Second, British officials and army officers treated this war as comparable to conflicts in Europe. They adopted a conventional strategy of capturing major American cities and defeating the rebel army decisively without suffering serious casualties themselves. Third, they assumed that a clear-cut military victory would achieve their goal of retaining the colonies' allegiance.

All three assumptions proved false. North and Germain vastly underestimated Americans' commitment to armed resistance. Battlefield defeats did not lead patriots to abandon their political aims and sue for peace. London officials also failed to recognize the significance of the American population's dispersal over an area 1,500 miles long and more than 100 miles wide. Although Britain would control each of the largest American ports

■ In 1775 an unknown artist painted the redcoats entering Concord. The fighting at North Bridge, which occurred just a few hours after this triumphal entry, signaled the start of open warfare between Britain and the colonies.   (Photography Courtesy of Concord Museum, Concord, Mass.)

at some time during the war, less than 5 percent of the population lived in those cities. Furthermore, the coast offered so many excellent harbors that essential commerce was easily rerouted. In other words, the loss of cities did little to damage the American cause, while British generals repeatedly squandered their resources to capture such ports.

Most of all, London officials did not initially understand that military triumph would not necessarily lead to political victory. Securing the colonies permanently would require hundreds of thousands of Americans to return to their original allegiance. After 1778 the ministry adopted a strategy designed to achieve that goal through the expanded use of loyalist forces and the restoration of civilian authority in occupied areas. But the new policy came too late. Britain's leaders never fully realized that they were fighting not a conventional European war but rather an entirely new kind of conflict: the first modern war of national liberation.

At least Great Britain had a bureaucracy ready to supervise the war effort. The Americans had only the Second Continental Congress, originally intended simply to consider the ministry's response to the Continental Association. Instead, the delegates who convened in Philadelphia on May 10, 1775, had to assume the mantle of intercolonial government. "Such a vast Multitude of objects, civil, political, commercial and military, press and crowd upon us so fast, that we know not what to do first," John Adams wrote a close friend early in the session. Yet as the summer passed, Congress slowly organized the colonies for war. It authorized the printing of money with which to purchase necessary goods, established a committee to supervise relations with foreign countries, and took steps to strengthen the militia. Most important, it created the Continental Army and appointed its generals.

SECOND CONTINENTAL CONGRESS

■ The plight of the redcoat soldiers besieged in Boston during the fall and winter of 1775–1776 attracted the sympathies of a British cartoonist. For "Six-Pence a Day," he noted, soldiers were exposed to "Yankees, Fire and Water, Sword and Famine," while their wives and children begged for assistance at home. The artist hoped to persuade men not to enlist in the British army.   (Courtesy of the British Museum, Department of Prints and Drawings, Satires)

Until Congress met, the Massachusetts provincial congress had taken responsibility for organizing the militiamen encamped at Boston. But that army, composed of men from all over New England, constituted a heavy drain on limited local resources. Consequently, Massachusetts asked the Continental Congress to assume the task of directing the army. As a first step, Congress had to choose a commander-in-chief, and many delegates recognized the importance of naming someone who was not a New Englander. John Adams later recalled that in mid-June he proposed the appointment of a Virginian "whose Skill and Experience as an Officer, whose independent fortune, great Talents and excellent universal Character, would command the Approbation of all America": George Washington. The Congress unanimously concurred.

Neither fiery radical nor a reflective political thinker, Washington had not played a prominent role in the prerevolutionary agitation. Devoted to the American cause, he was dignified, conservative, and respectable—a man of unimpeachable integrity. The younger son of a Virginia planter, Washington did not expect to inherit substantial property, planning to make his living

WASHINGTON AS LEADER

as a surveyor. But the early death of his older brother and his marriage to the wealthy widow Martha Custis made George Washington one of the largest slaveholders in Virginia. Though unmistakably an aristocrat, he was unswervingly committed to representative government and—thanks to his service in the Seven Years War—he had military experience. He also had remarkable stamina. In more than eight years of war, Washington never had a serious illness and took only one brief leave of absence. Moreover, he both looked and acted like a leader. More than six feet tall in an era when most men were five inches shorter, he displayed a stately and commanding presence. Other patriots praised his judgment, steadiness, and discretion, and even a loyalist admitted that Washington could "atone for many demerits by the extraordinary coolness and caution which distinguish his character."

Washington needed all the coolness and caution he could muster when he took command of the army outside Boston in July 1775. It took him months to impose hierarchy and discipline on the unruly troops and to bring order to the supply system. But by

BRITISH EVACUATION OF BOSTON

March 1776, when the arrival of cannon from Ticonderoga finally enabled him to put direct pressure on the redcoats in the city, the army was prepared to act. Yet an assault on Boston proved unnecessary. Sir William Howe, the new commander, had been considering an evacuation; he wanted to transfer his troops to New York City. The patriots' cannon decided the matter. On March 17, the British and more than a thousand of their loyalist allies abandoned Boston forever.

That spring of 1776, as the British fleet left Boston for the temporary haven of Halifax, the colonies were moving inexorably toward a declaration of independence. Though they had been engaged in combat for months, American leaders denied seeking a break with Great Britain until a pamphlet published in January 1776 advocated such a step.

Thomas Paine's *Common Sense* exploded on the American scene, quickly selling tens of thousands of copies. The author, a radical English printer who had lived in America only since 1774, called stridently for independence. Paine also challenged many common American assumptions about government and the colonies' relationship to Britain. Rejecting the notion that only a balance of monarchy, aristocracy, and democracy could preserve freedom, he advocated the establishment of a republic, a government by the people with no king or nobility. Instead of acknowledging the benefits of links to the mother country, Paine insisted that Britain had exploited the colonies unmercifully. And for the frequently heard assertion that an independent America would be weak and divided, he substituted an unlimited confidence in America's strength once freed from European control.

COMMON SENSE

He expressed these striking sentiments in equally striking prose. Scorning the rational style of most other pamphleteers, Paine adopted an enraged tone, describing the king as a "royal brute," a "wretch" who only pretended concern for the colonists' welfare. His pamphlet reflected the oral culture of ordinary folk. Couched in everyday language, it relied heavily on the Bible—the only book familiar to most Americans—as a primary source of authority. No wonder the pamphlet had a wider distribution than any other political publication of its day.

It is unclear how many people were converted to the cause of independence by reading *Common Sense*. But by the late spring independence had become inevitable. On May 10, the Second Continental Congress formally recommended that individual colonies form new governments, replacing their colonial charters with state constitutions. Perceiving the trend, the few loyalists still connected with Congress severed their ties to that body.

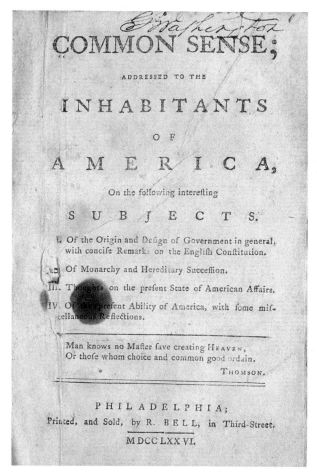

■ That America's patriot leaders read Thomas Paine's inflammatory *Common Sense* soon after it was published in early 1776 is indicated by this first edition, owned by George Washington himself.   (Boston Athenaeum)

Then on June 7 came confirmation of the movement toward independence. Richard Henry Lee of Virginia, seconded by John Adams of Massachusetts, introduced the crucial resolution: "that these United Colonies are, and of right ought to be, free and independent States, that they are absolved of all allegiance to the British Crown, and that all political connection between them and the State of Great Britain is, and ought to be, totally dissolved." Congress debated but did not immediately adopt Lee's resolution. Instead, it postponed a vote until early July, to allow time for consultation and public reaction. In the meantime, a five-man committee—including Thomas Jefferson, John Adams, and Benjamin Franklin—was directed to draft a declaration of independence.

The committee assigned primary responsibility for writing the declaration to Jefferson, who was well known for his eloquent style. Years later John Adams recalled that Jefferson had modestly protested his selection, suggesting that Adams prepare the initial draft. The Massachusetts revolutionary recorded his frank response: "You can write ten times better than I can."

JEFFERSON AND THE DECLARATION OF INDEPENDENCE The thirty-four-year-old Thomas Jefferson, a Virginia lawyer, had been educated at the College of William and Mary and in the law offices of a prominent attorney. A member of the House of Burgesses, he had read widely in history and political theory. That broad knowledge was evident not only in the declaration but also in his draft of the Virginia state constitution, completed just a few days before his appointment to the committee. Jefferson, an intensely private man, loved his home and family deeply. This early stage of his political career was marked by his beloved wife Martha's repeated difficulties in childbearing. While he wrote and debated in Philadelphia, she suffered a miscarriage at their home, Monticello. Not until after her death in 1782, from complications following the birth of their sixth (but only third surviving) child in ten years of marriage, did Jefferson fully commit himself to public service.

The draft of the declaration was laid before Congress on June 28, 1776. The delegates officially voted for independence four days later, then debated the wording of the declaration for two more days, adopting it with some changes on July 4. Since Americans had long ago ceased to see themselves as legitimate subjects of Parliament, the Declaration of Independence concentrated on George III (see the appendix). That focus also provided an identifiable villain. The document accused the king of attempting to destroy representative government in the colonies and of oppressing Americans through the unjustified use of excessive force.

The declaration's chief long-term importance, however, did not lie in its lengthy catalogue of grievances against George III (including, in a section deleted by Congress, Jefferson's charge that the British monarchy had forced slavery on America). It lay instead in the ringing statements of principle that have served ever since as the ideal to which Americans aspire: "We hold these truths to be self-evident: That all men are created equal; that they are endowed by their Creator with certain unalienable rights; that among these are life, liberty and the pursuit of happiness; that, to secure these rights, governments are instituted among men, deriving their just powers from the consent of the governed; that whenever any form of government becomes destructive of these ends, it is the right of the people to alter or to abolish it, and to institute new government." These phrases have echoed down through American history like no others.

The delegates in Philadelphia who voted to accept the Declaration of Independence could not predict the consequences of their audacious act. When they adopted the declaration, they were committing treason. Therefore, when they concluded with the assertion that they "mutually pledge[d] to each other our lives, our fortunes, and our sacred honor," they spoke no less than the truth. The real struggle still lay before them, and few had Thomas Paine's boundless confidence in success.

The Struggle in the North

In late June 1776, the first ships carrying Sir William Howe's troops from Halifax appeared off the coast of New York (see Map 6.1). On July 2, the day Congress voted for independence, redcoats landed on Staten Island. Washington marched his army of seventeen thousand south from Boston to defend Manhattan. Because Howe waited until more troops arrived from England before attacking, Americans could prepare to defend the city.

But Washington and his men, still inexperienced in fighting and maneuvering, made major mistakes, losing

Map 6.1   The War in the North, 1775–1777

The early phase of the Revolutionary War was dominated by British troop movements in the Boston area, the redcoats' evacuation to Nova Scotia in the spring of 1776, and the subsequent British invasion of New York and New Jersey.

NEW YORK AND NEW JERSEY

battles at Brooklyn Heights and on Manhattan Island. The city fell to the British, who captured nearly three thousand American soldiers. (Those men spent most of the rest of the war on British prison ships anchored in New York harbor, where many died of smallpox and other diseases.) Washington then slowly retreated across New Jersey into Pennsylvania, and British forces took control of most of New Jersey. Occupying troops met little opposition; the revolutionary cause appeared to be in disarray. "These are the times that try men's souls," wrote Thomas Paine in his pamphlet *The Crisis*. "The summer soldier and the sunshine patriot will, in this crisis, shrink from the service of his country; . . . yet we have this consolation with us, that the harder the conflict, the more glorious the triumph."

The British then forfeited their advantage as redcoats stationed in New Jersey went on a rampage of rape and plunder. Washington determined to strike back. Moving quickly, he crossed the Delaware River at night to attack a Hessian encampment at Trenton early in the morning of December 26, while the redcoats were still recuperating from their Christmas celebration. The patriots captured more than nine hundred Hessians and killed another thirty; only three Americans were wounded. A few days later, Washington attacked again at Princeton. Having gained command of the field and buoyed American spirits with the two swift victories, Washington set up winter quarters at Morristown, New Jersey.

British strategy for 1777, sketched in London over the winter, aimed to cut New England off from the other colonies. General John Burgoyne, a subordinate of Howe and one of the planners, would lead an invading force of redcoats and Indians down the Hudson River from Canada to rendezvous near Albany with a similar force that would move east along the Mohawk River valley. The combined forces would then presumably link up with Sir William Howe's troops in New York City. But in New York Howe simultaneously prepared his own plan to capture Philadelphia. Consequently, in 1777 the British armies in America would operate independently; the result would be disaster (see Map 6.2).

CAMPAIGN OF 1777

Howe took Philadelphia, but he did so in inexplicable fashion, delaying for months before beginning the campaign, then taking six weeks to transport his troops by sea instead of marching them overland. Incredibly, at the end of the lengthy voyage, he ended up only 40 miles closer to Philadelphia than when he started. By the time Howe advanced on Philadelphia, Washington had had time to prepare its defenses. Twice, at Brandywine Creek

and again at Germantown, the two armies clashed near the patriot capital. Although the British won both engagements, the Americans handled themselves well. The redcoats captured Philadelphia in late September, but to little effect. The campaign season was nearly over; the revolutionary army had gained confidence in itself and its leaders; and, far to the north, Burgoyne was going down to defeat.

Burgoyne and his men had set out from Montreal in mid-June, traveling first by boat on Lake Champlain, then later marching slowly overland toward the Hudson, forced as they went to clear giant trees felled across their path by patriot militiamen. An easy triumph at Fort Ticonderoga in July was followed in August by two setbacks—the redcoats and Indians marching east along the

Map 6.2   Campaign of 1777

The crucial campaign of 1777 was fought on two fronts: along the upper Hudson and Mohawk River valleys, and in the vicinity of Philadelphia. The rebels won in the north; the British triumphed—at least nominally—in the south. The capture of Philadelphia, however, did the redcoats little good, and they abandoned the city the following year.

■ George Washington at the Battle of Princeton, 1779, by Charles Willson Peale. Two years after the battle, Peale created this heroic image of the Continental Army's commander, intended (as were all his portraits of revolutionary leaders) to instill patriotic sentiments and pride in its viewers.   (Courtesy of the Pennsylvania Academy of Fine Arts, Philadelphia. Gift of Maria McKean Allen and Phoebe Warren)

Mohawk River turned back after a battle at Oriskany, New York; and in a clash near Bennington, Vermont, American militiamen nearly wiped out eight hundred of Burgoyne's German mercenaries. The general's dawdling gave American troops time to prepare for his arrival. After several skirmishes with an American army commanded by General Horatio Gates, Burgoyne was surrounded near Saratoga, New York. On October 17, 1777, he surrendered his entire force of more than six thousand men.

The August 1777 battle at Oriskany divided the Iroquois Confederacy. The Six Nations had formally

IROQUOIS CONFEDERACY SPLINTERS

pledged to remain neutral in the war. But two influential Mohawk leaders, the siblings Mary and Joseph Brant, believed that the Iroquois should ally themselves with the British to protect their territory from land-hungry colonists. The Brants won over the Senecas, Cayugas, and Mohawks, all of whom contributed warriors to the 1777 expedition. But the Oneidas—who had been converted to Christianity by Protestant missionaries—preferred the American side and brought the Tuscaroras with them. The Onondagas split into three factions, one on each side and one supporting neutrality. At Oriskany, some Oneidas and Tuscaroras joined patriot militiamen in fighting their Iroquois brethren, shattering a league of friendship that had survived for over three hundred years.

The collapse of Iroquois unity and the confederacy's abandonment of neutrality had significant consequences. In 1778 Iroquois warriors allied with the British raided frontier villages in Pennsylvania and New York. To retaliate, the Americans the following summer dispatched an expedition under General John Sullivan to burn Iroquois crops, orchards, and settlements. The resulting devastation led many bands to seek food and shelter north of the Great Lakes during the winter of 1779–1780. A large number of Iroquois people never returned to New York but settled permanently in Canada.

Burgoyne's surrender at Saratoga brought joy to patriots, discouragement to loyalists and Britons. In exile in London, Thomas Hutchinson wrote of "universal dejection" among loyalists there. "Everybody in a gloom," he commented; "most of us expect to lay our bones here." The disaster prompted Lord North to authorize a peace commission to offer the Americans what they had requested in 1774—in effect, a return to the imperial system of 1763. That proposal came far too late: the patriots rejected the overture, and the peace commission sailed back to England empty-handed in mid-1778.

Most important, the American victory at Saratoga drew France formally into the conflict. Ever since 1763, the French had sought to avenge their defeat in the Seven Years War, and the American Revolution gave them that opportunity. Even before Benjamin Franklin arrived in Paris in late 1776, France covertly supplied the revolutionaries with military necessities. Indeed, 90 percent of the gunpowder used by the Americans during the war's first two years came from France, transported via the French Caribbean island of Martinique.

Benjamin Franklin worked tirelessly to strengthen ties between the two nations. He adopted a plain style of dress that made him conspicuous amid the luxury of the

■ Joseph Brant, the Iroquois leader who helped to persuade the Mohawks, Senecas, and Cayugas to support the British in the latter stages of the Revolution, as painted by Charles Willson Peale in 1797.
(Independence National Historic Park Collection)

arms, ammunition, clothing, and blankets. Second, Britain could no longer focus solely on the American mainland, for it had to fight France in the Caribbean and elsewhere. Spain's entry into the war in 1779 as an ally of France (but not of the United States) magnified Britain's problems, for the Revolution then became a global war. The French aided the Americans throughout the conflict, but in its last years that assistance proved vital.

Life in the Army and on the Home Front

*O*nly in the first months of the war was the revolutionaries' army manned primarily by the semi-mythical "citizen soldier," the militiaman who exchanged his plow for a gun to defend his homeland. After a few months or at most a year, the early arrivals went home. They reenlisted, if at all, only briefly and only if the contending armies came close to their farms and towns. Even then, such men could avoid service if they hired replacements.

After 1776 the ranks of the Continental Army—those who enlisted for long periods or for the war's duration—were filled primarily by young, single, or propertyless men who signed up to earn monetary bonuses or allotments of land after the war. As the fighting dragged on, those bonuses and land grants grew larger. To meet their quotas of enlistees, towns and states eagerly signed up everyone they could, including slaves and indentured servants (who were promised freedom after the war) and recent immigrants. Regiments from the middle states contained an especially large proportion of foreign-born troops; about 45 percent of Pennsylvania soldiers were of Irish origin and about 13 percent were German, some serving in German-speaking regiments.

DIVERSITY IN THE RANKS

Recruiters in northern states turned increasingly to African Americans, both slave and free. Southern states initially resisted the trend, but later all but Georgia and South Carolina also enlisted black soldiers. Approximately five thousand African Americans eventually served in the Continental Army, most winning their freedom as a result. They commonly served in racially integrated units but were assigned tasks that others shunned, such as cooking, foraging for food, and driving wagons. Overall, it appears that at any given time they composed about 10 percent of the regular army, though they seldom served in militia units.

Also attached to the American forces were a number of women, the wives and widows of poor soldiers, who

FRANCO-AMERICAN ALLIANCE OF 1778

court of King Louis XVI. Presenting himself as a representative of American simplicity, Franklin played on the French image of Americans as virtuous farmers. His efforts culminated in 1778 when the countries signed two treaties. In the Treaty of Amity and Commerce, France recognized American independence, establishing trade ties with the new nation. In the Treaty of Alliance, France and the United States promised—assuming that France would declare war on Britain, which it soon did—that neither would negotiate peace with the enemy without consulting the other. France also formally abandoned any claim to Canada and to North American territory east of the Mississippi River. In the years that followed, the most visible symbol of Franco-American cooperation was the Marquis de Lafayette, a young nobleman who volunteered for service with George Washington in 1777 and fought with American forces until the conflict ended.

The French alliance had two major benefits for the patriot cause. First, France began to aid the Americans openly, sending troops and naval vessels in addition to

■ Barzillai Lew, a free African American born in Groton, Massachusetts, in 1743, served in the Seven Years War before enlisting with patriot troops in the American Revolution. An accomplished fifer, Lew fought at the Battle of Bunker Hill. Like other freemen in the north, he cast his lot with the revolutionaries, in contrast to southern bonds-people, who tended to favor the British.   (Courtesy of Mae Theresa Bonitto)

came to the army with their menfolk because they were too impoverished to survive alone. Such camp followers—estimated overall to be about 3 percent of the number of troops—worked as cooks, nurses, and launderers in return for rations and low wages. The women, as well as civilian commissaries and militiamen who floated in and out of camp at irregular intervals, made up an unwieldy assemblage that officers found difficult to manage. Yet the army's shapelessness also reflected its greatest strength: an almost unlimited reservoir of manpower and womanpower.

The officers of the Continental Army developed an intense sense of pride and commitment to the revolutionary cause. The hardships they endured, the battles they fought, the difficulties they

OFFICER CORPS

overcame all helped to forge an esprit de corps that outlasted the war. The realities of warfare were often dirty, messy, and corrupt, but the officers drew strength from a developing image of themselves as professionals who sacrificed personal gain for the good of the entire nation. When Benedict Arnold, an officer who fought heroically for the patriot cause early in the war, defected to the British, they made his name a metaphor for villainy. "How black, how despised, loved by none, and hated by all," wrote one officer.

The officers' wives, too, prided themselves on their and their husbands' service to the nation. Unlike poor women, they did not travel with the army but instead came for extended visits while the troops were in camp (usually during the winters). Martha Washington and other officers' wives, for example, lived at Valley Forge in the winter of 1777–1778. They brought with them food, clothing, and household furnishings to make their stay more comfortable, and they entertained each other and their menfolk at teas, dinners, and dances. Socializing and discussing current events created friendships later renewed in civilian life when some of their husbands became the new nation's leaders.

Life in the American army was difficult for everyone, although ordinary soldiers endured more hardships than their officers. Wages, even when paid, were small, and often the army could not meet the payroll. Rations (a daily standard allotment of bread, meat, vegetables, milk, and beer) did not always appear, and men had to forage for their own food. Clothing and shoes the army supplied were often of poor quality; soldiers had to make do, or find their own. While in camp, soldiers occasionally hired themselves out as laborers to nearby farmers to augment their meager rations or earnings. When conditions deteriorated, troops threatened mutiny (though only a few carried out that threat) or, more often, simply deserted. One study shows that more than 80 percent of the wartime courts-martial charged soldiers with desertion.

Endemic disease in the camps—especially dysentery, various fevers, and, early in the war, smallpox—made matters worse, sometimes discouraging recruiting. Most native-born colonists had neither been exposed to smallpox nor been inoculated against the disease, and so soldiers and civilians were vulnerable when smallpox spread through the northern countryside after the early months of 1774. The disease ravaged residents of Boston during the British occupation, the troops attacking Quebec in 1775–1776, and the African Americans who fled to join Lord Dunmore (1775) or Lord Cornwallis

HARDSHIP AND DISEASE

Measles, typhus, diphtheria, dysentery, and other diseases ravaged military encampments, so medicine chests like the one shown here were essential equipment for the army. Doctors used crude remedies that often did more harm than good, for little was known about the causes of such afflictions. Smallpox was one of the few epidemics that eighteenth-century doctors could combat: inoculation was known to be an effective preventive measure as early as the 1720s. (The West Point Museum Collection, U.S. Military Academy, West Point, N.Y. Photo by Josh Nefsky)

(1781). Because most British soldiers had already survived smallpox (which was endemic in Europe), it did not pose a significant threat to redcoat troops.

Washington recognized that smallpox could potentially decimate the revolutionaries' ranks, especially after it helped cause the failure of the 1775 Quebec expedition. Thus in Morristown in early 1777 he ordered that entire regular army and all new recruits be inoculated, although some would die from the risky procedure and survivors would be incapacitated for weeks. Those dramatic measures, coupled with the increasing numbers of foreign-born (and thus already immune) men who enlisted, helped to protect Continental soldiers later in the war, contributing significantly to the eventual American victory.

Men who enlisted in the army or served in Congress were away from home for long periods of time. In their absence their womenfolk, who previously had handled only the "indoor affairs" of the household, shouldered the responsibility for "outdoor affairs" as well. As the wife of

HOME FRONT

a Connecticut soldier later recalled, her husband "was out more or less during the remainder of the war [after 1777], so much so as to be unable to do anything on our farm. What was done, was done by myself." Similarly, John and Abigail Adams took great pride in Abigail's developing skills as a "farmeress." Like other female contemporaries, Abigail Adams stopped calling the farm "yours" in letters to her husband and began referring to it as "ours"—a revealing change of pronoun. Most women did not work in the fields themselves, but they supervised field workers and managed their families' resources.

Wartime disruptions affected the lives of all Americans. Even far from the battlefields, people suffered from shortages of necessities like salt, soap, and flour. Small luxuries like new clothing or even ribbons or gloves were essentially unavailable. Severe inflation added to the country's woes, eroding the value of any income. For those who lived near the armies' camps or lines of march, difficulties were compounded. Soldiers of both sides plundered farms and houses, looking for food or salable items; they burned fence rails in their fires and took horses and oxen to transport their wagons. Moreover, they carried smallpox and other diseases with them wherever they went. In such circumstances and in the absence of their husbands, women had to make the momentous decision whether to deliberately risk their children's lives by inoculating them with smallpox or to take the chance of the youngsters' contracting the disease "in the natural way," with its even greater risk of death. Many, including Abigail Adams, chose the former course of action and were relieved when their children survived.

Victory in the South

In early 1778, in the wake of the Saratoga disaster, Lord George Germain and British military leaders reassessed their strategy. The loyalist exiles in London persuaded them to shift the field of battle southward, contending that loyal southerners would welcome the redcoat army as liberators. Once the South had been pacified and returned to friendly civilian control, it could then serve as a base for once again attacking the middle and northern states.

Sir Henry Clinton, who replaced Sir William Howe, oversaw the regrouping of British forces in America. He

SOUTH CAROLINA AND THE CARIBBEAN

ordered the evacuation of Philadelphia in June 1778 and sent a convoy that successfully captured the French Caribbean island of St. Lucia, which thereafter served as a key base for Britain.

He also dispatched a small expedition to Georgia at the end of the year. When Savannah and then Augusta fell easily into British hands, Clinton became convinced that a southern strategy would succeed. In late 1779 he sailed down the coast from New York to besiege Charleston, the most important city in the South (see Map 6.3). Although afflicted by smallpox, the Americans trapped in the city held out for months. Still, on May 12, 1780, General Benjamin Lincoln was forced to surrender the entire southern army—5,500 men—to the invaders. In the following weeks, the redcoats spread through South Carolina, establishing garrisons at key points in the interior. Hundreds of South Carolinians renounced allegiance to the United States, proclaiming their renewed loyalty to the Crown. Clinton organized loyalist regiments, and the process of pacification began.

Map 6.3 The War in the South

The southern war—after the British invasion of Georgia in late 1778—was characterized by a series of British thrusts into the interior, leading to battles with American defenders in both North and South Carolina. Finally, after promising beginnings, Cornwallis's foray into Virginia ended with disaster at Yorktown in October 1781.

Yet the triumph was less complete than it appeared. The success of the southern campaign depended on control of the seas, for the British armies were so widely dispersed and travel by land was so difficult that only through British naval vessels could the armies coordinate their efforts. For the moment, the Royal Navy safely dominated the American coastline, but French naval power posed a threat to the entire southern enterprise. American privateers infested Caribbean waters, seizing valuable cargoes bound to and from the British West Indies. Furthermore, after late 1778 France picked off British islands one by one, including Grenada—second only to Jamaica in sugar production—and, in 1781, St. Christopher as well. Even though in early 1781 the British captured and plundered St. Eustatius (the Dutch island that after French entry into the war served as the main conduit for the movement of military supplies from Europe to America), the victory did them little good. Indeed, it might well have cost them the war, for Admiral Sir George Rodney, occupied with securing the victory (and his personal profits from the plunder), failed to pursue the French fleet under Admiral François de Grasse when it subsequently sailed from the Caribbean to Virginia, where it played a major role in the battle at Yorktown (see page 161).

Then, too, the redcoats never managed to establish full control of the areas they seized in South Carolina. Patriot bands operated freely, and loyalists could not be adequately protected. The fall of Charleston failed to dishearten the patriots; instead, it spurred them to greater exertions. As one Marylander declared confidently, "The Fate of America is not to be decided by the Loss of a Town or Two." Patriot women in four states formed the Ladies Association, which collected money to purchase shirts for needy soldiers. Recruiting efforts were stepped up.

Nevertheless, the war in South Carolina went badly for the patriots throughout most of 1780. At Camden in August, forces under Lord Cornwallis, the new British commander in the South, crushingly defeated a reorganized southern army led by Horatio Gates. Thousands of enslaved African Americans joined the redcoats, seeking the freedom promised by Lord Dunmore and later by Sir Henry Clinton. Running away from their patriot masters individually and as families, they seriously disrupted planting and harvesting in the Carolinas in 1780 and 1781. More than fifty-five thousand slaves were lost to their owners as a result of the war. Not all of them joined the British or won their freedom if they did, but their flight had exactly the effect the British sought. Many served the redcoats well as scouts, guides, and laborers.

■ "A View from the Two-Gun Battery," St. Lucia, 1780, by Charles Forrest. Forrest, a British officer stationed in the West Indies during the Revolution, sketched this scene showing some of the island's defenses against a possible attack by the American or French Navy. (William L. Clements Library)

After the Camden defeat, Washington (who had to remain in the North to contain the British army occupying New York) appointed General Nathanael Greene to command the southern campaign. Appalled by conditions in South Carolina, Greene told a friend that "the word difficulty when applied to the state of things here . . . is almost without meaning, it falls so far short" of reality. His troops needed clothing, blankets, and food, but "a great part of this country is already laid waste and in the utmost danger of becoming a desert." Incessant guerrilla warfare had, he commented, "so corrupted the principles of the people that they think of nothing but plundering one another."

GREENE AND THE SOUTHERN CAMPAIGN

In such dire circumstances, Greene had to move cautiously. He adopted a conciliatory policy toward loyalists and neutrals, persuading South Carolina to pardon those who had fought for the British if they would now join patriot militias. He also ordered his troops to treat captives fairly and not to loot loyalist property. Recognizing that the patriots needed to convince a war-weary populace that they could bring stability to the region, he helped the shattered provincial congresses of Georgia and South Carolina to reestablish civilian authority in the interior—a goal the British were never able to accomplish. Since he had so few regulars (only sixteen hundred when he took command), Greene had to rely on western volunteers and could not afford to have frontier militia companies occupied in defending their homes from Indian attack. He accordingly pursued diplomacy aimed at keeping the Indians out of the war. Although royal officials cooperating with the redcoat invaders initially won some Indian allies, Greene's careful maneuvers eventually proved successful. By war's end, only the Creeks remained allied with Great Britain.

Even before Greene took command of the southern army in December 1780, the tide had begun to turn. In October, at King's Mountain, a force from the backcountry defeated a large party of redcoats and loyalists. Then in January 1781 Greene's trusted aide Daniel Morgan brilliantly routed the crack British regiment Tarleton's Legion at Cowpens. Greene himself confronted the main body of British troops under Lord Cornwallis at Guilford Court House, North Carolina, in March. Although Cornwallis controlled the field at the end of the day, most of his army had been destroyed. He had to retreat to Wilmington, on the coast, to receive supplies and fresh troops from New York by sea. Meanwhile, Greene returned to South Carolina, where, in a series of swift strikes, he forced the redcoats to abandon their interior posts and retire to Charleston.

Cornwallis headed north into Virginia, where he joined forces with a detachment of redcoats commanded by the American traitor Benedict Arnold. Instead of acting decisively with his new army of 7,200 men, Cornwallis withdrew to the peninsula between the York and James Rivers, where he fortified Yorktown and awaited supplies and reinforcements. Seizing the opportunity, Washington quickly moved more than 7,000 French and American troops south from New York City. When De Grasse's fleet arrived from the Caribbean just in time to defeat the Royal Navy vessels sent to relieve Cornwallis, the British general was trapped (see Map 6.3). On October 19, 1781, Cornwallis surrendered.

SURRENDER AT YORKTOWN

When news of the defeat reached London, Lord North's ministry fell. Parliament voted to cease offensive operations in America, authorizing peace negotiations. Washington returned with the main army to the environs of New York, where his underpaid—and, they thought, underappreciated—officers grew restive. In March 1783 they threatened to mutiny unless Congress guaranteed them adequate compensation for their services. Washington, warned in advance of the so-called Newburgh Conspiracy, met the challenge brilliantly. Summoning his officers, he defused the crisis with a well-reasoned but emotional speech drawing on their patriotism. How could they, he asked, "open the flood Gates of Civil discord, and deluge our rising Empire in Blood"? When at one point he fumbled for glasses, remarking in passing that "I have grown gray in your service and now find myself growing blind," eyewitnesses reported that many of the rebellious officers began to cry. At the end of the year, he stood before Congress and formally resigned his commission as commander-in-chief. Through such actions at the end of the conflict, Washington established an enduring precedent: civilian control of the American military.

The war had been won, but at terrible cost. More than twenty-five thousand American men died in the war, only about one-quarter of them from wounds suffered in battle. The rest were declared missing in action or died of disease or as prisoners of war. In the South, years of guerrilla warfare and the loss of thousands of runaway slaves shattered the economy. Indebtedness soared, and local governments were crippled for lack of funds, since few people could afford to pay their taxes. In the 1780s in Charles County, Maryland, for example, men commonly refused to serve in elective or appointive office because their personal estates would become liable for any taxes or fines they were unable to collect. Many of the county's formerly wealthy planters descended into insolvency, and in the 1790s a traveler observed that "the country . . . wears a most dreary aspect," remarking on the "old dilapidated mansions" that had once housed well-to-do slaveowners.

Yet Charles County residents and Americans in general "all rejoiced" when they learned of the signing of the preliminary peace treaty at Paris in November 1782. The American diplomats—Benjamin Franklin, John Jay, and John Adams—ignored their instructions from Congress to be guided by France and instead negotiated directly with Great Britain. Their instincts were sound: the French government was more an enemy to Britain than a friend to the United States. In fact, French ministers worked secretly behind the scenes to try to prevent the establishment of a strong, unified government in America. Spain's desire to lay claim to the region between the Appalachian Mountains and the Mississippi River further complicated the negotiations. But the American del-

TREATY OF PARIS

egates proved adept at power politics, achieving their main goal: independence as a united nation. Weary of war, the new British ministry, headed by Lord Shelburne (formerly an outspoken critic of Lord North's American policies), made numerous concessions—so many, in fact, that Parliament ousted the ministry shortly after peace terms were approved.

The treaty, signed formally on September 3, 1783, granted the Americans unconditional independence. Generous boundaries delineated the new nation: to the north, approximately the present-day boundary with Canada; to the south, the 31st parallel (about the modern northern border of Florida); to the west, the Mississippi River. Florida, which Britain had acquired in 1763, reverted to Spain. The Americans also gained unlimited fishing rights off Newfoundland. In ceding so much land to the United States, Great Britain ignored the territorial rights of its Indian allies, sacrificing their interests to the demands of European politics. British diplomats also poorly served loyalists and British merchants. The treaty's ambiguously worded clauses pertaining to the payment of prewar debts and the postwar treatment of loyalists caused trouble for years to come, proving impossible to enforce.

Summary

The long war finally over, the victorious Americans could look back on their achievement with satisfaction and awe. Having unified the disparate mainland colonies, they had claimed their place in the family of nations and forged a successful alliance with France. With an inexperienced ragtag army, they had taken on the greatest military power in the world—and eight years later they had won. They accomplished their goal more through persistence and commitment than through brilliance on the battlefield. Actual victories were few, but their army always survived defeats and standoffs to fight again. Ultimately, the Americans simply wore their enemy down.

In winning the war, the Americans reshaped the physical and mental landscapes in which they lived. They abandoned the British identity once so important to them, excluding from their new nation all those unwilling to make a break with the mother country. In the families of Continental Army soldiers in particular they began the process of creating loyalty to an entity that had no prior existence—a nation they named "the United States of America." They also laid claim to most of the territory east of the Mississippi River and south of the

Great Lakes, thereby greatly expanding the land potentially open to their settlements and threatening the traditional Indian dominance of the continent's interior.

In achieving independence, Americans surmounted formidable challenges. But in the future they faced perhaps even greater ones: establishing stable republican governments at the state and national levels to replace the monarchy they had rejected, and ensuring their government's continued existence in a world of bitter rivalries among the major powers—Britain, France, and Spain. Those European rivalries worked to the Americans' advantage during the war, but in the decades to come they would pose significant threats to the survival of the new nation.

LEGACY FOR A PEOPLE AND A NATION
Revolutionary Origins

The United States was created in an event universally termed the "American Revolution." Yet many historians would contend today that it was not truly "revolutionary," if a revolution means overturning an earlier power structure. The nation won its independence and established a republic, both radical events in the context of the eighteenth century, but essentially the same men who had led the colonies also led the new country (with the exception of British officials and appointees). In sharp contrast, the nearly contemporary French Revolution witnessed the execution of the monarch and many aristocrats, and consequently a significant redistribution of authority. So the legacy of the "American Revolution" appears ambiguous, at once radical and conservative.

Throughout the more than two hundred years since the "revolution," groups of widely varying political views have claimed to represent its true meaning. From far left to far right, Americans frequently declare that they are acting in the spirit of the Revolution. People protesting discriminatory policies against women and minorities (usually "liberals") invoke the "created equal" language of the Declaration of Independence. Left-wing organizations rail against concentrations of wealth and power in the hands of a few, again citing the Revolution's egalitarian thrust. Those protesting higher taxes (usually "conservatives" wanting a reduced role for government) often adopt the symbolism of the Boston Tea Party. Right-wing militias arm themselves, preparing to defend their homes and families against a malevolent government, just as they believe the minutemen did in 1775. The message of the Revolution can be evoked to support extralegal demonstrations of any description, from invasions of military bases by antiwar protestors to demonstrations outside abortion clinics, all of which may be analogized to the demonstrations against British policies in the 1760s. But the Revolution can also be evoked to oppose such street protests, because—some would argue—in a republic change should come peacefully, via the ballot box, not the streets.

Just as Americans in the eighteenth century disagreed over the meaning of their struggle against the mother country, so the legacy of revolution remains contested in the first decade of the twenty-first century, both for the nation thus created and for today's American people.

The **history companion** powered by Eduspace®
Your primary source for interactive quizzes, exercises, and more to help you learn efficiently.
http://history.college.hmco.com/students

CHAPTER 7

*F*ORGING A NATIONAL REPUBLIC 1776–1789

*O*n December 26, 1787, a group of Federalists—supporters of the proposed Constitution—gathered in Carlisle, a town on the Pennsylvania frontier. The men planned to fire a cannon to celebrate their state convention's ratification vote two weeks earlier, but a large crowd of Antifederalists prevented them from doing so. First the Antis stood in front of the cannon, refusing to budge even though the Federalists threatened to fire the gun anyway. Then, moving from passive to active resistance, they attacked the Federalists, who eventually fled the scene as the angry Antis publicly burned a copy of the Constitution.

The next day, the Federalists returned in force to fire their cannon and to read the convention's ratification proclamation. Choosing not to create another violent confrontation, Antifederalists instead paraded around the town effigies of two supporters of the Constitution, then burned them. When Federalist officials later arrested several Antifederalists on riot charges, the Antifederalist-dominated militia mustered to break the men out of jail. Only a flaw in the warrant—which freed the arrestees legally—prevented another bloody brawl.

For several weeks thereafter, the participants in these events argued back and forth in the Carlisle newspaper about the meaning of the demonstrations. Pro-Federalist authors proclaimed that the respectable initial celebrants acted with "good order and coolness"; their Antifederalist opponents, by contrast, were "obscure" men, nothing but "a few worthless ragamuffins." In response, "One of the People" pronounced the Federalists "an unhallowed riotous mob." Although the Constitution's supporters had declared themselves to be "friends of government," he wrote, in fact they were not: through their support of a form of government that aimed to suppress the people's liberties, they had revealed their true identity as secret aristocrats.

The Carlisle riots presaged violent disputes over the new Constitution in Albany (New York), Providence (Rhode Island), and other cities. In late 1787,

◀ Detail of **The Ramsay-Polk Family at Carpenter's Point, Cecil County, Maryland,** painted by James Peale about 1793. The sumptuous dresses and elaborate hats and hairdos mark these republican women as ladies of leisure. On the river wharf in the background, ready for shipping, are the hogsheads of tobacco (produced by slave labor) that made their leisure possible. (Courtesy, Hirschl & Adler Galleries, New York)

Carlisle witnessed one incident in an ongoing struggle that began in 1775 and continued until the end of the eighteenth century. In that contest, Americans argued continually—in print and in person—over how to implement republican principles and over who represented the people's will. Easterners debated with westerners; in both regions, elites contended with ordinary folk. Public celebrations, like those in the small Pennsylvania town, played an important part in the struggle. After all, in a world in which only relatively few property-holding men had the right to vote, other people (and even voters themselves) expressed their political opinions in the streets rather than at the ballot box.

Republicanism—the idea that governments should be based wholly on the consent of the people—originated with political theorists in ancient Greece and Rome. Republics, theorists declared, were desirable yet fragile forms of government. Unless their citizens were especially virtuous—that is, sober, moral, and industrious—and largely in agreement on key issues, republics were doomed to failure. When Americans left the British Empire, they abandoned the idea that the best system of government balanced monarchy, aristocracy, and democracy—or, to put it another way, that a stable polity required participation by a king, the nobility, and the people. They substituted a belief in the superiority of republicanism, in which the people, not Parliament, were sovereign. During and after the war, Americans had to deal with the potentially unwelcome consequences of that decision, such as those evident in the Carlisle demonstrations. How could they ensure political stability? How could they foster consensus among the populace? How could they create and sustain a virtuous republic?

America's political and intellectual leaders worked hard to inculcate virtue in their fellow countrymen and countrywomen. After 1776, American literature, theater, art, architecture, and education all pursued explicitly moral goals. The education of women was considered particularly important, for as the mothers of the republic's children, they were primarily responsible for ensuring the nation's future. On such matters Americans could agree, but they disagreed on many other critical issues. Almost all white men assumed that women, Indians, and African Americans should have no formal role in politics, but they found it difficult to reach a consensus on how many of their own number should be included, how often elections should be held, or how their new governments should be structured.

Republican citizens had to make many other decisions as well. Should a republic's diplomacy differ from that of other nations? (For example, should the United States work to advance the cause of republicanism elsewhere?) And then there were Thomas Jefferson's words in the Declaration of Independence: "all men are created equal." Given that bold statement of principle, how could white republicans justify holding African Americans in perpetual bondage? Some answered that question by freeing their slaves or by voting for state laws that abolished slavery. Others responded by denying that blacks were "men" in the same sense as whites.

The most important task facing Americans in these years was the construction of a genuinely national government. Before 1765 the British mainland colonies had rarely cooperated on common endeavors. Many circumstances separated them: their diverse economies, varying religious traditions and ethnic compositions, competing land claims (especially in the West), and different political systems. But fighting the Revolutionary War brought them together and created a new nationalistic spirit, especially among those who served in the Continental Army or the diplomatic corps. Wartime experiences broke down at least some of the boundaries that previously had divided Americans, replacing loyalties to state and region with loyalties to the nation.

Still, forging a national republic (as opposed to a set of loosely connected state republics) was neither easy nor simple. America's first such government, under the Articles of Confederation, proved too weak and decentralized. But some of the nation's political leaders learned from their experiences and tried another approach when they drafted the Constitution in 1787. Some historians have argued that the Articles of Confederation and the Constitution reflect opposing political philosophies, the Constitution representing an "aristocratic" counterrevolution against the "democratic" Articles. The two documents are more accurately viewed as successive attempts to solve the same problems—for instance, the relationship of states and nation and the extent to which authority should be centralized. Both applied theories of republicanism to practical problems of governance; neither was entirely successful in resolving those difficulties. ■

Creating a Virtuous Republic

*W*hen the colonies declared their independence from Great Britain, John Dickinson recalled many years later, "there was no question concerning forms of Government, no enquiry whether a Republic or a limited Monarchy was best. . . . We knew that the people of this country must unite themselves under some form of Government and that this could be no other than the republican form"—in short, self-government by the people. But how should that goal be implemented?

Three different definitions of republicanism emerged in the new United States. Ancient history and political theory informed the first, held chiefly by members of the

VARIETIES OF REPUBLICANISM educated elite (such as the Adamses of Massachusetts). The histories of popular governments in Greece and Rome suggested that republics could succeed only if they were small in size and homogeneous in population. Unless a republic's citizens were willing to sacrifice their own private interests for the good of the whole, the government would collapse. A truly virtuous man, classical republican theory insisted, had to forgo personal profit and work solely for the best interests of the nation. In return for sacrifices, though, a republic offered its citizens equality of opportunity. Under such a government, rank would be based on merit rather than on inherited wealth and status. Society would be governed by members of a "natural aristocracy," men whose talent had elevated them from what might have been humble beginnings to positions of power and privilege. Rank would not be abolished but instead would be founded on merit.

A second definition, advanced by other members of the elite but also by some skilled craftsmen, drew more on economic theory than on political thought. Instead of perceiving the nation as an organic whole composed of people nobly sacrificing for the common good, this version of republicanism followed the Scottish theorist Adam Smith in emphasizing individuals' pursuit of rational self-interest. The huge profits some men reaped from patriotism by selling supplies to the army underscored such an approach. The nation could only benefit from aggressive economic expansion, argued men such as Alexander Hamilton. When republican men sought to improve their own economic and social circumstances, the entire nation would benefit. Republican virtue would be achieved through the pursuit of private interests, rather than through subordination to some communal ideal. Such thinking decisively abandoned the old notion of the Puritan covenant, which the first definition perpetuated in its emphasis on consensus though not in its stress on an aristocracy of talent rather than birth (see pages 51–52).

The third notion of republicanism was less influential but more egalitarian than the other two, which both contained considerable potential for inequality. Many of its illiterate or barely literate proponents could write little to promote their beliefs. Men who advanced the third version of republicanism, the most prominent of whom was Thomas Paine, called for widening men's participation in the political process. They also wanted government to respond directly to the needs of ordinary folk, rejecting any notion that the "lesser sort" should automatically defer to their "betters." They were, indeed, democrats in more or less the modern sense. For them,

■ When the great French sculptor Jean-Antoine Houdon prepared this bust of George Washington in 1785, he chose to show the revolutionary leader in classical garb rather than in contemporary clothing. Such images linked the aspirations of the new nation to the ancient republics American thinkers revered. (Collection of Dr. Gary Milan)

As citizens of the United States set out to construct their republic, they believed they were embarking on an

VIRTUE AND THE ARTS

unprecedented enterprise. With great pride in their new nation, they expected to replace the vices of monarchical Europe—immorality, selfishness, and lack of public spirit—with the sober virtues of republican America. They wanted to embody republican principles not only in their governments but also in their society and culture. They looked to painting, literature, drama, and architecture to convey messages of nationalism and virtue to the public, focusing on such themes until after the turn of the century.

Americans faced a crucial contradiction at the very outset of their efforts. To some republicans, the fine arts themselves were manifestations of vice. Their existence in a virtuous society, many contended, signaled the arrival of luxury and corruption. What need did a frugal yeoman have for a painting—or, worse yet, a novel? Why should anyone spend hard-earned wages to see a play in a lavishly decorated theater? The first American artists, playwrights, and authors thus confronted an impossible dilemma. They wanted to produce works embodying virtue, but those very works, regardless of their content, were viewed by many as corrupting.

Still, they tried. William Hill Brown's *The Power of Sympathy* (1789), the first novel written in the United States, was a lurid tale of seduction intended as a warning to young women. In Royall Tyler's *The Contrast* (1787), the first successful American play, the virtuous conduct of Colonel Manly was contrasted (hence the title) with the reprehensible behavior of the fop Billy Dimple. The most popular book of the era, Mason Locke Weems's *Life of Washington*, published in 1800 shortly after George Washington's death, was intended by its author to "hold up his great Virtues . . . to the imitation of Our Youth." Weems could hardly be accused of subtlety. The famous tale he invented—six-year-old George bravely admitting cutting down his father's favorite cherry tree—ended with George's father exclaiming, "Run to my arms, you dearest boy. . . . Such an act of heroism in my son, is worth more than a thousand trees, though blossomed with silver, and their fruit of purest gold."

Painting and architecture, too, were expected to embody high moral standards. Two of the most prominent artists of the period, Gilbert Stuart and Charles Willson Peale, painted innumerable portraits of upstanding republican citizens. John Trumbull's vast canvases depicted milestones of American history such as the Battle of Bunker Hill, Burgoyne's surrender at Saratoga, and Cornwallis's capitulation at Yorktown. Such portraits

republican virtue was embodied in the untutored wisdom of the people as a whole, rather than in the special insights of a natural aristocracy or the pronouncements of wealthy individuals.

Despite the differences, the three strands of republicanism shared many of the same assumptions. For example, all three contrasted the industrious virtue of America to the corruption of Britain and Europe. In the first version, that virtue manifested itself in frugality and self-sacrifice; in the second, it would prevent self-interest from becoming vice; in the third, it was the justification for including even propertyless free men in the ranks of voters. "Virtue, Virtue alone . . . is the basis of a republic," asserted Dr. Benjamin Rush of Philadelphia, an ardent patriot, in 1778. His fellow Americans concurred, even if they defined virtue differently. Most agreed that a virtuous country would be composed of hard-working citizens who would dress simply and live plainly, elect wise leaders to public office, and forgo the conspicuous consumption of luxury goods.

The citizens of the United States, fiercely patriotic and proud of achieving political independence from Great Britain, also sought intellectual and cultural independence. In novels, poems, paintings, plays, and histories they explored aspects of their new national identity. Ironically, though, the standards against which they measured themselves and the models they followed were European, primarily British.

That was especially true of the most widely read form of literature in the new United States, the novel. Susanna Haswell Rowson's *Charlotte: A Tale of Truth*, the most popular early "American" novel, was actually composed in England, where the novel, as a literary form, originated. In the mid-eighteenth century Samuel Richardson had composed the first works of fiction that today are called novels, the very name revealing their "newness," or novelty. Written in epistolary style (that is, through letters drafted by the various characters) Richardson's novels—*Pamela* (1740), *Clarissa* (1748), and *Sir Charles Grandison* (1753)—all revolved around the courtship and sexual relationships of young adults. The same themes permeated *Charlotte* and Richardson's other American imitators, and for good reason. Changing social mores in the late eighteenth century largely freed English and American young people from parental supervision of their marital decisions. While giving them greater individual choice, that freedom also rendered girls particularly vulnerable to new dangers of deception and seduction by unscrupulous suitors. And these same young women, as a group, were the most avid readers of novels, especially as expanded women's education increased female literacy rates.

William Hill Brown's *Power of Sympathy* (1789) and Hannah Foster's *Coquette* (1797), fictional versions of true "seduction and abandonment" tales, had avid readerships, but neither matched the sales of *Charlotte*, which despite its subtitle, *A Tale of Truth*, had no known factual basis. Rowson, born in England but raised in Massachusetts as the daughter of a customs officer in the British service, lived with her family in England during the Revolution but permanently returned to the United States in 1793. Her popular novel, first published in London in 1791, was reprinted in Philadelphia three years later and eventually went through more than 160 editions. *Charlotte* (later titled *Charlotte Temple*) narrates the story of a naive young woman who elopes, pregnant and unmarried, with her seducer, only to be deserted when a beautiful, rich, and virtuous rival appears on the scene. After giving birth to her baby, Charlotte dies in her father's arms, with her last breath directing him to care for the child. "Oh my dear girls," Rowson cautions her readers, "pray for fortitude to resist the impulses of inclination, when it runs counter to the precepts of religion and virtue."

Generations of young American women sobbed over Charlotte's fate, visiting Trinity churchyard in lower Manhattan, where a real-life counterpart of the fictional heroine was reputed to be buried. Their tears and women's preference on both sides of the Atlantic for such sentimental novels linked the young readers and their nation to the former mother country from which they were nominally so eager to separate.

This "Eighth American Edition" (such statements on the title pages of early novels can rarely be trusted because some printings were pirated) of Susanna Rowson's *Charlotte Temple* included a "portrait" of its entirely fictional heroine. That engraving thus reinforced the subtitle, *A Tale of Truth.* (Courtesy, American Antiquarian Society)

and historical scenes were intended to instill patriotic sentiments in their viewers. Architects likewise hoped to convey in their buildings a sense of the young republic's ideals. When the Virginia government asked Thomas Jefferson, then minister to France, for advice on the design of the state capitol in Richmond, Jefferson unhesitatingly recommended copying a Roman building, the Maison Carrée at Nîmes. "It is very simple," he explained, "but it is noble beyond expression." Jefferson set forth ideals that would guide American architecture for a generation to come: simplicity of line, harmonious proportions, a feeling of grandeur.

Despite the artists' efforts (or, some would have said, because of them), some Americans began to detect signs of luxury and corruption by the mid-1780s. The resumption of European trade after the war brought a return to fashionable clothing for both men and women and abandonment of the simpler homespun garments patriots had once worn with pride. Elite families again attended balls and concerts. Parties no longer seemed complete without gambling and cardplaying. Social clubs for young people multiplied; Samuel Adams worried in print about the opportunities for corruption lurking behind plans for tea drinking and genteel conversation among Boston youths. Especially alarming to fervent republicans was the establishment in 1783 of the Society of the Cincinnati, a hereditary association for Revolutionary War officers and their male descendants. Although the organizers hoped to advance the notion of the citizen-soldier, opponents feared that the group would become the nucleus of a native-born aristocracy. All these developments directly challenged the United States's self-image as a virtuous republic.

Americans' deep-seated concern for the future of the infant republic focused their attention on their children, the "rising generation." Education had previously been seen as a private means to personal advancement, a concern only for individual families. Now schooling would serve a public purpose. If young people were to resist the temptations of vice and become useful citizens prepared for self-government, they would need a good education. In fact, the very survival of the nation depended on it. The 1780s and 1790s thus witnessed two major changes in educational practice.

EDUCATIONAL REFORM

First, some northern states began to use tax money to support public elementary schools. In 1789 Massachusetts became one of the first states to require towns to offer their citizens free public elementary education. Second, schooling for girls was improved. Americans' recognition of the importance of the rising generation led to the realization that mothers would have to be properly educated if they were to instruct their children adequately. Therefore, Massachusetts insisted in its 1789 law that town elementary schools be open to girls as well as boys. Throughout the United States, private academies were founded to give teenage girls from well-to-do families an opportunity for advanced schooling. No one yet proposed opening colleges to women, but a few fortunate girls could study history, geography, rhetoric, and mathematics. The academies also trained female students in fancy needlework—the only artistic endeavor considered appropriate for genteel women.

The chief theorist of women's education in the early republic was Judith Sargent Murray of Gloucester, Massachusetts. In a series of essays published in the 1780s and 1790s, Murray argued that women and men had equal intellectual capacities, although women's inadequate education might make them seem less intelligent. "We can only reason from what we know," she declared, "and if an opportunity of acquiring knowledge hath been denied us, the inferiority of our sex cannot fairly be deduced from thence." Therefore, concluded Murray, boys and girls should be offered equivalent scholastic training. She further contended that girls should be taught to support themselves by their own efforts: "Independence should be placed within their grasp."

JUDITH SARGENT MURRAY

Murray's direct challenge to the traditional colonial belief that, as one man put it, girls "knew quite enough if they could make a shirt and a pudding" was part of a general rethinking of women's position that occurred as a result of the Revolution. Both men and women realized that female patriots had made vital and important contributions to winning the war through their work at home and that their notions of proper gender roles had to be rethought. Americans began to develop new ideas about the role women should play in a republican society.

The best-known expression of those new ideas appears in a letter Abigail Adams addressed to her husband in March 1776. "In the new Code of Laws which I suppose it will be necessary for you to make I desire you would Remember the Ladies," she wrote. "Remember all Men would be tyrants if they could. . . . If perticuliar care and attention is not paid to the Laidies [sic] we are determined to foment a Rebelion, and will not hold ourselves bound by any Laws in which we have no voice, or Representation." With these words, Abigail Adams took a step that was soon to be duplicated by other disfranchised Americans. She deliberately applied the ideology developed to combat parliamentary supremacy to purposes revolutionary leaders had never

WOMEN AND THE REPUBLIC

Judith Sargent Stevens (later Murray), by John Singleton Copley, c. 1770-1772. The eventual author of tracts advocating improvements in women's education sat for this portrait two decades earlier, during her first marriage. Her clear-eyed gaze suggests both her intelligence and her seriousness of purpose.   (Terra Museum of American Art, Chicago, Illinois. Daniel J. Terra Collection)

was evidence of their altered perception of their place in the political life of the country.

Such dramatic episodes were unusual. After the war, European Americans still viewed women in traditional terms, continuing to believe that women's primary function was to be good wives, mothers, and mistresses of households. They perceived significant differences between the male and female characters. That distinction eventually enabled Americans to resolve the conflict between the two most influential strands of republican thought and led to new roles for some women. Because wives could not own property or participate directly in economic life, women in general came to be seen as the embodiment of self-sacrificing, disinterested republicanism. Through new female-run charitable associations founded after the war, better-off women assumed public responsibilities, in particular through caring for poor widows and orphaned children. Thus men were freed from the naggings of conscience as they pursued their economic self-interest (that other republican virtue), secure in the knowledge that their wives and daughters were fulfilling the family's obligation to the common good. The ideal republican man, therefore, was an individualist, seeking advancement for himself and his family. The ideal republican woman, by contrast, always put the well-being of others ahead of her own.

Together European American men and women established the context for the creation of a virtuous republic. But nearly 20 percent of the American population was of African descent. How did approximately 700,000 African Americans fit into the developing national plan?

The First Emancipation and the Growth of Racism

Revolutionary ideology exposed one of the primary contradictions in American society. Both European and African Americans saw the irony in slaveholders' claims that they sought to prevent Britain from "enslaving" them. Many revolutionary leaders voiced the theme. In 1773 Dr. Benjamin Rush called slavery "a vice which degrades human nature," warning ominously that "the plant of liberty is of so tender a nature that it cannot thrive long in the neighborhood of slavery." Common folk also pointed out the contradiction. When Josiah Atkins, a Connecticut soldier, saw Washington's plantation, he observed in his journal: "Alas! That persons who pretend to stand for the rights of mankind for the liberties of society, can delight in oppression, & that even of the worst kind!"

intended. Since men were "Naturally Tyrannical," she argued, the United States should reform colonial marriage laws, which made wives subordinate to their husbands.

Abigail Adams did not ask that women be allowed to vote, but others claimed that right. The men who drafted the New Jersey state constitution in 1776 defined voters carelessly as "all free inhabitants" who met certain property qualifications. They thereby unintentionally gave the vote to property-holding white spinsters and widows, as well as to free black landowners. Qualified women and African Americans regularly voted in New Jersey's local and congressional elections until 1807, when they were disfranchised by the state legislature, which falsely alleged that they had engaged in widespread vote fraud. Yet the fact that women voted at all

African Americans did not need revolutionary ideology to tell them that slavery was wrong, but they quickly took advantage of that ideology. In 1779 a group of slaves from Portsmouth, New Hampshire, asked the state legislature "from what authority [our masters] assume to dispose of our lives, freedom and property," pleading "that the name of slave may not more be heard in a land gloriously contending for the sweets of freedom." The same year several bondspeople in Fairfield, Connecticut, petitioned the legislature for their freedom, characterizing slavery as a "dreadful Evil" and "flagrant Injustice." How could men who were "nobly contending in the Cause of Liberty," they asked, continue "this detestable Practice"?

Both legislatures responded negatively, but the postwar years witnessed the gradual abolition of slavery in the North, a process that has become known as "the first emancipation." Ver-

Emancipation and Manumission

mont banned slavery in its 1777 constitution. Massachusetts courts decided in the 1780s that a clause in the state constitution prohibited slavery. Most of the other states north of Maryland adopted gradual emancipation laws between 1780 (Pennsylvania) and 1804 (New Jersey). Although New Hampshire did not formally abolish slavery, only eight slaves were reported on the 1800 census, and none remained a decade later. No southern state adopted similar general emancipation laws, but the legislatures of Virginia (1782), Delaware (1787), and Maryland (1790 and 1796) altered laws that earlier had restricted slaveowners' ability to free their bondspeople. South Carolina and Georgia never considered adopting such acts, and North Carolina insisted that all manumissions (emancipations of individual slaves) be approved by county courts.

Revolutionary ideology thus had limited impact on the well-entrenched economic interests of large slaveholders. Only in the North, where slaves were relatively few, could state legislatures vote to abolish slavery. Even there, legislators' concern for the property rights of owners of human chattel—the Revolution, after all, was fought for *property* as well as life and liberty—led them to favor gradual emancipation over immediate abolition. For example, New York's law freed children born into slavery after July 4, 1799, but only after they had reached their mid-twenties (by then having through their labor more than paid back the cost of their upbringing). The laws failed to emancipate the existing slave population, thereby leaving the owners' current human property largely intact. For decades, then, African Americans in the North lived in an intermediate stage between slav-

ery and freedom. Although the emancipation laws forbade the sale of slaves to jurisdictions in which the institution remained legal, slaveowners regularly circumvented such provisions. The 1840 census still recorded the presence of slaves in several northern states; not until later that decade did Rhode Island and Connecticut, for instance, abolish all vestiges of slavery.

Despite the slow progress of abolition, the number of free people of African descent in the United States grew dramatically in the first years af-

Growth of Free Black Population

ter the Revolution. Before the war they had been few in number; in 1755, for example, only 4 percent of African Americans in Maryland were free. Most slaves emancipated before the war were mulattos, born of unions between bondswomen and their masters, who then manumitted the children. But wartime disruptions radically augmented the freed population. Slaves who had escaped from plantations during the war, others who had served in the American army, and still others who had been emancipated by their owners or by state laws were now free. By 1790 nearly 60,000 free people of color lived in the United States; ten years later they numbered more than 108,000, nearly 11 percent of the total African American population.

In the Chesapeake, manumissions were speeded by economic changes such as declining soil fertility and the shift from tobacco to grain production, as well as by the rising influence of antislavery Baptists and Methodists. Since grain cultivation was less labor-intensive than tobacco growing, planters began to complain about "excess" slaves. They occasionally solved that problem by freeing some of their less productive or more favored bondspeople. The enslaved also seized the opportunity to negotiate agreements with their owners allowing them to live and work independently until they could purchase themselves with their accumulated earnings. The free black population of Virginia more than doubled between 1790 and 1810, and by the latter year nearly one-quarter of Maryland's African American population was no longer in legal bondage.

In the 1780s and thereafter, freed people from rural areas often made their way to northern port cities. Boston and Philadelphia, where slavery

Migration to Northern Cities

was abolished sooner than in New York City, were popular destinations. Women outnumbered men among the migrants by a margin of three to two, for they had better employment opportunities in the cities, especially in domestic service. Some freedmen also worked in domestic service, but larger numbers were employed as unskilled laborers and sailors. A few of the women and a sizable proportion of men (nearly one-third of those in Philadelphia in 1795) were skilled workers or retailers. These people chose new names for themselves, exchanging the surnames of former masters for names like Newman or Brown, and as soon as possible they established independent two-parent nuclear families instead of continuing to live in their employers' households. They also began to occupy distinct neighborhoods, probably as a result of discrimination.

Emancipation did not bring equality. Even whites who recognized African Americans' right to freedom were unwilling to accept them as equals. Laws discriminated against freed people as they had against slaves. South Carolina, for example, did not permit free blacks to testify against whites in court. New Englanders attempted through indenture contracts to maintain control of freed youths. Public schools often refused to educate children of color. Freedmen found it difficult to purchase property and find good jobs. And though in many areas African Americans were accepted as members—even ministers—of evangelical churches, they were rarely allowed an equal voice in church affairs.

Gradually, freed people developed their own institutions, often based in their own neighborhoods. In Charleston mulattos formed the Brown

FREED PEOPLE'S INSTITUTIONS

Fellowship Society, which provided insurance coverage for its members, financed a school, and helped to support orphans. In 1794 former slaves in Philadelphia and Baltimore founded societies that eventually became the African Methodist Episcopal (AME) denomination. AME churches later sponsored schools in a number of cities and, along with African Baptist, African Episcopal, and African Presbyterian churches, became cultural centers of the free black community. Freed people quickly learned that, to survive and prosper, they had to rely on their own collective efforts rather than on the benevolence or goodwill of their white compatriots.

Their endeavors were all the more important because the postrevolutionary years witnessed the development of a formal racist theory in the United

DEVELOPMENT OF RACIST THEORY

States. European Americans had long regarded their slaves as inferior, but the most influential writers attributed that inferiority to environmental factors. They argued that African slaves' seemingly debased character derived from their enslavement, rather than enslavement being the consequence of inherited inferiority. In the Revolution's aftermath, though, slaveown-

■ A sailor of African descent posed proudly for this portrait around 1790. Unfortunately, neither the name of the sailor nor the name of the artist is known today.   (Private collection, photograph courtesy of Hirschl & Adler Galleries, New York)

ers needed to defend holding other human beings in bondage against the notion that "all men are created equal." Consequently, they began to argue that people of African descent were less than fully human and that the principles of republican equality applied only to European Americans. In other words, to avoid having to confront the contradiction between their practice and the egalitarian implications of revolutionary theory, they redefined the theory so that it would not apply to African Americans.

Simultaneously, the very notion of "race" appeared in coherent form, applied to groups defined by skin color as "whites" and "blacks." The rise of egalitarian thinking among European Americans both downplayed status distinctions within their own group and differentiated all "whites" from people of color—Indians and African Americans. (That differentiation soon manifested itself in new miscegenation laws adopted in both northern and southern states to forbid intermarriage between whites and blacks or Indians.) Meanwhile, a generation or two of experience as slaves on American soil forged the identity "African" or "black" from the various ethnic and national affiliations of people who had survived the transatlantic crossing. Strikingly, among the first to term themselves "Africans" were oceanic sailors—men whose wide-ranging contacts with Europeans caused them to construct a unified (and separate) identity for themselves. Thus in the revolutionary era "whiteness" and "blackness"—along with the superiority of the former, the inferiority of the latter—developed as contrasting terms in tandem with each other.

Such racism had several intertwined elements. First came the assertion that, as Thomas Jefferson insisted in 1781, blacks were "inferior to the whites in the endowments both of body and mind." There followed the belief that blacks were congenitally lazy and disorderly, even though owners had often argued, conversely, that slaves were "natural" workers. (No one seemed to notice the inherent contradiction.) Third was the notion that all blacks were sexually promiscuous and that African American men lusted after European American women. The specter of interracial sexual intercourse involving black men and white women haunted early American racist thought. Significantly, the more common reverse circumstance—the sexual exploitation of enslaved women by their masters—aroused little comment or concern.

African Americans did not allow these developing racist notions to go unchallenged. Benjamin Banneker, a free black surveyor, astronomer, and mathematical genius, directly disputed Thomas Jefferson's belief in Africans' intellectual inferiority. In 1791 Banneker sent Jefferson a copy of his latest almanac (which included his astronomical calculations) as an example of blacks' mental powers. Jefferson's response admitted Banneker's intelligence but indicated that he regarded Banneker as exceptional; Jefferson insisted that he needed more evidence before he would change his mind.

At its birth, then, the republic was defined by its leaders as an exclusively white male enterprise. Indeed, some historians have argued that the

A REPUBLIC FOR WHITE MEN ONLY

subjugation of blacks and women was a necessary precondition for theoretical equality among white men. They have pointed out that identifying a common racial antagonist helped to create white solidarity and to lessen the threat to gentry power posed by the enfranchisement of poorer white men. Moreover, excluding women from the political realm preserved all power for men, specifically those of the "better sort." Some schol-

ars have pointed out that it was less dangerous to allow white men with little property to participate formally in politics than to open the possibility that they might join with former slaves to question the rule of elites. That was perhaps one reason why after the Revolution the division of American society between slave and free was transformed into a division between blacks—some of whom were free—and whites. The white male wielders of power ensured their continued dominance in part by substituting race for enslavement as the primary determinant of African Americans' status.

Designing Republican Governments

In May 1776, even before adoption of the Declaration of Independence, the Second Continental Congress directed states to devise new republican governments to replace the provincial congresses and committees that had met since 1774. Thus American men initially concentrated on drafting state constitutions and devoted little attention to their national government—an oversight they later had to remedy.

At the state level, political leaders immediately faced the problem of defining a "constitution." Americans wanted to create tangible documents specifying the fundamental structures of government, but at first legislators could not decide how to accomplish that goal. States eventually concluded that their constitutions should not be drafted by regular legislative bodies. Following the lead established by Vermont in 1777 and Massachusetts in 1780, they began to elect conventions for the sole purpose of drafting constitutions. Thus states sought direct authorization from the people—the theoretical sovereigns in a republic—before establishing new governments. After preparing new constitutions, delegates submitted them to voters for ratification.

STATE CONSTITUTIONS

The framers of state constitutions concerned themselves primarily with outlining the distribution of and limitations on government power—both crucial to the survival of republics. If authority was not confined within reasonable limits, the states might become tyrannical, as Britain had. Americans' experience with British rule permeated every provision of their new constitutions. States experimented with different solutions to the problems the framers perceived, and the early constitutions varied considerably in specifics while remaining broadly comparable in outline.

Under their colonial charters, Americans had learned to fear the power of the governor—usually, the appointed agent of the king or proprietor—and to see the legislature as their defender. Accordingly, the first state constitutions typically provided for the governor to be elected annually (commonly by the legislature), limited the number of terms he could serve, and gave him little independent authority. Simultaneously, the constitutions expanded the legislature's powers. Every state except Pennsylvania and Vermont retained a two-house structure, with members of the upper house having longer terms and being required to meet higher property-holding standards than members of the lower house. But they also redrew electoral districts to reflect population patterns more accurately, and they increased the number of members in both houses. Finally, most states lowered property qualifications for voting. As a result the legislatures came to include some members who before the war would not have been eligible to vote. Thus the revolutionary era witnessed the first deliberate attempt to broaden the base of American government, a process that has continued to the present day.

But the state constitutions' authors knew that governments designed to be responsive to the people would not necessarily provide sufficient protection if tyrants were elected to office. They consequently included explicit limitations on government authority in the documents they composed, attempting to protect what they regarded as the inalienable rights of individual citizens. Seven of the constitutions contained formal bills of rights, and the others had similar clauses. Most guaranteed citizens freedom of the press, the right to a fair trial, the right of consent to taxation, and protection against general search warrants. An independent judiciary was charged with upholding such rights. Most states also guaranteed freedom of religion, but with restrictions. For example, seven states required that all officeholders be Christians, and some continued to support churches with tax money. (Not until 1833 did Massachusetts become the last state to remove all vestiges of a religious establishment.)

LIMITING STATE GOVERNMENTS

In general, the constitution makers put greater emphasis on preventing state governments from becoming tyrannical than on making them effective wielders of political authority. Their approach to shaping governments was understandable, given the American experience with Great Britain. But establishing such weak political units, especially in wartime, practically ensured that the constitutions soon would need revision. Soon some states began to rewrite constitutions they had drafted in 1776 and 1777.

Invariably, the revised versions increased the powers of the governor and reduced the scope of the legislature's authority. In the mid-1780s, some American political leaders started to develop a theory of checks and balances as the primary means of controlling government power. (In the mid-1770s, constitutions prescribed powerful legislatures to ensure good government, but wartime experiences led many to conclude that such arrangements often failed.) Americans sought to balance the powers of the legislative, executive, and judicial branches against one another. The national constitution they drafted in 1787 also embodied that principle.

REVISING STATE CONSTITUTIONS

Yet the constitutional theories that Americans applied at the state level did not at first influence their conception of national government. Since American officials initially focused on organizing the military struggle against Britain, the powers and structure of the Continental Congress evolved by default early in the war. Not until late 1777 did Congress send the Articles of Confederation to the states for ratification, and those Articles simply wrote into law the unplanned arrangements of the Continental Congress.

The chief organ of national government was a unicameral (one-house) legislature in which each state had one vote. Its powers included conducting foreign relations, mediating disputes between states, controlling maritime affairs, regulating Indian trade, and valuing state and national coinage. The Articles did not give the national government the ability to raise revenue effectively or to enforce a uniform commercial policy. The United States of America was described as "a firm league of friendship" in which each state "retains its sovereignty, freedom and independence, and every Power, Jurisdiction and right, which is not by this confederation expressly delegated to the United States, in Congress assembled."

ARTICLES OF CONFEDERATION

The Articles required unanimous consent of state legislatures for ratification or amendment, and a clause concerning western lands proved troublesome. The draft accepted by Congress allowed states to retain all land claims derived from their original charters. But states with definite western boundaries in their charters (such as Maryland and New Jersey) wanted other states to cede to the national government their landholdings west of the Appalachian Mountains. Otherwise, they feared, states with large claims could expand and overpower their smaller neighbors. Maryland refused to accept the Articles until 1781, when Virginia finally promised to surrender its western holdings to national jurisdiction (see Map 7.1). Other states followed suit, establishing the principle that unorganized lands would be held by the nation as a whole.

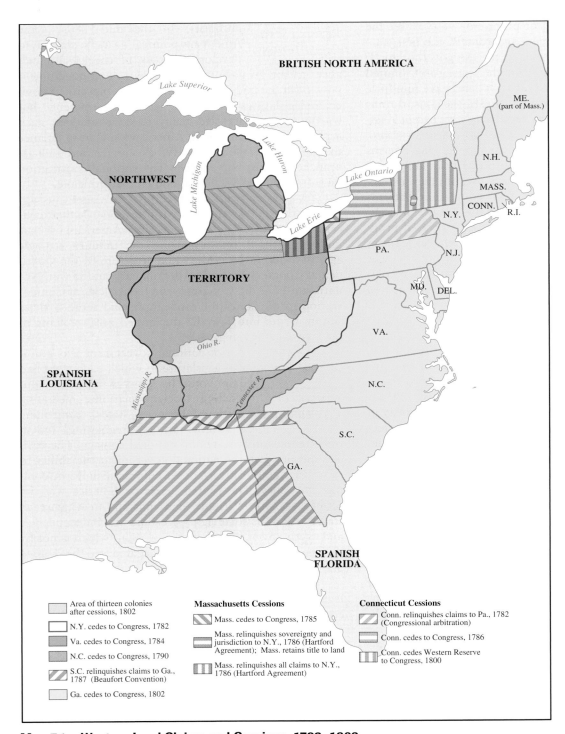

BRITISH NORTH AMERICA

Lake Superior

ME.
(part of Mass.)

N.H.

NORTHWEST

Lake Michigan

Lake Huron

Lake Ontario

MASS.

Lake Erie

CONN.

N.Y.

R.I.

PA.

N.J.

TERRITORY

MD.

DEL.

Ohio R.

VA.

SPANISH
LOUISIANA

Mississippi R.

Tennessee R.

N.C.

S.C.

GA.

SPANISH
FLORIDA

	Area of thirteen colonies after cessions, 1802
	N.Y. cedes to Congress, 1782
	Va. cedes to Congress, 1784
	N.C. cedes to Congress, 1790
	S.C. relinquishes claims to Ga., 1787 (Beaufort Convention)
	Ga. cedes to Congress, 1802

Massachusetts Cessions

	Mass. cedes to Congress, 1785
	Mass. relinquishes sovereignty and jurisdiction to N.Y., 1786 (Hartford Agreement); Mass. retains title to land
	Mass. relinquishes all claims to N.Y., 1786 (Hartford Agreement)

Connecticut Cessions

	Conn. relinquishes claims to Pa., 1782 (Congressional arbitration)
	Conn. cedes to Congress, 1786
	Conn. cedes Western Reserve to Congress, 1800

Map 7.1   Western Land Claims and Cessions, 1782–1802

After the United States achieved independence, states competed with each other for control of valuable lands to which they had possible claims under their original charters. That competition led to a series of compromises among the states or between individual states and the new nation, which are indicated on this map.

The capacity of a single state to delay ratification for three years portended the fate of American government under the Articles of Confederation. The unicameral legislature, whether it was called the Second Continental Congress (until 1781) or the Confederation Congress (thereafter), was too inefficient and unwieldy to govern effectively. The Articles' authors had not given adequate thought to the distribution of power within the national government or to the relationship between the Confederation and the states. The Congress they created was simultaneously a legislative body and a collective executive (there was no judiciary), but it had no independent income and no authority to compel the states to accept its rulings. Under the Articles, national government lurched from crisis to crisis. (See the Appendix for the text of the *Articles of Confederation.*)

Trials of the Confederation

inance posed the most persistent problem faced by both state and national governments. Because legislators at all levels levied taxes only reluctantly, both Congress and the states at first tried to finance the war simply by printing currency. Even though the money was backed only by good faith, it circulated freely and without excessive depreciation during 1775 and most of 1776. Demand for military supplies and civilian goods was high, stimulating trade (especially with France) and local production. Indeed, the amount of money issued in those years was probably no more than what a healthy economy required as a medium of exchange.

But in late 1776, as the American army suffered reverses in New York and New Jersey, prices began to rise and inflation set in. The currency's value rested on Americans' faith in their government, a faith that was sorely tested in the years that followed, especially during the dark days of British triumphs in the South (1779 and 1780). State governments fought inflation by controlling wages and prices and requiring acceptance of paper currency on an equal footing with hard money. States also borrowed funds, established lotteries, and even levied taxes. Their efforts were futile. So too was Congress's attempt to stop printing currency altogether and to rely solely on money contributed by the states. By early 1780 it took forty paper dollars to purchase one silver dollar. Soon, Continental currency was worthless (see Figure 7.1).

In 1781, faced with total collapse of the monetary system, the congressmen undertook ambitious reforms. After establishing a department of finance under the

FINANCIAL
AFFAIRS

Figure 7.1 Depreciation of Continental Currency, 1777–1780

The depreciation of Continental currency accelerated in 1778, as is shown in this graph measuring its value against one hundred silver dollars. Thereafter, its value dropped almost daily. (Source: Data from John J. McCusker, "How Much Is That in Real Money? A Historical Price Index for Use as a Deflator of Money Values in the Economy of the United States," *Proceedings of the American Antiquarian Society,* Vol. 101, Pt. 2 [1991], Table C-1.)

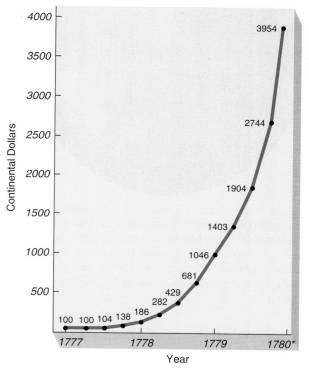

* Currency abandoned in April 1780

wealthy Philadelphia merchant Robert Morris, they asked the states to amend the Articles of Confederation to allow Congress to levy a duty of 5 percent on imported goods. Morris put national finances on a solid footing, but the customs duty was never adopted. First Rhode Island and then New York refused to agree to the tax. The states' resistance reflected fear of a too-powerful central government. As one worried citizen wrote in 1783, "If permanent Funds are given to Congress, the aristocratical Influence, which predominates in more than a major part of the United States, will fully establish an arbitrary Government." But states too needed revenue, and found it just as hard to come by. When they enacted new, heavy taxes after the war, farmers resisted their authority.

■ Because of their citizens' resistance to taxation, the early state governments found it hard to raise sufficient revenues. Some, like Massachusetts, turned to state-run lotteries to make up the shortfall. Here a New Englander proudly poses with a lottery ticket, demonstrating his support for the state.   (Milwaukee Art Museum Purchase, Layton Art Collection)

Because the Articles denied Congress the power to establish a national commercial policy, the realm of foreign trade also exposed the new government's weaknesses. Immediately after the war, Britain, France, and Spain restricted American trade with their colonies. Americans, who had hoped independence would bring about trade with all nations, were outraged but could do little to change matters. Members of Congress watched helplessly as British manufactured goods flooded the United States while American produce could no longer be sold in the British West Indies, once its prime market. Although Americans reopened commerce with other European countries and started a profitable trade with China in 1784, neither substituted for access to closer and larger markets.

FOREIGN AFFAIRS

Congress furthermore had difficulty dealing with the Spanish presence on the nation's southern and western borders. Determined to prevent the republic's expansion, Spain in 1784 closed the Mississippi River to American navigation, thereby depriving the growing settlements west of the Appalachians of their access to the Gulf of Mexico. Congress, through its Department of Foreign Affairs, opened negotiations with Spain in 1785, but even John Jay, one of the nation's most experienced diplomats, could not win the necessary concessions. The talks collapsed the following year after Congress divided sharply: southerners and westerners insisted on navigation rights on the Mississippi, whereas northerners were willing to abandon that claim in order to win commercial concessions in the West Indies. The impasse made some congressmen question the possibility of a national consensus on foreign affairs.

Provisions of the 1783 Treaty of Paris too caused serious problems. Article Four, which promised the repayment of prewar debts (most of them owed by Americans to British merchants), and Article Five, which recommended that states allow loyalists to recover their confiscated property, aroused considerable opposition. States passed laws denying British subjects the right to sue for recovery of debts or property in American courts, and town meetings decried the loyalists' return. As residents of Norwalk, Connecticut, put it, few Americans wanted to permit the "Tory Villains" to return "while filial Tears are fresh upon our Cheeks and our Murdered Brethren scarcely cold in their Graves." State governments also had reason to oppose enforcement of the treaty. Sales of loyalists' land, houses, and other possessions had helped finance the war. Since most of the purchasers were prominent patriots, states had no desire to raise questions about the legitimacy of their property titles.

PEACE TREATY PROVISIONS

The refusal of state and local governments to comply with Articles Four and Five gave Britain an excuse to maintain military posts on the Great Lakes long after its troops were supposed to have withdrawn. Furthermore, Congress's inability to convince states to implement the treaty disclosed its lack of power, even in an area—foreign affairs—in which it had authority under the Articles of Confederation. Concerned nationalists argued publicly that enforcement of the treaty, however unpopular, was a crucial test of the republic's credibility in foreign affairs. "Will foreign nations be willing to undertake anything with us or for us," asked Alexander Hamilton, "when they find that the nature of our governments will allow no dependence to be placed on our engagements?"

Order and Disorder in the West

ongressmen also confronted knotty problems when they considered the status of land beyond the Appalachians. Although British and American diplomats did not discuss tribal claims, the United States assumed that the Treaty of Paris cleared its title to all land east of the Mississippi except the area still held by Spain. Still, recognizing that land cessions should be obtained from the most powerful tribes, Congress initiated negotiations with both northern and southern Indians (see Map 7.2).

At Fort Stanwix, New York, in 1784, American diplomats negotiated a treaty with chiefs who said they represented the Iroquois; and at Hopewell, South Carolina, in late 1785 and early 1786, they did the same with emissaries from the Choctaw, Chickasaw, and Cherokee nations. In 1786 the Iroquois formally repudiated the Fort Stanwix treaty, denying that the men who attended the negotiations had been authorized to speak for the Six Nations. The confederacy threatened new attacks on frontier settlements, but everyone knew the threat was empty; the flawed treaty stood by default. At intervals until the end of the decade New York State purchased large tracts of land from individual Iroquois nations. By 1790 the once-dominant confederacy was confined to a few scattered reservations. In the South too the United States took the treaties as confirmation of its sovereignty, authorizing settlers to move onto the territories in question. European Americans poured over the southern Appalachians, provoking the Creeks—who had not agreed to the Hopewell treaties—to defend their territory by declaring war. Only in 1790 did they come to terms with the United States.

INDIAN RELATIONS

Western nations such as the Shawnees, Chippewas, Ottawas, and Potawatomis had already started to reject Iroquois hegemony as early as the 1750s (see page 118). After the collapse of Iroquois power, they formed their own confederacy and demanded direct negotiations with the United States. They intended to present a united front so as to avoid the piecemeal surrender of land by individual bands and villages. But they faced a difficult task. In the postwar world, Indian nations could no longer pursue the diplomatic strategy that had worked so well for so long: playing off European and American powers against one another. France was gone; Spanish territory lay far to the west and south; and British power was confined to Canada, north of the Great Lakes. Only the United States remained.

Map 7.2   Cession of Tribal Lands to the United States, 1775–1790

The land claims of the United States meant little as long as Indian nations still controlled vast territories within the new country's formal boundaries. A series of treaties in the 1780s and 1790s opened some lands to white settlement.
(Source: From Lester J. Cappon et al., eds., *Atlas of Early American History: The Revolutionary Era, 1760–1790.* Copyright © 1976 by Princeton University Press. Reprinted by permission of Princeton University Press.)

At first the national government ignored the western confederacy. Shortly after state land cessions were completed, Congress began to organize the Northwest Territory, bounded by the Mississippi River, the Great Lakes, and the Ohio River (see Map 7.1). Ordinances passed in 1784, 1785, and 1787 outlined the process through which the land could be sold to settlers and formal governments could be organized.

ORDINANCES OF 1784 AND 1785

■ In 1784 Thomas Jefferson proposed a scheme for organizing the new nation's western lands. His plan would have divided the region on a grid pattern, yielding fourteen new states (with names such as "Metropotamia" and "Pelisipia") composed of 10-mile-square "hundreds." After a year of debate, Jefferson's plan was replaced by the one adopted in the Land Ordinance of 1785, which is described in the text.   (Clements Library, University of Michigan)

To ensure orderly development, Congress in 1785 directed that the land be surveyed into townships 6 miles square, each divided into thirty-six sections of 640 acres (1 square mile). Revenue from the sale of the sixteenth section of each township was to be reserved for the support of public schools—the first instance of federal aid to education in American history. One dollar was the minimum price per acre; the minimum sale was one section. Thus Congress showed little concern for the small farmer: the resulting minimum outlay, $640, lay beyond the reach of ordinary Americans, except those veterans who received part of their army pay in land warrants. Proceeds from western land sales constituted the first independent revenues available to the national government.

The most important of the three land policies—the Northwest Ordinance of 1787—contained a bill of rights guaranteeing settlers freedom of religion and the right

NORTHWEST ORDINANCE to a jury trial, forbidding cruel and unusual punishments, and nominally prohibiting slavery. Eventually, that prohibition became an important symbol for antislavery northerners, but at the time it had little effect. Some residents of the territory already held slaves, and Congress did not intend to deprive them of their property. Moreover, the ordinance also contained a provision allowing slaveowners to "lawfully reclaim" runaway bondspeople who took refuge in the territory—the first national fugitive slave law. The ordinance prevented slavery from taking deep root by discouraging slaveholders from moving into the territory with their human chattel, but not until 1848 was enslavement abolished throughout the region, now known as the Old Northwest. And by omission Congress implied that slavery would be legal in the territories south of the Ohio River.

■ The two chief antagonists at the Battle of Fallen Timbers and negotiators of the Treaty of Greenville (1795). On the left, Little Turtle, the leader of the Miami Confederacy; on the right, General Anthony Wayne. Little Turtle, in a copy of a portrait painted two years later, appears to be wearing a miniature of Wayne on a bear-claw necklace.   (Left: Courtesy, Chicago Historical Society. Right: Independence National Historic Park)

The ordinance of 1787 also specified the process by which residents of the territory could organize state governments and seek admission to the Union "on an equal footing with the original States." Early in the nation's history, therefore, Congress laid down a policy of admitting new states on the same basis as the old and assuring residents of the territories the same rights held by citizens of the original states. Having suffered under the rule of a colonial power, congressmen understood the importance of preparing the new nation's first "colony" for eventual self-government. Nineteenth- and twentieth-century Americans were to be less generous in their attitudes toward residents of later territories, many of whom were non-European or non-Protestant. But the nation never fully lost sight of the egalitarian principles of the Northwest Ordinance.

In a sense, though, in 1787 the ordinance was purely theoretical. Miamis, Shawnees, and Delawares in the region refused to acknowledge American sovereignty. They opposed settlement violently, attacking unwary pioneers who ventured too far north of the Ohio River. In 1788 the Ohio Company, to which Congress had sold a large tract of land at reduced rates, established the town of Marietta at the juncture of the Ohio and Muskingum Rivers. But Indians prevented the company from extending settlement very far into the interior. After General Arthur St. Clair, the Northwest Territory's first governor, failed to negotiate a meaningful treaty with the Indians in early 1789, the United States could not avoid clashing with the western confederacy, composed of eight nations and led by the Miamis.

Little Turtle, the able war chief of the Miami Confederacy, defeated first General Josiah Harmar (1790) and then St. Clair himself (1791) in major battles near the present border between Indiana and Ohio. More than six hundred of St. Clair's men died, and scores more were wounded, in the United States's worst defeat in the entire history of the American frontier. In 1793 the Miami Confederacy declared that peace could

WAR IN THE OLD NORTHWEST

be achieved only if the United States recognized the Ohio River as its northwestern boundary. But the national government refused to relinquish its claims in the region. A new army under the command of General Anthony Wayne, a Revolutionary War hero, attacked and defeated the confederacy in August 1794 at the Battle of Fallen Timbers (near present-day Toledo, Ohio; see Map 7.2). Peace negotiations began after the victory.

By the summer of 1795, Wayne reached agreement with the Miami Confederacy. The Treaty of Greenville gave each side a portion of what it wanted. The United States gained the right to settle much of what was to become Ohio, the indigenous peoples retaining only the northwest corner of the region. Indians, though, received the acknowledgment they had long sought: American recognition of their rights to the soil. At Greenville, the United States formally accepted the principle of Indian sovereignty, by virtue of residence, over all lands the native peoples had not ceded. Never again would the United States government claim that it had acquired Indian territory solely through negotiation with a European or North American country.

The problems the United States encountered in ensuring safe settlement of the Northwest Territory revealed the basic weakness of the Confederation government. Not until after the Articles of Confederation were replaced with a new constitution could the United States muster sufficient force to implement the Northwest Ordinance. Thus, although the ordinance is often viewed as one of the few lasting accomplishments of the Confederation Congress, it must be seen within a context of political impotence.

From Crisis to the Constitution

*a*mericans involved in finance, overseas trade, and foreign affairs became acutely aware of the inadequacies of the Articles of Confederation. In those areas the Articles had obvious deficiencies: Congress could not levy taxes, nor could it impose its will on the states to establish a uniform commercial policy or to ensure the enforcement of treaties. Partly as a result, the American economy slid into a depression less than a year after war's end. Exporters of staple crops (especially tobacco and rice) and importers of manufactured goods suffered from the postwar restrictions European powers imposed on American commerce. Although recovery began by 1786, the war's effects proved impossible to erase, particularly in the Lower South. Some estimates suggest

that between 1775 and 1790 America's per capita gross national product declined by nearly 50 percent.

The war, indeed, wrought permanent change in the American economy. The near-total cessation of foreign commerce in nonmilitary items during the war stimulated domestic manufacturing. Consequently, despite the influx of European goods after 1783, the postwar period witnessed the stirrings of American industrial development.

ECONOMIC CHANGE AND COMMERCIAL REFORM

For example, the first American textile mill began production in Pawtucket, Rhode Island, in 1793. Because of continuing population growth, the domestic market assumed greater relative importance in the overall economy. Moreover, foreign trade patterns shifted from Europe and toward the West Indies, continuing a trend that had begun before the war. Foodstuffs shipped to the French and Dutch Caribbean islands became America's largest single export, replacing tobacco (and thus accelerating the Chesapeake's conversion from tobacco to grain production). South Carolina resumed importing slaves on a large scale, as planters sought to replace workers lost to wartime disruptions. Yet without British subsidies American indigo could not compete with that produced in the Caribbean, and even rice planters struggled to find new markets.

Recognizing the Confederation Congress's inability to deal with commercial matters, representatives of Virginia and Maryland met at Mt. Vernon (George Washington's plantation) in March 1785 to negotiate an agreement about trade on the Potomac River, which divided the two states for much of its length. The successful meeting led to an invitation to other states to discuss trade policy generally at a convention in Annapolis, Maryland. Although nine states named representatives to the meeting in September 1786, only five delegations attended. Those present realized that so few people could not have any significant impact on the political system. They issued a call for another convention, to be held in Philadelphia nine months later, "to devise such further provisions as shall . . . appear necessary to render the constitution of the federal government adequate to the exigencies of the Union."

The other states did not respond immediately. But then an armed rebellion in Massachusetts did what a polite invitation could not: convince doubters that reform was needed. Farmers from the western part of the state, many of them veterans, violently opposed the high taxes that had been levied by the east-

SHAYS'S REBELLION

ern-dominated legislature to pay off war debts. Courts had also begun to foreclose on the lands of tax defaulters. Daniel Shays, a former officer in the Continental Army, assumed the nominal leadership of the disgruntled western farmers. On January 25, 1787, he led about fifteen hundred men in an assault on the federal armory at Springfield, attempting to capture the military stores housed there. The militiamen mustered to defend the armory fired on their former comrades in arms, who then withdrew after suffering twenty-four casualties.

The westerners did not confine to the battlefield their challenge to the legitimacy of a government controlled by eastern merchants. Terming Massachusetts "tyranni-cal," they insisted that "whenever any encroachments are made either upon the liberties or properties of the people, if redress cannot be had without, it is virtue in them to disturb government." They thereby explicitly linked their rebellion to the earlier independence struggle.

Such explosive assertions convinced many political leaders that the nation's problems extended far beyond trade policy. To some, the rebellion confirmed the need for a much stronger federal government. After most of the states had already appointed delegates, the Confederation Congress belatedly endorsed the proposed convention, "for the sole and express purpose

CONSTITUTIONAL CONVENTION

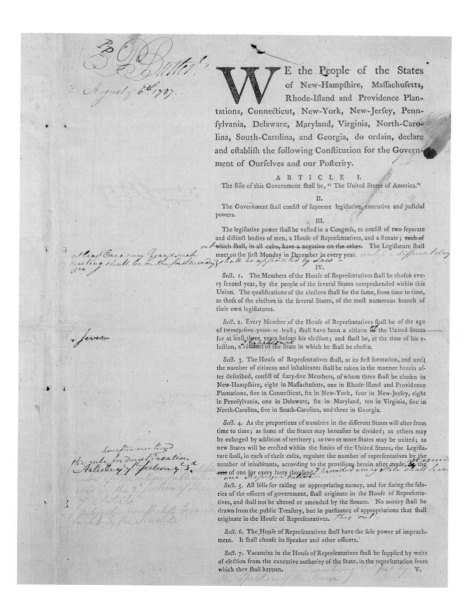

■ In August 1787 a first draft of the Constitution was secretly printed in Philadelphia for the use of convention members. Wide margins left room for additions and amendments, such as those made on this copy by the South Carolina delegate Pierce Butler. Note that in this early version the preamble does not yet read "We the people of the United States," but instead begins by listing the individual states. (The Gilder Lehrman Collection, © Collection of the New York Historical Society)

of revising the Articles of Confederation." In mid-May 1787, fifty-five men, representing all the states but Rhode Island, assembled in Philadelphia to begin their deliberations.

The vast majority of delegates to the Constitutional Convention were men of property and substance. They all favored reform; otherwise, they would not have come to Philadelphia. Most wanted to invigorate the national government and to give it new authority over taxation and foreign commerce. Many had been members of state legislatures, and some had helped to draft state constitutions. All were influenced in their Philadelphia deliberations by their understanding of the success or failure of those constitutions' provisions. Their ranks included merchants, planters, physicians, generals, governors, and especially lawyers—twenty-three had studied the law. Most had been born in America, and many came from families that had arrived in the seventeenth century. Most were Congregationalists, Presbyterians, or Angli-

■ James Madison (1751–1836), the youthful scholar and skilled politician who earned the title "Father of the Constitution." (Library of Congress)

cans. In an era when only a tiny proportion of the population had any advanced education, more than half of the delegates had attended college. A few had been educated in Britain, but most had graduated from American institutions: Princeton, with ten, counted the most alumni participants. The youngest delegate was twenty-six, the oldest—Benjamin Franklin—eighty-one. Like George Washington, whom they elected their presiding officer, most were in their vigorous middle years. A dozen men did the bulk of the convention's work. Of these, James Madison of Virginia was by far the most important; he deserves the title "Father of the Constitution."

The frail, shy James Madison was thirty-six years old in 1787. A Princeton graduate raised in western Virginia, he served on the local Committee of Safety and was elected successively to the provincial convention, the state's lower and upper houses, and the Continental Congress (1780–1783). Although Madison returned to Virginia to serve in the state legislature in 1784, he remained in touch with national politics, partly through his continuing correspondence with his close friend Thomas Jefferson. A promoter of the Annapolis Convention, he strongly supported its call for further reform.

MADISON AND THE CONSTITUTION

Madison stood out among the delegates for his systematic preparation for the Philadelphia meeting. Through Jefferson in Paris he bought more than two hundred books on history and government, carefully analyzing their accounts of past confederacies and republics. A month before the Constitutional Convention began, he summed up the results of his research in a lengthy paper entitled "Vices of the Political System of the United States." After listing the flaws he perceived in the current structure of the government (among them "encroachments by the states on the federal authority" and lack of unity "in matters where common interest requires it"), Madison revealed the conclusion that would guide his actions over the next few months. What the government most needed, he declared, was "such a modification of the sovereignty as will render it sufficiently neutral between the different interests and factions, to controul one part of the society from invading the rights of another, and at the same time sufficiently controuled itself, from setting up an interest adverse to that of the whole Society."

Thus Madison set forth the principle of checks and balances. The government, he believed, had to be constructed in such a way that it could not become tyrannical or fall wholly under the influence of a particular faction. He regarded the large size of a potential national republic as an advantage in that respect. Rejecting the common assertion that republics had to be small to survive, Madison asserted that a large, diverse republic should be preferred. Because the nation would include many different factions, no one of them would be able to control the government. Political stability would result from compromises among the contending parties.

The so-called Virginia Plan, introduced on May 29 by Edmund Randolph, embodied Madison's conception

VIRGINIA AND NEW JERSEY PLANS

of national government. The plan provided for a two-house legislature, the lower house elected directly by the people and the upper house selected by the lower; representation in both houses proportional to property or population; an executive elected by Congress; a national judiciary; and congressional veto over state laws. The Virginia Plan gave Congress the broad power to legislate "in all cases to which the separate states are incompetent." Had it been adopted intact, it would have created a government in which national authority reigned unchallenged and state power was greatly diminished. Proportional representation in both houses (however reckoned) would also have given large states a dominant voice in the national government.

The convention included many delegates who recognized the need for change but believed the Virginia Plan went too far in the direction of national consolidation. After two weeks of debate on Randolph's proposal, disaffected delegates—particularly those from small states—united under the leadership of William Paterson of New Jersey. On June 15 Paterson presented an alternative scheme, the New Jersey Plan, calling for strengthening the Articles rather than completely overhauling the government. Paterson proposed retaining a unicameral congress in which each state had an equal vote, but giving Congress new powers of taxation and trade regulation. Earlier Paterson had made his position clear in debate. Asserting that the Articles were "the proper basis of all the proceedings of the convention," he contended that the delegates' proper task was "to mark the orbits of the states with due precision and provide for the use of coercion" by the national government. Although the convention initially rejected Paterson's position, he and his allies won a number of victories in the months that followed.

The delegates began their work by discussing the structure and functions of Congress. They readily agreed that the new national government should have a two-

DEBATES OVER CONGRESS

house (bicameral) legislature. In addition, they concurred, in accordance with Americans' long-standing opposition to virtual representation (see pages 124–125), that "the people" (however that term was defined) should be directly represented in at least one house of Congress. But they discovered that they differed widely in their answers to three key questions: Should representation in both houses of Congress be proportional to population? How was representation in either or both houses to be apportioned among the states? And, finally, how were the members of the two houses to be elected?

The last issue proved the easiest to resolve. To quote John Dickinson, the delegates thought it "essential" that members of the lower branch of Congress be elected directly by the people and "expedient" that members of the upper house be chosen by state legislatures. Since legislatures had selected delegates to the Confederation Congress, they would expect a similar privilege in the new government. If the convention had not agreed to allow state legislatures to elect senators, the Constitution would have run into significant opposition among state political leaders. The plan also had the virtue of placing the election of one house of Congress one step removed from the "lesser sort," whose judgment the wealthy convention delegates did not wholly trust.

The possibility of representation proportional to population in the Senate caused considerably greater disagreement. The delegates accepted without much debate the principle of proportional representation in the House of Representatives. But small states, through their spokesman Luther Martin of Maryland, argued for equal representation in the Senate. Such a scheme, they rightly supposed, would give them relatively more power at the national level. Large states, on the other hand, supported a proportional plan, for they would then be allotted more votes in the upper house. For weeks the convention deadlocked, neither side able to obtain a majority. A committee appointed to work out a compromise recommended equal representation in the Senate, coupled with a proviso that all appropriation bills originate in the lower house. But not until the convention accepted a suggestion that a state's two senators vote as individuals rather than as a unit was a breakdown averted.

The remaining critical question divided the nation along sectional lines rather than by size of state: how was representation in the lower house to be

SLAVERY AND THE CONSTITUTION

apportioned among states? Delegates concurred that a census should be conducted every ten years to determine the nation's actual population, and they agreed that Indians who paid no taxes should be excluded for purposes of representation. Delegates from states with large numbers of slaves wanted African and European inhabitants to be counted equally; delegates from states with few slaves wanted only free people counted. Slavery thus became inextricably linked to the foundation of the new government. Delegates resolved the dispute by using a formula developed by the Confederation Congress in 1783 to allocate financial assessments among states: three-fifths of slaves would be included in population totals. (The formula reflected delegates' judgment that slaves were less efficient producers of wealth than free people, not that they were 60 percent human and 40 percent property.) The three-fifths compromise on representation won unanimous approval. Only two delegates, Gouverneur Morris of New York and George Mason of Virginia, later spoke out against the institution of slavery.

Although the words *slave* and *slavery* do not appear in the Constitution (the framers used euphemisms such as "other persons"), the document contained both direct and indirect protections for slavery. The three-fifths clause, for example, assured white southern male voters not only congressional representation out of proportion to their numbers but also a disproportionate influence on the selection of the president, since the number of each state's votes in the electoral college (see below) was determined by the size of its congressional delegation. In return for southerners' agreement that commercial regulations could be adopted by a simple majority vote in Congress (rather than two-thirds), New Englanders agreed that Congress could not end the importation of slaves for at least twenty years. Further, the fugitive slave clause required all states to return runaways to their masters. By guaranteeing that the national government would aid any states threatened with "domestic violence," the Constitution promised aid in putting down future slave revolts, as well as incidents like Shays's Rebellion.

Once delegates agreed on the knotty, conjoined problems of slavery and representation, they readily achieved consensus on the other issues confronting them. All concurred that the national government needed the authority to tax and to regulate commerce. But instead of giving Congress the nearly unlimited scope proposed in the Virginia Plan, delegates enumerated congressional powers and then provided for flexibility by granting it all authority "necessary and proper" to carry out those

CONGRESSIONAL AND PRESIDENTIAL POWERS

powers. Discarding the congressional veto contained in the Virginia Plan, the convention implied but did not explicitly authorize a national judicial veto of state laws. The Constitution plus national laws and treaties would constitute "the supreme law of the land; and the judges in every state shall be bound thereby," Article VI declared ambiguously. As another means of circumscribing state powers, delegates drafted a long list of actions forbidden to states. And—contrary to many state constitutions—they provided that religious tests could never be required of U.S. officeholders.

The convention placed primary responsibility for conducting foreign affairs in the hands of the president, who was also designated commander-in-chief of the armed forces. That decision raised the question, left unspecified in the Constitution's text, of whether the president (or Congress, for that matter) acquired special powers in times of war. With the consent of the Senate, the president could appoint judges and other federal officers. To select the president, delegates established an elaborate mechanism, the electoral college, whose members would be chosen in each state by legislatures or qualified voters. This system, they hoped, would ensure that the executive would be independent of the national legislature—and of the people. They also agreed that the chief executive should serve a four-year term but be eligible for reelection.

The final document still showed signs of its origins in the Virginia Plan, but compromises created a system of government less powerful at the national level than Madison and Randolph had envisioned. The key to the Constitution was the distribution of political authority—that is, separation of powers among executive, legislative, and judicial branches of the national government, and division of powers between states and nation. Two-thirds of Congress and three-fourths of the states, for example, had to concur on amendments. The branches balanced one another, their powers deliberately entwined to prevent each from acting independently. The president could veto congressional legislation, but that veto could be overridden by two-thirds majorities in both houses, and his treaties and major appointments required the Senate's consent. Congress could impeach the president and federal judges, but courts appeared to have the final say on interpreting the Constitution. These checks and balances would make it difficult for the government to become tyrannical. At the same time, though, the elaborate system would sometimes prevent the government from acting quickly and decisively. Furthermore, the Constitution drew such a vague line between state and national powers that the United States fought a civil war in the next century over that very issue.

The convention held its last session on September 17, 1787. Of the forty-two delegates present (others had returned home weeks earlier), only three refused to sign the Constitution, two of them in part because of the lack of a bill of rights. Benjamin Franklin had written a speech calling for unity; because his weak voice could not be heard, another delegate read it for him. "I confess that there are several parts of this constitution which I do not at present approve," Franklin admitted. Yet he urged its acceptance "because I expect no better, and because I am not sure, that it is not the best." Only then was the Constitution made public. The convention's proceedings had been entirely secret—and remained so until the delegates' private notes were published in the nineteenth century. (See the Appendix for the full text of the Constitution.)

Opposition and Ratification

*L*ater the same month, the Confederation Congress submitted the Constitution to the states but did not formally recommend approval. The ratification clause provided for the new system to take effect once it was approved by special conventions in at least nine states, with delegates being elected by qualified voters. Thus the national Constitution, unlike the Articles of Confederation, would rest directly on popular authority (and the presumably hostile state legislatures would be circumvented).

As states began to elect delegates to the special conventions, discussion of the proposed government grew more heated. Newspaper essays and pamphlets vigorously defended or attacked the Philadelphia convention's decisions. The extent of the debate was unprecedented. Every newspaper in the country printed the full text of the Constitution, and most supported its adoption. It quickly became apparent, though, that disputes within the Constitutional Convention had been mild compared to divisions of opinion within the populace as a whole. Although most citizens concurred that the national government should have more power over taxation and foreign commerce, some believed that the proposed government held the potential for tyranny. As happened in Carlisle, Pennsylvania, the vigorous debate between the two sides frequently spilled out into the streets.

Those supporting the proposed Constitution called themselves Federalists. They built on the notions of

FEDERAL HALL·

LET Trumpets found, and fwift wing'd Fame,
Thefe glorious tidings far proclaim ;
On Virtue's bafe, by Wifdom plann'd ;
And rear'd by Union's facred hand ;
The FEDERAL DOME, is rais'd fublime :
Its PILLARS folid, ftrong as time ;
Rife ! Commerce ! rife ! unfurl the fail,
Rich Golden harvefts blefs the vale :
Arts ! Science ! Genius ! fpring to light ;
And Freedom burft on realms of Night

■ *The Federal Almanack* for 1789 trumpeted the virtues of the new Constitution. Not all Americans were so certain that the national government, here symbolized as an edifice supported by thirteen pillars, was as "solid, strong as time" as the printer proclaimed. (American Antiquarian Society)

FEDERALISTS AND ANTIFEDERALISTS

classical republicanism, holding forth a vision of a virtuous, collectivist, self-sacrificing republic vigorously led by a manly aristocracy of talent. Claiming that the nation did not need to fear centralized authority when good men drawn from the elite were in charge, they argued that the carefully structured government would preclude the possibility of tyranny. A republic could be large, they declared, if the government's design prevented any one group from controlling it. The separation of powers among legislative, executive, and judicial branches, and the division of powers between states and nation, would accomplish that goal. Thus people did not need to be protected from the powers of the new government in a formal way. Instead, their liberties would be guarded by "distinguished worthies"— men of the "better sort" whose only goal (said George Washington) was "to merit the approbation of good and virtuous men."

The Federalists termed those who opposed the Constitution Antifederalists, thus casting them with a negative tag. Antifederalists, while recognizing the need for a national source of revenue, feared a too-powerful central government. They saw the states as the chief protectors of individual rights; consequently, weakening the states could bring the onset of arbitrary power. Antifederalist arguments against the Constitution often consisted of lists of potential abuses of government authority.

Heirs of the Real Whig ideology of the late 1760s and early 1770s, Antifederalists stressed the need for constant popular vigilance to avert oppression. Indeed, some of the Antifederalists had originally promulgated those ideas—Samuel Adams, Patrick Henry, and Richard Henry Lee led the opposition to the Constitution. Such older Americans, whose political opinions had been shaped prior to the centralizing, nationalistic Revolution, peopled the Antifederalist ranks. Joining them were small farmers preoccupied with guarding their property against excessive taxation, backcountry Baptists and Presbyterians, and ambitious, upwardly mobile men who would benefit from an economic and political system less tightly controlled than that the Constitution envisioned. Federalists denigrated such men as disorderly, licentious, and even "unmanly" and "boyish" because they would not follow the elites' lead in supporting the Constitution.

As public debate continued, Antifederalists focused on the Constitution's lack of a bill of rights. Even if the new system weakened the states, critics believed, people could still be protected from tyranny by specific guarantees of rights. The Constitution did contain some prohibitions on congressional power. For example, the writ of habeas corpus, which prevented arbitrary imprisonment, could not be suspended except in dire emergencies. But Antifederalists found such constitutional provisions to be few and inadequate. Nor were they reassured by Federalist assertions that the new government could not violate

BILL OF RIGHTS

people's rights because it had only limited powers. Opponents wanted the national governing document to incorporate a bill of rights, as had most state constitutions.

Letters of a Federal Farmer, perhaps the most widely read Antifederalist pamphlet, listed the rights that should be protected: freedom of the press and religion, trial by jury, and guarantees against unreasonable searches. From Paris, Thomas Jefferson added his voice to the chorus. Replying to Madison's letter conveying a copy of the Constitution, Jefferson declared, "I like much the general idea" but not "the omission of a bill of rights. . . . A bill of rights is what the people are entitled to against every government on earth, general or particular, and what no just government should refuse, or rest on inference."

As state conventions considered ratification, the lack of a bill of rights loomed ever larger as a flaw in the proposed government. Four of the first five states to ratify did so unanimously, but serious disagreements then surfaced. Massachusetts, in which Antifederalist forces had been bolstered by a backlash against the state government's heavy-handed treatment of the Shays rebels, ratified by a majority of only 19 votes out of 355 cast. In June 1788, when New Hampshire ratified, the requirement of nine states was satisfied. But New York and Virginia had not yet voted, and everyone realized the new Constitution could not succeed unless those key states accepted it.

RATIFICATION

Despite a valiant effort by the Antifederalist Patrick Henry, pro-Constitution forces won by 10 votes in the Virginia convention. In New York, James Madison, John Jay, and Alexander Hamilton campaigned for ratification by publishing *The Federalist,* a political tract that explained the theory behind the Constitution and masterfully answered its critics. Their reasoned arguments, coupled with Federalists' promise to add a bill of rights to the Constitution, helped win the battle. On July 26, 1788, New York ratified the Constitution by the slim margin of 3 votes. Although the last states—North Carolina and Rhode Island—did not join the Union until November 1789 and May 1790, respectively, the new government was a reality.

Americans in many cities celebrated ratification (somewhat prematurely) with a series of parades on July 4, 1788. The carefully planned processions dramatized the history and symbolized the unity of the new nation, seeking to counteract memories of the dissent that had so recently engulfed such towns as Carlisle, Pennsylvania. Like pre-Revolution protest

CELEBRATING RATIFICATION

■ The Philadelphia State House (the building now known as Independence Hall, but without its familiar tower), on the left; and, to its right, Congress Hall, where Congress met when Philadelphia served as the U.S. capital. Portrayed in front of the state house in this 1792 watercolor is the 33-foot-long vessel *Union,* an elaborately constructed ship carried through the city streets in the grand ratification parade of July 4, 1788.   (Philadelphia Museum of Art, Lent by the Dietrich American Foundation)

meetings, the parades served as political lessons for literate and illiterate Americans alike. The processions aimed to educate men and women about the significance of the new Constitution and to instruct them about political leaders' hopes for industry and frugality on the part of a virtuous American public.

Symbols expressing those goals filled the Philadelphia parade, planned by the artist Charles Willson Peale. About five thousand people participated in the procession, which featured floats portraying such themes as "The Grand Federal Edifice" and stretched for a mile and a half. Marchers representing the first pioneers and Revolutionary War troops paraded with groups of farmers and artisans dramatizing their work. More than forty groups of tradesmen, including barbers, hatters, printers, cloth manufacturers, and clockmakers, sponsored floats. Lawyers, doctors, clergymen of all denominations, and

congressmen followed the artisans. A final group of marchers symbolized the nation's future: students from the University of Pennsylvania and other city schools bore a flag labeled "The Rising Generation."

Summary

During the 1770s and 1780s the nation took shape as a political union. It began to develop an economy independent of the British Empire and attempted to chart its own course in the world in order to protect the national interest, defend the country's borders, and promote beneficial trade. Some Americans prescribed rules for the cultural and intellectual life they thought appropriate for a republic, outlining artistic and educational goals for a properly virtuous people. An integral part of the formation of the Union was the systematic formulation of American racist thought. Emphasizing race (rather than status as slave or free) as a determinant of African Americans' standing in the nation, and defining women as nonpolitical, allowed men who now termed themselves "white" to define republicanism to exclude all people but themselves and to ensure that they would dominate the country for the foreseeable future.

The experience of fighting a war and of struggling for survival as an independent nation altered the political context of American life in the 1780s. At the outset of the war, most Americans believed that "that government which governs best governs least," but by the late 1780s many had changed their minds. They were the drafters and supporters of the Constitution, who concluded from the republic's vicissitudes under the Articles of Confederation that a more powerful central government was needed. During ratification debates they contended that their proposals were just as "republican" in conception (if not more so) as the Articles.

Both sides concurred in a general adherence to republican principles, but they emphasized different views of republicanism. Federalists advanced a position based on the principles of classical republicanism, stressing the community over the individual. Antifederalists, fearing that elected leaders would not subordinate personal gain to the good of the whole, wanted a weak central government, formal protection of individual rights, and a loosely regulated economy. The Federalists won their point when the Constitution was adopted, however narrowly. The process of consolidating the states into a national whole was thereby formalized. The 1790s, the first decade of government under the Constitution, would witness hesitant steps toward the creation of a true nation, the United States of America.

LEGACY FOR A PEOPLE AND A NATION
Women's Education

Women today constitute a majority of the students enrolled in U.S. colleges and universities. Because women were denied all access to collegiate education in this country until the middle of the nineteenth century, that is a remarkable development. Moreover, it differentiates the United States from other nations, where the majority of university students are male. The origins of women's higher education lie deep, in the republican ideology of the 1770s and 1780s.

Once the United States had established republican forms of government at both state and national levels, its citizens began to worry about sustaining those governments—thought to be fragile and easily disrupted—for the decades and centuries to come. The future, everyone knew, lay in the hands of the nation's children, especially its sons. And theorists concluded that those sons could successfully perpetuate the republic only if they learned the lessons of patriotism from their mothers. Male and female reformers therefore began to contend that women in the United States should be better educated than those who lived under other forms of government. If American women were ignorant of the nation's history or principles of government, or if they did not know enough basic reading or arithmetic to assist their husbands in running farms or businesses, the republic was doomed to collapse. Mary Wollstonecraft made a similar argument on behalf of women's education in England, but without the rationale of republicanism, her words had little impact.

Some American reformers founded private academies (roughly equivalent to modern high schools) to teach young women from leading families such subjects as history, geography, mathematics, and languages. Some of the women who attended those academies later started educational establishments of their own—including Mary Lyon, who in 1837 founded Mt. Holyoke College in western Massachusetts, the first institution of higher education for women in the

United States. A few years later, some colleges for men (such as Oberlin, in Ohio) and state universities (for example, Michigan) admitted women as students, and a number of women's colleges were established. Not until the second half of the twentieth century, however, did American women gain truly equal access to higher education. In the 1970s such Ivy League universities as Yale and Princeton finally opened their doors to women students, and others (such as Cornell) that had restricted women's enrollment through quotas removed all constraints.

Along with the existence of the nation itself, increased educational opportunity for women is therefore one of the most important legacies of the revolutionary era for the American people.

The **history companion** *powered by Eduspace®*

Your primary source for interactive quizzes, exercises, and more to help you learn efficiently.
http://history.college.hmco.com/students

THE EARLY REPUBLIC: CONFLICTS AT HOME AND ABROAD 1789–1800

*I*n the last months of 1798, the wealthy Philadelphia matron Deborah Norris Logan became the target of widespread public criticism. Her husband, the Jefferson supporter Dr. George Logan, had undertaken a personal peace mission to France, fearing the looming prospect of war between the United States and its former ally. In his absence his wife loyally defended her husband's actions, and she in turn had to endure a campaign unlike any an American woman had ever previously experienced. That such an episode could occur at all suggested simultaneously the political symbolism now embodied by women, the growing division between the factions known as Federalists and Democratic-Republicans, and the significance of foreign affairs in the early republic.

First to attack was "Peter Porcupine," the Federalist newspaper editor William Cobbett, who observed with sly sexual innuendo in his *Porcupine's Gazette* in July that "it is said that JEFFERSON went to his friend Doctor Logan's farm and spent three days there, soon after the Doctor's departure for France. *Query:* What did he do there? Was it to arrange the Doctor's *valuable manuscripts?*" Later Cobbett suggested that both George and Deborah Logan should be placed in a pillory and publicly shamed for their actions—him, presumably, for treason (for that was the crime of which Federalists accused him) and her, Cobbett implied, for adultery. Understanding the symbolic significance of women's virtuous conduct in the fragile young republic, Democratic-Republican newspapers leaped to Deborah's defense. They attacked the vulgarity of the suggestions about her and Vice President Jefferson and insisted that not even a corrupt Londoner could have written "a greater libel upon public virtue or national morals."

Deborah Logan remained resolute in the face of such publicity. Although at first she secluded herself at her country estate, on Jefferson's advice she returned

◀ George and Deborah Logan, whose activities caused so much political controversy in 1798. Their elegant house, Stenton, where Jefferson visited her in her husband's absence, is still preserved as a historic site. (Left: Historical Society of Pennsylvania. Collection Atwater Kent Museum of Philadelphia. Right: Courtesy of the National Society of Colonial Dames of America in the Commonwealth of Pennsylvania at Stenton, Philadelphia)

CHRONOLOGY

1789 • Washington inaugurated as first president
- Judiciary Act of 1789 organizes federal court system
- French Revolution begins

1790 • Hamilton's *Report on Public Credit* proposes assumption of state debts

1791 • First ten amendments (Bill of Rights) ratified
- First national bank chartered

1793 • France declares war on Britain, Spain, and the Netherlands
- Washington's neutrality proclamation keeps the United States out of war
- Democratic-Republican societies founded, the first grassroots political organizations

1794 • Whiskey Rebellion in western Pennsylvania protests taxation

1795 • Jay Treaty with England
- Pinckney's Treaty with Spain

1796 • First contested presidential election: Adams elected president, Jefferson vice president

1798 • XYZ affair arouses American opinion against France
- Sedition Act penalizes dissent
- Virginia and Kentucky Resolutions protest suppression of dissent

1798–99 • Quasi-War with France

1800 • Franco-American Convention ends Quasi-War
- Gabriel's Rebellion threatens Virginia slaveowners

to Philadelphia to prove to the world George's "innocence and honor" and to show that she was "not afraid nor ashamed to meet the public eye." As reports emerged that her husband had been cordially received by French leaders, and that he had had some success in quelling hostilities, she reveled in the praise subsequently showered on him, later recalling that "almost every day, wishes for his safety and speedy return greeted my ears." George Logan was indeed enthusiastically welcomed home, at least by Jeffersonian partisans. Congress, controlled by Federalists, was less impressed. In January 1799 it adopted the so-called Logan Act, still in effect, which forbids private citizens from undertaking diplomatic missions.

The controversy caused by the Logans' actions was but one of many such battles in the 1790s. The fight over ratifying the Constitution turned out to presage an even wider division over the major political, economic, and diplomatic questions confronting the young republic: the extent to which authority (especially fiscal authority) should be centralized in the national government; the relationship of national power and states' rights; the formulation of foreign policy in an era of continual warfare in Europe; and the limits of dissent. Americans did not anticipate the acrimonious disagreements that rocked the 1790s. Believing that the Constitution would resolve the problems that had arisen under the Confederation, they mistakenly expected the new government to rule largely by consensus. And no one predicted the difficulties that would develop as the United States attempted to deal with Indian nations now wholly encompassed within its borders.

Most important of all, perhaps, Americans could not understand or fully accept the division of the nation's political leaders into two factions (not yet political parties), believing that only monarchies should experience such factional disputes. In republics, they believed, the rise of factions signified decay and corruption. As the decade closed, Americans still had not come to terms with the implications of partisan politics. ■

Building a Workable Government

*a*t first consensus appeared possible, as the nationalistic spirit expressed in the processions celebrating ratification of the Constitution carried over to the first session of Congress. Only a few Antifederalists ran for office in the congressional elections held late in 1788, and even fewer were elected. Thus the First Congress consisted chiefly of men who supported a strong national government. The drafters of the Constitution had deliberately left many key issues undecided, so the nationalists' domination of Congress meant that their views on those points quickly prevailed.

Congress faced four immediate tasks when it convened in April 1789: raising revenue to support the new government, responding to states' calls for a bill of rights, setting up executive departments, and organizing the federal judiciary. The last task was especially important. The Constitution established a Supreme Court but left it to Congress to decide whether to have other federal courts as well.

FIRST CONGRESS

James Madison, who had been elected to the House of Representatives, soon became as influential in Congress as he had been at the Constitutional Convention. A few months into the first session, he persuaded Congress to adopt the Revenue Act of 1789, imposing a 5 percent tariff on certain imports. Thus the First Congress quickly achieved what the Confederation Congress never had: an effective national tax law. The new government would have problems in its first years, but lack of revenue was not one of them.

Madison also took the lead with respect to constitutional amendments. At the convention and thereafter, he had consistently opposed additional limitations on the national government. He believed it unnecessary to guarantee people's rights explicitly when the government was one of limited powers. But Madison recognized that Congress should respond to public opinion as expressed in state ratifying conventions. Accordingly, he placed nineteen proposed amendments before the House. The states soon ratified ten, which officially became part of the Constitution on December 15, 1791 (see the Appendix for the Constitution and all amendments, including the Twenty-seventh, which was one of Madison's nineteen). Their adoption defused Antifederalist opposition and rallied support for the new government.

BILL OF RIGHTS

The First Amendment specifically prohibited Congress from passing any law restricting the right to freedom of religion, speech, press, peaceable assembly, or petition. The next two amendments arose directly from the former colonists' fear of standing armies as a threat to freedom. The Second Amendment guaranteed the right "to keep and bear arms" because of the need for a "well-regulated Militia." Thus the constitutional right to bear arms was based on the expectation that most able-bodied men would serve the nation as citizen-soldiers, and there would be little need for a standing army. The Third Amendment limited the conditions under which troops could be quartered in private homes. The next five pertained to judicial procedures. The Fourth Amendment prohibited "unreasonable searches and seizures"; the Fifth and Sixth established the rights of accused persons; the Seventh specified the conditions for jury trials in civil (as opposed to criminal) cases; and the Eighth forbade "cruel and unusual punishments." The Ninth and Tenth Amendments reserved to the people and the states other unspecified rights and powers. In short, the amendments' authors made clear that, in listing some rights, they did not mean to preclude the exercise of others.

While debating proposed amendments, Congress also considered the organization of the executive branch. It readily agreed to continue the three administrative departments established under the Articles of Confederation: War, Foreign Affairs (renamed State), and Treasury. Congress instituted two lesser posts: the attorney general—the nation's official lawyer—and the postmaster general. Controversy arose over whether the president alone could dismiss officials whom he originally had appointed with the Senate's consent. After some debate, the House and Senate agreed that he had such authority. Thus was established the important principle that the heads of executive departments are accountable solely to the president.

EXECUTIVE AND JUDICIARY

Aside from constitutional amendments, the most far-reaching piece of legislation enacted by the First Congress was the Judiciary Act of 1789, which defined the jurisdiction of the federal judiciary and established a six-member Supreme Court, thirteen district courts, and three circuit courts of appeal. Its most important provision, Section 25, allowed appeals from state courts to federal courts when cases raised certain types of constitutional issues. Section 25 thus implemented Article VI of the Constitution, which stated that federal laws and treaties were to be considered "the supreme Law of the Land." For Article VI to be enforced uniformly, the national judiciary had to be able to overturn state court decisions in cases involving the Constitution, federal laws, or treaties. Yet nowhere did the Constitution explicitly permit such action by federal courts. The Judiciary Act of 1789 presumed that the wording of Article VI implied the right of appeal from state to federal courts. In the nineteenth century, however, judges and legislators committed to states' rights challenged that interpretation.

During its first decade, the Supreme Court handled few cases of any importance, and several members resigned. (John Jay, the first chief justice, served only six years.) But in a significant 1796 decision, *Ware v. Hylton*, the Court for the first time declared a state law unconstitutional. That same year it also reviewed the constitutionality of an act of Congress, upholding its validity in the case of *Hylton v. U.S.* The most important case of the decade, *Chisholm v. Georgia* (1793), established that states could be sued in federal courts by citizens of other states. This decision, unpopular with state governments, was overturned five years later by the Eleventh Amendment to the Constitution.

Despite the constitutional provisions forbidding Congress from prohibiting the importation of slaves for twenty years, in early 1790 three groups of Quakers submitted petitions to Congress calling for an end to the foreign slave trade and favoring abolition in general. In the ensuing debates, the nation's first political leaders directly addressed the questions they had suppressed in euphemisms in the Constitution itself. Southerners vigorously asserted that not only should Congress reject the petitions, it should not even *discuss* them seriously. Had southern states thought that the federal government would consider interfering with the institution of slavery, their congressmen argued, they would never have ratified the Constitution. The legislators went on to develop a positive defense of slavery that presaged almost all the arguments offered on the subject during the next seven decades, insisting that slavery formed an integral part of the Union and that abolition would cause more problems than it solved, primarily by confronting the nation with the question of how to deal with a sizable population of freed people.

DEBATE OVER SLAVERY

Some northern congressmen—and, in his last published essay, Benjamin Franklin—contested the southerners' position, but a consensus soon emerged to quash such discussions in the future. Congress accepted a committee report denying it the power either to halt the slave trade before 1808 or to effect the emancipation of any slaves at any time, that authority "remaining with the several States alone." The precedent thereby established held until the Civil War.

Domestic Policy Under Washington and Hamilton

George Washington did not seek the presidency. In 1783 he returned to Mount Vernon eager for the peaceful life of a Virginia planter. But his fellow countrymen never regarded Washington as just another private citizen. Unanimously elected to preside at the Constitutional Convention, he did not participate in debates but consistently voted for a strong national government. After the adoption of the new governmental structure, Americans concurred that only George Washington had sufficient stature to serve as the republic's first president, an office designed largely with him in mind. The unanimous vote of the electoral college merely formalized that consensus.

Reluctant to return to public life, George Washington nevertheless knew he could not ignore his country's call. Awaiting the summons to New York City, the nation's capital, he wrote to an old friend, "My movements to the chair of Government will be accompanied by feelings not unlike those of a culprit who is going to the place of his execution. . . . I am sensible, that I am embarking the voice of my Countrymen and a good name of my own, on this voyage, but what returns will be made for them, Heaven alone can foretell."

Washington acted cautiously during his first months in office in 1789, knowing that whatever he did would set precedents for the future. When the title by which he should be addressed aroused controversy (Vice President John Adams favored "His Highness, the President of the United States of America, and Protector of their Liberties"), Washington said nothing. The accepted title soon became a plain "Mr. President." By using the heads of the executive departments collectively as his chief advisers, he created the cabinet. As the Constitution required, he sent Congress an annual State of the Union message. Washington also concluded that he should exercise his veto power over congressional legislation very sparingly—only, indeed, if he became convinced a bill was unconstitutional.

WASHINGTON'S FIRST STEPS

Early in his term, Washington undertook elaborately organized journeys to all the states. At each stop, he was ritually welcomed by uniformed militia units, young women strewing flowers in his path, local leaders, groups of Revolutionary War veterans, and respectable

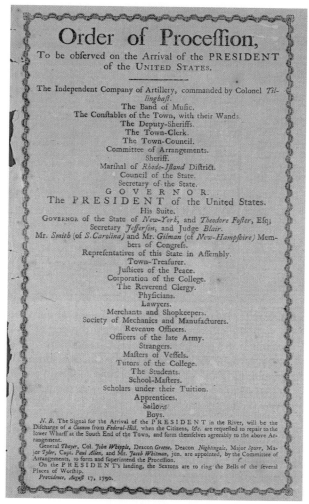

Order of Proceſſion,

To be obſerved on the Arrival of the PRESIDENT
of the UNITED STATES.

The Independent Company of Artillery, commanded by Colonel *Til-
lingaſt*.
The Band of Muſic.
The Conſtables of the Town, with their Wands.
The Deputy-Sheriffs.
The Town-Clerk.
The Town-Council.
Committee of Arrangements.
Sheriff.
Marſhal of *Rhode-Iſland* Diſtrict.
Council of the State.
Secretary of the State.
G O V E R N O R.
The P R E S I D E N T of the United States.
His Suite.
GOVERNOR of the State of *New-York*, and *Theodore Foſter*, Eſq;
Secretary *Jefferſon*, and Judge *Blair*.
Mr. *Smith* (of *S. Carolina*) and Mr. *Gilman* (of *New-Hampſhire*) Mem-
bers of Congreſs.
Repreſentatives of this State in Aſſembly.
Town-Treaſurer.
Juſtices of the Peace.
Corporation of the College.
The Reverend Clergy.
Phyſicians.
Lawyers.
Merchants and Shopkeepers.
Society of Mechanics and Manufacturers.
Revenue Officers.
Officers of the late Army.
Strangers.
Maſters of Veſſels.
Tutors of the College.
The Students.
School-Maſters.
Scholars under their Tuition.
Apprentices.
Boys.

N. B. The Signal for the Arrival of the P R E S I D E N T in the River, will be the
Diſcharge of *a Cannon* from *Federal-Hill*, when the Citizens, &c. are requeſted to repair to the
lower Wharff at the South End of the Town, and form themſelves agreeably to the above Ar-
rangement.
General *Thayer*, Col. *John Whipple*, Deacon *Greene*, Deacon *Nightingale*, Major *Spurr*, Ma-
jor *Tyler*, Capt. *Paul Allen*, and Mr. *Jacob Whitman*, jun. are appointed, by the Committee of
Arrangements, to form and ſuperintend the Proceſſion.
On the P R E S I D E N T's landing, the Sextons are to ring the Bells of the ſeveral
Places of Worſhip.
Providence, Auguſt 17, 1790.

■ When George Washington toured the nation during his first term in office, he was greeted by local leaders in elaborately orchestrated rituals. The organizers of the ceremony at Providence, Rhode Island, on August 17, 1790, issued this broadside to inform participants of their plans for a formal procession. While some Americans gloried in such displays of pomp, others feared they presaged the return of monarchy. (The Huntington Library & Art Collections, San Marino, California)

citizens who presented him with formal addresses reaffirming their loyalty to the United States. The president thus personally came to embody national unity, simultaneously drawing ordinary folk into the sphere of national politics.

Washington's first major task as president was to choose the heads of the executive departments. For the War Department he selected an old comrade-in-arms, Henry Knox of Massachusetts, who had been his reliable general of artillery during much of the Revolution. His choice for the State Department was his fellow Virginian Thomas Jefferson, who had just returned to the United States from his post as minister to France. And for the crucial position of secretary of the treasury, the president chose the brilliant, intensely ambitious Alexander Hamilton.

The illegitimate son of a Scottish aristocrat and a woman whose husband had divorced her for adultery and desertion, Hamilton was born in the British West Indies in 1757. His early years were spent in poverty; after his mother's death when he was eleven, he worked as a clerk for a mercantile firm. In 1773 Hamilton enrolled in King's College (later Columbia University) in New York City. Only eighteen months later, in late 1774, the precocious seventeen-year-old contributed a pamphlet to the prerevolutionary publication wars. Devoted to the patriot cause, Hamilton volunteered for service in the American army, where he came to Washington's attention. In 1777 Washington appointed the young man as one of his aides, and the two developed great mutual affection.

ALEXANDER HAMILTON

The general's patronage helped the poor youth of dubious background to marry well. At twenty-three he took as his wife Elizabeth Schuyler, daughter of a wealthy New York family. After the war, Hamilton practiced law in New York City and served as a delegate first to the Annapolis Convention and then to the Constitutional Convention. Although he exerted little influence at either gathering, his contributions to *The Federalist* in 1788 revealed him as one of the chief political thinkers in the republic.

In his dual role as secretary of the treasury and one of Washington's major advisers, Hamilton exhibited two traits that distinguished him from most of his contemporaries. First, he displayed an undivided loyalty to the nation as a whole. As a West Indian who had lived on the mainland only briefly before the war, Hamilton had no ties to a particular state. He showed little sympathy for, or understanding of, demands for local autonomy. Thus the aim of his fiscal policies was always to consolidate power at the national level. Further, he never feared the exercise of centralized executive authority, as did older counterparts who had clashed repeatedly with colonial governors, nor was he afraid of maintaining close political and economic ties with Britain.

Second, Hamilton regarded his fellow human beings with unvarnished cynicism. Perhaps because of his

■ John Trumbull, known primarily for his larger-than-life portraits of patriot leaders, painted this miniature (c. 1792–1794) of George Washington, who posed for it during his presidency. (Division of Political History, Smithsonian Institution, Washington, D.C.)

■ Alexander Hamilton, by James Sharpless, about 1796. This profile of Hamilton, painted near the end of Washington's presidency, shows the secretary of the treasury as he looked during the years of his first heated partisan battles with Thomas Jefferson and James Madison. (National Portrait Gallery, Smithsonian Institution/Art Resource, N.Y.)

difficult early life and his own overriding ambition, Hamilton believed people to be motivated primarily by self-interest—particularly economic self-interest. He placed no reliance on people's capacity for virtuous and self-sacrificing behavior. This outlook set him apart from those Americans who foresaw a rosy future in which public-spirited citizens would pursue the common good rather than their own private advantage. Although other Americans (for example, Madison) also stressed the role of private interests in a republic, Hamilton went beyond them in his emphasis on self-interest as the major motivator of human behavior. And his beliefs significantly influenced the way in which he tackled the monumental task before him: straightening out the new nation's tangled finances.

In 1789, Congress ordered the new secretary of the treasury to assess the public debt and to submit recommendations for supporting the government's credit. Hamilton found that the country's remaining war debts fell into three categories: those owed by the nation to foreign governments and investors,

NATIONAL AND STATE DEBTS

mostly to France (about $11 million); those owed by the national government to merchants, former soldiers, holders of revolutionary bonds, and the like (about $27 million); and, finally, similar debts owed by state governments (roughly $25 million). With respect to the national debt, few disagreed: Americans recognized that if their new government was to succeed, it would have to repay at full face value those financial obligations incurred by the nation while winning independence.

The state debts were another matter. Some states—notably Virginia, Maryland, North Carolina, and Georgia—already had paid off most of their war debts by levying taxes and handing out land grants in lieu of monetary payments. They would oppose the national government's assumption of responsibility for other states' debts because their citizens would be taxed to pay such obligations. Massachusetts, Connecticut, and South Carolina, by contrast, still had sizable unpaid debts and would welcome a system of national assumption. The possible assumption of state debts also had political implications. Consolidating the debt in the hands of the national government would help to concentrate economic and political power at the national level. A contrary policy would reserve greater independence of action for the states.

Hamilton's first *Report on Public Credit,* sent to Congress in January 1790, stimulated lively debate. The
**HAMILTON'S
FINANCIAL PLAN**
treasury secretary proposed that Congress assume outstanding state debts, combine them with national obligations, and issue new securities covering both principal and accumulated unpaid interest. Hamilton thereby hoped to ensure that holders of the public debt—many of them wealthy merchants and speculators—had a significant financial stake in the new government's survival. The opposition coalesced around James Madison, who opposed the assumption of state debts for two reasons. Not only had his state of Virginia already paid off most of its obligations, but he also wanted to avoid rewarding wealthy speculators who had purchased state and national debt certificates at a small fraction of their face value from needy veterans and farmers.

Prompted in part by Madison, the House initially rejected the assumption of state debts. The Senate, however, adopted Hamilton's plan largely intact. A series of compromises followed, in which the assumption bill became linked to the other major controversial issue of that congressional session: the location of the permanent national capital. Several related political deals were struck. A southern site—on the Potomac River—was selected for the capital, and the first part of Hamilton's financial program became law in August 1790.

Four months later Hamilton submitted to Congress a second report on public credit, recommending the
**FIRST BANK
OF THE UNITED
STATES**
chartering of a national bank modeled on the Bank of England. This proposal too aroused much opposition, primarily after Congress had already voted to establish the bank.

The Bank of the United States, to be chartered for twenty years, was to be capitalized at $10 million. Just $2 million would come from public funds, while private investors supplied the rest. The bank would act as collecting and disbursing agent for the Treasury and its notes would circulate as the nation's currency. Most political leaders recognized that such an institution would be beneficial, especially because it would solve the problem of America's perpetual shortage of an acceptable medium of exchange. But another issue loomed large: did the Constitution give Congress the power to establish such a bank?

James Madison answered that question with a resounding no. He pointed out that Constitutional

**INTERPRETING
THE
CONSTITUTION**
Convention delegates had specifically rejected a clause authorizing Congress to issue corporate charters. Consequently, he argued, that power could not be inferred from other parts of the Constitution. Madison's contention disturbed President Washington, who decided to request other opinions before signing the bill into law. Edmund Randolph, the attorney general, and Thomas Jefferson, the secretary of state, agreed with Madison that the bank was unconstitutional. Jefferson referred to Article I, Section 8, of the Constitution, which gave Congress the power "to make all Laws which shall be necessary and proper for carrying into Execution the foregoing Powers." The key word, Jefferson argued, was *necessary:* Congress could do what was needed but without specific constitutional authorization could not do what was merely desirable. Thus Jefferson formulated the strict-constructionist interpretation of the Constitution.

Washington asked Hamilton to reply to the negative assessments of his proposal. Hamilton's *Defense of the Constitutionality of the Bank,* presented to the president in February 1791, brilliantly expounded a broad-constructionist view of the Constitution. Hamilton argued forcefully that Congress could choose any means not specifically prohibited by the Constitution to achieve a constitutional end. He reasoned thus: if the end was constitutional and the means was not *un*constitutional, then the means was constitutional.

Washington concurred, and the bill became law. The bank proved successful, as did the scheme for funding the national debt and assuming the states' debts. The new nation's securities became desirable investments for its own citizens and for wealthy foreigners, especially those in the Netherlands, who rushed to purchase American debt certificates. The influx of new capital, coupled with the high prices American produce now commanded in European markets, eased farmers' debt burdens and contributed to a new prosperity. But two other aspects of Alexander Hamilton's wide-ranging financial scheme did not fare so well.

In December 1791, Hamilton presented to Congress his *Report on Manufactures,* the third and last of his
**REPORT ON
MANUFACTURES**
prescriptions for the American economy. In it he outlined an ambitious plan for encouraging and protecting the United States's infant industries, such as shoemaking and textile manufacturing. Hamilton argued that the nation could never be truly independent as long as it relied heavily on Europe for manufactured goods. He thus urged Congress to promote the

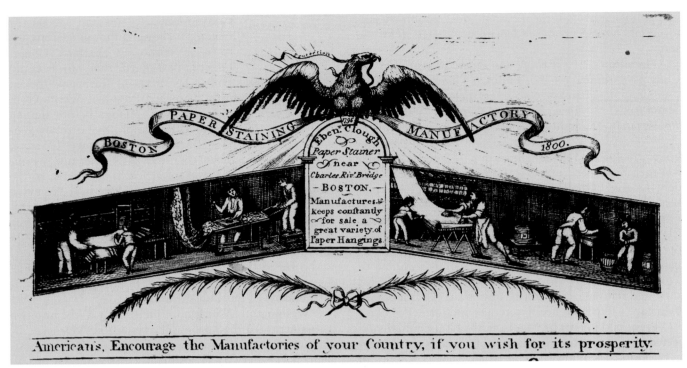

■ Although Congress did not react positively to the arguments in Hamilton's *Report on Manufactures,* the owners of America's burgeoning industries recognized the importance of the policy Hamilton advocated. Ebenezer Clough, a Boston maker of wallpaper, incorporated into his letterhead the exhortation "Americans, Encourage the Manufactories of your Country, if you wish for its prosperity." (American Antiquarian Society)

immigration of technicians and laborers and to support industrial development through a limited use of protective tariffs. Many of Hamilton's ideas were implemented in later decades, especially after the United States greatly increased its cultivation of cotton and could therefore amply supply its textile mills, but few congressmen in 1791 could see much merit in his proposals. They firmly believed that America's future lay in agriculture and the carrying trade and that the mainstay of the republic was the virtuous small farmer. Therefore, Congress rejected the report.

That same year Congress accepted another feature of Hamilton's financial program, levying a tax on whiskey produced within the United States. Although proceeds from the Revenue Act of 1789 covered the interest on the national debt, the decision to fund state debts meant that the national government required additional income. A tax on whiskey affected relatively few farmers—those west of the mountains who sold their grain in the form of distilled spirits as a means of avoiding the high cost of transportation—and might also reduce the consumption

of whiskey. (Eighteenth-century Americans, notorious for their heavy drinking, consumed about twice as much alcohol per capita as today's rate.) Moreover, Hamilton knew that those western farmers were Jefferson's supporters, and he saw the benefits of taxing them rather than the merchants who supported his own policies.

News of the tax set off protests in frontier areas of Pennsylvania, where residents were already dissatisfied

WHISKEY REBELLION

with the army's as yet unsuccessful attempts to defeat the Miami Confederacy (see pages 181–182). To their minds, the same government that protected them inadequately was now proposing to tax them disproportionately. Unrest continued for two years on the frontiers of Pennsylvania, Maryland, and Virginia. Large groups of men drafted petitions protesting the tax, deliberately imitated crowd actions of the 1760s, and occasionally harassed tax collectors.

President Washington responded with restraint until violence erupted in July 1794, when western Pennsylvania farmers resisted a federal marshal and a tax collector trying to enforce the law. Three rioters were killed and several militiamen wounded. About seven thousand rebels convened on August 1 to plot the destruction of Pittsburgh but decided not to face the heavy guns of the fort guarding the town. Washington then took decisive action to prevent a crisis reminiscent of Shays's Rebellion. On August 7, he called on the insurgents to disperse and summoned nearly thirteen thousand militia from Pennsylvania and neighboring states. By the time federal forces marched westward in October and November (led at times by Washington himself), the disturbances had ceased. The troops met no resistance and arrested only twenty suspects. Two, neither of them prominent leaders of the rioters, were convicted of treason, but—continuing his policy of restraint—Washington pardoned both. The leaderless and unorganized rebellion ended with little bloodshed.

The chief importance of the Whiskey Rebellion lay not in military victory over the rebels—for there was none—but in the forceful message it conveyed to the American people. The national government, Washington had demonstrated, would not allow violent resistance to its laws. In the republic, change would be effected peacefully, by legal means. People dissatisfied with the law should try to amend or repeal it, not take extralegal action as they had during the colonial era.

The French Revolution and the Development of Partisan Politics

By 1794, some Americans were already beginning to seek change systematically through electoral politics, even though traditional political theory regarded organized opposition—especially in a republic—as illegitimate. In a monarchy, formal opposition groups were to be expected. In a government of the people, by contrast, serious and sustained disagreement was taken as a sign of corruption and subversion. Such negative judgments, while widely held, still did not halt the growth of partisan sentiment.

Jefferson and Madison became convinced as early as 1792 that Hamilton's policies of favoring wealthy commercial interests at the expense of agriculture aimed at imposing a corrupt, aristocratic government on the United States. Characterizing themselves as the true heirs of the Revolution, they charged that Hamilton was plotting to subvert re-

DEMOCRATIC-REPUBLICANS AND FEDERALISTS

MAD TOM in A RAGE

■ A Federalist political cartoon from the 1790s shows "Mad Tom" Paine "in a rage," trying to destroy the federal government as carefully constructed (in classical style) by President Washington and Vice President Adams. That Paine is being aided by the Devil underscores the hostility to partisanship common in the era.   (The Huntington Library & Art Collections, San Marino, California)

publican principles. To dramatize their point, Jefferson, Madison, and their followers in Congress began calling themselves Democratic-Republicans. Hamilton in turn accused Jefferson and Madison of the same crime: attempting to destroy the republic. Hamilton and his supporters began calling themselves Federalists, to legitimize their claims and link themselves with the Constitution. Each group accused the other of being an illicit faction working to sabotage the republican principles of the Revolution. (In the traditional sense of the term, a faction was by definition dangerous and opposed to the public good.) Newspapers aligned with the two sides fanned the flames of partisanship, publishing virulent attacks on their political opponents.

At first, President Washington tried to remain aloof from the political dispute that divided Hamilton and

Jefferson, his chief advisers. Yet the growing controversy helped persuade him to seek a second term of office in 1792 in hopes of promoting political unity. But in 1793 and thereafter, developments in foreign affairs magnified the disagreements, for France—America's wartime ally—and Great Britain—America's most important trading partner—resumed the periodic hostilities that had originated a century earlier (see page 83).

In 1789 Americans welcomed the news of the French Revolution. The French people's success in limiting, and

FRENCH REVOLUTION then overthrowing, an oppressive monarchy seemed to vindicate the United States's own revolution. Americans saw themselves as the vanguard of an inevitable historical trend that would reshape the world in a republican mold. But by the early 1790s the reports from France were disquieting. Outbreaks of violence continued, and ministries succeeded each other with bewildering rapidity. Executions mounted; the king himself was beheaded in early 1793. Although many Americans,

■ Citizen Edmond Genêt's visit caused the first major diplomatic crisis in the new nation. His attempts to enlist Americans in support of the French Revolution raised troubling questions about the international role of the United States.   (Collection of the Albany Institute of History and Art. Bequest of George Genêt)

including Jefferson and Madison, retained a sympathetic view of the revolution, others began to cite France as a prime example of the perversion of republicanism. As might be expected, Alexander Hamilton spoke for the latter group.

Debates within the United States intensified when the newly republican France became enmeshed in conflict with other European nations. Both because French leaders feared that neighboring monarchies would intervene to crush the revolution and because they sought to spread the republican gospel throughout the continent, they declared war first on Austria and then, in 1793, on Britain, Spain, and Holland. That confronted the Americans with a dilemma. The 1778 Treaty of Alliance with France bound them to that nation "forever," and a mutual commitment to republicanism created ideological bonds. Yet the United States was connected to Great Britain as well. In addition to their shared history and language, America and Britain had again become important economic partners. Americans still purchased most of their manufactured goods from Great Britain. Indeed, since the financial system of the United States depended heavily on import tariffs as a source of revenue, the nation's economic health in effect required uninterrupted trade with the former mother country.

The political and diplomatic climate grew even more complicated in April 1793, when Citizen Edmond Genêt,

CITIZEN GENÊT a representative of the French government, landed in Charleston, South Carolina. As Genêt made his way north to New York City, he recruited Americans for expeditions against British and Spanish colonies in the Western Hemisphere, freely distributing privateering commissions. Genêt's arrival raised troubling questions for President Washington. Should he receive Genêt, thus officially recognizing the French revolutionary government? Should he acknowledge an obligation to aid France against Britain under the terms of the 1778 Treaty of Alliance? Or should he proclaim American neutrality?

For once, Hamilton and Jefferson saw eye to eye. Both told Washington that the United States could not afford to ally itself with either side. Washington concurred. He received Genêt but also issued a proclamation informing the world that the United States would adopt "a conduct friendly and impartial toward the belligerent powers." In deference to Jefferson's continued support for France, though, the word neutrality did not appear in the declaration.

Genêt himself was removed from politics when his faction fell from power in Paris; he subsequently sought political asylum in the United States. But his disappearance from the diplomatic scene did not diminish the impact of the French Revolution in America. The domestic divisions Genêt helped to widen were perpetuated by clubs called Democratic-Republican societies, formed by Americans sympathetic to the French Revolution and worried about the policies of the Washington administration. Such societies reflected a growing grassroots concern about the same developments that troubled Jefferson and Madison.

More than forty Democratic-Republican societies organized between 1793 and 1800. Their members saw

DEMOCRATIC-REPUBLICAN SOCIETIES

themselves as heirs of the Sons of Liberty, seeking the same goal as their predecessors: protection of people's liberties against encroachments by corrupt and self-serving rulers. To that end, they publicly protested government fiscal and foreign policy and repeatedly proclaimed their belief in "the equal rights of man," particularly the rights to free speech, free press, and assembly. Like the Sons of Liberty, the Democratic-Republican societies chiefly comprised artisans and craftsmen, although professionals, farmers, and merchants also joined.

The rapid growth of such groups, outspoken in their criticism of the Washington administration for its failure to come to the aid of France and for its domestic economic policies, deeply disturbed Hamilton and eventually Washington himself. Some newspapers charged that the societies were subversive agents of a foreign power. Their "real design," one asserted, was "to involve the country in war, to assume the reins of government and tyrannize over the people." The counterattack climaxed in the fall of 1794, when Washington accused the societies of having fomented the Whiskey Rebellion.

In retrospect, Washington and Hamilton's reaction to the Democratic-Republican societies seems disproportionately hostile. But it must be recalled that factional disputes were believed to endanger the survival of republics. As the first organized political dissenters in the United States, the Democratic-Republican societies alarmed elected officials, who had not yet accepted the idea that one component of a free government was an organized loyal opposition.

Partisan Politics and Relations with Great Britain

*Z*n 1794 George Washington dispatched Chief Justice John Jay to London to negotiate four unresolved questions in Anglo-American relations. The first point at issue was recent British seizures of American merchant ships trading in the French West In-

dies. The United States wanted to establish the principle of freedom of the seas and to assert its right, as a neutral nation, to trade freely with both combatants. Second, in violation of the 1783 peace treaty, Great Britain had not yet evacuated its posts in the American Northwest. Settlers there believed that the British were responsible for the renewed warfare in the region (see pages 181–182), and they wanted that threat removed. The Americans also hoped for a commercial treaty and sought compensation for the slaves who left with the British army at the end of the war.

The negotiations in London proved difficult, since Jay had little to offer in exchange for the concessions he

JAY TREATY

sought. Britain did agree to evacuate the western forts and ease restrictions on American trade to England and the West Indies. (Some limitations were retained, however, violating the Americans' desire for open commerce.) The treaty established two arbitration commissions—one to deal with prewar debts Americans owed to British creditors and the other to hear claims for captured American merchant ships—but Britain adamantly refused slaveowners compensation for their lost bondspeople. Under the circumstances, Jay did remarkably well: the treaty averted war with England at a time when the United States, which lacked an effective navy, could not have won such a conflict. Nevertheless, most Americans, including the president, expressed dissatisfaction with at least some parts of the treaty.

The Senate debated the Jay Treaty in secret, so members of the public did not learn its provisions until after Senate ratification (by the exact two-thirds vote needed, 20 to 10) in June 1795. The Democratic-Republican societies led protests against the treaty. Especially vehement opposition arose in the South, as planters criticized the failure to obtain compensation for runaway slaves and objected to the commission on prewar debts, which might make them pay off obligations to British merchants dating back to the 1760s. Once President Washington had signed the treaty, though, there seemed little the Democratic-Republicans could do to prevent it from taking effect. Just one opportunity remained: Congress had to appropriate funds to carry out the treaty provisions and, according to the Constitution, appropriation bills had to originate in the House of Representatives.

When the House debated the issue in March 1796, members opposing the treaty tried to prevent approval of the appropriations. To that end, they asked Washington to submit to the House all documents pertinent to the negotiations. In successfully resisting the House's request, Washington established the doctrine of executive privilege—the power of the president to withhold information from Congress if he believes circumstances warrant doing so.

The treaty's opponents initially appeared to be in the majority, but pressure for appropriating the necessary funds built as time passed. Frontier residents eagerly sought Britain's evacuation of its remaining outposts, for they feared a new outbreak of Indian war despite the signing of the Treaty of Greenville. Merchants wanted to reap benefits from expanded trade. Furthermore, in 1795 Thomas Pinckney of South Carolina had negotiated a treaty with Spain giving the United States navigation privileges on the Mississippi River, which would be an economic boost to the West and South. The popularity of Pinckney's Treaty (the Senate ratified it unanimously) helped to overcome opposition to the Jay Treaty. For all these reasons, the House appropriated the money by the narrow margin of 51 to 48.

Analysis of the vote reveals both the regional nature of the division and the growing cohesion of the Democratic-Republican and Federalist factions in Congress. Voting for the appropriations were 44 Federalists and 7 Democratic-Republicans; voting against were 45 Democratic-Republicans and 3 Federalists. The final tally also divided by region. Southerners (including those three Federalists, who were Virginians) cast the vast majority of votes against the bill. Except for two South Carolina Federalists, no one representing a state south of Maryland voted "yes."

PARTISAN DIVISIONS IN CONGRESS

The small number of defectors on both sides reveals a new force at work in American politics: partisanship. Voting statistics from the first four Congresses show the ever-increasing tendency of members of the House of Representatives to vote as cohesive groups, rather than as individuals. If factional loyalty is defined as voting together at least two-thirds of the time on national issues, the percentage of nonaligned congressmen dropped from 42 percent in 1790 to just 7 percent in 1796. Significantly, this trend toward party cohesion occurred even though Congress experienced heavy turnover. Most congressmen served only one or two terms in office, and fewer than 10 percent were reelected more than three times. During the 1790s the majority slowly shifted from Federalist to Democratic-Republican. Federalists controlled the first three Congresses, through the spring of 1795. Democratic-Republicans gained ascendancy in the Fourth Congress. Federalists returned to power with slight majorities in the Fifth and Sixth Congresses, but the Democratic-Republicans took over—more or less for good—in the Seventh Congress in 1801.

To describe these shifts is easier than to explain them. The terms used by Jefferson and Madison (aristocrats versus the people) or by Hamilton and Washington (true patriots versus subversive rabble) do not adequately explain the growing divisions. Simple economic differences between agrarian and commercial interests do not provide the answer either, since more than 90 percent of Americans still lived in rural areas. Moreover, Jefferson's vision of a prosperous agrarian America rested on commercial farming, not rural self-sufficiency. Nor did the divisions in the 1790s simply repeat the Federalist-Antifederalist debate of 1787–1788. Even though most Antifederalists became Democratic-Republicans, the party's leaders, Madison and Jefferson, had supported the Constitution.

BASES OF PARTISANSHIP

Yet certain distinctions can be made. Democratic-Republicans, especially prominent in the southern and middle states, tended to be self-assured, confident, and optimistic about both politics and the economy. Southern planters, firmly in control of their region and of a class of enslaved laborers, did not fear instability, at least among the European American population. They foresaw a prosperous future based partly on continued westward expansion, a movement they expected to dominate. Democratic-Republicans employed democratic rhetoric to win the allegiance of small farmers south of New England. Members of non-English ethnic groups—especially Irish, Scots, and Germans—found Democratic-Republicans' words attractive. Artisans also joined the coalition; they saw themselves as the urban equivalent of small farmers and valued their independence from domineering bosses. Democratic-Republicans of all descriptions emphasized developing America's own resources, worrying less than Federalists did about the nation's place in the world. Democratic-Republicans also remained sympathetic to France in international affairs.

By contrast, Federalists, concentrated among the commercial interests of New England, came mostly from English stock. Insecure and uncertain of the future, they stressed the need for order, authority, and regularity in the political world. Federalists had no grassroots political organization and put little emphasis on involving ordinary people in government. Wealthy New England merchants aligned themselves with the Federalists, but so too did the region's farmers who, prevented from expanding agricultural production because of New England's poor soil, gravitated toward the more conservative party. Federalists, like Democratic-Republicans, assumed that southern and middle-state interests would dominate the land west of the mountains, so they had little incentive to work actively to develop that potentially rich territory. In Federalist eyes, potential enemies—both internal and external—perpetually threatened the nation, which required a continuing alliance with Great Britain for its own protection. Their vision of international affairs may have been more accurate than that of the Democratic-Republicans, given the warfare in Europe, but it was also narrow and unattractive. Since the Federalist view held out little hope of a better future to the voters of any region, it is not surprising that the Democratic-Republicans prevailed in the end.

The presence of the two organized groups actively contending for office made the presidential election of

WASHINGTON'S FAREWELL ADDRESS

1796 the first serious contest for the position. Wearied by the criticism to which he had been subjected, George Washington decided to retire. (Presidents had not yet been limited to two terms, as they have been since the adoption of the Twenty-second Amendment in 1951.) In September Washington published his Farewell Address, most of which had been written by Hamilton. In it Washington outlined two principles that guided American foreign policy at least until the late 1940s: to maintain commercial but not political ties to other nations and to enter no permanent alliances. He also drew sharp distinctions between the United States and Europe, stressing America's uniqueness—its exceptionalism—and the need for independent action in foreign affairs, today called unilateralism.

Washington lamented the existence of factional divisions among his countrymen. Historians have often interpreted his call for an end to partisan strife as the statement of a man who could see beyond political affiliations to the good of the whole. But in the context of the impending presidential election, the Farewell Address appears rather as an attack on the legitimacy of the Democratic-Republican opposition. Washington advocated unity behind the Federalist banner, which he viewed as the only proper political stance. The Federalists (like the Democratic-Republicans) continued to see themselves as the sole guardians of the truth and the only true heirs of the Revolution. Both sides perceived their opponents as misguided, unpatriotic troublemakers who sought to undermine revolutionary ideals.

To succeed Washington, the Federalists in Congress put forward Vice President John Adams, with the diplomat

ELECTION OF 1796

Thomas Pinckney as his running mate. Congressional Democratic-Republicans chose Thomas Jefferson as their presidential candidate; the lawyer, Revolu-

tionary War veteran, and active Democratic-Republican politician Aaron Burr of New York agreed to run for vice president.

That the election was contested does not mean that the people decided its outcome. Voters could cast their ballots only for electors, not for the candidates themselves, and not all electors publicly declared their preferences. State legislatures, not a popular vote, selected more than 40 percent of the members of the electoral college; some electors had been picked even before Federalists and Democratic-Republicans named their presidential candidates. Moreover, the method of voting in the electoral college did not take into account the possibility of party slates. The Constitution's drafters had not foreseen the development of competing national political organizations, so the Constitution provided no way to express support for one person for president and another for vice president. The electors simply voted for two

■ John Adams, painted in 1798 by the English artist William Winstanley. Adams wears the same suit and sword he donned for his inauguration as the second president in March 1797. The open books and quill pen on the table suggest his lifelong love of reading and writing.
(U.S. Department of the Interior, National Park Service, Adams National Historic Site)

people. The man with the highest total became president; the second highest, vice president.

This procedure proved to be the Federalists' undoing. Adams won the presidency with 71 votes, but a number of Federalist electors (especially those from New England) failed to cast ballots for Pinckney. Thomas Jefferson won 68 votes, 9 more than Pinckney, to become vice president. The incoming administration was thus politically divided. During the next four years the new president and vice president, once allies and close friends, became bitter enemies.

John Adams and Political Dissent

John Adams took over the presidency peculiarly blind to the partisan developments of the previous four years. As president he never abandoned an outdated notion discarded by George Washington as early as 1794: that the president should be above politics, an independent and dignified figure who did not seek petty factional advantage. Thus Adams kept Washington's cabinet intact, despite its key members' allegiance to his chief rival, Alexander Hamilton. Adams often adopted a passive posture, letting others (usually Hamilton) take the lead when the president should have acted decisively. As a result, his administration gained a reputation for inconsistency. When Adams's term ended, the Federalists were severely divided, and the Democratic-Republicans had won the presidency. But Adams's detachment from Hamilton's maneuverings did enable him to weather the greatest international crisis the republic had yet faced: the Quasi-War with France.

The Jay Treaty improved America's relationship with Great Britain, but it provoked the French government to retaliate by ordering its ships to seize American vessels carrying British goods. In response, Congress increased military spending, authorizing the building of ships and the stockpiling of weapons and ammunition. President Adams also sent three commissioners to Paris to negotiate a settlement. For months, the American commissioners sought talks with Talleyrand, the French foreign minister, but Talleyrand's agents demanded a bribe of $250,000 before negotiations could begin. The Americans retorted, "No, no; not a sixpence," and reported the incident in dispatches that the president received in early March 1798. Adams informed Congress of the impasse and recommended further increases in defense appropriations.

XYZ Affair

Convinced that Adams had deliberately sabotaged the negotiations, congressional Democratic-Republicans insisted that the dispatches be turned over to Congress. Adams complied, aware that releasing the reports would work to his advantage. He withheld only the names of the French agents, referring to them as X, Y, and Z. The revelation that the Americans had been treated with contempt stimulated a wave of anti-French sentiment in the United States. A journalist's version of the commissioners' reply, "Millions for defense, but not a cent for tribute," became the national slogan. Cries for war filled the air. Congress formally abrogated the Treaty of Alliance and authorized American ships to seize French vessels.

Thus began an undeclared war with France. Warships of the U.S. Navy and French privateers seeking to capture American merchant vessels fought the Quasi-War in Caribbean waters. Although Americans initially suffered heavy losses of merchant shipping, by early 1799 the U.S. Navy had established its superiority in the West Indies. Its ships captured eight French privateers and naval vessels, easing the threat to America's vital Caribbean trade.

Quasi-War with France

The Democratic-Republicans, who opposed war and continued to sympathize with France, could do little to stem the tide of anti-French feelings. Since Agent Y had boasted of the existence of a "French party in America," Federalists flatly accused Democratic-Republicans (including the eccentric envoy George Logan) of traitorous designs. A New York newspaper declared that anyone who remained "lukewarm" after reading the XYZ dispatches was a "criminal—and the man who does not warmly reprobate the conduct of the French must have a soul black enough to be fit for treason Strategems and spoils." John Adams wavered between calling the Democratic-Republicans traitors and acknowledging their right to oppose administration measures. His wife was less tolerant. "Those whom the French boast of as their Partizans," Abigail Adams declared, should be "adjudged traitors to their country." If Jefferson had been president, she added, "we should all have been sold to the French."

Federalists saw this climate of opinion as an opportunity to deal a death blow to their Democratic-Republican opponents. Now that the country seemed to see the truth of what they had been saying ever since the Whiskey Rebellion in 1794—that Democratic-Republicans were subversive foreign agents—Federalists sought to codify that belief into law. In 1798

Alien and Sedition Acts

■ This cartoon drawn during the XYZ affair depicts the United States as a maiden being victimized by the five leaders of the French government's directorate. In the background, John Bull (England) watches from on high, while other European nations discuss the situation.
(The Lilly Library, Indiana University, Bloomington, Indiana)

the Federalist-controlled Congress adopted a set of four laws known as the Alien and Sedition Acts, intended to suppress dissent and to prevent further growth of the Democratic-Republican faction.

Three of the acts targeted recently arrived immigrants, whom Federalists accurately suspected of being Democratic-Republican in their sympathies. The Naturalization Act lengthened the residency period required for citizenship and ordered all resident aliens to register with the federal government. The two Alien Acts, though not immediately implemented, provided for the detention of enemy aliens in time of war and gave the president authority to deport any alien he deemed dangerous to the nation's security.

The fourth statute, the Sedition Act, sought to control both citizens and aliens. It outlawed conspiracies to prevent the enforcement of federal laws, setting the maximum punishment for such offenses at five years in prison and a $5,000 fine. The act also tried to control speech. Writing, printing, or uttering "false, scandalous and malicious" statements against the government or the

president "with intent to defame . . . or to bring them or either of them, into contempt or disrepute" became a crime punishable by as much as two years' imprisonment and a fine of $2,000. Today any such law punishing speech alone would be considered unconstitutional. But in the eighteenth century, when organized political opposition was by definition suspect, many Americans supported the Sedition Act's restrictions on free speech.

The Sedition Act led to fifteen indictments and ten convictions. Outspoken Democratic-Republican newspaper editors who failed to mute their criticism of the administration composed most of the accused. But the first person found guilty—whose story exemplifies the others—was a Democratic-Republican congressman from Vermont, Matthew Lyon. The Irish-born Lyon, a former indentured servant who had purchased his freedom and fought in the Revolution, was indicted for declaring in print that John Adams had displayed "a continual grasp for power" and "an unbounded thirst for ridiculous pomp, foolish adulation, and selfish avarice." Though convicted, fined $1,000, and sent to prison for four months, Lyon did not lapse into silence. He conducted his reelection campaign from jail, winning an overwhelming majority. Leading Democratic-Republicans from around the country contributed to pay his fine.

Faced with prosecutions of their supporters, Jefferson and Madison sought an effective means of combating the acts. Petitioning the Federalist-controlled Congress to repeal the laws would clearly fail. Furthermore, Federalist judges refused to allow accused individuals to question the Sedition Act's constitutionality. Accordingly, the Democratic-Republican leaders turned to the only other forum available for protest: state legislatures. Carefully concealing their own role—the vice president and congressman wanted to avoid being indicted for sedition—Jefferson and Madison drafted somewhat different sets of resolutions that were introduced into the Kentucky and Virginia legislatures, respectively, in the fall of 1798. Since a compact among the states created the Constitution, the resolutions contended, people speaking through their states had a legitimate right to judge the constitutionality of actions taken by the federal government. Both sets of resolutions pronounced the Alien and Sedition Acts unconstitutional, asking other states to join in a concerted protest against them.

VIRGINIA AND KENTUCKY RESOLUTIONS

Although no other state endorsed them, the Virginia and Kentucky Resolutions nevertheless had considerable influence. First, they constituted superb political propaganda, rallying Democratic-Republican opinion throughout the country. They placed the opposition party squarely in the revolutionary tradition of resistance to tyrannical authority. Second, the theory of union they proposed inspired southern states' rights advocates in the 1830s and thereafter. Jefferson and Madison had identified a key constitutional issue: How far could states go in opposing the national government? How could a conflict between the two be resolved? These questions would not be definitively answered until the Civil War.

Just as the Sedition Act was being implemented and northern state legislatures were rejecting the Virginia and Kentucky Resolutions, Federalists split over the course of action the United States should take toward France. Hamilton and his supporters called for a declaration legitimizing the undeclared naval war. But Adams received a number of private signals—among them George Logan's report—that the French government regretted its treatment of the American commissioners. Acting on such assurances, Adams dispatched the envoy William Vans Murray to Paris to negotiate

CONVENTION OF 1800

with Napoleon Bonaparte, France's new leader, who was consolidating his hold on the country and eager to end messy foreign conflicts. The United States sought two goals: compensation for ships the French had seized since 1793 and abrogation of the treaty of 1778. The Convention of 1800, which ended the Quasi-War, provided for the latter but not the former. Still, it freed the United States from its only permanent alliance, thus allowing it to follow the independent diplomatic course George Washington had urged in his Farewell Address.

The results of the negotiations did not become known in the United States until after the presidential election of 1800. Even so, since Hamilton and many of his followers wanted to widen the Quasi-War, Adams's decision to seek a peaceful settlement probably cost him reelection because of the divisions it caused in Federalist ranks.

Indians and African Americans at the End of the Century

By the end of the eighteenth century, the nation had added three states (Vermont, Kentucky, and Tennessee) to the original thirteen and more than 1 million people to the nearly 4 million counted by the 1790 census. Nine-tenths of the approximately 1 million resident African Americans—most still enslaved—lived in the Chesapeake or the Lower South. After the signing of the Treaty of Greenville in 1795 (see page 182), all the Indian nations residing in U.S. territory east of the Mississippi River had made peace with the republic. Even though many Indian peoples still lived independently of federal authority, they came increasingly within the orbit of U.S. influence.

The new nation's policymakers, all of European American descent, could not ignore such large proportions of the population. How should the republic deal with eastern Indians, who no longer posed a military threat to the country? Did the growing population of bondspeople (augmented by more than ninety thousand imports directly from Africa before Congress ended the slave trade in 1808) present new hazards? The second question took on added significance after 1793, when in the French colony of St. Domingue (Haiti), mulattos and blacks under the leadership of Toussaint L'Ouverture overthrew European rule in a bloody revolt characterized by numerous atrocities on both sides.

In 1789 Henry Knox, Washington's secretary of war, proposed that the new national government assume the task of "civilizing" America's indigenous population.

Although many European Americans initially welcomed the news of the French Revolution in 1789, few expressed similar sentiments about the slave rebellion that broke out soon thereafter in the French colony of St. Domingue (later Haiti), which shared the island of Hispaniola with Spanish Santo Domingo. The large number of refugees who soon flowed into the new United States from that nearby revolt brought with them consequences deemed undesirable by most political leaders. Less than a decade after winning independence, the new nation confronted its first immigration crisis.

Among the approximately 600,000 residents of St. Domingue in the early 1790s were about 100,000 free people, almost all of them slaveowners; half were whites, the rest mulattos. When in the wake of the French Revolution those free mulattos split the slaveholding population by seeking greater social and political equality, the slaves seized the opportunity to revolt. By 1793, they had triumphed under the leadership of a former slave, Toussaint L'Ouverture, and in 1804 they finally ousted the French, thereafter establishing the republic of Haiti. Thousands of whites and mulattos, accompanied by as many slaves as they could readily transport, sought asylum in the United States during those turbulent years.

Although willing to offer shelter to refugees from the violence, American political leaders nonetheless feared the consequences of their arrival. Southern plantation owners shuddered at the thought that slaves so familiar with ideas of freedom and equality would mingle with their own bondspeople. Many were uncomfortable with the immigration of numerous free people of color, even though the immigrants were part of the slaveholding class. Most of the southern states adopted laws forbidding the entry of Haitian slaves and free mulattos, but the laws were difficult if not impossible to enforce, as was a later congressional act to the same effect. And so more than 15,000 refugees—white, black, and of mixed race origins—flooded into the United States and Spanish Louisiana. Many ended up in Virginia (which did not pass an exclusion law) or the cities of Charleston, Savannah, and New Orleans.

There they had a considerable impact on the existing population. In both New Orleans and Charleston the influx of mulattos gave rise to heightened color consciousness that placed light-skinned people at the top of a hierarchy of people of color. Not coincidentally, the Charleston Brown Fellowship Society, composed exclusively of free mulattos, was founded in 1793. After the United States purchased Louisiana in 1803, the number of free people of color in the territory almost doubled in three years, largely because of a final surge of immigration from the new Haitian republic. And in Virginia, stories of the successful revolt helped to inspire local slaves in 1800 when they planned the action that has become known as Gabriel's Rebellion.

The Haitian refugees thus linked both European and African Americans to current events in the West Indies, indelibly affecting both groups of people.

A free woman of color in Louisiana early in the nineteenth century, possibly one of the refugees from Haiti. Esteban Rodriguez Miró, named governor of Spanish Louisiana in 1782, ordered all slave and free black women to wear head wraps rather than hats—which were reserved for whites—but this woman and many others subverted his order by nominally complying, but nevertheless creating elaborate headdresses. (Louisiana State Museum)

■ In 1805, an unidentified artist painted Benjamin Hawkins, a trader and U.S. agent to the Indians of the Southeast, at the Creek agency near Macon, Georgia. Hawkins introduced European-style agriculture to the Creeks, who are shown here with vegetables from their fields. Throughout the eastern United States, Indian nations had to make similar adaptations of their traditional lifestyles in order to maintain their group identity. (Collection of the Greenville County Art Museum, South Carolina)

"CIVILIZING" THE INDIANS

"Instead of exterminating a part of the human race," he contended, the government should "impart our knowledge of cultivation and the arts to the aboriginals of the country." The first step in such a project, Knox suggested, should be to introduce to Indian peoples "a love for exclusive property"; to that end, he proposed that the government give livestock to individual Indians. Four years later, the Indian Trade and Intercourse Act of 1793 codified Knox's plan, promising that the federal government would supply Indians with animals and agricultural implements and would also provide appropriate instructors.

The well-intentioned plan reflected federal officials' blindness to the realities of native peoples' lives. Not only did it incorrectly posit that the Indians' traditional commitment to communal notions of landowning (see page 44) could easily be overcome, it also ignored the centuries-long agricultural experience of eastern Indian peoples. The policymakers focused only on Indian men: since they hunted, male Indians were "savages" who had to be "civilized" by being taught to farm. That in these societies women traditionally did the farming was irrelevant because in the eyes of the officials, Indian women—like those of European descent—should properly confine themselves to child rearing, household chores, and home manufacturing.

Indian nations at first responded cautiously to the "civilizing" plan. The Iroquois Confederacy had been devastated by the war; its people in the 1790s lived in what one historian has called "slums in the wilderness." Restricted to small reservations increasingly surrounded by Anglo-American farmlands, men could no longer hunt and often spent their days in idle carousing. Quaker missionaries started a demonstration farm among the Senecas, intending to teach men to plow, but they quickly learned that women showed greater interest in their message. The same was true among the Cherokees of Georgia, where Indian agents found that

IROQUOIS AND CHEROKEES

women eagerly sought to learn both new farming methods and textile-manufacturing skills. As their southern hunting territories were reduced, Cherokee men did begin to raise cattle and hogs, but they startled the reformers by treating livestock like wild game, allowing the animals to run free in the woods and simply shooting them when needed, in the same way they had once killed deer. Men also started to plow the fields, although Cherokee women continued to bear primary responsibility for cultivation and harvest.

Iroquois men became more receptive to the Quakers' lessons after the spring of 1799, when a Seneca named Handsome Lake experienced a remarkable series of visions. Like other prophets stretching back to Neolin (see page 123), Handsome Lake preached that Indian peoples should renounce alcohol, gambling, and other destructive European customs. Even though he directed his followers to reorient men's and women's work assignments as the Quakers advocated, Handsome Lake aimed above all to preserve Iroquois culture by doing so. He recognized that, since men could no longer obtain meat through hunting, only by adopting a sexual division of labor that had originated in Europe could the Iroquois retain an autonomous existence.

African Americans had long been forced to conform to European American notions of proper gender roles and, unlike Indians, they had embraced Christianity as well during the Great Awakening. Yet, just as Cherokees and Iroquois adapted the reformers' plans to their own purposes, so too enslaved blacks found new meanings in the dominant society's ideas. Like their white compatriots, African Americans (both slave and free) became familiar with concepts of liberty and equality during the Revolution. They also witnessed the benefits of fighting collectively for freedom, rather than resisting individually or running away—a message reinforced by the dramatic news of the successful slave revolt in St. Domingue in 1793. And, as white evangelicals by the end of the century began to back away from the earlier racial egalitarianism of their movement, African Americans increasingly formed their own separate Baptist and Methodist congregations in the Chesapeake, as they did in Philadelphia and other urban centers (see page 173).

Such congregations near Richmond became the seedbeds of revolt. Gabriel, an enslaved blacksmith who argued that African Americans should fight for their freedom, carefully planned a large-scale revolt. Often accompanied by his brother Martin, a preacher, he visited Sunday church services, where blacks gathered outside of the watchful eyes of their owners. Gabriel first recruited to his cause other skilled African

GABRIEL'S REBELLION

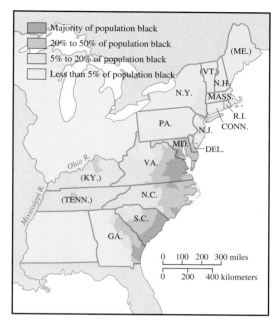

Map 8.1

African American Population, 1790: Proportion of Total Population   The first census clearly indicated that the African American population was heavily concentrated in just a few areas of the United States, most notably in coastal regions of South Carolina, Georgia, and Virginia. Although there were growing numbers of blacks in the backcountry—presumably taken there by migrating slaveowners—most parts of the North and East, with the exception of the immediate vicinity of New York City, had few African American residents.   (Source: From Lester J. Cappon et al., eds. *Atlas of Early American History: The Revolutionary Era, 1760–1790.* Copyright © 1976 by Princeton University Press. Reprinted by permission of Princeton University Press.)

Americans who like himself lived in semifreedom under minimal supervision. Next he enlisted rural slaves (see Map 8.1). The conspirators planned to attack Richmond on the night of August 30, 1800, set fire to the city, seize the state capitol, and capture the governor, James Monroe. At that point, Gabriel believed, other slaves and possibly sympathetic poor whites would join in.

The plan showed considerable political sophistication, but heavy rain forced a postponement. Several planters then learned of the plan from slave informers and spread the alarm. Gabriel avoided arrest for some weeks, but militia troops quickly apprehended and interrogated most of the other leaders of the rebellion. Twenty-six conspirators, including Gabriel himself, were hanged. Ironically, only those slaves who betrayed their fellows won their freedom as a consequence of the conspiracy.

■ Richmond, Virginia, at the time of Gabriel's Rebellion. This was the city as Gabriel knew it. The state capitol, the rebels' intended target, dominates the city's skyline as it dominated Gabriel's thinking.   (Maryland Historical Society)

That disastrous outcome did not end the unrest among Virginia's slaves. In 1802 a waterman named Sancho—a peripheral participant in Gabriel's plot—revived the plans for a revolt. This time word spread along Virginia and North Carolina rivers, carried by slaves who, like Sancho, worked on the boats that plied the two states' interconnected waterways. The incomplete plans disintegrated when the plots were revealed prematurely. Again, trials and executions followed, and twenty-five more African Americans lost their lives on the gallows.

At his trial two years earlier, one of Gabriel's followers had made explicit the links that so frightened Chesapeake slaveholders. He told his judges that, like George Washington, "I have adventured my life in endeavouring to obtain the liberty of my countrymen, and am a willing sacrifice in their cause." Southern state legislatures responded to such claims by increasing the severity of the laws regulating slavery. Before long, all talk of emancipation ceased in the South, and slavery became even more firmly entrenched as an economic institution and way of life.

Summary

*A*s the nineteenth century began, inhabitants of the United States faced changed lives in the new republic. Indian peoples east of the Mississippi River found that they had to give up some parts of their traditional culture to preserve others. Some African Americans struggled unsuccessfully to free themselves from the inhuman bonds of slavery, then subsequently confronted more constraints than ever because of increasingly restrictive laws.

European Americans too adjusted to changed circumstances. The first eleven years of government under the Constitution established many enduring precedents for congressional, presidential, and judicial action—among them establishment of the cabinet, interpretations of key clauses of the Constitution, and stirrings of judicial review of state and federal legislation. Building on successful negotiations with Spain (Pinckney's Treaty), Britain (the Jay Treaty), and France (the Convention of 1800), the United States developed its diplomatic independence, striving to avoid entanglement with European countries and their continental wars. Yet especially after 1793 internal political consensus proved elusive. The 1790s spawned vigorous debates over foreign and domestic policy and saw the beginnings of a system of organized political factionalism, if not yet formal parties. The Whiskey Rebellion, instigated by westerners outraged at tax policies formulated by eastern elites, showed that regional conflicts continued even under the new government. And the waging of an undeclared war against France proved extremely contentious, splitting one faction and energizing another.

At the end of the 1790s, after more than a decade of struggle, the Jeffersonian view of the future of republicanism prevailed over Alexander Hamilton's vision of a powerful centralized economy and a strong national government. As a result, for decades to come the country would be characterized by a decentralized economy, minimal government (especially at the national level), and maximum freedom of action and mobility for individual white men. Jeffersonian Democratic-Republicans, like other white men before them, failed to extend to white women, Indian peoples, and African Americans the freedom and individuality they recognized as essential for themselves.

LEGACY FOR A PEOPLE AND A NATION
Dissent During Wartime

The Quasi-War with France in 1798 and 1799, the nation's first overseas conflict, brought the first attempt to suppress dissent. By criminalizing dissenting speech, the Sedition Act of 1798 tried to quiet the Democratic-Republicans' criticism of the war in general and President John Adams in particular. Fifteen men (including a member of Congress) were fined and jailed after being convicted under the statute's provisions.

Although Americans might assume that their right to free speech under the First Amendment, more fully accepted now than it was two hundred years ago, today protects dissenters during a war, the history of the nation suggests otherwise. Each major conflict fought under the Constitution—the Civil War, World War I,

World War II, and Vietnam—has stimulated efforts by both government and individual citizens to suppress dissenting voices. For example, during the Civil War, the Union jailed civilian Confederate sympathizers, holding them under martial law for long periods. During the First World War, a Sedition Act allowed the government to deport immigrant aliens who too vocally criticized the war effort, among them several outspoken Socialists and anarchists. Moreover, citizens who objected to government policies were subjected to a variety of formal and informal sanctions by their neighbors. World War II brought the silencing of isolationists' voices, as those who had opposed American entry into the war were denied public outlets for their ideas. The consequences of antiwar protests in the Vietnam era still affect the nation today, for the American people remain divided over whether the proper course of action in the 1960s and 1970s was dissent from, or acquiescence in, government policy. Although during the first Persian Gulf war (1991) and the Afghanistan campaign (2001), military officials restricted reporters' access to the battlefront, during the war against Iraq (2003) that policy was reversed, with mixed results.

Freedom of speech is never easy to maintain, and wartime conditions make it much more difficult. When the nation comes under attack, whether from a foreign country or from terrorists, many patriotic Americans argue that the time for dissent has ceased and that all citizens should support the government. Others contend that, if freedom in the nation is to mean anything, people must have the right to speak their minds freely at all times. Events in the United States since the attacks of September 11, 2001, suggest that this legacy remains extremely contentious for the American people.

The **history companion** powered by Eduspace®

Your primary source for interactive quizzes, exercises, and more to help you learn efficiently.
http://history.college.hmco.com/students

HISTOIRE
DE
BARBARIE, ET DE SES
CORSAIRES.

Par R.P.F. PIERRE DAN, Bachelier en Theologie de la
Faculté de Paris, M.ʳᵉ et Superieur du Conuent de l'ordre de la S.
Trinité et Redemption des Captifs fondé au Chasteau de Fontaine-bleau.

SECONDE EDITION.
Reueuë et augmentée.

Partisan Politics and War: The Democratic-Republicans in Power 1801–1815

John Foss, captured by "pirates" off the Barbary Coast of North Africa in the 1790s, wrote of the "hellish tortures and punishments" inflicted "on the unfortunate Christians." Marched through Algiers, the party of nine ragged sailors heard shouts from the Islamic crowds praising the victories over "Christian dogs," and in prison they learned of ten other American vessels recently captured. In Algiers they became white slaves under African masters. Eventually the United States ransomed the captives, and four of the nine made it back to America; the others died of plague.

In the early nineteenth century, the Barbary captivity stories had the drama of modern gothic novels. "Pirates" took American men and women hostage from ships, held them in confinement, stripped and beat them as Christians, and humiliated them as Americans. In telling of white slaves with black masters, the tales turned American assumptions on their heads. Firsthand descriptions of Africa projected negative images of a despotic, depraved people, so very different from Americans. In the end, the Americans—at least those who survived to tell their stories—prevailed, and so the stories became epic affirmations of Western culture over "barbarians."

Americans loved to read these harrowing stories. John Foss's account of his captivity was reprinted twice in 1798. The fictional account of a woman held a slave in Algiers from 1800 to 1806, *History of the Captivity and Sufferings of Mrs. Maria Martin,* titillated Americans and went through twelve editions following its 1807 printing. Chained in prison, Martin described how "the enormous iron round my neck pained me," and how "her mind sunk under this accumulation of miserable sufferings." Finally, she wrote, "my liberty had been purchased by my country," and she heard the door of the dungeon slam shut

◀ Christian monks purchase the freedom of Barbary Coast captives, held in chains, from their Muslim captors. (Photograph courtesy of the James Ford Bell Library, University of Minnesota)

C H R O N O L O G Y

1800 • Jefferson elected president, Burr vice president

1801 • Marshall becomes chief justice of the United States
• Jefferson inaugurated as first Democratic-Republican president

1801–05 • United States defeats Barbary pirates in Tripoli War

1803 • *Marbury v. Madison* establishes judicial review
• United States purchases Louisiana Territory from France

1804 • Burr kills Hamilton in a duel
• Jefferson reelected president, Clinton vice president

1804–06 • Lewis and Clark explore Louisiana Territory

1805 • Prophet emerges as Shawnee leader

1807 • *Chesapeake* affair almost leads to war with Great Britain
• Embargo Act halts foreign trade

1808 • Congress bans importation of slaves to the United States
• Madison elected president, Clinton vice president

1808–13 • Prophet and Tecumseh organize Native American tribal resistance

1808–15 • Embargoes and war stimulate domestic manufacturing

1812 • Madison reelected president, Gerry vice president

1812–15 • United States and Great Britain fight the War of 1812

1813 • Death of Tecumseh ends effective pan-Indian resistance

1814 • Jackson's defeat of Creeks at Battle of Horseshoe Bend begins Indian removal from the South
• Treaty of Ghent ends the War of 1812

1814–15 • Hartford Convention undermines Federalists

1815 • Battle of New Orleans makes Jackson a national hero

behind her. As a Christian, in chains and afterward, she felt morally superior to her captors.

In reality the "pirates"—from what Europeans called the Barbary states and Africans the Maghreb—had challenged the United States in a most fundamental way: was this new nation an independent, sovereign state that could protect its citizens and commerce abroad?

The issue was money. In 1801 the *bashaw* of Tripoli, angry over the United States's refusal to pay tribute for safe passage of its ships, sailors, and passengers through the Mediterranean, declared war on the United States. President Thomas Jefferson responded by sending a naval squadron to protect American ships in the area. The only other alternative was to abandon the Mediterranean Sea, which would have damaged American trade. After two years of stalemate, Jefferson ordered a blockade of Tripoli, but the American frigate *Philadelphia* ran aground in its harbor and three hundred American officers and sailors were captured. Jefferson refused to ransom them. With the blockade still in place, seven marines and four hundred soldiers of fortune marched overland from Egypt to seize the port of Derne, on the shores of Tripoli. Finally, by treaty with Tripoli in 1805, the United States paid $60,000 to free the *Philadelphia* prisoners, and the war was over. But the United States continued to pay tribute to the other three Barbary states (Algiers, Morocco, and Tunis) until 1815. Was the United States an independent sovereign nation? The question rankled, especially as Great Britain seemed to think not, and continued to treat the new nation as a colony.

In replacing John Adams as president, Thomas Jefferson piloted the young nation in new directions at home as well as abroad. In the tradition of the Revolution, Jefferson and his Democratic-Republican successor presidents soon sought to restrain the national government, believing that limited government would foster republican virtue. The Federalists, in contrast, advocated a strong national government with centralized authority to promote economic development. As factions competed for popular support, they laid the basis for a national political culture. Factionalism did not spring only from politics, however. Americans also divided along other lines: by class, race, ethnicity, gender, religion, and region.

Events abroad and in the West both encouraged and threatened Americans. Seizing one opportunity, the

United States purchased the Louisiana Territory, adding a vast land from which new states would soon be carved. But even as American interests turned westward, events in Europe and on the high seas of the Atlantic wrenched an about-face. Caught between the warring British and French, the United States found its ships seized, its foreign commerce interrupted, its sailors forcibly drafted, and its rights as a neutral and independent nation violated. In what some have called the second war for independence, the United States fought Great Britain to a standoff, while on another front routing Indian resistance and shattering Native American unity. A peace treaty restored the prewar status quo, but the war and the treaty affirmed U.S. sovereignty and strengthened America's determination to steer clear of further European conflicts. The war also stimulated industry and nationalism. In 1815 a secure, independent, and self-confident nation looked to the future with optimism. ■

The Jefferson Presidency and Marshall Court

*I*n later years Thomas Jefferson would always refer to his winning the presidency as the "Revolution of 1800." The Democratic-Republicans, he believed, would restore government to its limited role, restrained and frugal. He stressed the republican virtues of independence, self-reliance, and equality, in contrast to the monarchical ambitions of the Federalists. To counter Federalist formality, Jefferson and his fellow Democratic-Republicans promoted simplicity, even in dress. They wore plain trousers instead of the wigs and knee breeches that George Washington and John Adams had favored.

Yet in his inaugural address in March 1801, Jefferson reached out to his opponents. Standing in the Senate chamber, the only part of the Capitol

JEFFERSON INAUGURAL

that had been completed, he appealed to the electorate not as party members but as citizens who shared common beliefs: "We are all republicans, we are all federalists." Nearly a thousand people strained to hear him lay out his vision of a restored republicanism: "A wise and frugal government, which shall restrain men from injuring one another, which shall leave them free to regulate their pursuits of industry and improvement, and shall not take from the mouth of labor the bread it has earned. This is the sum of good government," he concluded.

■ This portrait of President Thomas Jefferson was painted by Rembrandt Peale in 1805. Charles Willson Peale (Rembrandt's father) and his five sons helped establish the reputation of American art in the new nation. Rembrandt Peale achieved fame for his presidential portraits; here he has captured Jefferson in a noble pose without the usual symbols of office or power, befitting the Republican age. (© Collection of The New-York Historical Society)

But outgoing president John Adams was not there to hear Jefferson's call for unity. He had left Washington before dawn to avoid the Democratic-Republican takeover. He and Jefferson had once been close friends but now disliked each other intensely. Both were thin-skinned, quick to take offense and quick to give it. Despite the spirit of Jefferson's inaugural address, the Democratic-Republicans and Federalists remained bitter opponents. Nonetheless presidential succession in 1801 took place by ballot rather than by arms, which some had feared.

To implement the restoration of republican values, Jefferson aggressively extended the Democratic-Republicans'

DEMOCRATIC-REPUBLICANS IN OFFICE

grasp on the national government. It was indeed a takeover. Virtually all of the 600 or so officials appointed during the administrations of Washington and Adams had been loyal Federalists; only 6 were known Democratic-Republicans. To bring into his administration men who shared his vision of an agrarian republic and individual liberty, Jefferson refused to recognize appointments that Adams had made in the last days of his presidency and dismissed Federalist customs collectors from New England ports. He awarded vacant treasury and judicial offices to Democratic-Republicans. By July 1803, Federalists held only 130 of 316 presidentially controlled offices. They accused Jefferson of "hunting the Federalists like wild beasts" and abandoning the olive leaf extended in his inaugural address.

The Democratic-Republican Congress, swept into office in the election of 1800, also proceeded to affirm its belief in limited government. Albert Gallatin, secretary of the treasury, and John Randolph of Virginia, Jefferson's ally in the House of Representatives, translated ideology into policy, putting the federal government on a diet. Congress repealed all internal taxes, including the whiskey tax. Gallatin cut the army budget in half and reduced the 1802 navy budget by two-thirds. He then moved to reduce the national debt from $83 million to $57 million, as part of a plan to retire it altogether by 1817. If Alexander Hamilton had viewed the national debt as the engine of economic growth, Jefferson saw it as the source of government corruption. Jefferson even closed two of the nation's five diplomatic missions abroad—at The Hague and Berlin—to save money.

More than frugality, however, distinguished Democratic-Republicans from Federalists. Before Jefferson's election, opposition to the Alien and Sedition Acts of 1798 had helped unite Democratic-Republicans (see pages 206–207). Jefferson now declined to use the acts against his opponents (as President Adams had done in suppressing Democratic-Republican editors) and pardoned those who had been convicted under the provisions. Congress let expire the Sedition Act in 1801 and the Alien Act in 1802. Congress also repealed the Naturalization Act of 1798, which had required fourteen years of residency for citizenship. The 1802 act that replaced it, while stipulating the registration of aliens, required of would-be citizens only five years of residency, loyalty to the Constitution, and the forsaking of foreign allegiance and titles. The new act would remain the basis of naturalized American citizenship into the twentieth century.

The Democratic-Republicans turned next to the judiciary, the last stronghold of Federalist power. To many Democratic-Republicans, the judiciary represented a centralizing force, one undemocratic by virtue of unelected judges appointed for life. Especially galling to Jefferson, John Marshall had become chief justice of the United States, appointed after Adams's defeat. During the 1790s not a single Democratic-Republican had occupied the federal bench; thus the judiciary became a battlefield following the revolution of 1800.

WAR ON THE JUDICIARY

The first skirmish erupted over repeal of the Judiciary Act of 1801, which had been passed in the final days of the Adams administration. The act, designed to maintain Federalist control over the courts, created fifteen new judgeships, which Adams filled by signing "midnight" appointments until his term was just hours away from expiring. The act also reduced by attrition the number of justices on the Supreme Court from six to five. Since that reduction would have denied Jefferson a Supreme Court appointment until two vacancies occurred, the new Democratic-Republican–dominated Congress repealed the 1801 act.

Partisan Democratic-Republicans created another front in the war for control of the judiciary by targeting opposition judges for removal. Democratic-Republicans were especially infuriated with the Federalist judges who had refused to review the Sedition Act under which Federalists had prosecuted critics of the Adams administration. At Jefferson's prompting, the House impeached (indicted) Federal District Judge John Pickering of New Hampshire, an elderly, emotionally disturbed alcoholic. He was an easy target, and in 1805 the Senate convicted him, removing him from office.

The day Pickering was ousted, the House impeached Supreme Court Justice Samuel Chase for judicial misconduct. A staunch Federalist, Chase had pushed for prosecutions under the Sedition Act, had actively campaigned for Adams in 1800, and repeatedly had denounced Jefferson's administration from the bench. The Democratic-Republicans, however, failed to muster the two-thirds majority of senators necessary to convict him. Chase's acquittal preserved the Court's independence at a critical time before the role of the judiciary as an equal branch of government had been established. In failing to remove Chase, the Senate established the precedent that criminal actions, not political disagreements, were the only proper grounds for impeachment. In his tenure as president, Jefferson appointed three new Supreme Court justices. Nonetheless, under Chief Justice John Marshall, the Court remained a Federalist stronghold.

Jefferson and Marshall shared much in common. They were fellow Virginians, even distant cousins, and Marshall was of the generation of Madison and Monroe, the bright young men who formed Jefferson's intellectual entourage. Jefferson, however, viewed Marshall as a traitor to republicanism after Marshall became a Federalist in the 1790s. President Adams had appointed him secretary of state and then, in his last weeks as a lame-duck president, named Marshall chief justice. Though an autocrat by nature, Marshall possessed a grace and openness of manner that comple-

JOHN MARSHALL

■ John Marshall (1755-1835) was chief justice of the United States from 1801 to 1835. This painting by John B. Martin captures Marshall's aristocratic bearing and strong will that would allow him to dominate the Court.   (Collection of the Supreme Court of the United States)

mented the new Republican political style. As a justice he adopted republican dress, wearing a plain black gown rather than the British robes of scarlet and ermine or the colorful academic garb worn by other justices. John B. Martin's portrait of Marshall in 1801 captures both his aristocratic bearing and his strong will. Under Marshall's domination, however, the Supreme Court retained a Federalist outlook even after Democratic-Republican justices achieved a majority in 1811. Throughout his tenure (1801–1835), the Court consistently upheld federal supremacy over the states and protected the interests of commerce and capital.

Marshall made the Court an equal branch of government in practice as well as theory. Judicial service became a coveted honor for ambitious and talented men. Previously people regarded it lightly, and justices had served only short terms. No judicial building was constructed in Washington; Congress considered it unessential, and the Court continued to meet in a chamber of the Capitol. Marshall unified the Court, influencing the justices to issue joint majority opinions rather than a host of individual concurring judgments. Marshall himself became the voice of the majority: from 1801 through 1805 he wrote twenty-four of the Court's twenty-six decisions; through 1810 he wrote 85 percent of the opinions, including every important one.

Marshall significantly increased the Supreme Court's power in the landmark case of *Marbury v. Madison* (1803), another skirmish in war over

MARBURY V. MADISON

the judiciary. William Marbury, one of Adams's midnight appointees, had been named a justice of the peace in the District of Columbia. James Madison, Jefferson's new secretary of state, declined to certify Marbury's appointment so that the president could instead appoint a Democratic-Republican. Marbury sued, requesting a writ of mandamus (a court order forcing the president to appoint him). The case presented a political dilemma. If the Supreme Court ruled in favor of Marbury and issued a writ of mandamus, the president probably would not comply with it, and the Court had no way to force him to do so. But if the Federalist-dominated bench refused to issue the writ, it would be handing the Democratic-Republicans a victory.

Marshall brilliantly recast the issue to avoid both pitfalls. Speaking for the Court, he ruled that Marbury had a right to his appointment but that the Supreme Court could not compel Madison to honor the appointment because the Constitution did not grant the Court power to issue a writ of mandamus. In the absence of any specific mention in the Constitution, Marshall ruled, the section of the Judiciary Act of 1789 that authorized the Court to issue such writs was unconstitutional. In *Marbury v. Madison,* the Supreme Court denied itself the power to issue writs of mandamus but established its far greater power to judge the constitutionality of laws passed by Congress.

In succeeding years Marshall fashioned the theory of judicial review, the power of the Supreme Court to decide the constitutionality of legislation and presidential acts. Since the Constitution was "the supreme law of the land," he reasoned in *Marbury v. Madison,* any federal or state act contrary to the Constitution must be null and void. The Supreme Court, whose duty it was to uphold the law, would decide whether or not a legislative act contradicted the Constitution. "It is emphatically the province and duty of the judicial department," Marshall ruled, "to say what the law is." The power of judicial review established in *Marbury v. Madison* permanently enhanced the independence of the judiciary and breathed life into the Constitution. "Marshall found the Constitution paper and made it power," President James A. Garfield later observed.

Louisiana and Lewis and Clark

*D*emocratic-Republicans and Federalists divided sharply over more than just the Court; Jefferson's acquisition of the Louisiana Territory in 1803 was another point of contention. Jefferson shared with many other Americans the belief that the United States was destined to expand its "empire of liberty," and his presidency made western expansion a national goal.

Since American independence, Louisiana had held a special place in the nation's expansionist dreams. Louisiana defined the western border of the United States, which stretched along the Mississippi River from the Gulf of Mexico to present-day Minnesota. Spain had acquired the Louisiana Territory from France in 1763, at the end of the Seven Years War (see page 122). By 1800 hundreds of thousands of Americans in search of land had settled in the rich Mississippi and Ohio River valleys, intruding on Indian lands. These settlers floated their farm goods down the Mississippi and Ohio Rivers to New Orleans for export. Whoever controlled the port of New Orleans had a hand on the throat of the American economy. Americans preferred Spanish control of Louisiana to control by France, a much stronger power.

In secret pacts with Spain in 1800 and 1801, however, France had acquired the territory once again. The United States learned of the transfer only in 1802, when Napoleon seemed poised to rebuild a French empire in the New World. "Every eye in the United States is now focused on the affairs of Louisiana," Jefferson wrote to Robert R. Livingston, the American minister in Paris. American concerns intensified in October of that year when Spanish officials, on the eve of ceding control to the French, violated Pinckney's Treaty (see page 204) by denying Americans the privilege of storing their products at New Orleans prior to transshipment to foreign markets. "The Mississippi," Secretary of State James Madison wrote, "is to them [western settlers] everything. It is the Hudson, the Delaware, the Potomac and all navigable rivers of the Atlantic States formed into one stream." Western farmers and eastern merchants thought a devious Napoleon had closed the port; they grumbled and talked war.

Jefferson personally took charge. To relieve the pressure for war and to win western farm support, Jefferson prepared for war while sending Virginia governor James Monroe as his personal envoy to join Robert Livingston in France. Their mission: to buy the port of New Orleans and as much of the Mississippi valley as possible. Meanwhile, Congress authorized the call-up of eighty thousand militiamen in case war be-

LOUISIANA
PURCHASE

came necessary. Arriving in Paris in April 1803, Monroe was astonished to learn that France already had offered to sell all 827,000 square miles of Louisiana to the United States for a mere $15 million. Napoleon had lost interest in the New World. Once he failed to recapture independent Haiti, the idea of a New World empire dissolved and Louisiana became superfluous. At the same time he needed money for renewed warfare against Britain. On April 30 Monroe and Livingston signed a treaty buying the vast territory whose exact borders and land were uncharted (see Map 9.1).

At one stroke of a pen, the Louisiana Purchase doubled the size of the nation and opened the way for continental expansion. It was the most popular achievement of Jefferson's presidency. But for Jefferson, the purchase presented a dilemma. For one thing, it conflicted with his commitment to debt reduction. And some questioned Jefferson's power to make such a move. To be sure, the purchase promised fulfillment of his dream of an agrarian republic "with room enough for our descendants to the hundredth and thousandth generation." It also facilitated the removal of eastern Indians by providing land for their exile. But was it constitutional? The Constitution nowhere authorized the president to acquire new territory and incorporate it into the nation.

Jefferson considered proposing a constitutional amendment to allow the purchase but decided against it. He believed that the president's implied powers to protect the nation justified the purchase. His long-standing interest in Louisiana and the West also allayed his constitutional concerns. As early as 1782, as an American envoy in France, Jefferson had suggested sending an exploratory mission across the continent to California. A naturalist and scientist, Jefferson seemed obsessed with the West— its geography, people, plants, and animals; he had long wanted to acquire, subdue, and exploit it. As secretary of state in the 1790s, he had been active in promoting a search for "the shortest & most convenient route of communications between the U.S. & the Pacific Ocean."

In 1803 Jefferson sent an expedition headed by Meriwether Lewis and William Clark to the Pacific coast via the Missouri and Columbia Rivers. The twenty-nine-year-old Lewis, a regular army officer in the 1790s, had exchanged rugged military life to be Jefferson's private secretary in 1801. As friend, teacher, role model, and father figure, Jefferson gave Lewis a "crash course" on the botany and the environment of the West, and he proved an exceptional student. The thirty-year-old Clark was an explorer and former soldier who had fought against and negotiated with native peoples. Aware of the risks as well as the scientific importance of

LEWIS AND
CLARK

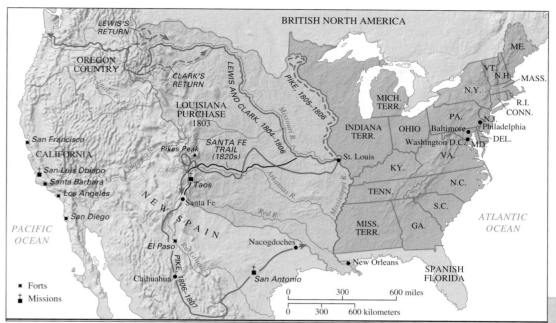

Map 9.1

Louisiana Purchase

The Louisiana Purchase (1803) doubled the area of the United States and opened the trans-Mississippi West for American settlement.

their mission, both were eager for the commission. The expedition also had political import, for the 1801 publication of Alexander MacKenzie's *Voyages from Montreal,* which described the first crossing of the continent in Canada in 1793, had raised fears that the British would dominate the West.

Lewis and Clark officially started their journey in May 1804. They traveled up the Missouri River and wintered at Fort Mandan in present-day North Dakota. There they selected their twenty-nine-member corps and were joined by Indian guides. In April 1805 they resumed their journey, traveling through present-day Montana. In August, having reached the navigable limits of the Missouri, they continued the journey with horses. Helped by a local Shoshone guide, they crossed the Bitterroot Mountains. Traversing the Rockies, "the most terrible mountains I ever beheld," wrote Sergeant Patrick Gass in his diary, proved their most dangerous and treacherous venture. At times they lost their way, tumbled down steep mountain trails, and slept in the snow, bone cold. Short of food, they had to kill a horse for meat. In November 1805 they reached the Pacific Ocean in present-day Oregon, where they wintered, and the following March began the return trek. Lewis and Clark split up to explore alternate routes and reunited in August 1806. They arrived back in St. Louis on September 23, 1806.

The original Corps of Discovery reflected American diversity. It included army regulars and young adventurers

■ This Charles M. Russell painting of the Lewis and Clark expedition depicts Sacagawea talking with Chinook Indians. A Shoshone, Sacagawea knew the land and the languages of the mountain Indians, and helped guide the Corps of Discovery. (Courtesy, Montana Historical Society, Gift of the artist)

CORPS OF DISCOVERY from Kentucky. Among them were two half-French and half-Omaha men and another who was son of a French Canadian father and a Shawnee mother. Clark brought his slave York, whom he inherited in 1799 from his father. Immigrants included an Irishman and a German. Later at the Mandan villages the French Canadian trader Toussaint Charbonneau and his pregnant, fifteen-year-old Shoshone wife, Sacagawea, joined the expedition. Lewis and Clark took Charbonneau because they wanted Sacagawea, who knew the languages of the mountain Indians. She proved invaluable as a guide and translator, and she knew the land and the people better than anyone else. The youngest member of the group was Jean Baptiste Charbonneau, son of Sacagawea, born on February 11, 1805.

Headed by army officers, the expedition followed military rules. At times, however, it was more informal and democratic than army regulations or even civilian society allowed. When trouble arose, Lewis and Clark held courts-martial to discipline corps members for such infractions as drunkenness. Contrary to army rules, enlisted men sat on the court. When Sergeant Charles Floyd died of a ruptured appendix at the beginning of the journey, the soldiers elected Private Patrick Gass as his successor, a most unusual move. In November 1805, to determine where to locate winter quarters on the Pacific coast, all voted, including the slave York and the Indian woman Sacagawea. Yet issues of race and gender were present. Along the way Indians were astonished at York; many had not seen a black man before. They were curious about his skin color, his "short, curling hair," and his strength. At the end of the journey the names of York and Sacagawea did not appear on the roster Lewis submitted to the War Department. Neither received pay for their work though their assistance had been indispensable.

Although some Americans still believed that the West was uninhabited, Lewis and Clark knew better. They anticipated a crowded wilderness and hoped to cement U.S. relations with Indians. The explorers carried with them twenty-one bags of gifts for Native American leaders, both to establish goodwill and to stimulate interest in trading for American manufactured goods. They brought back stories not only of various peoples, but also of fauna and flora unknown to the western scientific community; they encountered the grizzly bear, bighorn sheep, and mountain goats. Lewis sent boxes of natural-history specimens to Jefferson, including plant and tree cuttings.

In time, the expedition became legendary and Lewis and Clark fabled American explorers. They mapped the West and, with their reports, promoted dreams of a continental empire. The corps members were well rewarded and basked in their renown. But one among them reaped few rewards: the slave York. In 1808 York demanded his freedom from Clark as a reward for his service to the expedition. York's wife, a slave, lived in Louisville, Kentucky, and he wished to join her. Clark let him visit her, and York proposed that he stay there, hiring himself out and sending money to Clark. Clark refused and in May 1809 York returned to Clark in St. Louis. Clark found

York "insolent and sulky. I gave him a severe trouncing the other Day, and he has much mended" his ways.

Other explorations followed Lewis and Clark's, further publicizing the land west of the Mississippi. In 1805 and 1806 Lieutenant Zebulon Pike sought the source of the continent-cutting river and a navigable water route west. When Pike and his men wandered into Spanish territory to the south, the Spanish held them captive for several months in Mexico. After his release, Pike wrote an account of his experiences that set commercial minds spinning. He described a potential commercial market in southwestern Spanish cities as well as bountiful furs and precious minerals. Over the next few decades, Americans avidly read accounts of western exploration. The vision of a road to the Southwest became a reality with the opening of the Santa Fe Trail in the 1820s, and settlement followed the trail.

EXPLORATION OF THE WEST

New Spain's Tejas (Texas) province bordered the Louisiana Territory. Provincial officials welcomed Americans interested in the land south of the territory, and American immigrants began to drift in. Some fought as volunteers with Indians and Mexican rebels in a twelve-year war with Spain that ended with Mexican independence in 1821. The establishment of an independent Mexico inspired these Americans to dream of an independent Texas nation—a place for white American settlers. Since they envisioned the West an uninhabited area, they did not imagine a place for Mexicans or indigenous peoples in the "empire of liberty."

A New Political Culture

*W*riting to English scientist Joseph Priestly in 1801, Jefferson described his presidency as the beginning of a new era. "The great extent of our republic is new. Its sparse habitation is new. The mighty wave of public opinion which has rolled over is new." Although the electorate was limited mostly to white males over twenty-one who held property, the Democratic-Republicans had taken their appeals to the people in the elections of 1800. While Federalists might think that for candidates to debate their own merits in front of voters was demeaning, a subversion of the natural political order, the Democratic-Republicans did not. Now in office they worked hard to keep public opinion on their side.

One way to control that "wave" of public opinion was through the press. The new president persuaded the *National Intelligencer* to move from Philadelphia to Washington, and during the ensuing Democratic-Republican ad-

THE PARTISAN PRESS

■ The German immigrant John Lewis Kimmell conveys the growing popular interest in elections in his 1815 painting, *Election Day in Philadelphia.* Elections combined civic duty with a party atmosphere, and even the disfranchised free blacks and women turned out to join the festivities.   (Courtesy, Winterthur Museum)

ministrations it served as the official voice. In 1801 Alexander Hamilton launched the *New-York Evening Post* as the Federalist vehicle to retake power. It boosted Federalists while often calling Jefferson a liar and depicting him as head of a slave harem. Newspapers circulated widely, linking parties, voters, and the government. Sold by subscription, the papers were readily available in taverns, coffeehouses, and hotels, where they were often read aloud. They not only helped build the party system but, like the parties, they also contributed to building a national political culture. In 1800 the nation had 260 newspapers; by 1810 it had 396. Editors were outrageously partisan.

After the Federalist defeat in 1800, a younger generation of Federalists began to imitate the popular appeals of the Democratic-Republicans. Led by such men as Josiah Quincy, a Massachusetts congressman, the Younger Federalists campaigned for popular support. Quincy cleverly presented the Federalists as the people's party, attacking Democratic-Republicans as autocratic planters. "Jeffersonian Democracy," Quincy gibed in

1804, was "an Indian word, signifying 'a great tobacco planter who had herds of black slaves.'" In attacking frugal government, the Younger Federalists played on fears of a weakened army and navy. Eastern merchants depended on a strong navy to protect ocean trade; westerners looked to the army to defend them as they encroached on the territory of Native Americans.

For Democratic-Republicans, distinctive regional interests inspired a new style of campaigning, symbolized by the political barbecue. In New York campaigners roasted oxen; on the New England coast they baked clams; in Maryland they served oysters; in Virginia they planked shad. Guests washed down their meals with beer and punch and sometimes competed in corn-shucking or horse-pulling contests. Voters demonstrated their allegiance by attending these events and displaying images of Democratic-Republican party leaders. Oratory became a popular form of entertainment, and candidates delivered lengthy and uninhibited speeches wherever crowds gathered. They attacked the character

GRASSROOTS CAMPAIGNING

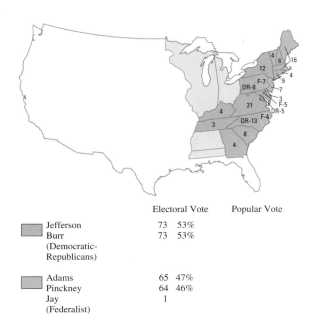

		Electoral Vote	Popular Vote
	Jefferson	73	53%
	Burr	73	53%
	(Democratic-Republicans)		
	Adams	65	47%
	Pinckney	64	46%
	Jay	1	
	(Federalist)		

Map 9.2 Presidential Election, 1800

The Democratic-Republicans, with their candidates Thomas Jefferson and Aaron Burr, won the electoral votes of the southern states, while the Federalists, the party of John Adams and Charles Cotesworth Pinckney, received votes primarily in New England. The parties split the votes of the middle states, but the Democratic-Republicans dominated the electoral-vote count there and won the election.

of their opponents, often making wild accusations that—given the slow speed of communications—might go unanswered until after the election. Slander and gossip were the rule of the day. Some historians have speculated that these developing party rituals helped contain more violent expression.

The opposition Federalists never mastered the art of campaigning. Older Federalists remained opposed to popular appeals. And though strong in Connecticut, Delaware, and a few other states, the Federalists were weak at the national level and could not manage sustained competition. Divisions among Federalists often undermined their success, and the extremism of some Older Federalists discredited most of the rest. A case in point was Timothy Pickering, a Massachusetts congressman and former secretary of state. Pickering opposed the Louisiana Purchase, feared Jefferson's reelection, and urged the secession of New England in 1803 and 1804. He won some support, but most Federalists balked at his plan for secession. Ever the opportunist, Vice President Aaron Burr, intrigued with Pickering's idea of northeastern independence, fantasized about leading New York

into secession, with other states following. But when Burr lost his bid to become governor of New York in 1804, dreams of a northern confederacy evaporated.

The controversies surrounding Burr illustrate the convergence of the political and the personal. In the election of 1800, he understood he was the vice-presidential candidate, but when all 73 of the Democratic-Republican electors cast ballots for both Jefferson and Burr (see Map 9.2), Burr challenged Jefferson for the presidency. The Constitution required that because neither had a plurality, the contest be decided in the House of Representatives, with each state's congressmen voting as a unit. It had taken thirty-five ballots for the House, still with a Federalist majority, to decide that Jefferson would be a lesser evil than Burr. In response to the tangle, the Twelfth Amendment to the Constitution (1804) changed the method of voting in the electoral college to allow for a party ticket.

BURR AND PERSONAL ANIMOSITY

For Burr, ever the opportunist, it was a short step from personal animosity into violence. He and the hothead Alexander Hamilton had long despised each other. Hamilton relentlessly blocked Burr's path. He thwarted Burr's attempt to steal the election of 1800 from Jefferson, and in the 1804 mudslinging New York gubernatorial race, he backed Burr's Democratic-Republican rival. Both Burr and Hamilton held grudges, and when Hamilton accused Burr of being a liar, Burr challenged him to a duel. With his honor at stake, Hamilton accepted even though his son Philip had died in 1801 from dueling wounds. Because New York had outlawed dueling, the two men met across the Hudson River at Weehawken, New Jersey, in July 1804. Hamilton did not fire, and he paid for that decision with his life. Burr was indicted for murder in New York and New Jersey and faced immediate arrest if he returned to either state.

Rather than preserving his honor, Burr's killing of Hamilton made him an outcast. His political career in ruins, Burr fled to start life anew in the West. He schemed to create in the Southwest a new empire carved out of the Louisiana Territory. With the collusion of General James Wilkinson, the U.S. commander in the Mississippi valley, Burr planned to raise a private army to grab land from the United States or from Spain (his exact plans remain unknown). Wilkinson switched sides and informed President Jefferson of Burr's devious intention. Jefferson personally assisted the prosecution in Burr's 1807 trial for treason, over which Chief Justice Marshall presided. Marshall construed treason narrowly, and the jury acquitted Burr, who fled to Europe.

Campaigning for reelection in 1804, Jefferson took credit for the restoration of republican values and the

ELECTION OF 1804

acquisition of the Louisiana Territory. The Democratic-Republicans claimed they ended the Federalist threat to liberty by repealing the Alien and Sedition and Judiciary Acts. They also boasted that they had reduced the size of government by cutting spending. American trade with Europe was flourishing, allowing Jefferson to demonstrate support for commerce too. Federalists had little to go on, though they did attack the president for paying too much for Louisiana and for exceeding his powers in buying it.

Jefferson's opponent in 1804 was Charles Cotesworth Pinckney, a wealthy South Carolina lawyer and former Revolutionary War aide to George Washington. As Adams's vice-presidential running mate in 1800, Pinckney had inherited the Federalist leadership. Jefferson dumped the disloyal Aaron Burr from the 1804 ticket, and he and his running mate, George Clinton of New York, swamped Pinckney and New Yorker Rufus King in the electoral college by 162 votes to 14, carrying fifteen of the seventeen states.

Indian Resistance

Lewis and Clark's account testified to the Indian presence in the West, and most Americans viewed Native Americans, no matter where they lived, as obstacles to American settlement. Violations of treaties and coerced new ones, forcing Indians to cede ever more land to the United States, continually shrunk Indian territory. With less land, Indians found hunting and agriculture more difficult. Not only their traditional ways but also their independence and existence were threatened. Encroachment by whites and the periodic ravages of disease—smallpox, measles, and influenza—brought further misery.

In the early 1800s two Shawnee brothers, Prophet (1775–1837) and Tecumseh (1768–1813), led a revolt against further American encroach-

THE PROPHET

ment by fostering a pan-Indian federation that stretched from the Old Northwest to the South. Prophet's early life typified the experiences of the Indians of the Old Northwest. Born in 1775 a few months after his father's death in battle, Prophet, called Lalawethika ("Noisemaker"), as a young man was expelled to Ohio along with other Shawnees under the 1795 Treaty of Greenville (see page 182), and he later moved to Indiana. Within Prophet and Tecumseh's own lifetimes the Shawnees had lost most of their Ohio land; by the 1800s they occupied scattered sites in Ohio and in the Michigan and Louisiana territories. Dis-

placement left Lalawethika forlorn, and like many other Native Americans he turned to whiskey for escape. He also turned to traditional folk knowledge and remedies and in 1804 became a tribal medicine man. His medicine, however, could not stop the white man's diseases from ravaging his village.

Lalawethika emerged from his own battle with illness in 1805 as a new man, called Tenskwatawa ("the Open Door"), or "the Prophet." Claiming to have died and been resurrected, he traveled widely in the Ohio River valley as a religious leader, attacking the decline of moral values among Native Americans, warning of damnation for those who drank whiskey, condemning intertribal battles, and stressing harmony and respect for elders. He urged Indians to return to the old ways and abandon white customs: to hunt with bows and arrows, not guns; to stop wearing hats; and to refrain from eating bread and instead cultivate corn and beans. Whiskey, he preached, was made for whites; the forest had been created for Indians.

Prophet was building a religious movement that offered reassurance to the Shawnees, Potawatomis, and other displaced western Indians. As a leader his power came from his eloquence, conviction, and performance of miracles. By timing his invocations to coincide with a solar eclipse, he even seemed to darken the sun. His outspoken opposition to federal Indian policy drew others into his camp, and as his message spread to southern tribes, the federal government and white settlers became alarmed.

By 1808 Prophet and his older brother Tecumseh talked less about spiritual renewal and more about

TECUMSEH

resisting American aggression. Together they invited Indians from all nations to settle in pan-Indian towns in Indiana, first at Greenville (1806–1808) on the Wabash, called Prophetstown by whites, and then at Tippecanoe (1808–1812). The new towns challenged the treaty-making process. The pan-Indian settlements denied the claims of Indians like Little Turtle and the Miamis, who had been guaranteed the land in exchange for enormous cessions. And the Americans viewed the new towns as places promoting Indian resistance. In effect Tecumseh was turning Prophet's religious movement into a political one. The British, who looked for alliances with Native Americans after renewed Anglo-American hostilities (see pages 232–233), encouraged Indians to defy the U.S. government. In repudiating land cessions to the government under the Treaty of Fort Wayne (1809), Tecumseh told Indiana's governor William Henry Harrison at Vincennes in 1810 that "the only way to check and stop this evil is, for all the red men to unite in claiming a

■ The Shawnee chiefs Tecumseh (*left*) and Prophet (*right*). The two brothers led a revival of traditional Shawnee culture and preached Native American federation against white encroachment. In the War of 1812 they allied themselves with the British, but Tecumseh's death at the Battle of the Thames (1813) and British indifference thereafter caused Native Americans' resistance and unity to collapse. (Tecumseh: Field Museum of Natural History, Chicago, FMNH Neg. #A93851; Prophet: Chicago Historical Society)

common and equal right in the land, as it was at first, and should be yet; for it . . . belongs to all, for the use of each. . . . No part has a right to sell, even to each other, much less to strangers."

Tecumseh, a towering six-foot warrior and charismatic orator, soon overshadowed his brother as Shawnee leader. He dressed as a chief from a century before, exchanging his European shirts and cloth trousers for soft deerskin suits with fringes. He replaced the bright beads and ribbons sold by whites with dyed porcupine quills. He returned to traditional diet as well, refusing foreign food. Younger Indians flocked to him. Warriors found his political visions more relevant than Prophet's spirituality in protecting themselves against the United States. Convinced that only an Indian federation could stop the advance of white settlement, Tecumseh sought to unify northern and southern Indians by traveling widely, from Canada to Georgia, preaching Indian resistance. And he warned Harrison that Indians would resist white occu-

pation of the 2.5 million acres on the Wabash River that they had ceded in the Treaty of Fort Wayne.

But the Indians could not match the armed might of the United States. In November 1811, while Tecumseh was recruiting support in the South, Harrison moved against the Prophet and his followers. In the battle of Tippecanoe, the army burned the town and dispersed Prophet's and Tecumseh's supporters. The spiritual and political movement initiated by the brothers began to unravel. Tecumseh's death two years later (see page 234) would end their movement for Indian unity.

American Shipping Imperiled

*P*eace, commerce, and honest friendship with all nations, entangling alliance with none," President Jefferson had proclaimed in his first inaugural address. Jefferson's efforts to stand aloof from

European conflict were successful until 1805. Thereafter the United States could not escape the web of European hostilities, and protection of American commerce and foreign relations occupied nearly all of Jefferson's second administration. The easy victory over the Barbary states would not be repeated against the British.

After the Senate ratified the Jay Treaty in 1795 (see pages 203–204), the United States and Great Britain appeared to reconcile their differences. Britain withdrew from its western forts and interfered less in American trade with France. Since the United States was Britain's best customer, and the British Empire in turn bought the bulk of American exports, both sides worked hard for good relations.

The economy of the early republic relied heavily on shipping, and the commercial fleet played a significant role in extending American trade not only to Britain but around the world. **U.S. COMMERCE** American fishermen explored the Atlantic, while whalers hunted for prey in the Atlantic and Pacific Oceans. Americans exported cotton, lumber, sugar, and other commodities to Europe, and brought back manufactured goods. The slave trade lured American sailing ships to Africa. Boston, Salem, and Philadelphia merchants opened trade with China, sending cloth and metal to swap for furs with Chinook Indians on the Oregon coast, then sailing to China to trade for porcelain, tea, and silk. Importing manufactured goods was more profitable than producing them at home.

Then in May 1803, two weeks after Napoleon sold Louisiana to the United States, renewal of the Napoleonic wars between France and Britain (and later Britain's continental allies, Prussia, Austria, and Russia) again trapped the United States between Britain and France on the high seas. For two years American commerce benefited from the conflict. As the world's largest neutral carrier, the United States became the chief supplier of grain to Europe. American merchants also gained control of most of the West Indian trade. But after defeating the French and Spanish fleets at the Battle of Trafalgar in October 1805, Britain's Royal Navy tightened its control of the oceans. Two months later Napoleon crushed the Russian and Austrian armies at Austerlitz. Stalemated, France and Britain launched a commercial war, blockading each other's trade. As a trading partner of both countries, the United States paid a high price.

All tension focused on the high seas, where Britain, commanding the world's largest navy, suffered a severe shortage of sailors. Too few men enlisted, and those in service frequently deserted, demoralized by harsh treatment. Some British sailors joined U.S. **IMPRESSMENT OF AMERICAN SAILORS** merchant ships, where conditions were better. The Royal Navy resorted to stopping American vessels and impressing, or forcibly detaining, British deserters, British-born naturalized American seamen, and other unlucky sailors suspected of being British. Perhaps six to eight thousand Americans were impressed in this way between 1803 and 1812. Moreover, alleged deserters—many of them American citizens—faced British courts-martial. Americans saw impressment as a direct assault on the independence of their new republic. The principle of "once a British subject, always a British subject" mocked U.S. citizenship and sovereignty.

The British violated other American rights as well. They interfered with U.S. trade with the West Indies by blocking goods the United States believed were part of neutral trade. They **NEUTRAL RIGHTS** also searched and seized U.S. vessels within American territory offshore.

In February 1806 Americans denounced British impressment as aggression and a violation of America's neutral rights. In protest, Congress passed the Non-Importation Act, barring British manufactured goods from entering American ports. Since the act exempted most cloth or metal articles, it had little impact on British trade; instead, it warned the British what to expect if they continued to violate American rights. In November Jefferson suspended the act temporarily while William Pinckney, a Baltimore lawyer, joined James Monroe in London to negotiate a settlement. But the treaty Monroe and Pinckney carried home violated their instructions—it did not so much as mention impressment—and Jefferson never submitted it to the Senate for ratification.

Anglo-American relations steadily deteriorated. Then in June 1807, the forty-gun frigate U.S.S. *Chesapeake* left Norfolk, Virginia, headed to protect American ships in the Mediterranean. About 10 miles from shore, still inside American territorial waters, **CHESAPEAKE AFFAIR** it met the fifty-gun British frigate *Leopard*. When the *Chesapeake* refused to be searched for deserters, the *Leopard* repeatedly fired its cannon broadside into the American ship. Three Americans were killed and eighteen wounded, including the ship's captain. The British seized four deserters from the Royal Navy—three of them American citizens; one of the deserters, British subject Jenkin Ratford, was hanged. Damaged and humiliated, the *Chesapeake* returned to port. Americans were outraged and united. "But one feeling pervades the nation," said a leading Democratic-Republican, former congressman Joseph Nicholson. "All distinctions of Federalism and Democracy are banished." The *Chesapeake* affair not only intensified the emotional impact

■ *Boarding and Taking of the American Ship* Chesapeake (1816) portrays crew from the British frigate *Leopard* fighting to search the *U.S.S. Chesapeake* for British navy deserters. The sailors of the *Chesapeake* resisted but the British overpowered them and seized four deserters, three of them American citizens. Americans were humiliated and angered by the British violation of American rights.   (William L. Clements Library)

of impressment but also exposed American military weakness.

Had the United States been better prepared militarily, the ensuing howl of public indignation might have brought about a declaration of war. But the still-fledgling country was ill equipped to defend its neutral rights with force; it was certainly no match for the British navy. With Congress in recess, Jefferson was able to avoid hostilities, choosing instead what he called "peaceable coercion." In July the president closed American waters to British warships to prevent similar incidents, and soon thereafter he increased military and naval expenditures. In December 1807 Jefferson again put economic pressure on Great Britain by invoking the Non-Importation Act, followed eight days later by a new restriction, the Embargo Act.

The Embargo Act was intended to avoid war. Jefferson thought of it as a short-term measure to prevent confrontation between American merchant vessels and British and French warships and to put pressure on France and England by denying them American products. The embargo forbade all exports from the United States to any country. Foreign ships delivering goods left American ports with empty holds. U.S. exports dropped some 80 percent in 1808, but smuggling blossomed overnight.

Few American policies were as well intentioned and as unpopular and unsuccessful as Jefferson's embargo.

EMBARGO ACT

Although "peaceable coercion" had been an enlightened concept in international affairs, some Democratic-Republicans felt uneasy about interfering with trade. Federalists opposed the embargo vociferously. Some feared its impact abroad. "If England [were to] sink," Federalist vice-presidential candidate Rufus King said in 1808, expressing Federalist pro-British sympathies, "her fall will prove the grave of our liberties." Mercantile New England, the heart of Federalist opposition to Jefferson, took the brunt of the resulting economic depression. In the winter of 1808–1809, talk of secession spread through New England port cities.

Although general unemployment soared, some individuals benefited from the embargo. Merchants with ships abroad (those not idled by the embargo) and merchants willing to risk the lax enforcement to trade illegally could garner enormous profits. U.S. manufacturers received a boost, since the domestic market became theirs exclusively, and merchants began to shift their capital from shipping to manufacturing.

DOMESTIC MANUFACTURING

Factories were still new in America. English immigrant Samuel Slater set up the first American textile mill in Rhode Island in the 1790s. It used water-powered spinning machines that he had built from memorized British models. Though Federalists like Alexander Hamilton, through his *Report on Manufactures* (see

Industrial Piracy

Though Americans pride themselves on inventiveness and hard work, their start in industrial development depended on importing technology, sometimes by stealth. Great Britain, which in the late eighteenth century had pioneered the invention of mechanical weaving and power looms, knew the value of its head start in the industrial revolution and prohibited the export of textile technology. But the British-born brothers Samuel and John Slater, their Scottish-born power-loom-builder William Gilmore, and Bostonians Francis Cabot Lowell and Nathan Appleton evaded British restrictions and patents to establish America's first textile factories.

As an apprentice and then a supervisor in a British cotton-spinning factory, Samuel Slater had mastered the machinery and the process. Britain forbade the export of textile technology, so Slater emigrated to the United States disguised as a farmer. In 1790 in Pawtucket, Rhode Island, on the Blackstone River, he opened the first water-powered spinning mill in America, rebuilding the complex machines from memory. With his brother John and their Rhode Island partners—Moses and Obadiah Brown and William Almy—Slater later built and oversaw mills in Rhode Island and Massachusetts. In 1815 he hired a recent immigrant, William Gilmore, to build a water-powered loom like those used in Britain. Later in the 1820s the Slaters introduced British steam-powered looms. Spinning and weaving would now be done in New England factories organized on British models.

In 1810, Francis Cabot Lowell had the same idea as the Slaters: to build modern mills with mechanical, water-powered looms. Lowell took a family vacation to Britain, and, in Edinburgh, Scotland, he met fellow Bostonian Nathan Appleton. Impressed by the textile mills they had seen in Britain, they laid plans to introduce water-powered mechanical weaving into the United States. They knew they had to acquire the "improved manufactures" from Britain that had made Manchester famous as a textile center. Lowell went to Manchester, during the day visiting and observing the factories and meeting the factory managers. At night, he returned to his hotel to sketch from memory the power looms and processes he saw. Back in the United States, he and others formed the Boston Associates, which created the Waltham-Lowell Mills based on Lowell's industrial piracy. The Lowell boarding houses, however, were intended as an alternative to the tenements and slums of Manchester. Within a few years, textiles would be a major American industry, and the Associates would dominate it.

Thus the modern American industrial revolution began with international links, not homegrown American inventions. Ingenuity and industrial piracy put the United States on the road to industrial advancement.

This contemporary painting shows the Boston Manufacturing Company's 1814 textile factory at Waltham, Massachusetts. All manufacturing processes were brought together under one roof, and the company built its first factories in rural New England to tap roaring rivers as a power source. (Courtesy of Gore Place Society, Waltham, Mass.)

page 199), had pushed the United States to promote manufacturing, Jefferson envisioned an "empire of liberty" that was agricultural and commercial, not industrial. Holding fast to frugal, limited government, the Democratic-Republican policy did not promote industry. Still, disruption in commerce made domestic manufactures profitable. In 1807 there were twenty cotton and woolen mills in New England; by 1813 there were more than two hundred. The embargo actually had little impact on Britain. The British most severely hurt—West Indians and factory workers in England—had no voice in policy. English merchants actually gained because they took over the Atlantic carrying trade from the stalled American ships. And because of a successful British blockade of Europe, the embargo had little practical effect on the French. Indeed, it gave France an excuse to set privateers against American ships that had evaded the embargo and were, possibly, heading to British ports. The French cynically claimed that such ships were British ships in disguise because the embargo prevented American vessels from sailing.

As the election of 1808 approached, the Democratic-Republicans were weakened by factional dissent and dissatisfaction in seaboard states hobbled by the embargo. Although nine state legislatures passed resolutions urging Jefferson to run again, the president followed Washington's lead in renouncing a third term. He supported James Madison, his secretary of state, as the Democratic-Republican standard-bearer. For the first time, however, the Democratic-Republican nomination was contested. Madison won the endorsement of the party's congressional caucus, but Virginia Democratic-Republicans put forth James Monroe, who later withdrew, and some easterners supported Vice President George Clinton. Madison and Clinton headed the ticket.

ELECTION OF 1808

Charles Cotesworth Pinckney and Rufus King again headed the Federalist ticket, but with new vigor. The Younger Federalists, led by Harrison Gray Otis and other Bostonians, made the most of the widespread disaffection with Republican policy, especially the embargo. Although Pinckney received only 47 electoral votes to Madison's 122, the Federalists offered genuine competition. Pinckney carried all of New England except Vermont, and he won Delaware and some electoral votes in two other states. Federalists also gained seats in Congress and captured the New York State legislature. The Federalist future looked promising.

Under the pressure of domestic opposition, the embargo eventually collapsed. In its place, the Non-Intercourse Act of 1809 reopened trade with all nations except Britain and France, and it authorized the president to

NON-INTERCOURSE ACT

resume trade with Britain or France if either of them ceased to violate neutral rights. On leaving office in March, Jefferson expressed the weight of his failure: "Never did a prisoner, released from his chains," he wrote, "feel such relief as I in shaking off the shackles of power."

The new act solved only the problems created by the embargo; it did not prevent further British and French interference with American commerce. For one brief moment it appeared to work. In June 1809 President Madison reopened trade with England after the British minister to the United States assured him that Britain would repeal restrictions on American trade. His Majesty's government in London, however, repudiated the minister's assurances, and Madison reverted to nonintercourse.

When the Non-Intercourse Act expired in 1810, Congress substituted a variant, Macon's Bill Number 2, that exchanged the proverbial stick for a carrot. The bill reopened trade with both Great Britain and France but provided that when either nation stopped violating American commercial rights, the president could suspend American commerce with the other. Madison, eager to avoid war, fell victim to French duplicity. When Napoleon accepted the offer, Madison declared nonintercourse with Great Britain in 1811. Napoleon, however, tricked him. The French continued to seize American ships, and nonintercourse failed a second time. But because the Royal Navy dominated the seas, Britain, not France, became the main focus of American hostility.

"Mr. Madison's War"

Though unprepared for war in 1812, the United States under President Madison seemed unable to avoid it. Economic pressure had failed to protect American ships and sailors. In truth, the United States had limited influence over British policy because the conflict was part of the ongoing wars between Britain with its continental allies, and France. Having exhausted all efforts to alter British policy, and fearing for the survival of American independence, the United States drifted toward war. The Democratic-Republican "War Hawks," elected to Congress in 1810, cried loudest for war. Pro-war newspapers, like the *National Intelligencer*, declared, "Our cause is just, and if we are decided and firm, success is inevitable." Britain's response was too little, too late. In spring 1812, the admiralty ordered British ships not to stop, search, or seize American warships.

Then in June 1812, Britain reopened the seas to American shipping. Hard times had hit the British Isles: the Anglo-French conflict had blocked much British commerce to the European continent, and exports to the United States had fallen 80 percent. But two days after the change in British policy, before word of it had crossed the Atlantic, Congress declared war.

In his message to Congress on June 1, 1812, President Madison enumerated familiar grievances: impressment, interference with neutral trading rights, and British alliances with western Indians. More generally, the Democratic-Republicans resolved to defend American independence and honor, but some Americans saw in the war an opportunity to conquer and annex British Canada. In Congress partisanship, regional loyalties, and personal bitterness dominated debate. Most militant were the War Hawks, land-hungry southerners and westerners, all Democratic-Republicans, led by John C. Calhoun of South Carolina and first-term congressman and House Speaker Henry Clay of Kentucky. John Randolph of Roanoke, an opponent of war, charged angrily, "Agrarian cupidity, not maritime rights, urges war." He heard "but one word" in Congress: "Canada! Canada! Canada!" Most representatives from the coastal states, and especially the Northeast, opposed war because armed conflict with the Royal Navy would interrupt American shipping. On June 4, the House voted 79 to 49 for war; two weeks later the Senate followed suit, 19 to 13. Republicans favored war by a vote of 98 to 23; Federalists opposed it 39 to 0. On June 19, President Madison signed the bill. Critics instantly called it "Mr. Madison's War."

DEBATE ON THE WAR

During these years politics and personal animosities were often so intense that civility dissolved. Political compromise and cooperation, essential to politics, seemed almost impossible. But social events at the Executive Mansion, dominated by the magnetic Dolley Madison, provided the site for political compromises. She had, said one observer, "the magic power of converting enemies into friends." Jefferson had used small dinners to guide domestic politics and relations with Great Britain, but Dolley Madison made hosting an art. At state dinners, she sat at the head of the table, and made socializing a state craft. Under Dolley Madison, the White House took on its modern role as the focus of presidential politics. She introduced the inaugural ball. Her Wednesday evening socials in the oval drawing room brought all political factions together, the only place where political enemies talked cordially. James Madison lacked the intellect of Jefferson, but with his

DOLLEY MADISON AND FEMALE POLITICAL WORK

wife in the lead, he was far more successful a politician than had been Jefferson.

The war unfolded as a series of scuffles and skirmishes, for which the U.S. Army and Navy and the state militias were unprepared. Officers executed campaigns poorly, and full-scale battles happened rarely (see Map 9.3). But the Americans had the advantage of fighting close to home.

RECRUITMENT

Jefferson's warning that "our constitution is a peace establishment—it is not calculated for war" proved true. Though the U.S. Navy had a corps of experienced officers who had proved their mettle in the Barbary War, it was no match for the Royal Navy. The U.S. Army had neither an able staff nor an adequate force of enlisted men. By 1812 the U.S. Military Academy at West Point, founded in 1802, had produced only eighty-nine regular officers. Senior army officers were aged Revolutionary War veterans or political hacks. The army depended on state militias to recruit volunteers, but not all states cooperated. The government offered enlistees a sign-up bonus of $16, monthly pay of $5, a full set of clothes, and a promise of three months' pay and rights to purchase 160 acres of western land upon discharge. Forty-two percent of the enlistees were illiterate.

At first, recruitment in the West went well. Civic spirit, desire for land, strong anti-Indian sentiment, and fear of Tecumseh's pan-Indian appeals and resistance stimulated thousands of frontiersmen to enlist. The army made itself more acceptable to new recruits by abolishing flogging as punishment in 1812. Within a year, however, frontier enlistments declined. Word spread that the War Department was six to twelve months behind in paying soldiers. Supplies were inadequate; troops often lacked shoes, uniforms, or blankets, and the rations they received were sometimes spoiled.

Raising an army proved even more difficult in New England, where many viewed the conflict as a Democratic-Republican affair—"Mr. Madison's War"—and Federalists discouraged enlistments. Even some New England Democratic-Republicans declined to raise volunteer companies. Those who accepted promised their men that they would serve only in a defensive role, as in Maine where they guarded the coastline. Indeed, the inability of the United States to mount a successful invasion of Canada was due in part to the army's failure to assemble an effective force. Militias in New England and New York often refused to fight outside their states.

Nonetheless, Canada was tempting, and Americans expected to take it quickly. The mighty Royal Navy could not reach the Great Lakes separating the United States and Canada because there was no direct access to

Map 9.3   Major Campaigns of the War of 1812

The land war centered on the U.S.-Canadian border, the Chesapeake Bay, and the Louisiana and Mississippi Territories.

INVASION OF CANADA

them from the Atlantic. Canada's population of just 0.5 million was a fraction of the United States's 7.5 million. Canada had 7,000 regulars in uniform; the United States, 12,000. And Americans hoped that the French in Canada might welcome U.S. forces.

Begun with high hopes, the invasion of Canada ended in disaster. The American strategy concentrated on the West, aiming to split Canadian forces and isolate the

pro-British Indians. At the outset of the war, Tecumseh joined the British, who promised him in return an Indian nation in the Great Lakes region. U.S. general William Hull, territorial governor of Michigan, marched his troops into Upper Canada, with the goal of conquering Montreal. More experienced as a politician than as a soldier, Hull had surrounded himself with newly minted colonels as politically astute and militarily ignorant as he was. Although his forces in the area outnumbered the

■ Michael Felice Corne depicts the U.S.S. *Constitution* engaging H.M.S. *Guerrière* in the Atlantic. The *Constitution*'s victories emboldened the U.S. Navy and earned the ship the nickname "Old Ironsides." (New Haven Colony Historical Society)

British and their Indian allies, Hull waged a timid campaign, retreating more than he attacked. His abandonment of Mackinac Island and Fort Dearborn in Chicago and his surrender of Fort Detroit left the entire Midwest exposed to the enemy. The only bright spot was the September 1812 defense of Fort Harrison in Indiana Territory by Captain Zachary Taylor, who provided the Americans with their first land victory. By the winter of 1812–1813, the British controlled about half of the Old Northwest.

The United States had no greater success on the Niagara front, where New York borders Canada. At the Battle of Queenstown, Canada, north of Niagara, the U.S. Army met defeat because the New York militia refused to leave New York. This frustrating scenario was repeated near Lake Champlain, when the New York militia's refusal to cross the border into Canada foiled American plans to attack Montreal. And the opposition proved tenacious; British regulars, their Indian allies, and Canadians, many who were loyalists who had fled to Canada at the time of the American Revolution, defeated the American invaders.

The navy provided the only good news in the first year of the war. The U.S.S. *Constitution,* the U.S.S. *Wasp,* and the U.S.S. *United States* all

NAVAL BATTLES bested British warships on the Atlantic Ocean. The *Constitution*'s 1812 rout of H.M.S. *Guerrière* in the Atlantic emboldened the U.S. Navy and earned the American ship the nickname "Old

Ironsides." In the first year of war the Americans lost 20 percent of their ships, while in defeat the British lost just 1 percent of their vessels. The United States, however, could ill afford to lose *any* ships. Democratic-Republican frugality had left the navy with only seventeen ships in 1812. It could not fight the British in a general naval war, and thus Britannia ruled the waves.

The Royal Navy blockaded the Chesapeake and Delaware Bays in December 1812, and by 1814 the blockade covered nearly all American ports along the Atlantic and Gulf coasts. After 1811, American trade overseas had declined nearly 90 percent, and the decline in revenues from customs duties threatened to bankrupt the federal government and prostrate New England.

The contest for control of the Great Lakes, the key to the war in the Northwest, evolved as a shipbuilding race.

GREAT LAKES CAMPAIGN Under Master Commandant Oliver Hazard Perry and shipbuilder Noah Brown, the United States outbuilt the British on Lake Erie and defeated them at the bloody Battle of Put-in-Bay on September 10, 1813. With this costly victory, the Americans gained control of Lake Erie.

General William Henry Harrison then began what proved to be among the United States's most successful land campaigns in the war. A ragged group of Kentucky militia volunteers who had been drafted into the regular army marched 20 to 30 miles a day to join Harrison's forces in Ohio. They were armed only with swords and

■ *Ballou's Pictorial Drawing-Room Companion* depicts the Battle of New Orleans, the last campaign of the War of 1812. Andrew Jackson's troops—army regulars, Tennessee and Kentucky volunteers, and two companies of African American volunteers from New Orleans—held off the better-trained British troops in January 1815. The battle made Andrew Jackson a national hero.   (Historic New Orleans Collection)

knives. Now 4,500 strong, Harrison's force attacked and took Detroit. Then they crossed to Canada, pursuing and defeating the British, Shawnee, and Chippewa forces on October 5 at the Battle of the Thames. In victory the United States captured 600 British troops and great amounts of war materiel; the United States regained control of the Old Northwest. Tecumseh died in the battle, and with his death expired Native American unity. Following the loss of their leader, some Indians joined the United States against Britain. After the Battle of the Thames, the Americans razed the Canadian capital of York (now Toronto). Though they did not have enough troops to hold the city, they looted and burned the Parliament building before withdrawing. The stunning land victory had the added effect of stopping the British on Lake Ontario and occupying British operations on Lake Erie.

After defeating Napoleon in Europe in April 1814, the British launched a land counteroffensive against the United States, concentrating on the Chesapeake Bay region. In retaliation for the burning of York—and to divert American troops from Lake Champlain, where the British planned a new offensive—royal troops occupied Washington, D.C., in August and set it ablaze, leaving the presidential mansion and parts of the city burning all night. Chaos ruled. The president and cabinet had planned to rendezvous in Frederick, Maryland, but Madison and his advisers fled to Virginia. Dolley Madison stayed in town long enough to oversee the removal of cabinet documents and—famously—save Gilbert Stuart's portrait of George Washington.

The British intended the attack on the capital only as a diversion. The major battle occurred in September 1814 at Baltimore, where the Americans held firm. Francis Scott Key, detained on a British ship, watched the bombardment of Fort McHenry from Baltimore harbor and the next morning wrote the verses of "The Star-Spangled Banner" (which became the national anthem in 1931). Although the British inflicted heavy damage both materially and psychologically, they achieved little militarily. Their offensive at Lake Champlain proved equally unsuccessful when American ships turned back a British flotilla at Plattsburgh. The British halted their offense; the war was stalemated.

The last campaigns of the war took place in the South, against the Creeks along the Gulf of Mexico and

BURNING OF WASHINGTON

CAMPAIGN AGAINST THE CREEKS

against the British around New Orleans (see Map 9.3). The Creeks had responded to the call of Tecumseh, whose mother was a Creek, to resist U.S. expansion. Some had died in Indiana Territory, at Prophetstown on Tippecanoe Creek, when General Harrison's troops routed Shawnee forces there in 1811. In December 1812 General Andrew Jackson raised his Tennessee militia to fight the Creeks. By late 1813 his anti-Creek campaign stalled for lack of supplies. His men, who had signed up for a year, muttered about going home. Jackson refused to discharge them; they could not, he said, abandon their posts on enemy ground. Officers repeatedly threatened to shoot any man who left. Indeed, in March 1814 Jackson executed John Woods, a militiaman, for disobedience and mutiny. This act broke the opposition within the ranks, and Jackson's men defeated the Creek nation at the Battle of Horseshoe Bend in Mississippi Territory in March 1814.

The victory began Jackson's rise to political prominence. In the 1814 Treaty of Fort Jackson, the Creeks ceded two-thirds of their land and withdrew to the southern and western part of Mississippi Territory (what is now Alabama); the removal of Indians from the South had begun. Jackson became a major general in the regular army and continued south toward the Gulf of Mexico. To forestall a British invasion at Pensacola Bay, which guarded an overland route to New Orleans, Jackson seized Pensacola—in Spanish Florida—in November 1814. Then, after securing Mobile, he marched on to New Orleans to defend it against the British.

The Battle of New Orleans was the last campaign of the war. Early in December the British fleet landed 1,500 men east of the city, hoping to seize the mouth of the Mississippi River and thus strangle the lifeline of the American West. They faced American regulars, Tennessee and Kentucky volunteers, and two companies of free African American volunteers from New Orleans. For three weeks the British under Sir Edward Pakenham and the Americans led by Jackson played cat-and-mouse. Finally, on January 8, 1815, the two forces met head-on. In fortified positions, Jackson's poorly trained army held its ground against two frontal assaults from a British contingent of 6,000. At day's end, more than 2,000 British soldiers lay dead or wounded; the Americans suffered only 21 casualties. Andrew Jackson emerged a national hero, and Americans memorialized the battle in song and paintings. The Battle of New Orleans actually took place two weeks after the end of the war. Unknown to the participants, a treaty had been signed in Ghent, Belgium, on December 24, 1814.

BATTLE OF NEW ORLEANS

Peace and Consequences

The U.S. government had gone to war reluctantly and throughout the conflict probed for a diplomatic end to hostilities. In 1813 President Madison eagerly accepted a Russian offer to mediate, but Great Britain balked. Three months later, British foreign minister Lord Castlereagh suggested opening peace talks. It took more than ten months to arrange meetings, but in August 1814 a team of American negotiators, including Henry Clay and John Quincy Adams, son of John and Abigail, began talks with the British in Ghent.

The Ghent treaty made no mention of the issues that had led to war. The United States received no satisfaction on impressment, blockades, or other maritime rights for neutrals. British demands for an independent Indian nation in the Northwest and territorial cessions from Maine to Minnesota likewise went unsatisfied. The Treaty of Ghent essentially restored the prewar status quo. It provided for an end to hostilities with the British and with Native Americans, release of prisoners, restoration of conquered territory, and arbitration of boundary disputes. Ironically, the treaty was concluded on December 24, 1814, but the news took 7 weeks to reach the United States and the war officially ended when the Senate ratified the treaty on February 17, 1815.

Why did the negotiators settle for so little? Events in Europe had made peace and the status quo acceptable at the end of 1814, as they had not been in 1812. Napoleon's defeat allowed the United States to abandon its demands, since peace in Europe made impressment and interference with American commerce moot issues. Similarly, war-weary Britain—its treasury nearly depleted—stopped pressing for a military victory.

The War of 1812 affirmed the independence of the American republic and ensured Canada's independence from the United States. Nearly 300,000 troops had taken up arms to maintain independence; almost 2,000 died for the cause, and 4,000 were wounded. Although conflict with Great Britain over trade and territory continued, it never again led to war. The experience strengthened America's resolve to steer clear of European politics because the Anglo-French conflagration had drawn the United States into war. At the same time, with Indian resistance broken, U.S. expansion would spread south and west, not north to Canada.

CONSEQUENCES

Conflict carried disastrous results for most Native Americans. Although they were not a party to the Treaty of Ghent, the ninth article of the pact pledged the United States to end hostilities and to restore "all the possessions, rights, and privileges" that Indians had enjoyed before the war. Midwestern Indians signed more than a dozen treaties with the United States in 1815, but they had little meaning. With the death of Tecumseh, the Indians had lost their most powerful political and military leader; with the withdrawal of the British, they had lost their strongest ally. The Shawnees, Potawatomis, Chippewas, and others had lost the means to resist American expansion.

The war exposed contradictions and American fears about its growing African American population. In the Deep South, fear of arming slaves kept them out of the military except in New Orleans, where a free black militia dated back to Spanish control of Louisiana. In the border states, in the Chesapeake area, and in the Midwest, the British army recruited slaves, offering them freedom in return for joining their side. Thus the British assault on Washington and Baltimore included former slaves. Ironically, the United States made the same offer to slaves in Canada, and both sides gave freedom to slaves in the Old Northwest who joined the military. New York State offered freedom to slaves who enlisted, and compensated their masters. In Philadelphia black leaders formed a "Black Brigade" to defend the city.

The war also exposed weaknesses in defense and transportation at home. American generals had found U.S. roads inadequate to move troops and supplies. In the Northwest, General Harrison's troops had depended on homemade cartridges and gifts of clothing from Ohio residents; in Maine, troops had melted down spoons to make bullets. Improved transportation and a well-equipped army became national priorities; both were vital for westward expansion. In 1815 President Madison responded by centralizing control of the military and building a line of forts for coastal defense, and Congress voted a standing army of ten thousand men—one-third of the army's wartime strength but three times the size of the army during Jefferson's administration. In 1818 the National Road reached Wheeling, Virginia (now West Virginia), from its Cumberland, Maryland, beginning and carried settlers westward (see page 249).

Perhaps most important of all, the war stimulated economic growth. The embargo, the Non-Importation and Non-Intercourse Acts, and the war itself spurred the production of manufactured goods because New England capitalists began to invest in home manufactures and factories. The effects of these changes were far-reaching (see Chapter 10).

Finally, the conflict sealed the fate of the Federalists. Realizing that they could not win a presidential election in wartime, the Federalists joined renegade Democratic-Republicans in supporting New York City mayor DeWitt Clinton for president in the election of 1812. Federalist organization peaked at the state level as the Younger Federalists campaigned hard. The Federalists nevertheless lost to President Madison and vice-presidential candidate Elbridge Gerry of Massachusetts by 128 to 89 electoral votes; areas that favored the war (the South and West) remained solidly Democratic-Republican. The Federalists gained some congressional seats and carried many local elections, but their star was waning.

With the war stalemated and the New England economy shattered by embargo and war, delegates from New England met in Hartford, Connecticut,

HARTFORD CONVENTION

for three weeks in the winter of 1814–1815 to discuss revising the national compact or pulling out of the republic. Moderates prevented a resolution of secession, but the twenty-six convention delegates condemned the war and the embargo and endorsed radical changes in the Constitution, such as restricting the presidency to one term and requiring a two-thirds congressional vote to admit new states to the Union. The delegates plotted preserving New England Federalist political power as electoral strength was shifting to the South and West.

The timing of the Hartford Convention proved lethal to the Federalists. The victory at New Orleans and news of the peace treaty made the convention look ridiculous, if not treasonous. Rather than harassing a beleaguered wartime administration, the Federalists found themselves in retreat before a rising tide of nationalism. Though the Federalists survived in a handful of states until the 1820s, the faction dissolved. The War of 1812, at first a source of revival as opponents of war flocked to the Federalist banner, helped speed its demise.

Summary

The 1800 election marked the peaceful transition in power from the Federalists to the opposition Democratic-Republicans. Thomas Jefferson replaced John Adams as president and sought both to unify the nation and to solidify Democratic-Republican control of the government. Jeffersonians favored frugal government, and they cut the budget, military forces, and diplomatic missions.

The Supreme Court under Chief Justice John Marshall remained a Federalist bastion. Both parties fought over the judiciary, and Marshall would ensure, until 1835, the dominance of Federalist principle: federal supremacy over the states and the protection of commerce and capital. In *Marbury v. Madison* (1803), the Supreme Court established its great power of judicial review.

Jefferson considered the acquisition of Louisiana Territory and the commissioning of Lewis and Clark's expedition among his significant presidential accomplishments. In a single act the United States doubled its size. Increasingly Americans looked westward, and Lewis and Clark's Corps of Discovery practiced "buckskin diplomacy" while exploring the land, flora, fauna, and people west of the Mississippi. Americans quickly moved to settle Louisiana.

With Jefferson and his successor James Madison, the Democratic-Republicans won every presidential election in this period. Though the electorate was limited only to males and mostly to whites, both the Federalists and the Democratic-Republicans competed at the grassroots level for popular support. Political conflict was bitter, and divisions were real. Sometimes they could prove fatal as in the Burr-Hamilton duel. Assisted by the partisan press and the social-politicking women, political intensity began to build a national political culture.

Despite internal divisions, the greatest threats came from abroad. In the war with the Barbary states, the United States sought to guard its commerce and ships on the high seas. The second war with Britain—the War of 1812—was fought for similar reasons but against a much more formidable power. The peace treaty reaffirmed American independence; thereafter the nation was able to settle disputes with Great Britain at the bargaining table. The war also dealt a serious blow to Indian resistance in the West and South. At the same time, embargoes and war forced Americans to look toward building domestic markets and jump-started American manufacturing. Military and diplomatic assertiveness brought Americans a sense of national identity and self-confidence.

LEGACY FOR A PEOPLE AND A NATION
States' Rights and Nullification

When the Constitution replaced the Articles of Confederation, the United States had a much stronger central government, but the exact nature of the relationship between the states and the central government was ambiguous, because Constitutional Convention delegates could not agree on whether states or nation should prevail in the event of irreconcilable conflict. The Tenth Amendment to the Constitution offered only a slight clarification: powers not delegated to the

central government, it said, were reserved to the states or to the people. The exact nature of the federal system's shared power, and in fact who would determine which powers had been delegated to which authority, remained to be defined.

When New England Federalists met in Hartford at the end of 1814 to prepare a list of grievances against "Mr. Madison's War," they drew on the doctrine of nullification, first announced sixteen years earlier in the Kentucky and Virginia Resolutions, written by Thomas Jefferson and James Madison, respectively. Opposing the Alien and Sedition Acts, these "founding fathers" had asserted that if the national government assumed powers not delegated to it by the Constitution, states could nullify federal actions—that is, declare them inoperative within state borders. At Hartford, Federalist representatives of New England states discussed taking nullification a step further by actually seceding, or withdrawing from the Union. They backed away from this extreme step, but their formulation of the rights of states to evaluate and nullify federal authority left a legacy for dissent that would be played out in crises to the present day.

In the following decade, South Carolina nullified federal tariffs that it opposed, and in 1861 southern states threatened by Abraham Lincoln's election to the presidency claimed the right of secession. Although the Civil War supposedly settled the issue—states could neither nullify federal law nor secede—southern states opposing the Supreme Court's 1954 ruling in favor of school integration again claimed the right to nullify "unauthorized" federal policy within their borders. In the 1990s, some western states sought to nullify federal environmental laws. The Hartford Convention's legacy for a people and a nation provides Americans who dissent from national policy a model for using state governments as vehicles for their protests.

The **history Companion** *powered by Eduspace®*

Your primary source for interactive quizzes, exercises, and more to help you learn efficiently.
http://history.college.hmco.com/students

THE OLD GRANITE STATE,

Judson   Abby.   John.   Asa.

A SONG,

Price 50 Cts Nett.

COMPOSED, ARRANGED AND SUNG, BY

THE HUTCHINSON FAMILY.

NATIONALISM, EXPANSION, AND THE MARKET ECONOMY 1816–1845

*T*he Hutchinson Family, also known as the Tribe of Jesse, was the most popular singing group in nineteenth-century America. Abby, Asa, Jesse, John, and Judson Hutchinson—five of a family of sixteen children from rural New Hampshire—performed the patriotic, religious, and sentimental songs that had dominated popular music since the Revolution. They initiated new musical styles, wrote lyrics full of social commentary, and made entertainment a commodity, promoted and performed in the market economy.

Unlike most musical groups, the Tribe of Jesse not only sang but also presented well-rehearsed and elaborately produced performances. They used folk tunes that the audiences found familiar and enjoyed, but their lyrics explored controversial topics such as abolition and temperance. Their 1844 "Get Off the Track!" used imagery from railroads, the newest form of transportation, to hail the unstoppable power of the antislavery movement.

The Hutchinson Family traveled by rail, too, performing across the expanding United States but drawing their largest audiences in the growing cities of the North. The family's fee for a single night in the 1840s reached $1,000, about four hundred times a worker's daily wage. They had an entourage of managers, agents, and publishers. Hawkers sold sheet music, portraits, and songbooks at the Hutchinsons' concerts. The Hutchinson Family made a business of music and entertainment, selling nostalgia and reform.

The Hutchinsons' off-stage lives, too, bridged the old and the new. They had come from the farms of New Hampshire, as they sang in "The 'Old Granite State.'" They left home, they explained in song, with the blessing of their "aged parents," to sing of liberty, traveling "round the World." Besides their musical talent, the Hutchinson Family offered their audiences reassurance in a time of rapid change. By setting their lyrics to familiar hymns (we are "good old fashioned singers"), they connected their advocacy of reform with the comfortable

◀ The Hutchinson Family celebrated their native rural New Hampshire in "The 'Old Granite State,'" their most popular song. They made a business of performing, and hawkers sold their sheet music at concerts.   (Courtesy, David Katzman)

CHRONOLOGY

1815 • Madison proposes internal improvements

1816 • Second Bank of the United States chartered
 • Tariff of 1816 imposes first substantial duties
 • Monroe elected president, Tompkins vice president

1817 • Rush-Bagot Treaty limits British and American naval forces on Lake Champlain and Great Lakes

1819 • *McCulloch v. Maryland* establishes supremacy of federal over state law
 • Adams-Onís Treaty with Spain gives Florida to the U.S. and defines Louisiana territorial border

1819–23 • Hard times bring unemployment

1820 • Missouri Compromise creates formula for admitting slave and free states
 • Monroe reelected president, Tompkins vice president

1820s • New England textile mills expand

1823 • Monroe Doctrine closes Western Hemisphere to European intervention

1824 • *Gibbons v. Ogden* affirms federal over state authority in interstate commerce
 • Monroe proposes Indian removal

1825 • Erie Canal completed

1830 • Railroad era begins
 • Congress passes Indian Removal Act

1830s • McCormick reaper, Deere steel plow patented

1830s–40s • Cotton production shifts to Mississippi valley

1831 • Trail of Tears begins with the forced removal of the Choctaws
 • Cherokees turn to courts to defend treaty rights in *Cherokee Nation v. Georgia*

1832 • Marshall declares Cherokee nation a distinct political community in *Worcester v. Georgia*

1834 • Women workers strike at Lowell textile mills

1835–42 • Seminoles successfully resist removal in Second Seminole War

1836 • Second Bank of the United States closes

1837 • *Charles River Bridge v. Warren Bridge* encourages new enterprises
 • Panic of 1837 begins economic downturn

1839–43 • Hard times strike again

1842 • *Commonwealth v. Hunt* declares strikes lawful

1844 • Government grant sponsors first telegraph line

past. And by describing a bucolic future, they reassured their audiences that the present, with all its turmoil, would turn out well.

The Hutchinsons' concert tours exemplified the market economy, in which goods and services sold in cash or credit transactions created a network of exchange that bound distant enterprises together. The family performed in western areas in the 1840s that had had no American settlements twenty years before. The canals and railroads that carried them also increasingly linked the nation's regions after the War of 1812. People moved inland from the seaboard, farmed the rich lands across the Appalachians, and sold their crops at home and abroad. Grain went east to coastal cities, slave-grown cotton went to Europe, and ready-made men's garments from New York and Cincinnati sold across the nation. Increasingly, farmers turned to staple-crop agriculture and city people worked not for themselves but for others, for wages. These large-scale enterprises needed capital, and new financial institutions amassed and loaned it. Mechanization took hold; factories and precision-made machinery put home workshops and handcrafters out of business; on farms, horse-drawn reapers replaced farmhands. In turn, the increased specialization in plantation and commercial agriculture, manufacturing, transportation, and finance further fired the engines of the new nationwide, capitalist, market-oriented economy.

The end of the War of 1812 unleashed this growth. A new nationalist spirit encouraged the economy and promoted western expansion at home, trade abroad, and assertiveness throughout the Western Hemisphere. Economic growth and territorial expansion, however, generated new problems. Sectional conflicts over slavery and economic development created divisions. Migration and changes in the ways people worked created new tensions. Not everyone profited in wealth and opportunity as the Hutchinson Family did. Journeyman tailors, displaced by retailers and cheaper labor, found their trades disappearing. New England farm daughters who became wage workers found their world changing no less radically. Moreover, boom-and-bust cycles, now on a national scale, wrenched livelihoods and lives. Mills, factories, roads, canals, and railroads altered or destroyed the landscape.

Everywhere Americans were on the move. Settlement, North and South, moved to the interior, and farms and cities, linked by rivers, then roads, canals, and railroads, stretched to the Ohio and Mississippi River valleys and beyond. The Indian inhabitants attempted to hold their ground but were in the end removed to the West, pushed off their lands by the same drive for profit— a nationalist spirit reshaping national politics and the dynamic American economy. ■

Postwar Nationalism

*N*ationalism surged after the War of 1812. Self-confident, Americans asserted themselves at home and abroad as Democratic-Republicans borrowed a page from the Federalists' agenda and encouraged economic growth. Though James Monroe would follow James Madison as the last of the presidents who had attended the Constitutional Convention, political power began to shift away from the founders of the republic. Congressional leaders Henry Clay and John C. Calhoun, and those who vied for the presidency in the 1820s—John Quincy Adams and Andrew Jackson— formed a new generation of political leaders with a national outlook.

James Madison inspired the postwar wave of nationalism. In his December 1815 message to Congress, he recommended economic development and military expansion. His agenda included a national bank (the charter of the first bank had expired in 1811) and improved transportation. To raise government revenues and foster manufacturing, Madison called for a protective tariff—a tax on imported goods designed to protect American manufactures. Yet his program acknowledged Jeffersonian republicanism; only a constitutional amendment, Madison argued, could authorize the federal government to build local roads and canals.

NATIONALIST PROGRAM

Congressional leaders saw Madison's program as a way of unifying the country. Democratic-Republican John C. Calhoun of South Carolina and House Speaker Henry Clay of Kentucky believed that the tariff would stimulate industry. The agricultural slave South and West would sell cotton to the churning mills of New England and food to its mill workers. Goods would move on roads and canals, and tariff revenues would provide money to build them. A national bank would handle the transactions.

In the last year of Madison's administration, the Democratic-Republican Congress enacted much of the nationalist program. In 1816 it chartered the Second Bank of the United States to assist the government and to issue currency. Like its predecessor, the bank mixed public and private ownership; the government provided one-fifth of the bank's capital and appointed one-fifth of its directors.

Congress also passed a protective tariff to aid industries that had flourished during the War of 1812 but were now threatened by the resumption of overseas trade. The Tariff of 1816 levied taxes on imported woolens and cottons, and on iron, leather, hats, paper, and sugar, in effect raising their prices in the United States. Foreshadowing a growing trend, support for the tariff divided along sectional lines: New England and the western and Middle Atlantic states stood to benefit and applauded it, but the South did not.

The South did press for better transportation. It was Congressman Calhoun of South Carolina, not the president, who promoted roads and canals to "bind the republic together." However, on March 3, 1817, the day before he left office, Madison vetoed Calhoun's internal improvements (public works) bill as unconstitutional, though he did approve funds for extending the National Road to Ohio, deeming it a military necessity.

James Monroe, Madison's successor, continued Madison's domestic program, supporting tariffs and vetoing internal improvements. Monroe was the third Virginian elected president since 1801. A former senator and twice governor of Virginia, he had served under Madison as secretary of state and of war and used his close association with Jefferson and Madison to attain the presidency.

JAMES MONROE

Among the nation's founders, Monroe was a most ordinary and colorless man who rarely had an original idea. But in 1816 he and his running mate, Daniel Tompkins, easily tromped the last Federalist presidential nominee, Rufus King, garnering all the electoral votes except those of the Federalist strongholds of Massachusetts, Connecticut, and Delaware. A Boston newspaper dubbed this one-party period the "Era of Good Feelings."

Led by Federalist chief justice John Marshall, the Supreme Court became the bulwark of a nationalist point of view. In *McCulloch v. Maryland* (1819), the Court struck down a Maryland law taxing banks within the state that were not chartered by the Maryland legislature—a law aimed at hindering the Baltimore branch of the federally chartered Second Bank of the United States. The Bank of the United States had refused to pay the tax and sued. At issue was state versus

McCULLOCH V. MARYLAND

federal jurisdiction. Speaking for a unanimous Court, Marshall asserted the supremacy of the federal government over the states. "The Constitution and the laws thereof are supreme," he declared. "They control the constitution and laws of the respective states and cannot be controlled by them."

In his opinion Marshall went on to consider whether Congress could issue a bank charter. The Constitution did not spell out such power, but Marshall noted that Congress had the authority to pass "all laws which shall be necessary and proper for carrying into execution" the enumerated powers of government. Marshall ruled that Congress could legally exercise "those great powers on which the welfare of the nation essentially depends." If the ends were legitimate and the means not prohibited, Marshall ruled, a law was constitutional. The Constitution was, in Marshall's words, "intended to endure for ages to come, and consequently, to be adapted to the various causes of human affairs." The Supreme Court declared the bank charter legal. *McCulloch v. Maryland* thus joined nationalism and economics. By asserting federal supremacy, Marshall protected the commercial and industrial interests that favored a national bank; this was federalism in the tradition of Alexander Hamilton (see page 199). The decision was only one in a series of rulings that cemented the federalist view.

Monroe's secretary of state, John Quincy Adams, matched the self-confident Marshall Court in assertiveness and nationalism. A small, austere man once described by a British official as a "bulldog among spaniels," Adams, the son of John and Abigail Adams, was a superb diplomat who spoke six languages. From 1817 to 1825 he brilliantly managed the nation's foreign policy, stubbornly pushing for expansion, fishing rights for Americans in Atlantic waters, political distance from the Old World, and peace. An ardent expansionist, he nonetheless believed that expansion must come through negotiations, not war, and that newly acquired territories must bar slavery. The United States, Adams said in an 1821 Fourth of July speech, "goes not abroad, in search of monsters to destroy. She is the well-wisher to the freedom and independence of all."

JOHN QUINCY ADAMS

But in navigating international waters, Adams faced major challenges. U.S. northern and southern borders were not clearly defined and were a potential source of conflict with Great Britain and Spain. Both war and peace had left many issues with Great Britain unresolved; continued hostility could necessitate an armed U.S.-Canadian border, something neither side could afford. Moreover Great Britain was the largest buyer of American exports, and British textile mills depended on American cotton; both sides looked to commerce to cement better relations. The United States also sought to prevent European conflicts from spilling over into the New World, both to ensure peace in the Western Hemisphere and to build closer commercial relations with the emerging Latin American states.

Though an Anglophobe, Adams worked to strengthen the peace with Great Britain negotiated at Ghent (1814). He found a willing partner in Lord Castlereagh of the British Foreign Office. Though Castlereagh opposed the spread of republicanism and was oriented toward Europe, he recognized the importance of peaceful relations with the United States. In 1817 the two nations agreed in the Rush-Bagot Treaty to limit their naval forces to one ship each on Lake Champlain and Lake Ontario and to two ships each on the four other Great Lakes. This first disarmament treaty of modern times led to the demilita-

■ John Quincy Adams (1767–1848), architect of the Monroe Doctrine, was secretary of state from 1817 to 1825. Thomas Sully's portrait, painted in 1825, captured Adams's determination and stubbornness. (New York State Office of Parks, Recreation, and Historic Preservation, Philipse Manor Hall State Historic Site)

Map 10.1

Missouri Compromise and the State of the Union, 1820

The compromise worked out by House Speaker Henry Clay established a formula that avoided debate over whether new states would allow or prohibit slavery. In the process, it divided the United States into northern and southern regions.

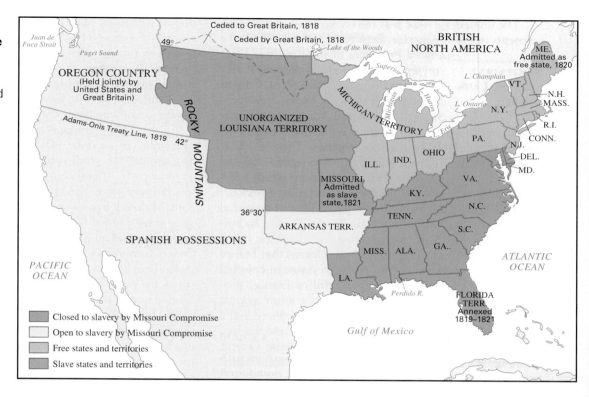

rization of the border between the United States and Canada. Adams then pushed for the Convention of 1818, which fixed the United States–Canadian border from Lake of the Woods in Minnesota westward to the Rockies along the 49th parallel (see Map 10.1). When they could not agree on the boundary west of the Rockies, Britain and the United States settled on joint occupation of Oregon for ten years (renewed indefinitely in 1827).

Adams next moved to settle long-term disputes with Spain. Although the 1803 Louisiana Purchase had omitted reference to Spanish-ruled West Florida, the United States claimed the territory as far east as the Perdido River (the present-day Florida-Alabama border) but occupied only a small finger of the area. During the War of 1812 the United States had seized Mobile and the remainder of West Florida. After the war Adams took advantage of Spain's preoccupation with domestic and colonial troubles to buy East Florida. During the 1818 talks, General Andrew Jackson occupied much of present-day Florida on the pretext of suppressing Seminole raids against American settlements across the border. Adams was furious with Jackson but defended his brazen act.

The following year, Don Luís de Onís, the Spanish minister to the United States, agreed to cede Florida to the United States without payment, while the United

States agreed to renounce its dubious claims to northern Mexico (Texas) and to assume $5 million of claims by American citizens against Spain. The Adams-Onís, or Transcontinental, Treaty also defined the southwestern boundary of the Louisiana Purchase and set the southern border of Oregon at the 42nd parallel (see Map 10.1). Expansion was achieved at little cost and without war.

When the Spanish flag was last lowered over St. Augustine on July 10, 1821, and at Pensacola on July 17, Florida residents differed in how they greeted the United States and its colonial governor, General Andrew Jackson. Some planter-slaveholders and traders welcomed the American flag, but Creeks and Seminoles, free blacks, runaway slaves, and Spanish-speaking town dwellers did not. Many feared Jackson, who had led raids against the Seminoles in Florida in 1814 and 1818. The Spanish encouraged residents to resettle in Mexico, Cuba, or Texas, but most stayed put though wary of the United States.

Conflict between the United States and European nations was temporarily resolved by the Rush-Bagot Treaty, the Convention of 1818, and the Adams-Onís Treaty, but events to the south still threatened American interests. John Quincy Adams's desire to insulate the United States and the Western Hemisphere from European conflict brought about his greatest achievement: the Monroe Doctrine.

The immediate issue was the recognition of new governments in Latin America. Between 1808 and 1822, the

INDEPENDENT STATES IN LATIN AMERICA

United Provinces of the Río de la Plata (present-day northern Argentina, Paraguay, and Uruguay), Chile, Peru, Colombia, and Mexico all broke free from Spain. Monroe and Adams moved cautiously, seeking to avoid conflict with Spain and to be sure of the stability of the new regimes. Then in 1822, shortly after the Adams-Onís Treaty was signed and ratified, the United States became the first nation outside Latin America to recognize the new states, including Mexico.

To the United States, Europe again offered potential threats to the stability of the New World. France, to bolster the weak Spanish monarchy against domestic rebellion, occupied Spain. The United States feared that France would return the new Latin American states to colonial rule. Great Britain, similarly distrustful of France, proposed a joint United States–British declaration against European intervention in the Western Hemisphere and a joint disavowal of territorial ambitions in the region. Adams rejected the British overture. Following George Washington's admonition to avoid foreign entanglements, he insisted that the United States act independently.

Despite clamors to take joint action with Great Britain, Adams refused to budge. Those who favored a multilateral move believed the United States needed British naval power to prevent French or Russian expansion in the New World. But Adams won. "It would be more candid, as well as more dignified," he argued, "to avow our principles explicitly to Russia and France, than to come in as a cockboat in the wake of the British man-of-war." Adams interpreted the British disavowal of territorial ambitions as an attempt to thwart American expansion.

President Monroe presented the American position— the Monroe Doctrine—to Congress in December 1823.

MONROE DOCTRINE

His message called for noncolonization of the Western Hemisphere by European nations, a principle that addressed American anxiety not only about Latin America but also about Russian expansion beyond Alaska and its settlements in California. He also demanded nonintervention by Europe in the affairs of independent New World nations, and he pledged noninterference by the United States in European affairs, including those of Europe's existing New World colonies.

The Monroe Doctrine proved popular at home. It tapped American nationalism and anti-British and anti-European feelings, and it eventually became the foundation of American policy in the Western Hemisphere. Monroe's words, however, carried no force. Indeed, the policy depended on the support of the British, who wanted to keep other European nations out of the hemisphere to protect their dominance in the Atlantic trade. Europeans ignored the Monroe Doctrine; it was the Royal Navy they respected, not American policy.

While nationalism brought Americans together, slavery divided them. Since the drafting of the Constitution,

"FIRE BELL IN THE NIGHT"

political leaders had tried to avoid the issue. The one exception was an act ending the foreign slave trade after January 1, 1808, which passed without much opposition. The act followed the expiration of the constitutional ban (Article I, Section 9) on ending the slave trade before 1808. In 1819, however, slavery crept onto the political agenda when Missouri residents petitioned Congress for admission to the Union as a slave state. Though slavery was dying out in the North, as ensured by gradual emancipation laws (see Chapter 13), border and southern states protected slavery, and Missouri wanted to enter the Union under those terms. For two and a half years the issue dominated Congress. "This momentous question," wrote Thomas Jefferson, fearful for the life of the Union, "like a fire bell in the night, awakened and filled me with terror" (see Map 10.1).

The debate transcended slavery in Missouri. The compromises that had kept the issue under wraps since the Constitutional Convention could collapse. Five new states had joined the Union since 1812: Louisiana (1812), Indiana (1816), Mississippi (1817), Illinois (1818), and Alabama (1819). Of these, Louisiana, Mississippi, and Alabama permitted slavery. Because Missouri was on the same latitude as free Illinois, Indiana, and Ohio (a state since 1803), its admission as a slave state would thrust slavery farther northward. It would also tilt the uneasy political balance in the Senate toward the slave states. In 1819 the Union consisted of eleven slave and eleven free states. If Missouri joined, slave states would have a two-vote edge in the Senate.

Moral issues made slavery an explosive question. Settlers from slave states—Kentuckians and Tennesseans—made up most of the new Missourians. But in the North slavery was slowly dying out, and many northerners had concluded that it was evil. When Representative James Tallmadge Jr. of New York proposed gradual emancipation in Missouri, a passionate and sometimes violent debate ensued. Southerners accused the North of threatening to destroy the Union. "If you persist, the Union will be dissolved," Thomas W. Cobb of Georgia shouted at Tallmadge. "Seas of blood can only extinguish" the fire Tallmadge was igniting, Cobb warned. "Let it come," retorted Tallmadge. The House, which had a northern majority, passed the Tallmadge Amendment, but the Senate rejected it. The two sides were deadlocked.

House Speaker Henry Clay promoted a compromise in 1820. Maine, carved out of Massachusetts, would become a free state balancing Missouri. In the rest of the Louisiana Territory north of latitude 36°30' (Missouri's southern boundary), slavery would be prohibited forever (see Map 10.1). The compromise carried, but the agreement almost unraveled in November when Missouri submitted a constitution that barred free blacks from entering the state. Opponents contended that Missouri would violate the federal constitutional provision that "the citizens of each State shall be entitled to all privileges and immunities of citizens in the several States." Proponents argued that many states, North and South, barred free blacks from entering. But, as historian Ira Berlin has noted, the United States was a slave society, and free people of color would not be equal to whites. In 1821 Clay produced a second compromise: Missouri guaranteed that none of its laws would discriminate against citizens of other states. (Once admitted to the Union, however, Missouri twice adopted laws barring free blacks.)

The Market Economy and Government's Role

Before canals and railroads, farmers had geared production to their own needs and to local and foreign, not national, markets. They lived in interdependent communities and exchanged labor and goods with their neighbors. Farm families produced much of what they needed—food, clothing, candles, soap, and the like—and traded for or purchased items they could not produce, such as cooking pots, horseshoes, coffee, tea, and sugar. The market for staple products—cotton, lumber, and sugar—was international, not domestic.

Increasingly in the years after the War of 1812, Americans became involved in the market economy—growing crops and producing goods specifically for cash and buying items produced by other people. Farms and slave plantations produced crops for market sales. Plantations raised rice, tobacco, sugar, or cotton; farmers grew only one or two crops or raised animals for market. Farm women gave up spinning and weaving and purchased cloth made by wage-earning farm girls in Massachusetts textile mills. Nonfarm men and women sold not goods but their labor for cash, working for wages. By buying goods at market, free farmers and workers increased the demand for manufactured things. Such a

system encouraged specialization. It also energized transportation, as both goods and entertainment, like the Hutchinsons, circulated nationally.

Mechanization, the division of labor, new methods of financing, and improvements in transportation all fueled the expansion of the economy. Goods and services multiplied. This growth, in turn, prompted new improvements and greater opportunities for wage labor. The effect was cumulative; by the 1840s the economy was growing faster than in the previous four decades. While per capita income increased 50 percent between 1800 and 1840, the price of manufactured goods and food fell.

The pace of economic growth, however, was uneven. Prosperity reigned during two long periods, from 1823 to 1835 and from 1843 to 1857. But there were long stretches of economic contraction as well. Contraction and deflation (decline in the general price level) occurred again during the hard times of 1819–1823 and 1839–1843. During these periods banks closed, businesses went under, wages and prices declined, and jobs were hard to find or to keep. Yet even during boom periods major industries like construction offered only cyclical employment. In the 1820s and 1830s, laborers in Baltimore, for example, typically found steady work only from March through October.

EFFECTS OF BOOM AND BUST

In 1819 the postwar boom collapsed. Expansion had been built on easy credit; state banks had printed notes freely, fueling speculative buying of western land. Speculators had bought acreage to sell at a profit rather than to farm. Foreign investment in the United States had soared. When manufacturing fell in 1818, prices spiraled downward. The Second Bank of the United States cut back on loans, thus further shrinking the economy. The United States had a net outflow of capital for the first time since 1813. With urban workers, farmers, and southern planters having less money to spend, the economy declined.

The contraction devastated workers and their families. As a Baltimore physician noted in 1819, working people felt hard times "a thousand fold more than the merchants." They could not build up savings during boom times to get them through the hard times; often they could not make it through the winter without drawing on charity for food, clothing, and firewood.

The 1820s and 1830s were boom times. Internal improvement projects—streets, turnpikes, canals, and railroads—made regular work plentiful, as did building construction. In the 1830s foreign investment soared; from 1832 through 1839, the United States had a net capital inflow of $189 million, or $12 for every man, woman, and child.

■ E. Didier painted *Auction in Chatham Street* in 1834. Auction houses in New York and other cities boomed during hard times. (Museum of the City of New York)

The Panic of 1837 and sustained contraction from 1839 through 1843 led to a bust cycle as workers were helpless to forces beyond their control. Money became tight. Internal savings and foreign investment, which had fueled economic expansion, declined sharply. In the Panic of 1837 many banks could not repay depositors, and states, facing deficits because of the decline in the economy, defaulted on their bonds. European, especially British, investors were furious, became suspicious of all U.S. loans, and withdrew money from the United States.

Hard times had come. New York countinghouses closed their doors. Hungry workers looted a flour merchant. Crowds of laborers gathered at closed banks demanding their deposits. Then, Philip Hone noted in his diary, "a deadly calm pervades this lately flourishing city. No goods are selling, no businesses stirring." In New York, the hungry formed bread lines in front of soup societies, and beggars crowded the sidewalks. In Baltimore in 1839, when hundreds of small manufacturers closed their doors, tailors, milliners, and shipyard and construction workers lost their jobs. Ninety miles to the north, Philadelphia took on an eerie aura. "The streets seemed

deserted," Sidney George Fisher observed in 1842. "The largest [merchant] houses are shut up and to rent, there is no business . . . no money, no confidence." Only auctions boomed, as sheriffs sold off seized property at a quarter of pre-hard-times prices, a dismal scene as portrayed by artist E. Didier in *Auction in Chatham Street* in nearby New York (see the painting above). In smaller cities like Lynn, Massachusetts, shoemakers weathered the hard times by fishing and tending gardens while laborers became scavengers, digging for clams and harvesting dandelions.

What caused the boom-and-bust cycles that brought about such suffering? Generally speaking, they were a direct result of the market economy. As with the expansion following the War of 1812, prosperity stimulated demand for finished goods such as clothing and furniture. Increased demand in turn led not only to higher prices and still higher production but also, because of business optimism and expectation of higher prices, to speculation in land. Investment money was plentiful as Americans saved regularly, and foreign, mostly British,

CAUSES OF BOOM AND BUST

investors, bought U.S. bonds and securities. Then, as with the hard times of 1819, production surpassed demand, causing prices and wages to fall; in response, land and stock values collapsed. Investment money then flowed out of the United States.

In the economic thinking of the time, some considered this process beneficial—a self-adjusting cycle that eliminated unprofitable economic ventures. In theory, people concentrated on the activities they did best, and the economy as a whole became more efficient. Believers in the self-adjusting system also argued that it enhanced individual freedom, since theoretically each seller, whether of goods or labor, determined the price. But in fact the system tied workers to a perpetual roller coaster; they became dependent on wages—and on the availability of jobs—for their very survival. The cycles that governed the market economy influenced every corner of the country as even small localities became tied, or handcuffed, to regional and national markets.

The market economy also ushered in another type of boom-and-bust cycle: harvest and destruction. Canals and railroads spurred demand for distant resources, then accelerated the destruction of forests, natural waterways, and any landscape features that represented obstacles. Railroads made possible large-scale lumbering of pinewood forests in Michigan and Wisconsin. During the 1840s, lumber companies deforested millions of acres, leaving most of that land unfit even for agriculture. The process of harvest and destruction would eventually change the ecology of the United States.

The idea of a market economy drew on eighteenth-century republicanism. Advanced by members of the elite as well as by craftsmen, it emphasized economic liberty and individualism (see page 166). Limited, not active, government, adherents argued, fostered economic expansion because individuals pursuing their own private interests benefited the nation as a whole.

GOVERNMENT ECONOMIC ROLE

Nonetheless, the federal government played an active role in technological and industrial growth. Federal arsenals pioneered new manufacturing techniques that helped to develop the machine-tool industry. The United States Post Office fostered the circulation of information, a critical element in a market economy. The number of post offices grew from three thousand in 1815 to fourteen thousand in 1845. The post office also played a brief but crucial role in the development of the telegraph, financing the first telegraph line, from Washington to Baltimore, in 1844. Invented by artist Samuel F. B. Morse, the telegraph allowed information to travel faster, almost instantaneously, over long distances. To create an atmo-sphere conducive to economic growth and individual creativity, the government protected inventions and domestic industries. Patent laws gave inventors a seventeen-year monopoly on their inventions, and tariffs protected American industry from foreign competition.

Government policy also fostered farm life. Republicanism associated farming with virtue, independence, and productivity, essential values in the new republic, and the federal government surveyed public land and opened it to settlement. Internal improvements such as harbors, roads, and canals—some underwritten by government—linked new farms in the West to markets in the East. When Indians got in the way of expansion, the federal government moved them across the Mississippi River (see pages 263–268).

The federal judiciary validated government promotion of the economy and encouraged business enterprise and risk taking. In *Gibbons v. Ogden* (1824), the Supreme Court overturned the New York State law that gave Robert Fulton and Robert Livingston a monopoly on the New York–New Jersey steamboat trade. Aaron Ogden, a successor, lost the monopoly when Chief Justice John Marshall ruled that the federal power to license new enterprises took precedence over New York's grant of monopoly rights. Marshall declared that Congress's power under the commerce clause of the Constitution extended to "every species of commercial intercourse," including transportation. Within a year, forty-three steamboats were plying Ogden's route.

LEGAL FOUNDATIONS OF COMMERCE

In defining interstate commerce broadly, the Marshall Court expanded federal powers over the economy while restricting the ability of states to control economic activity within their borders. Its action was consistent with *Dartmouth College v. Woodward* (1819), which protected the sanctity of contracts against interference by the states, and with *Fletcher v. Peck* (1810), which voided a Georgia law that violated individuals' rights to make contracts. "If business is to prosper," Marshall wrote, "men must have assurance that contracts will be enforced."

Federal and state courts, in conjunction with state legislatures, also encouraged the proliferation of corporations—organizations entitled to hold property and transact business as if they were individuals. Corporation owners, called shareholders, were granted *limited liability*, or freedom from responsibility for the company's debts beyond their original investments. Limited liability encouraged investors to back new business ventures. Shareholders elected managers who ran the corporation, though often managers controlled a majority of the voting stock.

CORPORATIONS

■ The Marshall Court encouraged business competition by ending state-licensed monopolies on inland waterways. *Gibbons v. Ogden* (1824) opened up the New York–New Jersey trade to new lines, and within a short time dozens of steamboats were ferrying passengers and freight across the Hudson River.   (© Collection of The New York Historical Society)

By 1817 the number of corporations in the United States had grown to two thousand, from three hundred in 1800. By 1830 the New England states alone had issued nineteen hundred charters, one-third to manufacturing and mining firms. At first each firm needed a special legislative act to incorporate, but after the 1830s applications became so numerous that states established routine procedures allowing businesses to incorporate easily.

Though legislative action created corporations, the courts played a critical role in extending their powers and

CHARLES RIVER
BRIDGE V.
WARREN BRIDGE

protecting them. Two Massachusetts cases in 1819, for instance, upheld the limited liability of stockholders. And the U.S. Supreme Court in *Charles River Bridge v. Warren Bridge* (1837) paved the way for new enterprises and technologies, favoring competition over monopoly and the public interest over implied privileges in old contracts.

The Massachusetts legislature had chartered the Charles River Bridge Company in 1785 and seven years later extended its charter for seventy years. In return for building a bridge between Charlestown and Boston, the owners received the right to collect tolls. In 1828 the legislature chartered another company to build the Warren

Bridge across the Charles nearby; the new bridge could collect tolls for six years, after which the bridge would be turned over to the state and be free of tolls. The Charles River Bridge Company sued in 1829, claiming that the new bridge breached the earlier charter, which was an exclusive contract, protected under *Dartmouth College v. Woodward.*

Speaking for a narrow 4-to-3 majority, Marshall's successor Roger Taney declared that the original charter did not confer the privilege of monopoly and that exclusivity could not therefore be implied. Taney ruled that charter grants should be interpreted narrowly and that ambiguities would be decided in favor of the public interest. New enterprises should not be restricted by old charters, and economic growth would best be served by narrowing the application of the *Dartmouth College* decision. In this way the judiciary promoted new technologies over old ones.

In promoting the economy, state governments far surpassed the federal government. From 1815 through the

STATES' SUPPORT
FOR THE
ECONOMY

1840s, for example, government money, mostly from the states, financed three-fourths of the nearly $200 million invested in canals. In the 1830s the states started to invest in rail construction.

Though the federal government played a larger role in constructing railroads than in building canals, state and local governments provided more than half of the capital for southern rail lines. State governments also invested in corporate and bank stocks, providing corporations and banks with much-needed capital. In fact, states actually equaled or exceeded private enterprise in their investments.

Pennsylvania, encompassing a vast area from the Delaware River to beyond the Appalachians, developed the nation's most extensive program of internal improvements to stimulate settlement and economic growth. The state invested $100 million in canals, railroads, banks, and manufacturing firms; its appointees sat on more than 150 corporate boards of directors. But Pennsylvania and other states did more than invest resources in industry. Through special acts and incorporation laws, they regulated the nature and activities of corporations and banks and used licensing to control industrial operations. Georgia, for example, regulated the grading and marketing of tobacco.

Largely as a result of these government efforts, the United States experienced uneven but sustained economic growth from the end of the War of 1812 until midcentury. Political controversy raged over questions of state versus federal activity—especially with regard to internal improvements and banking—but all parties agreed on the general goal of economic expansion. Indeed, during these years the major restraint on government action was not philosophical but financial: the public purse was small. As the private sector grew more vigorous, entrepreneurs looked less to government for financial support, and the states played less of a role in investment.

Transportation Links

Improved transportation facilitated economic growth. Outside the South, state governments invested heavily in roads, canals, and railroads, with much of the financing borrowed from Europe. With regional and national financial institutions increasingly concentrated in New York, Boston, and Philadelphia, northeastern seaboard cities became the center of American commerce. New York financial and commercial houses dominated the American export trade, not only of New England textiles but also, through affiliates in southern port cities, of southern cotton. The South's staple crop was marketed to, and through, the North. The Deep South, with most of its capital invested in slave labor and land, built fewer canals, railroads, and factories and remained mostly rural.

Water routes provided the cheapest and most available transportation. Before the War of 1812 nearly all commerce moved on navigable rivers, and bulk shipments—cotton in the South and grain in the West—continued to move to ocean port cities by water. Increasingly, however, settlement extended beyond the river links, and the federal and state governments, followed by private corporations, invested heavily in alternative transportation.

In the 1820s new arteries opened up east-west travel. The National Road—a stone-based, gravel-topped highway originating in Cumberland, Maryland—reached Columbus, Ohio, in 1833. More important, the Erie Canal, completed in 1825, linked the Great Lakes with New York City and the Atlantic Ocean. The canal carried easterners and then immigrants to settle the Old Northwest and the frontier beyond; in the opposite direction, it transported western grain to the large and growing eastern markets. Railroads and later the telegraph would strengthen these east-west links. Other than the coastal cotton trade, links between the Deep South and the North were rare.

EAST-WEST LINKS

The 363-mile-long Erie Canal was a visionary enterprise. When the state of New York authorized its construction in 1817, the longest American canal was only 28 miles long. Vigorously promoted by Governor DeWitt Clinton, the Erie cost $7 million, much of it borrowed from British investors. The canal shortened the journey between Buffalo and New York City from twenty to six days and reduced freight charges from $100 to $5 a ton. By 1835 traffic was so heavy that the canal had to be widened from 40 to 70 feet and deepened from 4 to 7 feet. Skeptics who had called the canal "Clinton's big ditch" had long since fallen silent.

CANALS

The success of the Erie Canal triggered an explosion of canal building. By 1840 canals crisscrossed the Northeast and Midwest, and total canal mileage reached 3,300—most of it built in the 1820s (see Map 10.2). None of the new canals enjoyed the financial success achieved by the Erie, however. As the high cost of construction combined with an economic contraction, investment in canals began to slump in the 1830s. By midcentury more miles were being abandoned than built; the canal era had ended.

Meanwhile, railroads boomed. The railroad era in the United States began in 1830 when Peter Cooper's locomotive, "Tom Thumb," first steamed along 13 miles of Baltimore and Ohio Railroad track. In 1833 the nation's second railroad ran 136 miles from Charleston to

RAILROADS

The United States as a Developing Nation

In the early nineteenth century, the United States was a "developing nation" as its economy slowly shifted from dependence on agriculture and raw materials to producing manufactured goods. In order to develop economically, the United States imported capital to finance international trade, internal improvements, and early factories.

American political and economic leaders in the early part of the nineteenth century talked as if they were masters of their own fate. In many ways, however, the United States remained economically dependent on its former mother country, Great Britain. The political independence that the United States won in the Revolutionary War and affirmed in the War of 1812 was not matched in the economic sphere.

Following the War of 1812, Americans depended on Britain for capital investment. Ninety percent of all U.S. foreign capital came from Britain, and around 60 percent of all British capital exports flowed to the United States. Americans used British capital to develop first the canals, then the railroads that facilitated American industrial development. For instance, from 1817 to 1825 the British invested $7 million in New York State bonds to finance the Erie Canal. Altogether, European investors provided 80 percent of the money to build the Erie, and the United States depended on mostly British capital to finance America's internal improvements.

As a developing nation, the United States imported more goods than it exported. In other words, Americans consumed more than they produced. It was able to do so because imported capital balanced the trade deficit. As in most developing countries, exports were concentrated in agricultural commodities; 50 percent of the value of all exports was in cotton. And British credit financed cotton sales.

As a developing nation, U.S. dependency on international capital was highlighted when imported capital was interrupted, as in the Panics of 1819 and 1837. Though the financial crises began in the United States, the hard times were made worse in both cases when British investors and creditors squeezed Americans. Economic crises in England led investors to pull out capital from the United States while merchants demanded that Americans pay what they owed to British creditors. Money became tight, and the economy declined.

Thus both economic development and hard times revealed the significance of international capital links to the United States, a developing nation.

In the 1820s canals like the Erie linked the West with eastern cities and the Atlantic Ocean, and thus world trade. U.S. exports were concentrated in agriculture, and the Erie and other canals carried grain to the world market. Charles Klackner published this view of a canal boat and its passengers, based on a contemporary painting by Edward Lamson Henry. Canal boats carried gentlemen and ladies as well as more modest citizens, many of them immigrants on their way to settling western lands. (Chicago Historical Society)

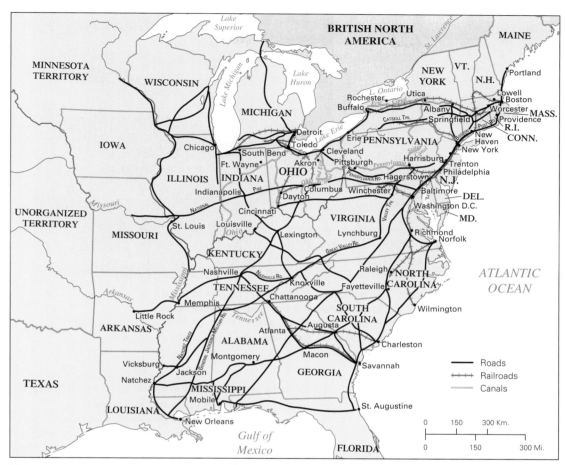

Map 10.2   Major Roads, Canals, and Railroads, 1850

A transportation network linked the seaboard to the interior. Settlers followed those routes westward, and they sent back grain, grain products, and cotton to the port cities.

Hamburg in South Carolina. By 1850 the United States had nearly 9,000 miles of railroad track.

The earliest railroads connected nearby cities, such as Philadelphia and Baltimore; not until the 1850s did railroads offer long-distance service at reasonable rates. The early lines had to overcome technical problems. Locomotives heavy enough to climb steep grades and pull long trains required strong rails and resilient track beds. Engineers met those needs by replacing wooden tracks with iron rails and by supporting the rails with ties embedded in gravel. A new wheel alignment—the swivel truck—permitted heavy engines to hold the track on sharp curves. Other problems persisted: the lack of a common standard for the width of track thwarted development of a national system. Pennsylvania and Ohio railroads, for instance, had no fewer than seven different

track widths. A journey from Philadelphia to Charleston, South Carolina, involved eight different gauges, which meant that passengers and freight had to change trains seven times. Only at Bowling Green, Kentucky, did northern and southern railroads connect directly with one another.

Technology and investments in transportation dramatically reduced travel time and shipping. Before 1815,

REDUCTION IN TRAVEL TIME AND COST

river transportation was the only feasible route for long-distance journeys. In 1815 a traveler took four days to go by stagecoach from New York City to Baltimore and nearly four weeks to reach Detroit. By 1830 the New York–Baltimore journey took a day and a half, while the Erie Canal reduced the New York–Detroit journey to two weeks. Before the War of

■ Railroads, introduced in the 1830s, soon surpassed canals. Easier, quicker, and cheaper to build than canals, they moved goods and people faster. David Matthews, the engineer of the Mohawk & Hudson's *John Bull,* drew this picture of his early locomotive. The Mohawk and Hudson offered competition to the slower Erie Canal boats. (© Collection of the New York Historical Society)

1812, wagon transportation cost 30 to 70 cents per ton per mile. By midcentury railroads brought the cost of land transportation down 95 percent and reduced the journey to one-fifth the time.

Commercial Farming

*a*lthough manufacturing increased steadily, agriculture remained the backbone of the economy and American exports. But increasingly the market economy altered farming. Though the plantation system had always been market oriented, self-sufficient farm households were becoming market oriented too. Equally important, the center of commercial farming moved westward. In the 1830s and after, the plantation South shifted toward the Mississippi River valley, while commercial farming came to dominate the Old Northwest and the Ohio River valley, then moved even farther westward to the prairies.

After the 1820s, northeastern agriculture began to decline. Eastern farmers had cultivated all the land available to them; expansion was impossible.
New England Agriculture Moreover, small New England farms with their uneven terrains did not lend themselves to the new labor-saving farm implements introduced in the 1830s—mechanical sowers, reapers, and threshers. As a result, many north-

ern farmers either moved west or gave up farming for jobs in the merchant houses and factories.

But neither the countinghouse nor the factory depleted New England agriculture. The farmers who remained proved as adaptable on the farm as were their children working at copy desks and water-powered looms. By the 1850s many New England and Middle Atlantic farm families had abandoned the commercial production of wheat and corn and stopped tilling poor land. Instead, they improved their livestock, especially cattle, and specialized in vegetable and fruit production and dairy farming. They financed these initiatives through land sales and debt. Indeed, increasing land values, not farming, promised the greatest profit.

Farm families everywhere gradually adjusted to market conditions and began to welcome new opportunities. In 1820 about one-third of all produce was intended for market. By 1850 the amount surpassed 50 percent. Farmers shifted toward specialization and market-oriented production. The rewards for such flexibility were great. Produce sold at market financed land and equipment purchases and made credit arrangements possible. Middlemen specializing in the grain and food trades replaced the rural storekeepers who had once handled all transactions for local farmers, acting both as retailers and as marketing and purchasing agents.

Farm families who owned their own land flourished, but the rising cost of land and of farming made it harder to start up. By the 1840s it took more than ten years for a rural laborer to save enough money to farm for himself. Thus the number of tenant farmers and hired hands increased. Previously farmers had relied mostly on the labor of unpaid family members or enslaved workers; now they had to secure waged farm labor.

Farm women had a distinctive role in the market economy aside from their work in fields and barnyards.

WOMEN'S PAID LABOR Many sold eggs, dairy products, and garden produce in local markets, and their earnings became essential to household incomes. Butter and cheese making replaced spinning and weaving; farm women now sold commodities and bought cloth. The work was physically demanding and did not replace regular home and farm chores but added to them. Yet women took pride in their work, often gaining from it a sense of independence that was as valuable as their profits. Esther Lewis, a widow who sent from 75 to 100 pounds of butter monthly to Philadelphia in the 1830s, even hired other women to increase production.

Women's success at butter and cheese making led some farms to specialize in dairy production. After the Erie Canal opened, Ohio dairy farms had access to New York's export trade. Ohio entrepreneurs turned cheese into factory production in the 1840s, contracting to buy curd from local dairy farmers. Canals and railroads took the cheese to eastern ports, where wholesalers sold the cheese around the world, shipping it to California, England, and China. In 1844 Britain imported more than 5 million pounds of cheese from the United States.

Individually and collectively, Americans still valued agrarian life. State governments energetically promoted commercial agriculture to spur economic growth and sustain the values of an agrarian-based republic. Massachusetts in 1817 and New York in 1819 began to subsidize agricultural prizes and county fairs. New York required contestants to submit written descriptions of how they grew their prize crops; the state then published the essays to encourage new methods and specialization. The post office circulated farm journals that helped familiarize farmers with developments in agriculture.

Gradually the Old Northwest replaced the Northeast as the center of American family agriculture. Farms

MECHANIZATION OF AGRICULTURE in the Old Northwest were much larger, flatter, and better suited to the new mechanized farming implements than were their northeastern counterparts. Cyrus McCormick, a Virginia farmer, had invented the reaper in 1831. In one continuous motion, a revolving drum on the horse-drawn reaper positioned grain stalks in front of a blade and the cut grain fell onto

■ Women tended cows and chickens and sold dairy products and eggs in the growing market economy. (Princeton University Library, Sinclair Hamilton Collection. Visual Materials Division, Department of Rare Books and Special Collections)

a platform. Though ridiculed by the *London Times* as "a cross between a flying machine, a wheelbarrow, and an Astly chariot," the reaper was a great success. McCormick patented his machine in 1834 and built a factory in Chicago that by 1847 sold a thousand reapers a year. Midwestern farmers bought reapers on credit and paid for them with the profits from their high yields. Similarly, John Deere's steel plow, invented in 1837, replaced the traditional iron plow; steel blades kept the soil from sticking and were tough enough to break the roots of prairie grass.

And just in time. The Midwest was becoming one of the leading agricultural regions of the world. Midwestern farms fed the growing cities in the East, bursting with growing immigrant populations, and still produced enough to export to Europe.

At the end of the eighteenth century, southern agriculture was diverse. The South grew sufficient grain to

THE COTTON SOUTH feed itself. Although debt plagued Virginia's tobacco growers, farther south, along the coast, slaves grew rice and some indigo for the market. Cotton was profitable only for the Sea Island planters in South Carolina and Georgia, who grew the luxurious long and silky variety. Short-staple cotton, which grew readily in the interior and in all kinds of soil, was unmarketable because its sticky seeds lay tangled in the fibers. Then, in 1793, Eli Whitney invented the cotton gin. The gin separated the cotton from the seeds fifty times faster than by hand and

■ This is a model of the reaper invented by McCormick in 1831. As Midwestern farmers mechanized in the 1840s, they bought factory-produced reapers. Increased production fed the growing eastern cities and led to grain export. (Smithsonian Institution, Washington, D.C.)

made possible the expansion of cotton production at the very time that new textile mills in England and New England were increasing demand for cotton cloth. The result transformed southern agriculture, revived and expanded slavery, and boosted export of both cotton and cloth.

After 1800 the cultivation of short-staple cotton spread rapidly. By the 1820s there were cotton plantations in the fertile lands of Louisiana, Mississippi, Alabama, Arkansas, and Tennessee, and the center of cotton production was moving west. From 1820 to 1840, South Carolina sank from first to fifth in cotton production, and Mississippi rose to first. In each decade after 1820, the total crop doubled. By 1825 the slave South was the world's dominant supplier of cotton, and the white fibers were America's largest export. Southerners with capital bought more land and more slaves and planted ever more cotton.

No region was more tied to international markets than the South, yet the region seemed immune to the transforming potential of foreign trade. The South produced cotton exclusively as a market crop. Though some cotton production became mechanized, with steam engines used in place of horses to power gins and presses, most southern capital remained concentrated in land and slaves. It could not shift easily to support manufacturing and commerce. In many ways the cotton economy resembled a colonial economy. Planters depended on distant agents, some in southern cities, many in the North, and even some in Europe, to represent them and handle finances, which often included loans. Thus critical market decisions were made by bankers, financiers, and brokers, all outside the South. The South was engaged in the new market economy, but at a distance.

The cotton boom, dependent on slave labor, defined both the southern economy and southern society as it moved westward. Slaveholders were oriented to the market economy, as were commercial farmers, merchants, and entrepreneurs in the North. But slaveholders did not pay wages for labor; they bought laborers. With capital tied to the slave system, the entire South—whites, free blacks, and slaves—were tied together and trapped by the cotton economy. Ultimately this "peculiar" system (see Chapter 13) would separate the South from the national economy and the nation.

The Rise of Manufacturing and Commerce

*T*hough at first Americans imported machines or copied British designs, they soon built their own. Matthew Baldwin made steam engines in Philadelphia in the 1820s, but in 1834, with railroads expanding, Baldwin turned to making steam locomotives. By 1839 he had produced 140 of them, or 45 percent of all American-made locomotives. A visitor to his shop in 1838 found twelve engines in various states of construction. "Those parts of the engine, such as the cylinder, piston, valves . . . in which good fitting and fine workmanship are indispensable to the efficient action of the machine, were very highly finished," the British visitor reported. By 1840 the United States exported railroad engines to Russia, some German states, and even Britain.

British visitors to the 1851 London Crystal Palace Exhibition, the first modern world's fair, were equally impressed by American design and fine tooling of working parts. American companies displayed hundreds of American machines and wares—from farm tools to exotic devices such as the reaper and an ice-cream freezer—that

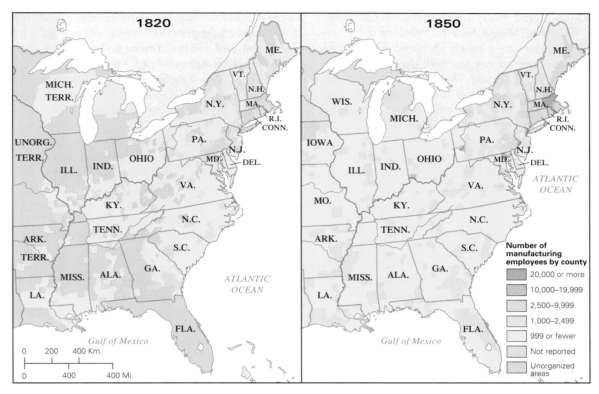

Map 10.3   U.S. Manufacturing Employment, 1820 and 1850

In 1820 manufacturing employment was concentrated mostly in the Northeast, where the first textile mills appeared. By 1850 the density of manufacturing in the Northeast had increased, but new manufacturing centers arose in Baltimore, Pittsburgh, and Cincinnati.   (Source: *Historical Atlas of the United States,* 2d ed. [Washington, D.C.: National Geographic Society, 1993], p. 148. Reprinted by permission of National Geographic Maps/National Geographic Society Image Collection.)

astonished observers. American manufacturers returned home with dozens of medals. Most impressive to the Europeans were three simple machines: Alfred C. Hobb's unpickable padlocks, Samuel Colt's revolvers, and Robbins and Lawrence's rifles fashioned with completely interchangeable parts. Like Baldwin's locomotives, all were machine-tooled rather than handmade, products of what the British called the American system of manufacturing.

AMERICAN SYSTEM OF MANUFACTURING

The American system of manufacturing used precision machinery to produce interchangeable parts that did not require individual adjustment to fit. Eli Whitney, inventor of the cotton gin, had promoted the idea of interchangeable parts in 1798 when he contracted with the federal government to make ten thousand rifles in twenty-eight months. By the 1820s the United States Ordnance Department had contracted with private firms to introduce machine-made interchangeable parts for firearms. The American system

quickly spread beyond the arsenals, producing the machine-tool industry—the manufacture of machines for the purposes of mass production. One outcome was an explosion in consumer goods. With the time and skill involved in manufacturing greatly reduced, the new system permitted mass production at low cost: Waltham watches, Yale locks, and other goods became household items, inexpensive yet of uniformly high quality.

TEXTILE MILLS

Even larger than the machine-tool industry was the textile industry. New England mills began processing and weaving slave-grown cotton in the same decade that Whitney patented his gin.

Boosted by embargo and war, then protected by the tariff, the textile industry boomed with the expansion of cotton cultivation after the war (see Map 10.3).

The Boston Manufacturing Company, chartered in 1813, radically transformed textile manufacturing. Francis Cabot Lowell and other Boston merchants capitalized the corporation at $400,000—ten times the amount behind the first Rhode Island mills. The owners erected their factories in Waltham, Massachusetts, bringing all the manufacturing processes to a single location. They employed a resident manager to run the mill, thus separating ownership from management. Workers received wages, and the cloth they produced was sold throughout the United States. By the 1840s a cotton mill resembled a modern factory, and textiles were the most important industry in the nation. Cotton cloth production rose from 4 million yards in 1817 to 323 million in 1840. The industry employed around eighty thousand workers in the mid-1840s, more than half of them women.

The industry's great innovation was that the machines, not the women, spun the yarn and wove the cloth. Workers monitored the machines. When a thread broke, the machine stopped automatically; a worker then found the break, pieced the ends together, and restarted the machine. The mills increasingly used specialized machines. Their application of the American system of manufacturing enabled American firms to compete successfully with British cotton mills.

The early mills, dependent on waterpower, sprung up in rural areas. By erecting dams and watercourses, mill owners diverted water from farmers and destroyed fishing, an important source of income and protein in rural and village America. To protect their customary rights, fishermen and farmers fought the manufacturers in New England state legislatures, but petitions from job seekers in the mill environs supported the manufacturers. The ensuing compromises promoted mill development.

Textile manufacturing changed New England and had its greatest impact on Lowell, Massachusetts. The population of Lowell, the "city of spindles" and the prototype of early American industrialization, grew from twenty-five hundred to thirty-three thousand between 1826 and midcentury. The largest of the cotton-mill towns and the front runner in technological change, Lowell boasted the biggest work force, the greatest output, and the most capital invested.

The cloth New England mills produced was so inexpensive that many women began to purchase it rather than make their own. The success of the textile factories also spawned the ready-made clothing industry. Before the 1820s, women sewed most clothing

READY-MADE CLOTHING

■ In the 1830s an unknown artist painted *Middlesex Company Woolen Mills,* portraying the hulking mass of the mill buildings. The company organized all the manufacturing processes at a single location, in Lowell, Massachusetts, on the Merrimack River. (Museum of American Textile History)

at home, and some people purchased used clothing. Tailors and seamstresses made wealthy men's and women's clothing to order. By the 1820s and 1830s, much clothing was mass-produced. Manufacturers used two methods, either separately or in combination. In one, the clothing was made in a factory; in the other, at home, through the putting-out system. In this arrangement, a journeyman tailor—a trained craftsman employed by a master tailor who owned the workshop—cut the fabric panels in the factory, and the masters "put out" the sewing at piece rates to women working in their own homes. In this way, women who formerly had spun their own yarn now received yarn from a master and returned finished cloth. The work itself was familiar, but the change was significant: women were operating their looms for wages and producing cloth for the market, not primarily for their families.

In 1832 Boston manufacturers employed three hundred journeyman tailors at $2 per day and thirteen hundred women and one hundred boys at 50 cents a day. Apprentices, if used at all, were no longer learning a trade; they were a permanent source of cheap labor. In the 1840s as many as a dozen different pairs of hands contributed to making a single pair of pants under the putting-out system.

Most of the early mass-produced clothes were made for men. Urban dwellers who lived in boarding and rooming houses, far from the female kin who previously would have made their garments, purchased the crudely made, loose-fitting clothing. Improvements in fit and changes in men's fashion eventually made ready-to-wear apparel more acceptable to clerks and professional men. In the 1840s the short sack coat, which did not taper at the waist, began to replace the embroidered waistcoat. This forerunner of the modern suit jacket fit loosely and needed little custom tailoring. Now even well-to-do men were willing to consider ready-made apparel. Most women made their own clothes, but those who could afford to do so employed seamstresses.

Retail clothing stores began to stock ready-made clothes in the 1820s. T. S. Whitmarsh of Boston advertised

RETAIL MERCHANTS in 1827 that "he keeps constantly for Sale, from 5 to 10,000 Fashionable ready-made Garments." Such merchants often bought goods wholesale, though many manufactured shirts and trousers in their own factories. Lewis and Hanford of New York City boasted of cutting more than one hundred thousand garments in the winter of 1848–1849. The New York firm sold most of its clothing in the South and owned its own retail outlet in New Orleans. Paul Tulane, a New Orleans competitor, owned a New York factory that made goods for his

■ F. B. Locke adapted to the new market for ready-made clothing by becoming a manufacturer, wholesaler, and retailer of men's shirts. Although he continued to make shirts to order, the staple of his Shirt Depot was mass-produced shirts, as this advertisement from the *Boston Directory* for 1848–1849 indicates.   (Warshaw Collection of Business Americana, Smithsonian Institution, Washington, D.C.)

Louisiana store. In the West, Cincinnati became the center of the new men's clothing industry. By midcentury, Cincinnati's ready-to-wear apparel industry employed fifteen hundred men and ten thousand women. As in Boston, most of the women did outwork.

Commerce expanded hand in hand with manufacturing. Cotton, for instance, had once been traded by

SPECIALIZATION OF COMMERCE plantation agents, who sold the raw cotton and bought manufactured goods that they then sold to plantation owners, extending them credit when necessary. Cotton exports rose from 83 million pounds in 1815 to 298 million in 1830 to more than a billion pounds for the first time in 1849. Gradually, some agents came to specialize in finance alone: they were cotton brokers, who for a commission brought together buyers and sellers. Similarly, wheat and hog brokers sprang up in the West—in Cincinnati, Louisville, and St. Louis. The distribution of finished goods also became more specialized as wholesalers bought large quantities of particular items from manufacturers, and jobbers broke down the wholesale lots for retail stores and country merchants.

General merchants persisted longer in small towns than in cities. They continued to exchange some goods with local farm women—trading flour or pots and pans for eggs or other produce. And local craftsmen continued to sell their own finished goods, such as shoes and clothing. In some rural areas and on the frontier, peddlers acted as general merchants. But as transportation improved and towns grew, even small-town merchants began to specialize.

Commercial specialization transformed some traders in big cities, especially New York, into virtual merchant princes. After the Erie Canal opened, New York City became a stop on every major trade route from Europe, the southern ports, and the West. New York traders were the middlemen for southern cotton and western grain. Merchants in other cities played a similar role within their own regions. Some traders in turn invested their profits in factories, further stimulating urban manufacturing. Some cities specialized: Rochester became a milling center, and Cincinnati—"Porkopolis"—became the first meatpacking center.

Merchants who engaged in complex commercial transactions required large office staffs, mostly all male. At the bottom of the office hierarchy were messenger boys, often preteens, who delivered documents. Above them were copyists, on high stools, who hand-copied as many documents as needed. Clerks processed documents and shipping papers and did translations. Above them were the bookkeeper and the confidential chief clerk. Those seeking employment in such an office, called a countinghouse, often took a course from a writing master to acquire a "good hand." All hoped to rise someday to the status of partner, although their chances of doing so were slim.

Financial institutions played a significant role in the expansion of manufacturing and commerce. Banks, insurance companies, and corporations linked savers—those who deposited money in banks—with producers and speculators who wished to borrow money. After 1816, the Second Bank of the United States injected a national perspective into finance, but many farmers, local bankers, and politicians denounced the bank as a monster, blaming it for serving national, not local, interests. Western landowners suffered severe losses when the Second Bank reduced loans in the western states during the Panic of 1819. In 1836 critics finally succeeded in killing the bank (see page 286).

BANKING AND CREDIT SYSTEMS

The closing of the Second Bank in 1836 caused a nationwide credit shortage, which, in conjunction with the Panic of 1837, led to fundamental reforms in banking. Michigan and New York introduced charter laws promoting what was called free banking. Many other states soon followed suit. Previously, every new bank needed a special legislative charter to operate; thus each bank incorporation involved a political process. Under the new laws, any proposed bank that met certain minimum conditions—amount of capital invested, number of notes issued, and types of loans to be offered—would receive a state charter automatically. Banks in Michigan, New York, and, soon, other states could incorporate more easily.

Free banking proved to be a significant stimulus to the economy in the late 1840s and 1850s. New banks sprang up everywhere, providing merchants and manufacturers with the credit they needed. Free-banking laws also served as a precedent for general incorporation statutes that allowed manufacturing firms to receive state charters without special legislative acts.

Workers and the Workplace

Loud the morning bell is ringing,
    Up, up sleepers, haste away;
Yonder sits the redbreast singing,
    But to list we must not stay.

. . . .

Sisters, haste, the bell is tolling,
    Soon will close the dreadful gate;
Then, alas! We must go strolling,
    Through the counting-room too late.

. . . .

Now the sun is upward climbing,
    And the breakfast hour has come;
Ding, dong, ding, the bell is chiming,
    Hasten, sisters, hasten home.

*T*he poet, writing in 1844 in the *Factory Girl's Garland*, uses the sound of the factory bell as a refrain to emphasize its incessant control, announcing when the workers are to wake, eat, begin and stop work, and go to sleep. Night and day the mill workers felt the stress of factory schedules.

But the first generation of young single women who left New England villages and farms to work in the mills had come with great optimism. The managers in rural Waltham recruited New England farm daughters with inducements including cash wages, company-run boarding houses, and cultural events such as evening lectures—none of which were available on the farm. This paternalistic approach, called the Waltham or Lowell system, spread to other mills erected alongside New England rivers. The mills offered steady work and good pay, airy rooms, prepared meals, and cultural activities. Though housekeepers enforced strict curfews, banned alcohol, and reported on workers' behavior and church attendance, mill work brought financial independence and friendship.

Sisters and cousins often worked and lived in the same mill and boarding house. They helped each other adjust, and their letters home drew kin to the mills. The benefits were not sufficient, however, to change their ambitions to be wives and mothers. Most arrivals were sixteen and stayed only about five years. When they left the mills to marry, other younger women interested in earning a wage took their places.

In the hard times from 1837 to 1842, demand for cloth declined, and most mills ran only part-time. Subsequently

BOOM AND BUST IN THE TEXTILE MILLS managers pressured workers by means of the speed-up, the stretch-out, and the premium system. The speed-up increased the speed of the machines; the stretch-out increased the number of machines each worker had to operate; and premiums paid overseers whose departments produced the most cloth encouraged them to pressure workers for greater output. The result: between 1836 and 1850 the number of spindles and looms in Lowell increased 150 and 140 percent, respectively, while the number of workers increased by only 50 percent. The corporation's goal of building an industrial empire and maximizing profits took precedence over its paternalistic concern for workers' living conditions. In the race for profits, owners lengthened hours, cut wages, tightened discipline, and packed the boarding houses. Some mill workers began to think of themselves as slaves.

New England mill workers responded to their deteriorating working conditions by organizing and striking.

PROTESTS In 1834, in reaction to a 25 percent wage cut, they unsuccessfully "turned out" (struck) against the Lowell mills. Two years later, when boarding house fees increased, they turned out again. As conditions continued to worsen, workers adopted new methods of resistance. In the 1840s, strikes gave way to a concerted effort to shorten the workday. Massachusetts mill women and other workers joined forces to press for state legislation mandating a ten-hour day. Eliza R. Hemingway, a three-year veteran of two different Lowell mills, told a Massachusetts House of Representatives committee in 1845 that workers' hours were too long. In the summer, work ran from 5:00 A.M. to 7:00 P.M., with time off for meals.

Women aired their complaints in worker-run newspapers: in 1842, the *Factory Girl* appeared in New Hampshire, the *Wampanoag and Operatives' Journal* in Massachusetts. Two years later they founded the *Factory Girl's Garland* and the *Voice of Industry,* nicknamed "the factory girl's voice." Even the *Lowell Offering,* the owner-sponsored paper that was the pride of mill workers and managers alike, became embroiled in controversy

■ This young mill girl at Waltham or Lowell, probably in the late 1840s, posed for an early daguerreotype. Her swollen and rough hands contrast with her youth, neat dress, and carefully tied, beribboned hair. Her hands suggest that she worked, as did most twelve- and thirteen-year-olds, as a warper, straightening the strands of cotton or wool as they entered the looms. (Courtesy of Jack Naylor)

when workers charged that its editors had suppressed articles criticizing working conditions.

The women's labor organizations were weakened by worker turnover. Few militant native-born mill workers stayed on to fight the managers and owners, and gradually fewer New England daughters entered the mills. In the 1850s, Irish immigrant women who lived at home replaced them. Technological improvements in the looms and other machinery had made the work less skilled and more routine. The mills could thus pay lower wages and draw from a reservoir of unskilled labor.

A growing gender division in the workplace, especially in the textile, clothing, and shoemaking industries,

GENDER DIVISIONS IN WORK was one important outcome of large-scale manufacturing. Although women and men in traditional agricultural and artisan households tended to perform different tasks, they worked as a family unit. As wage work spread, however, men's and women's work cultures became increasingly separate. The women and girls who left home for jobs in textile mills worked and lived in a mostly female world. In the clothing and shoemaking industries, whose male artisans had once worked at home assisted by unpaid family labor, men began working outside the home while women continued to work at home through the putting-out system. Tasks and wages, too, became rigidly differentiated: women sewed, whereas men shaped materials and finished products, receiving higher wages in shops employing men only.

The market economy had an impact on unpaid household labor as well. As home and workplace became separate and labor came to be defined in terms of wages (what could be sold in the marketplace) rather than production (what could be made by hand), the unpaid labor of women was devalued. Cash exchanged was the measure, and as families increasingly recorded their incomes and expenditures in account books, there was no category for women's unpaid services. Yet those labors were extensive; indeed, the family depended on women's work within the household, ever more so as sons and even daughters found wage work outside the home and had less time for household tasks. Thus gender defined household labor, and in the market economy it went unrecorded. Inevitably, it seemed to be worth little and was taken for granted.

The new textile mills, shoe factories, iron mills, and railroads were the antithesis of traditional workshop and household production. In factories, authority was hierarchically organized. Factory workers lost their sense of autonomy as impersonal market forces seemed to dominate their lives. Their jobs were insecure, as competition frequently led to layoffs and replacement by cheaper, less-skilled workers or children. Moreover, the formal rules of the factory contrasted sharply with the informal atmosphere of artisan shops and farm households. Journeymen recognized that the new system of manufacturing threatened them. When master craftsmen became managers in shoemaking and textiles as they turned their workshops into small factories, journeymen became factory operatives. In large factories, the workers never saw the owners, working under paid supervisors. The division of labor and the use of machines narrowed the skills required. Mill workers had to tolerate the roar of the looms, and all workers on power machines risked accidents that could maim or even kill. Perhaps most demoralizing, opportunities for advancement in the new system were virtually nil. And the bell, the steam whistle, or the clock governed the flow of work, as the *Factory Girl's Garland* poem anxiously described.

CHANGES IN THE WORKPLACE

As a sense of distance from their employers took hold, so did deep-seated differences among workers. Initially, mill women drew on kinship, village, and gender ties to build supportive networks in factories. But in the 1840s, as recently arrived Irish immigrant women entered the mills, many workers found themselves working with total strangers. Wage workers felt distanced from traditional culture as well. As wage work became common, the republican virtues associated with independent craft traditions eroded. The rigid rules of factory work and the swings in employment brought on by boom-and-bust cycles restricted individual freedom. At every turn, workers were hemmed in by formidable forces.

In response, some workers organized to resist changes wrought by the market economy and factories and to regain control of their work and their lives. Women textile workers organized into unions and demonstrated for better wages and conditions or lobbied legislatures for relief. Male workers, like shoemakers, also organized and protested, but because they were eligible to vote, they also organized political parties. Labor parties first formed in Pennsylvania, New York, and Massachusetts in the 1820s and then spread elsewhere; they advocated free public education and abolishing imprisonment for debt and opposed banks and monopolies. The interests of workers' parties often coincided with those of middle-class reformers: temperance, observance of the Sabbath, and suppression of vice (see Chapter 11). Ironically, however, reform politics also tended to divide workers. Many reforms—moral education, temperance, Sabbath closings—served the interests of merchants and industrialists seeking a more disciplined work force. Temperance and Sabbath closings pitted Protestants against Catholics who celebrated Sunday at public beer gardens. Anti-immigrant and anti-Catholic movements further divided workers.

LABOR PARTIES

Organized labor's greatest achievement during this period was to gain relief from the threat of conspiracy laws. When journeyman shoemakers organized during the first decade of the century, their employers accused them of criminal conspiracy. The cordwainers' (shoemakers') cases between 1806 and 1815 left labor organizations in an uncertain position. Although the courts acknowledged the journeymen's right to organize, judges viewed strikes as illegal until a Massachusetts case, *Commonwealth v. Hunt* (1842), ruled that Boston journeyman bootmakers could strike "in such manner as best to subserve their own interests."

EMERGENCE OF A LABOR MOVEMENT

Yet workers found permanent labor organizations difficult to sustain. Most workers outside the crafts were unskilled or semiskilled at best. Moreover, religion, race, ethnicity, and gender divided workers, and labor organizations excluded African Americans and women. (Massachusetts mill women organized their own unions.) The first unions arose among urban journeymen in printing, woodworking, shoemaking, and tailoring. They tended to be local; the strongest resembled medieval guilds in that members sought to protect themselves against the competition of inferior workmen by regulating apprenticeship and establishing minimum wages. Umbrella organizations composed of individual craft unions, like the National Trades Union (1834), arose in several cities in the 1820s and 1830s. But the movement fell apart amid wage reductions and unemployment in the hard times of 1839–1843.

Labor organizations remained weak; individual producers—craftsmen, factory workers, and farmers—lost economic power; and workers increasingly forfeited control over their own work. While mill owners, corporate investors, large-scale landowners, and slaveholding planters reaped benefits from economic growth, workers' share of the national wealth declined after 1830.

Americans on the Move

*A*fter the War of 1812 the United States grew in size and population. The Louisiana Purchase (1803) doubled the land area of the United States, and acquisitions in the 1840s nearly doubled it again. Throughout the Atlantic world, population soared, and

that of the United States grew by a third in each decade. Between 1820 and 1845, the U.S. population expanded by 10.6 million people, with immigration accounting for only a small percentage of this number; 89 percent of the population growth was from natural increase. In 1845, 20.2 million people lived in the United States.

The United States spread outward, mostly westward, from its original seaboard base (see Map 10.4). The admission of new states tells the story: Indiana (1816), Mississippi (1817), Illinois (1818), Alabama (1819), Maine (1820), and Missouri (1821) brought the Union to twenty-four states in the 1820s. Arkansas (1836) and Michigan (1837) soon followed, as did Florida and Texas (1845), Iowa (1846), and Wisconsin (1848) in the following decade.

WESTWARD MOVEMENT

Southerner and easterner, cotton raiser and grain farmer, black and white, slave and free person, owner and renter, investor and speculator, settler and transient marched across the Appalachians. In the first two decades of the century Americans poured into the Ohio River valley; then, starting in the 1820s they moved into the Mississippi River valley and beyond, doubling the population living beyond the Appalachians. By midcentury two-thirds of Americans lived west of the Appalachians. Mostly young and hard working, they had visions of establishing family farms and achieving economic security.

Some 5 to 10 percent of Americans moved each year, their travel made ever faster and easier by the expanding

■ Women who traveled west with their husbands found their domestic skills in great demand. In this watercolor entitled *Laying Out of Karns' City, Minnesota* (1856), E. Whitefield shows a woman preparing a meal out of her lean-to kitchen for her husband and their guests. (Chicago Historical Society)

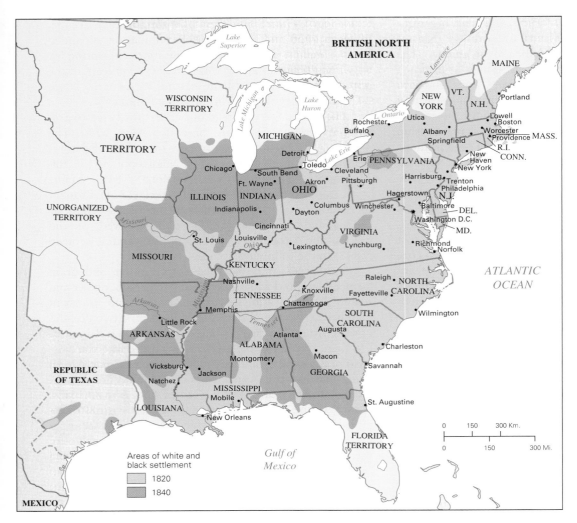

Map 10.4

Westward Movement, 1820 and 1840

Removal of Indians and a growing transportation network opened up land to white and black settlers in the West and in the Southeast, as the U.S. population grew from 9.6 million in 1820 to 17.1 million in 1840.

transportation networks. Restless, they settled only temporarily and then moved on. "There is more travelling in the United States than in any part of the world," observed a commentator in 1828. "Here the whole population is in motion, whereas, in old countries, there are millions who have never been beyond the sound of the parish bell." People tended to move short distances; thus long moves were made in stages. Though most people lived on farms, there was also a steady rural-to-urban migration.

After the 1820s the heart of cotton cultivation and the slave-based plantation system shifted from the coastal states to Alabama and the newly settled Mississippi valley—Tennessee, Louisiana, Arkansas, and Mississippi. Southerners brought their institutions with them; they forced slaves to move with them to the newer areas of the South, and yeoman farmers followed.

THE SOUTH

The shift was dramatic. The population of Mississippi soared from 73,000 in 1820 to 607,000 in 1850, with African American slaves in the majority. Across the Mississippi River, the population of Arkansas went from 14,000 in 1820 to 210,000 in 1850. Indian removal made this expansion possible. After the United States acquired Florida and attempted to colonize and suppress the Indian peoples there, southerners poured into the new territory.

The South and cotton continued westward into Texas. In 1830 the 7,000 American immigrants living in northwest Mexico outnumbered Mexicans there two to one. By 1835 the American population reached 35,000, including 3,000 slaves. The American settlers were restless for independence or U.S. annexation and chafed at Mexico's resistance toward Anglo domination in Texas. Independence in 1836 spurred further American immigration into Texas. By 1845 "Texas fever" had boosted the Anglo population to 125,000. Statehood that year opened the floodgates.

Not all moves were westward. A steady stream drifted from the Upper South to the Ohio valley, from slave to free states. Abraham Lincoln's family, for example, took this path in moving from Kentucky to Indiana Territory and, later, to Illinois. Though northern black people moved westward as well, thousands of free people of color moved to northern states and Canada in the 1830s following the adoption of black codes and mob violence in the South (see pages 321–322). Fugitives from slavery too went north. Hispanics in the Southwest continued to move north into areas of Texas and present-day New Mexico and Utah. Hispanics and Indians competed for control of the land, but when the U.S. Army suppressed the Comanches, Apaches, Navajos, and Utes, Hispanic migration spread.

MOVES NORTH

Settlers needed land and credit. Reflecting the nationalist outlook, the federal government served as real estate agent, transferring land to private hands, filling the West with non-Indian peoples, and promoting republican virtue. Some public lands were granted as rewards for military service; veterans of the War of 1812 received 160 acres. Until 1820, civilians could buy government land at $2 an acre (a relatively high price) on a liberal four-year payment plan, but the minimum purchase had been reduced in 1817 to 80 acres. After 1819 the government discontinued credit sales but reduced the price to an affordable $1.25 an acre.

LAND GRANTS TO STATES

Some eager pioneers settled land before it had been surveyed and offered for sale. Such illegal settlers, or squatters, then had to buy the land at auction and faced the risk of being unable to purchase it. In 1841, to facilitate settlement and end property disputes, Congress passed the Pre-emption Act, which legalized settlement prior to surveying.

Since most settlers needed to borrow money, private credit systems arose: banks, private investors, country storekeepers, and speculators loaned money to farmers. Nearly all economic activity in the West involved credit, from land sales to produce shipments to railroad construction. In 1816 and 1836 easy credit boosted land prices. When tight credit, high interest, low prices, or destructive weather squeezed farmers' income, land values collapsed, ending the speculative bubble. Mortgage bankers and speculators then purchased land cheaply. As a consequence, many farmers became renters instead of owners of land; tenancy became more common in the West than it had been in New England.

CREDIT

■ A painting after William James Bennett's depiction of the busy, growing western port city of Detroit in 1836. It highlights the role cities played in western settlement and growth. The view is from Canada (present-day Windsor), looking south to Detroit, and the mostly rural Canadian shore contrasts sharply with booming Detroit. (Detroit Institute of Arts)

From the start, newly settled western areas depended on their links with towns and cities. Ohio River cities—Louisville and Cincinnati—and the old French settlements—Detroit on the Great Lakes, St. Louis on the Mississippi River—predated and promoted the earliest western settlements. So too in the South, from New Orleans to Natchez to Memphis, towns spearheaded settlement and economic growth. Steamboats connected the river cities with eastern markets and ports, carrying grain east and returning with finished goods. Like cities in the Northeast, these western cities eventually developed into manufacturing centers as merchants shifted their investments from commerce to industry. Louisville, for instance, became a textile center. Smaller cities specialized in flour mills, and all produced consumer goods for the hinterlands. As commerce, urban growth, and industrialization overtook the farmers' frontier, the West was wed to the Northeast.

FRONTIER CITIES

American Indian Resistance and Removal

Indians were also on the move, but in forced migrations. To make way for white expansion, the indigenous cultures of the eastern and southern woodlands were uprooted. Perhaps 100,000 eastern and southern Indian people were removed between 1820 and

1850; about 30,000 died in the process. Those who remained became virtually invisible.

In theory, under the U.S. Constitution, the federal government recognized Indian sovereignty and treated

TREATY MAKING

Indian nations as foreign nations. Indeed the United States received Indian delegations with pomp and ceremony, exchanging presents as tokens of friendship. Agreements between Indian nations and the United States were signed, sealed, and ratified like other international treaties. In practice, however, treaty making and Indian sovereignty were fictions. The United States imposed conditions on Indian representatives, and as the United States expanded, new treaties replaced old ones, shrinking Indian land holdings. Eventually, under President Andrew Jackson, wholesale removal would be the order of the day.

Indians could delay but not prevent removal. Though Indian resistance persisted after the War of 1812, it only slowed the inevitable. In the 1820s native peoples in Ohio, southern Indiana and Illinois, southwestern Michigan, most of Missouri, central Alabama, and southern Mississippi ceded lands under federal pressure. They gave up nearly 200 million acres for pennies an acre.

To maintain independence and preserve traditional ways, many Indian nations tried to accommodate to the

INDIANS IN THE MARKET ECONOMY

expanding market economy. In the first three decades of the century, the Choctaw, Creek, and Chickasaw peoples in the lower Mississippi became suppliers and traders. Under treaty provisions, Indian commerce took place through trading posts and stores that provided Indians with supplies and purchased or bartered Indian-produced goods. Indians exchanged hides, skins, and beeswax for cloth, ammunition, manufactured goods, and illegal liquor. The trading posts extended credit to chiefs, and increasingly they fell into debt. With pelt prices falling, the debts grew enormously and often could be paid off only by selling land to the federal government. The Choctaws, Creeks, and Chickasaws found themselves in a cycle of trade debt and land cessions. By 1822 the Choctaw nation had sold 13 million acres but still carried a debt of $13,000. The Indians struggled to adjust, increasing agricultural production and hunting, working as farmhands and craftsman, and selling produce at market stalls in Natchez and New Orleans. Over time, however, they could not prevent the spread of the cotton economy that arose on their lands. With loss of land came dependency. The Choctaws came to rely on white Americans not only for manufactured goods but also for food.

Dependency facilitated removal of American Indian peoples to western lands. While the population of other groups increased by leaps and bounds, the Indian population fell. Alexis de Tocqueville noticed the contrast. "Not only have these wild tribes receded, but they are destroyed," Tocqueville concluded, after personally observing the tragedy of forced removal, "and as they give way or perish, an immense and increasing people fill their place. There is no instance upon record of so prodigious a growth or so rapid a destruction." War, forced removal, disease, especially smallpox, and malnutrition reduced many Indian nations by 50 percent. More than half of the Pawnees, Omahas, Otoes, Missouris, and Kansas died in the 1830s alone.

The wanderings of the Shawnees, the people of Prophet and Tecumseh (see pages 225–226), illustrate

SHAWNEES

the uprooting of Indian people. After giving up 17 million acres in Ohio in the 1795 Treaty of Greenville (see page 182), the Shawnees scattered to Indiana and eastern Missouri. After the War of 1812, Prophet's Indiana group withdrew to Canada under British protection. In 1822 other Shawnees sought Mexican protection and moved from Missouri to present-day eastern Texas. As the U.S. government promoted removal to Kansas, Prophet returned from Canada to lead a group to the new Shawnee lands in eastern Kansas in 1825. When Missouri achieved statehood in 1821, Shawnees living there were also forced to move to Kansas, where in the 1830s other Shawnees removed from Ohio or expelled from Texas joined them. By 1854 Kansas was open to white settlement, and the Shawnees had to cede seven-eighths of their land, or 1.4 million acres.

Removal had a profound impact on all Shawnees. The men lost their traditional role as providers; their methods of hunting and their knowledge of woodland animals were useless on the prairies of Kansas. As grain became the tribe's dietary staple, Shawnee women played a greater role as providers, supplemented by government aid under treaty provisions. (Typically, treaties required annual government distributions of grain, blankets, and cash payments.) Remarkably, the Shawnees preserved their language and culture in the face of these drastic changes. Although resistance proved incapable of protecting their lands, it did help maintain their culture.

Ever since the early days of European colonization, whites had sought the assimilation of American Indians

ASSIMILATION AND EDUCATION

through education and Christianity. This goal took on renewed urgency as the United States expanded westward. "Put into the hand of [Indian] children

■ Southern Indians attempted to remain in their ancestral lands in the South. Karl Bodmer's watercolor portrayed a Choctaw camp on the Mississippi River near Natchez, before the Indians were forced out of Mississippi and Alabama in 1830.   (Joslyn Art Museum, Omaha, Nebraska. Gift of the Enron Art Foundation)

the primer and the hoe," the House Committee on Indian Affairs recommended in 1818, "and they will naturally, in time, take hold of the plough; and, as their minds become enlightened and expand, the Bible will be their book, and they will grow up in habits of morality and industry . . . and become useful members of society." In 1819, in response to missionary lobbying, Congress appropriated $10,000 annually for "civilization of the tribes adjoining the frontier settlements." Protestant missionaries administered the "civilizing fund" and established mission schools. Catholic missions were already established in the Southwest and California.

Within five years thirty-two boarding schools enrolled Indian students. They substituted English for American Indian languages and taught agriculture alongside the Christian Gospel. The emphasis on agriculture taught the value of private property, hard work, adaptation to the market economy, and the nuclear family. But to settlers eyeing Indian land, assimilation through education seemed too slow a process. At the program's peak, schools across the United States enrolled fewer than fifteen hundred students; at that rate it would take centuries to assimilate all Indians. Thus wherever native peoples lived, illegal settlers disrupted their lives. Though obligated to protect the integrity of treaty lands, the federal government did so only halfheartedly. With government supporting westward expansion, legitimate Indian land rights gave way to the advance of white civilization.

In the 1820s it became apparent that neither economic dependency nor education nor Christianity could persuade Indians to cede enough acreage to satisfy land-hungry whites. Attention focused on southeastern tribes—Cherokees, Creeks, Choctaws, Chickasaws, and Seminoles—because much of their land remained intact after the War of 1812 and because they aggressively resisted white encroachment. Possessing some formal political institutions, they were better organized than the northern tribes to resist.

In his last annual message to Congress in late 1824, President James Monroe suggested that all Indians be

INDIAN REMOVAL AS FEDERAL POLICY

moved beyond the Mississippi River. Three days later he sent a special message to Congress proposing removal. Monroe described his proposal as an "honorable" one that would protect Indians from invasion and provide them with independence for "improvement and civilization." Force would be unnecessary, he believed; Indians would willingly accept western land free from white encroachment.

Monroe's proposition targeted the Cherokees, Creeks, Choctaws, and Chickasaws, and they unanimously rejected it. Between 1789 and 1825 they had negotiated thirty treaties with the United States, and they had reached their limits. Most wished to remain on what little was left of their ancestral land.

Pressure from Georgia had prompted Monroe's policy. Cherokees and Creeks lived in northwestern

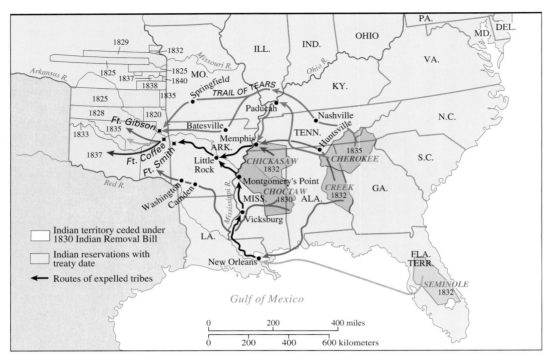

Map 10.5 Removal of Native Americans from the South, 1820–1840

Over a twenty-year period, the federal government and southern states forced Native Americans to exchange their traditional homes for western land. Some tribal groups remained in the South, but most settled in the alien western environment. (Acknowledgment is due to Martin Gilbert and George Weidenfeld and Nicholson Limited for permission to reproduce this map, taken from *American History Atlas*)

Georgia, and in the 1820s the state accused the federal government of not fulfilling its 1802 promise to remove the Indians in return for the state's renunciation of its claim to western lands. Georgia remained unsatisfied by Monroe's removal messages and by further cessions by the Creeks. In 1826, under federal pressure, the Creek nation ceded all but a small strip of its Georgia acreage. Georgians were unmoved. Only the removal of the Georgia Creeks to the West could resolve the conflict between the state and the federal government.

For the Creeks the outcome was devastating. In an ultimately unsuccessful attempt to hold fast to the remainder of their traditional lands, which were in Alabama, they radically altered their political structure. In 1829, at the expense of traditional village autonomy, they centralized tribal authority and forbade any chief from ceding land. In the end, they lost not only their land but also their traditional forms of social and political organization.

Adapting to American ways seemed no more successful than resistance in forestalling removal. No people _____ met the challenge of civilizing themselves by American standards more

CHEROKEES

thoroughly than the Cherokees, whose traditional home centered on eastern Tennessee and northern Alabama and Georgia. Between 1819 and 1829 the tribe became economically self-sufficient and politically self-governing; during this Cherokee renaissance the twelve to fifteen thousand adult Cherokees came to think of themselves as a nation, not a collection of villages. In 1821 and 1822 Sequoyah, a self-educated Cherokee, devised an eighty-six-character phonetic alphabet that made possible a Cherokee-language Bible and a bilingual tribal newspaper, *Cherokee Phoenix* (1828). Between 1820 and 1823 the Cherokees created a formal government with a bicameral legislature, a court system, and a salaried bureaucracy. In 1827 they adopted a written constitution, modeled after that of the United States. Cherokee land laws, however, differed from U.S. law. The tribe collectively owned all Cherokee land and forbade land sales to outsiders. Nonetheless, the Cherokees assimilated American cultural patterns. Economic change paralleled political adaptation. Many became individual farmers and slaveholders; by 1833 they held fifteen hundred black slaves. They transformed their economy from hunting,

■ *The Trail of Tears,* by twentieth-century Pawnee artist Brummet Echohawk. About twenty thousand Cherokees were evicted in 1838–1839, and about one-quarter of them died on the forced march to present-day Oklahoma. (Thomas Gilcrease Institute of American History and Art)

gathering, and subsistence agriculture to commodity trade based on barter, cash, and credit.

But Cherokees' political and economic changes failed to win respect or acceptance from southerners. In the 1820s, Georgia pressed them to sell the 7,200 square miles of land they held in the state. Congress appropriated $30,000 in 1822 to buy the Cherokee land in Georgia, but the Cherokees preferred to stay where they were. Impatient with their refusals to negotiate cession, Georgia annulled the Cherokees' constitution, extended the state's sovereignty over them, prohibited the Cherokee National Council from meeting except to cede land, and ordered their lands seized. The discovery of gold on Cherokee land in 1829 whetted Georgia's appetite for Cherokee territory.

Backed by sympathetic whites but not by the new president, Andrew Jackson, the Cherokees under Chief John Ross turned to the federal courts to defend their treaty with the United States and to prevent Georgia from seizing more land. Their legal strategy reflected their growing political sophistication. In *Cherokee Nation v. Georgia* (1831), Chief Justice John Marshall ruled that under the federal Constitution an Indian tribe was neither a foreign nation nor a state and therefore had no standing in federal courts. Nonetheless, said Marshall, the Indians had an unquestionable right to their lands; they could lose title only by

CHEROKEE NATION V. GEORGIA

voluntarily giving it up. A year later, in *Worcester v. Georgia,* Marshall defined the Cherokee position more clearly. The Indian nation was, he declared, a distinct political community in which "the laws of Georgia can have no force" and into which Georgians could not enter without permission or treaty privilege. The Cherokees cheered. *Phoenix* editor Elias Boudinot called the decision "glorious news." But Georgia refused to comply.

President Andrew Jackson, whose reputation had been built as an Indian fighter, refused to interfere because the case involved a state action. Newspapers widely reported that Jackson had said, "John Marshall has made his decision: now let him enforce it." Keen to open up new lands for settlement, Jackson favored expelling the Cherokees. In the Removal Act of 1830 Congress had provided Jackson with the funds he needed to negotiate new treaties and resettle the resistant tribes west of the Mississippi (see Map 10.5).

The Choctaws went first; they made the forced journey from Mississippi and Alabama to the West in the winter of 1831 and 1832. Alexis de Tocqueville was visiting Memphis when they passed through: "The wounded, the sick, newborn babies, and the old men on the point of death. . . . I saw them embark to cross the great river," he wrote, "and the sight will never fade from my memory. Neither sob nor complaint rose from that silent assembly. Their afflictions were of long standing, and they

TRAIL OF TEARS

felt them to be irremediable." Other tribes soon joined the forced march. The Creeks in Alabama resisted removal until 1836, when the army pushed them westward. A year later the Chickasaws followed.

Having fought removal in the courts, the Cherokees were divided. Some believed that further resistance was hopeless and accepted removal as the only chance to preserve their civilization. The leaders of this minority agreed in 1835 to exchange their southern home for western land in the Treaty of New Echota. Most, though, wanted to stand firm. John Ross, with petitions signed by fifteen thousand Cherokees, lobbied the Senate against ratification of the treaty. They lost. But when the time for evacuation came in 1838, most Cherokees refused to move. President Martin Van Buren sent federal troops to round them up. About twenty thousand Cherokees were evicted, held in detention camps, and marched to Indian Territory in present-day Oklahoma under military escort. Nearly one-quarter of them died of disease and exhaustion on what came to be known as the Trail of Tears.

When the forced march to the West ended, the Indians had traded about 100 million acres east of the Mississippi for 32 million acres west of the river plus $68 million. Only a few scattered remnants, among them the Seminoles in Florida and the Cherokees in the southern Appalachian Mountains, remained in the East and South.

Forced removal had a disastrous impact on the Cherokees and other displaced Indian nations. In the West they encountered an alien environment; lacking traditional ties, few felt at peace with the land. The animals and plants they found were unfamiliar. Unable to live off the land, many became dependent on government payments for survival. Removal also brought new internal conflicts. The Cherokees in particular struggled over their tribal government. In 1839 followers of John Ross assassinated the leaders of the protreaty faction. Violence continued sporadically until a new treaty in 1846 imposed a temporary truce.

Conflicts also arose among migrating American Indian groups from the South and East and Indians already living in the West, as they were forced to share land and scarce resources. Nearly one hundred thousand newcomers settled west of the Mississippi, and the existing game could not support them all. The Osages and Pawnees grittily fought the newcomers who, under U.S. Army escort, were invading their land and homes.

In Florida a small band of Seminoles continued to resist. Some Seminole leaders agreed in the 1832 Treaty of Payne's Landing to relocate to the West within three years, but others opposed the treaty, and some probably did not

SECOND
SEMINOLE WAR

know it existed. A minority under Osceola, a charismatic leader, refused to vacate their homes and fought the pro-treaty group. When federal troops were sent to impose removal in 1835, Osceola waged a fierce guerrilla war against them.

The Florida Indians were a varied group that included many Creeks and mixed Indian–African Americans (ex-slaves or descendants of runaway slaves). The U.S. Army, however, considered them all Seminoles, subject to removal. General Thomas Jesup believed that the runaway slave population was the key to the war. "This, you may be assured, is a Negro, not an Indian war," he wrote a friend in 1836, "and if it be not speedily put down, the South will feel the effects of it on their slave population before the end of the next season."

Osceola was captured under a white flag of truce and died in an army prison in 1838, but the Seminoles fought on under Chief Coacoochee (Wild Cat) and other leaders. In 1842 the United States abandoned the removal effort. Most of Osceola's followers agreed to move west to Indian Territory in 1858, but many Seminoles remained in the Florida Everglades, proud of having resisted conquest.

Summary

*N*ationalism and self-confidence accompanied the end of the War of 1812. Under the Democratic-Republicans the federal government fostered expansion and economic growth through internal improvements, tariffs, the Second Bank of the United States, land sales, and Indian removal. The Supreme Court and American diplomats, too, asserted nationalism. John Quincy Adams negotiated peace and secure borders with Great Britain and Spain, and through the Monroe Doctrine insulated the Western Hemisphere from European conflict.

But sectionalism accompanied nationalism and geographical expansion. Conflicts over tariffs, economic hard times, and slavery brought discord. The Missouri Compromise, in preserving a balance between slave and free states, was a stopgap measure to avoid the explosive issue of slavery.

From 1816 through 1845 the United States experienced explosive growth. Population increased sixfold and moved westward. New farms grew cotton and grain for the market, and cities followed. In the process, Indians were pushed aside.

Agriculture remained the dominant industry, though by midcentury a booming manufacturing sector challenged farming. And agriculture itself was becoming market-oriented and mechanized. The market economy brought sustained growth; it also ushered in cycles of boom and bust. Americans became familiar with hard times and unemployment. The growing economy also meant larger-scale destruction of the environment: mills exploited New England waterways as a source of power.

Large-scale manufacturing also altered traditional patterns of production and consumption. Farm families began to purchase goods formerly made by wives and daughters and geared production to faraway markets. Farm women increasingly contributed income from market sales to the household purse. In New England many young women left the family farm to become the first factory workers in the new textile industry. As workshops and factories replaced home-based production, and the master-journeyman-apprentice system faded away, workplace relations became more impersonal, working conditions grew harsher, and men's and women's work became increasingly distinct. Industrial jobs began to attract large numbers of immigrants, and some workers organized labor unions.

LEGACY FOR A PEOPLE AND A NATION
A Mixed Economy

How active should the U.S. government be? Should it run, regulate, or leave to the market system healthcare, Social Security and private pensions, corporate concentration, and stock trading and investments? In other words, to what degree should the government be responsible for the well-being of the economy and individuals?

The Articles of Confederation limited government, the Constitution empowered it, and the Bill of Rights restricted it in specific areas. While Americans have continuously debated the appropriate role of government, the United States has generally occupied a middle ground: a mixed economy.

In the early nineteenth century, government played an active role in economic and social expansion. Federal and state governments built roads and canals, developed harbors, and operated post offices and the early telegraph. More commonly the government intervened to stimulate and regulate the private sector. In chartering corporations and banks and in land sales and grants, the United States created an infrastructure that laid the way for the market economy and industrialization.

In the late nineteenth century advocates of laissez-faire or hands-off government challenged the pre–Civil War traditions of an active government. Laissez faire dominated briefly until the 1880s and 1890s, when large corporations and trusts accumulated so much power that governments stepped in to regulate railroads and business concentration. After the turn of the century the federal government extended regulation to food, drugs, the environment, working conditions, and fair business practices. Probably the most innovative example of the mixed economy was the creation in 1913 of the Federal Reserve System—a public system for overseeing currency and banking that left control in private hands. After a revival of laissez faire in the 1920s, the crisis of the Great Depression of the 1930s and World War II would lead the federal government to establish the modern welfare state, which operates through a mixed public/private structure.

As the United States begins the twenty-first century, its people again debate the appropriate role of government. Conservatives view government as the problem rather than the solution, arguing that government regulation hampers individual freedom and distorts the law of supply and demand. Advocates of an activist government argue that only the government has the power and resources to check economic concentration and to protect health, safety, and the environment. The framework of this debate is a legacy from before the Civil War.

The **history companion** *powered by Eduspace®*

Your primary source for interactive quizzes, exercises, and more to help you learn efficiently.

http://history.college.hmco.com/students

REFORM AND POLITICS IN THE AGE OF JACKSON 1824–1845

I proceed, Gentlemen, briefly to call your attention to the present state of Insane persons confined within this Commonwealth," Dorothea Dix petitioned the 1843 Massachusetts legislature, "in cages, closets, stalls, pens! Chained, naked, beaten with rods and lashed into obedience."

Dix revealed the netherworld she had uncovered in her two-year investigation of the treatment of the insane. She found appalling conditions in Massachusetts: men and women in cages, chained to walls, in dark dungeons, brutalized and held in solitary confinement. In a visit to a Newburyport almshouse in the summer of 1842, Dix expressed surprise at the comfortable conditions for the "one idiotic" and seven insane inhabitants. On the grounds she discovered, however, one man residing in a shed whose door opened to the local "dead room" or morgue; his only companions were corpses. Shocked, she heard from an attendant about another insane inmate of whom no one spoke openly: "a woman in a cellar."

Dix asked to see her. The superintendent warned Dix that the woman "was dangerous to be approached; that 'she had lately attacked his wife,' and was often naked." Dix pressed on. "If you will not go with me," she said, "give me the keys and I will go alone." They unlocked the doors and entered an underground cell. Beneath the staircase was a tiny door. In the shadows Dix saw "a female apparently wasted to a skeleton, partially wrapped in blankets." She was withered, wrote Dix, "not by age, but by suffering." When the inmate saw the visitors, she wailed with despair: "Why am I consigned to hell? dark—dark—I used to pray, I used to read the Bible—I have done no crime in my heart. I had friends; why have all forsaken me!—my God! my God! why hast thou forsaken me?"

Dix described in the most personal and vivid terms her visits to jails, almshouses, and private homes, and the cruel treatment of the insane. Her petition to the General Court of Massachusetts was so graphic and shocking that

◀ Dorothea Dix's powerful personal descriptions of the brutal treatment of the mentally ill propelled her from reform to politics. This painting of Dix portrays a sense of humanity and determination. (Trenton Psychiatric Hospital Photo by John Nefsky)

271

C H R O N O L O G Y

1790s–1840s • Second Great Awakening spreads religious fervor

1820s • Reformers in New York and Pennsylvania establish model penitentiaries

1824 • No presidential candidate wins a majority in the electoral college

1825 • House of Representatives elects Adams president

1826 • American Society for the Promotion of Temperance founded
• Morgan affair is catalyst for Antimasonry movement

1828 • Tariff of Abominations passed
• Jackson elected president

1830 • Webster-Hayne debate explores the nature of the Union

1830s–40s • Democratic-Whig competition gels in second party system

1831 • Garrison begins abolitionist newspaper *The Liberator*
• First national Antimason convention

1832 • Jackson vetoes rechartering of the Second Bank of the United States
• Jackson reelected president

1832–33 • South Carolina nullifies Tariffs of 1828 and 1832, prompting nullification crisis

1836 • Republic of Texas established after breaking from Mexico
• Specie Circular ends credit purchase of public lands
• Van Buren elected president

1837 • *Caroline* affair sparks Anglo-U.S.-Canadian hostility
• Financial panic ends boom of the 1830s

1838–39 • United States and Canada mobilize their militias over Maine–New Brunswick border dispute

1839–43 • Hard times spread unemployment and deflation

1840 • Whigs win presidency under Harrison

1841 • Tyler assumes the presidency after Harrison's death
• "Oregon fever" attracts settlers to the Northwest and intensifies expansionism

1843 • Dix petitions Massachusetts legislature regarding deplorable condition of insane asylums

1844 • Polk elected president

1845 • Texas admitted to the Union

1848 • Woman's Rights Convention at Seneca Falls, New York, calls for women's suffrage

the legislature voted to reprint it as a government pamphlet: *Memorial to the Massachusetts Legislature* (1843). Part petition, part sermon, and part autobiography, it made riveting reading.

The first-person narrative—"I tell what I have seen"—gave Dix's message power. She seemed, however, an unlikely herald. Reared in Massachusetts, she began teaching in Worcester at age fourteen in 1816. She wrote an elementary science text and children's devotional verse and poetry. Her appearance was somber: she wore dark dresses with starched white collars and pulled her hair back tightly. She never married and seemed aloof to other Bostonians, but she became an impassioned crusader for asylum reform, advocating hospitals for the mentally ill. In the 1840s she traveled more than 40,000 miles, exposing the inhumane treatment of the insane and petitioning state legislatures. From 1848 through 1856 she lobbied Congress annually to set aside 5 million acres to fund insane asylums. During the Civil War Dix recruited and supervised nurses for the federal government; afterward she resumed her efforts on behalf of the mentally ill. She died in 1887 in a hospital she had founded.

Dix epitomized much of early-nineteenth-century reform. She started with a religious belief in individual self-improvement and human perfectibility that led her to advocate collective responsibility, especially on behalf of those dependent on the kindness of others. She made reform her career, fearlessly entering the public arena. Investigating asylums, petitioning the Massachusetts legislature, and lobbying other states and Congress, Dix moved from reform to politics, and she helped create a new public role for women, in the process broadening the base of political participation.

The religious and reform fervor of the period arose both as part of the spiritual renewal known as the Second Great Awakening and as a response to the enormous transformation that the United States experienced after the War of 1812. Immigration, the market economy, growing inequality, the westward advance of settlement, and territorial expansion all contributed to remaking the United States. Many Americans had difficulty keeping up with the rapid pace of change and felt they no longer controlled their own fates.

Anxieties wrought by rapid change drove the impulse to reform society. Men and women organized to end the abuses of alcohol and prostitution, to improve conditions in prisons and asylums, to oppose secret and antidemocratic societies, to end slavery, and to achieve equal rights for women. Inevitably reform movements pushed men and women into politics, though only men voted. Opponents of reform, however, were equally concerned about social problems. What distinguished them from reformers was their skepticism about human perfectibility and their distrust of institutions and the exercise of power, both public and private. To them, government coercion was the greater evil. They sought to reverse, not shape, change.

Two issues in particular bridged reform and politics: the short-lived Antimasonry frenzy against secret societies; and the intense, uncompromising crusade for an immediate end to slavery. Though Antimasons organized the first third-party movement, abolition eventually overrode all other concerns. No single issue evoked the passion that slavery did. It pitted neighbor against neighbor and region against region.

The Jacksonians, too, saw themselves as reformers. They opposed special privileges and the Second Bank of the United States with the same vigor with which reformers opposed sin. President Andrew Jackson believed that a strong federal government restricted individual freedom by favoring one group over another. Social and religious reformers disagreed. Wanting a more active federal role, they rallied around the new Whig Party, which allied itself with humanitarian reform. Democrats and Whigs constituted a new party system, characterized by strong organizations, intense loyalty, and energetic religious and ethnic competition.

Both parties eagerly promoted expansionism during the prosperous 1840s. Democrats saw the agrarian West as an antidote to urbanization and industrialization; Whigs focused on the new commercial opportunities it offered. Expanding the nation to the Pacific seemed to be the manifest destiny of the United States. Texas, California, and Oregon, unknown to most Americans in 1800, had become familiar places by the 1830s and 1840s, and to annex them, the United States would challenge its neighbors north and south. ■

From Revival to Reform

R eligion was probably the strongest motivation behind organized benevolence and reform. Beginning in the late 1790s religious revivals galvanized Protestants, especially women, into social action. The most famous was at Cane Ridge, Kentucky, in 1801, and it became legendary. One report estimated twenty-five thousand people attended the August meetings, at a time when Kentucky's largest city, Lexington, had fewer than two thousand inhabitants. Revivals spread in waves, finding ready audiences in the countryside. At camp meetings, sometimes lasting a week with thousands in attendance, preachers exhorted sinners to repent and become genuine Christians. They offered salvation to all through personal conversion. At a time when only a minority could read and write, itinerant evangelists were democratizing American religion, making it available to all.

Resembling the Great Awakening of the eighteenth century (see pages 110–111), the movement came to be

SECOND GREAT AWAKENING

called the Second Great Awakening. It raised people's hopes for the Second Coming of the Christian messiah and the establishment of the Kingdom of God on earth. Revivalists resolved to speed the Second Coming by combating the forces of evil and darkness. Some believed that the United States had a special mission in God's design and a special role in eliminating evil. Under revivalist influence, the role of churches and ministers in community life diminished as lay participation increased, and evangelical Christians across the country tried to right the wrongs of the world. Visiting the United States in the 1830s, Alexis de Tocqueville noted that "there is no country in the world where the Christian religion retains greater influence" than in America.

In the South, huge numbers of people attended revivals, but they especially drew women and African Americans, free and slave. The call to personal repentance and conversion invigorated Protestantism, giving southern churches an evangelical base and giving evangelicalism a southern accent. In essence, the Second Great Awakening turned the South into the Bible belt. It also mostly ignored slavery, thus accommodating to it. In the North, New York lawyer Charles G. Finney led the revival movement. After his 1821 soul-shaking conversion, which he interpreted as "a retainer from the Lord Jesus Christ to plead his cause," Finney abandoned the law to convert souls, staging three- to four-day camp meetings in western New York, a region that experienced such continuous and heated waves of revivalism that it became known as "the burned-over district."

ing "the democratic art of persuasion." Persuasion was at the core of democracy, of religious appeals to the heart, and of reform's influence on the head and the heart. Even nonevangelical Protestants and Catholics practiced persuasion in this era. Roman Catholics elevated the sermon to a central place in the church service, while in words and song, black preachers recalled the biblical exodus and the promise of escape from the land of slavery. Among Jews, Isaac Lesser, in a Philadelphia Sephardic congregation, introduced regular sermons in 1829, and Rabbi Isaac Meyer Wise, a German immigrant in 1846, later made it the hallmark of Reform Judaism.

As Methodists and Baptists moved west, migration patterns spread not only religion but also the impulse for moral reform. All revivalists shared a belief in individual self-improvement. The doctrine of perfectibility demanded that Christians actively organize and convert others. Thus the Second Great Awakening bred reform, and evangelical Protestants became missionaries for both religious and secular salvation. Wherever they preached, evangelists generated new religious groups and voluntary reform societies. New sects like the Mormons arose out of this ferment. So did associations to address the pressing issues of the day: temperance, education, Sabbath observance, dueling, and later slavery. Among the organizations created in the wake of revival were the American Sunday School Union (1824), the American Temperance Society (1826), the American Peace Society (1828), and the American Anti-Slavery Society (1833). Religious zeal led believers to support missionaries abroad, particularly in Asia and Africa. Collectively these groups constituted a national web of benevolent and moral-reform societies, and strengthened by numbers, they moved into the public sphere.

■ Samuel Waldo and William Jewett's oil portrait of Charles Finney around 1834 captures Finney at his peak. The charismatic Finney mesmerized his audiences, and contemporaries credited him with converting 500,000 people. (Oberlin College Archives, Oberlin, OH)

Salvation could be achieved, Finney preached, through spontaneous conversion like his own. He mesmerized his audiences. In everyday language, Finney preached that "God has made man a moral free agent." In other words, evil was avoidable: Christians were not doomed by original sin, and anyone could achieve salvation. Finney's brand of revivalism transcended sects, class, and race. At first a Presbyterian, he eventually found his home in Methodism with its doctrine of perfectibility. Revivalism had a particularly strong base among Methodists and Baptists, and in the 1820s the Methodists surpassed the Baptists as the most numerous denomination. These denominations grew the most because their structure maximized democratic participation and drew their ministers from ordinary folk.

Revivalist ministers and lay leaders were powerful preachers. Historian Nathan O. Hatch has called preach-

More women than men answered the call of Christianity, sustaining the Second Great Awakening and invigorating local churches. Pious middle-class women in Rochester, New York, for instance, responded to Finney by spreading the word to other women while their husbands were at work. Gradually women brought their families and sometimes their husbands into church and reform. Although many businessmen recruited their employees to benevolent work, women more than men tended to feel personally responsible for counteracting the increasingly secular orientation of the expanding market economy. Emotionally charged conversions could return women to what they believed was the right path. It also offered them communal ties with other women.

EVANGELICAL WOMEN

Female missionary societies motivated organized religious and benevolent activity on an unprecedented scale.

For women and some men, reform represented their first political involvement at a time when women did not vote. In reform organizations women represented themselves; by participating directly in service activities, they pioneered new, visible, public roles for women. Within churches and society, they dissented and opposed traditional political leaders.

An exposé of prostitution in New York City illustrates how reform led to political action. John R. McDowall, a divinity student, published a report in 1830 documenting the prevalence of prostitution in New York City. Philip Hone, a prominent civic leader (see page 311), denounced McDowall's report as "a disgraceful document," and New York businessmen and politicians defended the city's good name against "those base slanders." Women, moved by the plight of "fallen women," revived the fight against prostitution in 1834. But whereas male reformers made prostitutes the target of their zeal, the newly organized Female Moral Reform Society focused on men who victimized young women, publicizing the names of brothel clients. They organized a shelter for refuge and an employment agency to find jobs for prostitutes.

FEMALE REFORM SOCIETIES

During the 1830s, the New York society expanded its activities and geographical scope, calling itself the American Female Moral Reform Society. By 1840 it had 555 affiliated chapters across the nation. The society also entered the political sphere. In New York State in the 1840s, it successfully lobbied for criminal sanctions against men who seduced women into prostitution, as well as against the prostitutes themselves.

One of the most successful reform efforts was the campaign against alcohol. Drinking was widespread in the early nineteenth century. American men gathered in public houses and rural inns to gossip, talk politics, play cards, escape work and home, and drink whiskey, rum, and hard cider. Contracts were sealed, celebrations commemorated, and harvests toasted with liquor. Respectable women did not drink in public, but many regularly tippled alcohol-based patent medicines promoted as cure-alls. Why then did temperance become such a vital issue? And why were women especially active in the movement? Like all nineteenth-century reform, temperance had a strong religious foundation.

TEMPERANCE

Evangelicals considered drinking sinful, and in many denominations, forsaking alcohol was part of conversion. Preachers condemned alcohol for violating the Sabbath; many workers labored six days and spent Sunday at the public house drinking and socializing. Alcoholism

■ As the temperance movement spread, the evils of alcohol became a major theme in popular culture. This 1830s lithograph, "Mortgaging the Farm," hints at drinking's potential destructiveness. Drunken, idyll farmers sit in the shadow of the gallows holding the tavern's signboard. (Old Sturbridge Village)

also destroyed families; it created poverty and crime. In the early 1840s thousands of ordinary women formed Martha Washington societies to protect families by reforming alcoholics, raising children as teetotalers, and spreading the temperance message. Popular culture of the time was laced with domestic images of the damage alcohol left: abandoned wives and children and drunken fathers. Timothy Shay Arthur dramatized these evils in *Ten Nights in a Barroom* (1853), a classic American melodrama, as did the lithograph "Mortgaging the Farm." Employers complained that drinkers took "St. Monday" as a holiday to recover from Sunday. In the new world of the factory, drinking was unacceptable.

As the temperance movement gained momentum, its goal shifted from moderation to voluntary abstinence and finally to prohibition. The American Society for the Promotion of Temperance, organized in 1826 to promote pledges of abstinence, became a pressure group for state prohibition legislation. By the mid-1830s five thousand state and local temperance societies touted teetotalism, and more than a million people had taken the pledge. Several hundred thousand children, for instance, enlisted in the Cold Water Army.

The temperance movement's success was reflected in a sharp decline in alcohol use. Per capita consumption fell from five gallons in 1800 to below two gallons in the 1840s. Success bred more victories. Maine prohibited the manufacture and sale of alcohol except for medicinal purposes in 1851, and by 1855 similar laws had been enacted throughout New England and in New York, Pennsylvania, and the Midwest.

Even as consumption declined, opposition to alcohol grew. From the 1820s on, many reformers expressed their prejudices by regarding alcohol as an evil introduced by Catholic immigrants. The Irish and Germans, the *American Protestant Magazine* complained in 1849, "bring the grog shops like the frogs of Egypt upon us." Demon rum became a prime target of reformers. Rum and immigrants defiled the Sabbath; rum and immigrants brought poverty; rum and immigrants supported the feared papacy. Many Catholics took the pledge of abstinence and formed their own organizations, such as the St. Mary's Mutual Benevolent Total Abstinence Society in Boston. But even Catholic teetotalers tended to oppose state regulation of drinking; temperance seemed to them a question of individual choice. They favored self-control, not state coercion.

As the career of Dorothea Dix demonstrated, moral reform also stimulated the construction of asylums and other institutions to house prisoners, the mentally ill, orphans, delinquent children, and the poor. Such institutions were needed, reformers argued, to shelter victims of society's turbulence and impose familial discipline on them. It was widely believed that criminals came from unstable families whose lack of restraint led to vice and drink. Idleness was both a symptom and a cause of crime; thus the clock governed a prisoner's day, and idleness was banished. Through discipline, inmates might become self-reliant and responsible. Even the most sinful could be redeemed.

PENITENTIARIES AND ASYLUMS

In the 1820s New York and Pennsylvania developed competing models for reforming criminals. Both rejected incarceration to punish criminals or to remove them from society, introducing instead disciplined regimens to rehabilitate them. New York's Auburn (1819–1823) and Ossining (1825) prisons placed prisoners in individual cells but brought them together in common workshops. Pennsylvania's Pittsburgh (1826) and Philadelphia (1829) prisons isolated prisoners completely, forcing them to eat, sleep, and work in their individual cells, allowing them contact only with guards and visitors.

Insane asylums, hospitals, and orphanages instituted similar approaches. Formerly the prescribed treatment removed disturbed individuals from society and isolated them among strangers, many with criminals. Dorothea Dix argued that this treatment was inhumane. The new asylums were clean and orderly. In response to Dix's crusade and reform societies, twenty-eight of thirty-three states had public institutions for the mentally ill by 1860.

Critical to reform movements was the building of networks. Reform and literary societies brought national speakers like Dorothea Dix, abolitionist Frederick Douglass, and hundreds of others to cities and towns to preach reform. Most reform organizations, like political parties, sponsored weekly newspapers, creating a virtual community of reformers. Annual conventions increased personal contacts and motivated supporters. Reformers made use of new technology—the new steam presses that permitted mass publication and the railroads that distributed their newspapers and pamphlets around the country—to spread their word.

ANTIMASONRY

More intense than moral reform movements but of shorter duration was the crusade against Freemasonry, a secret fraternity that had come to the United States from England in the eighteenth century. Sons of the Enlightenment such as Benjamin Franklin and George Washington were attracted to Masonry because it emphasized individual belief in a deity (as opposed to organized religion or a single church's doctrine). In the early nineteenth century Freemasonry attracted middle- and upper-class men prominent in commerce and civic affairs. For the ambitious, the Masons offered access to community leaders. Monumental lodges called attention to the Masons' affluence and prominence.

Opponents of Masonry believed that its secrecy and elite appeal were antidemocratic and antirepublican. Publications such as the *Anti Masonic Almanac* attacked Masonic initiation rites. Evangelicals labeled the order satanic. Antimasons argued that Masonry threatened the family because it excluded women and encouraged men to neglect their families for alcohol and ribald entertainment at Masonic lodges. As the temperance movement sought to liberate individuals from drink, Antimasons sought to liberate society from the grip of what they considered a powerful, antirepublican secret fraternity. To Antimasons, as penitentiaries and asylums would rehabilitate the criminal and insane, the abolition of Masonry would reestablish moral discipline. The political arena quickly absorbed Antimasonry, and its short life illustrates the close association of politics and reform in the period.

MORGAN AFFAIR

The catalyst for Antimasonry as an organized movement was the suspected murder of William Morgan, a disillusioned Mason who published an exposé in 1826, *The Illustration of Ma-*

№ IV.
ANTI MASONIC ALMANAC,
FOR THE YEAR
1831:
BY EDWARD GIDDINS.

The above plate represents "a poor blind candidate" taking the oath of an entered apprentice mason. He is divested of all clothing but a shirt, drawers, and one slipper; he kneels before the masonic altar on his naked knee, with a halter round his neck, and a hoodwink over his eyes; his left arm and breast are also bare: and in this humiliating posture he receives his oaths from the "worshipful master," wherein he binds himself to keep all masonic secrets, under the penalty of having his throat cut, his tongue torn out, and his body buried in the ocean. He is then taught the sign, grip, and word of that degree, and is presented with a little sheepskin apron, told he must wear it with the flap up, and that it is more honorable than the Star and Garter, or any other order that could be conferred upon him, except in a masonic lodge! and that it had been worn by kings, princes, and potentates, who were not ashamed to wear it. He is finally permitted to put his clothes on, and thank the worshipful master, wardens, and brethren, for the honor they had conferred upon him!

■ Antimasonic publications, such as this 1831 almanac, made much of the allegedly sinister initiation rites that bound a new member "to keep all Masonic secrets, under the penalty of having his throat cut, his tongue torn out, and his body buried in the ocean." (Print collection, Miriam and Ira D. Wallach Division of Art, Prints, and Photographs, New York Public Library, Astor, Lenox and Tilden Foundations)

sonry, *By One of the Fraternity Who Has Devoted Thirty Years to the Subject.* Even before the book appeared, a group of Masons abducted Morgan in Canandaigua, New York. It was widely believed that his kidnappers murdered him, though his body was never found.

Events seemed to confirm Masonry's antidemocratic character. Prosecutors who were Masons appeared to obstruct the investigation of Morgan's abduction. The public pressed for justice, and a series of notorious trials from 1827 through 1831 led many to suspect a conspiracy. The cover-up became as much of an issue as Masonry itself, and the movement spread to other states. Antimasonry coalesced overnight in the burned-over district of western New York, and it quickly became a political movement.

With growing popular support, the Antimasons held conventions in 1827 to select candidates to oppose Masons running for office. The next year the conventions supported, for president, John Quincy Adams, and opposed Andrew Jackson because he was a Mason. The Antimasons held the first national political convention in Baltimore in 1831, and a year later they nominated William Wirt as their presidential candidate. Thus the Antimasons became a rallying point for anti-Jacksonians. Their electoral strength lay in New England and New York: in Vermont the Antimasons became the dominant party for a brief time in 1833; in Massachusetts they replaced the Democrats as the second major party. Antimasonry found little support, however, in the slave South.

CONVENTION SYSTEM

By the mid-1830s, Antimasonry had faded as a moral and political movement. A single-issue party, Antimasons declined along with Freemasonry. Yet Antimasonry left its mark on the politics of the era. As a moral crusade focused on public officeholders, it inspired broad participation in the political process. It drew new white voters into politics at a time when male suffrage was being extended, and it attracted the lower and middle classes by opposing the Masonic elite, exploiting their distrust of local political leaders. The Antimasons also changed party organization by pioneering the convention, rather than the caucus, for nominating candidates and by introducing the party platform.

Abolitionism and the Women's Movement

*A*ntimasonry foreshadowed and had much in common with abolitionism. Indeed, as Antimasonry waned, the antislavery movement gathered momentum. Abolitionist William Lloyd Garrison at first ignored the frenzy over the Morgan affair, but in 1832 he joined the ranks of Antimasons. Echoing his stand on emancipation, Garrison wrote: "I go for the immediate, unconditional and total abolition of Freemasonry." In his eyes, both slavery and Masonry undermined republican values. Eventually the issue of slavery became so compelling that it consumed all other reforms and threatened the nation itself. Those who advocated immediate emancipation saw slavery as, above all, a moral issue—the ultimate sin.

Free blacks in the North had demanded an end to slavery since the Revolution. Richard Allen, the first

■ Women played an activist role in reform, especially in abolitionism. A rare daguerreotype from August 1850 shows women and men, including Frederick Douglass, on the podium at an abolitionist rally in Cazenovia, New York. (Collection of J. Paul Getty Museum, Los Angeles, California)

stages), whites took little interest in the issue. Antislavery sentiment appeared strongest in the Upper South, though northern involvement grew after the War of 1812. The American Colonization Society, founded in 1816, advocated gradual, voluntary emancipation and resettlement of former slaves in Africa, establishing the colony of Liberia for that purpose in the 1820s. Society members did not believe that free blacks had a place in the United States, and its members included Jefferson and other slaveholders, some evangelicals and Quakers, and (briefly) a few blacks.

During the 1830s, however, a small number of white reformers, driven by moral urgency, joined the black crusade for immediate emancipation. Soon the immediatists, who demanded immediate, complete, and uncompensated emancipation, surpassed the gradualists as the dominant strand of abolitionism. The most prominent and uncompromising immediatist, was the incendiary William Lloyd Garrison, a talented journalist who broke with moderate abolitionists in 1831. That year he began publishing *The Liberator,* which for thirty-five years would be his major weapon against slavery. He declared in its first issue, "I am in earnest—I will not equivocate—I will not excuse—I will not retreat a single inch—and *I will be heard.*"

Garrison's refusal to work with anyone who tolerated the delay of emancipation isolated him from other white opponents of slavery. He even forswore political action on the grounds that it was government that permitted slavery. Garrison burned a copy of the Constitution on July 4, 1854, proclaiming, "So perish all compromises with tyranny." By his actions and rhetorical power, Garrison helped to push antislavery onto the national agenda, though he had no specific plan for abolishing it. In essence, what Garrison called for was conversion of those who held slaves or cooperated with institutions that supported slavery; they must repent.

It is difficult to differentiate between those whites who became immediatists and those who did not. But

IMMEDIATISTS immediatists like Garrison, Elizabeth Chandler, Amos Phelps, and Theodore Weld had much in common. They were young evangelicals active in benevolent societies in the 1820s; many became ordained ministers; and many had personal contact with free blacks and were sympathetic to African American rights. They were convinced that slaveholding was a sin. Motivated to abolish sin, they sought to change the institutions that harbored slavery. Finally, they shared great moral intensity. Because they were unwilling to compromise, their zeal made them forceful political activists. Their main organizational

AFRICAN AMERICAN ABOLITIONISTS bishop of the African Methodist Episcopal (AME) Church, was outspoken on the issues. In 1800, for instance, he eulogized former president George Washington for freeing his slaves, and his sermon on immediatism—an immediate end to slavery—was widely circulated as a pamphlet. To free blacks slavery was both a moral issue and a personal one; while slavery was legal, they were always at risk of being seized as fugitives, and many had relatives who were slaves. David Walker's *Appeal . . . to the Colored Citizens* (1829), in language later imitated by Garrison, was a clarion call for immediatism and helped politicize many abolitionists. Walker, a southern-born free black, was Boston's leading abolitionist until his death in 1830. When Walker died, there were fifty black abolitionist societies in the United States assisting fugitive slaves, lobbying for emancipation, and exposing slavery as evil. African American newspapers spread the word.

Few whites, however, advocated the abolition of slavery before the 1830s. In the North, where by 1820

GRADUAL EMANCIPATION slavery had been virtually abolished (five states still had gradual emancipation plans that were freeing slaves in

The International Antislavery Movement

The heart of the international antislavery movement had been in Great Britain, but in the 1830s many of Britain's local antislavery societies thought they had accomplished their mission and disbanded. In 1833 Parliament ended slavery in the British Empire, and over the previous three decades the international slave trade had greatly diminished. At the same time, however, abolitionism in the United States was on the rise, and now American black abolitionists extended their work across the Atlantic. They revived the international movement to end slavery where it still existed—in Spanish possessions like Cuba, in independent and colonial South America, in Africa and Asia, and in the United States.

American abolitionism in the 1830s was invigorated by the militancy of these black abolitionists and by the conversion of William Lloyd Garrison to immediatism. Seeking to raise money and to put international pressure on the United States to abolish slavery, African American abolitionists in the 1840s toured Britain regularly. On the lecture circuit and in published narratives, they appealed for support. Especially effective were ex-slaves, who recounted their firsthand experiences of slavery and bared their scarred bodies.

Black abolitionists spoke in small towns and villages and in Britain's industrial centers. After fugitive slave Moses Gandy toured England, he published his autobiography, the first of dozens of slave narratives published in London. The next year, 1845, Frederick Douglass began a nineteen-month tour, giving three hundred lectures in Britain.

In 1849 black abolitionists William Wells Brown, Alexander Crummell, and J. W. C. Pennington were among the twenty American delegates at the international Paris Peace Conference. There Brown likened war and slavery, telling the eight hundred delegates from western Europe and the United States that "it is impossible to maintain slavery without maintaining war." His scheduled brief lecture tour in Britain turned into a five-year exile because, after passage of the 1850 Fugitive Slave Law, he feared being seized and sent back to slavery if he returned to the United States. In 1854 he became free when British abolitionists purchased his freedom from his former master.

Gandy, Douglass, Brown, and dozens of other former slaves helped revive abolitionism as an international issue. They energized the British and Foreign Anti-Slavery

■ William Wells Brown's autobiography stirred abolitionists in the United States and England. In 1849 Brown was among the American delegates to the Paris Peace Conference, then spent the next five years as an exile in Britain, fearing being sent back to slavery under the 1850 Fugitive Slave Act. He returned to the United States only after British abolitionists purchased his freedom from his former master. (Southern Historical Collection, The Library of the University of North Carolina, Chapel Hill)

Society, founded in 1839, and hundreds of more militant, local societies. By the early 1850s national abolitionist movements succeeded in abolishing slavery in Columbia, Argentina, Venezuela, and Peru. Though the United States continued to resist internal and international pressure, its black abolitionists were instrumental not only in reviving the worldwide antislavery movement but also, as advocates of woman's rights, international peace, temperance, and other reforms, in linking Americans to reform movements around the world.

vehicle was the American Anti-Slavery Society, founded in 1833.

In the 1840s escaped slaves Frederick Douglass and Harriet Tubman joined forces with white reformers in the American Anti-Slavery Society. Their militant and unrelenting campaign also won European support. "Brethren, arise, arise, arise!" Henry Highland Garnet commanded the 1843 National Colored Convention. "Strike for your lives and liberties. Now is the day and hour. Let every slave in the land do this and the days of slavery are numbered. Rather die freemen than live to be slaves."

Those who knew the experience of slavery firsthand, like Douglass and Sojourner Truth, wrote personal narratives that mobilized northerners. Most benevolent workers and reformers, however, kept their distance from the immediatists. They shared with immediatists the view that slavery was a sin but believed in gradual emancipation. They feared that if they moved too fast, attacked sinners too harshly, or interfered aggressively in time-honored customs and beliefs, they would destroy the harmony and order they sought to bring about through peaceful reform. But peace was at a premium: unlike temperance, the antislavery movement faced fierce opposition, even mob violence.

Immediatists' greatest recruitment successes resulted from defending their own constitutional rights, not the rights of slaves. Wherever they went, immediatists found their free speech threatened by hostile crowds. At Utica, New York, in 1835, merchants and professionals broke up the state Anti-Slavery Convention that had welcomed blacks and women. Mob violence peaked that year, with more than fifty riots aimed at abolitionists or African Americans. In 1837 in Alton, Illinois, a mob murdered abolitionist editor Elijah P. Lovejoy, who had been driven out of slaveholding Missouri, and rioters sacked his printing office. But public outrage at Lovejoy's murder only increased antislavery support in the North.

OPPOSITION TO ABOLITIONISTS

In the South, mobs blocked the distribution of antislavery tracts. Technological developments in mechanized papermaking and in steam-powered presses in the 1830s made it possible for the American Anti-Slavery Society to publish and distribute millions of pamphlets. The state of South Carolina intercepted and burned abolitionist literature, and President Andrew Jackson proposed a law prohibiting the mailing of antislavery tracts. In 1835 proslavery assailants killed four abolitionists in South Carolina and Louisiana and forty supposed insurrectionists in Mississippi and Louisiana that summer. Riots in the South, unchecked by authorities, were violent and deadly.

At a rally in Boston's Faneuil Hall in 1835, former Federalist Harrison Gray Otis portrayed abolitionists as subversives. Attacking Garrison's American Anti-Slavery Society as "revolutionary," he accused it of having women "turn their sewing parties into abolition clubs." Soon, Otis charged, school primers would teach "that A stands for abolition." Abolitionists, he predicted, would turn to politics, causing unforeseeable calamity. "What will become of the nation?" Otis asked. "What will become of the Union?"

But the furor between the abolitionists and their opponents had already entered the House of Representatives. Abolitionists bombarded Congress with petitions to abolish slavery and the slave trade in the District of Columbia, which Congress governed. The House in 1836 adopted what abolitionists labeled the "gag rule," which automatically tabled abolitionist petitions, effectively preventing debate on them. When the immediatists, in response, flooded Congress with nearly seven hundred thousand petitions, the gag rule gave new energy to the antislavery movement. In a dramatic defense of the right of petition, former president John Quincy Adams, now a representative from Massachusetts, took to the floor again and again to speak against the gag rule. (Its repeal in 1844 was anticlimactic.)

GAG RULE

The Missouri Compromise, censorship of the mails, and the gag rule represented attempts to keep the issue of slavery out of the political arena. Yet the more national leaders, especially Democrats, worked to avoid the issue, the more antislavery forces hardened their resolve. The unlawful and violent tactics used by opponents of abolition actually unified the movement by forcing factions to work together in mutual defense.

Abolition was highly factionalized, and its adherents fought one another as often as they fought the defenders of slavery. They were divided over Garrison's emphasis on "moral suasion"—winning over the hearts of slaveowners rather than coercing them—versus the practical politics of James G. Birney, the Liberty Party's candidate for president in 1840 and 1844, who sought to end slavery by electing abolitionists. They also disagreed about the place of free blacks in American society. And the movement split over support for other reforms, especially the roles and rights of women.

Women had been prominent in the antislavery movement from the start. They joined local female antislavery societies through their churches as part of the network of moral reform. In 1833 women in Boston founded the Female Anti-Slavery Society, and in many

WOMEN ABOLITIONISTS

antislavery organizations women were as active and politically involved as men. Lydia Maria Child, Maria Chapman, and Lucretia Mott served on the American Anti-Slavery Society's executive committee; Child edited its official paper, the *National Anti-Slavery Standard,* from 1841 to 1843, and Chapman coedited it from 1844 until 1848. Garrison's moral suasion attracted many women because it gave them a platform from which to oppose slavery. Yet some politically active societies excluded women because they could not vote and opposed women's roles in reform. In Boston in 1832, African American Maria Stewart was harshly criticized for addressing a mixed audience of abolitionist men and women. Opponents of such roles for women found her boldness—and her message that listeners should improve their own lives, their children's lives, and their communities—offensive. Stewart had to leave Boston for New York.

Later in the 1830s abolitionists Angelina and Sarah Grimké were similarly attacked for speaking to mixed audiences. One pastoral letter declared that women should obey, not lecture, men. This reaction turned the Grimkés' attention from the condition of slavers to the condition of women. Born into a Charleston, South Carolina, slaveholding family, both sisters had experienced conversion, became outspoken abolitionists, moved north, and found a home in Garrison's immediatism. Now they confronted the concept of "subordination to man," insisting that men and women had the "same rights and same duties." Sarah Grimké's *Letters on the Equality of the Sexes and the Condition of Women* and Angelina Grimké's *Letters to Catharine E. Beecher,* both published in 1838, initiated a new reform movement to secure legal and social equality of women.

Public participation in religious revival and reform had led some women to reexamine their positions in

WOMEN'S RIGHTS

society. As the predominant group in the Second Great Awakening, women began to challenge male domination in religion. During revivals women made public declarations of their faith and recounted their conversion experiences. Revivals brought ordinary women into the public sphere. Female societies and reform networks, convention participation, and advocacy opened new roles to women. The market economy also created new occupations for women outside their homes. Those factors, together, help explain why women's rights became an issue.

Women abolitionists were among the leaders on behalf of women's rights. In July 1848 Elizabeth Cady Stanton, Lucretia Mott, and Lucy Stone organized the Woman's Rights Convention at Seneca Falls, New York.

■ Elizabeth Cady Stanton posed in 1848 with two of her sons, Henry Jr., left, and Neil. Stanton, one of the organizers of the Seneca Falls Woman's Rights Convention, traveled widely and agitated for women's equality while raising five children. (Collection of Rhoda Jenkins)

Three hundred women and men reformers gathered to demand political, social, and economic equality for women. They protested women's legal disabilities—limited property rights and inability to vote—and their social restrictions, such as exclusion from advanced schooling and from many occupations. Their Declaration of Sentiments, modeled after the Declaration of Independence, broadcast the injustices suffered by women and launched the women's rights movement. "All men and women are created equal," the declaration proclaimed.

Advocates of women's rights were slow to garner support, especially from men, who held most of the political and legal power. In the 1840s the question of women's suffrage split the antislavery movement. Some men joined the ranks, notably Garrison and Frederick Douglass, but most men actively opposed a vote for women. Not everyone at Seneca Falls signed the resolution on women's suffrage. Of the one hundred who did, only two would live to see the passage of the Nineteenth Amendment to the Constitution seventy-two years later.

Jacksonianism and Party Politics

In the 1820s, reform pushed its way into politics. No less than reformers, politicians sought to control the direction of change in the expanding nation. The 1824 presidential election ignited a political barn fire that reformers, abolitionists, and expansionists would continuously stoke. By the 1830s, politics had become the great nineteenth-century American pastime.

The election of 1824, in which John Quincy Adams and Andrew Jackson faced off for the first time, heralded a more open political system. From 1800 through 1820 the system in which a congressional caucus (House and Senate members of the political party) chose Jefferson, Madison, and Monroe as the Democratic-Republican nominees had worked well. That it limited voters' involvement in choosing candidates was not an anomaly because in 1800 only five of the sixteen states selected presidential electors by popular vote. In most of the others, state legislatures selected the electors who voted for president. By 1824, however, eighteen out of twenty-four states chose electors at the polls.

The Democratic-Republican caucus in 1824 chose William H. Crawford of Georgia, secretary of the treasury,

ELECTION OF 1824 as its presidential candidate. But other Democratic-Republicans, emboldened by the chance to appeal directly to voters, put themselves forward as sectional candidates. John Quincy Adams drew support from New England, while westerners backed House Speaker Henry Clay of Kentucky. Secretary of War John C. Calhoun looked to the South for support and hoped to win Pennsylvania as well. The Tennessee legislature nominated Andrew Jackson, a popular military hero whose political views were unknown. Jackson had the most widespread support, but Crawford led in the party caucus. By boycotting the caucus and by attacking it as undemocratic, the four other candidates and their supporters ended the role of Congress in nominating presidential candidates.

In the four-way presidential election of 1824, Andrew Jackson led in both electoral and popular votes, but no candidate received a majority in the electoral college (see Map 11.1). Adams finished second, and Crawford and Clay trailed far behind (Calhoun had dropped out of the race before the election). Under the Constitution, the House of Representatives, voting by state delegation, one vote to a state, would select the next president from among the leaders in electoral votes. Clay, who had the fewest votes, was dropped. Crawford, who had a stroke

■ Presidential candidate Andrew Jackson is portrayed on a trinket or sewing box in 1824. This is an example of how campaigns entered popular culture and also illustrates the active role of women, excluded from voting, in politics. (Collection of David J. and Janice L. Frent)

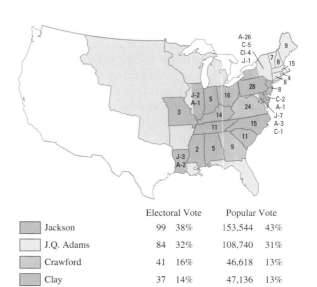

	Electoral Vote		Popular Vote	
Jackson	99	38%	153,544	43%
J.Q. Adams	84	32%	108,740	31%
Crawford	41	16%	46,618	13%
Clay	37	14%	47,136	13%

Map 11.1   Presidential Election, 1824

Andrew Jackson led in both electoral and popular votes but failed to win a majority of electoral college votes. The House elected John Quincy Adams president.

after the election, never received serious consideration. The influential Clay—Speaker of the House and leader of the Ohio valley states—backed Adams, who won with the votes of thirteen of the twenty-four state delegations. Clay became Adams's secretary of state, the traditional steppingstone to the presidency.

Angry Jacksonians denounced the outcome of the election as a "corrupt bargain" that had stolen the office. Jackson's bitterness reinforced his opposition to elitism and fueled his later emphasis on the people's will. The Democratic-Republican Party split. The Adams wing emerged as the National Republicans, and the Jacksonians became the Democrats; they immediately began planning for 1828.

After taking the oath of office, Adams proposed a strong nationalist policy incorporating Henry Clay's "American System," a program of protective tariffs, a national bank, and internal improvements. Adams believed the federal government should take an active role not only in the economy but also in education, science, and the arts. He proposed establishing a national university in Washington, D.C. Brilliant as a diplomat and secretary of state, Adams was an inept president. The political skills he had demonstrated in winning the office eluded him as chief executive. He underestimated the lingering effects of the Panic of 1819 and the resulting staunch opposition to a national bank and protective tariffs. Meanwhile, supporters of Andrew Jackson sabotaged Adams's administration at every opportunity.

The 1828 election pitted Adams against Jackson in a rowdy campaign. Voters displayed their enthusiasm for

ELECTION OF 1828

Jackson with badges, medals, and other campaign paraphernalia, which were mass-produced for the first time. The contest was also intensely personal. Mudslinging was the order of the day. Jackson's supporters accused Adams of stealing the 1824 election and, when he was envoy to Russia, of having secured prostitutes for the czar. Anti-Jacksonians published reports that Rachel Jackson had had an affair with Jackson and married the young officer before her first husband divorced her in 1793; she was, they sneered, an adulterer and a bigamist. In 1806 Jackson had killed John Dickinson in a Kentucky duel defending Rachel's integrity, and the cry of murderer was revived in the election. After the election Rachel Jackson discovered a pamphlet defending her, and she was shocked by the extent of the charges. When she died of a heart attack in December 1828, Jacksonians charged that she was "murdered."

Although Adams kept the states he won in 1824, the opposition was unified, and Jackson swamped him (see

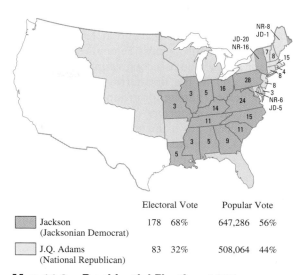

		Electoral Vote		Popular Vote	
▩	Jackson (Jacksonian Democrat)	178	68%	647,286	56%
▢	J.Q. Adams (National Republican)	83	32%	508,064	44%

Map 11.2   Presidential Election, 1828

Andrew Jackson avenged his 1824 loss of the presidency, sweeping the election in 1828.

Map 11.2). Jackson polled 56 percent of the popular vote and won in the electoral college by 178 to 83 votes. He and his supporters believed that the will of the people had finally been served. Through a lavishly financed coalition of state parties, political leaders, and newspaper editors, a popular movement had elected the president, and a new era began. The Democratic Party became the first well-organized national political party in the United States, and tight party organization became the hallmark of nineteenth-century American politics.

Nicknamed "Old Hickory" after the toughest of American hardwoods, Andrew Jackson was a rough-and-

ANDREW JACKSON

tumble, ambitious man. Born in South Carolina in 1767, he rose from humble beginnings to become a wealthy Tennessee planter and slaveholder. Jackson was the first American president from the West and the first born in a log cabin; he was at ease among both frontiersmen and southern planters. Though vindictive and given to violent displays of temper, he could charm opposition into assent. A natural leader, Jackson inspired immense loyalty. He had an instinct for politics and picked both issues and supporters shrewdly.

Few Americans have been as celebrated as Jackson. Having served in the Revolution as a boy, he claimed a connection to the founding generation. In the Tennessee militia General Jackson led the campaign to remove Creeks from the Alabama and Georgia frontier (see pages

234–235). He burst onto the national scene in 1815 as the hero of the Battle of New Orleans and in 1818 enhanced his glory in an expedition against Seminoles in Spanish Florida. Jackson also served as a congressman and senator from Tennessee, and as the first territorial governor of Florida (1821), before running for president in 1824.

Jackson and his supporters offered an alternative to the strong federal government advocated by John Quincy Adams. The Democrats represented a wide range of views but shared a fundamental commitment to the Jeffersonian concept of an agrarian society. They viewed the central government as the enemy of individual liberty. The 1824 "corrupt bargain" had strengthened their suspicion of Washington politics. Jackson himself, a backwoodsman and farmer, symbolized simpler times.

DEMOCRATS

Jacksonians feared the concentration of economic and political power. They believed that government intervention in the economy benefited special-interest groups and created corporate monopolies that favored the rich. They sought to restore the independence of the individual—the artisan and the ordinary farmer—by ending federal support of banks and corporations and restricting the use of paper currency, which they distrusted. Their definition of the proper role of government tended to be negative, and Jackson's political power was largely expressed in negative acts. He exercised the veto more than all previous presidents combined.

Jackson and his supporters also opposed reform as a movement. Reformers eager to turn their programs into legislation called for a more active government. But Democrats tended to oppose programs like educational reform and the establishment of a public education system. They believed, for instance, that public schools restricted individual liberty by interfering with parental responsibility and undermined freedom of religion by replacing church schools. Nor did Jackson share reformers' humanitarian concerns. He had no sympathy for American Indians, initiating the removal of the Cherokees along the Trail of Tears (see pages 267–268).

Jacksonians considered themselves reformers in a different way. By restraining government and emphasizing individualism, they sought to restore traditional republican virtues, such as prudence and economy. No less zealous than reformers, Jackson sought to encourage self-discipline and self-reliance, traits undermined by economic and social change. In doing so, Jackson looked to Jefferson and the generation of the founders as models of traditional values. "My political creed," Jackson wrote to Tennessee congressman James

JACKSONIANS
AS REFORMERS

K. Polk in 1826, "was formed in the old republican school."

Like Jefferson, Jackson strengthened the executive branch of government even as he weakened the federal role. Given his popularity and the strength of his personality, this concentration of power in the presidency was perhaps inevitable, but in combining the roles of party leader and chief of state, he centralized power in the White House. Jackson relied on political friends, his "Kitchen Cabinet," for advice; he rarely consulted his official cabinet. Enamored of power, Jackson never hesitated to confront opponents with all the weapons at his disposal. He commanded enormous loyalty, and he rewarded his followers handsomely. Rotating officeholders, Jackson claimed, made government more responsive to the public will, but it allowed him to introduce a spoils system to appoint loyal Democrats to office. He removed fewer than one-quarter of the federal officeholders he inherited, but he used patronage to strengthen party organization and loyalty.

Jackson stressed rejection of elitism and special favors, rotation of officeholders—political appointees rather than a permanent bureaucracy—and belief in popular government. Time and again he declared that sovereignty resided with the people, not with the states or the courts. In this respect Jackson was a reformer; he returned government to majority rule. Yet it is hard to distinguish between Jackson's belief in himself as the instrument of the people and simple egotism and demagogic arrogance. After all, his opponents, too, claimed to represent the people.

Animosity grew year by year between Jacksonians and their opponents. Massachusetts senator Daniel Webster feared the men around the president; Henry Clay most feared Jackson himself. Rotation in office, they contended, corrupted government because appointments were based on political loyalty, not competency. Opponents mocked Jackson as "King Andrew I," charging him with abuse of power by ignoring the Supreme Court's ruling on Cherokee rights (see page 267), by using the spoils system, and by consulting his Kitchen Cabinet. Critics rejected his claim of restoring republican virtue and accused him of recklessly destroying the economy.

Amid this agitation, Jackson pursued his agenda. He invigorated the philosophy of limited government. In 1830 he vetoed the Maysville Road bill—which would have funded construction of a 60-mile turnpike from Maysville to Lexington, Kentucky. A federally subsidized internal improvement confined to one state was unconstitutional, he charged; such projects were properly a state responsibility. The veto undermined Henry Clay's nationalist program and personally embarrassed Clay because the project was in his home district. Such federal-state issues were to loom even larger in the nullification crisis.

Federalism at Issue: The Nullification and Bank Controversies

Soon Jackson had to face directly the question of the proper division of sovereignty between state and central governments. The slave South feared federal power, no state more so than South Carolina, where the planter class was strongest and slavery most concentrated. Southerners also resented protectionist tariffs, one of the foundations of Clay's American System, which in 1824 and 1828 protected manufactures by imposing import duties on manufactured cloth and iron. But in protecting northern factories, the tariff raised the costs of these goods to southerners, who quickly labeled the high tariff of 1828 the Tariff of Abominations.

South Carolina's political leaders went so far as to reject the 1828 tariff, invoking the doctrine of nullification, according to which a state had the right to overrule, or nullify, federal legislation. Nullification was based on the idea expressed in the Virginia and Kentucky Resolutions of 1798 (see page 208)—that the states, representing the people, have a right to judge the constitutionality of federal actions. Jackson's vice president, John C. Calhoun of South Carolina, argued in his unsigned *Exposition and Protest* that in any disagreement between the federal government and a state, a special state convention—like the conventions called to ratify the Constitution—should decide the conflict by either nullifying or affirming the federal law. Only the power of nullification, Calhoun asserted, could protect the minority against the tyranny of the majority.

NULLIFICATION

In public, Calhoun let others advance nullification. As Jackson's running mate in 1828, he had avoided endorsing nullification and thus embarrassing the Democratic ticket; he also hoped to win Jackson's support as the Democratic presidential heir apparent. Thus in early 1830 Calhoun presided silently over the Senate and its packed galleries when Senator Daniel Webster of Massachusetts and Senator Robert Y. Hayne of South Carolina debated states' rights. The debate started over a resolution to restrict western land sales and engaged the tariff issue by exploring sectional differences. It quickly

WEBSTER-HAYNE DEBATE

turned to the nature of the Union, with nullification a subtext. With Vice President Calhoun nodding in agreement, Hayne charged that the North was threatening to bring disunity, as it had done fifteen years earlier at the Hartford Convention (see pages 236, 237). Hayne accused reformers of wanting in "the spirit of false philanthropy" to destroy the South.

For two days Webster eloquently defended New England and the republic as he kept nullification on the defense. Though debating Hayne, he aimed his remarks at Calhoun. At the climax of the debate, Webster invoked two powerful images. One was the outcome of nullification: "states dissevered, discordant, belligerent; on a land rent with civil feuds, or drenched . . . in fraternal blood!" The other was a patriotic vision of a great nation flourishing under the motto "Liberty and Union, now and forever, one and inseparable."

Though sympathetic to states' rights and distrustful of the federal government, Jackson rejected the idea of state sovereignty. He strongly believed that sovereignty rested with the people. Believing deeply in the Union, he shared Webster's dread of nullification. Soon after the Webster-Hayne debate, the president made his position clear at a Jefferson Day dinner with the toast "Our Federal Union, it must and shall be preserved." Vice President Calhoun, when his turn came, toasted "The Federal Union—next to our liberty the most dear." Thus Calhoun revealed his adherence to states' rights. Calhoun and Jackson grew apart, and Jackson looked to Secretary of State Martin Van Buren, not Calhoun, as his successor.

Tension resumed when Congress passed a new tariff in 1832, reducing some duties but retaining high taxes on imported iron, cottons, and woolens. Though a majority of southern representatives supported the new tariff, South Carolinians refused to go along. In their eyes, the constitutional right to control their own destiny had been sacrificed to the demands of northern industrialists. More than the duties, they feared that the act could set a precedent for congressional legislation on slavery. In November 1832 a South Carolina state convention nullified both the 1828 and 1832 tariffs, declaring it unlawful for federal officials to collect duties in the state.

NULLIFICATION CRISIS

Old Hickory responded quickly. Privately he threatened to invade South Carolina and hang Vice President Calhoun; publicly he took measured steps. In December Jackson issued a proclamation opposing nullification. He moved troops to federal forts in South Carolina and prepared U.S. marshals to collect the required duties. At Jackson's request, Congress passed the Force Act, authorizing the president to call up troops but also offering a way to avoid force by collecting duties before foreign ships reached Charleston's harbor. At the same time, Jackson extended an olive branch by recommending tariff reductions.

Calhoun, disturbed by South Carolina's drift toward separatism, resigned as vice president and soon won election to represent South Carolina in the U.S. Senate. There he worked with Henry Clay to draw up the compromise Tariff of 1833. Quickly passed by Congress and signed by the president, the new tariff lengthened the list of duty-free items and reduced duties over nine years. Satisfied, South Carolina's convention repealed its nullification law. In a final salvo, it also nullified Jackson's Force Act. Jackson ignored the gesture.

Nullification offered a genuine debate on the nature and principles of the republic. Each side believed it was upholding the Constitution. Both sides felt they were opposing special privilege and subversion of republican values. South Carolina opposed the tyranny of the federal government and manufacturers that sought tariff protection. Jackson fought the tyranny of South Carolina, whose refusal to bow to federal authority threatened to split the republic. Neither side won a clear victory, though both claimed to have done so. It took another crisis, over a central bank, to define the powers of the federal government more clearly.

At stake was survival of the Second Bank of the United States, whose twenty-year charter was scheduled to expire in 1836. Like its predecessor, the bank served as a depository for federal funds and provided credit for businesses. Its bank notes circulated as currency throughout the country; they could be readily exchanged for gold, and the federal government accepted them as payment in all transactions. Through its twenty-five branch offices, the Second Bank acted as a clearing-house for state banks, keeping them honest by refusing to accept bank notes of any state bank lacking sufficient gold in reserve. Most state banks resented the central bank's police role: by presenting a state bank's notes for redemption all at once, the Second Bank could easily ruin a state bank. Moreover, with less money in reserve, state banks found themselves unable to compete on an equal footing with the Second Bank.

Many state governments also regarded the national bank as unresponsive to local needs. Westerners and urban workers remembered with bitterness the bank's conservative credit policies during the Panic of 1819 (see page 245). As a private, profit-making institution, its policies reflected the interest of its owners, especially its

SECOND BANK OF THE UNITED STATES

president, Nicholas Biddle, who controlled the bank completely. An eastern patrician, Biddle symbolized all that westerners found wrong with the bank.

Rechartering was a volatile issue in the 1832 presidential campaign. The bank's charter was valid until 1836, but Henry Clay, the National Republican presidential candidate, persuaded Biddle to ask Congress to approve an early rechartering. This strategy was designed to pressure Jackson to sign the rechartering bill or to override his veto of it. The plan backfired, however. The president vetoed the bill, and the Senate failed to override. Jackson's veto message was an emotional attack on the undemocratic nature of the bank. "It is to be regretted," he wrote, "that the rich and powerful too often bend the acts of government to their selfish purposes."

The bank became the prime issue in the presidential campaign of 1832, with Jackson denouncing special privilege and economic power. With every state but South Carolina now choosing electors by popular vote, the Jacksonians used their party organization to mobilize voters by advertising the presidential election as the central event of the political system. When the Antimasons adopted a party platform, the first in the nation's history, the Democrats and the National Republicans quickly followed suit. The Democratic convention nominated Jackson and Martin Van Buren, Jackson's first secretary of state and then American minister to Great Britain; the National Republican convention selected Clay and John Sergeant. South Carolina nominated its own candidate, John Floyd. Jackson was reelected easily in a Democratic Party triumph.

After his sweeping victory and second inauguration, Jackson moved in 1833 to dismantle the Second Bank of the United States. He deposited federal funds in state-chartered banks (critics called them his "pet banks"). Without federal money, the Second Bank shriveled. When its federal charter expired in 1836, it became just another Pennsylvania-chartered private bank. Five years later it closed its doors.

JACKSON'S SECOND TERM

As Congress allowed the Bank of the United States to die, it passed the Deposit Act of 1836 with Jackson's support. The act authorized the secretary of the treasury to designate one bank in each state and territory to provide the services formerly performed by the Bank of the United States. The act provided that the federal surplus in excess of $5 million be distributed to the states as interest-free loans beginning in 1837. These loans were never repaid— a fitting Jacksonian restraint on the federal purse.

The surplus had derived from wholesale speculation in public lands: speculators borrowed money to purchase

■ This 1830 Ralph E. W. Earl oil painting of President Andrew Jackson, entitled *Tennessee Gentleman,* captures the complexity of Jackson's image. The first president from the West and the first born in a log cabin, Jackson nonetheless poses as an aristocrat with his plantation house, The Hermitage, in the background.   (Courtesy, The Hermitage—The Home of Andrew Jackson)

public land, used the land as collateral for credit to buy additional acreage, and repeated the cycle. Between 1834 and 1836 federal receipts from land sales rose from $5 million to $25 million. The state banks providing the loans issued bank notes. Jackson, an opponent of paper money, feared that the speculative craze threatened the stability of state banks and undermined the interests of settlers, who could not compete with speculators in bidding for the best land.

In keeping with his hard-money instincts and opposition to paper currency, the president ordered Treasury Secretary Levi Woodbury to issue the Specie Circular. It

SPECIE CIRCULAR provided that after August 1836 only specie—gold or silver—or Virginia scrip (paper money) would be accepted as payment for land. By ending credit sales, it significantly reduced purchases of public land and the federal budget surplus. As a result the government suspended payments to the states soon after they began.

The policy was a disaster. Although federal land sales fell sharply, speculation continued as land available for sale became scarce. The increased demand for specie squeezed banks, and many suspended the redemption of bank notes for specie. Credit contracted further as banks issued fewer notes and made fewer loans. Jackson aggravated the situation by instinctively pursuing a tight money policy. More important, the Specie Circular was similar to a bill defeated in the Senate just three months earlier. Jackson's opponents thus saw King Andrew at work. In the waning days of Jackson's administration, Congress voted to repeal the circular, but the president pocket-vetoed the bill by holding it unsigned until Congress adjourned. Finally in May 1838, a joint resolution of Congress overturned the circular. Sales of land resumed, but the speculative fervor had ended.

From George Washington to John Quincy Adams, the first six presidents had vetoed nine bills; Jackson alone vetoed twelve. Previous presidents believed that vetoes were justified only on constitutional grounds, but Jackson considered policy disagreements legitimate grounds as well. He made the veto an effective weapon for controlling Congress, since representatives and senators had to weigh the possibility of a presidential veto as they deliberated. In effect, Jackson made the executive for the first time a rival branch of government, equal in power to Congress.

USE OF THE VETO

The Whig Challenge and the Second Party System

*M*ost historians view the 1830s and 1840s as an age of reform and popularly based political parties. As the passions of reformers and abolitionists spilled over into politics, party differences became paramount and party loyalties solidified. For the first time in American history, grassroots political groups, organized from the bottom up, set the tone of political life. And both parties were national, drawing voters and winning counties in every region.

Opponents of the Democrats, including remnants of the National Republican Party, found shelter under a

WHIG PARTY   common umbrella, the Whig Party, in the 1830s. Resentful of Jackson's domination of Congress, the Whigs borrowed the name of the British party that had opposed the tyranny of Hanoverian monarchs in the eighteenth century. From 1834 through the 1840s, the Whigs and the Democrats competed on a nearly equal footing. They fought at the city, county, state, and national levels and achieved a stability previously unknown in American politics. The political competition of this period—known as the second party system—was more intense and well organized than that of the first party system of Democratic-Republicans versus Federalists.

Reform and the party system changed politics. As political interest broadened, states expanded white male voting. By 1840 only seven of twenty-six states had property restrictions for male suffrage, though most excluded convicted felons. Some even allowed immigrants who had taken out citizenship papers to vote. Hotly contested elections further stimulated public interest in politics. The net effect was a sharp increase in the number of votes cast in presidential elections. Between 1824 and 1828 that number increased threefold, from 360,000 to over 1.1 million. In 1840, 2.4 million men cast votes. The proportion of eligible voters who cast ballots also increased, from about 27 percent in 1824 to more than 80 percent in 1840.

Increasingly the parties diverged. Whigs favored economic expansion through an activist government, Democrats through limited central government. Whigs supported corporate charters, a national bank, and paper currency; Democrats were opposed to all three. Whigs also favored more humanitarian reforms than did Democrats, including public schools, abolition of capital punishment, prison and asylum reform, and temperance. Whigs were more optimistic than Democrats, generally speaking, and more enterprising. They did not object to helping a specific group if doing so would promote the general welfare. The chartering of corporations, they argued, expanded economic opportunity for everyone, laborers and farmers alike. Democrats, distrustful of concentrated economic power and of moral and economic coercion, held fast to the Jeffersonian principle of limited government.

WHIGS AND REFORMERS

Religion and ethnicity, not economics and class, most influenced party affiliation. The Whigs' support for energetic government and humanitarian and moral reform won the favor of evangelical Protestants, especially those involved in religious revivals. Methodists and Baptists were overwhelmingly Whigs, as were the small number of free black voters. The Whig Party was the vehicle of revivalist Protestantism. In many locales the membership rolls of reform societies overlapped those of the party. Indeed, Whigs practiced a kind of political revivalism. Their rallies resembled camp meetings; in their speeches they employed pulpit rhetoric; their programs embodied the perfectionist beliefs of reformers. This potent blend of religion and politics—"intimately united" in America, according to Tocqueville—greatly intensified political loyalties.

In their appeal to evangelicals, Whigs alienated members of other faiths. The evangelicals' ideal Christian state had no room for nonevangelical Protestants, Catholics, Mormons, Unitarians, Universalists, or religious freethinkers. Those groups opposed Sabbath laws and temperance legislation in particular and state interference in moral and religious questions in general. In fact, they preferred to keep religion and politics separate. As a result, more than 95 percent of Irish Catholics, 90 percent of Reformed Dutch, and 80 percent of German Catholics voted Democratic.

Vice President Martin Van Buren, handpicked by Jackson, headed the Democratic ticket in the 1836 presidential election. Van Buren was a shrewd politician who had built a political machine—the Albany Regency—in New York and then left to join Jackson's cabinet in 1829. Having helped found the Democratic Party, Van Buren was a professional politician; he made his career in party politics.

ELECTION OF 1836

Because the Whigs in 1836 had not yet coalesced into a national party, they entered three sectional candidates: Daniel Webster of New England, Hugh White of the South, and William Henry Harrison of the West. By splintering the vote, they hoped to throw the election into the House of Representatives. Van Buren, however, comfortably captured the electoral college even though he had only a 25,000-vote edge out of a total of 1.5 million votes cast. No vice-presidential candidate received a majority of electoral votes, and for the only time in American history the Senate decided a vice-presidential race, selecting Democratic candidate Richard M. Johnson of Kentucky.

Van Buren took office just weeks before the American credit system collapsed. In response to the impact of the Specie Circular, New York banks stopped redeeming paper currency with gold in mid-1837. Soon all banks suspended payments in hard coin. Thus began a downward economic spiral that curtailed bank loans and strangled business confidence. Credit contraction made things worse; after a brief recovery, hard times persisted from 1839 until 1843.

VAN BUREN AND HARD TIMES

Ill advisedly, Van Buren followed Jackson's hard-money policies. He cut federal spending, which caused prices to drop further, and he opposed a national bank, which would have expanded credit. Even worse, the president proposed a new regional treasury system for government deposits. The proposed treasury branches would accept and pay out only gold and silver coin; they would not accept paper currency or checks drawn on state banks. Van Buren's independent treasury bill became law in 1840. By increasing the demand for hard coin, it deprived banks of gold and further accelerated price deflation. Whigs and Democrats faced off at the state level over these issues. Whigs favored new banks, more paper currency, and readily available corporate and bank charters. As the party of hard money, Democrats favored eliminating paper currency altogether. Increasingly the Democrats became distrustful even of state banks, and by the mid-1840s a majority favored eliminating all bank corporations.

With the nation in the grip of hard times, the Whigs prepared confidently for the election of 1840. Their

WILLIAM HENRY HARRISON AND THE ELECTION OF 1840

strategy was simple: hold on to loyal supporters and win over independents by blaming hard times on the Democrats. The Whigs rallied behind a military hero, General William Henry Harrison, conqueror of the Shawnees at Tippecanoe Creek in 1811 (see page 226). The Democrats renominated President Van Buren at a somber convention.

Harrison, or "Old Tippecanoe," and his running mate, John Tyler of Virginia, ran a "log cabin and hard cider" campaign—a people's crusade—against the aristocratic president in "the Palace." Though descended from a Virginia plantation family, Harrison presented himself as an ordinary farmer. The Whigs wooed supporters and independents alike with huge rallies, parades, songs, posters, campaign mementos, and a party newspaper, *The Log Cabin*. Harrison took the position that a presidential candidate should not be involved in the issues, earning himself the nickname "General Mum," but party hacks bluntly blamed the hard times on the Democrats. In a huge turnout, 80 percent of eligible voters cast ballots. Harrison won the popular vote by a narrow margin but swept the electoral college by 234 to 60.

Immediately after taking office in 1841, President Harrison convened a special session of Congress to pass the Whig program: repeal of the independent treasury system, a new national bank, and a higher protective tariff. But the sixty-eight-year-old Harrison caught pneumonia and died within a month of his inauguration. His successor, John Tyler, who had left the Democratic Party to protest Jackson's nullification proclamation, now found himself the first vice president to move up to the presidency on the death of a president.

In office, Tyler turned out to be more of a Democrat than a Whig. As critical of the Whigs' economic nationalism as he had been of Jackson's use of executive power, Tyler consistently opposed his own party's

■ Using patriotic and emotional images that look familiar to people today, General William Henry Harrison in 1840 ran a "log cabin and hard cider" campaign against Jackson's heir, President Martin Van Buren. The cotton bandana, presumably widely distributed given its practical use, shows Harrison, before a log cabin, welcoming a disabled veteran while another person draws hard cider. (Collection of Janice L. and David J. Frent)

PRESIDENT
TYLER
congressional agenda. He repeatedly vetoed Henry Clay's protective tariffs, internal improvements, and bills aimed at reviving the Bank of the United States. The only important measures that became law during his term were repeal of the independent treasury system and passage of a higher tariff. Two days after Tyler's second veto of a bank bill, the entire cabinet except Secretary of State Daniel Webster resigned; Webster, busy negotiating a new treaty with Great Britain, left shortly thereafter. Tyler became a president without a party, and the Whigs lost the presidency without losing an election. Disgusted Whigs referred to Tyler as "His Accidency."

Hard times in the late 1830s and early 1840s deflected attention from a renewal of Anglo-American tensions that had multiple sources: northern commercial rivalry with Britain, the default of state governments and corporations on British-held debts during the Panic of 1837, rebellion in Canada, boundary disputes, southern alarm over West Indian emancipation, and American expansionism.

One of the most troublesome disputes arose from the *Caroline* affair. A U.S. citizen, Amos Durfee, had been

ANGLO-
AMERICAN
TENSIONS
killed when Canadian militia set afire the privately owned steamer *Caroline* in the Niagara River. (The *Caroline* had supported an unsuccessful uprising against Great Britain in 1837.) Britain refused to apologize, and American newspapers called for revenge. Fearing that popular support for the Canadian rebels would ignite war, President Van Buren posted troops at the border to discourage raids. Tensions subsided in late 1840 when New York arrested Alexander McLeod, a Canadian deputy sheriff, for the murder of Durfee. McLeod eventually was acquitted. Had he been found guilty and executed, Lord Palmerston, the British foreign minister, might have sought war.

At almost the same time an old border dispute between Maine and New Brunswick disrupted Anglo-American relations. Great Britain had accepted an 1831 arbitration decision fixing a new boundary, but the U.S. Senate rejected it. Thus when Canadian lumbermen cut trees in the disputed region in the winter of 1838–1839, the citizens of Maine attempted to expel them. The lumbermen captured the Maine land agent and posse, both sides mobilized their militias, and Congress authorized a call-up of fifty thousand men. Ultimately, no blood was spilled. General Winfield Scott, who had patrolled the border during the *Caroline* affair, was dispatched to Aroostook, Maine, where he arranged a truce. The two sides compromised on their conflicting land claims in the Webster-Ashburton Treaty (1842).

These border disputes with Great Britain prefigured the conflicts that were to erupt in the 1840s over the expansion of the United States. With Tyler's succession to power in 1841 and James K. Polk's Democratic victory in the presidential election of 1844, federal activism in the domestic sphere ended for the rest of the decade, as attention turned to territorial expansion. Reform, however, was not dead. Its passions would resurface before the decade was over in the debate about slavery in the territories.

Manifest Destiny and Expansionism

*T*he belief that American expansion westward and southward was inevitable, just, and divinely ordained was first labeled "manifest destiny" in 1845, by John L. O'Sullivan, editor of the *United States Magazine and Domestic Review*. The annexation of Texas, O'Sullivan wrote in 1845, was "the fulfillment of our manifest destiny to overspread the continent allotted by Providence for the free development of our yearly multiplying millions." Armed with such sentiments, expansionism reached a new fervor in the 1840s.

Since colonial days Americans had hungered for more land. Acquisition of the Louisiana Territory (1803) and Florida (1819) (see Map 9.1) and Indian removal (see pages 263–268) had set the process in motion. As the proportion of Americans living west of the Appalachians grew from one-quarter to one-half between 1830 and 1860, both national parties joined the popular clamor for expansion. Agrarian Democrats sought western land to balance urbanization. Enterprising Whigs looked to the new commercial opportunities the West offered. Southerners envisioned the extension of slavery and more slave states.

Fierce national pride spurred the quest for land. Subdued during hard times, it reasserted itself after 1843 when the economy recovered, and during the decade expansionism reached a new fervor. Americans were convinced that theirs was the greatest country on earth, with a special role to play in the world. As reform sought to perfect American society, so too expansion promised to extend the benefits of America's republican system of government to the unfortunate and the inferior.

In part, racism contributed to manifest destiny as well. The impulse to colonize and develop the West was based on the belief that Euro-Americans could use the land more productively than American Indians or Hispanics. Euro-Americans viewed Indians and Hispanics as inferior peoples, best controlled or conquered. Thus the same racial attitudes that justified discrimination against black people and slavery supported expansion in the West.

The desire to secure the nation from perceived external threats also fed expansionist fever. The internal enemies of the 1830s—banks, corporations, paper currency, alcohol—seemed pale in comparison to the opportunities Americans saw along their borders in the 1840s. Expansion, some believed, was necessary to preserve American independence, and no other nation should stop its westward movement.

Among the long-standing objectives of expansionists was Texas, Mexico's remote northern province that in

REPUBLIC OF TEXAS addition to present-day Texas included parts of Oklahoma, Kansas, Colorado, Wyoming, and New Mexico (see Map 11.3). After winning its independence from Spain in 1821, Mexico had encouraged the development of Texas, offering large tracts of land virtually free to U.S. settlers called *empresarios*. The settlers in turn agreed to become Mexican citizens, adopt the Catholic religion, and bring hundreds of American families into the area. Moses and Stephen Austin, who had helped to formulate the policy, responded eagerly.

By 1835 thirty-five thousand Americans, including many slaveholders, lived in Texas. As the new settlers' numbers and power grew, they tended to ignore their commitments to the Mexican government. In response, dictator General Antonio López de Santa Anna tightened control over the region. In turn, the Anglo immigrants and *Tejanos*—Mexicans living in Texas—rebelled. At the Alamo mission in San Antonio in 1836, fewer than two hundred Texans made a heroic but unsuccessful stand against three thousand Mexicans under General Santa Anna. "Remember the Alamo" became the Texans' rallying cry. By the end of the year the Texans had won independence, delighting most Americans. Some saw the victory as a triumph of Protestants over Catholic Mexico; others cheered that proslavery Texans had defeated antislavery Mexicans.

Texas established the independent Lone Star Republic but soon sought annexation to the United States. Sam Houston, president of the Texas republic, opened negotiations with Washington, but the issue quickly became politically explosive. Southerners favored annexing proslavery Texas; abolitionists, many northerners, and most Whigs opposed annexation. In recognition of the political dangers, President Jackson had reneged on his promise to recognize Texas, and President Van Buren ignored annexation. Rebuffed by the United States, Texans talked about closer ties with the British and extending their republic to the Pacific coast. With Britain control-

■ Texans believed that their war for independence paralleled the Revolutionary War. The lady of liberty on this banner, carried by Texans in 1836, brings to mind similar images that stirred patriots during the American Revolution. (Archives Division, Texas State Library)

ling Canada, the prospect of a rival republic to the south caused some Americans to fear encirclement. If Texas reached the ocean and became an English ally, would not American independence be threatened?

President Tyler, committed to expansion, pushed for annexation. Eager to gain the 1844 Democratic nomination, Tyler hoped his position would build a political base in the South. Southerners also pressed for annexation. Former president Jackson agreed, stating that the United States must have Texas, "peacefully if we can, forcibly if we must." But the Senate rejected annexation in 1844. A letter from Secretary of State Calhoun to the British minister, justifying annexation to protect slavery, so outraged senators that the treaty was defeated 16 to 35.

As southerners sought expansion in the Southwest, northerners looked to the Northwest. "Oregon fever"

OREGON FEVER struck thousands in 1841. Lured by the glowing reports of missionaries who seemed as enthusiastic about the Northwest's riches and beauty as about conversion of Indians, migrants in wagon trains took to the Oregon Trail. Their

Map 11.3 Westward Expansion, 1800–1860

Through exploration, purchase, war, and treaty, the United States became a continental nation, stretching from the Atlantic to the Pacific.

■ An unknown artist depicted, in rich detail, the election campaign of 1844. A team of Polk supporters offers a campaign handbill to the seated voter. Passions were so high and party organization was so extensive that door-to-door politicking became the norm. (Courtesy, Nathan Liverant & Son)

enthusiasm was tempered by apprehension. Lavinia Porter feared that her husband did not have "the training to make a living on the plains of the West or the crossing of the continent in an ox team a successful venture." The 2,000-mile journey took six months or more, but within a few years five thousand settlers had arrived in the fertile Willamette valley south of the Columbia River.

Britain and the United States had jointly occupied the disputed Oregon Territory since the Convention of 1818 (see pages 242–243). Beginning with the administration of President John Quincy Adams, the United States had tried to fix the boundary at the 49th parallel, but Britain was determined to maintain access to Puget Sound and the Columbia River. Time only increased the American appetite. In 1843 a Cincinnati convention of expan-

sionists demanded the entire Oregon Country for the United States, up to its northernmost border at latitude 54°40'. Soon "Fifty-four Forty or Fight" became the rallying cry of American expansionists.

Expansion into Oregon and rejection of the annexation of Texas, both favored by antislavery forces, worried southern leaders. Anxious about their diminishing ability to control the debate over slavery, they persuaded the 1844 Democratic convention to adopt a rule requiring the presidential nominee to receive two-thirds of the convention votes. In effect, the southern states acquired a veto, and they wielded it to block Van Buren as the nominee; most southerners objected to his opposition to slavery and

POLK AND THE ELECTION OF 1844

Texas annexation. Instead, the party chose "Young Hickory," House Speaker James K. Polk, a hard-money Jacksonian, avid expansionist, and slaveholding cotton planter from Tennessee. The Whig leader Henry Clay, who opposed annexation, won his party's nomination handily. The Democratic platform called for occupation of the entire Oregon Territory and annexation of Texas. The Whigs, while favoring annexation, argued that the Democrats' belligerent nationalism would lead the nation into war with Great Britain or Mexico or both. Clay favored expansion through negotiation.

With a well-organized campaign, Polk and the Democrats won the election by 170 electoral votes to 105. (They won the popular vote by just 38,000 out of 2.7 million votes cast.) Polk won New York's 36 electoral votes by just 6,000 popular votes. Abolitionist James G. Birney, the Liberty Party candidate, had drawn almost 16,000 votes away from Clay, handing New York and the election to Polk. Abolitionist forces thus unwittingly brought about the choice of a slaveholder as president, but they viewed Polk as more moderate than Clay on slavery and the lesser of two evils.

Interpreting Polk's victory as a mandate for annexation, President Tyler proposed in his final days in office that Texas be admitted by joint resolution of Congress. The usual method of annexation, by treaty negotiation,

ANNEXATION OF TEXAS

required a two-thirds vote in the Senate—which expansionists clearly did not have, since there were sufficient opponents to slavery who would vote against annexation. Joint resolution required only a simple majority in each house. The resolution passed the House by 120 to 98 and the Senate by 27 to 25. Three days before leaving office, Tyler signed the measure. Mexico, which had never recognized Texas independence, immediately broke relations with the United States. In October the citizens of Texas ratified annexation, and Texas joined the Union in December 1845.

Summary

*R*eligion, reform, and expansionism shaped politics from 1824 through the 1840s. As the Second Great Awakening spread through villages and towns, the converts, especially women, organized to reform a rapidly changing society. Religion imbued men and women with zeal to right the wrongs of American society and the world. Reformers pursued perfectionism and republican virtue by battling with the evils of slavery, prostitution, and alcohol. As reformers, they sought to improve insane asylums and penitentiaries. In the process, women entered the public sphere as advocates of reform. Two issues elicited particular intensity: the comet of Antimasonry and the smoldering fire of abolitionism. The passions that both aroused were so potent, and success so elusive, that Antimasons and abolitionists transformed their moral crusades into political movements. Women's rights and nationalism contributed to the brew, and the new mixture made politics far more important, critical, and engaging than just voting at elections.

Reform remade politics, and politics remade public discourse. So too did American nationalism and economic cycles. As did reformers, President Adams raised expectations about an expanded governmental role. The organized parties of the 1820s and the struggles between the National Republicans and the Democrats, then between the Democrats and the Whigs, stimulated even greater interest in campaigns and political issues. The Democrats, who rallied around Andrew Jackson, and Jackson's opponents, who found shelter under the Whig tent, competed almost equally for the loyalty of voters. Both parties built strong organizations that faced off in national and local elections. And both parties favored economic expansion. Their world-views, however, were fundamentally different. Whigs were more optimistic and favored greater centralized government initiative. Democrats harbored a deep-seated belief in limited government. The controversies over the Second Bank of the United States and nullification allowed Americans to debate the principles of the republic. Jackson, however, did not hesitate to use presidential authority, and his opponents called him King Andrew.

Many Americans had caught the fever of expansionism. Euro-Americans wanted to colonize the continent, farmers sought land, slaveholders wished to extend slavery, and millions itched to move westward. The admission of Texas into the Union in 1845 seemed to fulfill one destiny—expansion—but brought divisiveness as well as the nation increasingly divided over the issue of slavery.

LEGACY FOR A PEOPLE AND A NATION
The Bible Belt

Had an eighteenth-century visitor to North America asked for the Bible belt, she would have been directed to New England, whose colonies were all founded for religious purposes. Early southerners tended to be more secular than religious. By the 1830s, however, the South was the most churched region, and southerners were the most devout. The Second Great Awakening, beginning with the Cane Ridge revival in 1801, spread like wildfire through the South. By the 1830s more than half of white and one-quarter of black southerners had undergone a conversion experience, and religion and the South formed a common identity. Embracing the Bible as the revealed word of God, the South became known as the Bible belt.

Religion helped define southern distinctiveness. Southern Protestant liturgy and cadences were as much African as European; thus southern and northern denominations grew apart. They formally separated in the 1840s when Southern Baptists and Methodists withdrew from the national organizations that had barred slaveowners from church offices. Presbyterians withdrew later. After the Civil War, evangelical denominations remained divided in northern and southern organizations.

Southern religion maintained tradition and resisted modern ways. Protestantism dominated, making the South more religiously homogeneous than other regions. Mostly evangelical, southern religion emphasized conversion and a personal battle against sin. By the twentieth century, fundamentalism, which stressed a literal reading of the Bible, reinforced resistance to modernism. Yet southern Protestantism lost ground as a political force in opposing evolution and in alliances with nativist, anti-immigrant groups.

But evangelicalism rose again in the 1960s, especially after a Catholic—John F. Kennedy—won the Democratic nomination for president. Many evangelicals began to vote their religion, moving to the Republican Party, and in 1964 Republican Barry Goldwater won the Bible belt states, breaking up the solid Democratic block. His conservative rhetoric resonated with southerners concerned about desegregation and erosion of religious values. *Time* called 1976 the "Year of the Evangelical" when born-again Southern Baptist Jimmy Carter was elected president.

In the 1980s and 1990s the Bible belt became the base of mobilized evangelical political action led by the Moral Majority. Religious and cultural issues rallied southern evangelicals: defending the traditional family, advocating prayer in schools, and opposing abortion, the Equal Rights Amendment, and gay rights legislation. In their own eyes, fundamentalist evangelical Protestants were defending biblical principles.

Thus the revivals that began in Kentucky in 1801 have rippled in ever wider circles across the South for two centuries, shaping the distinctive southern blend of culture and politics.

The **history companion** *powered by Eduspace®*

Your primary source for interactive quizzes, exercises, and more to help you learn efficiently.
http://history.college.hmco.com/students

PEOPLE AND COMMUNITIES IN THE NORTH AND WEST 1830–1860

*a*t eight o'clock on a snowy St. Patrick's Day morning in Lowell, Massachusetts, in 1841, more than one hundred members of the Irish Benevolent Society pinned on large green and white flowers as they and a brass band prepared to march through the mill town. Across the United States—in Boston, New York, Philadelphia, Charleston, New Orleans, St. Louis— and around the world in Ireland, England, Canada, Argentina, and Australia, Irish settlers and their descendants expressed their Irish pride by celebrating.

St. Patrick's Day celebrations meant many things to different people. In colonial America, mostly Scots-Irish Protestants toasted Ireland and their mother country Britain at banquets. In the 1760s, in probably the first St. Patrick's Day parade in America, Irish Protestant soldiers in the British army marched with local residents in New York City. After the War of 1812, the banqueters and marchers, mostly middle-class Irish, represented charities, and they raised money to assist immigrants. New arrivals were mostly Catholic, and the parades and banquets brought together Catholics and Protestants.

But events in Ireland made the American Irish community increasingly Catholic. A failed revolution against Britain in 1798, inspired by the American and French Revolutions, and the 1800 Act of Union, which merged Ireland into the United Kingdom, eliminated the Irish Parliament and disfranchised Catholics, making them powerless. Declining farm sizes and a population explosion made them impoverished. When Alexis de Tocqueville visited Ireland in 1835, four years after his trip to the United States, the contrast stunned him. "You cannot imagine," he wrote his father from Ireland, "what a complexity of miseries five centuries of oppression and disorders and religious hostility have piled up on this poor people."

While many struggled in Ireland for equal rights and economic survival, others left their country. In England, industrial Manchester and London offered

◄ New Yorkers celebrated St. Patrick's Day Parade in 1853, during the peak period of Irish immigration. Led by the mayor, the crowd reviewed the militia and the parading Irish marchers. Spectators came from all classes, including ordinary folk like the woman and child fruit sellers in the foreground. (Culver Pictures)

CHRONOLOGY

1827 • *Freedom's Journal,* first African American newspaper, appears

1830 • Smith founds Mormon Church
• First National Negro Convention

1830s–50s • Urban riots commonplace

1832 • Rice debuts in New York minstrel show

1835 • Arkansas passes first women's property law

1837 • Emerson delivers "The American Scholar" address
• Boston employs paid policemen

1837–48 • Mann heads the Massachusetts Board of Education

1838 • Mormons driven out of Missouri

1841–47 • Brook Farm combines spirituality, work, and play in a utopian rural community

1842 • Knickerbocker baseball club formed

1844 • Nativist riots peak in Philadelphia
• Smith brothers murdered in Illinois

1845 • Irish potato blight begins
• *Narrative of the Life of Frederick Douglass* appears

1846–47 • Mormon trek to the Great Salt Lake

1847–57 • Immigration at peak pre–Civil War levels

1848 • Abortive revolution in German states
• United States acquires Alta California in Treaty of Guadalupe Hidalgo
• Gold discovered in California

1849 • California gold rush transforms the West Coast

1852 • Stowe's *Uncle Tom's Cabin* published

1854 • Railroad reaches the Mississippi River
• Large-scale Chinese immigration begins
• Germans replace Irish as largest group of new arrivals

1855 • New York establishes Castle Garden as immigrant center

jobs, but more distant America offered political and religious freedom as well as economic opportunities. To the Irish, the United States offered the best hope.

Thus, in the 1820s and 1830s, in Lowell and elsewhere, St. Patrick's Day increasingly became identified with Irish Catholics. As a Catholic holiday, parades became more important than the banquets; recent immigrants were poorer, and they could not pay for banquets. But parades were an opportunity to express their solidarity as well as their appreciation for America. They marched against the British and its established Anglican Church, and for equal rights in Ireland. Increasingly they wore red, white, and blue as well as green, to demonstrate their identity. Both Americans and the Irish had suffered, they pointed out, from British tyranny. St. Patrick's Day speakers reminded audiences that "republicanism" was both an American and Irish principle. In 1837, on St. Patrick's Day, Dr. William James McNeven, who had been imprisoned following the 1798 insurrection, told his New York audience that the Irish sought only the rights Americans already possessed. Editor Thomas O'Connor, who described himself as an "Irishman by birth" and an "American by adoption," toasted "America as she is, Ireland as she ought to be." St. Patrick's Day linked American and Irish causes.

But increasingly American Irish Protestants stayed away from such events. They identified with Britain, not the Irish opposition. In the 1820s they began to skip St. Patrick's Day parades and march on July 12, commemorating English ascendancy—the victory of William of Orange in the Battle of the Boyne in 1690. They purposefully distanced themselves from the new immigrants, becoming Whigs while the new immigrants gravitated to Andrew Jackson. Then, in the 1840s and 1850s, as potato blight and famine stalked Ireland, nearly 2 million Irish immigrants—almost all Catholics—arrived in the United States. Now St. Patrick's Day marches attracted not hundreds but thousands, and nativists jeered the marchers, occasionally assaulting them. By the 1850s contingents of police had to accompany the paraders to protect them.

The huge Irish immigration was only part of a worldwide population movement. From the 1830s through the 1850s, millions of Europeans arrived on America's shores.

Immigration added to the rapidly growing population and transformed the American nation. Within large cities and in the countryside, whole districts became ethnic and religious enclaves.

What it meant to be an American was changing. The Revolution and early years of nation building diminished as sources of American identity. The cultural traditions of European immigrants differed from those in the American colonial past, and increasingly some white Americans came to see the differences as racial rather than cultural. Black Americans became racial outsiders, as did Hispanics in the Southwest. In a society growing ever more diverse and complex, conflict became common.

The market economy both energized and accentuated the differences among Americans. In the nation's cities, opulent mansions rose within sight of notorious slums, and both wealth and poverty reached extremes unknown in the countryside. Ethnicity, race, religion, and class divided Americans as well. Farm families attempted to maintain cohesive, rural villages, while utopians and groups like the Mormons sought to create self-governing communal havens.

The market economy altered family life too. As commerce and industry grew, the home lost its function as a workplace. Goods formerly made at home were now mass-manufactured in factories and bought in stores. Public schools took over much of the family's traditional role as prime educator. Leisure became a commodity to be purchased by those who could afford it. Families shrank in size, and more people lived outside family units. In the North and West, urban growth and immigration challenged economic and social conventions. ■

Country Life

*R*ural life changed significantly in the first half of the nineteenth century. Farm population in the coastal states declined as towns grew and manufacturing expanded. Farm families—native-born whites, blacks, and immigrants—sought more fertile and cheaper land in the West. Market-oriented communities arose there, linked to eastern markets by the new transportation networks. But not all accepted the market economy. The religious fervor of the Second Great Awakening inspired some to seek spiritual regeneration, rather than cash-crop profits, through the establishment of utopian communities.

In the 1850s, western settlement, technological improvements, competition, economic recovery, and a desire for national unity prompted development of regional and, eventually, national rail networks. By 1853 rail lines linked eastern cities to Chicago, and a year later track reached the Mississippi River. By 1860 rails stretched as far west as St. Joseph, Missouri, as railroad track tripled during the 1850s, reaching 30,600 miles in 1860.

RAILROAD LINKS

The railroad depot and post office in the farm village linked farmers with the world. But in these villages, with their churches, general stores, and taverns, communal values still ruled. Families gathered on one another's farms to accomplish as a community what they could not manage individually. Barn-raisings regularly brought people together. A farm family with the help of an itinerant carpenter would prepare the walls. The neighbors would come by buggy to help the family raise walls into position and build a roof. Afterward everyone celebrated with a hearty communal feast and sang, danced, and played games. They might compete in foot races, wrestling, or marksmanship, and on occasion they raced horses. Similar gatherings took place at harvest time and on special occasions.

FARM COMMUNITIES

Farm men and women had active social lives. Men met frequently at general stores, weekly markets, and taverns, and hunted and fished together. Some women also attended market, especially those engaged in dairy farming. More typically they met at after-church dinners, prayer groups, sewing and corn-husking bees, and quilting parties. These were cherished opportunities to exchange experiences, thoughts, and spiritual support, and to swap letters, books, and news.

Irene Hardy, who grew up in rural Ohio in the 1840s, left a memoir of the gatherings she had attended as a girl. Fifty years later she recalled apple bees at which neighbors gathered to make apple butter or preserves. After the day's work, Hardy remembered, the elders gossiped while the youngsters joked and teased each other and flirted. "Then came supper, apple and pumpkin pies, cider, doughnuts, cakes, cold chicken and turkey," Hardy wrote, "after which games, 'Forfeits,' 'Building a Bridge,' 'Snatchability,' even 'Blind Man's Bluff' and 'Pussy Wants a Corner.'" Traditional country bees had their town counterparts. Fredrika Bremer, a Swedish visitor, described a sewing bee in Cambridge, Massachusetts, in 1849, at which neighborhood women made clothes for

BEES

■ *The Lackawanna Valley* (1855) by George Inness. Hired by the Lackawanna Railroad to paint a picture showing the company's new roundhouse at Scranton, in northeastern Pennsylvania, Inness combined landscape and locomotive technology into an organic whole. Industrialism, Inness seems to say, belonged to the American landscape; it would neither overpower nor obliterate the land. (Gift of Mrs. Huttleston Rogers, © 1996 Board of Trustees, National Gallery of Art, Washington, D.C.)

"a family who had lost all their clothing by fire." Yet town bees were not the all-day family affairs of the countryside, and when the Hardy family moved to Eaton, Ohio, Irene missed the country gatherings. The families of Eaton seldom held bees; instead, they purchased the goods country people made. They were wage earners and consumers, and the market economy shaped and controlled their daily lives.

Most Americans came to accept these changes as inevitable, but some tried to resist. One opposition path was to restore traditional work tasks and social cohesion by living in rural utopian communities. Some groups, like the Shakers, had originated in eighteenth-century Europe, while others, like the Mormons, arose in the wake of the religious ferment of the Second Great Awakening (see pages 273–274). What they shared in common was a commitment to rural communal living

as members experimented with innovative (sometimes shocking) family arrangements and more egalitarian gender roles in a cooperative rather than competitive environment.

The Shakers, the largest of the communal utopian experiments, reached their peak between 1820 and 1860.

SHAKERS

In those years six thousand members lived in twenty settlements in eight states. Shaker communities emphasized agriculture and handcrafts; most managed to become self-sufficient and profitable enterprises. Shaker furniture became famous for its simplicity, beauty of design, and excellent construction. The community's craft tradition contrasted with the new factory regime.

But the Shakers were essentially a spiritual community. Founded in England in 1736 by Mother Ann Lee, they got their name from their worship service, which included singing and dancing. Ann Lee's children had died in infancy, and she believed that their deaths were retribution for her sin of intercourse; thus she advocated celibacy. After imprisonment in England in 1773–1774, she fulfilled a vision by settling in America.

In religious practice and social relations, Shakers offered an alternative to changes in urban and rural life. Shakers lived communally, abolishing individual families. Leadership tended to be in the hands of women. The settlements, however, depended on constant enlistment of new recruits, not only because the practice of celibacy meant that they could not reproduce themselves but also because most members only stayed a short time. Many Shaker settlements became temporary refuges for orphans, runaways, abused wives, and unemployed workers during hard times. And some families found themselves unsuited to communal living. Those who were not committed to the Shakers' spiritual message also moved on. In the middle of the nineteenth century, Shaker communities began a slow but steady decline.

The Church of Jesus Christ of Latter-day Saints, whose members were known as the Mormons, was the most

MORMONS
successful communitarian experiment, and it, like the Shakers, restructured family life. During the religious ferment of the 1820s in western New York, Joseph Smith, a young farmer, reported that an angel called Moroni had given him divine engraved gold plates. Smith published his revelations as the *Book of Mormon* and organized a church in 1830. The next year the community moved west to Ohio to build a "New Jerusalem" and await the second coming of Jesus.

But angry mobs drove the Mormons from Ohio, and they settled in Missouri. There, too, the Mormons' rapid growth created antagonism, as did their claim that only Mormons would be saved upon Jesus' return. Anti-Mormons charged that Mormonism was fraudulent, a scam by Joseph Smith. Opponents also feared Mormon political power. In 1838 the governor of Missouri charged Smith with fomenting insurrection and gathered evidence to indict him and other leaders for treason.

Smith and his followers resettled in Nauvoo, Illinois. The state legislature gave them a city charter that made them self-governing and authorized a local militia. But again the community met antagonism, especially after Smith introduced the practice of polygamy in 1841, allowing men to have several wives at once. The next year Smith became mayor, and this consolidation of religious and political power, as well as Nauvoo's petition to the federal government to be a self-governing territory, further antagonized opponents, who now included some

former Mormons. After Smith and his brother were charged with treason and jailed, and then murdered, the Mormons left Illinois to seek security in the wilderness. In the Great Salt Lake valley, in the unorganized territory of Utah, they established a patriarchal, cooperative "community of saints." Now led by Brigham Young, they achieved religious freedom and political autonomy.

In Utah the Mormons distributed agricultural land according to family size. An extensive irrigation system, constructed by men who contributed their labor in proportion to the quantity of land they received and the amount of water they expected to use, transformed the arid valley into a rich oasis. As the colony developed, the church elders gained control of water, trade, industry, and eventually the territorial government of Utah.

Religious conviction fortified the Latter-day Saints to withstand persecution. The Mormons offered success and community in this world and salvation in the next to anyone who would join. Indeed, many recruits were poor and uneducated. To those who rejected existing churches, the Mormons also offered fellowship and religious certainty within a tight-knit society and cooperative economic system.

Not all utopian communities sought wilderness. Brook Farm cooperative in West Roxbury, Massachusetts, near

■ Violence stalked the Mormons until they found safety in the Great Salt Lake valley. Here a Mormon family—a father, three wives, and five children—poses for a photographer in the 1850s in Salt Lake City. (Church of Jesus Christ of Latter-Day Saints)

BROOK FARM Boston, had a lasting impact although its achievements were more artistic than economic. Inspired by transcendentalism—the belief that the physical world is secondary to the spiritual realm, which human beings can reach not by custom and experience but only by intuition—Brook Farm's members rejected materialism. Their rural communalism combined spirituality, manual labor, intellectual life, and play. Founded in 1841 by the Unitarian minister George Ripley, a literary critic and friend of transcendentalist lecturer and essayist Ralph Waldo Emerson, Brook Farm attracted farmers, craftsmen, and writers, among them the novelist Nathaniel Hawthorne. Indeed, the fame of Brook Farm rested on the intellectual achievements of its members. Its school drew students from outside the community, and its residents contributed regularly to the *Dial,* the leading transcendentalist journal. In 1845 Brook Farm's hundred members organized themselves into model phalanxes (working-living units) suggested by French utopian Charles Fourier. Rigid regimentation replaced individualism, and membership dropped. After a disastrous fire in 1846, the experiment collapsed in 1847.

Though short-lived, Brook Farm played a significant role in the flowering of a national literature. During these years Hawthorne, Emerson, and *Dial* editor Margaret Fuller joined Henry David Thoreau, Herman Melville, and others in a literary outpouring known today as the American Renaissance. In philosophical intensity and moral idealism, their work was both distinctively American and an outgrowth of the European romantic movement. Their themes were universal, their settings and characters American. Hawthorne, for instance, used Puritan New England as a backdrop, and Melville wrote of great spiritual quests as seafaring adventures.

AMERICAN RENAISSANCE

The essayist Ralph Waldo Emerson was the prime mover of the American Renaissance and a pillar of the transcendental movement. Emerson had followed his father and grandfather into the ministry but quit his Boston Unitarian pulpit in 1831. After a two-year sojourn in Europe, he returned to lecture and write, preaching individualism and self-reliance. "We live in succession, in division, in parts, in particles," Emerson wrote. "We see the world piece by piece, as the sun, the moon, the animal, the tree; but the whole, of which these are the shining parts, is the soul." Intuitive experience of God is attainable, insisted Emerson, because "the Highest dwells" within every individual in the form of the "Over-soul." What gave Emerson's writings force was,

for his times, a simple, direct prose. In his first book, *Nature* (1836), and in "The American Scholar" (1837), a Phi Beta Kappa address at Harvard, Emerson explored human nature and American culture. Widely admired, he influenced Thoreau, Fuller, Hawthorne, and other members of Brook Farm.

Whether intellectual, spiritual, or economic in their origins, utopian communities can be seen as attempts to recapture the cohesiveness of traditional agricultural and artisan life in the face of the competitive pressures of the market economy and urbanization. Utopians resembled Puritan perfectionists; like the Separatists of seventeenth-century New England (see pages 49–50), they sought to begin anew in their own colonies.

The West

In the 1840s a trickling stream of migrants followed the Oregon Trail to the West Coast. Then, in 1848, gold was discovered in California. The next year a pioneer observed that the Oregon Trail "bore no evidence of having been much traveled." Traffic flowed south instead, and California drew population to the Pacific slope. One measure of this shift was the overland mail routes. In the 1840s the Oregon Trail had been the main communications link between the Midwest and the Pacific. Ten years later the post office routes terminated in California, not Oregon; in fact, in the 1850s there was no mail route north of Sacramento.

When the United States acquired Alta California from Mexico in the 1848 Treaty of Guadalupe Hidalgo (see page 358), the province was inhabited mostly by Indians, with some Mexicans living on large estates. A chain of small settlements surrounded military forts (*presidios*) and missions. That changed almost overnight after James Marshall, a carpenter, spotted gold particles in the millrace at Sutter's Mill (now Coloma, California, northwest of Sacramento) in January 1848. Word of the discovery spread, and Californians rushed to scrabble for instant fortunes. When the military explorer John C. Frémont reached San Francisco five months later, he found that "all its male inhabitants had gone to the mines." The town, "which a few months before was so busy and thriving, was then almost deserted."

GOLD RUSH

By 1849 the news had sped around the world, and hundreds of thousands of fortune seekers, mostly young men, streamed in from Mexico, England, Germany, France, Ireland, and from all over the United States, including some African Americans. They mined the lodes

Gold in California

When James Marshall discovered gold in Sutter's Mill, California, in January 1848, word spread quickly—and quite literally around the world. Hundreds of millions of people thus learned of California for the first time. Within a year tens of thousands of adventurers from other countries had rushed to California, the new "land of opportunity." Soon it was as cosmopolitan as any other American place.

In an era before the telegraph crossed the oceans, it is surprising how fast the news traveled. Mexicans heard of the gold strike first. Next word spread to Chile, Peru, and throughout South America; then across the Pacific to Hawai'i, China, and Australia; and then to Europe—Ireland, France, and the German states. How did the news travel? Overland travelers brought the news south to Baja California and Sonora in Mexico. By spring 1849 some six thousand Mexicans were panning for gold around the newly established town of Sonora, California. Many of the Mexicans came north seasonally to seek gold, spreading news of California on every trip home.

Sailing ships brought news of California gold to Hawai'i. The newspaper *Honolulu Polynesian* announced it in the kingdom on June 24, 1848. "Honolulu has never before witnessed such an excitement as the gold fever has created," the *Polynesian* reported later that summer. Gold seekers and merchants sailed from Hawai'i to California, and their letters home recruited others to come. The constant traffic led to the introduction of regular steamship service between Hawai'i and California as early as 1853.

A ship brought news of California gold discoveries to Valparaiso, Chile, in August 1848. More dramatically, a few weeks later, another sailing vessel landed with $2,500 in gold dust aboard. Although Chilean newspapers initially ignored the discovery, the people in Chile's cities talked about nothing but gold. By November the newspapers were reporting rumors of overnight riches in California. Before the end of the year, two thousand Chileans had left for California, and many Chilean merchants opened branch stores in San Francisco.

Word of gold and California reached Australia in December 1848. Gold seekers quickly made travel arrangements, and by 1850 every ship in Sydney harbor was destined for California. News had already reached China in mid-1848. A San Francisco merchant headed for the gold fields, Chum Ming, had written a cousin about his hopes for wealth. Four months later the cousin arrived in San Francisco, with fellow villagers he had recruited. After the upheavals of the Taiping Revolution in 1850, Chinese migration soared. By the mid-1850s, one in five gold miners was Chinese.

Californians, new and old, foreign and native-born, expressed amazement at the ethnic variety. One described it as "the most curious Babel of a place imaginable." In 1850 the new state of California had nearly 40 percent foreign-born inhabitants, the majority non-European. Through word of mouth, rumor, letters home, and newspaper reports, the discovery of gold in 1848 linked California to millions of ordinary people around the globe.

This 1855 Frank Marryat drawing of a San Francisco saloon dramatizes the international nature of the California gold rush. Like theater performers, the patrons of the saloon dress their parts as Yankees, Mexicans, Asians, and South Americans. (© Collection of the New York Historical Society)

and washed away the surface soil with hydraulic works, leaving the land unsuitable for anything after they abandoned it.

Gold mining seemed to offer instant riches, and indeed, some made fortunes. In 1848 a California male servant earned $2,000 mining for gold and returned to Monterey a rich man. Peter Brown, a black man from Ste. Genevieve, Missouri, went to California alone, as did most "forty-niners." He wrote his wife in 1851 that "California is the best country in the world to make money. It is also the best place for black folks on the globe." He had earned $300 in two months.

Most forty-niners, however, never found enough gold to pay their expenses. "The stories you hear frequently in the States," one gold seeker wrote home, "are the most extravagant lies imaginable—the mines are a humbug." Another gold seeker called gold mining "Nature's Great Lottery scheme." Many found work in California's cities and agricultural districts more profitable. Meanwhile, enterprising merchants rushed to supply, feed, and clothe the new settlers. One such merchant was Levi Strauss, a German Jewish immigrant, whose tough mining pants found a ready market among the prospectors.

San Francisco, the former *presidio* and mission of Yerba Buena, had in 1848 been a small settlement of about a thousand Mexicans, Anglos, soldiers, friars, and Indians. As the West Coast gateway to the interior, it became an instant city, ballooning to thirty-five thousand people in 1850. Ships bringing people and supplies continuously jammed the harbor. A French visitor in that year wrote, "At San Francisco, where fifteen months ago one found only a half dozen large cabins, one finds today a stock exchange, a theater, churches of all Christian cults, and a large number of quite beautiful homes."

The forty-niners had their eyes on gold nuggets, but they had to be fed. Thus began the great California agricultural boom. Farmers preferred wheat; it required minimal investment, was easily planted, and offered a quick return at the end of a relatively short growing season. California farmers eagerly imported horse-drawn machines, since labor was scarce (and expensive). By the mid-1850s, California exported wheat and had become firmly linked, through commerce, to the rest of the United States. Farmers on the West Coast cleared the land and constructed log cabins. Success often depended on their access to water, and they sought to divert the streams and rivers of the West to irrigate their land.

FARMERS

In contrast to the Midwest, where family farms were the basic unit of production, in California men dominated mining, grazing, and large-scale wheat farming.

Most men came alone, drawn by a sense of adventure and personal opportunity. Women who accompanied their husbands—only one-seventh of the travelers on the overland trails were women—experienced migration differently. Their lives drastically changed as they left behind networks of friends and kin to journey, often with children, along an unknown and hazardous path to a strange environment. Yet in the West their domestic skills were in great demand. They received high fees for cooking, laundering, and sewing, and they ran boarding houses and hotels (men shunned domestic work).

City Life

Irish and other European immigrants and rural migrants made cities, especially northern ones, expand geometrically. The nation's population increased during this period from 12.9 million to 31.4 million. Europeans spread westward, and small rural settlements quickly became towns. In 1830 the nation had only 23 cities with 10,000 or more people and only 7 with more than 25,000. By 1860, 93 towns exceeded 10,000, 35 towns had more than 25,000, and 9 exceeded 100,000 (see Map 12.1). The Northeast was most heavily urban, and the percentage of people living in urban areas there grew from 14 to 35 percent between 1830 and 1860.

Some cities became great metropolitan centers. By 1830 New York City had been the nation's most populous city and major commercial center for twenty years. At midcentury, Baltimore and New Orleans dominated the South, and San Francisco was the leading West Coast city. In the Midwest, the new lake cities (Chicago, Detroit, and Cleveland) began to pass the frontier river cities (Cincinnati, Louisville, and Pittsburgh) founded a generation earlier. The largest cities of the North anchored a nationwide network linked by canals, roads, railroads, and the telegraph (see Chapter 10).

As the nation's premier city, New York grew from 202,000 people in 1830 to over 814,000 in 1860. The immigrant port city was mostly Irish and German by the 1850s. Across the East River, Brooklyn tripled in size between 1850 and 1860, becoming the nation's third-largest city, with a population of 279,000. Many people were short-term residents of the two cities; the majority did not stay ten years. Thus New York was ever changing, full of energy, reeking of sweat, horse dung, and garbage—and above all, teeming with people.

NEW YORK CITY

New York City literally had burst its boundaries around 1830. Until then New Yorkers could walk from

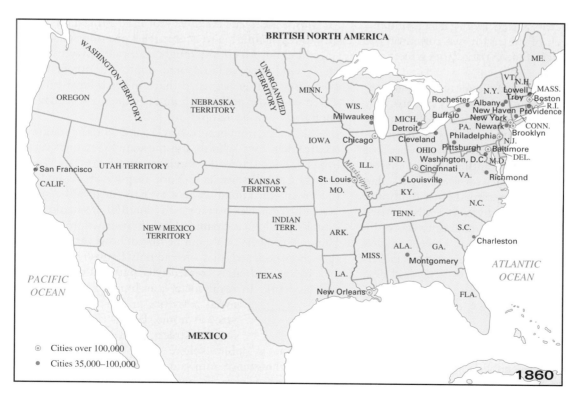

Map 12.1

Major American Cities in 1830 and 1860

The number of Americans who lived in cities increased rapidly between 1830 and 1860, and the number of large cities grew as well. In 1830 only New York City had a population exceeding one hundred thousand; thirty years later, eight more cities had surpassed that level.

one end to the other in an hour. In 1825, 14th Street was the city's northern boundary. By 1860, 400,000 people lived above that divide, and 42nd Street was the city's northern limit. Gone were the cow pastures, kitchen gardens, and orchards of the eighteenth century. George Templeton Strong, a New York lawyer, recorded in his diary in 1856 that he had attended a party on 37th Street: "It seems but the other day that thirty-seventh Street was an imaginary line running through a rural district and grazed over by cows." Mass transit made city expansion possible. Horse-drawn omnibuses appeared in New York in 1827, and the Harlem Railroad, completed in 1832, ran the length of Manhattan. By the 1850s all big cities had horse-drawn streetcars.

By modern standards nineteenth-century cities were disorderly, unsafe, and unhealthy. Expansion occurred so

URBAN PROBLEMS

rapidly that few cities could handle the problems it brought. For example, migrants from rural areas were accustomed to relieving themselves outside and throwing refuse in vacant areas. In the city, such waste smelled, spread disease, and polluted water. New York City partially solved the problem in the 1840s by abandoning wells in favor of reservoir water piped into buildings and outdoor fountains. In some districts, scavengers and refuse collectors carted away garbage and human waste, but in much of the city it just rotted on the ground. Only one-quarter of New York City's streets had sewers by 1857.

Cities lacked adequate taxing power to provide services for all. The best cities could do was to tax property adjoining new sewers, paved streets, and water mains. Thus new services and basic sanitation depended on residents' ability to pay. As a result, those most in need of services got them last. Another solution was to charter private companies to sell basic services. This plan worked well with gas service used for lights. Baltimore first chartered a private gas company in 1816; New York did so in 1842. By midcentury every major city was lit by a private gas supplier. The private sector, however, failed to supply the water the cities needed. Private firms lacked the capital to build adequate systems, and they laid pipe only in commercial and well-to-do residential areas, ignoring the poor. As population grew, city governments had to take over.

Cities led in offering public education. In 1800 only New England had public education; by 1860 every state offered some public education to whites.

HORACE MANN AND PUBLIC SCHOOLS

Under Horace Mann, secretary of the state board of education from 1837 to 1848, Massachusetts led the way. It established a minimum school year of six months and formalized the training of teachers.

Mann, an evangelist for public education and school reform, advocated free, state-sponsored education. "If we do not prepare children to become good citizens," Mann argued, "if we do not develop their capacities, imbue their hearts with the love of truth and duty, and a reverence for all things sacred and holy, then our republic must go down to destruction." Universal education, Mann proposed, would end misery and crime. Mann and others responded to the changes wrought by the market economy, urbanization, and immigration. The typical city dweller was a newcomer, whether from abroad or from the country. Public schools would take the children of strangers and give them shared values. But the system was distinctly racialized; few states included free black children in public schools.

Free public schools altered the scope of education. Schooling previously had focused on literacy, religious training, and discipline. Under Mann's leadership, the curriculum became more secular and appropriate for future American clerks, farmers, and workers. Students studied geography, American history, arithmetic, and science. Schools retained moral education, but they dropped direct religious indoctrination. Nonetheless, primers like *McGuffey's Eclectic Readers* still used Protestant Scripture to teach children to accept their positions in society. A good child, *McGuffey* taught, does not envy the rich: "It is God who makes some poor and others rich." *McGuffey* further preached that "the rich have troubles which we know nothing of; and . . . the poor, if they are good, may be very happy."

Catholics, immigrants, blacks, and workers sought to control their own schools, but the state legislatures established secular statewide standards under Protestant educators. Catholics in New York responded by building their own educational system over the next half-century. When Los Angeles became a city in 1850, it attempted to establish bilingual Spanish-English instruction. Trained bilingual teachers could not be found, however, and when the schools opened, they offered only English instruction.

Towns and cities created new patterns of leisure as well as work. In rural society, as Irene Hardy recalled,

LEISURE

social activities and work often took place at home. But in cities, dedicated spaces—streets, theaters, sports fields—constituted a public sphere for people to socialize. Through the sale of admission tickets or membership in associations, leisure became a commodity to be purchased. As the population became more diverse, leisure associations reflected ethnic, racial, and class divisions.

Traditional rural pursuits continued in the city. Men frequented taverns and spent spare time drinking and playing games of skill and strength—arm wrestling, ninepins, and pitching coins. Though city dwellers had less opportunity than their rural counterparts to ride and hunt, fishing remained popular among both men and women. Churches continued to serve as social centers, and the Second Great Awakening increased women's involvement. Church clubs combined socializing with good works.

Americans read more too. Thanks to the expansion of public education, the vast majority of native-born white Americans were literate by the 1850s. In cities, urban newspapers and magazines proliferated and bookstores spread. Power printing presses and better transportation made possible wide distribution of books and periodicals. The religious press—of both traditional sects and dissenters—produced pamphlets, hymnals, Bibles, and religious newspapers. Americans also read secular publications. Newspapers and magazines—political organs, literary journals, and the voices of specialized groups like mill workers—abounded in the 1830s and after. In Brookfield, Massachusetts, in 1798, the mails brought one weekly newspaper; fifty years later, in 1848, the post office delivered to subscribers fifty different newspapers and fifty-five monthly magazines.

READING

Fiction and autobiographies competed with religious tracts as popular literature. Newspapers and magazines printed fiction, and bookstores and stationers in large cities sold novels and autobiographies. Frederick Douglass's powerful attack on slavery in the *Narrative of the Life of Frederick Douglass, an American Slave, Written by Himself* (1845) sold widely. Many popular novels, some written by women, often for women, were set in the home and upheld Christian values. They reflected growing gender differences in American society in their exploration of the divisions between home and work, between emotion and authority, and between sentimentality and power. Yet in their support of traditional female moral roles, they also can be read as a challenge to prevailing values. Although Susan Warner's *The Wide, Wide, Wide World* (1850), Nathaniel Hawthorne's *The House of the Seven Gables* (1851), and Fanny Fern's *Ruth Hall* (1855) did not challenge women's traditional domestic roles, they gave women a special moral bearing. In giving a positive cast to notions of community and republican virtue, they implicitly criticized the growing market economy. By the 1850s popular fiction circulated widely. Harriet Beecher Stowe's antislavery novel, *Uncle Tom's Cabin, or Life Among the Lowly* (1852), which appeared serially in 1851–1852, sold 300,000 copies in book form in its first year.

A major attraction, theater provided a social sphere in which both men and women gathered. A theater was often the second public building constructed in a town—after a church. Large cities boasted two or more theaters catering to different classes. In New York City the Park Theater enjoyed the patronage of the carriage trade, the Bowery drew the middle class, and the Chatham attracted workers. Some plays cut across class lines. Shakespeare was performed so often and appreciated so widely that even illiterate theatergoers knew his plays well. In the 1840s musical and dramatic presentations took on a more professional tone; like the Hutchinson Family (see pages 239–240), newly popular minstrel shows and traveling circuses offered carefully rehearsed routines. Dancing and music remained popular and took new forms, as in blackfaced minstrelsy.

THEATER

By the 1840s hundreds of traveling minstrel troupes performed a complete evening's entertainment in American theaters. Minstrel acts had first appeared two decades earlier, when white men, in burnt-cork makeup, imitated African Americans in song, dance, and patter. In the early 1830s Thomas D. Rice of New York became famous for his role as Jim Crow, an old southern slave. In ill-fitting patched clothing and torn shoes, the blackface Rice shuffled, danced, and sang on stage. Another stereotyped image soon joined him: Zip Coon, a black Bowery Boy. What minstrels presented was a European version of African American culture.

MINSTREL SHOWS

Minstrelsy combined contradictory elements. At one level, performers masked as people of color told jokes mocking economic and political elites. At the same time the actors stereotyped black people by exaggerating physical features. They also presented blacks as sensual and lazy, thus stoking the fires of racism with ridicule. In blending black culture with white humor, African dance with English folk tunes, and the African banjo with the Irish fiddle, minstrelsy seemed to represent the new urban potpourri. In portraying foils to sexual purity and work discipline, minstrelsy also constituted a resistance to the moral demands and factory regimens of the era. Ultimately, minstrelsy furthered growing racial divisions in the United States. The fictional representation of blacks on stage not only defined "blackness" but also defined "whiteness." Whiteness as a racial category took on meaning as laughing white audiences distinguished themselves from the black characters.

■ Thomas D. Rice playing "Jim Crow" in blackface at the Bowery Theater in New York City, 1833. The rowdy audience climbed on to the stage, leaving Rice little room to perform. In representing African Americans on stage, Rice and other minstrels contributed to establishing both black and white as racial categories. (© Collection of the New York Historical Society)

Increasingly, urban recreation and sports became more formal commodities to be purchased. One had to buy a ticket to go to the theater, the circus, P. T. Barnum's American Museum in New York City, the racetrack, or the ballpark. Spectator sports surged. From 1831 enthusiasts could read the all-sports newspaper, *Spirit of the Times*. By 1849 news of boxing was so much in demand that a round-by-round account of a Maryland boxing match was telegraphed throughout the East. Horseracing, walking races, and, in the 1850s, baseball began to attract large urban male crowds.

Sports

Organized leagues replaced spontaneity. A group of Wall Street office workers formed the Knickerbocker Club in 1842 and in 1845 drew up rules for the game of baseball. Their rules were widely adopted and continue to serve as the basis for the game.

Ironically, public leisure soon developed a private dimension. Exclusive private clubs and associations provided space and occasions for leisure apart from the crowds and rowdiness in the public sphere. As cities grew, their pop-

City Culture

ulations seemed increasingly fragmented. Finding people similar to oneself required more of a conscious effort. The new associations that evolved served as a bulwark against the cultures of other groups—immigrants, migrants, blacks, and artisans. Middle- and upper-class New Yorkers who felt alienated in the city of their birth joined exclusive clubs. Some joined the Masonic order, which offered everything the bustling, chaotic city did not: an elaborate hierarchy, an orderly code of deference between ranks, harmony, and shared values. Members knew one another. Masons played a political role as well: they recruited officeholders and marched in the parades that were a regular feature of the city's life.

Ethnic, racial, and religious groups shared traditions in their own clubs and societies. The Irish formed the Hibernian Society and the Sons of Erin; Germans brought Turnvereine physical-cultural clubs from across the Atlantic; Jews founded B'nai B'rith as a men's club; and African Americans had chapters of the Prince Hall Masons in their communities. Women, too, organized their own associations, ranging from literary clubs to benevolent societies. Americans of all sorts—native- and foreign-born, black and white—also formed churches and church-associated clubs. Associations brought together like people, but they also formalized divisions.

Divisions seemed to occur naturally on city streets. In the 1840s, a youth culture developed on the Bowery, one of New York's entertainment strips. In the evenings the lamp-lit promenade, lined with theaters, dance halls, and cafés, became an urban midway. Older New Yorkers feared the "Bowery boys and gals," whose ostentatious dress and behavior seemed threatening to them. Around 1847 artist Nicholino Calyo depicted three Bowery boys in a watercolor painting (see below). A Bowery boy had long hair, often greased into a roll. He wore a broad-brimmed black hat, an open shirt collar, a black frock coat that reached below the knee, and as much jewelry as he could afford. His swaggering gait, especially when he had a girlfriend on his arm, frightened many in the middle class. Equally disturbing to old New Yorkers were the young working women who strolled the Bowery. They came in groups to enjoy each other's company and to meet Bowery boys. Unlike more genteel ladies who wore modest veils or bonnets, Bowery "gals" drew attention to themselves with outlandish costumes and ornate hats.

Much more than on the stage, racial, ethnic, and class divisions were played out in public space. Most working people spent much of their lives outdoors; they worked in the open air as laborers, shopped in public markets, paraded on city streets, and socialized on sidewalks. Young people courted, neighbors argued, and ethnic and racial groups defended their turf in public places. Urban streets served as a political arena as crowds listened to speakers, demonstrated, and sometimes took mob action.

Competition for jobs, often between native-born Americans and new immigrants, turned into violence on city streets. In the 1830s riots became commonplace as economic, political, social, racial, and ethnic conflict erupted and professionals, merchants, craftsmen, and laborers vented their rage against political and economic rivals. "Gentlemen of property and standing," unnerved by antislavery proponents, sacked abolitionist and antislavery organizations, even murdering newspaper editor Elijah Lovejoy in Alton, Illinois, in 1837. In the 1840s "respectable" citizens drove the Mormons out of Missouri and Illinois. In Philadelphia native-born workers attacked Irish weavers in 1828, and whites and blacks fought on the docks in 1834 and 1835. Residents of North Philadelphia took to the streets continuously from 1840 to 1842 until the construction of a railroad through their neighborhood was abandoned. These disturbances came to a head in the Philadelphia riots of 1844, in which Protestant skilled workers attacked Irish Catholics. Smaller cities, too, became battlegrounds as nativist riots

URBAN RIOTS

■ Nicholino Calyo's watercolor *Soap-Locks, or Bowery Boys* (c. 1847) captured the bold body language and showy dress of the youths who controlled the sidewalks of the Bowery.   (© Collection of The New York Historical Society)

peaked in the 1850s; Louisville, for instance, witnessed an anti-German riot in 1855. By 1840 more than 125 people had died in urban riots, and by 1860 fatalities exceeded 1,000.

As public disorder spread, Boston hired uniformed policemen in 1837 to supplement its part-time watchmen and constables, and New York in 1845 established a uniformed force. Nonetheless, middle-class city dwellers did not venture out alone at night. The police tried to control and suppress street activity. They used local laws against vagrancy and disturbing the peace to suppress free blacks and immigrants. The continuing inflow of immigrants to the cities worsened social tensions by pitting groups against one other in the contest for jobs, housing, and street space. In the midst of so much noise, crime, and conflict, the lavish uptown residences of the very rich rose like an affront to those struggling to survive.

Extremes of Wealth

After visiting all twenty-four states in 1831 and 1832, Alexis de Tocqueville characterized the United States as primarily a place of equality and opportunity for white males. He opened *Democracy in America,* his classic analysis of the American people and

nation, with this observation: "No novelty in the United States struck me more vividly during my stay there than the equality of conditions."

Tocqueville attributed American equality—the relative fluidity of the social order—to Americans' mobility and restlessness. Geographic mobility, he felt, offered people a chance to start anew regardless of where they came from or who they were. Wealth and family mattered little; a person could be known by deeds alone. Indeed, Americans seemed driven by ambition and an itch to move. "An American will build a house in which to pass his old age," Tocqueville wrote, "and sell it before the roof is on; he will plant a garden and rent it just as the trees are coming into bearing; he will clear a field and leave others to reap the harvest; he will take up a profession and leave it, settle in one place and soon go off elsewhere with his changing desires."

Others disagreed with the egalitarian view of American life. *New York Sun* publisher Moses Yale Beach believed a new aristocracy based on wealth and power was forming. Author of twelve editions of *Wealth and Biography of the Wealthy Citizens of New York City,* Beach listed 750 New Yorkers with assets of $100,000 or more in 1845. John Jacob Astor, with a fortune of $25 million, led the list of 19 millionaires. Ten

GREAT
FORTUNES

■ This gouache, attributed to Nicholino Calyo, depicts the Haight family in their drawing room in 1848. Richard K. Wright was a wealthy New York City merchant, trading internationally, as the globe in the foreground suggests. Sarah Rogers Haight was a famous beauty and socialite, and the family's clothing, art, library, and furniture all stand in sharp contrast to the poverty, homelessness, and orphans found on the city's streets. (Museum of the City of New York. Bequest of Elizabeth Cushing Iselin)

years later, Beach reported more than 1,000 New Yorkers worth $100,000, among them 28 millionaires. Combining gossip-column items with wild guesses at people's wealth, Beach's publications suggest the enormous wealth of New York's upper class. Tocqueville himself, sensitive to conflicting trends in American life, had described the new industrial wealth. The rich and well educated "come forward to exploit industries," Tocqueville wrote, and become "more and more like the administrators of a huge empire. . . . What is this if not an aristocracy?"

Wealth throughout the United States was becoming concentrated in the hands of a relatively small number of people. In New York City between 1828 and 1845, the richest 4 percent of the city's population increased their holdings from an estimated 63 percent to 80 percent of all individual wealth. Meanwhile, the holdings of many ordinary people virtually disappeared. In Brooklyn between 1810 and 1841, the share of wealth held by the bottom two-thirds of families decreased from 10 percent to almost nothing. By 1860 the top 5 percent of American families owned more than half of the nation's wealth, and the top 10 percent owned nearly three-quarters.

From 1826 until his death in 1851 Philip Hone, one-time mayor of New York, kept a diary, meticulously recording the life of an American aris-

URBAN ELITE tocrat. On February 28, 1840, Hone attended a masked ball at the Fifth Avenue mansion of Henry Breevoort Jr. and Laura Carson Breevoort. The ball began at the fashionable hour of 10 P.M., and the five hundred invited ladies and gentlemen wore costumes adorned with ermine and gold. For more than a week, Hone believed, the affair "occupied the minds of people of all stations, ranks, and employments." Similar parties were held in Boston, Philadelphia, Baltimore, and Charleston. Hone regularly attended elegant dinners graced by fine cuisine and imported wines. The New York elite who filled the pages of Hone's diary—the 1 percent of the population who owned half of the city's wealth—lived in mansions attended by servants. Country estates, ocean resorts, mineral spas, and grand tours of Europe offered relief from the winter and spring social seasons and escape from the heat and smells of the summer.

Much of this wealth was inherited. For every John Jacob Astor who made millions in the western fur trade or George Law who left a farm to become a millionaire contractor and investor, ten others had inherited or married money. Andrew H. Mickle, a poor Irish immigrant who became a millionaire and mayor of New York City, derived his fortune from marrying the daughter of his

employer. Many of the wealthiest New Yorkers bore the names of the colonial commercial elite: Breevoort, Roosevelt, Van Rensselaer, and Whitney. These rich New Yorkers were not idle; they worked at increasing their fortunes and power. Urban capitalists like Philip Hone and the fashionable society, like their Boston counterparts who founded the Lowell mills, invested in and profited enormously from commerce and manufacturing. Wealth begat wealth, and marriage cemented upper-crust family ties.

But just a short walk from Hone's wealthy district were urban slums. There poor working men and women were continually anxious that hard times were imminent. They dreaded poverty, chronic illness, disability, old age, widowhood, and desertion. With good reason women did fear raising children without a spouse, as few women's jobs paid enough to support a family.

On crowded streets, the working poor jostled with newly arrived immigrants as well as free blacks, thieves, beggars, and prostitutes. New York

URBAN SLUMS City's Five Points, a few blocks from City Hall, lacked running water and sewers and was notorious for its physical and moral squalor. "I do think I saw more drunk folks, men and women, that day," frontiersman Davy Crockett recalled in 1835 of his visit to Five Points a year earlier, "than I ever saw before." Dominated by the Old Brewery, which had been converted to housing in 1837, the neighborhood was overwhelmingly immigrant, predominantly Irish but also with a few free black people. Contemporaries estimated that more than a thousand people lived in the Old Brewery's rooms and cellars. Throughout the city, workers' housing was at a premium. Houses built for two families often held four; tenements built for six families held twelve. Families took in lodgers to help pay the rent.

Meanwhile, a distinct middle class appeared on the urban scene. Small in number, they were the city businessmen, traders, and profession-

MIDDLE CLASS als in the market economy. The growth and specialization of trade rapidly increased their numbers. Middle-class families enjoyed the new consumer items: wool carpeting, fine wallpaper, and rooms full of furniture replaced the bare floors, whitewashed walls, and relative sparseness of eighteenth-century homes. Houses were large, often having from four to six rooms. Middle-class children slept one to a bed, and by the 1840s and 1850s middle-class families used indoor toilets. When Philadelphia publishing agent Joseph Engles died in 1861, an inventory of his estate indicated that his parlor contained two sofas, thirteen

A visible sign of urban poverty in the 1850s was the homeless and orphaned children, most of them immigrants, who wandered the streets of New York City. The Home for the Friendless Orphanage, at Twenty-ninth Street and Madison Avenue, provided shelter for some of the orphan girls. (© Collection of The New York Historical Society)

chairs, three card tables, a fancy table, a piano, a mirror, and a fine carpet. Other rooms were similarly furnished.

Middle-class families formed the backbone of the clubs and societies that Tocqueville had observed in America. They filled the family pews in church on Sundays; their male children went to college. They were as distant from Philip Hone's world as they were from the milieu of the working class and the poor. Increasingly they looked to the family and home as the core of middle-class life.

Family Life

Once primarily an economic unit, urban families in the nineteenth-century market economy began to lose their role as producers (see Chapter 10). The result was sweeping changes in the household economy as it adjusted to the market economy. As men increasingly worked for wages outside the home, and so did their offspring, the urban workplace and home became separate entities.

In the home men were economically dominant. English common law gave husbands absolute control over the family. Men owned their wives' personal property; they were legal guardians of the children; and they owned whatever family members produced or earned. A father still had the legal authority to oppose his daughter's choice of husband. Nonetheless, most American women, with their parents' blessing, chose their own marriage partners.

LEGAL RIGHTS

But the legal rights within families were beginning to change. Although married women still had limited legal rights and standing, they made modest gains in property and spousal rights from the 1830s on. Arkansas in 1835 passed the first married women's property law, and by 1860 sixteen more states had followed suit. In those states, women—single, married, or widowed—could own and convey property. When a wife inherited, earned, or acquired property, it was hers, not her husband's; and she could write a will. In the 1830s states began to liberalize divorce, adding cruelty and desertion as grounds for divorce. Nonetheless divorce was rare.

In working-class families, women left their parental homes as early as age twelve, earning wages most of their lives, with only short respites for bearing and rearing children. Primarily unmarried girls and women worked as domestic servants in other women's homes; married and widowed women worked as laundresses, seamstresses, and cooks. Some hawked food and wares on city streets; others did piecework sewing at home, earning wages in the putting-out system; and some became prostitutes. Few of these occupations enabled women to support themselves or a family at a respectable level.

WORKING WOMEN

Middle-class Americans, however, sought to keep women close to home. They idealized the family as a moral institution characterized by selflessness and cooperation, while the world of work—the market economy—was increasingly seen as an arena of conflict increasingly identified with men and dominated by base self-interest. If young girls left home to work—in New England's textile mills, in new urban stores as clerks—it was only for a brief interval before marriage.

The domestic ideal restricted the paying jobs available to middle-class women, but one occupation was considered consistent with genteel femininity: teaching. In 1823 the Beecher sisters, Catharine and Mary, established the Hartford Female Seminary and offered history and science in addition to the traditional women's curriculum of domestic arts and religion. A decade later Catharine Beecher successfully campaigned for teacher-training schools for women. By 1850 schoolteaching had become a woman's profession. "Females govern with less resort to physical force," Horace Mann asserted, "and exert a more kindly, humanizing and refining influence upon the dispositions and manners of their pupils." Many women worked for a time as teachers, usually for two to five years. Unmarried women earned about half the salary of male teachers.

TEACHERS

The market economy brought economic insecurity and altered family life. As the American population moved west, kin became separated and multigenerational families in the same household became less common. And all families, regardless of class or region, were shrinking in size. In 1830 American women bore an average of almost six children; by 1860 the figure had dropped to five. This decline occurred even though many immigrants with large-family traditions were settling in the United States; thus the birth rate among native-born women declined even more steeply. Although rural families re-

FAMILY SIZE

mained larger than their urban counterparts, birth rates among both groups declined comparably.

A number of factors account for reduced family size. Small families were viewed as increasingly desirable in an economy in which the family was a unit of consumption rather than production. In urban areas, children tended to become an economic burden rather than an asset as the family lost its role as a producer of goods. Children in smaller families, however, would have greater opportunities: parents could give them more attention, better

■ Rebecca Lukens pioneered in an unusual role for a woman in early-nineteenth-century America: she ran the Lukens Steel Company in eastern Pennsylvania from 1825 until she died in 1854. The deaths of her father in 1823 and of her husband in 1825 left her with the mill and large debts. She revived the steel company and soon was shipping iron plates as far away as Europe.   (Courtesy of Lukens, Inc., Coatesville, Pa.)

education, and more financial help. Evidence suggests many wives and husbands made deliberate decisions to limit the size of families. Where farmland was relatively expensive in eastern states, for instance, family size was smaller than in cheaper agricultural districts to the west.

The demographic data suggest that changes in child-bearing reduced family size. Average age at marriage rose, thus shortening the period of potential childbearing. The age at which women bore their last child dropped from around forty in the mid-eighteenth century to around thirty-five in the mid-nineteenth.

But couples also limited their family size through birth control. Traditional practices continued—coitus interruptus (withdrawal of the male before completion of the sexual act), breast-feeding to prolong infertile periods, and rhythm methods. Traditional folk remedies from American Indian folk medicine to African societies spread as well. Although animal-skin condoms imported from France were too expensive for popular use, cheap rubber condoms became available in the 1850s. Douching after intercourse was also practiced. None of the methods was particularly reliable.

BIRTH CONTROL

As formerly private concerns began to be discussed publicly, women shared and purchased information on limiting reproduction. Reproductive controls were considered part of women's responsibilities. If all else failed, women resorted to abortions, especially after 1830. Ineffective folk methods of self-induced abortion had been around for centuries, but in the 1830s abortionists, mostly women, advertised surgical services in large cities. To protect women from unqualified abortionists, and in response to reformers opposed to abortion, states began to regulate the procedure. Between 1821 and 1841, ten states and one territory either restricted late-term abortions or prohibited abortion altogether; by 1860 twenty states had adopted such restrictions.

ABORTION

Smaller families and fewer births changed the family. At one time birth and infant care had occupied nearly the entire span of women's adult lives, and few mothers lived to see their youngest child reach maturity. In smaller families, individual children received greater attention, and childhood gradually came to be perceived as a distinct period in the life span. The expansion of public education in the 1830s and the policy of grouping schoolchildren by age reinforced this perspective.

Not everyone lived in traditional families. Many single men lived and worked outside of families. In urban areas rooming and boarding houses provided them with places to sleep and eat. The expansion of cities and the market economy led more women to live outside families as well. Lowell and other mill towns provided boarding houses for the single farm daughters who did factory work for a few years before marriage. Other women, like Louisa May Alcott (1832–1888), author of *Little Women* (1868), who lived most of her life in Massachusetts, followed an independent path. Her father, the philosopher Bronson Alcott, never adequately supported his family. Not even the family's participation in Brook Farm put enough food on the table. Louisa May Alcott supported the family by working as a seamstress, governess, teacher, and housemaid before her writing brought her success. "I think I shall come out right, and prove that though an Alcott, I can support myself," she wrote her father in 1856. "I like the independent feeling; and though not an easy life, it is a free one, and I enjoy it. I can't do much with my hands; so I will make a battering-ram of my head and make a way through this rough-and-tumble world."

SINGLE MEN AND WOMEN

Louisa May Alcott forswore marriage and a family. It was not easy in a society that considered family the foundation of a moral life and appropriate for women. But she and other unmarried women managed to pursue careers and lives defined by female relationships. Given the difficulty women had finding ways to support themselves, they undertook independence at great risk. Nonetheless, the proportion of single women in the population increased significantly in the nineteenth century. In Massachusetts in 1850, 17 percent of native-born women never married—a far larger percentage than in colonial days. Independent white women, in sum, were taking advantage of new opportunities offered by the market economy and urban expansion. At the same time communitarian ventures in rural America—exemplified by the Shakers, Mormons, and Brook Farm—offered experimentation in new family relationships.

Immigrant Lives in America

The United States continued to be a nation of newcomers. The 5 million immigrants who came to the United States between 1830 and 1860 outnumbered the entire population of the country recorded in the first census in 1790. The vast majority were European (see Figure 12.1). During the peak period of pre–Civil War immigration, from 1847 through 1857, 3.3 million immigrants entered the United States: 1.3 million from

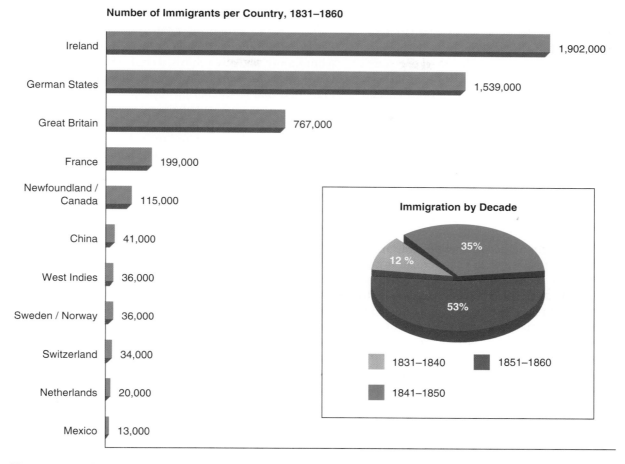

Number of Immigrants per Country, 1831–1860

Ireland	1,902,000
German States	1,539,000
Great Britain	767,000
France	199,000
Newfoundland / Canada	115,000
China	41,000
West Indies	36,000
Sweden / Norway	36,000
Switzerland	34,000
Netherlands	20,000
Mexico	13,000

Immigration by Decade

35%
12 %
53%

1831–1840   1851–1860
1841–1850

Figure 12.1   Major Sources of Immigration to the United States, 1831–1860

Most immigrants came from two areas: Great Britain, of which Ireland was a part, and the German states. These two areas sent more immigrants between 1830 and 1860 than the inhabitants of the United States enumerated at the first census in 1790. By 1860, 15 percent of the white population was of foreign birth.

(Source: Data from Stephan Thernstrom, ed., *Harvard Encyclopedia of American Ethnic Groups* [Cambridge, Mass., and London: Harvard University Press, 1980], 1047.)

Ireland and 1.1 million from the German states. By 1860, 15 percent of the white population was foreign-born.

This massive migration had been set in motion decades earlier. At the turn of the nineteenth century, the Napoleonic wars gave rise to one of the greatest population shifts in history; ultimately it lasted more than a century. War, revolution, famine, religious persecution, and the lure of industrialization led many Europeans to leave home. From the other side of the world, Asian immigration to the United States was just beginning; 41,000 Chinese, nearly all men, entered the United States from 1854 through 1860 to work mostly in heavy construction. The

United States attracted immigrants as the market economy offered jobs and its Constitution protected religious freedom. Not all planned to stay permanently, and many, like the Irish, saw themselves as exiles from their homeland.

The market economy needed workers. Large construction projects and mining operations sought strong young men, and textile mills sought young women. To fill these jobs both private firms and governments recruited European immigrants. Midwestern and western states lured potential settlers to promote economic growth. Two transplanted New Yorkers, Augustus and

PROMOTION OF IMMIGRATION

Joe Kirby Allen, for instance, in 1836 set themselves up in what became Houston, Texas, and advertised in newspapers for settlers. In the 1850s Wisconsin appointed a commissioner of emigration, who advertised the state's advantages in European newspapers. Wisconsin also opened an office in New York and hired European agents to compete with other states and with firms like the Illinois Central Railroad in recruiting immigrants. Europeans' awareness of the United States grew as employers, states, and shipping companies promoted opportunities across the Atlantic. Often the message was stark: work and prosper in America or starve in Europe. The price of a ticket on the regularly scheduled sailing ships crossing the ocean after 1848 was within easy reach of millions of Europeans.

Success in America stimulated further emigration. "I wish, and do often say that we wish you were all in this

LETTERS HOME happy land," wrote shoemaker John West of Germantown, Pennsylvania, to his kin in Corsley, England, in 1831, adding: "A man nor woman need not stay out of employment one hour here." John Down, a weaver from Frome, England, who immigrated to New York without his family, described for his wife in 1830 the bountiful meals he shared with a farmer's family. The farmhands sat at the same table with their masters and ate a banquet of puddings, pies, fruits and vegetables of the season, and preserves. Though Down sorely missed his family, he wrote, "I do not repent of coming, for you know that there was nothing but poverty before me." Such testimonials to the success of pauper immigrants in America circulated widely in Europe.

Immigrants endured the hardships of travel and of living in a strange land. The average transatlantic crossing took six weeks; in bad weather it could take three months. Disease spread unchecked among people packed together like cattle in steerage. More than seventeen thousand immigrants, mostly Irish, died from "ship fever" in 1847 alone. On arrival, con artists and swindlers preyed on newcomers. Boarding house and employment agents tried to lure them from their chosen destinations. In response, New York State established Castle Garden as an immigrant center in 1855. There, at the tip of Manhattan Island, the major port for European entry, immigrants were somewhat sheltered from fraud. Authorized transportation companies maintained offices in the large rotunda and assisted new arrivals with their travel plans.

Most immigrants gravitated toward cities, and many stayed in New York City itself. By 1855, 52 percent of its 623,000 inhabitants were immigrants, 28 percent from Ireland and 16 percent from the German states. Boston,

SETTLING IN another major entry port for the Irish, took on a European tone; throughout the 1850s the city was about 35 percent foreign-born, of whom more than two-thirds were Irish. In the West, St. Louis's population was 61 percent foreign-born, and San Francisco had a foreign-born majority. Southern cities like Charleston and Savannah had significant Irish settlements. Many sought ethnic neighborhoods where their countrymen and women and their descendants lived.

Only a few immigrants had farming experience or the means to purchase land, but those who did settled in rural areas—though they tended to avoid the rural South, with its predominance of slave labor. German, Dutch, and Scandinavian farmers, in particular, headed toward the Midwest. Greater percentages of Scandinavians and Netherlanders took up farming than did other nationalities; both groups came mostly as religious dissenters and migrated in family units. The Dutch who founded colonies in western Michigan and Wisconsin, for instance, had seceded from the official Reformed Church of the Netherlands, fleeing persecution in their native land to establish new and more pious communities such as Holland and Zeeland in Michigan.

Not all new arrivals found success in the United States; hundreds of thousands returned to their homelands

IMMIGRANT DISENCHANTMENT disappointed. Before the famine of the late 1840s hit Ireland, American recruiters had lured many Irish to swing picks and shovels on American canals and railroads and to work in construction. The promise that "he should soon become a wealthy man" lured Michael Gaugin, who had worked for thirteen years as an assistant engineer in the construction of a Dublin canal. The Irish agent for a New York firm convinced him to quit his job, which included a house and an acre of ground, to come to America. But Gaugin landed in New York City during the financial panic of 1837. He could not find work, and within two months he was broke, struggling to find the means to return to Ireland.

Before the great famine, caused by a blight that turned the potato crop—Ireland's food staple—rotten

IRISH IMMIGRANTS and inedible, there had been a substantial outmigration from Ireland, mostly to English cities, but also a steady stream to the United States. From 1845 to 1849, death from starvation, malnutrition, and typhus spread in Ireland. In all, 1 million died and about 1.5 million scattered around the world, two-thirds of them to the United States. Ireland's major export became its people. At the peak of Irish immigration, from 1847 to 1854, 1.2 million Irish men and women entered the

United States. In every year but one between 1830 and 1854, the Irish constituted the largest group of immigrants. By the end of the nineteenth century there would be more Irish in the United States than in Ireland.

Though most Irish made an economic decision to leave their homeland, they often viewed themselves as political exiles, forced to flee because of British tyranny. While nature caused the potato blight, they blamed British misrule for the events that led to famine. Thus settlers of the Irish diaspora—in the United States, Canada, Australia, South Africa, Argentina, and even England— tended to be politically active. In the United States especially, as in St. Patrick's Day parades, they displayed their two national identities.

Most of the new immigrants from Ireland were young, female, poor, from rural districts, and Roman Catholic. In America, the women found work in textile mills and households. Young Irishmen worked in transportation and construction. The Irish supported their families back home and in Irish enclaves in cities, built Catholic churches and schools, and established networks of charitable and social organizations.

This wave of Irish immigrants, descended from the ancient Celts who spoke Gaelic, differed greatly from the Irish who had migrated earlier to the American colonies. In the eighteenth century (see page 92), the Protestant Scots-Irish predominated; they were considered British. But the Celts were considered inferior. The British had thought them barbaric, and they carried those views to America. Dr. Robert Knox of the Edinburgh College of Surgeons believed the British stood for liberty, whereas "the source of all evil lies in the race, the Celtic race of Ireland." "Race is everything," he declared in an 1850 study published in Philadelphia; "literature, science, art, in a word, civilization, depends upon it." Many Americans agreed, describing Irish immigrants in negative, racial terms. They talked about Celtic racial characteristics: a small upturned nose, high forehead, and black tint of skin. As scientists like Knox began to classify peoples into biological types, scientific theory buttressed the developing notion of race.

With the immigration of new groups to the United States (Celts, Jews, Catholics, and Chinese, for instance), with the black population growing, and with territorial expansion bringing Hispanics and more Indians into the United States as well, native-born white Americans were increasingly confronted with people who did not look like them. Many considered these non-British, non-European, non-Protestant people separate races, distinct from their own. Ralph Waldo Emerson, while rejecting the extremes

RACIAL IDEAS

■ Though the popular slogan "No Irish Need Apply" excluded Irish immigrants from jobs and housing, it was used by Kathleen O'Neil to attack such exclusion in her lyrics and spirited melody. In the song the Irishman meets discrimination head on, and "No Irish Need Apply" is banished. (Special Collections, Milton S. Eisenhower Library, The Johns Hopkins University)

of Dr. Knox's argument, asserted the importance of race in *English Traits* (1856). To Emerson, as a son inherits his ancestors' "every mental and moral property," so too does a race pass on to its members its physical, intellectual, and moral characteristics. "Race avails . . . that all Celts are Catholics," Emerson wrote. "Race is a controlling influence in the Jew. . . . Race in the negro [sic] is of appalling importance. The French in Canada, cut off from all intercourse with the parent people, have held their national traits."

Were the Irish part of the white majority? In the 1840s and 1850s native-born white Americans and British and German immigrants often treated Irish men and women as if they were nonwhites. Posting placards warning "No Irish Need Apply," they excluded the Irish from many occupations. The Irish immigrants who lived with blacks in Five Points seemed to many observers to be much closer to black than white.

Closely related to racial stereotyping in its causes and nasty effects was anti-Catholicism, which became strident in the 1830s and was most overt and cruel in Boston, where a great many Irish had settled. Anti-Catholic riots were almost commonplace. In Charlestown, Massachusetts, a mob burned a convent in 1834; in Philadelphia a crowd attacked priests and nuns and vandalized churches in 1844; and in Lawrence, Massachusetts, a mob leveled the Irish neighborhood in 1854.

ANTI-
CATHOLICISM

The native-born whites who rejected the Irish and hated Catholics were motivated in part by economic competition and anxiety. Competition was stiffest among the lowest-paid and least desirable jobs, from women's textile mill work to men's day-laboring jobs. To apprehensive workers, racializing the Irish as Celts was a way of keeping them out of the running. Irish Catholics were also blamed for nearly every social problem, from immorality and alcoholism to poverty and economic upheaval. Impoverished native-born workers complained to the Massachusetts legislature in 1845 that the Irish displaced "the honest and respectable laborers of the State . . . and from their manner of living . . . work for much less per day . . . being satisfied with food to support the animal existence alone." American workers, they claimed, "not only labor for the body but for the mind, the soul, and the State."

In emphasizing "the soul, and the State," native-born workers added a political dimension to their racial expression. Republicanism depended on broad participation and the consent of the governed, and it seemed to American nativists that the Irish, a nonwhite, non-British "race," were not fit to participate. The Know-Nothings turned these attitudes into a political movement in the 1850s (see page 368).

The experience of German immigrants differed from that of the Irish. By and large Americans viewed most Germans, especially the majority Protestant group, as white. They shared a racial stock with the English, who according to Emerson, "come mainly from the Germans." Americans stereotyped Germans as hard working, self-reliant, and intelligent, attributes also applied to white people. Many believed that Germans fit more easily than the Irish into American culture.

GERMAN
IMMIGRANTS

In the ten years from 1846 to 1855, 977,000 immigrants from the German states entered the United States. In 1854 Germans replaced the Irish as the largest group of new arrivals. Potato blight also prompted emigration from the German states in the 1840s; other hardships added to the steady stream. Many came from regions where small landholdings made it hard to eke out a living. Craftsmen displaced by the industrial revolution sought jobs in the American expanding market economy. Political refugees—liberals, freethinkers, socialists, communists, and anarchists—fled to the United States after the abortive revolutions of 1848.

Germans shared the same language, though neither a single German state nor a common culture united them. While New York's sizable German population made it the world's third largest German-speaking city—after Vienna and Berlin—Germans settled elsewhere in the United States as well. In the South they were peddlers and merchants; in the North and West they worked as farmers, urban laborers, and businessmen. Their tendency to migrate as families and groups helped them maintain German customs and institutions. Many settled in small towns and rural areas where they could preserve their language and regional German cultures. In larger cities immigrants from the same German states tended to cluster together. Their presence transformed the tone of cities like Cincinnati and Milwaukee, as they became major producers of German beer and sausage and built shops and factories based on German craft skills, from cigar making to tool works.

Non-Protestant Germans did not fare so well, frequently encountering hostility fed by religious and racial prejudice. A significant number of German immigrants were Jewish, and Jews were considered a separate race. Anti-Catholics attacked the German immigrants who were Catholic. The Sunday tradition of urban German families gathering at beer gardens to eat and drink, to dance and sing, and sometimes to play cards outraged evangelical Protestants, who viewed this behavior as violating the sanctity of the Lord's day.

From Florida to Texas and the Southwest to California, Hispanic inhabitants of the borderlands became "immigrants" without actually moving; treaties placed them in the United States. Some Mexicans were unhappy to find themselves in a new country, while others welcomed the political self-government that the United States seemed to promise.

HISPANICS

But reality did not live up to promise. In Nueces County, Texas, at the time of the Texas Revolution (1836), Mexicans held all the land; twenty years later, they had lost it. The new Anglo owners produced crops for the market economy; *rancheros* and *vaqueros*—cowboys—became obsolete. Although many Texas Mexicans, called *Tejanos*, had fought for Texas's independence, new Anglo settlers tended to treat them as inferiors and foreigners. They became second-class citizens on land where they had lived for generations. Still they retained their culture. They held fast to their language, Roman Catholic religion, and cultural traditions. San Antonio, Mexican from 1821 to 1836 and thereafter a Texas city, illustrates *Tejano* persistence. The church, free public schools (established in 1827), newspapers, mutual aid societies, public holidays, and celebrations of life-cycle events from baptism to marriage to funerals all perpetuated *Tejano* culture.

In California—unlike in Texas, New Mexico, and Arizona—Hispanic society and political power quickly gave way to American and European culture. *Californios*, the Mexican population, numbered 10,000 in 1848, or two-thirds of the non-Indian population. By the end of the century the Hispanic population was 15,000 out of 1.5 million, and Hispanic culture was only a remnant, though Mexican immigrants would reestablish it in the twentieth century.

White Americans considered Hispanics, a group descended from Indians and Spaniards, as a separate, non-white race. Anglo-Americans also inherited the British view of Spaniards as inferior, lazy, and decadent, stereotypes they applied to Hispanics. Racializing Hispanics helped to justify the attitudes and actions of aggressive whites, who pushed aside any who stood in the way of expansion and settlement.

Free People of Color

*a*s Irish Americans marched on St. Patrick's Day, declaring their identities as Irish and Americans and demanding Ireland's liberation from the yoke of British colonialism, so too did African Americans celebrate freedom holidays, commemorating emancipation (where it took place) and protesting their own inequality and the persistence of slavery. Thus from 1834 through the Civil War, free people of color across the United States, from big cities like Boston, New York, Philadelphia, Cincinnati, and 1850s San Francisco to small towns like Troy, New York; Harrisburg, Ohio; and Niles, Michigan, celebrated August 1, the anniversary of West Indian emancipation, as a major holiday. "To many of us," Frederick Douglass said, "the first of August is like the white man's 4th of July." Celebrations were held in at least thirteen states, and New Bedford, Massachusetts's 1855 regional event topped them all with seven thousand attendees. And as on St. Patrick's Day, many whites saw such parades as provocative.

Blacks, slave and free, were the most visible non-white group in the early nineteenth century. As their

■ This painting (c. 1840) of Saint Isadore of Madrid, patron saint of farmers, is attributed to Rafael Aragon. Hispanic farmers in the Southwest sought the aid of Saint Isadore as they struggled to raise crops and preserve their culture.   (Courtesy of Dr. and Mrs. Ward Alan Minge)

GROWTH OF THE BLACK POPULATION numbers grew, from 2.3 million in 1830 to 4.4 million in 1860, whites increasingly viewed them as a racial group, a people apart from Europeans. In law and society most black people found themselves as outsiders in the land of their birth.

The free African American population grew from 320,000 in 1820 to almost 500,000 in 1860. Nearly half lived in the urban North, and almost an equal number in the Upper South, where outside of Baltimore—the nation's largest black community—most were rural. A scattering of free people of color lived in the Deep South. An estimated 60,000 free blacks lived in Canada as exiles from the United States. Despite differences in occupation, wealth, education, religion, and social status, the need for self-defense promoted solidarity among free blacks.

Ex-slaves constantly increased the ranks of free people of color in the North. Some, like Frederick Douglass and Harriet Tubman, were fugitives. Douglass, a Baltimore ship caulker, escaped in 1838 by bluffing his way to Philadelphia and freedom. Tubman, a slave in Maryland, escaped to Philadelphia in 1849 when it was rumored that she would be sold out of the state. Over the next two years she returned twice to free her two children, her sister, her mother, and her brother and his family. Some slaves received freedom in owners' wills when masters sought, at death, to rid themselves of the stain of owning slaves. Some owners released elderly slaves rather than support them in old age. Others freed their children, offspring of liaisons and forced relations with slaves. After Nat Turner's slave revolt in Virginia in 1831, when Upper South states further eroded the line between free and

■ Black churches—especially the African Methodist Episcopal Church, run by and for free people of color—were central in the communal and religious life of free people of color. Mrs. Juliann Jane Tillman, an AME minister in Philadelphia, was a popular preacher. Peter S. Duval printed this 1844 life drawing of Tillman by Alfred Hoffy. (Library of Congress)

slave by barring free blacks from learning to read, many families from the cities of Virginia moved to the Midwest. Even in the Midwest they were not full citizens: they could not vote, but at least they were free to educate their children.

Black people, free and slave, forged their own communities and culture in the early nineteenth century. Swept up by the Second Great Awakening, blacks turned increasingly to religion, most often to Christianity. But as they founded their own churches and independent denominations, like the African Methodist Episcopal (AME) Church (1816), they reshaped ritual and practice. Services reflected black musical traditions, from the "shout and call" to the spirituals, and they gave theological prominence to themes of equality, exodus, and freedom (see chapter 13). By 1846 there were 296 AME congregations in the United States and Canada. Black churches and preachers, both male and female, played central roles in their communities. Chapels and social halls functioned as town hall and school buildings. Ministers were political leaders, and their halls housed political forums, conventions, and protest meetings. Above all else they were abolitionists, united in their opposition to the enslavement of other black people, sometimes their own kin.

AFRICAN AMERICAN COMMUNITIES

A network of voluntary associations became the hallmark of black communities. Besides the churches and reform societies—from abolition to temperance—men and women organized benevolent associations, literary societies, and schools. In Philadelphia in the 1840s, more than half of the black population belonged to mutual beneficiary societies. The Prince Hall Masons had more than fifty lodges in seventeen states by 1860. Many black leaders believed that these mutual aid societies would encourage thrift, industry, and morality, thus assisting their members to improve themselves. But no amount of effort could completely counteract the burden of white racism, which impinged on every aspect of their lives. For example, blacks in effect paid double for education: their taxes supported white public schools, which excluded black children; then they raised additional funds to educate their own children.

In the majority of states where free blacks were excluded from voting, they formed organizations to fight for equal rights. Among the early efforts to organize for self-defense was the Negro Convention movement. From 1830 to 1835, and irregularly thereafter, free blacks held national conventions with delegates drawn from city and state organizations. Under

POLITICAL ACTIVISM

middle-class leadership, which included the Philadelphia sail manufacturer James Forten and the orator Reverend Henry Highland Garnet, the convention movement served as a forum to attack slavery and agitate for equal rights. Militant new black newspapers joined the struggle. *Freedom's Journal,* the first black weekly, appeared in 1827; in 1837 the *Weekly Advocate* began publication in New York City. Both papers circulated throughout the North, disseminating African American political analysis and promoting activism.

Activists fought their second-class status and the continuation of slavery. The Constitution acknowledged

DISCRIMINATION
AND EXCLUSION

slavery, but the Bill of Rights seemed to apply to free African Americans. The Fifth Amendment specified that "no person shall . . . be deprived of life, liberty, or property, without due process of law." But eighteenth-century political theory had defined the republic as being for whites only (see Chapter 7), and early federal legislation excluded blacks from common rights. The first naturalization law in 1790 limited citizenship to "free white persons." Thus from the start, legislation excluded free people of color from citizenship rights. When Congress created militias in 1792, they included only whites. After the admission of Missouri in 1821, every new state admitted until the Civil War, free and slave, banned blacks from voting. When Congress organized the Oregon and New Mexico Territories, it reserved public land grants for whites. Free people of color were defined as an alien race; they could not participate in the republican ideal that government rested on the consent of the governed.

Even in the North, states attempted to exclude African Americans. Many northern and western states barred free blacks from entering or required them to post bonds ranging from $500 to $1,000 to guarantee their good conduct, as did Illinois (1819), Michigan (1837), and Oregon (1857). Only in Massachusetts, New Hampshire, Vermont, and Maine could blacks vote on an equal basis with whites throughout the early nineteenth century. In 1842 African Americans gained the right to vote in Rhode Island (where all voters faced restrictive property qualifications), but they had lost it earlier in Pennsylvania and Connecticut. Only Massachusetts permitted blacks to serve on juries. Four midwestern states and California did not allow African Americans to testify against whites. In Oregon blacks could not own real estate, make contracts, or sue in court. The laws were meant to render African Americans powerless.

Black people also faced economic restrictions. They were excluded from the new factory and clerical jobs of the expanding market economy. In the North and Upper South, black women, who were more likely to work for wages than white women, whether married or single, worked as house servants, cooks, washerwomen, and child nurses. Men worked as servants, waiters, cooks, barbers, janitors, and sailors. In service work wages were low but relatively immune from boom-and-bust cycles. Most black men, however, were construction workers, porters, longshoremen, and day laborers; all suffered frequent unemployment.

Some black men and women turned service occupations into businesses. In the growing cities blacks opened restaurants, taverns, hotels, barber shops, and employment agencies for domestic servants. Some became caterers. Others sold used clothing or were junk dealers or small-job contractors, especially in the Upper South. A few became very successful economically, like sail maker James Forten (Philadelphia), barbers William Johnson (Natchez) and Samuel Mordechai (St. Louis), and ship captain Paul Cuffee. They became wealthy, invested in real estate, and loaned money. With professionals—ministers, teachers, physicians and dentists, lawyers, and newspaper editors—they formed a growing black middle class.

While free people of color sought economic and political security, they forged their own cultural identity.

AFRICAN
AMERICAN
CULTURE

They began to call themselves "Colored Americans" rather than "Africans," reflecting their growing participation in public life. Like the Irish who wore red, white, and blue on St. Patrick's Day, they acknowledged a dual consciousness, a dual identity, as African descendants and as Americans. There is much evidence that they mixed African and American cultures in distinct ways. They dressed up for church, wearing their "Sunday go-to-meetin' clothes." They modified African hairstyles in cutting, wrapping, and braiding their hair. Africans brought the banjo and drum to the New World, introducing new rhythms to Europeans. Black brass bands created what Walt Whitman called "grand American opera."

Most expressive was African American dance. From Congo Square in New Orleans on Sundays to the integrated "dives" in Five Points, New York, visitors observed African-based dance movements unknown to Europeans. European dance used arm and leg movements; but African dancers moved their entire bodies. "Single shuffle, double shuffle, cut and cross-cut; snapping his fingers, rolling his eyes, turning in his knees . . . , spinning about on his toes and heels like nothing but the man's fingers on the tambourine; dancing with two left legs, two right legs, two wooden legs, two wire legs, two spring legs—all sorts of legs and no legs," was Charles Dickens's 1842 attempt (in *American Notes*) to describe the flowing motion of Mr. Juba (William Henry Lane), "the greatest dancer known," in Five Points in 1842. Frederick Bremer in South Carolina in 1850 saw similar physical movements in a black church. They sang "with all their souls and with all their bodies in unison, for their bodies wagged, their heads nodded, their feet stamped, their knees shook, their elbows and their hands beat time to the tune." Here were the African traditions of polyrhythms, of improvisation, and intensive physicality. Over time, some white churches came to incorporate this style in their worship. And when whites parodied black styles in minstrel shows, they were acknowledging black culture.

In the late 1840s and 1850s the mood of many free blacks turned pessimistic. They felt frustrated by the failure of the abolitionist movement and angered by the passage of the stringent Fugitive Slave Act of 1850 (see page 362). Some fled to Canada, others became more militant, and a few joined John Brown in his plans for a slave uprising (see page 374). Many more were swept up in a wave of black nationalism that stressed racial solidarity, self-help, and a growing interest in Africa. Before this time, efforts to send African Americans "back to Africa" had originated with whites seeking to rid the United States of blacks, and nearly all African American leaders had been opposed. But in the 1850s some participated in emigrationist conventions led by abolitionists Martin Delany and Henry Bibb. Delany led an exploration party to the Niger valley as the emissary of a black convention, signing a treaty with Yoruba rulers to allow American settlers in their African kingdom.

Nothing better illustrates the difficult and ironic condition of free blacks in the United States than their flight to Canada and Africa in search of freedom while millions of European migrants came to the United States for liberty and opportunity. With the coming of the Civil War, the status of blacks would move onto the national political agenda.

Summary

*T*he American people and communities in the North and West were far more diverse and turbulent in the 1850s than they had been in the 1820s. The market economy and westward movement altered rural and urban life and class structure; heavy immigration, growing racial ideas, and the anguished position of free

people of color added to the tensions. Inequality increased, as did the gap between the haves and the have-nots. As the nation grew more populous and the market economy upset work and social relations, many felt a loss of tradition and community. Some longed to return to old values. Utopians like the Shakers, Mormons, and Brook Farmers sought to counter isolation and individualism.

Increasingly cities became the center of American life, with New York the predominant metropolis. Growing populations brought new problems, however, and cities struggled to provide adequate public health, safety, and education for their residents. Large cities offered rich leisure activities, from entertainment to sporting events. Increasingly, however, people divided along class, ethnic, and racial lines. Whether formal, as in the Masonic order, or informal as in the youth culture of the Bowery, divisions became more rigid. The gap between rich and poor widened.

In the midst of these changes, families adapted to the urban, market economy. They became consumers rather than producers, and they shrunk in size as women had fewer children. Middle-class families sought to insulate their homes from the competition of the market economy. Increasingly cities offered opportunities for people to live outside of families.

Famine and oppression in Europe propelled millions of people across the Atlantic, most from Ireland and the German states. American expansion added Hispanics to the nation. Diversity, competition, and religious and scientific thought fueled racial ideas. Many European descendants began to view and treat the Irish, Hispanics, and African Americans as inferior races rather than as cultural groups.

LEGACY FOR A PEOPLE AND A NATION

White Fascination with and Appropriation of Black Culture

White Americans' fascination with and appropriation of black culture blossomed in the early nineteenth century. Whites performed songs and dances from blackface minstrel reviews, while urban young people imitated black language, dress, and hairstyles. In the 1850s white songwriter Stephen Foster's "Old Folks at Home," "Susanna," and "Camptown Races" were enormously popular. Whites believed they were traditional black folk songs, though they romanticized the slave South.

American popular culture combined African, European, and African American traditions. Its emphasis on performance, improvisation, strong rhythms, vernacular language, multiple meanings, and integration into everyday life is evident of strong African ties. These elements appealed to whites because of their expressive powers. Whites also believed that black cultural forms were "exotic" and offered "natural" forms of expression.

Black traditions continue to influence twenty-first-century popular culture. Minstrelsy turned into vaudeville and Broadway theater, which gave birth to American popular music. Popular dance and music, performed mostly by whites, drew heavily on black gospel, slave spirituals, the blues, and jazz and spread through live performance, recorded music, and later radio and television. Black traditions influenced the swing bands of the 1930s, and after World War II, they shaped rhythm and blues, rock 'n' roll, and, later, rap, hip-hop, and ska.

Until recently, most whites experienced black culture as appropriated by whites. Minstrels in blackface and Stephen Foster's songs modified black culture for white audiences. But in the late twentieth century, a synthesis of black and white traditions became notable. In the early 1950s Bill Haley and the Comets, a white country-western group, combined black rhythm and blues with white country and western music. Their 1954 sensation, "Shake, Rattle & Roll," for instance, was a sanitized version of Big Joe Turner's rhythm and blues hit. White audiences responded enthusiastically, and when Haley and the Comets played "Rock Around the Clock" in the 1955 movie *Blackboard Jungle,* rock 'n' roll took off. Elvis Presley too synthesized rhythm and blues and gospel with country music and middle-of-the-road popular music. Rap and hip-hop built on the talking blues, call and response, and urban black and Chicano/a dance styles of the 1970s. White suburban youth made them dominant popular forms.

Popular music and dance, with its African American roots, is uniquely American. Young people fostered this popular culture and used its expressive elements to define themselves. Thus African American culture has given the people and nation a unique cultural legacy.

The **history companion** *powered by Eduspace®*
Your primary source for interactive quizzes, exercises, and more to help you learn efficiently.
http://history.college.hmco.com/students

PEOPLE AND COMMUNITIES IN A SLAVE SOCIETY: THE SOUTH 1830–1860

a slaveholder in debt was a dangerous man. Pierce Butler was broke. It was late winter of 1859, fear of disunion dominated national life, and Butler's slave auction had all of coastal Georgia and South Carolina talking. Butler was the grandson of Major Pierce Butler, a framer of the Constitution, a senator from South Carolina, and a wealthy planter. Butler the younger divided his time between the family's ostentatious home in Philadelphia and 1,500 acres of cotton plantations on Butler Island and St. Simons Island in Georgia, worked by eight hundred slaves. His marriage to the famous British actress Fanny Kemble had ended in divorce; she could not bear the realities of slavery on her husband's cotton plantations, and he could not bear her protests. By 1859 Butler had squandered a fortune of $700,000 through speculation and gambling. Allegedly, he blew $25,000 on one hand of cards.

Most of Butler's properties and possessions in Philadelphia were sold to satisfy his creditors. Then came the largest slave auction in American history. In the last week of February, 436 Butler slaves were taken to Savannah by railroad and steamboat. They were housed for several days in horse-and-carriage sheds at the Ten Broeck racetrack. People of all ages—infants, husbands, wives, children, grandparents—huddled in fearful expectation. Joseph Bryan, a slave broker and auctioneer, managed the sale. Among the planters and speculators who were there to buy was an undercover *New York Tribune* reporter who left a detailed account of the event. The auction, held in the racecourse's grandstand, lasted an agonizing two days in a driving rainstorm.

◀ Thomas S. Noble's painting *The Last Sale of Slaves* depicts the public drama and family horror of slave auctions. Noble's work stimulated a heated newspaper debate in St. Louis over its abolitionist message. The sight of people treated as property, and bills of sale signed on the table, leave slavery's most haunting images. (Missouri Historical Society)

CHRONOLOGY

1810–20 • 137,000 slaves are forced to move from the Upper South to Alabama, Mississippi, and other western regions

1822 • Vesey's insurrection plot is discovered in South Carolina

1830s • Vast majority of African American slaves are native-born in America

1830s–40s • Cotton trade grows into largest source of commercial wealth and America's leading export

1831 • Turner leads a violent slave rebellion in Virginia

1832 • Virginia holds the last debate in the South about the future of slavery; gradual abolition is voted down
• Publication of Dew's proslavery tract *Abolition of Negro Slavery*

1836 • Arkansas gains admission to the Union as a slave state

1839 • Mississippi's Married Women's Property Act gives married women some property rights

1845 • Florida and Texas gain admission to the Union as slave states
• Publication of Douglass's *Narrative of the Life of Frederick Douglass, An American Slave, Written by Himself*

1850 • Planters' share of agricultural wealth in the South is 90 to 95 percent

1850–60 • Of some 300,000 slaves who migrate from the Upper to the Lower South, 60 to 70 percent go by outright sale

1857 • Publication of Helper's *The Impending Crisis*, denouncing the slave system
• Publication of Fitzhugh's *Southern Thought,* an aggressive defense of slavery

1860 • 405,751 mulattos in the United States, 12.5 percent of the African American population
• Three-quarters of all southern white families own no slaves
• South produces largest cotton crop ever

If possible, families were sold intact for group prices; thus the old and infirm could still be liquidated, while the closest kin stayed together. A seventeen-year-old "Prime woman" named Dorcas and her three-month-old son, Joe, went for $2,200. A nineteen-year-old "prime young man," Abel, netted $1,295. Some families of four, such as Goin and Cassander and their two daughters, Emiline and Judy, brought only $1,600 together. At the end of the second day of what blacks in the region called the "weeping time," Butler had amassed $303,850 by selling 436 human beings. It would have been impossible to convince the numbed and despairing African Americans who traveled away from Savannah in wagons or railcars that their enslavement was not at the heart of the crisis dividing the nation.

As long as slavery was perceived as a peculiarly southern institution, even the ownership of humans as property, the threat of slave rebellion, and the divisions in southern society fostered by slave ownership did not seem to bother many northerners at first glance. But as slavery spread westward, its worst elements, such as the Butler auction, threatened and disturbed growing numbers of restless Americans. And on the ground in the South, as slaves' bodies, labor, and lives came to be defined more and more as chattel, they struggled to survive and resist, sometimes overtly, but more often in daily life and cultural expression.

By the 1830s the North was an emerging market economy embarking on an industrial revolution. Meanwhile, the South, with a different kind of growth and prosperity, also participated in the market revolution. New lands were settled, new states peopled, and steadily the South emerged as the world's most extensive and vigorous slave economy, linked to an international cotton trade and textile industry. Slavery had a far-reaching influence on all of southern society. The Old South's wealth came from export crops, land, and slaves; and its population was almost wholly rural. In the land where cotton became king, racial slavery affected not only economics but values, customs, laws, class structure, and the region's relationship to the nation. ■

The "Distinctive" South?

The South, the section composed of the slaveholding states from the Chesapeake region of Maryland and Virginia to Missouri and from Florida to Texas, has often been considered America's most distinctive region. Historians and other commentators have long asked the question: how was the Old South like or unlike the rest of the nation? Because of its unique history, has the South, in the words of poet Allen Tate, always been "Uncle Sam's other province"? Or as the southern writer W. J. Cash wrote in 1940, is the South "a tree with many age rings, with its limbs and trunk bent and twisted by all the winds of the years, but with its tap root in the Old South?" Figuring out just why the South seems more religious, more conservative, or more tragic than other regions of America has been an enduring practice in American thought.

Certain American values such as materialism, individualism, and faith in progress have been associated with the North in the nineteenth century, and values such as tradition, intolerance, and family loyalty with the South. The South, so the stereotype has it, was static, even "backward," and the North dynamic in the decades leading up to the Civil War. There are many measures of just how different South was from North in the antebellum era, and at the same time there were many Souths: low-country rice and cotton regions with dense slave populations; mountainous regions of small farmers, plantation culture, and subsistence agriculture; semitropical wetlands in the southeast; Texas grasslands; cities with bustling ports and merchants; and rural areas with only the rare homestead of hillfolk.

The South was distinctive because of its commitment to slavery, but it also shared much in common with the rest of the nation. The geographic sizes of the South and the North were roughly the same. By the 1830s, white southerners shared a heritage of heroes and ideology from the era of the American Revolution with their fellow free citizens in the North. With varying accents, southerners spoke the same language and worshiped the same Protestant God as northerners. Southerners lived under the same cherished Constitution as northerners, and they shared a common mixture of nationalism and localism in their attitudes toward government. Down to the 1840s, northerners and southerners invoked the doctrine of states' rights against federal authority with nearly equal frequency. A faith in the future fueled by a sense of American mission and the dreams inspired by the westward movement were as much a part of southern as of northern experience.

SOUTH-NORTH SIMILARITY

Indeed, some of the most eloquent visions of America as a land of independent, self-sufficient farmers expanding westward had come from a southerner, Thomas Jefferson. Jefferson believed that "virtue" rested in those who tilled the soil, that farmers made the best citizens. In 1804 Jefferson declared his "moral and physical preference of the agricultural over the manufacturing man." But as slavery and the plantation economy expanded (see Map 13.1), the South did not become a land of individual opportunity in the same manner as the North.

During the thirty years before the Civil War, the South shared in the nation's economic booms and busts. Research has shown that despite its enormous cruelties, slavery was a profitable labor system for planters. Southerners and northerners shared an expanding capitalist economy. As it grew, the slave-based economy of money-crop agriculture reflected the rational choices of planters. More land and more slaves generally converted into more wealth. By the eve of the Civil War in 1860, the distribution of wealth and property in the two sections was almost identical: 50 percent of free adult males owned only 1 percent of real and personal property, while the richest 1 percent owned 27 percent of the wealth. One study comparing Texas and Wisconsin in 1850 shows that the richest 2 percent of families in each state owned 31 to 32 percent of the wealth. So, both North and South had ruling classes, even if their wealth was invested in different kinds of property. Entrepreneurs in both sections, whether forging plantations out of Mississippi Delta land or shoe factories and textile mills in New England river towns, sought their fortunes in an expanding market economy.

But there were also important differences between the North and the South. The South's climate and longer growing season gave it an unmistakable rural and agricultural destiny. Its people, white and black, developed an intense attachment to place, to the ways people were related to the land and to one another. The South developed as a biracial society of brutal inequality, where the liberty of one race directly depended on the enslavement of another. White wealth was built on highly valued black labor.

SOUTH-NORTH DISSIMILARITY

Cotton growers spread out over as large an area as possible to maximize production and income. Population density was low; by 1860 there were only 2.3 people per square mile in vast and largely unsettled Texas, 15.6 in Louisiana, and 18.0 in Georgia. By contrast,

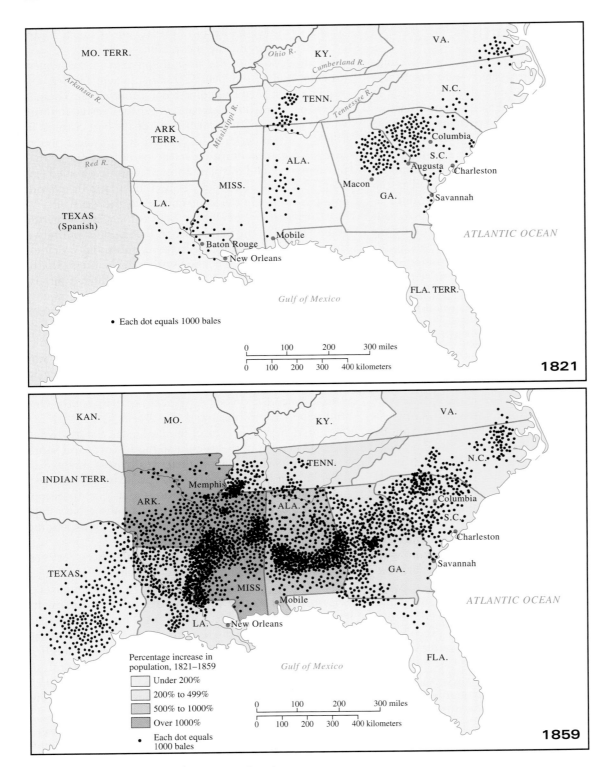

Map 13.1   Cotton Production in the South

These two maps reveal the rapid westward expansion of cotton production and its importance to the antebellum South.

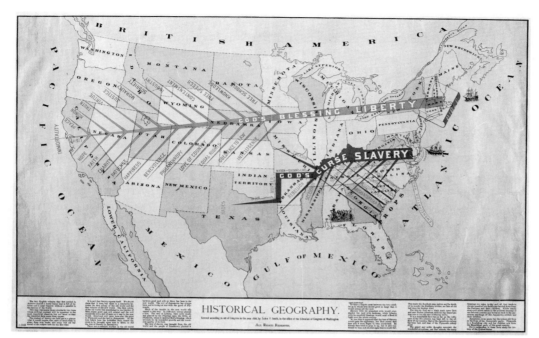

■ A map, entitled "Historical Geography," produced in the 1850s, demonstrates from an abolitionist perspective the notion of historical and cultural differences between North and South. With the values of "liberty" emanating from Plymouth, and the values of slavery emanating from Jamestown, such simplistic but graphic depictions helped fuel sectional animosity.   (Library of Congress)

population density in the nonslaveholding states east of the Mississippi River was almost three times higher. The Northeast had an average of 65.4 people per square mile. Massachusetts had 153.1 people per square mile, and New York City compressed 86,400 people into each square mile. When in the 1850s young Frederick Law Olmsted of Connecticut, later renowned as a landscape architect, toured the South as a journalist, he traveled mostly on horseback along primitive trails. Between Columbus, Georgia, and Montgomery, Alabama, Olmsted found "a hilly wilderness, with a few dreary villages, and many isolated cotton farms." For the designer of Central Park in New York City, this was just too much ruralness.

Where people were scarce, it was difficult to finance and operate schools, churches, libraries, or even inns and restaurants. Southerners were strongly committed to their churches, and some believed in the importance of universities, but all such institutions were far less developed than those in the North. Factories were rare be-

cause planters invested most of their capital in slaves. A few southerners did invest in iron or textiles on a small scale. But the largest southern "industry" was lumbering, and the largest factories used slave labor to make cigars. More decisively, the South was slower than the North to develop a unified market economy and a regional transportation network. Despite concerted efforts, the South had only 35 percent of the nation's railroad mileage in 1860.

The South lagged way behind the North in nearly any measure of industrial growth. It always had its reformist voices, however, who advocated commercial development. The South did have urban centers, especially ports like New Orleans and Charleston, which became crossroads of commerce and small-scale manufacturing. But slavery slowed urban growth. As a system of labor and racial control, slavery did not work well in cities. As one historian has said, southern urban centers were small market towns, dependent on agricultural trade—"urbanization without cities." Likewise, because of a lack of jobs, the South did not attract immigrants as readily as the North. By 1860 only 13 percent of the nation's foreign-born population lived in the slave states.

Like most northerners, antebellum southerners were adherents to evangelical Christianity. Americans from all regions held in common a faith in a personal God and in conversion and piety as the means to salvation. But southern evangelicalism was distinct from its northern practice. In the South, Baptists and Methodists concentrated on personal rather than social improvement. By the 1830s in the North, evangelicalism was a major wellspring of reform movements (see Chapter 11); but in the states where blacks were so numerous and unfree, and where the very social structure was under increasingly aggressive attacks from abolitionists, religion, as one scholar has written, preached "a hands-off policy concerning slavery." Although blacks themselves began to convert to Christianity in the early-nineteenth-century South, many southern whites feared a reform impulse that would foster what one historian has called an "interracial communion" in their churches and in their communities. Moreover, those women who may have been reform minded were prevented from developing frequent associations because of the sparse population. The only reform movements that did take hold in the emerging Bible belt of the South, such as temperance, focused on personal behavior, not social reform.

Within an inherently conservative social structure, antebellum southern law restricted the authority of the courts, reinforcing a tradition of planter control. Penitentiaries tended to house only whites, as most blacks were under the authority of personal masters. Law-breaking in the South tended to be crimes of violence rather than crimes against property. Similarly, the rural character of the South and the significance of the plantation as a self-sufficient social unit meant that the section put few resources into improving disease control and public health. So, in a host of ways, the South was distinct.

Perhaps in no way was the South more distinctive than in its embrace of a particular world-view, a system of thought and meaning held especially by the planter class, but also influencing all groups of whites. Like those of all people, southerners' values, beliefs, and rationalizations for slavery were not so different from those of any civilization trying to defend the institutions it inherits. But at the heart of the proslavery argument was a deep and abiding racism. The persistence of modern racism in all sections of the United States

A SOUTHERN WORLD-VIEW AND THE PROSLAVERY ARGUMENT

is all the more reason to comprehend antebellum southerners' justifications for human slavery.

By 1830 white southerners defended slavery as a "positive good," and not merely a "necessary evil." They used the Bible and its many references to slaveholding, as well as the ancient roots of slavery, to foster a historical argument for bondage. Slavery, they deemed, was the natural status of blacks. Whites were the more intellectual race and blacks the race more inherently physical, and therefore destined for labor. Whites were the creators of civilizations, blacks the appointed hewers of wood and drawers of water. Proslavery writers did not mince words. In a proslavery tract written in 1851, John Campbell confidently declared that "there is as much difference between the lowest tribe of negroes and the white Frenchman, Englishman, or American, as there is between the monkey and the negro."

Some southerners defended slavery in practical terms; they simply saw their bondsmen as economic necessity and as symbols of their quest of prosperity. In 1845, James Henry Hammond of South Carolina argued that slaveholding was essentially a matter of property rights. He spoke for many southerners in his unwillingness to "deal in abstractions" about the "right and wrong" of slavery: property was sacred, protected by the Constitution, and slaves were legal property—end of argument.

The deepest root of the proslavery argument was a hierarchical view of the social order as slavery's defenders believed God or nature had prescribed it. Southerners cherished stability, duty, and honor, believing social change should come only in slow increments, if at all. As the Virginia legislature debated the gradual abolition of slavery in 1831–1832, in the wake of Nat Turner's rebellion, Thomas R. Dew, a slaveholder and professor of law and history at the College of William and Mary, contended that "that which is the growth of *ages* may require *ages* to remove." Dew's widely read work, *Abolition of Negro Slavery* (1832), ushered in an outpouring of proslavery writing that would intensify in volume and depth of commitment over the next thirty years. Until Turner's bloody rebellion, Dew admitted, emancipation in the South had "never been seriously discussed." But as slavery expanded westward and fueled national prosperity, Dew cautioned southerners that any degree of gradual abolition or colonization was impossible and threatened the whole region's "irremediable ruin." Writing one year after William Lloyd Garrison began publishing the antislavery *Liberator* in Boston, Dew declared black slavery part of the "order of nature," an indispensable part of the "deep and solid foundations of society," and the basis of the "well-ordered, well-established lib-

■ A slave woman with inventory number, unidentified photographer, c. 1860. This woman's humanity seems to survive in her expression despite the dehumanization represented in her worn clothing and her number.   (The Burns Archive)

erty" of white Americans. Dew's well-ordered society also included his conception of the proper division of men and women into separate spheres and functions.

Proslavery advocates held very different views from those of northern reformers on the concepts of freedom, progress, and equality. They turned natural-law doctrine to their favor, arguing that the natural state of mankind was inequality of ability and condition, not equality. A former U.S. senator in South Carolina, William Harper, charged in 1837 that Jefferson's famous dictum about equality in the Declaration of Independence was no more than a "sentimental phrase." "Is it not palpably nearer the truth to say that no man was ever born free," Harper argued, "and that no two men were ever born equal?" Proslavery writers believed that people were born to certain stations in life; they stressed dependence over autonomy, and duty over rights, as the human condition. As the Virginia writer George Fitzhugh put it in 1854, "Men are not born entitled to equal rights. It would be far nearer

the truth to say, that some were born with saddles on their backs, and others booted and spurred to ride them."

Hence, however differently their slaves may have interpreted the relationship, many slaveholders believed that their ownership of people bound them to a set of paternal obligations. They saw themselves as guardians of a familial relationship between masters and slaves. Although contradicted by countless examples of slave resistance and escape, as well as by slave sales, planters needed to believe in, and exerted great energy in constructing, the idea of the contented slave. Slaveholders needed to endlessly justify how much the freedom and profits of whites depended on the bondage of blacks.

What the South had become by the 1830s, and grew even more fully into by 1860, was not merely a society with slaves, but a *slave society* (see pages 72–73). In this way, the region was most distinct within the larger American nation. Slavery and race affected everything in the Old South. Whites and blacks alike grew up, were socialized, married, reared children, worked, conceived of property, and honed their most basic habits of behavior under the influence of slavery. This was true of slaveholding and nonslaveholding whites, as well as of blacks who were slave and free. Slavery shaped the social structure of the South, fueled almost anything meaningful in its economy, and came to dominate its politics.

A SLAVE SOCIETY

The South was interdependent with the North, the West, and even with Europe in a growing capitalist market system. Southerners relied on northern banks, northern steamship companies working the great western rivers, and northern merchants to keep the cotton trade flowing. But there were elements of that system that southerners increasingly rejected during the antebellum era, especially urbanism, the wage labor system, a broadening right to vote, and any threats to the racial and class order on which they so depended.

In the antebellum era, as later, there were many Souths, but Americans have always been determined to define what one historian called the "Dixie difference." "The South is both American and something different," writes another historian, "at times a mirror or magnifier of national traits and at other times a counterculture." This was most acutely true in the decades before the Civil War.

Culturally, the South developed a proclivity to tell its own story. Its ruralness and its sense of tradition may have given southerners a special habit of telling tales. "Southerners . . . love a good tale," says Mississippi writer Eudora Welty. "They are born reciters, great memory retainers, diary keepers, letter exchangers, and letter savers, history tracers, and debaters, and—outstaying all the rest—great talkers." The South's tragic and distinct story begins in the Old South. The story was distinctive and national all at once.

Free Southerners: Farmers, Free Blacks, and Planters

a large majority of white southern families (three-quarters in 1860) owned no slaves. Some lived in towns and ran stores or businesses, but most were yeoman farmers who owned their own land and grew their own food. The social distance between different groups of whites was great. Still greater was the distance between whites and blacks.

These farmers were individualistic and hard working. Unlike their northern counterparts, their lives were not being transformed by improvements in transportation. They could be independent thinkers as well, but their status as a numerical majority did not mean that they set the political or economic direction of the slave society. Self-reliant and often isolated, always absorbed in the work of their farms, they operated both apart from and within the slave-based staple-crop economy.

YEOMAN FARMERS

Yeomen pioneered the southern wilderness, moving into undeveloped regions—or Indian land after removal—and building log cabins. After the War of 1812 they moved in successive waves down the southern Appalachians into the Gulf lands. In large sections of the South, especially inland from the coast and away from large rivers, small, self-sufficient farms were the norm. Lured by stories of good land, many men uprooted their wives and children repeatedly. So many shared the excitement over new lands that one North Carolinian wrote in alarm, "The Alabama Fever rages here with great violence. . . . I am apprehensive if it continues to spread as it has done, it will almost depopulate the country."

On the southern frontier men worked hard to clear fields and establish farms while their wives labored in the household economy and patiently re-created the social ties—to relatives, neighbors, fellow churchgoers—that enriched everyone's experience. Women seldom shared the men's excitement about moving. They dreaded the isolation and loneliness of the frontier. "We have been [moving] all our lives," lamented one woman. "As soon as ever we git comfortably settled, it is time to be off to something new."

Some yeomen acquired large tracts of level land, purchased slaves, and became planters. They forged part of the new wealth of the boom states of Mississippi and Louisiana, the region to which the southern political power base shifted by the 1840s and 1850s. Others clung to familiar mountainous areas or kept moving as independent farmers because, as one frontiersman put it, he disliked "seeing the nose of my neighbor sticking out between the trees." As one historian has put it, while they owned no slaves, yeomen were jealous of their independence, and "the household grounded their own claims to masterhood."

The yeomen enjoyed a folk culture based on family, church, and local region. Their speech patterns and inflections recalled their Scots-Irish and Irish backgrounds. They flocked to religious revivals called camp meetings, and in between they got together for house-raisings, logrollings, quilting bees, corn-shuckings, and hunting for both food and sport. Such occasions combined work with fun and fellowship, offering food in abundance, and usually liquor as well.

YEOMAN FOLK CULTURE

A demanding round of work and family responsibilities shaped women's lives in the home. They worked in the fields to an extent that astonished travelers such as Frederick Law Olmsted or Frances Trollope, who believed yeomen had rendered their wives "slaves of the soil." Throughout the year the care and preparation of food consumed much of women's time. Household tasks continued during frequent pregnancies and childcare. Primary nursing and medical care also fell to mothers, who often relied on folk wisdom. Women too wanted to be masters of their households, although it came at the price of their health.

Among the men there were many who aspired to wealth, eager to join the scramble for slaves and cotton profits. North Carolinian John F. Flintoff kept a diary of his struggle for success. At age eighteen in 1841, Flintoff went to Mississippi to seek his fortune. Like other aspiring yeomen, he worked as an overseer of slaves but often found it impossible to please his employers. At one point he gave up and returned to North Carolina, where he married and lived for a while in his parents' house. But Flintoff was "impatient to get along in the world," so he tried Louisiana next and then Mississippi again.

YEOMAN LIVELIHOODS

Flintoff's health suffered in the Gulf region and, routinely, "first rate employment" alternated with "very low wages." Moreover, as a young man working on isolated plantations, Flintoff often felt lonely. Even a revival

■ Eastman Johnson's *Fiddling His Way* (1866) depicts rural life by representing the visit of an itinerant black musician to a farm family. Expressions and gestures suggest remarkable ease between the races at the yeoman level of southern society.   (The Chrysler Museum of Art, Norfolk, Virginia. Bequest of Walter P. Chrysler, Jr.)

meeting in 1844 proved "an extremely cold time" with "little warm feeling." His uncle and other employers found fault with his work, and in 1846 Flintoff concluded in despair that "managing negroes and large farms is soul destroying."

But a desire to succeed at this very economic proposition kept him going. At twenty-six, even before he owned any land, Flintoff bought his first slave, "a negro boy 7 years old." Soon he had purchased two more children, the cheapest slaves available. Conscious of his status as a slaveowner, Flintoff resented the low wages he was paid. In 1853, with nine young slaves and a growing family, Flintoff faced "the most unhappy time of my life." Fired by his uncle, he returned to North Carolina, sold some of his slaves, and purchased 124 acres with help from his in-laws. By 1860 he owned three horses, twenty-six hogs, ten head of cattle, and several slaves and was paying off his debts. As the Civil War approached, he looked forward to freeing his wife from labor, and possibly sending his sons to college. Although Flintoff demonstrated that a farmer could move in and out of the

slaveholding class, he never achieved the cotton planter status he desired.

Probably more typical of the southern yeoman was Ferdinand L. Steel, who as a young man moved from North Carolina to Tennessee to work as a river boatman but eventually took up farming in Mississippi. Steel rose every day at five and worked until sundown. He and his family raised staple crops while cotton was his cash product: he sold five or six bales (about two thousand pounds) a year to obtain money for sugar, coffee, salt, calico, gunpowder, and a few other store-bought goods.

Thus Steel entered the market economy as a small farmer, but with mixed results. He picked his own cotton and complained that cotton cultivation was brutal work and not profitable. He felt like a serf in cotton's kingdom. When cotton prices fell, a small grower like Steel could be driven into debt and lose his farm.

Steel's life in Mississippi in the 1840s retained much of the flavor of the frontier. He made all the family's shoes; his wife and sister sewed dresses, shirts, and "pantaloons."

The Steel women also rendered their own soap and spun and wove cotton into cloth; the men hunted game. Steel doctored his illnesses with boneset tea and other herbs. As the nation fell deeper into crisis over the future of free or slave labor, this independent southern farmer never came close to owning a slave.

The focus of Steel's life was family and religion. Family members prayed together daily, and he studied Scripture for an hour after lunch. "My Faith increases, & I enjoy much of that peace which the world cannot give," he wrote in 1841. Seeking to prepare himself for Judgment Day, Steel borrowed histories, Latin and Greek grammars, and religious books from his church. Eventually he became a traveling Methodist minister. "My life is one of toil," he reflected, "but blessed be God that it is as well with me as it is."

Toil with even less security was the lot of two other groups of free southerners: landless whites and free

■ This formal photograph, ca. 1855, of a black woman attending to two mulatto children indicates how common mixed-race children were in domestic relations in the Old South.   (Photograph by James P. Bau; collection of Matthew Isenburg)

LANDLESS
WHITES

blacks. A sizable minority of white southern workers—from 25 to 40 percent, depending on the state—were unskilled laborers who owned no land and worked for others in the countryside and towns. Their property consisted of a few household items and some animals—usually pigs—that could feed themselves on the open range. The landless included some immigrants, especially Irish, who did heavy and dangerous work such as building railroads and digging ditches.

In the countryside, white farm laborers struggled to purchase land in the face of low wages or, if they rented, unpredictable market prices for their crops. By scrimping and saving and finding odd jobs, some managed to climb into the ranks of yeomen. When James and Nancy Bennitt of North Carolina succeeded in their ten-year struggle to buy land, they decided to avoid the unstable market in cotton; thereafter they raised extra corn and wheat as sources of cash. People like the Bennitts were both participants in and victims of an economy dominated by cotton producers who relied on slave labor.

Herdsmen who viewed pigs and livestock as a major economic asset always had a desperate struggle to succeed. By 1860, as the South anticipated war to preserve its society, between 300,000 and 400,000 white people in the four states of Virginia, North and South Carolina, and Georgia lived in genuine poverty, approximately one-fifth of the total white population. Their lives were harsh, to say the least. An early antebellum traveler in central South Carolina described the white folk he encountered in the countryside: "The people looked yellow, poor, and sickly. Some of them lived the most miserably I ever saw any poor people live." Land and slaves determined wealth in the Old South, and many whites possessed neither.

For the nearly quarter-million free blacks in the South in 1860, conditions were generally worse than the

FREE BLACKS

yeoman's and often little better than the slave's. The free blacks of the Upper South were usually descendants of men and women manumitted by their owners in the 1780s and 1790s. A remarkable number of slaveholders in Virginia and the Chesapeake region had freed their slaves because of religious principles and revolutionary ideals in the wake of American independence (see Chapter 7). Many free blacks also became free as runaways, especially by the 1830s, disappearing into the southern population; a few made their way northward.

White southerners were increasingly desperate to restrict this growing free black presence in their midst. "It seems the number of free Negroes," complained a Virginia slaveholder, "always exceeds the number of Negroes freed." Some free blacks worked in towns or cities, but most lived in rural areas and struggled to survive. They usually did not own land and had to labor in someone else's fields, often beside slaves. By law free blacks could not own a gun, buy liquor, violate curfew, assemble except in church, testify in court, or (throughout the South after 1835) vote. Despite these obstacles, a minority bought land, and others found jobs as skilled craftsmen.

A few free blacks prospered and bought slaves, most of them purchasing their own wives and children (whom they could not free, since laws required newly emancipated blacks to leave their states). In 1830 there were 3,775 free black slaveholders in the South; 80 percent lived in the four states of Louisiana, South Carolina, Virginia, and Maryland, and approximately one-half of the total lived in the two cities of New Orleans and Charleston. Hundreds of petitions survive in which black slaveholders asked to be exempted from antimanumission laws passed in most southern states. At the same time, a few mulattos in New Orleans were active slave traders in its booming market.

In the cotton and Gulf regions, a large proportion of free blacks were mulattos, the privileged offspring of wealthy white planters. Not all planters freed their mixed-race offspring, but those who did often recognized a moral obligation and gave their children a good education and financial backing. In a few cities like New Orleans, Charleston, and Mobile, extensive interracial sex, as well as migrations from the Caribbean, had produced a mulatto population that was recognized as a distinct class.

FREE BLACK COMMUNITIES

In many southern cities by the 1840s, free black communities formed, especially around an expanding number of churches. By the late 1850s, Baltimore had fifteen churches, Louisville nine, and Nashville and St. Louis four each, and most of them were African Methodist Episcopal. Class and race distinctions were important to southern free blacks, but outside a few cities, which developed fraternal orders of skilled craftsmen and fellowships of light-skinned people, most mulattos experienced hardship. In the United States, "one drop" of black "blood" (any observable racial mixture to white people's eyes) made them black, and potentially enslaveable.

At the top of the southern social pyramid were slaveholding planters. As a group they lived well, but most lived in comfortable farmhouses, not on the opulent scale that legend suggests. The grand plantation mansions, with fabulous gardens and long rows of out-

PLANTERS

lying slave quarters, are an enduring symbol of the Old South. But a few statistics tell the fuller story: in 1850, 50 percent of southern slaveholders had fewer than five slaves; 72 percent had fewer than ten; 88 percent had fewer than twenty. Thus the average slaveholder was not a wealthy aristocrat but an aspiring farmer, usually a person of humble origins.

Consider the Louisiana cotton planter Bennet Barrow, a newly rich planter of the 1840s who was preoccupied with moneymaking. He worried constantly over his cotton crop, filling his diary with weather reports and gloomy predictions of his yields. Yet Barrow also strove to appear above such worries. He hunted frequently and had a passion for racing horses and raising hounds. He could report the loss of a slave without feeling, but emotion broke through his laconic manner when illness afflicted his sporting animals. "Never was a person more unlucky than I am," he mourned. "My favorite pup never lives." His strongest feelings surfaced when his horse Jos Bell—equal to "the best Horse in the South"—"broke down running a mile . . . ruined for Ever." The same day the distraught Barrow gave his human property a "general Whipping." In 1841 diary entries he worried about a rumored slave insurrection. He gave a "severe whipping" to several of his slaves when they disobediently killed a hog. And when a slave named Ginney Jerry "sherked" his cotton-picking duties and was rumored "about to run off," Barrow whipped him one day, and the next, recorded matter-of-factly: "took my gun found him in the Bayou behind the Quarter, shot him in his thigh—etc. raining all around."

The richest planters used their wealth to model genteel sophistication. Extended visits, parties, and balls to which women wore the latest fashions provided opportunities for friendship, courtship, and display. Such parties were held during the Christmas holidays, but also on such occasions a molasses stewing, a Bachelor's Ball, a horserace, or the crowning of the May Queen. These entertainments were especially important as diversions for plantation women, and at the same time they sustained a rigidly gendered society. Young women relished social events to break the monotony of their domestic lives. In 1826 a Virginia girl was ecstatic about the "week . . . I was in Town." "There were five beaux and as many belles in the house constantly," she declared, and all she and her companions did was "eat, visit, romp, and sleep."

Most of the planters in the cotton-boom states of Alabama and Mississippi were newly rich by the 1840s. As one historian put it, "a number of men mounted from log cabin to plantation mansion on a stairway of cotton

"King Cotton" in the World Economy

The economy of the Old South was deeply intertwined with international trade. Cash crops such as cotton were export, and the fate of this slave society depended on world trade, especially with Europe. Cotton planters and slaveholders constantly had their eyes on export prices.

The American South so dominated the world's supply of cotton that the size of the U.S. crop normally determined the price in an international market where demand continued to skyrocket. This circumstance gave southern planters enormous confidence that the cotton boom was permanent, and that the industrializing nations of England and France in particular would always bow to "King Cotton."

American cotton doubled in yield each decade after 1800 and provided three-fourths of the world's supply by the 1840s. Southern staple crops were fully three-fifths of all American exports by 1850, and one of every seven workers in England depended on American cotton for a job. Indeed, cotton production made slaves the single most valuable financial asset in the United States—greater in dollar value than all of America's banks, railroads, and manufacturing combined.

The Old South never developed its own banking and shipping capacity to any degree. If it had, its effort to be an international cartel might have succeeded longer. Most southern bank deposits were in the North, and southern cotton planters became ever more dependent on New York for shipping. As early as 1822 one-sixth of all southern cotton cleared for Liverpool or Le Havre from the port of New York and constituted two-fifths of all that city's exports.

A collapse of cotton prices in the Panic of 1837 prompted some southerners to try to establish more direct trade relations between themselves and Europe. In a series of economic conventions held from 1837 to 1839, delegates debated the nature of foreign trade, dependence on northern importers and financiers, and other alleged threats to their commercial independence and security. But nothing, save rhetoric, came of these conventions; it was the last time southern planters would organize to break from their Yankee middlemen and shippers.

"Cotton is King," the *Southern Cultivator* declared in 1859, "and wields an astonishing influence over the world's commerce." Until 1840 the cotton trade furnished much of the export capital to finance northern economic growth. After that date, however, the northern economy expanded without dependence on cotton profits. Nevertheless, southern planters and politicians continued to boast of King Cotton's supremacy. "Our cotton is the most wonderful talisman in the world," announced a planter in 1853. "By its power we are transmuting whatever we choose into whatever we want." "No power on earth dares . . . to make war on cotton," James Hammond lectured the U.S. Senate in 1858; "Cotton is king." Although the South produced 4.5 million bales in 1861, its greatest cotton crop ever, this link to the world was about to collapse in a civil war. Thereafter cotton was more a shackle to the South than a king.

■ Cotton traded to England would be returned to the United States in fabric collections called sample books, such as this Norwich Textile Sample Book. Orders were placed and then shipped to Americans. (Courtesy, The Henry Francis du Pont Winterthur Library: Joseph Downs Collection of Manuscripts & Printed Ephemera)

bales, accumulating slaves as they climbed." And many did not live like rich men. They put their new wealth into cotton acreage and slaves even as they sought refinement and high social status.

William Faulkner immortalized the new wealthy planter in a fictional character, Thomas Sutpen, in his novel *Absalom, Absalom!* (1936). Sutpen arrives in a Mississippi county in the 1830s, buys a huge plantation he calls Sutpen's Hundred, and with his troop of slaves converts it into a wealthy enterprise. Sutpen marries a local woman, and although he is always viewed as a mysterious outsider by many earlier residents of the county, he becomes a pillar of the slaveholding class, eventually an officer in the Confederate Army. But Sutpen is a self-made man of indomitable will and slave-based wealth. Although his ambition is ultimately his undoing, one of the earliest lessons he had learned about success in the South was that "you got to have land and niggers and a fine house. . . ."

The cotton boom in the Mississippi valley created one-generation aristocrats. A nonfictional case in point is Greenwood Leflore, a Chocktaw chieftain who owned a plantation in Mississippi with four hundred slaves. After selling his cotton on the world market, he spent $10,000 in France to furnish one room of his mansion with hand-woven carpets, furniture upholstered in gold leaf, tables and cabinets ornamented with tortoise-shell inlay, a variety of mirrors and paintings, and a clock and candelabra in brass and ebony.

Slaveholding men dominated society and, especially among the wealthiest and oldest families, justified their dominance over white women and black slaves through a paternalistic ideology.

SOUTHERN PATERNALISM Instead of stressing the profitable aspects of commercial agriculture, they focused on their obligations, viewing themselves as custodians of the welfare of society in general, and of the black families they owned in particular. The paternalistic planter saw himself not as an oppressor but as the benevolent guardian of an inferior race. Even yeomen who moved in and out of the slaveowning class shared this attitude of racial paternalism.

Paul Carrington Cameron, who was North Carolina's largest slaveholder, exemplifies this mentality. After a period of sickness among his one thousand North Carolina slaves (he had hundreds more in Alabama and Mississippi), Cameron wrote, "I fear the Negroes have suffered much from the want of proper attention and kindness under this late distemper . . . no love of lucre shall ever induce me to be cruel. . . ." On another occasion he described to his sister the sense of responsibility he felt:

"Do you remember a cold & frosty morning, during [our mother's] illness, when she said to me 'Paul my son the people ought to be shod' this is ever in my ears, whenever I see any ones shoes in bad order; and in my ears it will be, so long as I am master."

It was comforting to rich planters to see themselves in this way, and slaves—accommodating to the realities of power—encouraged their masters to think their benevolence was appreciated. Paternalism also served as a defense against abolitionist criticism. Still, paternalism was often a matter of style, covering harsher assumptions. As talk of paternalistic duties increased, theories about the complete and permanent inferiority of blacks multiplied. In reality, paternalism grew as a give-and-take relationship between masters and slaves, each extracting from the other what they desired—owners took labor from the bondsmen, while slaves obligated masters to provide them a measure of autonomy and living space. But it also evolved as a theory of black slavery and white dominance. As one historian has argued, paternalism "grew out of the necessity to discipline and morally justify a system of exploitation, . . . a fragile bridge across the intolerable contradictions inherent" in a slave society dependent on "the willing reproduction and productivity of its victims."

Even Paul Cameron's benevolence vanished with changed circumstances. After the Civil War, he bristled at African Americans' efforts to be free and made sweeping economic decisions without regard to their welfare. Writing on Christmas Day 1865, Cameron showed little Christian charity (but a healthy profit motive) when he declared, "I am convinced that the people who gets rid of the free negro first will be the first to advance in improved agriculture. Have made no effort to retain any of mine [and] will not attempt a crop beyond the capacity of 30 hands." With that he turned off his land nearly a thousand black people, rented his fields to several white farmers, and invested in industry.

Relations between men and women in the planter class were similarly paternalistic. The upper-class southern woman was raised and educated to be a wife, mother, and subordinate companion to men. South Carolina's Mary Boykin Chesnut wrote of her husband, "He is master of the house. To hear is to obey. . . . All the comfort of my life depends upon his being in a good humor." In a social system based on the coercion of an entire race, women were not allowed to challenge society's rules on sexual or racial relations.

Planters' daughters usually attended one of the South's rapidly multiplying boarding schools. There they formed friendships with other girls and received an education.

Typically the young woman could entertain suitors whom her parents approved. But very soon she had to choose a husband and commit herself for life to a man whom she generally had known for only a brief time. Young women were often alienated and emotionally unfulfilled. They had to follow the wishes of their families, especially fathers. "It was for me best that I yielded to the wishes of papa," wrote a young North Carolinian in 1823. "I wonder when my best will cease to be painful and when I shall begin to enjoy life instead of enduring it."

Upon marriage, a planter-class woman ceded to her husband most of her legal rights, becoming part of his family. Most of the year she was isolated on a large plantation, where she had to oversee the cooking and preserving of food, manage the house, supervise care of the children, and attend sick slaves. All these realities were more rigid and confining on the frontier, where isolation was even greater. Women sought refuge in their extended families and associations with other women. In 1821 a Georgia woman wrote to her brother of the distress of a cousin's wife: "They are living . . . in the frontiers of the state and [a] perfectly uncivilized place. Cousin W. gets a good practice [the husband] but she is almost crazy to get to Alabama where one of her sisters is living." Men on plantations could occasionally escape into the public realm—to town, business, or politics. Women could retreat from rural plantation culture only into kinship.

It is not surprising that a perceptive young white woman sometimes approached marriage with anxiety.

MARRIAGE AND FAMILY AMONG PLANTER CLASS

Women could hardly help viewing their wedding day, as one put it in 1832, as "the day to fix my fate." Lucy Breckinridge, a wealthy Virginia girl of twenty, lamented the autonomy she surrendered at the altar. In her diary she recorded this unvarnished observation on marriage: "If [husbands] care for their wives at all it is only as a sort of servant, a being made to attend to their comforts and to keep the children out of the way. . . . A woman's life after she is married, unless there is an immense amount of love, is nothing but suffering and hard work."

Lucy loved young children but knew that childbearing often involved grief, poor health, and death. In 1840 the birth rate for white southern women in their childbearing years was almost 30 percent higher than the national average. The average southern white woman could expect to bear eight children in 1800; by 1860 the figure had decreased to only six, with one or more miscarriages likely. For those women who wanted to plan their fami-

■ Portrait of a planter's family and slave, New Market, Virginia, photographer unidentified, c. 1859-1864. The structure of life on a small plantation is vividly indicated here: the young black woman holding the baby, the white mistress with shawl and fan, and the planter as patriarch.   (Collection of William A. Turner)

lies, methods of contraception and medical care were uncertain. Complications of childbirth were a major cause of death, occurring twice as often in the hot, humid South as in the Northeast.

Sexual relations between planters and slaves were another source of problems that white women had to endure but were not supposed to notice. "Violations of the moral law . . . made mulattos as common as blackberries," protested a woman in Georgia, but wives had to play "the ostrich game." "A magnate who runs a hideous black harem," wrote Mrs. Chesnut, ". . . poses as the model of all human virtues to these poor women whom God and the laws have given him."

Southern men tolerated little discussion by women of the slavery issue. In the 1840s and 1850s, as abolitionist attacks on slavery increased, southern men published a barrage of articles stressing that women should restrict their concerns to the home. The *Southern Quarterly Review* declared, "The proper place for a woman is at home. One of her highest privileges, to be politically merged in the existence of her husband."

But some southern women were beginning to seek a larger role. A study of women in Petersburg, Virginia, a large tobacco-manufacturing town, revealed behavior that valued financial autonomy. Over several decades before 1860, the proportion of women who never married, or did not remarry after the death of a spouse, grew to exceed 33 percent. Likewise the number of women who worked for wages, controlled their own property, and ran millinery or dressmaking businesses increased. In managing property, these and other women benefited from legal changes such as the Mississippi Married Women's Property Act of 1839; to protect families from the husband's indebtedness during business panics and recessions, such reforms gave married women some property rights.

Slave Life and Labor

For African Americans, slavery was a burden that destroyed some people and forced others to develop modes of survival. Slaves knew a life of poverty, coercion, toil, and resentment. They provided the physical strength, and much of the know-how, to build an agricultural empire. But their daily lives embodied the nation's most basic contradiction: in the world's model republic, they were on the wrong side of a brutally unequal power relationship.

Southern slaves enjoyed few material comforts beyond the bare necessities. Although they generally had

SLAVES' EVERYDAY CONDITIONS

enough to eat, their diet was plain and monotonous, lacking in nutrition. Clothing too was plain, coarse, and inexpensive. Few slaves received more than one or two changes of clothing for hot and cold seasons and one blanket each winter. Children of both sexes ran naked in hot weather and wore long cotton shirts in winter. Many slaves had to go without shoes until December, even as far north as Virginia. The bare feet of slaves were often symbolic of their status, and one reason why, after freedom, many black parents were so concerned to provide their children with shoes.

Some of the richer plantations provided substantial houses, but the average slave lived in crude accommodations, usually one-room cabins. The gravest drawback of slave cabins was not lack of comfort but their unhealthfulness. Each dwelling housed one or two entire families. Crowding and lack of sanitation fostered the spread of infection and contagious diseases such as typhoid fever, malaria, and dysentery.

Hard work was the central fact of slaves' existence. The long hours and large work gangs that characterized

SLAVE WORK ROUTINES

Gulf Coast cotton districts operated almost like factories in the field. Overseers rang the morning bell before dawn, and black people of varying ages, tools in hand, walked toward fields. Slaves who cultivated tobacco in the Upper South worked long hours picking the sticky, sometimes noxious, leaves under harsh discipline. And, as one woman recalled when interviewed in the 1930s, "it was way after sundown fore they could stop that field work. Then they had to hustle to finish their night work [such as watering livestock or cleaning cotton] in time for supper, or go to bed without it."

Working "from sun to sun" became a norm in much of the South. As one planter put it, slaves were the best labor because "you could command them and make them do what was right." Profit took precedence over paternalism. Slave women did heavy fieldwork, often as much as the men and even during pregnancy. Old people were kept busy caring for young children, doing light chores, or carding, ginning, and spinning cotton. The black abolitionist orator Frances Ellen Watkins captured this grinding economic reality of slavery in an 1857 speech, charging that slaveholders had "found out a fearful alchemy by which . . . blood can be transformed into gold. Instead of listening to the cry of agony, they listen to the ring of dollars and stoop down to pick up the coin."

Slave children were the future of the system and were widely valued as potential labor. "A child raised every

■ George Fuller, an itinerant painter from Massachusetts, worked from 1856 to 1858 in Alabama, where he made this sketch in ink and pencil of a mistress joining her slave at work on washday. (Pocumtuck Valley Memorial Association)

two years," wrote Thomas Jefferson, "is of more profit than the crop of the best laboring man." And in 1858, an unidentified slaveowner writing in an agricultural magazine calculated that a slave girl he purchased in 1827 for $400 had borne three sons now worth $3,000 as his working field hands. Slave children gathered kindling, carried water to the fields, swept the yard, lifted cut sugar-cane stalks into carts, stacked wheat, chased birds away from sprouting rice plants, and labored at many levels of cotton and tobacco production. "Work," wrote one historian, "can be rightly called the thief who stole the childhood of youthful bond servants."

Incentives had to be part of the labor regime and the master-slave relationship as well. Planters in the South Carolina and Georgia low country used a task system whereby slaves were assigned measured amounts of work to be performed in a given amount of time. So much cotton on a daily basis was to be picked from a designated field, so many rows hoed or plowed in a particular slave's specified section. When the task system worked best, slaves and masters alike embraced it, fostering a degree of reciprocal trust.

By the 1830s slaveowners found that labor could be regulated and motivated by the clock. When their task and "clock time" was up, slaves' time was their own, for working in garden plots, tending to hogs, or even hiring out their own extra labor. The system's incentives afforded many slave families life-sustaining material and psychological benefits. From this experience and personal space, many slaves developed their own sense of property ownership.

Slaves could not demand much autonomy, of course, because the owner enjoyed a monopoly on force and violence. Whites throughout the South believed that slaves "can't be governed except with the whip." One South Carolinian frankly explained to a northern journalist that he whipped his slaves regularly, "say once a fortnight; . . . the fear of the lash kept them in good order." Evidence suggests that whippings were less frequent on small farms than on large plantations. But beatings symbolized authority to the master and tyranny to the slaves, who made them a benchmark for evaluating a master. In the words of former slaves, a good owner was one who did not "whip too much," whereas a bad owner "whipped till he's bloodied you and blistered you."

VIOLENCE AGAINST SLAVES

As these reports suggest, terrible abuses could and did occur. The master wielded virtually absolute authority on his plantation, and courts did not recognize the word of chattel. Slaveholders rarely had to answer to the law or to the state. Pregnant women were whipped, and there were burnings, mutilations, tortures, and murders. Yet physical cruelty may have been less prevalent in the United States than in other slaveholding parts of the New World. Especially in some of the sugar islands of the Caribbean, treatment was so poor and death rates were so high that the heavily male slave population shrank in size. In the United States, by contrast, the slave population experienced a steady natural increase as births exceeded deaths and each generation grew larger. Indeed, the North American slave population was the only one in the New World to naturally reproduce itself.

The worst evil of American slavery was not its physical cruelty but the nature of slavery itself: coercion, belonging to another person, virtually no hope for mobility or change. Recalling their time in bondage, some former slaves emphasized the physical abuse, or the "bullwhip days," as one woman described her past. But memories of physical punishment focused on the tyranny of whipping as much as the pain. Delia Garlic made the essential point: "It's bad to belong to folks that own you soul an' body. I could tell you 'bout it all day, but even then you couldn't guess the awfulness of it." Thomas Lewis put it this way: "There was no such thing as being good to slaves. Many people were better than others, but a slave belonged to his master and there was no way to get out of it." To be a slave was to be the object of another person's will and material gain, to be owned, as the saying went, "from the cradle to the grave."

As these comments reveal, the great majority of American slaves retained their mental independence and self-respect despite their bondage. Contrary to popular belief at the time, they were not loyal partners in their own oppression. They had to be subservient and speak honeyed words to their masters, but they talked and behaved quite differently among themselves. The evidence of their resistant attitudes comes from their actions and their own life stories. In *Narrative of the Life of Frederick Douglass, an American Slave, Written by Himself* (1845), Douglass wrote that most slaves, when asked about "their condition and the character of their masters, almost universally say they are contented, and that their masters are kind." Slaves did this, said Douglass, because they were governed by the maxim that "a still tongue makes a wise head," especially in the presence of unfamiliar people. Because they were "part of the human family," slaves often quarreled over who had the best master. But at the end of the day, Douglass remarked, when one had a bad master, he sought a better master; and when he had a better one, he wanted to "be his own master."

Some former slaves remembered warm feelings between masters and slaves, but the prevailing attitudes were distrust and antagonism. Slaves saw through acts of kindness. One woman said her mistress was "a mighty good somebody to belong to" but only " 'cause she was raisin' us to work for her." A man recalled that his owners took good care of their slaves, "and Grandma Maria say, 'Why shouldn't they—it was their money.' " Slaves also resented being used as beasts of burden. One man observed that his master "fed us reg'lar on good, 'stantial food, just like you'd tend to your horse, if you had a real good one."

Slaves were alert to the thousand daily signs of their degraded status. One man recalled the general rule that slaves ate cornbread and owners ate biscuits. If blacks did get biscuits, "the flour that we made the biscuits out of was the third-grade sorts." A former slave recalled, "Us catch lots of 'possums," but "the white folks at 'em." If the owner took his slaves' garden produce to town and sold it for them, the slaves often suspected him of pocketing part of the profits.

Suspicion often grew into hatred. When a yellow fever epidemic struck in 1852, many slaves saw it as God's retribution. An elderly ex-slave named Minnie Fulkes cherished the conviction that God was going to punish white people for their cruelty to blacks. She described the whippings that her mother had to endure, and then she exclaimed, "Lord, Lord, I hate white people and the flood waters goin' to drown some more."

On the plantation, of course, slaves had to keep such thoughts to themselves. Often they expressed one feeling to whites, another within their own households. In their daily lives slaves created many ways to survive and to sustain their humanity in this world of repression.

Slave Culture

a people is always "more than the sum of its brutalization," wrote the African American novelist Ralph Ellison in 1967. What people create in the face of hard luck and oppression is what provides hope. The resource that enabled slaves to maintain such defiance was their culture: a body of beliefs, values, and practices born of their past and maintained in the present. As best they could, they built a community knitted together by stories, music, a religious world-view, leadership, the smells of their cooking, the sounds of their own voices, and the tapping of their feet. "The values expressed in folklore," wrote the African American poet Sterling Brown, provided a "wellspring to which slaves . . . could return in times of doubt to be refreshed." That they endured and found loyalty and strength among themselves is a tribute to their courage and triumph of the human spirit.

Slave culture changed significantly after 1800, as fewer and fewer slaves were African-born. For a few

AFRICAN CULTURAL SURVIVAL

years South Carolina reopened the international slave trade, but after 1808 Congress banned further importations. By the 1830s, the vast majority of slaves in the South were native-born Americans. Many blacks, in fact, can trace their American ancestry back further than most white Americans.

Despite lack of firsthand memory, African influences remained strong, especially in appearance and forms of expression. Some slave men plaited their hair into rows and fancy designs; slave women often wore their hair "in string"—tied in small bunches secured by a string or piece of cloth. A few men and many women wrapped their heads in kerchiefs of the styles and colors of West Africa. Some could remember the names of African ancestors passed on to them by family lore. In burial practices, slaves used jars and other glass objects to decorate graves, following similar African traditions.

Music, religion, and folktales were parts of daily life for most slaves. Borrowing partly from their African background, as well as forging new American folkways, they developed what scholars have called a "sacred world-view," which affected all aspects of work, leisure, and self-understanding. Slaves made musical instruments with carved motifs that resembled African stringed instruments. Their drumming and dancing followed African patterns that made whites marvel. One visitor to Georgia in the 1860s described a ritual dance of African origin: "A ring of singers is formed. . . . They then utter a kind of melodious chant, which gradually increases in strength, and in noise, until it fairly shakes the house, and it can be heard for a long distance." This observer of the "ring shout" also noted the agility of the dancers and the African call-and-response pattern in their chanting.

Many slaves continued to believe in spirit possession. Whites, too, believed in ghosts and charms, but the slaves' belief resembled the African concept of the living dead—the idea that deceased relatives visit the earth for many years until the process of dying is complete. Slaves also practiced conjuration and quasi-magical root medicine. By the 1850s the most notable conjurers and root doctors were reputed to live in South Carolina, Georgia, Louisiana, and other isolated coastal areas with high slave populations. But even in Maryland, a young Frederick Douglass carried a special root that had to be positioned "always on the right side," given him by an "old advisor" who lived alone in the woods.

These cultural survivals provided slaves with a sense of their separate past. Such practices and beliefs were not static "Africanisms" or mere "retentions." They were cultural adaptations, living traditions re-formed in the Americas in response to new experience. African American slaves in the Old South were a people forged by two centuries of cultural mixture in the Atlantic world; and the South itself was a melding of many African and European cultural forces.

As they became African Americans, slaves also developed a sense of racial identity. In the colonial period, Africans had arrived in America from many different states and kingdoms, represented in distinctive languages, body markings, and traditions. Planters had used ethnic differences to create occupational hierarchies. By the early antebellum period, however, old ethnic identities gave way as American slaves increasingly saw themselves as a single group unified by race. Africans had arrived in the New World with virtually no concept of "race"; by the antebellum era, their descendants had learned through bitter experience that race was now the defining feature of their lives. They were a transplanted and transformed people.

As African culture gave way to a maturing African American culture, more and more slaves adopted

SLAVES' RELIGION AND MUSIC

Christianity. But they fashioned Christianity into an instrument of support and resistance. Theirs was a religion of justice and deliverance, quite unlike their masters' religious propaganda directed at them as a means of control. "You ought to have heard that preachin'," said one man. "'Obey your master and mistress, don't steal chickens and eggs and meat,' but nary a word about havin' a soul to save." Slaves believed that Jesus cared about their souls and their plight. In their interpretations of biblical stories, as one historian has said, they were "literally willing themselves reborn." They rejected the idea that in heaven whites would have "the colored folks . . . there to wait on 'em." Instead, slaveholders would be "broilin' in hell for their sin" when God's justice came.

For slaves, Christianity was a religion of personal and group salvation. Devout men and women worshiped every day, "in the field or by the side of the road," or in special "prayer grounds" that afforded privacy. Some slaves held fervent secret prayer meetings that lasted far into the night. Many slaves nurtured an unshakable belief that God would enter history and end their bondage.

This faith—and the joy and emotional release that accompanied worship—sustained them.

Slaves also adapted Christianity to African practices. In West African belief, devotees are possessed by a god so thoroughly that the god's own personality replaces the human personality. In the late antebellum era, Christian slaves experienced possession by the Protestant "Holy Spirit." The combination of shouting, singing, and dancing that seemed to overtake black worshipers formed the heart of their religious faith. "The old meeting house caught fire," recalled an ex-slave preacher. "The spirit was there. . . . God saw our need and came to us. I used to wonder what made people shout but now I don't. There is a joy on the inside and it wells up so strong that we can't keep still. It is fire in the bones. Any time that fire touches a man, he will jump." Out in brush arbors or in meetinghouses, slaves took in the presence of God and sang away their woes. Some travelers observed "bands" of "Fist and Heel Worshippers." "He who could sing loudest and longest led the 'Band,'" said a suspicious black bishop from the North who opposed emotional religion, "a handkerchief in hand with which he kept time, while his feet resounded on the floor like the drumsticks of a bass drum." Many post-slavery black choirs could not perform properly without a good wooden floor to use as their "drum."

Rhythm and physical movement were crucial to slaves' religious experience. In their own preachers' chanted sermons, which reached out to gather the sinner into a narrative of meanings and cadences along the way to conversion, an American tradition was born. The chanted sermon was both a message from Scripture and a patterned form that required audience response punctuated by "yes sirs!" and "amens!" But it was in song that the slaves left their most sublime gift to American culture.

Through the spirituals, slaves tried to impose order on the chaos of their lives. Many themes run through the lyrics of slave songs. Often referred to later as the "sorrow songs," they also anticipate imminent rebirth. Sadness could give way immediately to joy: "Did you ever stan' on a mountain, wash yo hands in a cloud?" Rebirth was at the heart as well of the famous hymn "Oh, Freedom": "Oh, Oh, Freedom / Oh, Oh, Freedom over me— / But before I'll be a slave, / I'll be buried in my grave, / And go home to my Lord, / And Be Free!"

This tension and sudden change between sorrow and joy animates many songs: "Sometimes I feel like a motherless chile . . . / Sometimes I feel like an eagle in the air, / Spread my wings and fly, fly, fly!" Many songs also express a sense of intimacy and closeness with God. Some songs display an unmistakable rebelliousness, such as the enduring "He said, and if I had my way / If I had my

■ Drawing by Lewis Miller of a "Lynchburg Negro Dance," Lynchburg, Virginia, August 18, 1853. This work of art shows the slaves' use of elaborate costumes, string instruments, and the bones. (Abby Aldrich Rockefeller Folk Art Collection, Colonial Williamsburg Foundation)

way, if I had my way, / I'd tear this building down!" And some spirituals reached for a collective sense of hope in the black community as a whole:

> O, gracious Lord! When shall it be,
> That we poor souls shall all be free;
> Lord, break them slavery powers—
> Will you go along with me?
> Lord break them slavery powers,
> Go sound the jubilee!

In many ways, American slaves converted the Christian God to themselves. They sought an alternative world to live in—a home other than the one fate had given them on earth. In a thousand variations on the 'Brer Rabbit folktales—in which the weak survive by wit, and power is reversed—and in the countless refrains of their songs, they fashioned survival and resistance out of their own cultural imagination.

American slaves clung tenaciously to the personal relationships that gave meaning to life. Although American law did not recognize slave families, masters permitted them; in fact, slaveowners expected slaves to form families and have children. As a result, even along the rapidly expanding edge of the cotton kingdom, there was a normal ratio of men to women, young to old. Studies have shown that on some of the largest cotton plantations of South Carolina, when masters allowed their slaves increased autonomy working on the task system, the property accumulation thus fostered led to more stable and healthier families.

THE BLACK FAMILY IN SLAVERY

■ This photograph of five generations of a slave family, taken in Beaufort, South Carolina, in 1862, is silent but powerful testimony to the importance that enslaved African Americans placed on their ever-threatened family ties.   (Library of Congress)

Following African kinship traditions, African Americans avoided marriage between cousins (commonplace among aristocratic slaveowners). By naming their children after relatives of past generations, African Americans emphasized their family histories. If they chose to bear the surname of a slaveowner, it was often the name of the owner under whom their family had begun their bondage in America. Kinship networks and broadly extended families are what held life together in many slave communities.

For slave women sexual abuse and rape by white masters were ever-present threats to themselves and their family lives. By 1860 there were 405,751 mulattos in the United States, comprising 12.5 percent of the African American population, and the majority were the offspring of involuntary relationships. White planters were sometimes open with their behavior toward slave women, but not in the way they talked about it. As Mary Chesnut remarked, sex between slaveholding men and their slave women was "the thing we can't name." Buying slaves for sex was all too common at the New Orleans slave market. In what was called the "fancy trade" (a "fancy" was a young attractive slave girl or woman), females were often sold for prices as much as 300 percent higher than the average. At such auctions for young women, slaveholders exhibited some of the ugliest values at the heart of the slave system—patriarchal dominance demonstrated in paying $3,000 to $5,000 for female "companions."

Slave women had to negotiate this confused world of desire, threat, and shame. Harriet Jacobs, who spent much of her youth and early adult years dodging her owner's relentless sexual pursuit, descried this circumstance as "the war of my life." In recollecting her desperate effort to protect her children and help them find a way north to freedom, Jacobs asked a haunting question that many slave women carried with them to their graves: "Why does the slave ever love? Why allow the tendrils of the heart to twine around objects which may at any moment be wrenched away by the hand of violence?"

Separation from those they loved by violence, sexual appropriation, and sale was what slave families feared and hated most. Many struggled for years to keep their children together and, after emancipation, to reestablish contact with loved ones lost by forced migration and sale. Between 1820 and 1860 an estimated 2 million slaves were moved into the region extending from western Georgia to eastern Texas. When the Union Army registered thousands of black marriages

THE DOMESTIC SLAVE TRADE

in Mississippi and Louisiana in 1864 and 1865, fully 25 percent of the men over forty reported that they had been forcibly separated from a previous wife. Thousands of black families were disrupted every year to serve the needs of the expanding cotton economy. The Butler auction of 1859, described in the chapter-opening vignette, was only one gruesome chapter of a very long story.

Many antebellum white southerners made their living from the slave trade. In South Carolina alone by the 1850s, there were over one hundred slave-trading firms selling an annual average of approximately 6,500 slaves to southwestern states. Although southerners often denied it, vast numbers of slaves moved west by outright sale and not by migrating with their owners. A typical trader's advertisement read: "NEGROES WANTED. I am paying the highest cash prices for young and likely NEGROES, those having good front teeth and being otherwise sound."

Slave traders were practical, roving businessmen. They were sometimes considered degraded by white planters, but many slaveowners did business with them. Market forces, as the Butler auction indicates, drove this commerce in humanity. At slave "pens" in cities such as New Orleans, traders promoted "a large and commodious showroom . . . prepared to accommodate over 200 Negroes for sale." Traders did their utmost to make their slaves appear young, healthy, and happy, cutting gray whiskers off men, using "paddles" as discipline so as not to scar their merchandise, and forcing people to dance and sing as buyers arrived for an auction. When transported to the southwestern markets, slaves were often chained together in "coffles," which made journeys of 500 miles or more on foot.

The complacent mixture of racism and business among traders is evident in their own language. "I refused a girl 20 year[s] old at 700 yesterday," one trader wrote to another in 1853. "If you think best to take her at 700 I can still get her. She is very badly whipped but good teeth." Some sales were transacted at owners' requests. "Bought a cook yesterday that was to go out of state," wrote a trader; "she just made the people mad that was all." Some traders demonstrated how deeply slavery and racism were intertwined. "I have bought the boy Isaac for 1100," wrote a trader in 1854 to his partner. "I think him very prime. . . . He is a . . . house servant . . . first rate cook . . . and splendid carriage driver. He is also a fine painter and varnisher and . . . says he can make a fine panl door. . . . Also he performs well on the violin. . . . He is a genius and its strange to say I think he is smarter than I am."

■ A slave coffle on the march toward newly settled states of the Southwest. (Collection of William Loren Katz)

Slave Resistance and Rebellion

Slaves brought to their efforts at resistance the same common sense and determination that characterized their struggle to secure their family lives. The scales weighed heavily against overt revolution, and the slaves knew it. But they seized opportunities to alter their work conditions. They sometimes slacked off when they were not being watched. Thus owners complained that slaves "never would lay out their strength freely." These slave attitudes caused many whites to doubt the success of black free labor after the Civil War.

Daily discontent and desperation were also manifest in sabotage of equipment, in wanton carelessness about work, in theft of food, livestock, or crops, or in getting drunk on stolen liquor. Some slaves who were hired out

STRATEGIES OF RESISTANCE

might show their anger by hoarding their earnings. Or, they might just fall into recalcitrance. "I have a boy in my employ called Jim Archer," complained a Vicksburg, Mississippi, slaveholder in 1843. "Jim does not want to be under anyones control and says . . . he wants to go home this summer." A woman named Ellen, hired as a cook in Tennessee in 1856, quietly put mercury poison into a roasted apple for her unsuspecting mistress. And some slave women resisted as best they could by trying to control their own pregnancy, either by avoiding it or by seeking it as a way to improve their physical conditions.

Many male, and some female, slaves acted out their defiance by violently attacking overseers or even their owners. Southern court records and newspapers are full of accounts of these resistant slaves who gave the lie to the image of the docile bondsmen. The price they paid was high. Such lonely rebels were customarily secured and flogged, sold away, or hanged. One Louisiana planter reported strapping two especially uncooperative slaves to a stake and delivering 15 lashes to one and 175 to the other.

Many individual slaves attempted to run away to the North, and some received assistance from the loose network known as the Underground Railroad (see pages 363–364). But it was more common for slaves to run off temporarily to hide in the woods. Approximately 80 percent of runaways were male; women simply could not flee as readily because of their responsibility for children. Fear, disgruntlement over treatment, or family separation might motivate slaves to risk all in flight. Only a minority of those who tried such escapes ever made it to freedom in the North or Canada, but these fugitives made slavery a very insecure institution by the 1850s.

American slavery produced some fearless revolutionaries. Gabriel's Rebellion involved as many as a thousand slaves when it was discovered in 1800, just before it exploded in Richmond, Virginia (see pages 211–212). According to controversial court testimony, a similar conspiracy existed in Charleston in 1822, led by a free black named Denmark Vesey. Born a slave in the Caribbean, Vesey won a lottery of $1,500 in 1799, bought his own freedom, and became a religious leader in the black community. According to one long-argued interpretation, Vesey was a heroic revolutionary determined to free his people or die trying. But in a recent challenge, historian Michael Johnson points out that the court testimony is the only reliable source on the alleged insurrection. Could the testimony reveal less of reality than of white South Carolina's fears of slave rebellion? The court, says Johnson, built its case on rumors and intimidated witnesses, and "conjured into being" an insurrection not about to occur in reality. Whatever the facts, when the arrests and trials were over, thirty-seven "conspirators" were executed and more than three dozen others were banished from the state.

The most famous rebel of all, Nat Turner, struck for freedom in Southampton County, Virginia, in 1831. The son of an African woman who passionately hated her enslavement, Nat Turner was a precocious child who learned to read when he was very young. Encouraged by his first owner to study the Bible, he enjoyed certain privileges but also endured hard work and changes of masters. His father successfully escaped to freedom.

NAT TURNER'S INSURRECTION

Eventually young Nat became a preacher with a reputation for eloquence and mysticism. After nurturing his plan for several years, Turner led a band of rebels from farm to farm in the predawn darkness of August 22, 1831. The group severed limbs and crushed skulls with axes or killed their victims with guns. Before

■ A bill of sale documents that this slave woman, Louisa, was owned by the young child whom she holds on her lap. In the future Louisa's life would be subject to the child's wishes and decisions. (Missouri Historical Society, St. Louis)

alarmed planters stopped them, Nat Turner and his followers had slaughtered sixty whites of both sexes and all ages in forty-eight hours. The rebellion was soon put down, and in retaliation, whites killed slaves at random all over the region, including in adjoining states. Turner was eventually caught and then hanged. As many as two hundred African Americans, including innocent victims of marauding whites, lost their lives as a result of the rebellion.

Nat Turner remains one of the most haunting symbols in America's unresolved history with racial slavery and discrimination. While in jail awaiting execution, Turner was interviewed by a Virginia lawyer and slaveholder, Thomas R. Gray. Their intriguing creation, *The*

Confessions of Nat Turner, became a bestseller within a month of Turner's hanging. Turner told of his early childhood, his religious visions, his zeal to be free; Gray called the rebel a "gloomy fanatic," but in a manner that made him fascinating and produced one of the most remarkable documents in the annals of American slavery. In the wake of Turner's insurrection, many states passed stiffened legal codes against black education and religious practice.

Most importantly, in 1832 the state of Virginia, shocked to its core, held a full-scale legislative and public debate over gradual emancipation as a means of ridding itself of slavery and of blacks. The plan debated would not have freed any slaves until 1858, and it provided that eventually all blacks would be colonized outside Virginia. But when the House of Delegates voted, gradual abolition lost, 73 to 58. In the end, Virginia opted to do nothing except reinforce its own moral and economic defenses of slavery. It was the last time white southerners would debate any kind of emancipation until war forced their hand.

Harmony and Tension in a Slave Society

From 1830 to 1860, slavery impinged on laws and customs, individual values, and, increasingly, every aspect of southern politics. In all things, from their workaday movements to Sunday worship, slaves fell under the supervision of whites. State courts held that a slave "has no civil right" and could not hold property "except at the will and pleasure of his master." Revolts like Nat Turner's tightened the legal straitjacket even more. As political conflicts between North and South deepened, fears of slave revolt grew, and restrictions on slaves increased accordingly.

State and federal laws aided the capture of fugitive slaves and required nonslaveholders to support the slave system. All white male citizens had a legal duty to participate in slave patrols. Ship captains, harbor masters, and other whites were required to scrutinize the papers of African Americans who might be attempting to escape bondage.

Slavery deeply affected southern values precisely because it was the main determinant of wealth. Ownership

SLAVERY, WEALTH, AND SOCIAL STATUS of slaves guaranteed the labor to produce cotton and other crops on a large scale. Slaves were a commodity and an investment, much like gold; people bought them on speculation, hoping

for a steady rise in their market values. Across the South, variations in wealth from county to county corresponded very closely to variations in slaveholding. Wealth in slaves also translated into political power: a solid majority of political officeholders were slaveholders, and the most powerful were usually large-scale planters.

Slavery's influence spread throughout the social system until even the values and mores of nonslaveholders bore its imprint. The availability of slave labor tended to devalue free labor: where strenuous work under supervision was reserved for an enslaved race, few free people relished it. When Alexis de Tocqueville crossed from Ohio into Kentucky in his travels of 1831, he observed "the effect that slavery produces on society. On the right bank of the Ohio [River] everything is activity, industry; labor is honoured; there are no slaves. Pass to the left bank and the scene changes so suddenly that you think yourself on the other side of the world; the enterprising spirit is gone. There, work is not only painful; it is shameful." Tocqueville's own class impulses found a home in the South, however. There he found a "veritable aristocracy which . . . combines many prejudices with high sentiments and instincts."

The values of the aristocrat—lineage, privilege, pride, and refinement of person and manner—commanded respect throughout the South. Many of those qualities were in short supply, however, in the recently settled portions of the cotton kingdom, where frontier values of courage and self-reliance ruled. Thus independence and defense of one's honor became important traits for planter and frontier farmer alike.

ARISTOCRATIC VALUES AND FRONTIER INDIVIDUALISM

Instead of gradually disappearing as it did in the North, the Code Duello, which required men to defend their honor through violence, lasted much longer in the South. In North Carolina in 1851 a wealthy planter named Samuel Fleming responded to a series of disputes with the lawyer William Waightstill Avery by "cowhiding" (whipping) him on a public street. According to the code, Avery had two choices: to redeem his honor violently or to brand himself a coward through inaction. Three weeks later Avery shot Fleming dead at point-blank range during a session of the Burke County Superior Court, with Judge William Battle and numerous spectators looking on. A jury later took only ten minutes to find Avery not guilty, and the spectators gave him a standing ovation.

Other aristocratic values of the planter class were less acceptable to less wealthy whites. In their pride, planters expected not only to wield power but to receive deference from poorer whites. But the sternly independent yeoman class resented infringements of their rights, and many belonged to evangelical faiths that exalted values of simplicity and condemned the planters' love of wealth. Also conscious of national democratic ideals, yeomen sometimes challenged or rejected the political pretensions of planters. And much of the planters' power and their claims to a republican ideal of white men leading other white men was built on a foundation of black slave labor.

Class tensions emerged in the western, nonslaveholding parts of the seaboard states by the 1830s. There

YEOMAN DEMANDS AND WHITE CLASS RELATIONS

yeoman farmers resented their underrepresentation in state legislatures and the corruption in local government. After vigorous debate, the reformers won many battles. Voters in the more recently settled states of the Old Southwest adopted white manhood suffrage and other electoral reforms, including popular election of governors, legislative apportionment based on white population only, and locally chosen county government. Slaveowners knew that a more open government structure could permit troubling issues to arise. In Virginia, it was nonslaveholding westerners who petitioned and initiated the debate over abolition in the wake of Nat Turner's Rebellion in 1832.

Given such tensions, it was perhaps remarkable that slaveholders and nonslaveholders did not experience more overt conflict. Why were class confrontations among whites so infrequent? Historians have given several answers. One of the most important factors was race. The South's racial ideology stressed the superiority of all whites to blacks. Thus slavery became the basis of equality among whites, and racism inflated the status of poor whites and gave them a common interest with the rich. Moreover, family ties linked some nonslaveholders to wealthy planters, especially on the expanding frontier.

At the same time, the potential for upward mobility blunted some class conflict. The "Old South" was a fluid society in which many people rose in status by acquiring land or slaves, and those who did not wished they could. Even in cotton-rich Alabama in the 1850s, fewer than half of the richest families in a typical county belonged to its elite ten years later. Most did not die or lose their wealth; they merely moved on to some new state. This constant mobility in an expanding plantation economy meant that southern society did not settle into an utterly rigid social pattern.

Most importantly, in their daily lives yeomen and slaveholders were seldom in conflict. Before the Civil War most yeomen were able to pursue unhindered their independent lifestyle. They worked their farms, avoided debt, and marked progress for their families that in their rural habitats was unrelated to slaveholding. Likewise, slaveholders pursued their goals quite independently of yeomen. Planters farmed for the market but also for themselves.

Suppression of dissent also played an increasing role. After 1830 white southerners who criticized the slave system out of moral conviction or class resentment were intimidated, attacked, or legally prosecuted. By the 1850s the defense of slavery's interests exerted an ever more powerful influence on southern politics and society.

Still, there were signs that the relative lack of conflict between slaveholders and nonslaveholders was

HARDENING OF CLASS LINES

coming to an end in the late antebellum period. As cotton lands filled up, nonslaveholders saw their opportunities beginning to narrow; meanwhile, wealthy planters enjoyed expanding profits. The risks of entering cotton production were becoming too great and the cost of slaves too high for many yeomen to rise in society. From 1830 to 1860 the percentage of white southern families holding slaves declined steadily from 36 to 25 percent. Although slaveowners accounted for this smaller portion of the population, planters' share of the South's agricultural wealth remained at between 90 and 95 percent.

Urban artisans and mechanics felt the pinch acutely. Their numbers were few, and in bad times they were often the first to lose work as markets collapsed. Moreover, they faced stiff competition from urban slaves, whose masters wanted to hire them out to practice trades. White workers in some port cities staged protests demanding that economic competition from slaves be forbidden, but they were ignored. Such angry protests of white workers resulted in harsh restrictions on free African American laborers and craftsmen. Pre–Civil War politics reflected these tensions as well. Anticipating possible secession and the prospect of a war to defend slavery, slaveowners expressed growing fear about the loyalty of nonslaveholders. Schemes to widen the ownership of slaves were discussed, including reopening the African slave trade. In North Carolina, a prolonged and increasingly bitter controversy erupted over the combination of high taxes on land and low taxes on slaves. When nonslaveholder Hinton R. Helper denounced the slave system in *The Impending Crisis*, published in 1857, discerning planters feared the eruption of such controversies in every southern state.

But for the moment slaveowners stood secure. In the 1850s they occupied from 50 to 85 percent of the seats in state legislatures and a similarly high percentage of the South's congressional seats. Planters' interests controlled all the other major social institutions. Professors who criticized slavery had been dismissed from colleges and universities; schoolbooks that contained "unsound" ideas had been replaced. And almost all the Methodist and Baptist clergy had become slavery's most vocal defenders.

Summary

During the thirty years before the Civil War the South grew as part of America's westward expansion. Ideologically and economically, the southern states developed in many distinctive ways; at the same time, they were also deeply enmeshed in the nation's heritage and political economy. Far more than the North, the antebellum South was a biracial society; whites grew up directly influenced by black folkways and culture, and blacks, the vast majority of whom were slaves, became predominantly native-born Americans and the cobuilders with whites of a rural, agricultural society. From the Old South on to modern times, white and black southerners have always shared a tragic, mutual history.

With the sustained cotton boom, the South grew fatefully into a much larger slave society than it had been early in the century. The coercive influence of slavery affected virtually every element of southern life and politics, and increasingly produced a leadership determined to preserve a conservative, hierarchical social and racial order. Despite the white supremacy that united them, the democratic values of yeomen often clashed with the profit motives of aristocratic planters. The benevolent self-image and paternalistic ideology of slaveholders had to ultimately stand the test of the slaves' own judgments. African American slaves responded by fashioning over time a rich, expressive folk culture and a religion of personal and group deliverance. Their experiences could be profoundly different from one region and kind of labor to another. Some blacks were crushed by bondage; many others transcended it in an epic of survival and resistance.

By 1850, through their own wits and on the backs of African labor, white southerners had aggressively built one of the last profitable, expanding slave societies on earth. North of them, deeply intertwined with them in the same nation, market economy, constitutional system, and history, a different kind of society had grown even faster—one driven by industrialism and free labor. The clash of these two deeply connected, yet mutually fearful and divided societies was about to explode in political storms over how the nation would define its future.

LEGACY FOR A PEOPLE AND A NATION
Reparations for Slavery

How should the United States come to terms with 250 years of racial slavery? Is this period best forgotten as a terrible passage that African Americans as well as the country transcended over time? Or does the nation owe a long-overdue debt to black people for their oppression?

In the wake of emancipation in 1865, and rooted in vague federal promises, many former slaves believed they were entitled to "forty acres and a mule," but these never materialized. As the leader of a planters' association put it in 1865, "the emancipated slaves own nothing, because nothing but freedom has been given to them."

In 1897, Callie House, born in 1865 in a contraband camp for ex-slaves and a poor mother of four children, organized the National Ex-Slave Pension and Bounty Association, modeled after the pension system established for soldiers. House traveled all over the South, recruiting 250,000 members at 10-cent dues. Her lobbying of the federal government for slave pensions failed, and she was accused of mail fraud and imprisoned for one year in 1916.

More recently a widespread debate over "reparations" for slavery has emerged. As the history of slavery has been rewritten since the 1960s, Americans have learned a great deal about how slave labor created American wealth: how insurance companies insured slaves, how complicitous the U.S. government was in slavery's defense and expansion, and how slaves built the U.S. Capitol while their owners received $5 a month for their labor. And since 1989 Representative John Conyers Jr. has annually submitted an unsuccessful bill in Congress to establish a commission to study the legacies of slavery and racism.

The debate is fueled by a wealth of analogies: the reparations paid to Japanese Americans interned in World War II; the reparations paid to several Native American tribes for their stolen land; the reparations paid to thousands of Holocaust survivors and victims of forced labor; and a suit settled in 1999 that will pay an estimated $2 billion to some twenty thousand black farmers for discrimination practiced by the Agriculture Department in the early twentieth century.

On the other side, some argue that because there are no living former slaves or slaveholders, reparations for slavery can never take the form of money. But in 2002 a lawsuit was filed against three major corporations who allegedly profited from slavery, and the National Reparations Coordinating Committee promises a suit against the U.S. government itself. Critics argue that resources would be better spent "making sure black kids have a credible education" and in rebuilding inner cities. Advocates contend that when "government participates in a crime against humanity," it is "obliged to make the victims whole." The movement for reparations has strong support in grassroots black communities, and the issue has become the subject of a broad public debate. The legacy of slavery for a people and a nation promises to become America's most traumatic test of how to reconcile its history with justice.

The **history companion** *powered by Eduspace*®
Your primary source for interactive quizzes, exercises, and more to help you learn efficiently.
http://history.college.hmco.com/students

PRIZE BANNER

OBTAINED BY THE REPUBLICANS OF THE TOWNSHIP OF PEQUANNOC,

Sept. 18*th*   1856.

FOR PRESIDENT
JOHN C. FREMONT,
FOR VICE PRESIDENT
WILLIAM L. DAYTON,

OUR STANDARD BEARER THEN,

THE BRAVE PATH FINDER BE!

FREE SPEECH, FREE PRESS, FREE SOIL,

FREE MEN,

FREMONT AND VICTORY.

E. Kranich, Pnt.

Morristown

SLAVERY AND AMERICA'S FUTURE: THE ROAD TO WAR 1845–1861

*a*s the delegates filed into the Musical Fund Hall in Philadelphia on June 17, 1856, they knew they had created something special in American politics. The first national nominating convention of the Republican Party met to approve a platform and select their presidential ticket. Formed just two years earlier, the party drew together a broad coalition of northern politicians who opposed the expansion of slavery, as well as the growing power of the South in the federal government. Most American political conventions in those years were raucous affairs; but at this gathering, according to a journalist, there was only "a slight quantity of liquor consumed, very little profane swearing . . . and . . . intense propriety." Republicans had come to Philadelphia for the solemn business of offering the American electorate a genuinely antislavery future.

Their coalition combined men who had been former Democrats; men who had been founding members of the American Party, a group that wanted to prohibit foreigners, especially Catholics, from settling in the United States; and many former Whigs, whose party had been shattered by the crisis over slavery and its expansion. They consisted of conservatives, moderates, and radicals; some believed slavery a moral evil, while others saw it as a political problem.

At this convention, a radical temper prevailed. The convention was only minutes old when the temporary chairman brought the delegates to their feet by using the Declaration of Independence to label slavery a great political danger to the nation's future. Permanent chairman Henry S. Lane of Indiana followed by declaring the "vital principle of the Republican party" to be "no more slave states," an aim he rooted in the "natural rights of man." Speaker after speaker declared that their party would render "freedom national" and "slavery sectional" by using the power of Congress to outlaw human bondage in all western territories.

◀ The Republican John C. Frémont's presidential campaign banner from Pequannoc Township, New Jersey, September 1856. The banner contains all the keywords of the Republican campaign except "free labor." (Smithsonian Institution, Washington, D.C.)

CHRONOLOGY

1846 • War with Mexico begins
• Oregon Treaty negotiated
• Wilmot Proviso inflames sectional divisions

1847 • Cass proposes idea of popular sovereignty

1848 • Treaty of Guadalupe Hidalgo gives United States new territory in the Southwest
• Free-Soil Party formed
• Taylor elected president

1849 • Gold discovered in California, which applies for admission to United States as free state

1850 • Compromise of 1850 passed in separate bills

1852 • Stowe publishes *Uncle Tom's Cabin*
• Pierce elected president

1854 • Publication of "Appeal of the Independent Democrats"
• Kansas-Nebraska Act wins approval and ignites controversy
• Republican Party formed
• Return of fugitive Burns from Boston to slavery in Virginia

1856 • Bleeding Kansas troubles nation
• Brooks attacks Sumner in Senate chamber
• Buchanan elected president, but Republican Frémont wins most northern states

1857 • *Dred Scott v. Sanford* endorses southern views on black citizenship and slavery in territories
• Economic panic and widespread unemployment begins

1858 • Kansas voters reject Lecompton Constitution
• Lincoln-Douglas debates attract attention
• Douglas proposes Freeport Doctrine

1859 • Brown raids Harpers Ferry

1860 • Democratic Party splits in two; southern Democrats demand "Slave Code for the Territories"
• Lincoln elected president
• Crittenden Compromise fails
• South Carolina secedes from Union

1861 • Six more Deep South states secede
• Confederacy established at Montgomery, Alabama
• Attack on Fort Sumter begins Civil War
• Four states in the Upper South join the Confederacy

The convention's platform committee was fittingly chaired by David Wilmot, a former Democrat who was no friend of black civil and political rights. But Wilmot, like others, was firmly opposed to slavery's expansion and endorsed the protection of free white men's labor and land ownership across the continent. The platform denounced the South's interest in the acquisition of Cuba, supported the building of a transcontinental railroad, and nodded gently against nativism. But these were all "like a tail to the antislavery kite," as one historian put it. At the heart of the platform was the short, direct credo calling upon Congress to "prohibit in the territories those twin relics of barbarism—polygamy and slavery." The Republicans nominated the famous western explorer and former California senator John C. Frémont for president. In the election that followed, Americans began to vote by section and not by party as never before. The Republican coalition began to unify the North around keeping the West free and alarmed the South, which now saw the future of its slave society endangered by a political movement determined to limit if not destroy slavery. Frémont would lose the 1856 election, but Republicans made the best showing in American history of a newly born party in its first presidential bid.

As the Republicans engaged in their near miss at winning the presidency in 1856, a larger drama of conflict and violence had begun to envelop the nation. In Kansas Territory, open warfare had exploded between proslavery and antislavery settlers. On the floor of the U.S. Senate a southern representative beat a northern senator senseless. A new fugitive slave law sent thousands of blacks fleeing into Canada in fear for their liberty and their lives. The tradition of compromise on political problems related to slavery teetered on the brink of complete collapse. Within a year the Supreme Court had issued a dramatic decision about slavery's constitutionality in westward expansion, and the status of African American citizenship—to the delight of most southerners and the dread of many northerners. And abolitionist John Brown was planning a raid into Virginia to start a slave rebellion.

The political culture of the American republic was disintegrating. As the 1850s advanced, slavery pulled

Americans, North and South, into a maelstrom of dispute that its best statesmen, ultimately, could not subdue. A prosperous nation, riven by stark contradictions, was on the road to a terrible war. Divergent economic and political aims, which had long been held in check, now flew apart over the issue of slavery. The old nationwide political parties fractured, and a realignment that reinforced sectional interests took their place. The means for compromise steadily slipped from the nation's grasp.

Slavery had aroused passions that could be neither contained nor resolved. What began as a dark cloud over the territories became a storm engulfing the nation. Between 1845 and 1853 the United States added Texas, California, Oregon Country, and the Southwest to its domain and launched the settlement of the Great Plains. During the administration of President James K. Polk alone (1845–1849), the nation increased its land mass by two-thirds. Each time the nation expanded, it confronted a thorny issue: should new territories and states be slave or free?

The ensuing political storms gave rise to a feeling in both North and South that America's future was at stake—the character of its economy, its labor system, its definition of liberty under the Constitution, and its racial self-definition. The new Republican Party believed that America's future depended on the unbounded labor of free men. They charged southerners with using the power of the federal government to make slavery legal throughout the Union. Southern leaders defended slavery and charged the North with unconstitutional efforts to destroy it.

For blacks, the growing dispute brought hope and despair. They could take heart that the country's political strife over slavery might somehow lead to their liberation. But in a nation now trying to define its future, blacks had to wonder whether they had a future at all in America. In 1855 Frederick Douglass spoke for slaves and former slaves when he wrote that "the thought of only being a creature of the present and the past, troubled me, and I longed to have a future—a future with hope in it." In those words, Douglass spoke as well to the nation's central dilemma. ∎

The War with Mexico and Its Consequences

In the 1840s, territorial expansion surged forward under the leadership of President James K. Polk of North Carolina. The annexation of Texas (see pages 293–294) just before his inauguration did not necessarily make war with Mexico inevitable, but by design and through a series of calculated decisions, Polk brought the conflict on. Mexico broke off relations with the United States, and during the annexation process, Polk urged Texans to seize all land to the Rio Grande and claim the river as their southern and western border. Mexico held that the Nueces River was the border; hence the stage was set for conflict. Nothing could weaken Polk's determination to fulfill the nation's "manifest destiny" to rule the continent. He wanted Mexico's territory all the way to the Pacific, and all of Oregon Country, since 1818 jointly occupied with Britain, as well. He and his expansionist cabinet achieved their goals but were largely unaware of the price in domestic harmony that expansion would exact.

During the 1844 campaign, Polk's supporters had threatened war with Great Britain to gain all of Oregon.

OREGON As president, however, Polk turned first to diplomacy. Not wanting to fight Mexico and Great Britain at the same time, he tried to avoid bloodshed in the Northwest, where America and Britain had for decades jointly occupied disputed territory. Dropping the demand for a boundary at latitude 54°40', he pressured the British to accept the 49th parallel. In 1846 Great Britain agreed. The Oregon Treaty gave the United States all of present-day Oregon, Washington, and Idaho and parts of Wyoming and Montana (see Map 14.1). Thus a new era of land acquisition and conquest had begun under the tenth president of the United States, the sixth to be a slaveholder, and one who secretly bought and sold slaves through an agent from the White House.

Toward Mexico, Polk was more aggressive. In early 1846, he ordered American troops under "Old Rough and Ready," General Zachary Taylor,

"MR. POLK'S WAR" to march south and defend the contested border of the Rio Grande across from the town of Matamoros (see Map 14.2). Polk especially desired California as the prize in his expansionist strategy, and he attempted to buy from Mexico a huge tract of land extending to the Pacific. When that effort failed, Polk waited for war. Negotiations between troops on the Rio Grande were awkwardly

Map 14.1   American Expansion in Oregon

The slogan of Polk's supporters had been "Fifty-four forty or fight," but negotiation of a boundary at the 49th parallel avoided the danger of war with Great Britain.

conducted in French because no American officer spoke Spanish and no Mexican spoke English. After a three-week standoff, the tense situation came to a head. On April 24, 1846, Mexican cavalry ambushed a U.S. cavalry unit on the north side of the river; eleven Americans were killed and sixty-three taken captive. On April 26 Taylor sent a dispatch overland to Washington, D.C., which took two weeks to arrive, announcing: "Hostilities may now be considered as commenced."

Polk now drafted a message to Congress: Mexico had "passed the boundary of the United States, had invaded our territory and shed American blood on American soil." In the bill accompanying the war message, Polk deceptively declared that "war exists by the act of Mexico itself" and summoned the nation to arms. Two days later, on May 13, the House recognized a state of war with Mexico by a vote of 174 to 14, and the Senate by 40 to 2, with numerous abstentions. Some antislavery Whigs had tried to oppose the war but were barely allowed to gain the floor of Congress to speak. Since Polk withheld key facts, the full reality of what had happened on the distant Rio Grande was not known. But the theory and practice of manifest destiny had

launched the United States into its first major war on foreign territory.

The idea of war unleashed great public celebrations. Huge crowds gathered in southern cities such as Richmond and Louisville to voice support for the war effort. Twenty thousand Philadelphians and even more New Yorkers rallied in the same spirit. After news came of General Taylor's first two battlefield victories at Palo Alto and Resaca de la Palma, volunteers swarmed recruiting stations. From his home in Lansingburgh, New York, the writer Herman Melville remarked that "the people here are all in a state of delirium. . . . A military ardor pervades all ranks. . . . Nothing is talked of but the 'Halls of the Montezumas.'" Publishers rushed books about Mexican geography into print; "Palo Alto" hats and root beer went on sale. And the advent of daily newspapers, printed on new rotary presses, boosted sales by giving the war a romantic appeal.

FOREIGN WAR AND THE POPULAR IMAGINATION

Here was an adventurous war of conquest in a far-off, exotic land. Here was the fulfillment of Anglo-Saxon–Christian destiny to expand and possess the North American continent and to take "civilization" to the "semi-Indian" Mexicans. For many, racism fueled the expansionist spirit. In 1846 an Illinois newspaper justified the war on the basis that Mexicans were "reptiles in the path of progressive democracy." For those who read newspapers, the War with Mexico became the first national event experienced with immediacy. The battles south of the border were reported by war correspondents. From Vera Cruz on the Gulf Coast of Mexico, ships carried news dispatches to New Orleans, whose nine daily newspapers ran a faster steamer out to meet them. With stories set in type before even reaching shore, the news was then sent by riders toward the North. Near the end of the war, news traveled by telegraph in only three days from New Orleans to Washington.

The war spawned an outpouring of poetry, song, drama, travel literature, and lithographs that captured the popular imagination and glorified the conflict. New lyrics to the tune "Yankee Doodle" proclaimed: "They attacked our men upon our land / and crossed our river too sir / now show them all with sword in hand / what yankee boys can do sir." Most of the war-inspired flowering in the popular arts was patriotic. But not everyone cheered. The abolitionist James Russell Lowell considered the war a "national crime committed in behoof of slavery, our common sin." Ralph Waldo Emerson confided to his journals in 1847: "The United States will conquer Mexico, but it will be as the man swallows ar-

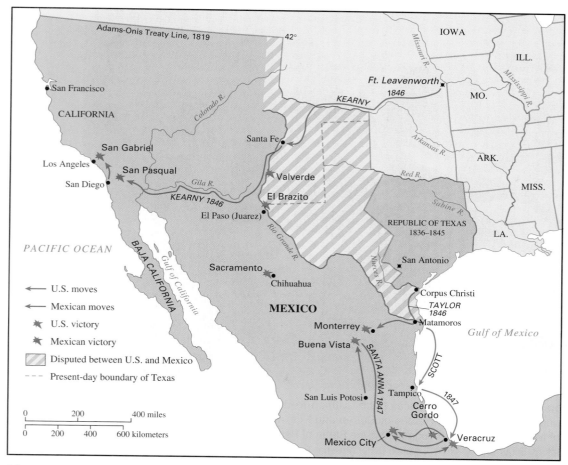

Map 14.2   The War with Mexico

This map shows the territory disputed between the United States and Mexico. After U.S. gains in northeastern Mexico and in New Mexico and California, General Winfield Scott captured Mexico City in the decisive campaign of the war.

senic, which brings him down in turn. Mexico will poison us." Even proslavery spokesman John C. Calhoun saw the perils of expansionism. Mexico, he said, was "the forbidden fruit; the penalty of eating it would be to subject our institutions to political death."

The troops proved unruly and undisciplined, and their politically ambitious commanders often quarreled among themselves. Nevertheless, progress was steady, and early in the war U.S. forces made significant gains. In May 1846 Polk ordered Colonel Stephen Kearny and a small detachment to invade the remote and thinly populated provinces of New Mexico and California. Taking Santa Fe without opposition, Kearny pushed into Cali-

CONQUEST

fornia, where he joined forces with rebellious American settlers led by Captain John C. Frémont and with a couple of U.S. naval units. General Zachary Taylor's forces attacked and occupied Monterrey, which surrendered in September, securing northeastern Mexico (see Map 14.2). And before the end of 1846 American soldiers had also established dominion over California. Because losses on the periphery of their large country had not broken Mexican resistance, General Winfield Scott carried the war to the enemy's heartland. Landing at Veracruz, he led fourteen thousand men toward Mexico City. This daring invasion proved the decisive campaign of the war. Scott's men, outnumbered and threatened by yellow fever, encountered a series of formidable Mexican

■ Enthusiastic publishers vied to furnish the American public with up-to-date news of the War with Mexico. This is one of three lithographs issued by Currier and Ives in 1846 to celebrate U.S. forces' capture of Mexico's General La Vega during the Battle of Resaca de la Palma, fought near the border of Texas and Mexico.   (Amon Carter Museum, Fort Worth, Texas)

defenses, but engineers repeatedly discovered flanking routes around their foes. After a series of hard-fought battles, U.S. troops captured the Mexican capital.

Representatives of both countries signed the Treaty of Guadalupe Hidalgo in February 1848. The United States gained California and New Mexico (including present-day Nevada, Utah, and Arizona, and parts of Colorado and Wyoming) and recognition of the Rio Grande as the southern boundary of Texas. In return, the American government agreed to settle the claims of its citizens against Mexico ($3.2 million) and to pay Mexico a mere $15 million. On the day Polk received the treaty from the Senate, a mob in Paris forced Louis Philippe to abdicate the throne of France, and a German writer, Karl Marx, published a pamphlet, *The Communist Manifesto*, in London. The enormous influence of Marx's work would be many years away, but as the 1848 nationalistic revolutions against

TREATY OF GUADALUPE HIDALGO

monarchy spread to Italy, Austria, Hungary, and Germany, republican America seized an empire.

The costs of the war included the deaths of thirteen thousand Americans (mostly from disease) and fifty thousand Mexicans. Moreover, enmity endured between Mexico and the United States into the twentieth century. The domestic cost to the United States was even higher. Public opinion was sharply divided, despite widespread hostility toward Mexicans. Southwesterners were enthusiastic about the war, as were most southern planters; New Englanders strenuously opposed it. Whigs in Congress charged that Polk, a Democrat, had "provoked" an unnecessary war and "usurped the power of Congress." The aged John Quincy Adams denounced the war; and an Illinois Whig named Abraham Lincoln called Polk's justifications the "half insane mumbling of a fever-dream." Abolitionists and a small minority of antislavery Whigs charged that the war was no less than a plot to extend slavery. Congressman Joshua Giddings of Ohio charged that Polk's purpose was "to render slavery secure in Texas" and to extend slavery's dominion over the West.

These charges fed northern fear of the so-called Slave Power. Abolitionists had long warned of a slaveholding

"SLAVE POWER CONSPIRACY"

oligarchy that intended to dominate the nation through its hold on federal power. Slaveholders had gained control of the South by persecuting critics of slavery and suppressing dissent. They had forced the gag rule on Congress in 1836 (see page 280) and threatened northern liberties. To many white northerners, even those who saw nothing wrong with slavery, it was the battle over free speech that first made the idea of a Slave Power credible. The War with Mexico deepened such fears. Had this questionable war, asked antislavery northerners, not been launched for vast, new slave territory?

Northern opinion on slavery expansion began to shift, but the impact of the war on southern opinion was even more dramatic. At first some southern leaders had criticized the War with Mexico. Southern Whigs attacked the Democratic president for causing the war, and few southern congressmen saw slavery as the paramount issue. Many whites in both North and South feared that large land seizures would bring thousands of nonwhite Mexicans into the United States and upset the racial order. An Indiana politician did not want "any mixed races in our Union, nor men of any color except white, unless they be slaves." And the *Charleston Mercury* of South Carolina asked if the nation expected "to melt into our population eight millions of men, at war with us by race, by language, by religion, manners and laws." Yet despite their racism, many statesmen soon saw other prospects in the outcomes of a war of conquest in the Southwest.

In August 1846, David Wilmot, a Pennsylvania Democrat, proposed an amendment, or proviso, to a military

WILMOT PROVISO

appropriations bill: that "neither slavery nor involuntary servitude shall ever exist" in any territory gained from Mexico. Although the proviso never passed both houses of Congress, its repeated introduction by northerners transformed the debate over the expansion of slavery. Southerners suddenly circled their wagons to protect the future of a slave society. Alexander H. Stephens, only recently "no defender of slavery," now declared that slavery was based on the Bible and above moral criticism, and John C. Calhoun took an aggressive stand. The territories, Calhoun insisted, belonged to all the states, and the federal government could do nothing to limit the spread of slavery there. Southern slaveholders had a constitutional right rooted in the Fifth Amendment, Calhoun claimed, to take their slaves (as property) anywhere in the territories.

This position, often called "state sovereignty," which quickly became a test of orthodoxy among southern politicians, was a radical reversal of history. In 1787 the Confederation Congress had excluded slavery from the Northwest Territory (see pages 180–181); Article IV of the federal Constitution had authorized Congress to make "all needful rules and regulations" for the territories; and the Missouri Compromise had barred slavery from most of the Louisiana Purchase. Now, however, southern leaders demanded future guarantees for slavery.

In the North, the Wilmot Proviso became a rallying cry for abolitionists. Eventually the legislatures of fourteen northern states endorsed it—and not because all its supporters were abolitionists. David Wilmot, significantly, was neither an abolitionist nor an antislavery Whig. He denied having any "squeamish sensitiveness upon the subject of slavery" or "morbid sympathy for the slave." Instead, his goal was to defend "the rights of white freemen" and to obtain California "for free white labor." Wilmot's involvement in antislavery controversy is a measure of the remarkable ability of the territorial issue to alarm northerners of many viewpoints.

As Wilmot demonstrated, it was possible, however, to be both a racist and an opponent of slavery. The vast majority of white northerners were not active abolitionists, and their desire to keep the West free from slavery was often matched by their desire to keep blacks from settling there. Fear of the Slave Power was thus building a potent antislavery movement that united abolitionists and antiblack voters. At stake was an abiding version of the American Dream: the free individual's access to social mobility through acquisition of land and jobs in the West. This sacred ideal of *free labor,* and its dread of concentrated power, fueled a new political persuasion in America. A man's ownership and sale of his own labor, wrote the British economist Adam Smith, was "the most sacred and inviolable foundation of all property." Slave labor, thousands of northerners had come to believe, would degrade the honest toil of free men and render them unemployed and propertyless. The West must therefore be kept free of slaves and open to free white men.

The divisive slavery question could not be kept out of national politics. After Polk renounced a second term

THE ELECTION OF 1848 AND POPULAR SOVEREIGNTY

as president, the Democrats nominated Senator Lewis Cass of Michigan for president and General William Butler of Kentucky for vice president. Cass, a party loyalist who had served in Jackson's cabinet, had devised in 1847 the

TABLE 14.1

New Political Parties

Party	Period of Influence	Area of Influence	Outcome
Liberty Party	1839–1848	North	Merged with other antislavery groups to form Free-Soil Party
Free-Soil Party	1848–1854	North	Merged with Republican Party
Know-Nothings (American Party)	1853–1856	Nationwide	Disappeared, freeing most to join Republican Party
Republican Party	1854–present	North (later nationwide)	Became rival of Democratic Party and won presidency in 1860

idea of "popular sovereignty"—letting residents in the western territories decide the question of slavery for themselves. His party's platform declared that Congress lacked the power to interfere with slavery's expansion. The Whigs nominated General Zachary Taylor, a southern slaveholder and war hero; Congressman Millard Fillmore of New York was his running mate. The Whig convention similarly refused to assert that Congress had power over slavery in the territories.

But the issue could not be avoided. Many southern Democrats distrusted Cass and eventually voted for Taylor because he was a slaveholder. Among northerners, concern over slavery led to the formation of a new party. New York Democrats committed to the Wilmot Proviso rebelled against Cass and nominated former president Martin Van Buren. Antislavery Whigs and former supporters of the Liberty Party then joined them to organize the Free-Soil Party, with Van Buren as its candidate (see Table 14.1). This party, whose slogan was "Free Soil, Free Speech, Free Labor, and Free Men," won almost 300,000 northern votes. For a new third party to win 10 percent of the national vote was a signal achievement. Taylor polled 1.4 million votes to Cass's 1.2 million and won the White House, but the results were more ominous than decisive.

American politics had split along sectional lines as never before. Religious denominations, too, were splitting into northern and southern wings. Many Protestants, North and South, began to fear that God had an appointment with America, either to destroy the national sin of slavery or to help the South defend it as part of his divine order. As the 1850s dawned, the legacies of the War with Mexico and the conflicts of 1848 dominated national life and threatened the nature of the Union itself.

1850: Compromise or Armistice?

The first sectional battle of the new decade involved California. More than eighty thousand Americans flooded into California during the gold rush of 1849 (see page 302). With Congress unable to agree on a formula to govern the territories, President Taylor urged these settlers to apply directly for admission to the Union. They promptly did so, proposing a state constitution that did not allow for slavery. Because California's admission as a free state would upset the sectional balance of power in the Senate (the ratio of slave to free states was 15 to 15), southern politicians wanted to postpone admission and make California a slave territory, or at least to extend the Missouri Compromise line west to the Pacific. Representatives from nine southern states, meeting in Nashville, asserted the South's right to part of the territory.

Henry Clay, the venerable Whig leader, sensed that the Union was in peril. Twice before—in 1820 and 1833—Clay, the "Great Pacificator," had taken the lead in shaping sectional compromise; now he struggled one last time to preserve the nation. To hushed Senate galleries Clay presented a series of compromise measures in the winter of 1850. At one point Clay held up what he claimed was a piece of George Washington's coffin as a means of inspiring unity. Over the weeks that followed, he and Senator Stephen A. Douglas of Illinois, the "Little Giant," steered their omnibus bill, or compromise package, through debate and amendment.

The problems to be solved were numerous and difficult. Would California, or part of it, become a free state?

DEBATE OVER SLAVERY IN THE TERRITORIES

How should the territory acquired from Mexico be organized? Texas, which allowed slavery, claimed large portions of the new land as far west as Santa Fe. Southerners complained that fugitive slaves were not being returned as the Constitution required, and northerners objected to the sale of human beings in the nation's capital. Eight years earlier, in *Prigg v. Pennsylvania* (1842), the Supreme Court had ruled that enforcement of the fugitive slave clause in the Constitution was a federal obligation, buttressing long-standing southern desires to bring this issue to a head. Most troublesome of all, however, was the status of slavery in the territories.

Clay and Douglas hoped to avoid a specific formula, and in Lewis Cass's idea of popular sovereignty they discovered what one historian called a "charm of ambiguity" that appealed to practical politicians. Ultimately Congress would have to approve statehood for a territory, but "in the meantime," said Cass, it should allow the people living there "to regulate their own concerns in their own way."

Those simple words proved all but unenforceable. When could settlers prohibit slavery? To avoid dissension within their party, northern and southern Democrats explained Cass's statement to their constituents in two incompatible ways. Southerners claimed that neither Congress nor a territorial legislature could bar slavery. Only late in the territorial process, when settlers were ready to draft a state constitution, could they take that step, thus allowing time for slavery to take root. Northerners, however, insisted that Americans living in a territory were entitled to local self-government and thus could outlaw slavery at any time, especially early in the process.

The cause of compromise gained a powerful supporter when Senator Daniel Webster committed his prestige and eloquence to Clay's bill. "I wish to speak today," Webster declaimed on March 7 in a scene of high drama, "not as a Massachusetts man, nor as a Northern man, but as an American. I speak today for the preservation of the Union." Abandoning his earlier support for the Wilmot Proviso, Webster urged northerners not to "taunt or reproach" the South with antislavery measures. To southern firebrands he issued a warning that disunion inevitably would cause violence and destruction. For his efforts at compromise, Webster was condemned by many former abolitionist friends in New England who accused him of going over to the "devil."

Only three days earlier, with equal drama, Calhoun had been carried from his sickbed to deliver a speech opposing the compromise. Unable to stand and speak, his

address was read for him by Senator James Mason of Virginia. Grizzled and dying, the South's intellectual defender warned that the "cords which bind these states" were "already greatly weakened." Calhoun did not address the specific measures in the bill; he predicted disunion if southern demands were not met, thereby frightening some into support of compromise.

Yet rising fear and Webster's influence were not enough. After months of labor, Clay and Douglas finally brought their legislative package to a vote, and lost. With Clay sick and absent from Washington, Douglas reintroduced the compromise measures one at a time. Though there was no majority for compromise, Douglas shrewdly realized that different majorities might be created for the separate measures. Because southerners favored some bills and northerners the rest, the small bloc for compromise could vote first with one section and then with the other. The strategy worked, and Douglas's resourcefulness alleviated the crisis as the Compromise of 1850 became law.

The compromise had five essential measures: California became a free state; the Texas boundary was set at

COMPROMISE OF 1850

its present limits (see Map 14.3) and the United States paid Texas $10 million in compensation for the loss of New Mexico territory; the territories of New Mexico and Utah were organized on a basis of popular sovereignty; the fugitive slave law was strengthened; and the slave trade was abolished in the District of Columbia. Jubilation greeted passage of the compromise; crowds in Washington and other cities celebrated the happy news. "On one glorious night," records a modern historian, "the word went abroad that it was the duty of every patriot to get drunk. Before the next morning many a citizen had proved his patriotism."

In reality, there was less cause for celebration than people hoped. At best, the Compromise of 1850 was an artful evasion. As one historian has argued, the legislation was more an "armistice," delaying greater conflict, than a compromise. Douglas had found a way to pass the five proposals without convincing northerners and southerners to agree on fundamentals. The compromise bought time for the nation, but it did not provide a real settlement of the territorial questions.

Furthermore, the compromise had two basic flaws. The first concerned the ambiguity of popular sovereignty. Southerners insisted there would be no prohibition of slavery during the territorial stage, and northerners declared that settlers could bar slavery whenever they wished. The compromise even allowed for the appeal of

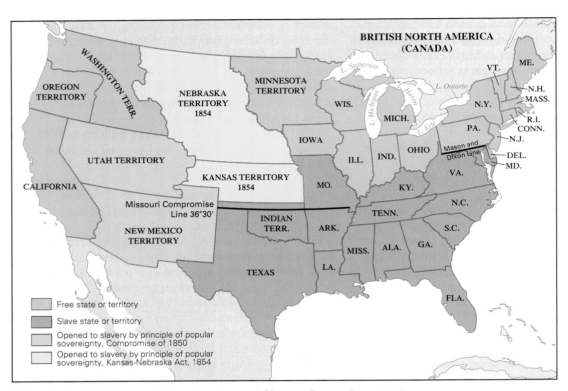

Map 14.3   The Kansas-Nebraska Act and Slavery Expansion, 1854

The vote on the Kansas-Nebraska Act (see also Table 14.2 on page 367) in the House of Representatives demonstrates the sectionalization of American politics due to the slavery question.

a territorial legislature's action to the Supreme Court. One witty politician remarked that the legislators had enacted a lawsuit instead of a law.

The second flaw lay in the Fugitive Slave Act, which gave new—and controversial—protection to slavery. The

FUGITIVE SLAVE ACT

law empowered slaveowners to go into court in their own states to present evidence that a slave who owed them service had escaped. The resulting transcript and a description of the fugitive would then serve as legal proof of a person's slave status, even in free states and territories. Specially appointed court officials adjudicated the identity of the person described, not whether he or she was indeed a slave. Penalties made it a felony to harbor fugitives, and the law stated that northern citizens could be summoned to hunt fugitives. The fees paid to U.S. marshals favored slaveholders: $10 if the alleged fugitive was returned to the slaveowner, $5 if not returned.

Abolitionist newspapers quickly attacked the Fugitive Slave Act as a violation of fundamental American

rights. Why were alleged fugitives denied a trial by jury? Why were they given no chance to present evidence or cross-examine witnesses? Why did the law give authorities a financial incentive to send suspected fugitives into bondage? These arguments convinced some northerners that all free blacks were vulnerable to kidnapping and enslavement. The "free" states were no longer a safe haven for black folk, whatever their origins.

Between 1850 and 1854, protests and violent resistance to slave catchers occurred in dozens of northern towns. Sometimes a captured fugitive was broken out of jail or from the clutches of slave agents by abolitionists, as in the case of Shadrach Minkins in 1851 in Boston, who was spirited by a series of wagons and trains across Massachusetts, up through Vermont, to Montreal, Canada. Also in 1851, a fugitive named Jerry McHenry was freed by an abolitionist mob in Syracuse, New York, and hurried into Canadian freedom. That same year as well, the small black community in Lancaster County, Pennsylvania, rose up in arms to defend four escaped slaves from a federal posse charged with reenslaving them. At this

"Christiana riot," the fugitives shot and killed Edward Gorsuch, the Maryland slaveowner who sought the return of his "property." Amid increasing border warfare over fugitive slaves, a headline reporting the Christiana affair screamed "Civil War, The First Blow Struck!"

Many abolitionists became convinced by their experience of resisting the Fugitive Slave Act that violence was a legitimate means of opposing slavery. In an 1854 column entitled "Is It Right and Wise to Kill a Kidnapper?" Frederick Douglass said that the only way to make the fugitive slave law "dead letter" was to make a "few dead slave catchers."

At this point a novel portrayed the humanity and suffering of slaves in a way that touched millions of

UNCLE TOM'S CABIN

northerners. Harriet Beecher Stowe, whose New England family had produced many prominent ministers, wrote *Uncle Tom's Cabin* out of deep moral conviction. Her story, serialized in 1851 and published as a book in 1852, conveyed the agonies faced by slave families and described a mother's dash to freedom with her child across the frozen Ohio River. Stowe also portrayed slavery's evil effects on slaveholders, indicting the institution itself more harshly than she indicted the southerners caught in its web. Moreover, Stowe exposed northern racism and complicity with slavery by making the worst slaveholder a man of New England birth, and a visiting relative on a plantation a squeamish Vermont woman who could hardly cope with the near presence of blacks.

In nine months the book sold over three hundred thousand copies, by mid-1853 over a million. Countless people saw *Uncle Tom's Cabin* performed as a stage play or heard the story in dramatic readings or read similar novels inspired by it. Stowe brought home the evil of slavery to many who had never given it much thought. Indeed, for generations, the characters in *Uncle Tom's Cabin*—Eliza, Little Eva, Simon Legree, and Uncle Tom himself—entered the American imagination as symbols of the entire era of slavery and the Civil War.

The popularity of *Uncle Tom's Cabin* alarmed anxious southern whites. In politics and now in popular literature they saw threats to their way of life. Behind the South's aggressive claims about territorial rights lay the fear that if nearby areas outlawed slavery, they would be used as bases from which to spread abolitionism into the slave states. To most white southerners, a moral condemnation of slaveholding anywhere meant the same thing everywhere.

To protect slavery in the arena of ideas, southerners needed to counter indictments of the institution as a moral wrong. Accordingly, some fifteen to twenty

■ The Webb Family toured the North, presenting dramatic readings of *Uncle Tom's Cabin.* Performances by the Webbs and others deepened the already powerful impact of Harriet Beecher Stowe's novel. (Harriet Beecher Stowe Center, Hartford, Conn.)

proslavery novels were published in the 1850s as responses to *Uncle Tom's Cabin.* Most of these anti–Uncle Tom books paled in comparison with Mrs. Stowe's masterpiece, but southern writers continued to defend their system as more humane than wage labor, and they blamed the slave trade on the "outside interference" of Yankee speculators. In awkward stories such as J. W. Page's *Uncle Robin in His Cabin and Tom Without One in Boston,* slaves were induced to run away by visiting abolitionists, and then all but starved in northern cities.

In reality, slaveholders were especially disturbed by the 1850s over what was widely called the Underground

THE UNDERGROUND RAILROAD

Railroad. This loose, illegal network of civil disobedience, spiriting runaways to freedom, had never been very organized. Thousands of slaves did escape by these routes, but largely through

■ In *Still Life of Harriet Tubman with Bible and Candle,* we see the youthful, calm, determined leader of the Underground Railroad. Appearing gentle, Tubman was in her own way a revolutionary who liberated nearly three hundred of her people. (© psihoyos.com)

their own wits and courage and through the assistance of black vigilance committees in some northern cities. Lewis Hayden in Boston, David Ruggles in New York, William Still in Philadelphia, John Parker in Ripley, Ohio, and Jacob Gibbs in Washington, D.C., were only some of the many black abolitionists who managed fugitive slave escapes through their regions.

Moreover, Harriet Tubman, herself an escapee in 1848, returned to her native Maryland and to Virginia nearly twenty times and through clandestine measures helped as many as three hundred slaves to freedom, some of them her own family members. Maryland planters were so outraged at her heroic success that they offered a $40,000 reward for her capture.

In Ohio numerous white abolitionists, often Quakers, joined with blacks as agents of slave liberation at various points along the river border between slavery and freedom. In the wake of the Fugitive Slave Act, an estimated twenty thousand blacks, most of them fugitive slaves, moved from the northern states into Canada seeking security. The Underground Railroad also had numerous maritime routes, as coastal slaves escaped aboard ship out of Virginia or the Carolinas, or from New Orleans. Many slaves who escaped by sea ended up in northern port cities, and some went to the Caribbean or to England. Many fugitive slaves from the Lower South and in Texas had escaped over the decades to Florida and across the Mexican border. In Mexico they entered a country that had abolished slavery; in Florida many were fully assimilated into the Seminole communities and fought with them against the U.S. Army in the Seminole Wars of 1835–1842 and 1855–1858.

This constant, dangerous flow of humanity was a testament to human courage and the will for freedom. It never reached the scale believed by some angry slaveholders nor that of the countless safe houses and hideaways claimed by hundreds of northern towns and local historical societies today. But in reality and in legend the Underground Railroad applied pressure to the slavery crisis and provided slaves with a focus for hope.

The 1852 election gave southern leaders hope that slavery would be secure under the administration of a new president. Franklin Pierce, a Democrat from New Hampshire, won an easy victory over the Whig presidential nominee, General Winfield Scott. Pierce defended each section's rights as essential to the nation's unity, and southerners hoped that his firm support for the Compromise of 1850 might end the season of crisis. Because Scott's views on the compromise had been unknown and the Free-Soil candidate, John P. Hale of New Hampshire, had openly rejected it, Pierce's victory suggested widespread support for the compromise.

ELECTION OF 1852 AND THE COLLAPSE OF COMPROMISE

Pierce's victory, however, derived less from his strengths than from the Whig Party's weakness. The Whigs were a congressional and state-based party that had never achieved much success in presidential politics. By 1852 sectional discord had rendered the Whig Party all but dead.

President Pierce's embrace of the compromise appalled many northerners. His vigorous enforcement of the Fugitive Slave Act provoked outrage and fear of the Slave Power, especially in the case of the fugitive slave Anthony Burns, who had fled Virginia by stowing away on a ship in 1852. In Boston, thinking he was safe in a city known for abolitionism, Burns began a new life. But in 1854 federal marshals found and placed him under guard in Boston's courthouse. An interracial crowd of abolitionists attacked the courthouse, killing a jailor in an unsuccessful attempt to free Burns, whose case attracted nationwide attention.

Pierce moved decisively to enforce the Fugitive Slave Act. He telegraphed local officials to "incur any expense to insure the execution of the law" and sent marines, cavalry, and artillery to Boston. U.S. troops marched Burns to Boston harbor through streets draped in black and hung with American flags at half-mast. At a cost of $100,000, a single black man was returned to slavery through the power of federal law.

The national will to sustain the future of slavery was now tested at every turn. This demonstration of federal support for slavery radicalized opinion, even among many conservatives. Textile manufacturer Amos A. Lawrence observed that "we went to bed one night old fashioned, conservative, Compromise Union Whigs & waked up stark mad Abolitionists." Juries refused to convict the abolitionists who had stormed the Boston courthouse, and New England states began to pass personal-liberty laws designed to impede or block federal enforcement. In such laws local judges were absolved from enforcing the Fugitive Slave Act, in effect nullifying federal authority. What northerners now saw as evidence of a dominating Slave Power, outraged slaveholders saw as the legal defense of their rights.

Pierce seemed unable to avoid sectional conflict in other arenas as well. His proposal for a transcontinental railroad derailed when congressmen fought over its location, North or South. His attempts to acquire foreign territory stirred more trouble. An annexation treaty with Hawai'i failed because southern senators would not vote for another free state, and efforts to acquire slaveholding Cuba angered northerners. Events in the Pacific also caused division at home over just how far American expansion should extend. With two orchestrated landings in the Bay of Tokyo, in 1853 and 1854, Commodore Matthew Perry established U.S. intentions to trade with Japan, whether that country sought such contact or not. Offended and intrigued, the Japanese were impressed with Perry's steam-powered warships, the first such black-smoke-belching floating machines they had seen. Perry's Treaty of Kanagawa in March 1854 negotiated two ports as coaling stations for American ships. The much-sought-after trading arrangements were slow in coming, although this did not stop merchants and bankers from lavishing on Perry a hero's honors when he returned to the United States. In his meetings with the Japanese, the pompous Perry had given his hosts, whom

he considered an inferior people, a telegraph system, a quarter-scale railroad train, a bound history of the War with Mexico, and one hundred gallons of Kentucky whiskey.

Soon back home another territorial bill threw Congress and the nation into even greater turmoil, and the Compromise of 1850 fell into complete collapse.

Slavery Expansion and Collapse of the Party System

*T*he new controversy began in a surprising way. Stephen A. Douglas, one of the architects of the Compromise of 1850, introduced a bill to establish the Kansas and Nebraska Territories. Talented and ambitious for the presidency, Douglas was known for compromise, not sectional quarreling. But he did not view slavery as a fundamental problem, and he was willing to risk some controversy to win economic benefits for Illinois, his home state. A transcontinental railroad would encourage settlement of the Great Plains and stimulate the economy of Illinois; but no company would build such a railroad before Congress organized the territories it would cross. Thus interest in promoting the construction of such a railroad drove Douglas to introduce a bill that inflamed sectional passions.

The Kansas-Nebraska bill exposed the conflicting interpretations of popular sovereignty. Douglas's bill left

THE KANSAS-NEBRASKA BILL

"all questions pertaining to slavery in the Territories . . . to the people residing therein." Northerners and southerners, however, still disagreed violently over what territorial settlers could constitutionally do. Moreover, the Kansas and Nebraska Territories lay within the Louisiana Purchase, and the Missouri Compromise prohibited slavery in all that land from latitude 36°30' north to the Canadian border. If popular sovereignty were to mean anything in Kansas and Nebraska, it had to mean that the Missouri Compromise was no longer in effect and that settlers could establish slavery there.

Southern congressmen, anxious to establish slaveholders' right to take slaves into any territory, pressed Douglas to concede this point. They demanded an explicit repeal of the 36°30' limitation as the price of their support. During a carriage ride with Senator Archibald Dixon of Kentucky, Douglas debated the point at length. Finally he made an impulsive decision: "By God, Sir, you are right. I will incorporate it in my bill, though I know it will raise a hell of a storm."

Annexation of Cuba

One of the most contentious issues in antebellum American foreign relations was the annexation of Cuba. As a strategic bulwark against Britain and France in the Western Hemisphere, for its massive sugar wealth, and as a slave society that might reinforce the security of southern slavery, the Spanish-controlled island fired the imagination of manifest destiny. In the early republic, Presidents Jefferson and Madison explored acquisition. "I have ever looked on Cuba as the most interesting addition which could . . . be made to our system of states," wrote Jefferson. John Quincy Adams, speaking as secretary of state in 1823, considered Cuba "indispensable to the continuance . . . of the Union."

Until the 1840s the United States officially supported Spanish rule for stability and the preservation of slavery. Southerners feared a "second Haiti" if Cuba became independent through revolution. The prospect of slave insurrection and the spread of abolitionism throughout the upper Caribbean and the rim of the Deep South drove many southerners and three Democratic administrations to shift course and pursue acquisition of Cuba. Slaveholding politicians viewed Cuba as critical to expansion; human bondage, they believed, had to expand southward and westward or it might die.

In 1848 President Polk authorized $100 million to purchase Cuba. The Spanish foreign minister, however, told Polk's emissary that his government would rather see Cuba "sunk in the ocean" than sell it to the United States. During the crisis over the Kansas-Nebraska Act in 1854, as President Pierce revived the annexation scheme, some southerners planned to seize Cuba by force. Although the expedition never embarked, its prospect outraged antislavery Republicans eager to halt slavery's expansion and protect their claims for free labor as the basis of America's future.

Yet another aggressive American design on Cuba emerged in the Ostend Manifesto in October 1854. Written after a meeting among the American foreign ministers to Britain, France, and Spain, the document advocated conquest of Cuba if it could not be purchased. The ministers predicted that Cuba "would be Africanized and become a second St. Domingo, with all its attendant horrors to the white race." But antislavery northerners saw schemes of the "Slave Power," whose "will is the law of this administration." The Ostend controversy forced temporary abandonment of annexation efforts, but as the fires in Bleeding Kansas subsided in 1858, President Buchanan reignited Cuba fever. A fierce Senate debate over yet another purchase offer in early 1859 ended in bitter division over the extension of slavery's domain.

The failure of Cuban annexation was deeply intertwined with the meaning of the United States as a slaveholding republic. "I want Cuba, and I know that sooner or later we must have it . . . for the planting or spreading of slavery," said Mississippian Albert G. Brown in 1858. Too many northerners, however, understood Brown's intentions. In America's links to the world, in this case only 90 miles from the Florida coast, just as in domestic affairs, the expansion of slavery poisoned the body politic.

■ Despite the failure of filibustering expeditions, the effort to annex Cuba continued throughout James Buchanan's presidential administration. This cartoon portrays Sam Houston, the famed Texan and proponent of American expansion, rowing the boat for a harpoonist in quest of the whale, Cuba. The dream of appropriating Cuba to the United States died very hard in the antebellum era. *Vanity Fair,* New York, June 1860.   (© Bettmann/Corbis)

TABLE 14.2

The Vote on the Kansas-Nebraska Act

The vote was 113–100 in favor.

	Aye	Nay
Northern Democrats	44	42
Southern Democrats	57	2
Northern Whigs	0	45
Southern Whigs	12	7
Northern Free-Soilers		4

Perhaps Douglas underestimated the storm because he believed that conditions of climate and soil would keep slavery out of Kansas and Nebraska. Nevertheless, his bill threw open to slavery land from which it had been prohibited for thirty-four years. Opposition from Free-Soilers and antislavery forces was immediate and enduring; many considered this turn of events a betrayal of a sacred trust. The titanic struggle in Congress lasted three and a half months. Douglas won the support of President Pierce and eventually prevailed: the bill became law in May 1854 by a vote that demonstrated the dangerous sectionalization of American politics (see Map 14.3 and Table 14.2).

But the storm was just beginning. Abolitionists charged sinister aggression by the Slave Power, and northern fears of slavery's influence deepened. Opposition to the Fugitive Slave Act grew dramatically; between 1855 and 1859 Connecticut, Rhode Island, Massachusetts, Michigan, Maine, Ohio, and Wisconsin passed personal-liberty laws. These laws enraged southern leaders by providing counsel for alleged fugitives and requiring trial by jury. More important was the devastating impact of the Kansas-Nebraska Act on political parties. The weakened Whig Party broke apart into northern and southern wings that could no longer cooperate nationally. The Democrats survived, but their support in the North fell drastically in the 1854 elections. Northern Democrats lost sixty-six of their ninety-one congressional seats and lost control of all but two free-state legislatures.

The beneficiary of northern voters' wrath was a new political party. During debate on the Kansas-Nebraska

BIRTH OF THE REPUBLICAN PARTY

bill, six congressmen had published an "Appeal of the Independent Democrats." Joshua Giddings, Salmon Chase, and Charles Sumner—the principal authors of this protest—attacked Doug-

■ Throughout the North the Kansas-Nebraska Act kindled fires of alarm over the Slave Power's "determination to extend its dominion" and "control the government of the nation." Public meetings like the one announced here, held in West Chester, Pennsylvania, aided the new Republican Party. (American Antiquarian Society)

las's legislation as a "gross violation of a sacred pledge" (the Missouri Compromise) and a "criminal betrayal of precious rights" that would make free territory a "dreary region of despotism." Their appeal tapped a reservoir of deep concerns in the North, cogently expressed by Illinois's Abraham Lincoln.

Although Lincoln did not personally condemn southerners—"They are just what we would be in their situation"—he exposed the meaning of the Kansas-Nebraska Act. Denying "that there can be moral right in the enslaving of one man by another," Lincoln argued that the founders, from love of liberty, had banned slavery from the Northwest Territory, kept the word *slavery* out of the Constitution, and treated it overall as a "cancer" on the republic. Rather than encouraging liberty, the Kansas-Nebraska Act put slavery "on the high road to extension and perpetuity," and that constituted a "moral wrong and injustice." America's future, Lincoln warned, was being mortgaged to slavery and all its influences.

Thousands of ordinary white northerners agreed. During the summer and fall of 1854, antislavery Whigs and Democrats, Free-Soilers, and other reformers throughout the Old Northwest met to form the new Republican Party, dedicated to keeping slavery out of the territories. The influence of the Republicans rapidly spread to the East, and they won a stunning victory in the 1854 elections. In their first appearance on the ballot, Republicans captured a majority of northern House seats. Antislavery sentiment had created a new party and caused roughly a quarter of northern Democrats to desert their party.

For the first time, too, a sectional party had gained significant power in the political system. Now the Whigs were gone, and only the Democrats struggled to maintain national membership. The Republicans absorbed the Free-Soil Party and grew rapidly in the North. Indeed, the emergence of the Republican coalition of antislavery interests is the most rapid transformation in party allegiance and voter behavior in American history. This fact alone attests to the centrality of slavery expansion in the causation of the Civil War.

Republicans also drew into their coalition a fast-growing nativist movement that called itself the American

KNOW-NOTHINGS

Party, or Know-Nothings (because its first members kept their purposes secret, answering "I know nothing" to all questions). This group exploited nativist fear of foreigners and Catholics. Between 1848 and 1860, nearly 3.5 million immigrants entered the United States—proportionally the heaviest inflow of foreigners ever in American history (see pages 314–319). Democrats courted the votes of these new citizens, but many native-born Anglo-Saxon Protestants believed that Irish and German Catholics would owe primary allegiance to the pope in Rome and not to the American nation.

In 1854 anti-immigrant fears gave the Know-Nothings spectacular success in some northern states. They triumphed especially in Massachusetts, electing 11 congressmen, a governor, all state officers, all state senators, and all but 2 of 378 state representatives. The temperance movement also gained new strength early in the 1850s with its promises to stamp out the evils associated with liquor and immigrants (a particularly anti-Irish campaign). In this context the Know-Nothings strove to reinforce Protestant morality and restrict voting and officeholding to the native-born. As the Whig Party faded from the scene, the Know-Nothings temporarily filled the void. But like the Whigs, the Know-Nothings could not keep their northern and southern wings together in the face of the slavery expansion issue, and they dissolved after 1856. The growing Republican coalition wooed the nativists with temperance ordinances and laws postponing suffrage for naturalized citizens (see Table 14.1).

With nearly half of the old electorate up for grabs, the demise of the Whig Party ensured a major realignment

PARTY REALIGNMENT AND THE REPUBLICANS' APPEAL

of the political system. The remaining parties made appeals to various segments of the electorate. Immigration, temperance, homestead bills, the tariff, internal improvements—all played important roles in attracting voters during the 1850s. The Republicans appealed strongly to those interested in the economic development of the West. Commercial agriculture was booming in the Ohio–Mississippi–Great Lake area, but residents of that region desired more canals, roads, and river and harbor improvements to reap the full benefit of their labors. Because credit was scarce, a homestead program attracted voters: its proponents argued that western land should be made available free to individual farmers. The Republicans seized on these political desires, promising internal improvements and land grants as well as backing higher tariffs for industrialists.

Partisan ideological appeals became the currency of the realigned political system. As Republicans preached "Free Soil, Free Labor, Free Men," they captured a self-image of many northerners. These phrases resonated with traditional ideals of equality, liberty, and opportunity under self-government—the heritage of republicanism. Invoking that heritage also undercut charges that the Republican Party was radical and unreliable.

"Free Soil, Free Labor, Free Men" seemed an appropriate motto for a northern economy that was energetic, expanding, and prosperous. Thousands of farmers had moved west to establish productive farms and growing communities. Midwesterners multiplied their yields by using new machines such as mechanical reapers. Railroads were carrying their crops to urban markets. And industry was beginning to perform wonders of production, making available goods that only recently had been beyond the reach of the average person. As northerners surveyed the general growth and prosperity, they thought they saw a reason for it.

The key to progress appeared, to many people, to be free labor—the dignity of work and the incentive of opportunity. Any hard-working and virtuous man, it was

REPUBLICAN IDEOLOGY

thought, could improve his condition and achieve economic independence by seizing opportunities that the country had to offer. Republicans argued that the South, with little industry and slave labor, was backward by comparison. Their arguments captured the spirit of the age in the North.

Traditional republicanism hailed the virtuous common man as the backbone of the country. In Abraham Lincoln, a man of humble origins who had become a successful lawyer and political leader, Republicans had a symbol of that tradition. They portrayed their party as the guardian of economic opportunity, giving individuals a chance to work, acquire land, and attain success. In the words of an Iowa Republican, the United States was thriving because its "door is thrown open to all, and even the poorest and humblest in the land, may, by industry and application, gain a position which will entitle him to the respect . . . of his fellow-men."

At stake in the enveloping crises of the 1850s were thus two competing definitions of "liberty": southern planters' claims to protection of their liberty in the possession and transport of their slaves anywhere in the land, and northern workers' and farmers' claims to protection of their liberty to seek a new start on free land, unimpeded by a system that defined labor as slave and black. Thus, a growing number of northerners expressed the fear that the rising political storm was an "irrepressible conflict."

Opposition to the extension of slavery had brought the Republicans into being, but party members carefully broadened their appeal by adopting the causes of other groups. Their coalition ideology consisted of many elements: resentment of southern political power, devotion to unionism, antislavery based on free-labor arguments, moral revulsion to slavery, and racial prejudice. As the *New York Tribune* editor Horace Greeley wrote in 1856, "It is beaten into my bones that the American people are not yet anti-slavery." Four years later, Greeley again observed that "an Anti-Slavery man per se cannot be elected." But, he added, "a Tariff, River-and-Harbor, Pacific Railroad, Free Homestead man, may succeed although he is Anti-Slavery." As these elements joined the Republican Party, they also grew to fear slavery even more.

In the South, the disintegration of the Whig Party had left many southerners at loose ends politically; they

SOUTHERN
DEMOCRATS

included a good number of wealthy planters, smaller slaveholders, and urban businessmen. Some gravitated to the American Party, but not for long. In the increasingly tense atmosphere of sectional crisis, these people were highly susceptible to strong states' rights positions and defense of slavery. The security of their own communities seemed at stake, and in the

1850s, most formerly Whig slaveholders converted to the Democrats.

Since Andrew Jackson's day, however, nonslaveholding small farmers had been the heart of the Democratic Party. Democratic politicians, though often slaveowners themselves, lauded the common man and argued that their policies advanced his interests. According to the southern version of republicanism, white citizens in a slave society enjoyed liberty and social equality because black people were enslaved. As Jefferson Davis put it in 1851, in other societies distinctions were drawn "by property, between the rich and the poor." But in the South, slavery elevated every white person's status and allowed the nonslaveholder to "stand upon the broad level of equality with the rich man." To retain the support of ordinary whites, southern Democrats emphasized this appeal to racism. The issue in the sectional crisis, they warned, was "shall negroes govern white men, or white men govern negroes?"

Southern leaders also portrayed sectional controversies as matters of injustice and insult to the South. The rights of all southern whites were in jeopardy, they argued, because antislavery and Free-Soil forces threatened an institution protected in the Constitution. The stable, well-ordered South was the true defender of constitutional principles, the rapidly changing North their destroyer.

Racial fears and traditional political loyalties helped keep the political alliance between yeoman farmers and planters largely intact through the 1850s. Across class lines, white southerners joined together in the interest of community security against what they perceived as the Republican Party's capacity to cause slave unrest in their midst. In the South no viable party emerged to replace the Whigs. The result was a one-party system that emphasized sectional issues and loyalty. In the South as in the North, political realignment sharpened sectional identities.

Political leaders of both sections used race in their arguments about opportunity, but northerners and southerners saw different futures. The *Montgomery* (Alabama) *Mail* warned southern whites in 1860 that the Republicans intended "to free the negroes and force amalgamation between them and the children of the poor men of the South. The rich will be able to keep out of the way of the contamination." Republicans warned northern workers that if slavery entered the territories, the great reservoir of opportunity for ordinary citizens would be poisoned.

In the territory of Kansas a succession of events, like hammer blows, deepened the conflict. The Kansas-Nebraska Act spawned hatred and violence as land-hungry partisans in the sectional struggle clashed repeatedly in Kansas Territory. Abolitionists and religious groups sent in armed Free-Soil settlers; southerners sent in their reinforcements to establish slavery and prevent "northern hordes" from stealing Kansas away. Conflicts led to bloodshed, and soon the whole nation was talking about "Bleeding Kansas."

Politics in the territory resembled war more than democracy. During elections for a territorial legislature in 1855, thousands of proslavery Missourians—known as Border Ruffians—invaded the polls and ran up a large but fraudulent majority for proslavery candidates. The resulting legislature legalized slavery, and in response Free-Soilers held an unauthorized convention at which they created their own government and constitution. In the spring of 1856, a proslavery posse sent to arrest the Free-Soil leaders sacked the Kansas town of Lawrence, killing several people. In revenge John Brown, a radical abolitionist with a band of followers, murdered five proslavery settlers living along Pottawatomie Creek. Soon, armed bands of guerrillas roamed the territory, battling over land claims as well as slavery.

BLEEDING KANSAS

These passions brought violence to the U.S. Senate in May 1856, when Charles Sumner of Massachusetts denounced "the Crime against Kansas." Radical in his antislavery views, Sumner bitterly assailed the president, the South, and Senator Andrew P. Butler of South Carolina. Soon thereafter Butler's cousin, Representative Preston Brooks, approached Sumner at the latter's Senate desk, raised his cane, and began to beat Sumner on the head. Trapped behind his desk, which was bolted in place, Sumner tried to rise, eventually wrenching the desk free before he collapsed, bleeding, on the floor.

Shocked northerners recoiled from what they saw as another southern assault on free speech and southerners' readiness to use violence. William Cullen Bryant, editor of the *New York Evening Post,* asked, "Has it come to this, that we must speak with bated breath in the presence of our southern masters?" As if in reply, the *Richmond Enquirer* denounced "vulgar Abolitionists in the Senate" who "have been suffered to run too long without collars. They must be lashed into submission." Popular opinion in Massachusetts strongly supported Sumner; South Carolina voters reelected Brooks and sent him dozens of commemorative canes. The country was becoming polarized.

The election of 1856 showed how extreme that polarization had become. When Democrats met to select a nominee, they shied away from prominent leaders whose views on the territories were well known. In-

■ Proslavery advocates and Free-Soilers clashed in open battle in Kansas Territory on September 13, 1856, captured in this sketch made by eyewitness S. J. Reader. (Kansas State Historical Society)

stead, they chose James Buchanan of Pennsylvania, whose chief virtue was that for the past four years he had been ambassador to Britain, uninvolved in territorial controversies. Superior party organization helped Buchanan win 1.8 million votes and the election, but he owed his victory to southern support. Hence, he was tagged with the label "a northern man with southern principles." Eleven of sixteen free states voted against him, and Democrats did not regain ascendancy in those states for decades. The Republican candidate, John C. Frémont, won those eleven free states and 1.3 million votes; Republicans had become the dominant party in the North after only two years of existence. The Know-Nothing candidate, Millard Fillmore, won almost 1 million votes, but this election was that party's last hurrah. The coming battle would pit a sectional Republican Party against an increasingly divided Democratic Party. With huge voter turnouts as high as 75–80 percent in many states, Americans were about to learn that elections really matter.

Slavery and the Nation's Future

*F*or years the issue of slavery in the territories had convulsed Congress, and Congress had tried to settle the issue with vague formulas. In 1857 a different branch of government stepped into the fray. The Supreme Court took up this emotionally charged subject and attempted to silence controversy with a definitive verdict.

A Missouri slave named Dred Scott had sued his owner for his freedom. Scott based his claim on the fact

DRED SCOTT CASE

that his former owner, an army surgeon, had taken him for several years into Illinois, a free state, and into the Wisconsin Territory, from which slavery had been barred by the Missouri Compromise. Scott first won and then lost his case as it moved on appeal through the state courts into the federal system and, finally, after eleven years, to the Supreme Court.

Normally Supreme Court justices were reluctant to inject themselves into political issues, and it seemed likely that the Court would stay out of this one. An 1851 decision had declared that state courts determined the status of Negroes who lived within their jurisdictions. The Supreme Court had only to follow this precedent to avoid ruling on substantive, and very controversial, issues: Was a black person like Dred Scott a citizen of the United States and thus eligible to sue in federal court? Had residence in a free state or territory made him free?

Did Congress have the power to prohibit slavery in a territory or to delegate that power to a territorial legislature?

After some initial reticence to take the case, the Supreme Court agreed to hear *Dred Scott v. Sanford* and decided to rule on the Missouri Compromise after all. Two northern justices indicated that they would dissent from the assigned opinion and argue for Scott's freedom and the constitutionality of the Missouri Compromise. Their decision emboldened southerners on the Court, who were growing eager to declare the 1820 geographical restriction on slavery unconstitutional. Southern sympathizers in Washington were pressing for a proslavery verdict, and several justices simply felt they should try to resolve sectional strife once and for all.

In March 1857, Chief Justice Roger B. Taney of Maryland delivered the majority opinion of a divided Court. Taney declared that Scott was not a citizen of either the United States or Missouri; that residence in free territory did not make Scott free; and that Congress had no power to bar slavery from any territory. The decision not only overturned a sectional compromise that had been honored for thirty-seven years; it also invalidated the basic ideas of the Wilmot Proviso and popular sovereignty as well.

The Slave Power seemed to have won a major constitutional victory. African Americans were especially dismayed, for Taney's decision asserted that the founders had never intended for black people to be citizens. At the nation's founding, the chief justice wrote, blacks had been regarded "as beings of an inferior order" with "no rights which the white man was bound to respect." Taney was mistaken, however. African Americans had been citizens in several of the original states, and had voted.

Nevertheless, the ruling seemed to shut the door permanently on black hopes for justice. After 1857, African Americans lived in the land of the *Dred Scott* decision. In northern black communities rage and despair prevailed. Many who were still fugitive slaves sought an uncertain refuge in Canada. Others considered emigration to the Caribbean or even to Africa. Mary Ann Shadd Cary, the leader of an emigration movement to Canada, advised her fellow blacks: "Your national ship is rotten and sinking, why not leave it?" Another black abolitionist said the *Dred Scott* decision had made slavery "the supreme law of the land and all descendants of the African race denationalized." In this state of social dislocation and fear, blacks contemplated whether they had any future in America.

Northern whites who rejected the decision's content were suspicious of the circumstances that produced it.

■ Dred Scott, a slave who brought suit in Missouri for his freedom, and Chief Justice Roger Taney, a descendant of Maryland's slaveholding elite, were principal figures in the most controversial Supreme Court decision of the nineteenth century. (Scott: Missouri Historical Society; Taney: Maryland Historical Society, Baltimore)

Five of the nine justices were southerners; three of the northern justices actively dissented or refused to concur in crucial parts of the decision. The only northerner who supported Taney's opinion, Justice Robert Grier of Pennsylvania, was known to be close to President Buchanan. In fact, Buchanan had secretly brought to bear improper but effective influence.

A storm of angry reaction broke in the North. The decision seemed to confirm every charge against the aggressive Slave Power. "There is such a thing as the slave power," warned the *Cincinnati Daily Commercial*. "It has marched over and annihilated the boundaries of the states. We are now one great homogenous slaveholding community." The *Cincinnati Freeman* asked, "What security have the Germans and the Irish that their children will not, within a hundred years, be reduced to slavery in this land of their adoption?" The poet James Russell Lowell expressed the racial and economic anxieties of poor northern whites when he had his Yankee character Ezekiel Biglow say in the language of the day:

> Wy, it's just ez clear ez figgers,
> Clear ez one an' one make two,
> Chaps thet make black slaves o' niggers,
> Want to make wite slaves o' you.

Republican politicians used these fears to strengthen their antislavery coalition. Abraham Lincoln stressed that the territorial question affected every citizen. "The whole nation," he had declared as early as 1854, "is interested that the best use shall be made of these Territories. We want them for homes of free white people. This they cannot be, to any considerable extent, if slavery shall be planted within them." The territories must be reserved, he insisted, "as an outlet for free white people everywhere" so that immigrants could come to America and "find new homes and better their condition in life."

ABRAHAM LINCOLN AND THE SLAVE POWER

More importantly, Lincoln warned of slavery's increasing control over the nation. The founders had created a government dedicated to freedom, Lincoln insisted. Admittedly they had recognized slavery's existence, but the public mind, he argued in 1858, had always rested in the belief that slavery would die either naturally or by legislation. The next step in the unfolding Slave Power conspiracy, Lincoln alleged, would be a Supreme Court decision "declaring that the Constitution does not permit a State to exclude slavery from its limits. . . . We shall lie down pleasantly, dreaming that the people of Missouri are on the verge of making their State free; and we shall awake to the reality instead, that the Supreme Court has made Illinois a slave State." This charge was not hyperbole, for lawsuits soon challenged state laws that freed slaves brought within their borders.

Lincoln's most eloquent statement against the Slave Power was his famous "House Divided" speech, delivered as he announced his campaign for the U.S. Senate in 1858. Using biblical metaphor and extraordinary grace, he declared:

> "A house divided against itself cannot stand." I believe this government cannot endure, permanently half slave and half free. I do not expect the Union to be dissolved— I do not expect the House to fall—but I do expect it to cease to be divided. It will become all one thing or all the other. Either the opponents of slavery will arrest the further spread of it, and place it where the public mind shall rest in the belief that it is in the course of ultimate extinction; or its advocates will push it forward, till it shall become alike lawful in all the States, old as well as new, North as well as South.

Countless northerners heeded Lincoln's warnings, and events convinced them that slaveholders were nearing their goal of making slavery a national institution. Southerners, fatefully, never forgot Lincoln's use of the direct words "ultimate extinction."

Politically, these forceful Republican arguments offset the difficulties that the *Dred Scott* decision posed. By endorsing the South's doctrine of state sovereignty, the Court had in effect declared that the central position of the Republican Party—no extension of slavery—was unconstitutional. Republicans could only repudiate the decision, appealing to a "higher law," or hope to change the personnel of the Court. They did both and gained politically as fear of the Slave Power grew. But fear also deepened among free blacks. Frederick Douglass continued to try to fashion hope among his people but concluded a speech in the wake of the *Dred Scott* decision bleakly: "I walk by faith, not by sight."

For northern Democrats like Stephen Douglas, the Court's decision posed an awful dilemma. Northern voters were alarmed by the prospect that the territories would be opened to slavery. To retain their support, Douglas had to find some way to reassure these voters. Yet, given his ambitions to lead the national Democratic Party and become president, Douglas could not afford to alienate southern Democrats.

THE LECOMPTON CONSTITUTION AND SECTIONAL DISHARMONY AMONG DEMOCRATS

Douglas chose to stand by his principle of popular sovereignty, even if the result angered southerners. In 1857 Kansans voted on a proslavery constitution that had been drafted at Lecompton. It was defeated by more than ten thousand votes in a referendum boycotted by most proslavery voters. The evidence was overwhelming that Kansans did not want slavery, yet President Buchanan tried to force the Lecompton Constitution through Congress in an effort to hastily organize the territory.

Never had the Slave Power's influence over the government seemed more blatant; the Buchanan administration and southerners demanded a proslavery outcome, contrary to the popular will of the majority in Kansas. Breaking with the administration, Douglas threw his weight against the Lecompton Constitution. He gauged opinion in Kansas correctly, for in 1858 voters there rejected the constitution again. But his action infuriated southern Democrats. After the *Dred Scott* decision, southerners like Senator Albert G. Brown of Mississippi believed that slavery was protected in the territories: "The Constitution as expounded by the Supreme Court awards it. We demand it; we mean to have it." Increasingly, many southerners believed their sectional rights and slavery would be safe only in a separate nation. And northern Democrats, led by Douglas, found it harder to support the territorial protection for slavery that southern Democrats insisted was theirs as a constitutional right. Thus, in North and South the issue of slavery in the territories continued to destroy moderation and promote militancy.

Meanwhile, as the territorial process floundered in Kansas, it also collapsed in Utah. For their practice of polygamy and their theocratic government, the Mormons who settled Utah were among the most persecuted peoples in America. Under the church-centered leadership of seer and prophet Brigham Young, the Mormons claimed the doctrine of popular sovereignty as their basis of independent rule while seeking recognition from Congress of territorial status and polygamy. But a series of corrupt territorial court justices appointed by Presidents Pierce and Buchanan failed to reign in the frontier society.

THE "MORMON WAR" IN UTAH

In 1857, Buchanan dispatched 2,500 troops, one-sixth of the U.S. Army, to suppress Young, who as one historian describes him, ruled "like a traitor in rebellion against the United States." Because of winter in the Rockies, the army never reached Utah. The massacre of a wagon train of 120 settlers by the Mormons and Indian allies notwithstanding, the "Mormon War" ended in Young withdrawing his forces and Buchanan sending peace commissioners and offering amnesty in 1858. The struggle over federal authority, as well as the Mormons' own "peculiar institution" in Utah, would continue for years.

Disunion

t is worth remembering that in the late 1850s most Americans were not caught up daily in the slavery crisis. They were preoccupied with personal affairs, especially coping with the effects of the economic panic that had begun in the spring of 1857. They were worried about widespread unemployment, the plummeting price of wheat, the declining wages at a textile mill, or sons who needed land. In the Midwest, clerks, mechanics, domestics, railroad hands, and lumber camp workers lost jobs by the thousands. Bankers were at a loss for what to do about a weak credit system caused by frenzied western land speculation that began early in the decade. In parts of the South, such as Georgia, the panic intensified class divisions between upcountry yeomen and coastal slaveholding planters. Farmers blamed the tight money policies of Georgia's budding commercial banking system on wealthy planters who controlled the state's Democratic Party.

The panic had been caused by several shortcomings of the unregulated American banking system, by frenzies of speculation in western lands and railroads, and by a weak and overburdened credit system. By 1858 Philadelphia had 40,000 unemployed workers, and New York City nearly 100,000. Fear of bread riots and class warfare gripped many cities in the North. True to form, blame for such economic woe became sectionalized, as southerners saw their system justified by the temporary collapse of industrial prosperity and northerners feared even more the incursions of the Slave Power on an insecure future.

Soon, however, the entire nation's focus would be thrown on a new dimension of the slavery question—

JOHN BROWN'S RAID ON HARPERS FERRY armed rebellion, led by the abolitionist who had killed proslavery settlers along Pottawatomie Creek in "Bleeding Kansas." Born in Connecticut in 1800, John Brown had been raised by staunchly religious and antislavery parents. Between 1820 and 1855, he engaged in some twenty business ventures, including farming, nearly all of them failures. But Brown had a distinctive vision of abolitionism. He relied on an Old Testament conception of justice—"an eye for an eye"—and he had a puritanical obsession with the wickedness of others, especially southern slaveowners. Brown believed that slavery was an "unjustifiable" state of war conducted by one group of people against another. He also believed that violence in a righteous cause was a holy act, even a rite of purification for those who engaged in it. To Brown, the destruction of slavery in America required revolutionary ideology and revolutionary acts.

On October 16, 1859, Brown led a small band of whites and blacks (eighteen men in all) in an attack on the federal arsenal at Harpers Ferry, Virginia. Hoping to trigger a slave rebellion, Brown failed miserably and was quickly captured. In a celebrated trial in November and a widely publicized execution in December, in Charles Town, Virginia, Brown became one of the most enduring martyrs, as well as villains, of American history. His attempted insurrection struck fear into the South.

Then it became known that Brown had received financial backing from several prominent abolitionists. When northern intellectuals such as Emerson and Henry David Thoreau praised Brown as a holy warrior who "would make the gallows as glorious as the cross," white southerners' outrage multiplied. The South almost universally interpreted Brown's attack at Harpers Ferry as an act of midnight terrorism, as the fulfillment of their long-stated dread of "abolition emissaries" who would infiltrate the region to incite slave rebellion.

Perhaps most telling of all was the fact that the pivotal election of 1860 was less than a year away when Brown went so eagerly to the gallows, handing a note to

■ The earliest known photograph of John Brown, probably taken in 1846 in Massachusetts, shows him pledging his devotion to an unidentified flag, possibly an abolitionist banner. Already Brown was aiding runaway slaves and pondering ways to strike at slavery.   (Ohio Historical Society)

his jailer with the famous prediction: "I John Brown am now quite certain that the crimes of this guilty land will never be purged away, but with blood." Most troubling to southerners, perhaps, was their awareness that while Republican politicians condemned Brown's crimes, they did so in a way that deflected attention onto the still greater crime of slavery.

Many Americans believed that the election of 1860 would decide the fate of the Union. The Democratic Party was the only party truly national in scope. "One after another," wrote a Mississippi editor, "the links which have bound the North and South together, have been severed . . . [but] the Democratic party looms gradually up . . . and waves the olive branch over the troubled waters of politics." But at its 1860 convention in Charleston, South Carolina, the Democratic Party split.

ELECTION OF 1860

Stephen Douglas wanted his party's presidential nomination, but he could not afford to alienate northern voters by accepting the southern position on the territories. Southern Democrats, however, insisted on recognition of their rights—as the *Dred Scott* decision had defined them—and they moved to block Douglas's nomination. When Douglas obtained a majority for his version of the platform, delegates from the Deep South walked out of the convention. After efforts at compromise failed, the Democrats presented two nominees: Douglas for the northern wing, and Vice President John C. Breckinridge of Kentucky for the southern.

The Republicans nominated Abraham Lincoln at a rousing convention in Chicago. The choice of Lincoln reflected the growing power of the Midwest, and he was perceived as more moderate on slavery than the early front runner, Senator William H. Seward of New York. A Constitutional Union Party, formed to preserve the nation but strong only in the Upper South, nominated John Bell of Tennessee.

Bell's only issue in the ensuing campaign was the urgency of preserving the Union; Constitutional Unionists hoped to appeal to history, sentiment, and moderation to hold the country together. Douglas desperately sought to unite his northern and southern supporters, while Breckinridge quickly backed away from the appearance of extremism and his supporters in several states stressed his unionism. Although Lincoln and the Republicans denied any intent to interfere with slavery in the states where it existed, they stood firm against the extension of slavery into the territories.

The election of 1860 was sectional in character, and the only one in American history in which the losers refused to accept the result. Lincoln won, but Douglas, Breckinridge, and Bell together received a majority of the votes. Douglas had broad-based support but won few states. Breckinridge carried nine southern states, all in the Deep South. Bell won pluralities in Virginia, Kentucky, and Tennessee. Lincoln prevailed in the North, but in the four border states that ultimately remained loyal to the Union (Missouri, Kentucky, Maryland, and Delaware) he gained only a plurality, not a majority (see Table 14.3). Lincoln's victory was won in the electoral college. He polled only 40 percent of the total vote and was not even on the ballot in ten slave states.

Opposition to slavery's extension was the core issue of the Republican Party, and Lincoln's alarm over slavery's growing political power was genuine. Moreover, abolitionists and supporters of free soil in the North worked to keep the Republicans from compromising on their territorial stand. Meanwhile in the South, proslavery advocates and secessionists whipped up public opinion and demanded that state conventions assemble to consider secession.

Lincoln made the crucial decision not to soften his party's position on the territories. He wrote of the necessity of maintaining the bond of faith between voter and

TABLE 14.3

Presidential Vote in 1860 (by State)

Lincoln (Republican)	Carried all northern states and all electoral votes except 3 in New Jersey
Breckinridge (Southern Democrat)	Carried all slave states except Virginia, Kentucky, Tennessee, and Missouri
Bell (Constitutional Union)	Carried Virginia, Kentucky, Tennessee
Douglas (Northern Democrat)	Carried only Missouri

Lincoln received only 26,000 votes in the entire South and was not even on the ballot in ten slave states.
Breckinridge was not on the ballot in three northern states.

candidate and of declining to set "the minority over the majority." Although many conservative Republicans—eastern businessmen and former Whigs who did not feel strongly about slavery—hoped for a compromise, the original and most committed Republicans—old Free-Soilers and antislavery Whigs—were adamant to stop the expansion of the peculiar institution.

In the winter of 1860–1861, Senator John J. Crittenden of Kentucky tried to craft a late-hour compromise. Hoping to don the mantle of Henry Clay and avert disunion, Crittenden proposed that the two sections divide the territories between them at latitude 36°30'. But the southerners would agree to this only if the Republicans did, too, for they wanted no less and knew that extremists in the South would demand much more. When Lincoln ruled out concessions on the territorial issue, Crittenden's peacemaking effort, based on old and discredited measures, collapsed.

Meanwhile, the Union was being destroyed. On December 20, 1860, South Carolina passed an ordinance of secession amid jubilation and cheering. This step marked the inaugural success of a strategy favored by secessionists: separate-state secession. Secessionists concentrated their efforts on the most extreme proslavery state, hoping that South Carolina's bold act would induce other states to follow, with each decision building momentum for disunion.

SECESSION AND THE CONFEDERATE STATES OF AMERICA

By reclaiming its independence, South Carolina raised the stakes in the sectional confrontation. No longer was secession an unthinkable step; the Union was broken. Secessionists now argued that other states should follow South Carolina and that those who favored compromise could make a better deal outside the Union than in it. Moderates found it difficult to dismiss such arguments, since most of them—even those who felt deep affection for the Union—were committed to defending southern rights and the southern way of life.

Southern extremists soon got their way in the Deep South. Overwhelming their opposition, they called separate state conventions and passed secession ordinances in Mississippi, Florida, Alabama, Georgia, Louisiana, and Texas. By February 1861 these states had joined South Carolina to form a new government in Montgomery, Alabama: the Confederate States of America. The delegates at Montgomery chose Jefferson Davis as their president, and the Confederacy began to function independently of the United States.

This apparent unanimity of action was deceiving. Confused and dissatisfied with the alternatives, many southerners who in 1860 had voted in the U.S. presidential election stayed home a few months later rather than vote for delegates who would decide on secession. Even so, in some state conventions the vote to secede was close, with secession decided by overrepresentation of plantation districts. Furthermore, the conventions were noticeably unwilling to let voters ratify their acts. Four states in

R. H. Howell, after Henry Cleenewerck, *The First Flag of Independence Raised in the South.* Lithograph, Savannah, Georgia, 1860. On the night of November 8, 1860, a huge crowd gathered in Johnson Square, Savannah, to protest Lincoln's election victory. The special banner on the obelisk reads "Our Motto Southern Rights, Equality of the States, Don't Tread on Me," drawing upon traditions from the Revolutionary War. (Library of Congress)

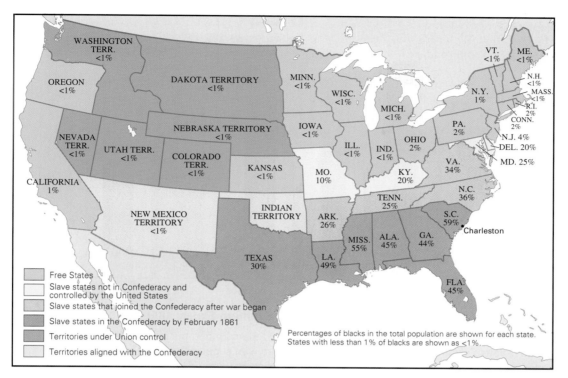

Map 14.4

The Divided Nation—Slave and Free Areas, 1861

After fighting began, the Upper South joined the Deep South in the Confederacy. How does the nation's pattern of division correspond to the distribution of slavery and the percentage of blacks in the population?

the Upper South—Virginia, North Carolina, Tennessee, and Arkansas—flatly rejected secession and did not join the Confederacy until after fighting had begun. In the border states, popular sentiment was deeply divided; minorities in Kentucky and Missouri tried to secede, but these slave states ultimately came under Union control, along with Maryland and Delaware (see Map 14.4).

Such misgivings were not surprising. Secession posed new and troubling issues for southerners, especially the possibility of war, where it would be fought, and who would die. Analysis of election returns from 1860 and 1861 indicates that slaveholders and nonslaveholders were beginning to part company politically. Heavily slaveholding counties strongly supported secession. But nonslaveholding areas that had favored Breckinridge in the presidential election proved far less willing to support secession: most counties with few slaves took an antisecession position or were staunchly Unionist (see Figure 14.1). With war on the horizon, yeomen were beginning to consider their class interests and to ask themselves how far they would go to support slavery and slaveowners.

As for why the Deep South bolted, we need look no further than the speeches and writings of the secession commissioners sent out by the seven seceded states to try to convince the other slave states to join them. Repeat-

edly they stressed independence as the only way to preserve white racial security and the slave system against the hostile Republicans. Upon "slavery," said the Alabama commissioner, Stephen Hale, to the Kentucky legislature, rested "not only the wealth and prosperity of the southern people, but their very existence as a political community." Only secession, Hale contended, could sustain the "heaven-ordained superiority of the white over the black race."

The dilemma facing President Lincoln on inauguration day in March 1861 was how to maintain the authority of

FORT SUMTER AND OUTBREAK OF WAR

the federal government without provoking war. Proceeding cautiously, he sought only to hold on to forts in the states that had left the Union, reasoning that in this way he could assert federal sovereignty while waiting for a restoration. But Jefferson Davis, who could not claim to lead a sovereign nation if the Confederate ports were under foreign (that is, United States) control, was unwilling to be so patient. A collision was inevitable.

It arrived in the early morning hours of April 12, 1861, at Fort Sumter in Charleston harbor. A federal garrison there ran low on food, and Lincoln notified the South Carolinians that he was sending a ship to resupply the fort. For the Montgomery government, the

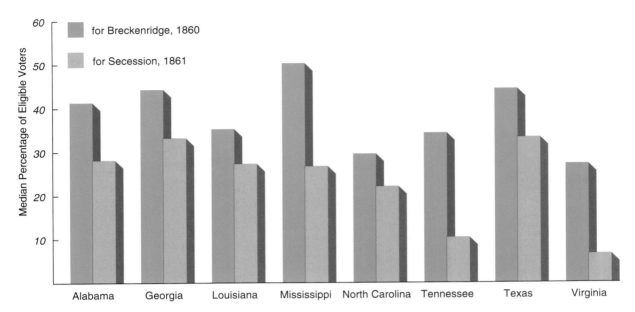

Figure 14.1   Voting Returns of Counties with Few Slaveholders, Eight Southern States, 1860 and 1861

This graph depicts voting in counties whose percentage of slaveholders ranked them among the lower half of the counties in their state. How does voters' support for secession in 1861 compare with support for John Breckinridge, the southern Democratic candidate in 1860? Why was their support for secession so weak? At this time counties with many slaveholders were giving increased support to secession.

alternatives were to attack the fort or to acquiesce to Lincoln's authority. After the Confederate cabinet met, the secretary of war ordered local commanders to obtain a surrender or attack the fort. After two days of heavy bombardment, the federal garrison finally surrendered. No one died in battle, though an accident during post-battle ceremonies killed two Union soldiers. Confederates permitted the U.S. troops to sail away on unarmed vessels while Charlestonians celebrated wildly. The Civil War—the bloodiest war in America's history—had begun.

Summary

Throughout the 1840s and 1850s many able leaders had worked diligently to avert this outcome. Most people, North and South, had hoped to keep the nation together. As late as 1858 even Jefferson Davis had declared, "This great country will continue united," saying that "to the innermost fibers of my heart I love it all, and every part." Secession dismayed northern editors and voters, and it also plunged some planters into depression. Paul Cameron, the largest slaveowner in North Carolina, confessed that he was "very unhappy. I love the Union." Many blacks, however, shared Frederick Douglass's outlook. "The contest must now be decided," he wrote in March 1861, "and decided forever, which of the two, Freedom or Slavery, shall give law to this Republic. Let the conflict come."

Why had war broken out? Why had all efforts to prevent it failed? The conflict slavery generated was fundamental. The emotions bound up in attacking and defending slavery's future were too powerful, and the interests it affected too vital, for compromise. Even if one excludes extreme views, North and South had fundamentally different attitudes toward the institution. The logic of Republican ideology tended in the direction of abolishing slavery, even though Republicans denied any such intention. The logic of southern arguments led toward establishing slavery everywhere, though southern leaders too denied such a motive.

These positions hardened in American political life during the decade and a half before secession. Lincoln put these facts succinctly. In a post-election letter to his old friend Alexander Stephens of Georgia, soon to be vice president of the Confederacy, Lincoln offered assurance that Republicans would not attack slavery in the states where it existed. But Lincoln continued, "You think slavery is right and ought to be expanded; while we think it is wrong and ought to be restricted. That I suppose is the rub."

A nation may face unresolvable issues yet manage to get past them. New events can capture people's attention; time can alter interests and attitudes—this is why historians always remind us of the importance of "contingency" in human affairs. Change can occur when we least expect it and the best experts have not predicted it. Advocates of compromise hoped that the tradition of conciliation and sectional adjustment would yet again save the Union in 1860. They tried to contain conflict and buy time for the nation, but their efforts were doomed to failure.

Territorial expansion generated disputes so frequently that the nation never enjoyed an extended breathing space during the 1850s. Every southern victory increased fear of the Slave Power, and each new expression of Free-Soil sentiment made alarmed slaveholders more insistent in their demands. Eventually even those opposed to war could see no way to avoid it. In the profoundest sense, slavery was the root of the war. But as the fighting began, this, the war's central issue, was shrouded in confusion. How would the Civil War affect slavery, its place in the law, and African Americans' place in society? Would the institution survive a short war, but not a long war? As a people and a nation, Americans had reached the most fateful turning point in their history. Answers would now come from the battlefield and from the mobilization of two societies to wage war on a scale they had not imagined.

LEGACY FOR A PEOPLE AND A NATION
Terrorist or Freedom Fighter?

The greatest significance of John Brown's raid on Harpers Ferry in 1859 rests in its long aftermath in American memory. "Men consented to his death," wrote Frederick Douglass of Brown, "and then went home and taught their children to honor his memory." Brown is as important as a symbol as he is for his deeds. He has been at once one of the most beloved and most loathed figures in American history. In the song that bears his name, "John Brown's Body," a popular marching tune during the Civil War, his "soul goes marching on." As the poet Stephen Vincent Benet

wrote: "You can weigh John Brown's body well enough, / But how and in what balance weigh John Brown?"

In the wake of his execution, in painting, song, and poetry people constructed a John Brown mythology. Was he a Christ-like figure who died for the nation's sins, who had to commit crimes in order to expose the nation's larger crime? Or was he a terrorist, who murdered in the name of his own peculiar vision of God's will? Brown can be inspiring and disturbing, majestic and foolish, a warrior saint or a monster. He represents the highest ideals and the most ruthless deeds. He killed for justice and was hanged as a traitor. Perhaps Brown was one of the avengers of history who does the work the rest of us won't, or couldn't, or shouldn't.

Over the years many organizations have adopted John Brown as their justifying symbol, from left-wing students opposing American foreign policy to current anti-abortion groups who target clinics and doctors. In today's world, terrorism and revolutionary violence are more often in the news: an airliner is blown up over Lockerbie, Scotland; suicide bombers attack buses and restaurants in Israel; a federal building explodes in Oklahoma City; the Irish Republican Army plants explosives in London subways; American embassies are attacked in Africa and Europe; and on September 11, 2001, four hijacked passenger airplanes are turned into weapons of death that bring terrorism to American soil as never before. The story of John Brown's raid in 1859 forces us to ask when and how revolutionary violence—violence in the name of a political or spiritual end—is justified. That is his legacy for a people and a nation.

The **history Companion** powered by Eduspace®

*T*RANSFORMING FIRE: THE CIVIL WAR 1861–1865

*H*e was an ordinary twenty-seven-year-old store clerk from a New England town. But he went off, as though directed by a manly compass, to seek the extraordinary experiences of comradeship and war. In the spring of 1861, Charles Brewster, a member of a militia unit in Northampton, Massachusetts, left his mother and two sisters behind and joined Company C of the Tenth Massachusetts Volunteers. At that moment, Brewster had no idea of his capacity for leadership or his ability to uphold such values as courage and manliness. But the war released him from the boredom and failure of his life.

On April 18, only three days after the surrender of Fort Sumter, a mustering of Company C turned into a large public rally. The next week seventy-five Northampton women committed their labor to sew uniforms for the company. Local poets came to the armory to recite patriotic verses to the would-be soldiers. Yesterday farmers, clerks, and mechanics, today they were the heroes who would "whip secesh." By June 10, after weeks of drilling, Brewster's company strode down Main Street amid a cheering throng of spectators. Flags waved everywhere, brass bands competed, and Brewster and his company boarded a train going south. En route the soldiers continued the joyous fervor of the day by singing "patriotic airs" to the accompaniment of a lone accordion.

Before their three-year enlistment ended, the Tenth Massachusetts participated in nearly every major battle fought by the Army of the Potomac from early 1862 to the summer of 1864. When the survivors of the Tenth were mustered out, only 220 of the nearly 1,000 in the original regiment were still on active duty. Their summer outing had transformed into the bloodiest war in history. They had seen thousands die of disease, practiced war upon civilians and the southern landscape, and loyally served the cause as variously defined, trying their best to fulfill their communities' expectations. In more than two hundred sometimes lyrical letters to his mother and sisters, Brewster, who rose to lieutenant and adjutant of his regiment, left a trove of commentary on the meaning

◀ War drastically altered the lives of millions of Americans. Many young men found in soldiering a combination of comradeship, devotion, boredom, and horror. Winslow Homer gave the ironic title *Home, Sweet, Home* to this painting of Union soldiers in camp about 1863.   (National Gallery of Art, Washington, D.C. Patron's Permanent Fund)

CHRONOLOGY

1861 • Battle of Bull Run
- McClellan organizes Union Army
- Union blockade begins
- U.S. Congress passes first confiscation act
- *Trent* affair

1862 • Union captures Fort Henry and Fort Donelson
- U.S. Navy captures New Orleans
- Battle of Shiloh shows the war's destructiveness
- Confederacy enacts conscription
- McClellan's Peninsula Campaign fails to take Richmond
- U.S. Congress passes second confiscation act, initiating emancipation
- Confederacy mounts offensive in Maryland and Kentucky
- Battle of Antietam ends Lee's drive into Maryland in September
- British intervention in the war on Confederate side is averted

1863 • Emancipation Proclamation takes effect
- U.S. Congress passes National Banking Act
- Union enacts conscription
- African American soldiers join Union Army
- Food riots occur in southern cities
- Battle of Chancellorsville ends in Confederate victory but Jackson's death
- Union wins key victories at Gettysburg and Vicksburg
- Draft riots take place in New York City
- Battle of Chattanooga leaves South vulnerable to Sherman's march into Georgia

1864 • Battles of the Wilderness and Spotsylvania produce heavy casualties on both sides in the effort to capture and defend Richmond
- Battle of Cold Harbor continues carnage in Virginia
- Lincoln requests Republican Party plank abolishing slavery
- Sherman captures Atlanta
- Confederacy begins to collapse on the home front
- Lincoln wins reelection, eliminating any Confederate hopes for a negotiated end to war
- Jefferson Davis proposes emancipation within the Confederacy
- Sherman marches through Georgia to the sea

1865 • Sherman marches through Carolinas
- U.S. Congress approves Thirteenth Amendment
- Lee abandons Richmond and Petersburg
- Lee surrenders at Appomattox Court House
- Lincoln assassinated
- Death toll in war reaches 620,000

of war, why slavery had to be destroyed, and especially the values of common, mid-nineteenth-century American men.

Brewster was as racist as many southerners in his perceptions of blacks. He was no "desperate hero" about battlefield courage, and he nearly died of dysentery twice. He was personally eager for rank and recognition, and eventually held only contempt for civilians who stayed at home. He was often miserably lonely and homesick, and he described battlefield carnage with an honest realism. The early romantic was transformed into a mature veteran by what he called the "terrible, terrible business" of war.

Most tellingly, Brewster's attitudes toward race transformed. In 1862 he defied orders and took in a seventeen-year-old ex-slave as his personal servant, patronizingly clothing him with his own old pants sent from home. In 1864, after surviving some of the worst battles of the war in Virginia, which destroyed his regiment, and frightened of civilian life, Brewster reenlisted to be a recruiter of black troops. In this new role, Brewster worked from an office in Norfolk, Virginia, where his principal job was writing "love letters" for illiterate black women to their soldier husbands at the front. In imagining Brewster sitting at a table with a lonely freedwoman, swallowing his prejudices toward blacks and women, and repeatedly writing or reciting the phrases "give my love to . . ." and "your Husband untall Death," we can glimpse the enormous potential for human transformation at work in this war.

The Civil War brought astonishing, unexpected changes to individuals everywhere in North and South. It obliterated the normal patterns of life. Millions of men were swept away into training camps and battle units. Armies numbering in the hundreds of thousands marched over the South, devastating once-peaceful countrysides. Families struggled to survive without their men; businesses tried to cope with the loss of workers. Women in both North and South took on extra responsibilities in the home and moved into new jobs in the work force. Many women joined the ranks of nurses and hospital workers. No sphere of life was untouched.

But southern soldiers, and their families, also experienced what few other groups of Americans have—utter defeat. For most of them, wealth changed to poverty and hope to despair as countless southern farms were ruined. Late in the war many southerners yearned only for an end to inflation, shortages, the escape of their slaves, and the death that visited nearly every family. Even the South's slaves, who hoped that they were witnessing the "coming of the jubilee," encountered unsympathetic liberators. When a Yankee soldier ransacked a slave woman's cabin, stealing her best quilts, she denounced him as a "nasty, stinkin' rascal" who had betrayed his cause of freedom. Angrily the soldier contradicted her, saying, "I'm fightin' for $14 a month and the Union."

Northern soldiers, though ultimately victorious, often resented the sacrifices demanded of them. Northern businessmen, however, viewed the economic effects of the war with optimism. The conflict ensured vast government expenditures, a heavy demand for goods, and lucrative federal contracts. *Harper's Monthly* reported that an eminent financier expected a long war, fostering huge purchases, paper money, active speculation, and rising prices. "The battle of Bull Run," predicted the financier, "makes the fortune of every man in Wall Street who is not a natural idiot."

Change was most drastic in the South, where secessionists had launched a conservative revolution for their section's national independence. Born of states' rights doctrine, the Confederacy now had to be transformed into a centralized nation to fight a vast war. Never were men more mistaken: their revolutionary means were fundamentally incompatible with their conservative purpose. Southern whites had feared that a peacetime government of Republicans would interfere with slavery and upset the routine of plantation life. Instead their own actions led to a war that turned southern life upside down and imperiled the very existence of slavery.

War altered the North as well, but less sharply. Because most of the fighting took place on southern soil, northern farms and factories remained largely unscathed and busy. Workers lost ground to inflation, but the economy hummed. A new pro-business atmosphere dominated Congress, where the seats of southern representatives were empty. To the alarm of many, the powers of the federal government and of the president increased during the war.

The war created social strains in both North and South. Disaffection was strongest in the Confederacy, where poverty and class resentment threatened the Confederacy from within as federal armies assailed it from without. In the North, dissent also flourished, and antiwar sentiment occasionally erupted into violence.

Ultimately, the Civil War forced on the nation a social and political revolution regarding race. Its greatest effect was to compel leaders and citizens to deal directly with the issue they had struggled over but had been unable to resolve: slavery. This issue, in a host of ways, had caused the war. Now the scope and demands of the war forced reluctant Americans to confront it. And blacks themselves embraced what was for them the most fundamental turning point in their experience as Americans. ■

America Goes to War, 1861–1862

Few Americans understood what they were getting into when the war began. The onset of hostilities sparked patriotic sentiments, optimistic speeches, and joyous ceremonies in both North and South. Northern communities, like Brewster's Northampton, raised companies of volunteers eager to save the Union and sent them off with fanfare. In the South, confident recruits boasted of whipping the Yankees and returning home before Christmas. Southern women sewed dashing uniforms for men who soon would be lucky to wear drab gray or butternut homespun. Americans went to war in 1861 with decidedly romantic notions of what they would experience.

Through the spring of 1861 both sides scrambled to organize and train their undisciplined armies. On July 21, 1861, the first battle took place outside Manassas Junction, Virginia, near a stream called Bull Run. General Irvin McDowell and 30,000 Union troops attacked General P. G. T. Beauregard's 22,000 southerners (see Map 15.1). As raw recruits struggled amid the confusion of their first battle, federal forces began to gain ground. Then they ran into a line of Virginia troops under General Thomas Jackson. "There is Jackson standing like a stone wall," shouted one Confederate. "Stonewall" Jackson's line held, and the arrival of 9,000 Confederate reinforcements won the day for the South. Union troops fled back to Washington, observed by shocked northern congressmen and spectators who had watched the battle; a few sightseers were actually captured for their folly.

FIRST BATTLE OF BULL RUN

■ In *Departure of the Seventh Regiment* (1861), flags and the spectacle of thousands of young men from New York marching off to battle give a deceptively gay appearance to the beginning of the Civil War. (Museum of Fine Arts, Boston; M. and M. Karolik Collection)

The unexpected rout at Bull Run gave northerners their first hint of the nature of the war to come. While the United States enjoyed an enormous advantage in resources, victory would not be easy. Pro-Union feeling was growing in western Virginia, and loyalties were divided in the four border slave states—Missouri, Kentucky, Maryland, and Delaware. But the rest of the Upper South—the states of North Carolina, Virginia, Tennessee, and Arkansas—had joined the Confederacy in the wake of the attack on Fort Sumter. Moved by an outpouring of regional loyalty, half a million southerners volunteered to fight, so many that the Confederate government could hardly arm them all. The United States therefore undertook a massive mobilization of troops around Washington, D.C.

Lincoln gave command of the army to General George B. McClellan, an officer who proved to be better at organization and training than at fighting. McClellan put his growing army into camp and devoted the fall and winter of 1861 to readying a formidable force of a quarter-million men whose mission would be to take Richmond, established as the Confederate capital by July 1861. "The vast preparation of the enemy," wrote one southern soldier, produced a "feeling of despondency" in the South for the first time. But southern morale remained high early in the war.

While McClellan prepared, the Union began to implement other parts of its overall strategy, which called for a blockade of southern ports and eventual capture of the Mississippi River. Like a constricting snake, this "Anaconda plan" would strangle the Confederacy (see Map 15.2). At first the Union Navy had too few ships to patrol 3,550 miles of coastline and block the Confederacy's avenues of supply. Gradually, however, the navy increased the blockade's effectiveness, though it never stopped southern commerce completely.

GRAND STRATEGY

Confederate strategy was essentially defensive. A defensive posture was not only consistent with the South's claim of independence, but acknowledged the North's advantage in resources (see Figure 15.1). Furthermore, communities all across the South demanded their defense. But Jefferson Davis called the southern strategy an "offensive defensive," taking advantage of opportunities to attack and using its interior lines of transportation to concentrate troops at crucial points. In its war aims, the

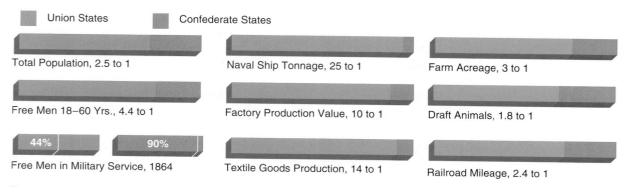

Figure 15.1   Comparative Resources, Union and Confederate States, 1861

The North had vastly superior resources. Although the North's advantages in manpower and industrial capacity proved very important, the South still had to be conquered, its society and its will crushed.

(Source: *The Times Atlas of World History.* Time Books, London, 1978. Used with permission.)

Confederacy did not need to conquer the North; the Union effort, however, as time would tell, required conquest of the South.

Strategic thinking on both sides slighted the importance of "the West," that vast expanse of territory between Virginia and the Mississippi River and beyond. Guerrilla warfare broke out in 1861 in the politically divided state of Missouri, and key locations along the Mississippi and other major western rivers would prove to be crucial prizes in the North's eventual victory. Beyond the Mississippi River, the Confederacy hoped to gain an advantage by negotiating treaties with the Creeks, Choctaws, Chickasaws, Cherokees, Seminoles, and smaller tribes of Plains Indians. Meanwhile the Republican U.S. Congress carved the West into territories in anticipation of state making. But what began during the Civil War was the start of nearly three decades of offensive warfare against Indians, an enveloping strategy of conquest, relocation, and slaughter. All Americans would soon know they were in a war the scale of which few people had ever imagined.

The last half of 1861 brought no major land battles, but the North made gains by sea. Late in the summer Union naval forces captured Cape Hatteras and then seized Hilton Head, one of the Sea Islands off Port Royal, South Carolina. A few months later, similar operations secured vital coastal points in North Carolina, as well as Fort Pulaski, which defended Savannah. Federal naval operations established significant beachheads along the Confederate coastline (see Map 15.2).

The coastal victories off South Carolina foreshadowed a revolution in slave society. At the federal gun-

UNION NAVAL CAMPAIGN

boats' approach, planters abandoned their lands and fled. For a while, Confederate cavalry tried to round up slaves and move them to the interior as well. But thousands of slaves greeted what they hoped to be freedom with rejoicing and broke the hated cotton gins. Some entered their masters' homes and took clothing and furniture, which they conspicuously displayed. A growing stream of runaways poured into the Union lines. Unwilling at first to wage a war against slavery, the federal government did not acknowledge the slaves' freedom—though it began to use their labor in the Union cause. This swelling tide of emancipated slaves, defined by many Union officers as "contraband" of war (confiscated enemy property), forced first a bitter and confused debate within the Union Army and government over how to treat the freedmen, and then a forthright attempt to harness their power.

The coastal incursions worried southerners, but the spring of 1862 brought even stronger evidence of the war's gravity. In March two ironclad ships—the *Monitor* (a Union warship) and the *Merrimack* (a Union ship seized by the Confederacy)—fought each other for the first time off the coast of Virginia; their battle, though indecisive, ushered in a new era in naval design. In April, Union ships commanded by Admiral David Farragut smashed through log booms blocking the Mississippi River and fought their way upstream to capture New Orleans.

Farther west three full Confederate regiments were organized, mostly of Cherokees, from Indian Territory, but a Union victory at Elkhorn Tavern, Arkansas, shattered southern control of the region. Thereafter, dissension within Native American groups and a

WAR IN THE FAR WEST

Union victory the following year at Honey Springs, Arkansas, reduced Confederate operations in Indian Territory to guerrilla raids.

In the westernmost campaign of the war, from February to May 1862, some 3,000 Confederate and 4,000 Union forces fought for control of New Mexico Territory. The military significance of the New Mexico campaign was limited, but the Confederate invasion had grander aims: access to the trade riches of the Santa Fe Trail and possession of gold mines in Colorado and California. If the campaign had endured long enough, the Confederacy would have been much stronger with a western empire. But Colorado and New Mexico Unionists fought for their region, and in a series of battles at Glorieta Pass, 20 miles east of Santa Fe, on March 26–28, they blocked the Confederate invasion. By May 1, Confederate forces straggled down the Rio Grande River back into Texas, ending their effort to take New Mexico.

Meanwhile, in February 1862 land and river forces in northern Tennessee won significant victories for the Union. A Union commander named Ulysses S. Grant saw the strategic importance of Fort Henry and Fort Donelson,

GRANT'S TENNESSEE CAMPAIGN AND THE BATTLE OF SHILOH

the Confederate outposts guarding the Tennessee and Cumberland Rivers. If federal troops could capture these forts, Grant realized, they would open two prime routes into the heartland of the Confederacy. In just ten days he seized the forts, cutting off the Confederates completely and demanding "unconditional surrender" of Fort Donelson. A path into Tennessee, Alabama, and Mississippi now lay open before the Union Army. Grant's achievement of such a surrender from his former West Point roommate, Confederate commander Simon Bolivar Buckner, inspired northern public opinion.

Grant moved on into southern Tennessee and the first of the war's shockingly bloody encounters, the Battle of Shiloh (see Map 15.2). On April 6 Confederate general Albert Sidney Johnston caught federal troops with their backs to the water awaiting reinforcements along the Tennessee River. The Confederates attacked early in the morning and inflicted heavy damage all day. Close to victory, General Johnston was shot from his horse and killed. Southern forces almost achieved a break-

■ Both armies experienced religious revivals during the war. This photograph shows members of a largely Irish regiment from New York celebrating Mass at the beginning of the war. Notice the presence of some female visitors in the left foreground. (Library of Congress)

through, but Union reinforcements arrived that night. The next day the tide of battle turned, and after ten hours of terrible combat, Grant's men forced the Confederates to withdraw.

Neither side won a victory at Shiloh, yet the losses were staggering. Northern troops lost 13,000 men (killed, wounded, or captured) out of 63,000; southerners sacrificed 11,000 out of 40,000. Total casualties in this single battle exceeded those in all three of America's previous wars combined. Now both sides were beginning to sense the true nature of the war. "I saw an open field," Grant recalled, "over which Confederates had made repeated charges . . . so covered with dead that it would have been possible to walk across the clearing, in any direction, stepping on dead bodies, without a foot touching the ground." Shiloh utterly changed Grant's thinking about the war. He had hoped that southerners soon would be "heartily tired" of the conflict. After Shiloh, "I gave up all idea of saving the Union except by complete conquest." Memories of the Shiloh battlefield, and many others to come, would haunt the soldiers who survived for the rest of their lives. Herman Melville's "Shiloh, A Requiem" captures the pathos of that spring day when armies learned the truth about war.

> Skimming lightly, wheeling still,
>   The swallows fly low
> Over the field in clouded days,
>   The forest-field of Shiloh—
> Over the field where April rain
> Solaced the parched ones stretched in pain
> Through the pause of night
> That followed the Sunday fight
>   Around the church of Shiloh—
> The church so lone, the log-built one,
> That echoed to many a parting groan
>   And natural prayer
>   Of dying foemen mingled there—
> Foemen at morn, but friends at eve—
>   Fame or country least their care:
> (What like a bullet can undeceive!)
>   But now they lie low,
> While over them the swallows skim,
>   And all is hushed at Shiloh.

On the Virginia front, President Lincoln had a different problem. General McClellan was slow to move.

McClellan and the Peninsula Campaign

Only thirty-six, McClellan had already achieved notable success as an army officer and railroad president. Habitually overestimating the size of enemy forces, he called repeatedly for reinforcements

Map 15.1   McClellan's Campaign

The water route chosen by McClellan to threaten Richmond during the peninsular campaign.

and ignored Lincoln's directions to advance. McClellan advocated war of limited aims that would lead to a quick reunion. He intended no disruption of slavery, nor war on noncombatants. McClellan's conservative vision of the war was practically outdated before he ever moved his army into Virginia. Finally he chose to move by a water route, sailing his troops down the Chesapeake, landing them on the peninsula between the York and James Rivers, and advancing on Richmond from the east (see Map 15.1).

After a bloody but indecisive battle at Fair Oaks on May 31–June 1, the federal armies moved to within 7 miles of the Confederate capital. They could see the spires on Richmond churches. The Confederate commanding general, Joseph E. Johnston, was badly wounded at Fair Oaks, and President Jefferson Davis placed his chief military adviser, Robert E. Lee, in command. The fifty-five-year-old Lee was an aristocratic Virginian, a lifelong military officer, and a veteran of distinction from the War with Mexico. Although he initially opposed secession, Lee loyally gave his allegiance to his state and became a staunch Confederate nationalist. He soon foiled McClellan's legions.

First, Lee sent Stonewall Jackson's corps of 17,000 northwest into the Shenandoah valley behind Union forces, where they threatened Washington, D.C., and with rapid-strike mobility drew some federal troops away from Richmond to protect their own capital. Further, in mid-June, in an extraordinary four-day ride around the entire Union Army, Confederate cavalry under J. E. B. Stuart, a self-styled Virginia cavalier, with red cape and plumed hat, confirmed the exposed position of a major portion of McClellan's army north of the rain-swollen Chickahominy River. Then, in a series of engagements known as the Seven Days Battles, June 26–July 1, Lee struck at McClellan's army. Lee never managed to close his pincers around the retreating Union forces, but the daring move of taking the majority of his army northeast and attacking the Union right flank, while leaving only a small force to defend Richmond, forced McClellan (always believing he was outnumbered) to retreat toward the James River.

During the sustained fighting of the Seven Days, the Union forces suffered 20,614 casualties, and the Confederates 15,849. After repeated rebel assaults against entrenched positions on high ground at Malvern Hill, an officer concluded: "It was not war, it was murder." By August 3 McClellan withdrew his army back to the Potomac and the environs of Washington. Richmond remained safe for almost two more years.

Buoyed by these results, Jefferson Davis conceived an ambitious plan to turn the tide of the war and gain recognition of the Confederacy by European nations. He ordered a general offensive, sending Lee north into Maryland and Generals Kirby Smith and Braxton Bragg into Kentucky. Calling on residents of Maryland and Kentucky, still slave states, to make a separate peace with his government, Davis also invited northwestern states like Indiana, which sent much of their trade down the Mississippi to New Orleans, to leave the Union. This was a coordinated effort to take the war to the North, and to try to force a turning point.

CONFEDERATE OFFENSIVE IN MARYLAND AND KENTUCKY

The plan was promising, but every part of the offensive failed. In the bloodiest day of the entire war, September 17, 1862, McClellan turned Lee back from Sharpsburg, Maryland. In this Battle of Antietam 5,000 men died, and another 18,000 were wounded. Lee was lucky to escape destruction, for McClellan had intercepted a lost battle order, wrapped around cigars for each Confederate corps commander and inadvertently dropped by a courier. But McClellan moved slowly, failed to use his larger forces in simultaneous attacks, and allowed Lee's stricken army to retreat to safety across the Potomac. In the wake of Antietam, Lincoln removed McClellan from command.

■ In October 1862 in New York City, photographer Mathew Brady opened an exhibition of photographs from the Battle of Antietam. Although few knew it, Brady's vision was very poor, and this photograph of Confederate dead was actually made by his assistants, Alexander Gardner and James F. Gibson. (Library of Congress)

In Kentucky Generals Smith and Bragg secured Lexington and Frankfurt, but their effort to force the Yankees back to the Ohio River was stopped at the Battle of Perryville on October 8. Bragg's army retreated back into Tennessee, where on December 31, 1862, to January 2, 1863, they fought an indecisive but much bloodier battle at Murfreesboro. Casualties exceeded even those of Shiloh, and many lives were sacrificed on a bitter winter landscape.

Confederate leaders had marshaled all their strength for a breakthrough but had failed. Outnumbered and disadvantaged in resources, the South could not continue the offensive. Profoundly disappointed, Davis admitted to a committee of Confederate representatives that southerners were entering "the darkest and most dangerous period we have yet had."

But 1862 also brought painful lessons to the North. Confederate general J. E. B. Stuart executed a daring cavalry raid into Pennsylvania in October. Then on December 13 Union general Ambrose Burnside, now in command of the Army of the Potomac, unwisely ordered his soldiers to attack Lee's army, which held fortified positions on high ground at Fredericksburg, Virginia. Lee's men performed so efficiently in killing northerners that Lee was moved to say, "It is well that war is so terrible. We should grow too fond of it." Burnside's repeated assaults up Marye's Heights shocked even the opponents. "The Federals had fallen like the steady dripping of rain from the eaves of a house," remarked Confederate general James Longstreet. And a Union officer observed the carnage of 1,300 dead and 9,600 wounded Union soldiers: "The whole plain was covered with men, prostrate and dropping. . . . I had never before seen fighting like that . . . the next brigade coming up in succession would do its duty, and melt like snow coming down on warm ground."

The rebellion was far from being suppressed. Both sides were learning that they would have to pay a terrible price. And people on both home fronts had now to decide just what they would endure to win a war of one society against the other.

War Transforms the South

*T*he war caused tremendous disruptions in civilian life and altered southern society beyond all expectations. One of the first traditions to fall was the southern preference for local and limited government. States' rights had been a formative ideology for the Confederacy, but state governments were weak operations. The average citizen, on whom the hand of government had rested lightly, probably knew county authorities

best. To withstand the massive power of the North, however, the South needed to centralize; like the colonial revolutionaries, southerners faced a choice of join together or die separately. Jefferson Davis quickly saw the necessity of centralization. If the states of the Confederacy insisted on fighting separately, said Davis, "we had better make terms as soon as we can."

Promptly Davis moved to bring all arms, supplies, and troops under his control. But by early 1862 the scope and duration of the conflict required something more. Tens of thousands of Confederate soldiers had volunteered for just one year's service, planning to return home in the spring to plant their crops. To keep southern armies in the field, the War Department encouraged reenlistments and called for new volunteers. However, as one official admitted, "the spirit of volunteering had died out." Finally, faced with a critical shortage of troops, in April 1862 the Confederate government enacted the first national conscription (draft) law in American history. Thus the war forced unprecedented change on states that had seceded out of fear of change.

THE CONFEDERACY AND CENTRALIZATION

Jefferson Davis was a strong chief executive. He adopted a firm leadership role toward the Confederate Congress, which raised taxes and later passed a tax-in-kind—paid in farm products. Almost three thousand agents dispersed to collect the tax, assisted by almost fifteen hundred appraisers. Where opposition arose, the government suspended the writ of habeas corpus (which prevented individuals from being held without trial) and imposed martial law. Despite Davis's unyielding stance, this tax system, however, proved inadequate to the South's war effort.

To replace the food that men in uniform would have grown, Davis exhorted state governments to require farmers to switch from cash crops to food crops. But the army remained short of food and labor. The War Department resorted to impressing slaves to work on fortifications, and after 1861 the government relied heavily on confiscation of food to feed the troops. Officers swooped down on farms in the line of march and carted away grain, meat, wagons, and draft animals. Such raids caused increased hardship for women managing farms in the absence of husbands and sons.

Soon the Confederate administration in Richmond gained virtually complete control over the southern economy. Because it controlled the supply of labor through conscription, the administration could compel industry to work on government contracts and supply the military's needs. The Confederate Congress also gave the central government almost complete control of the

■ Five Texans in the Confederate cavalry sitting for a formal photograph. Three have the "lone star" on their hats. Like thousands of others, these men posed to send their images to the folks back home, but also perhaps as an act of comradeship at the war front. (The Panhandle-Plains Historical Society, Canyon, Texas)

railroads. A large bureaucracy sprang up to administer these operations: over seventy thousand civilians staffed the Confederate administration. By the war's end, the southern bureaucracy was larger in proportion to population than its northern counterpart.

Historians have long argued over whether the Confederacy itself was a "rebellion," a "revolution," or the genuine creation of a "nation." Whatever label we apply, Confederates created a culture and an ideology of nationalism. Immediately, southerners tried to forge their own national symbols and identity. In flags, songs, language, seals, school readers, and other forms of "national characteristics," Confederates created their own story.

CONFEDERATE NATIONALISM

In its conservative crusade to preserve states' rights, the social order, and racial slavery, southerners believed the Confederacy was the true legacy of the American Revolution—in continuity with the War of American Independence and a bulwark against centralized power. In this view, southern "liberty" was no less a holy cause than that of the patriots of 1776. To southerners, theirs was a continuing revolution against the excesses of Yankee democracy; George Washington on horseback formed the center of the official seal of the Confederacy.

Also central to Confederate nationalism was a refurbished defense of slavery as a benign, protective institu-

tion. In wartime schoolbooks children were instructed in the divinely inspired, paternalistic character of slavery. And the idea of the "faithful slave" was key to southerners' nationalist cause. A poem popular among whites captured an old slave's rejection of the Emancipation Proclamation:

> Now, Massa, dis is berry fine, dese words
>> You've spoke to me,
> No doubt you mean it kindly, but ole Dinah
>> Won't be free . . .
> Ole Massa's berry good to me—and though I am
>> His slave,
> He treats me like I'se kin to him—and I would
>> Rather have
> A home in Massa's cabin, and eat his black
>> Bread too,
> Dan leave ole Massa's children and go and
>> Lib wid you.

In the face of defeat and devastation, this and other forms of Confederate nationalism collapsed in the final year of the war. But much of the spirit and substance of Confederate nationalism would revive in the postwar period in a new ideology of the Lost Cause.

Clerks and subordinate officials crowded the towns and cities where Confederate departments set up their offices. Clerks had always been males, but now "government girls" staffed the Confederate bureaucracy.

SOUTHERN CITIES AND INDUSTRY The sudden population booms that resulted overwhelmed the housing supply and stimulated new construction. The pressure was especially great in Richmond, whose population increased 250 percent. Mobile's population jumped from 29,000 to 41,000; Atlanta began to grow; and 10,000 people poured into war-related industries in little Selma, Alabama.

As the Union blockade disrupted imports of manufactured products, the traditionally agricultural South forged industries. Many planters shared Davis's hope that industrialization would bring "deliverance, full and unrestricted, from all commercial dependence" on the North or the world. Indeed, beginning almost from scratch, the Confederacy achieved tremendous feats of industrial development. Chief of Ordnance Josiah Gorgas increased the capacity of Richmond's Tredegar Iron Works and other factories to the point that by 1865 his Ordnance Bureau was supplying all Confederate small arms and ammunition. Meanwhile, the government constructed new railroad lines and ironworks, much of the labor for which consisted of slaves relocated from farms and plantations.

White women, restricted to narrow roles in antebellum society, gained substantial new responsibilities in wartime. The wives and mothers of soldiers now headed households and performed men's work, including raising crops and tending animals. Women in nonslaveowning families cultivated fields themselves, while wealthier women suddenly had to perform as overseers and manage field work. In the cities, white women—who had been virtually excluded from the labor force—found a limited number of respectable paying jobs, and female schoolteachers appeared in the South for the first time.

CHANGING ROLES OF WOMEN

Women experienced both confidence and agony from their new responsibilities. Among them was Janie Smith, a young North Carolinian. Raised in a rural area by prosperous parents, she now faced grim realities as the war reached her farm and troops turned her home into a hospital. "It makes me shudder when I think of the awful sights I witnessed that morning," she wrote to a friend. "Ambulance after ambulance drove up with our wounded. . . . Under every shed and tree, the tables were carried for amputating the limbs. . . . The blood lay in puddles in the grove; the groans of the dying . . . were horrible." But Janie Smith learned to cope with crisis. She ended her account with the proud words, "I can dress amputated limbs now and do most anything in the way of nursing wounded soldiers."

Patriotic sacrifice appealed to some women, but others resented their new burdens. A Texas woman who had struggled to discipline slaves pronounced herself "sick of trying to do a man's business." Others grew angry over shortages and resented cooking and unfamiliar contact with lower-class women. Some women grew scornful of the war and demanded that their men return to help provide for families.

For millions of ordinary southerners, change brought privation and suffering. Mass poverty descended for the first time on a large minority of the white population. Many yeoman families had lost their breadwinners to the army. As a South Carolina newspaper put it, "The duties of war have caled away from home the sole supports of many, many families. . . . Help must be given, or the poor will suffer." Women on their own sought help from relatives, neighbors, friends, anyone. Sometimes they pleaded their cases to the Confederate government. "In the name of humanity," begged one woman, "discharge my husband he is not able to do your government much good and he might do his children some good . . . my poor children have no home nor no Father." To the extent that the South eventually lost the will to fight in the face of defeat, women played a key role in demanding an end to the war.

HUMAN SUFFERING, HOARDING, AND INFLATION

The South was in many places so sparsely populated that the conscription of one skilled craftsman could work a hardship on the people of an entire county. Often they begged in unison for the exemption or discharge of the local miller or the neighborhood tanner or wheelwright. Physicians also were in short supply. Most serious, however, was the loss of a blacksmith. As a petition from Alabama explained, "Our Section of County [is] left entirely Destitute of any man that is able to keep in order any kind of Farming Tules."

The blockade of Confederate shipping created shortages of important supplies—salt, sugar, coffee, nails—and speculation and hoarding made the shortages worse. Greedy businessmen cornered the supply of some commodities; prosperous citizens stocked up on food. The *Richmond Enquirer* criticized a planter who purchased so many wagonloads of supplies that his "lawn and paths looked like a wharf covered with a ship's loads." North Carolina's Governor Zebulon Vance worried about "the cry of distress . . . from the poor wives and children of our soldiers. . . . What will become of them?"

Inflation raged out of control, fueled by the Confederate government's heavy borrowing and inadequate taxes, until prices had increased almost 7,000 percent. Inflation particularly imperiled urban dwellers without their own sources of food. As early as 1861 and 1862, newspapers reported that "want and starvation are staring thousands in the face," and troubled officials predicted that "women and children are bound to come to suffering if not starvation." Some families came to the aid of their neighbors, and "free markets," which disbursed goods as charity, sprang up in various cities. But hoarding continued, and a rudimentary relief program organized by the Confederacy failed to meet the need.

As their fortunes declined, people of once-modest means looked around and found abundant evidence that all classes were not sacrificing equally.

INEQUITIES OF THE CONFEDERATE DRAFT

And they noted that the Confederate government enacted policies that favored the upper class. Until the last year of the war, for example, prosperous southerners could avoid military service by hiring substitutes. Prices for substitutes skyrocketed until it cost a man $5,000 or $6,000 to send someone to the front in his place. Well over 50,000 upper-class southerners purchased such substitutes. Mary Boykin Chesnut knew of one young aristocrat who "spent a fortune in substitutes. . . . He is at the end of his row now, for all able-bodied men are ordered to the front. I hear he is going as some general's courier." The rich traded on their social connections to avoid danger.

Anger at such discrimination exploded in October 1862 when the Confederate Congress exempted from military duty anyone who was supervising at least twenty slaves. "Never did a law meet with more universal odium," observed one representative. "Its influence upon the poor is most calamitous." Protests poured in from every corner of the Confederacy, and North Carolina's legislators formally condemned the law. Its defenders argued, however, that the exemption preserved order and aided food production, and the statute remained on the books. The twenty-slave law is indicative of the racial fears many Confederates felt as the war threatened to overturn southern society.

Dissension spread, and alert politicians and newspaper editors warned of class warfare. The bitterness of letters to Confederate officials suggests the depth of the people's anger. "If I and my little children suffer [and] die while there Father is in service," threatened one woman, "I invoke God Almighty that our blood rest upon the South." Another woman swore to the secretary of war that unless help was provided to poverty-stricken wives and mothers "an allwise god . . . will send down his fury . . . [on] those that are in power." War magnified existing social tensions in the Confederacy, and created a few new ones.

Wartime Northern Economy and Society

With the onset of war, a tidal wave of change rolled over the North as well. Factories and citizens' associations geared up to support the war, and the federal government and its executive branch gained new powers. The energies of an industrializing society were harnessed to serve the cause of the Union. Idealism and greed flourished together, and the northern economy proved its awesome productivity. Unlike the experience of the South, northern farms and factories came through the war unharmed.

At first the war was a shock to business. Northern firms lost their southern markets, and many companies had to change their products and find new customers to remain open. Southern debts became uncollectable, jeopardizing not only northern merchants but also many western banks. In farming regions, families struggled with an aggravated shortage of labor caused by army enlistments. A few enterprises never pulled out of the tailspin caused by the war. Cotton mills lacked cotton; construction declined; shoe manufacturers sold few of the cheap shoes that planters had bought for their slaves.

NORTHERN BUSINESS, INDUSTRY, AND AGRICULTURE

But certain entrepreneurs, such as wool producers, benefited from shortages of competing products, and soaring demand for war-related goods swept some businesses to new success. To feed the hungry war machine, the federal government pumped unprecedented sums into the economy. The Treasury issued $3.2 billion in bonds and paper money called "greenbacks," and the War Department spent over $360 million in revenues from new taxes, including the nation's first income tax. Government contracts soon totaled more than $1 billion.

Secretary of War Edwin M. Stanton's list of the supplies needed by the Ordnance Department indicates the scope of government demand: "7,892 cannon, 11,787 artillery carriages, 4,022,130 small-arms, . . . 1,022,176,474 cartridges for small-arms, 1,220,555,435 percussion caps, . . . 26,440,054 pounds of gunpowder, . . . and 90,416,295 pounds of lead." Stanton's list covered only weapons; the government also purchased huge quantities of uniforms, boots, food, camp equipment, saddles, ships, and other necessities. War-related spending revived business in many northern states. In 1863 a merchants' magazine examined the effects of the war in Massachusetts: "Seldom, if ever, has the business of Massachusetts been more active or profitable than during the past year. . . . In every department of labor the government has been, directly or indirectly, the chief employer and paymaster." Government contracts saved Massachusetts shoe manufacturers from ruin.

Nothing illustrated the wartime partnership between business and government better than the work of Jay Cooke, a wealthy New York financier. Cooke threw himself into the marketing of government bonds to finance the war effort. With imagination and energy, he convinced both large investors and ordinary citizens to invest enormous sums, and in the process earning hefty commissions for himself. But the financier's profit served the Union cause, as the interests of capitalism and government merged.

War aided some heavy industries in the North as well, especially iron and steel production. Although new railroad construction slowed, repairs helped the manufacture of rails to increase. Of considerable significance for the future was the railroad industry's adoption of a standard gauge (width) for track, which eliminated the unloading and reloading of boxcars and created a unified transportation system.

The northern economy also grew because of a complementary relationship between agriculture and industry. Mechanization of agriculture had begun before the war. Wartime recruitment and conscription, however, gave western farmers an added incentive to purchase labor-saving machinery. The shift from human labor to machines created new markets for industry and expanded the food supply for the urban industrial work force. The boom in the sale of agricultural tools was tremendous. Cyrus and William McCormick built an industrial empire in Chicago from the sale of their reapers. Between 1862 and 1864 the manufacture of mowers and reapers doubled to 70,000 yearly; by war's end 375,000 reapers were in use, triple the number in 1861. Thus northern farm families whose breadwinners went to war did not suffer as much as their counterparts did in the South. "We have seen," one magazine observed, "a stout matron whose sons are in the army, cutting hay with her team . . . and she cut seven acres with ease in a day, riding leisurely upon her cutter."

Northern industrial and urban workers did not fare as well. After the initial slump, jobs became plentiful, but inflation ate up much of a worker's paycheck. The price of coffee had tripled; rice and sugar had doubled; and clothing, fuel, and rent had all climbed. Between 1860 and 1864 consumer prices

NORTHERN
WORKERS'
MILITANCY

rose at least 76 percent, while daily wages rose only 42 percent. Workers' families consequently suffered a substantial decline in their standards of living.

As their real wages shrank, industrial workers lost job security. To increase production, some employers replaced workers with labor-saving machines. Other employers urged the government to promote immigration to secure cheap labor. Workers responded by forming unions and sometimes by striking. Skilled craftsmen organized to combat the loss of their jobs and status to machines; women and unskilled workers, who were excluded by the craftsmen, formed their own unions. Indeed, thirteen occupational groups—including tailors, coal miners, and railway engineers—formed national unions during the Civil War, and the number of strikes climbed steadily.

Employers reacted with hostility to this new labor independence. Manufacturers viewed labor activism as a threat to their freedom of action and accordingly formed statewide or craft-based associations to cooperate and pool information. These employers shared blacklists of union members and required new workers to sign "yellow dog" contracts (promises not to join a union). To put down strikes, they hired strikebreakers from among blacks, immigrants, and women, and sometimes used federal troops to break the will of unions.

Labor militance, however, did not prevent employers from making profits, nor from profiteering on government contracts. Unscrupulous businessmen took advantage of the suddenly immense demand for army supplies by selling clothing and blankets made of "shoddy"— wool fibers reclaimed from rags or worn cloth. Shoddy goods often came apart in the rain; most of the shoes purchased in the early months of the war were worthless. Contractors sold inferior guns for double the usual price and passed off tainted meat as good. Corruption was so widespread that it led to a year-long investigation by the House of Representatives. Those who romanticize the Civil War era rarely learn of these historical realities in the daily lives of Americans.

Legitimate enterprises also made healthy profits. The output of woolen mills increased so dramatically that dividends in the industry nearly tripled.

ECONOMIC NATIONALISM AND GOVERNMENT-BUSINESS PARTNERSHIP

Some cotton mills made record profits on what they sold, even though they reduced their output. Brokerage houses worked until midnight and earned unheard-of commissions. Railroads carried immense quantities of freight and passengers, increasing their business to the point that railroad stocks skyrocketed in value.

Railroads also were a leading beneficiary of government largesse. With southern representatives absent from Congress, the northern route of the transcontinental railroad quickly prevailed. In 1862 and 1864 Congress chartered two corporations, the Union Pacific Railroad and the Central Pacific Railroad, and assisted them financially in connecting Omaha, Nebraska, with Sacramento, California. For each mile of track laid, the railroads received a loan of from $16,000 to $48,000 in government bonds plus 20 square miles of land along a free 400-foot-wide right of way. Overall, the two corporations gained approximately 20 million acres of land and nearly $60 million in loans.

Other businessmen benefited handsomely from the Morrill Land Grant Act (1862). To promote public education in agriculture, engineering, and military science, Congress granted each state 30,000 acres of federal land for each of its congressional districts. The states could sell the land, as long as they used the income for the purposes Congress had intended. The law eventually fostered sixty-nine colleges and universities, but one of its immediate effects was to enrich a few prominent speculators. At the same time, the Homestead Act of 1862 offered cheap, and sometimes free, land to people who would settle the West and improve their property.

Before the war, there was no adequate national banking, taxation, or currency. Banks operating under state charters issued no fewer than seven thousand different kinds of notes, which were difficult to distinguish from forgeries. During the war, Congress and the Treasury Department established a national banking system empowered to issue national bank notes, and by 1865 most state banks were forced to join the national system by means of a prohibitive tax. This process created sounder currency, but also inflexibility in the money supply and an eastern-oriented financial structure that, later in the century, pushed farmers in need of credit and cash to revolt.

In response to the war, the Republicans created an activist federal government. They converted the sale of war bonds into a crusade, affirming that the country could absorb any level of debt or expense for the cause of union. Indeed, with agricultural legislation, the land grant colleges, higher tariffs, and railroad subsidies, the federal government entered the economy forever. Moreover, Republican economic policies bonded people to the nation as never before. Economic nationalism eventually helped buttress public opinion for the controversial cause of slave emancipation.

The powers of the federal government and the president grew steadily during the crisis. Abraham Lincoln,

EXPANSION OF PRESIDENTIAL POWER

like Jefferson Davis, found that war required active presidential leadership. At the beginning of the conflict, Lincoln launched a major shipbuilding program without waiting for Congress to assemble. The lawmakers later approved his decision, and Lincoln continued to act in advance of Congress when he deemed such action necessary. In one striking exercise of executive power, Lincoln suspended the writ of habeas corpus for everyone living between Washington, D.C., and Philadelphia. There was scant legal justification for this act, but the president's motive was practical: to ensure the loyalty of Maryland, which surrounded the capital on three sides. Later in the war, with congressional approval, Lincoln repeatedly suspended habeas corpus and invoked martial law. Between fifteen and twenty thousand U.S. citizens were arrested on suspicion of disloyal acts. Through such measures Lincoln expanded the powers of wartime presidents.

On occasion Lincoln used his wartime authority to bolster his own political fortunes. He and his generals proved adept at furloughing soldiers so they could vote in close elections; those whom Lincoln furloughed, of course, usually voted Republican. He also came to the aid of other officeholders in his party. When the Republican governor of Indiana, who was battling Democrats in his legislature that sought a negotiated end to the war, ran short of funds, Lincoln had the War Department supply $250,000. This procedure lacked constitutional sanction, but it advanced the Union cause.

In thousands of self-governing towns and communities, northern citizens felt a personal connection to representative government. Secession

THE UNION CAUSE

threatened to destroy their system, and northerners rallied to its defense. Secular and church leaders supported the cause, and even ministers who preferred to separate politics and pulpit denounced "the iniquity of causeless rebellion." In the first two years of the war, northern morale remained remarkably high for a cause that today may seem abstract—the Union—but at the time meant the preservation of a social and political order that people cherished.

But in the excitement of moneymaking, an eagerness to display one's wealth flourished in the largest cities. *Harper's Monthly* reported that "the suddenly enriched contractors, speculators, and stock-jobbers . . . are spending money with a profusion never before witnessed in our country. . . . The men button their waistcoats with diamonds . . . and the women powder their hair with gold and silver dust." The *New York Herald* summarized that city's atmosphere: "This war has entirely changed the American character. . . . The individual who makes the most money—no matter how—and spends the most—no matter for what—is considered the greatest man."

Yet idealism coexisted with ostentation. Many churches endorsed the Union cause as God's cause. One

Methodist newspaper described the war as a contest between "equalizing, humanizing Christianity" and "disunion, war, selfishness, [and] slavery." Abolitionists campaigned to turn the war into a crusade against slavery. Free black communities and churches both black and white responded to the needs of slaves who flocked to the Union lines, sending clothing, ministers, and teachers to aid the freedpeople. Indeed, northern blacks gave wholehearted support to the war, volunteering by the thousands at first and in spite of the initial rejection they received from the Lincoln administration.

Thus northern society embraced strangely contradictory tendencies. Materialism and greed flourished alongside idealism, religious conviction, and self-sacrifice. In decades to come Americans would commemorate and build monuments to soldiers' sacrifice and idealism, not to opportunism, and sometimes not even to the causes for which they fought, which was a way of forgetting the deeper nature of the conflict.

Northern women, like their southern counterparts, took on new roles. Those who stayed home organized over ten thousand soldiers' aid soci-

NORTHERN WOMEN ON HOME FRONT AND BATTLEFRONT

eties, rolled bandages, and raised $3 million to aid injured troops. Women were instrumental in pressing for the first trained ambulance corps in the Union armies, and they formed the backbone of the U.S. Sanitary Commission, a civilian agency officially recognized by the War Department in 1861. The Sanitary Commission provided crucial nutritional and medical aid to soldiers. Although most of its officers were men, the bulk of its volunteers who ran its seven thousand auxiliaries were women. Women organized elaborate "Sanitary Fairs" all across the North to raise money and awareness for soldiers' health and hygiene.

Approximately 3,200 women also served as nurses in frontline hospitals, where they pressed for better care of the wounded. Yet women had to fight for a chance to serve at all; the professionalization of medicine since the Revolution had created a medical system dominated by men, and many male physicians did not want women's aid. Even Clara Barton, famous for her persistence in working in the worst hospitals at the front, was ousted from her post in 1863. But with Barton, women such as the stern Dorothea Dix (see pages 271–272), well known for her efforts to reform asylums for the insane, and an Illinois widow, Mary Ann Bickerdyke, who served tirelessly in Sherman's army in the West, established a heroic tradition for Civil War nurses. They also advanced the professionalization of nursing as several schools of nursing were established in northern cities during or after the war.

Women also wrote popular fiction about the war. In sentimental war poetry, short stories, and novels, and in printed war songs that reached thousands of readers, women produced a commercial literature in illustrated weeklies, monthly periodicals, and special "story papers." In many stories women characters seek recognition for their loyalty and service to the Union, while countless others probed the suffering and death of loved ones at the front. And by 1863, women writers found the liberation of slaves an irresistible subject. At its heart, what one historian has called a "feminized war literature," explored the relationship between individual and national needs, between "home" and the "cause."

The poet Walt Whitman left a record of his experiences as a volunteer nurse in Washington, D.C. As

WALT WHITMAN'S WAR

he dressed wounds and tried to comfort suffering and lonely men, Whitman found "the marrow of the tragedy concentrated in those Army Hospitals." But despite "indescribably horrid wounds," he also found inspiration in such suffering and a deepening faith in American democracy. Whitman cel-

ebrated the "incredible dauntlessness" and sacrifice of the common soldier who fought for the Union. As he had written in the preface to his great work *Leaves of Grass* (1855), "The genius of the United States is not best or most in its executives or legislatures, but always most in the common people." Whitman worked this idealization of the common man into his poetry, which also explored homoerotic themes and rejected the lofty meter and rhyme of European verse to strive for a "genuineness" that would appeal to the masses.

In "The Wound Dresser," Whitman meditated unforgettably on the deaths he witnessed on both sides:

> On, on I go, (open doors of time! open hospital doors!)
> The crush'd head I dress, (poor crazed hand tear not
>   the bandage away,)
> The neck of the cavalry-man with the bullet through
>   and through I examine,
> Hard the breathing rattles, quite glazed already the eye,
>   yet life struggled hard,
> (Come sweet death! be persuaded O beautiful death!
>   In mercy come quickly.)

Whitman mused for millions in the war who suffered the death of a husband, brother, father, or friend. Indeed, the scale of death in this war shocked many Americans into believing that this conflict had to be for purposes larger than themselves.

The Advent of Emancipation

*D*espite the sense of loyalty to cause that animated soldiers and civilians on both sides, the governments of the United States and the Confederacy lacked clarity about the purpose of the war. Throughout the first several months of the struggle, both Davis and Lincoln studiously avoided references to slavery. Davis realized that emphasis on the issue could increase class conflict in the South. To avoid identifying the Confederacy only with the interests of slaveholders, he articulated a broader, traditional ideology. Davis told southerners that they were fighting for constitutional liberty: northerners had betrayed the founders' legacy, and southerners had seceded to preserve it. As long as Lincoln also avoided making slavery an issue, Davis's line seemed to work.

Lincoln had his own reasons for not mentioning slavery. It was crucial at first not to antagonize the Union's border slave states, whose loyalty was tenuous. Also for many months Lincoln hoped that a pro-Union majority would assert itself in the South. It might be pos-

■ Walt Whitman, now America's most celebrated wartime poet. His *Drum Taps* series, part of his evolving masterpiece *Leaves of Grass,* left some of the most haunting and moving poetic images of both the death and new life wrought by the war.   (National Portrait Gallery, Smithsonian Institution, Washington, D.C.)

sible, he thought, to coax the South back into the Union and stop the fighting, short of what he later called "the result so fundamental and astounding"—emancipation. Raising the slavery issue would severely undermine both goals. Powerful political considerations also dictated Lincoln's reticence. The Republican Party was a young and unwieldy coalition. Some Republicans burned with moral outrage over slavery; others were frankly racist, dedicated to protecting free whites from the Slave Power and the competition of cheap slave labor. A forthright stand by Lincoln on the subject of slavery could split the party. No northern consensus on what to do about slavery existed early in the war.

The president's hesitancy ran counter to some of his personal feelings. Lincoln was a compassionate man

LINCOLN AND EMANCIPATION

whose humility and moral anguish during the war were evident in his speeches and writings. But as a politician, Lincoln distinguished between his own moral convictions and his official acts. His political positions were studied and complex, calculated for maximum advantage.

Many blacks furiously attacked Lincoln during the first year of the war for his refusal to convert the struggle into an "abolition war." When Lincoln countermanded General John C. Frémont's order of liberation for slaves owned by disloyal masters in Missouri in September 1861, the *Anglo-African* declared that the president, by his actions, "hurls back into the hell of slavery thousands . . . rightfully set free." As late as July 1862, Frederick Douglass condemned Lincoln as a "miserable tool of traitors and rebels," and characterized administration policy as reconstruction of "the old union on the old and corrupting basis of compromise, by which slavery shall retain all the power that it ever had." Douglass wanted the old union destroyed and a new one created in the crucible of a war that would destroy slavery and rewrite the Constitution in the name of human equality. To his own amazement, within a year, just such a profound result began to take place.

Lincoln first broached the subject of slavery in a substantive way in March 1862, when he proposed that the states consider emancipation on their own. He asked Congress to promise aid to any state that decided to

■ A group of "contrabands" (liberated slaves), photographed at Cumberland Landing, Virginia, May 14, 1862, at a sensitive point in the war when their legal status was still not fully determined. The faces and generations of the women, men, and children represent the human drama of emancipation.   (Library of Congress)

emancipate, appealing especially to border state representatives. What Lincoln proposed was gradual emancipation, with compensation for slaveholders and colonization of the freed slaves outside the United States. To a delegation of free blacks he explained that "it is better for us both . . . to be separated."

Until well into 1864 Lincoln's administration promoted an impractical scheme to colonize blacks in Central America or the Caribbean. Lincoln saw colonization as one option among others in dealing with the impending freedom of America's 4.2 million slaves. As yet, he was unconvinced that America had any prospect as a truly biracial society, and he desperately feared that white northerners might not support a war for black freedom. Led by Frederick Douglass, black abolitionists vehemently opposed these machinations by the Lincoln administration.

Other politicians had much greater plans for a struggle against slavery. A group of Republicans in Congress, known as the Radicals and led by men such as George Julian, Charles Sumner, and Thaddeus Stevens, dedicated themselves to a war for emancipation. They were instrumental in creating a special House-Senate committee on the conduct of the war, which investigated Union reverses, sought to make the war effort more efficient, and prodded the president to take stronger measures against slavery.

In August 1861, at the Radicals' instigation, Congress passed its first confiscation act. Designed to punish the Confederates, the law confiscated *CONFISCATION* all property used for "insurrectionary *ACTS* purposes." Thus if the South used slaves in a hostile action, those slaves were declared seized and liberated as contraband of war. A second confiscation act (July 1862) went much further: it confiscated the property of anyone who supported the rebellion, even those who merely resided in the South and paid Confederate taxes. Their slaves were declared "forever free of their servitude." These acts stemmed from the logic that in order to crush the southern rebellion, the government had to use extraordinary powers.

Lincoln refused to adopt that view in the summer of 1862. He stood by his proposal of voluntary gradual emancipation by the states and made no effort to enforce the second confiscation act. His stance provoked a public protest from Horace Greeley, editor of the powerful *New York Tribune*. In an open letter to the president entitled "The Prayer of Twenty Millions," Greeley pleaded with Lincoln to "execute the laws" and declared, "On the face of this wide earth, Mr. President, there is not one . . . intelligent champion of the Union cause who does not feel that all attempts to put down the Rebellion

and at the same time uphold its inciting cause are preposterous and futile." Lincoln's reply was an explicit statement of his calculated approach to the question. He disagreed, he said, with all those who would make slavery the paramount issue of the war. "I would save the Union," announced Lincoln. "If I could save the Union without freeing any slave I would do it, and if I could save it by freeing all the slaves I would do it; and if I could save it by freeing some and leaving others alone I would also do that. What I do about slavery, and the colored race, I do because I believe it helps to save the Union." Lincoln closed with a personal disclaimer: "I have here stated my purpose according to my view of official duty; and I intend no modification of my oft-expressed personal wish that all men everywhere could be free."

When he wrote those words, Lincoln had already decided to boldly issue a presidential Emancipation Proclamation. He was waiting, however, for a Union victory so that it would not appear to be an act of desperation. Yet the letter to Greeley was not simply an effort to stall; it was an integral part of Lincoln's approach to the future of slavery, as the text of the Emancipation Proclamation would show. Lincoln was concerned to condition public opinion as best he could for the coming social revolution, and he needed to delicately consider international opinion as well.

On September 22, 1862, shortly after Union success at the Battle of Antietam, Lincoln issued the first part of his two-part proclamation. Invoking his *EMANCIPATION* powers as commander-in-chief of the *PROCLAMATIONS* armed forces, he announced that on January 1, 1863, he would emancipate the slaves in the states "in rebellion." Lincoln made plain that he would judge a state to be in rebellion in January if it lacked bona fide representatives in the U.S. Congress. Thus his September proclamation was less a declaration of the right of slaves to be free than a threat to southerners: unless they put down their arms and returned to Congress, they would lose their slaves. "Knowing the value that was set on the slaves by the rebels," said Garrison Frazier, a black Georgia minister, "the President thought that his proclamation would stimulate them to lay down their arms . . . and their not doing so has now made the freedom of the slaves a part of the war." Lincoln had little expectation that southerners would give up their effort, but he was careful to offer them the option, thus trying to put the onus of emancipation on them.

In the fateful January 1 proclamation, Lincoln excepted (as areas in rebellion) every Confederate county or city that had fallen under Union control. Those areas, he declared, "are, for the present, left precisely as if this proclamation were not issued." Nor did Lincoln liberate slaves in the border slave states that remained in the Union. "The President has purposely made the proclamation inoperative in all places where . . . the slaves [are] accessible," charged the anti-administration *New York World*. "He has proclaimed emancipation only where he has notoriously no power to execute it." Partisanship aside, even Secretary of State Seward said sarcastically, "We show our sympathy with slavery by emancipating slaves where we cannot reach them and holding them in bondage where we can set them free." A British official, Lord Russell, commented on the "very strange nature" of the document, noting that it did not declare "a principle adverse to slavery." Russell may have missed the point.

Lincoln was worried about the constitutionality of his acts. Making the liberation of the slaves "a fit and necessary war measure" raised a variety of legal questions. How long did a war measure remain in force? Did it expire with the suppression of a rebellion? The proclamation did little to clarify the status or citizenship of the freed slaves, although it did open the possibility of military service for blacks. How indeed would this change the character and purpose of the war?

Thus the Emancipation Proclamation was an ambiguous document. But if as a legal document it was wanting, as a moral and political document it had great meaning. Because the proclamation defined the war as a war against slavery, radicals could applaud it, even if the president had not gone as far as Congress. Yet at the same time it protected Lincoln's position with conservatives, leaving him room to retreat if he chose and forcing no immediate changes on the border slave states. It was a delicate balancing act, but one from which there was no real turning back.

Most important, though, thousands of slaves had already reached Union lines in various sections of the South. They had "voted with their feet" for emancipation, as many said, well before the proclamation. And now, every advance of federal forces into slave society was a liberating step. This Lincoln knew in taking his own initially tentative, and then forthright, steps toward emancipation.

Across the North and in Union-occupied sections of the South, blacks and their white allies celebrated the Emancipation Proclamation with unprecedented fervor. Full of praise songs, these celebrations demonstrated that whatever the fine print of the proclamation, black folks knew that they had lived to see a new day. At a large "contraband camp" in Washington, D.C., some six hundred black men, women, and children gathered at the superintendent's headquarters on New Year's Eve and sang through the night. In chorus after chorus of "Go Down, Moses," they announced the magnitude of their painful but beautiful exodus. One newly supplied verse concluded with "Go down, Abraham, away down in Dixie's land, tell Jeff Davis to let my people go!"

The need for men soon convinced the administration to recruit northern and southern blacks for the Union Army. By the spring of 1863, African American troops were answering the call of a dozen or more black recruiters barnstorming the cities and towns of the North. Lincoln came to see black soldiers as "the great available and yet unavailed of force for restoring the Union." African American leaders hoped that military service would secure equal rights for their people. Once the black soldier had fought for the Union, wrote Frederick Douglass, "there is no power on earth which can deny that he has earned the right of citizenship in the United States." If black soldiers turned the tide, asked another man, "would the nation refuse us our rights?"

In June 1864 Lincoln gave his support to a constitutional ban on slavery. On the eve of the Republican national convention, Lincoln called the party's chairman to the White House and instructed him to have the party "put into the platform as the keystone, the amendment of the Constitution abolishing and prohibiting slavery forever." The party promptly called for the Thirteenth Amendment. Republican delegates probably would have adopted such a plank without his urging, but Lincoln demonstrated his commitment by lobbying Congress for quick approval of the measure. The proposed amendment passed in early 1865 and was sent to the states for ratification. The war to save the Union had also become the war to free the slaves.

It has long been debated whether Abraham Lincoln deserved the label (one he never claimed for himself) of "Great Emancipator." Was Lincoln ultimately a reluctant emancipator, following rather than leading Congress and public opinion? Or did Lincoln give essential presidential leadership to the most transformative and sensitive aspect of the war by going slow on emancipation, but once moving, never backpedaling on black freedom. Once he had realized the total character of the war and decided to prosecute it to the unconditional surrender of the Confederates, Lincoln made the destruction of slavery central to the war's purpose.

Others have argued, however, that the slaves themselves are the central story in the achievement of their own freedom. When they were in proximity to the war zones, or had opportunities as traveling laborers, slaves fled for their freedom by the thousands. Some worked as

WHO FREED THE SLAVES?

camp laborers for the Union armies, and eventually more than 180,000 black men served in the Union Army and Navy. Sometimes freedom came as a combination of confusion, fear, and joy in the rural hinterlands of the South. Some found freedom as individuals in 1861, and some not until 1865 as members of trains of refugees trekking great distances to reach contraband camps.

However freedom came to individuals, emancipation was a historical confluence of two essential forces: one, a policy directed by and dependent on the military authority of the president in his effort to win the war; and two, the will and courage necessary for acts of self-emancipation. In his annual message in December 1862, Lincoln asserted that "in giving freedom to the slave, we assure freedom to the free." Likewise, most blacks understood the long-term meaning in those words—in the midst of total war they comprehended their freedom as both given and taken, but also as their fundamental human right.

Before the war was over, the Confederacy, too, addressed the issue of emancipation. Jefferson Davis himself

A CONFEDERATE PLAN OF EMANCIPATION

offered a proposal for black freedom of a kind. Late in the war he was willing to sacrifice slavery to achieve independence. He proposed that the Confederate government purchase forty thousand slaves to work for the army as laborers, with a promise of freedom at the end of their service. Soon Davis upgraded the idea, calling for the recruitment and arming of slaves as soldiers, who likewise would gain their freedom at war's end. The wives and children of these soldiers, he made plain, must also receive freedom from the states. Davis and his advisers envisioned an "intermediate" status for ex-slaves of "serfage or peonage." Thus at the bitter end, a few southerners were willing to sacrifice some of the racial, if not class, destiny for which they had launched their revolution.

Bitter debate over Davis's plan resounded through the Confederacy. When the Confederate Congress approved slave enlistments without the promise of freedom in March 1865, Davis insisted on more. He issued an executive order to guarantee that owners would emancipate slave soldiers and eventually their families.

The war ended before much could come of these desperate policy initiatives on the part of the Confederacy. By contrast, Lincoln's Emancipation Proclamation stimulated a vital infusion of forces into the Union armies. Before the war was over, 134,000 former slaves (and 52,000 free blacks) had fought for freedom and the Union. Their participation was pivotal in northern victory. As both policy and process, emancipation had profound practical and moral implications for the new nation to be born out of the war.

The Soldiers' War

The intricacies of policymaking and social revolutions were far from the minds of most ordinary soldiers. Military service completely altered their lives. Enlistment took young men from their homes and submerged them in large organizations whose military discipline ignored their individuality. Army life meant tedium, physical hardship, and separation from loved ones. Yet the military experience had powerful attractions as well. It molded men on both sides so thoroughly that they came to resemble one another far more than they resembled civilians back home. Many soldiers forged amid war a bond with their fellows and a connection to a noble purpose that they cherished for years afterward.

Union soldiers may have sensed most clearly the massive scale of modern war. Most were young; the average soldier was between eighteen and twenty-one. Many went straight from small towns and farms into large armies supplied by extensive bureaucracies. By late 1861 there were 640,000 volunteers in arms, a stupendous increase over the regular army of 20,000 men.

Soldiers benefited from certain new products, such as canned condensed milk, but blankets, clothing, and

HOSPITALS AND CAMP LIFE

arms were often of poor quality. Hospitals were badly managed at first. Rules of hygiene in large camps were scarcely enforced; latrines were poorly made or carelessly used. One investigation turned up "an area of over three acres, encircling the camp as a broad belt, on which is deposited an almost perfect layer of human excrement." Water supplies were unsafe and typhoid epidemics common. About 57,000 men died from dysentery and diarrhea; in fact, 224,000 Union troops died from disease or accidents, far more than the 140,000 who died as a result of battle. Confederate troops were less well supplied, especially in the latter part of the war, and they had no sanitary commission. Still, an extensive network of hospitals, aided by many white female volunteers and black women slaves, sprang up to aid the sick and wounded.

On both sides troops quickly learned that soldiering was far from glorious. "The dirt of a camp life knocks all its poetry into a cocked hat," wrote a North Carolina volunteer in 1862. One year later he marveled at his earlier innocence. Fighting had taught him "the realities of a soldier's life. We had no tents after the 6th of August, but slept on the ground, in the woods or open fields. . . . I learned to eat fat bacon raw, and to like it. . . . Without time to wash our clothes or our persons . . . the whole army became lousy more or less with body lice." Union troops "skirmished" against lice by boiling their clothes but, reported one soldier, "I find some on me in spite of all I can do."

Few had seen violent death before, but war soon exposed them to the blasted bodies of their friends and comrades. "Any one who goes over a battlefield after a battle," wrote one Confederate, "never cares to go over another. . . . It is a sad sight to see the dead and if possible more sad to see the wounded—shot in every possible way you can imagine." Many men died gallantly; there were innumerable striking displays of courage. But more often soldiers gave up their lives in mass sacrifice, in tactics that made little sense.

Still, Civil War soldiers developed deep commitments to each other and to their task. As campaigns dragged on, most soldiers who did not desert grew determined to see the struggle through. "We now, like true Soldiers go determined not to yield one inch," wrote a New York corporal. When at last the war was over, "it seemed like breaking up a family to separate," one man observed. Another admitted, "We shook hands all around, and

laughed and seemed to make merry, while our hearts were heavy and our eyes ready to shed tears."

Advances in technology made the Civil War particularly deadly. By far the most important were the rifle and the "minie ball." Bullets fired from a smoothbore musket tumbled and wobbled as they flew through the air and thus were not accurate at distances over 80 yards. Cutting spiraled grooves inside the barrel gave the projectile a spin and much greater accuracy, but rifles remained difficult to load and use until the Frenchman Claude Minie and the American James Burton developed a new kind of bullet. Civil War bullets were sizable lead slugs with a cavity at the bottom that expanded upon firing so that the bullet "took" the rifling and flew accurately. With these bullets, rifles were accurate at 400 yards and useful up to 1,000 yards.

THE RIFLED MUSKET

This meant, of course, that soldiers assaulting a position defended by riflemen were in greater peril than ever before. Even though Civil War rifles were cumbersome to load, the defense gained a significant advantage. While artillery now fired from a safe distance, there was no substitute for the infantry assault or the popular turning movements aimed at an enemy's flank. Thus advancing soldiers had to expose themselves repeatedly to accurate rifle fire. Because medical knowledge was rudimentary, even minor wounds often led to amputation, and to death through infection. Never before in Europe or America had such massive forces pummeled each other with weapons of such destructive power. As losses mounted, many citizens wondered at what Union soldier (and future Supreme Court justice) Oliver Wendell Holmes Jr. called "the butcher's bill."

At the outset of the war, racism in the Union Army was strong. Most white soldiers wanted nothing to do with black people and regarded them as inferior. "I never came out here for to free the black devils," wrote one soldier, and another objected to fighting beside African Americans because "We are a too superior race for that." For many, acceptance of black troops grew only because they could do heavy labor and "stop Bullets as well as white people." A popular song celebrated "Sambo's Right to Be Kilt" as the only justification for black enlistments.

THE BLACK SOLDIER'S FIGHT FOR MANHOOD

But among some a change occurred. While recruiting black troops in Virginia in late 1864, Charles Brewster sometimes denigrated the very men he sought to enlist. But he was delighted at the sight of a black cavalry unit because it made the local "secesh" furious, and he praised black soldiers who "fought nobly" and filled hospitals with "their wounded and mangled bodies." White officers who volunteered to lead black units only to gain promotion found that experience altered their opinions. After just one month with black troops, a white captain informed his wife, "I have a more elevated opinion of their abilities than I ever had before. I know that many of them are vastly the superiors of those . . . who would condemn them all to a life of brutal degradation." One general reported that his "colored regiments" possessed "remarkable aptitude for military training," and another observer said, "They fight like fiends."

Black troops created this change through their own dedication. They had a mission to destroy slavery and demonstrate their equality. "When Rebellion is crushed," wrote a black volunteer from Connecticut, "who will be more proud than I to say, 'I was one of the first of the despised race to leave the free North with a rifle on my shoulder, and give the lie to the old story that the black man will not fight.'" Corporal James Henry Gooding of Massachusetts's black Fifty-fourth Regiment explained that his unit intended "to live down all prejudice against its color, by a determination to do well in any position it is put." After an engagement he was proud that "a regiment of white men gave us three cheers as we were passing them," because "it shows that we did our duty as men should."

Through such experience under fire the blacks and whites of the Fifty-fourth Massachusetts forged deep bonds. Just before the regiment launched its costly as-

■ Company E, 4th U.S. Colored Infantry, photographed at Fort Lincoln, Virginia, in 1864. Nothing so symbolized the new manhood and citizenship among African Americans in the midst of the war as such young black men in blue.
(Chicago Historical Society)

sault on Fort Wagner in Charleston harbor, in July 1863, a black soldier called out to abolitionist Colonel Robert Gould Shaw, who would perish that day, "Colonel, I will stay by you till I die." "And he kept his word," noted a survivor of the attack. "He has never been seen since." Indeed, the heroic assault on Fort Wagner was celebrated for demonstrating the valor of black men. This bloody chapter in the history of American racism proved many things, not least of which was that black men had to die in battle to be acknowledged as men.

Such valor emerged despite persistent discrimination. Off-duty black soldiers were sometimes attacked by northern mobs; on duty, they did most of the heavy labor. The Union government, moreover, paid white privates $13 per month plus a clothing allowance of $3.50, whereas black privates earned only $10 per month less $3 for clothing. Outraged by this injustice, several regiments refused to accept any pay whatsoever, and Congress eventually remedied the inequity. In this instance, at least, the majority of legislators agreed with a white private that black troops had "proved their title to manhood on many a bloody field fighting freedom's battles."

1863: The Tide of Battle Turns

The fighting in the spring and summer of 1863 did not settle the war, but it began to suggest the outcome. The campaigns began in a deceptively positive way for Confederates, as Lee's army performed brilliantly in battles in central Virginia.

For once, a large Civil War army was not slow and cumbersome but executed tactics with speed and precision.

BATTLE OF CHANCELLORSVILLE On May 2 and 3, west of Fredericksburg, Virginia, some 130,000 members of the Union Army of the Potomac bore down on fewer than 60,000 Confederates. Boldly, Lee and Stonewall Jackson divided their forces, ordering 30,000 men under Jackson on a day-long march westward to prepare a flank attack.

This classic turning movement was carried out in the face of great numerical disadvantage. Arriving at their position late in the afternoon, Jackson's seasoned "foot cavalry" found unprepared Union troops laughing, smoking, and playing cards. The Union soldiers had no idea they were under attack until frightened deer and rabbits bounded out of the forest, followed by gray-clad troops. The Confederate attack drove the entire right side of the Union Army back in confusion. Eager to press his advantage, Jackson rode forward with a few officers to study the ground. As they returned at twilight, south-

ern troops mistook them for federals and fired, fatally wounding their commander. The next day Union forces left in defeat. Chancellorsville was a remarkable southern victory but costly because of the loss of Stonewall Jackson, who would forever remain a legend in Confederate memory.

July brought crushing defeats for the Confederacy in two critical battles—Vicksburg and Gettysburg—that severely damaged Confederate hopes for independence. Vicksburg was a vital western citadel, the last major fortification on the Mississippi River in southern hands (see Map 15.2). After months of searching through swamps and bayous, General Ulysses S. Grant found an advantageous approach to the city. He laid siege to Vicksburg in May, bottling up the defending army of General John Pemberton. If Vicksburg fell, Union forces would control the river, cutting the Confederacy in two and gaining an open path into its interior. To stave off such a result, Jefferson Davis gave command of all other forces in the area to General Joseph E. Johnston and beseeched him to go to Pemberton's aid. Meanwhile, at a council of war in Richmond, General Robert E. Lee proposed a Confederate invasion of the North. Although such an offensive would not relieve Vicksburg directly, it could stun and dismay the North and, if successful, possibly even lead to peace. By invading the North a second time, Lee hoped to take the war out of war-weary Virginia, garner civilian support in Maryland, win a major victory on northern soil, threaten major cities, and thereby force a Union capitulation on his terms.

As Lee's emboldened army advanced through western Maryland and into Pennsylvania, Confederate prospects to the south along the Mississippi darkened. Davis repeatedly wired General Johnston, urging him to concentrate his forces and attack Grant's army. Johnston, however, did little, telegraphing back, "I consider saving Vicksburg hopeless." Grant's men, meanwhile, were supplying themselves from the abundant crops of the Mississippi River valley and could continue their siege indefinitely. Their rich meat-and-vegetable diet became so tiresome, in fact, that one day, as Grant rode by, a private looked up and muttered, "Hardtack," referring to the dry biscuits that were the usual staple of soldiers' diets. Soon a line of soldiers was shouting "Hardtack! Hardtack!" demanding respite from turkey and sweet potatoes.

In such circumstances the fall of Vicksburg was inevitable, and on July 4, 1863, its commander surrendered.

BATTLE OF GETTYSBURG The same day a battle that had been raging for three days concluded at Gettysburg, Pennsylvania (see Map 15.3).

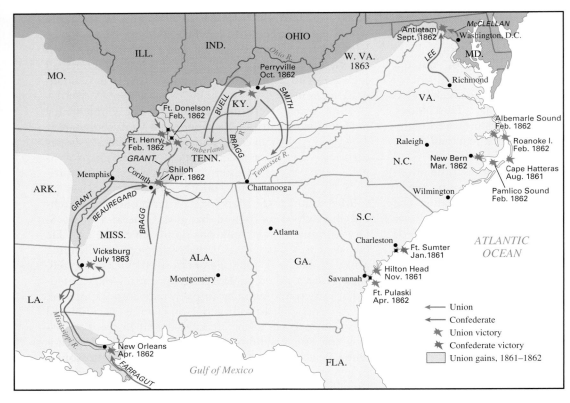

Map 15.2 War in the West, 1861–1863

Here is an overview of the Union's successful campaigns in the West and its seizure of key points on the Mississippi River, as well as along the Atlantic coast in 1862 and 1863. These actions were decisive in paving the way for ultimate northern victory.

On July 1 Confederate forces hunting for a supply of shoes had collided with part of the Union Army. Heavy fighting on the second day over two steep hills left federal forces in possession of high ground along Cemetery Ridge, running more than a mile south of the town. There they enjoyed the protection of a stone wall and a clear view of their foe across almost a mile of open field.

Undaunted, Lee believed his reinforced troops could break the Union line, and on July 3 he ordered a direct assault. Full of foreboding, General James Longstreet warned Lee that "no 15,000 men ever arrayed for battle can take that position." But Lee stuck to his plan. Virginians under General George E. Pickett and North Carolinians under General James Pettigrew methodically marched up the slope in a doomed assault known as Pickett's Charge. For a moment a few hundred Confederates breached the enemy's line, but most fell in heavy slaughter. On July 4 Lee had to withdraw, having suffered almost 4,000 dead and about 24,000 missing and wounded. The Confederate general reported to President Davis that "I am alone to blame" and offered to resign. Davis replied that to find a more capable commander was "an impossibility." The Confederacy had reached what many consider its "high water mark" on that ridge at Gettysburg.

Southern troops displayed unforgettable courage and dedication at Gettysburg, and the Union Army, which suffered 23,000 casualties (nearly one-quarter of the force), under General George G. Meade exhibited the same bravery in stopping the Confederate invasion. But the results there and at Vicksburg were disastrous for the South. The Confederacy was split in two; west of the Mississippi General E. Kirby Smith had to operate on his own, virtually independent of Richmond. Moreover, the heartland of Louisiana, Tennessee, and Mississippi lay exposed to invasion. Far to the north, Lee's defeat spelled the end of major southern offensive actions. Too weak to prevail in attack, the Confederacy henceforth would have to conserve its limited resources and rely on a prolonged defense. By refusing to be beaten, and wearing down northern morale, the South might yet win, but its prospects were darker than ever before.

Disunity, South, North, and West

Both northern and southern governments waged the final two years of the war in the face of increasing opposition at home. Dissatisfactions that had surfaced earlier grew more intense and sometimes vi-

Map 15.3   Battle of Gettysburg

In the war's greatest battle, fought around a small market town in southern Pennsylvania, Lee's invasion of the North was repulsed. Union forces had the advantage of high ground, shorter lines, and superior numbers. The casualties for the two armies—dead, wounded, and missing—exceeded 50,000 men.

olent. The gigantic costs of a civil war that neither side seemed able to win fed the unrest. But protest also arose from fundamental stresses in the social structures of North and South.

The Confederacy's problems were more deeply rooted than the North's. Vastly disadvantaged in industrial capacity, natural resources, and labor, southerners felt the cost of the war more directly and more painfully than northerners. But even more fundamental were the Confederacy's internal problems; the southern class system threatened the Confederate cause.

DISINTEGRATION OF CONFEDERATE UNITY

One ominous development was the planters' increasing opposition to their own government. Not only did the Richmond government impose new taxes but Con-

federate military authorities also impressed slaves to build fortifications. And when Union forces advanced on plantation areas, Confederate commanders burned stores of cotton that lay in the enemy's path. Such interference with plantation routines and financial interests was not what planters had expected of their government, and they complained bitterly.

Nor were the centralizing policies of the Davis administration popular. The increasing size and power of the Richmond government startled and alarmed planters who had condemned federal usurpations. In fact, the Confederate constitution had granted substantial powers to the central government, especially in time of war. But many planters assumed with R. B. Rhett, editor of the *Charleston Mercury,* that the Confederate constitution "leaves the States untouched in their Sovereignty, and commits to the Confederate Government only a few simple objects, and a few simple powers to enforce them." Governor Joseph E. Brown of Georgia took a similar view of the importance of the states. During the brief interval between Georgia's secession from the Union and its admission to the Confederacy, Brown sent an ambassador to Europe to seek recognition for the sovereign republic of Georgia from Queen Victoria, Napoleon III, and the king of Belgium.

Years of opposition to the federal government within the Union had frozen southerners in a defensive posture. Now they erected the barrier of states' rights as a defense against change, hiding behind it while their capacity for creative statesmanship atrophied. Planters sought, above all, a guarantee that their plantations and their lives would remain untouched. As secession revolutionized their world, and hard war took so many lives, some never could fully commit to the cause.

Confused and embittered planters struck out at Jefferson Davis. Conscription, thundered Governor Brown, was "subversive of [Georgia's] sovereignty, and at war with all the principles for the support of which Georgia entered into this revolution." Searching for ways to frustrate the law, Brown bickered over draft exemptions and ordered local enrollment officials not to cooperate with the Confederacy. The *Charleston Mercury* told readers that "conscription . . . is . . . the very embodiment of Lincolnism, which our gallant armies are today fighting." In a gesture of stubborn selfishness, Robert Toombs of Georgia, a former U.S. senator, refused to switch from cotton to food crops, defying the wishes of the government, the newspapers, and his neighbors' petitions. His action bespoke the inflexibility of the southern elite at a crucial point in the Confederacy's struggle to survive.

The southern courts ultimately upheld Davis's power to conscript. Despite his cold formality and inability to

■ The impoverishment of nonslaveholding white families was a critical problem for the Confederacy. The sale of this sheet music was intended not only to boost morale but also to raise money that could be used to aid the hungry and needy. This effort and larger government initiatives, however, failed to solve the problem. (Chicago Historical Society)

disarm critics, Davis possessed two important virtues: iron determination and total dedication to independence. These qualities kept the Confederacy afloat. But his actions earned him the hatred of influential and elite citizens.

Meanwhile, for ordinary southerners, the dire predictions of hunger and suffering were becoming a reality.

FOOD RIOTS IN SOUTHERN CITIES

Food riots occurred in the spring of 1863 in Atlanta, Macon, Columbus, and Augusta, Georgia, and in Salisbury and High Point, North Carolina. On April 2 a crowd assembled in Richmond to demand relief. A passerby, noticing the excitement, asked a young girl, "Is there some celebration?" "We celebrate our right to live," replied the girl. "We are starving. As soon as enough of us get together we are going to the bakeries and each of us will take a loaf of bread." Soon they did just that, sparking a riot that Davis ordered quelled at gunpoint.

Throughout the rural South, ordinary people resisted more quietly—by refusing to cooperate with conscription, tax collection, and impressments of food. "In all the States impressments are evaded by every means which ingenuity can suggest, and in some openly resisted," wrote a high-ranking commissary officer. Farmers who did provide food for the army refused to accept payment in certificates of credit or government bonds, as required by law. Conscription officers increasingly found no one to draft. "The disposition to avoid military service is general," observed one of Georgia's senators in 1864. In some areas tax agents were killed in the line of duty.

Jefferson Davis was ill equipped to deal with such discontent. Austere and private by nature, he failed to communicate with the masses. Often he buried himself in military affairs or administrative details. His class perspective also distanced him from the sufferings of the common people. While his social circle in Richmond dined on duck and oysters, ordinary southerners recovered salt from the drippings on their smokehouse floors and went hungry. Davis failed to reach out to the plain folk and thus lost their support.

Such discontent was certain to affect the Confederate armies. "What man is there that would stay in the army and no that his family is sufring

DESERTIONS FROM THE CONFEDERATE ARMY

at home?" an angry citizen wrote anonymously to the secretary of war. Worried about their loved ones and resentful of what they saw as a rich man's war, large numbers of men did indeed leave the armies. Their friends and neighbors gave them support. Mary Chesnut observed a man being dragged back to the army as his wife looked on. "Desert agin, Jake!" she cried openly. "You desert agin, quick as you kin. Come back to your wife and children."

Desertion did not become a serious problem for the Confederacy until mid-1862, and stiffer policing solved the problem that year. But from 1863 on, the number of men on duty fell rapidly. By mid-1863, John A. Campbell, the South's assistant secretary of war, wondered whether "so general a habit" as desertion could be considered a crime. Campbell estimated that 40,000 to 50,000 troops were absent without leave and that 100,000 were evading duty in some way. Furloughs, amnesty proclamations, and appeals to return had little effect; by November 1863 Secretary of War James Seddon admitted that one-third of the army could not be accounted for.

The defeats at Gettysburg and Vicksburg dealt a heavy blow to Confederate morale. When the news reached Josiah Gorgas, the genius of Confederate ordnance operations, he confided to his diary, "Today absolute ruin seems our portion. The Confederacy totters to its destruction." In desperation President Davis and several state governors resorted to threats and racial scare tactics to drive southern whites to further sacrifice. Defeat, Davis warned, would mean "extermination of yourselves, your wives, and children." Governor Charles Clark of Mississippi predicted "elevation of the black race to a position of equality—aye, of superiority, that will make them your masters and rulers."

From this point on, the internal disintegration of the Confederacy quickened. A few newspapers began to call openly for peace. "We are for peace," admitted the *Raleigh* (North Carolina) *Daily Progress,* "because there has been enough of blood and carnage, enough of widows and orphans." Similar proposals were made in several state legislatures, though they were presented as plans for independence on honorable terms. Confederate leaders began to realize that they were losing the support of the common people. Governor Zebulon Vance of North Carolina wrote privately that victory would require more "blood and misery . . . and our people will not pay this price I am satisfied for their independence."

In North Carolina a peace movement grew under the leadership of William W. Holden, a popular Democratic

ANTIWAR
SENTIMENT,
SOUTH AND
NORTH

politician and editor. Over one hundred public meetings took place in the summer of 1863 in support of peace negotiations, and many seasoned political observers believed that Holden had the majority of the people behind him. In Georgia early in 1864, Governor Brown and Alexander H. Stephens, vice president of the Confederacy, led a similar effort. Ultimately, however, these movements came to naught. The lack of a two-party system threw into question the legitimacy of any criticism of the government; even Holden and Brown could not entirely escape the taint of dishonor and disloyalty.

The results of the 1863 congressional elections strengthened dissent in the Confederacy. Everywhere secessionists and supporters of the administration lost seats to men not identified with the government. In the last years of the war, Davis's support in the Confederate Congress dwindled. Only a few editors and a core of courageous, determined soldiers, especially in Lee's Army of Northern Virginia, kept the Confederacy alive in spite of disintegrating popular support.

By 1864 much of the opposition to the war had moved entirely outside the political sphere. Southerners were simply giving up the struggle and withdrawing their cooperation from the government. Deserters dominated whole towns and counties. Active dissent was particularly common in upland and mountain regions. "The condition of things in the mountain districts of North Carolina, South Carolina, Georgia, and Alabama," admitted Assistant Secretary of War Campbell, "menaces the existence of the Confederacy as fatally as either of the armies of the United States." The government was losing the support of its citizens.

In the North, opposition to the war was similar but less severe. Alarm intensified over the growing centralization of government, and by 1863 war-weariness was widespread. Resentment of the draft sparked protest, especially among poor citizens, and the Union Army struggled with a desertion rate as high as the Confederates'. But the Union was so much richer than the South in human resources that none of these problems ever threatened the effectiveness of the government. Fresh recruits were always available, especially after black enlistments in 1863.

Also, Lincoln possessed a talent that Davis lacked: he knew how to stay in touch with the ordinary citizen. Through letters to newspapers and to soldiers' families, he reached the common people and demonstrated that he had not forgotten them. The daily carnage, the tortuous political problems, and the ceaseless criticism weighed heavily on him. But this president—a self-educated man of humble origins—was able to communicate his suffering. His moving words helped to contain northern discontent, though they could not remove it.

Much of the wartime protest in the North was political in origin. The Democratic Party fought to regain

PEACE
DEMOCRATS

power by blaming Lincoln for the war's death toll, the expansion of federal powers, inflation and the high tariff, and the emancipation of blacks. Appealing to tradition, its leaders called for an end to the war and reunion on the basis of "the Constitution as it is and the Union as it was." The Democrats denounced conscription and martial law and defended states' rights. They charged repeatedly that Republican policies were designed to flood the North with blacks, depriving white males of their status, their jobs, and their women. In the 1862 congressional elections, the Democrats made a strong comeback, and peace Democrats—who would go much further than others in their party to end the war— had influence in New York State and majorities in the legislatures of Illinois and Indiana.

Led by outspoken men like Representative Clement L. Vallandigham of Ohio, the peace Democrats made themselves highly visible. Vallandigham criticized Lincoln as a "dictator" who had suspended the writ of habeas corpus without congressional authority and had arrested thousands of innocent citizens. He condemned both conscription and emancipation and urged voters to use their power at the polls to depose "King Abraham." Vallandigham stayed carefully within legal bounds, but his attacks seemed so damaging to the war effort that military authorities arrested him for treason. Lincoln wisely decided against punishment—and martyr's status—for the Ohioan and exiled him to the Confederacy. (Eventually Vallandigham returned to the North through Canada.)

Lincoln believed that antiwar Democrats were linked to secret organizations that harbored traitorous ideas. These societies, he feared, encouraged draft resistance, discouraged enlistment, sabotaged communications, and plotted to aid the Confederacy. Likening such groups to a poisonous snake, Republicans sometimes branded them—and by extension the peace Democrats—as "Copperheads." Although some Confederate agents were active in the North and Canada, they never genuinely threatened the Union war effort.

More violent opposition to the government arose from ordinary citizens facing the draft, which became law in 1863. While some soldiers risked their lives willingly out of a desire to preserve the Union or extend freedom, many others openly sought to avoid service. Under the law, a draftee could stay at home by providing a substitute or paying a $300 commutation fee. Many wealthy men chose these options, and in response to popular demand, clubs, cities, and states provided the money for others to escape conscription. In all, 118,000 substitutes were provided and 87,000 commutations paid before Congress ended the commutation system in 1864.

NEW YORK CITY DRAFT RIOTS

The urban poor and immigrants in strongly Democratic areas were especially hostile to conscription. Federal enrolling officers made up the lists of eligibles, a procedure open to personal favoritism and prejudice. Many men, including some of modest means, managed to avoid the army by hiring a substitute or paying commutation, but the poor viewed the system as discriminatory, and many immigrants suspected (wrongly, on the whole) that they were called in disproportionate numbers. (Approximately 200,000 men born in Germany and 150,000 born in Ireland served in the Union Army.)

As a result, there were scores of disturbances. Enrolling officers received rough treatment in many parts of the North, and riots occurred in New Jersey, Ohio, Indiana, Pennsylvania, Illinois, and Wisconsin. By far the most serious outbreak of violence occurred in New York City in July 1863. The war was unpopular in that Democratic stronghold, and racial, ethnic, and class tensions

■ Mobs in the New York City draft riots directed much of their anger at African Americans. Rioters burned an orphanage for black children and killed scores of blacks. This wood engraving, which appeared in the *Illustrated London News* on August 8, 1863, depicts a lynching in Clarkson Street.   (Chicago Historical Society)

ran high. Shippers had recently broken a longshoremen's strike by hiring black strikebreakers to work under police protection. Working-class New Yorkers feared an inflow of black labor from the South and regarded blacks as the cause of the war. Poor Irish workers resented being forced to serve in the place of others who could afford to avoid the draft.

Military police officers came under attack first, and then mobs crying "Down with the rich" looted wealthy homes and stores. But blacks became the special target. Those who happened to be in the rioters' path were beaten; soon the mob rampaged through African American neighborhoods, destroying an orphan asylum. At least seventy-four people died in the violence, which raged out of control for three days. Only the dispatch of army units directly from Gettysburg ended this tragic episode of racism and class resentment.

East and West, and over race, land, and culture, America was a deeply divided country. A civil war of another kind raged on the Great Plains and in the Southwest. By 1864 U.S. troops under the command of Colonel John Chivington waged full-scale war against the Sioux, Arapaho, and Cheyennes in order to eradicate Indian title to all of eastern Colorado. Indian chiefs sought peace, but American

WAR AGAINST INDIANS IN THE FAR WEST

commanders had orders to "burn villages and kill Cheyennes whenever and wherever found." A Cheyenne chief, Lean Bear, was shot from his horse as he rode toward U.S. troops, holding in his hand papers given him by President Lincoln during a visit to Washington, D.C. Another chief, Black Kettle, was told by the U.S. command that by moving his people to Sand Creek, Colorado, they would find a safe haven. But on November 29, 1864, 700 cavalrymen, many drunk, attacked the Cheyenne village. With most of the men absent hunting, the slaughter included 105 Cheyenne women and children and 28 men. American soldiers scalped and mutilated their victims, carrying women's body parts on their saddles or hats back to Denver. The Sand Creek Massacre, and the retaliation against white ranches and stagecoaches by Indians in 1865, would live in western historical memory forever.

In New Mexico and Arizona Territories an authoritarian and brutal commander, General James Carleton, waged war on the Apaches and the Navajos. Both tribes had engaged for generations in raiding the Pueblo Indians and Hispanic peoples of the region to maintain their security and economy. During the Civil War years, Anglo-American farms also became Indian targets. In 1863, the New Mexico Volunteers, commanded in the field by former mountain man Kit Carson, defeated the Mescalero Apaches and forced them onto a reservation at Bosque Redondo in the Pecos River valley.

But the Navajos, who lived in a vast region of canyons and high deserts, resisted. In a "scorched earth" campaign, Carson destroyed the Navajos' livestock, orchards, and crops. On the run, starving and demoralized, the Navajos began to surrender for food in January 1864. Three-quarters of the twelve thousand Navajos were rounded up and forced to march 400 miles (the "Long Walk") to the Bosque Redondo Reservation, suffering malnutrition and death along the way. When General William T. Sherman visited the reservation in 1868 he found the Navajos "sunk into a condition of absolute poverty and despair." Permitted to return to a fraction of their homelands later that year, the Navajos carried with them searing memories of the federal government's ruthless policies of both removal and eradication of Indian peoples.

Back east, war-weariness reached a peak in the summer of 1864, when the Democratic Party nominated the

ELECTION OF 1864

popular General George B. McClellan for president and inserted a peace plank into its platform. The plank, written by Vallandigham, called for an armistice, and spoke vaguely about preserving the Union. The Democrats made racist appeals to white insecurity, calling

Lincoln "Abe the nigger-lover" and "Abe the widow-maker." Lincoln concluded that it was "exceedingly probable that this Administration will not be reelected." No incumbent president had been reelected since 1832, and no nation had ever held a general election in the midst of all-out civil war. Some radical Republicans worked to dump Lincoln from their ticket in favor of either Salmon P. Chase or John C. Frémont, although little came of either effort. Even a relatively unified Republican Party, declaring itself for "unconditional surrender" of the Confederacy and a constitutional amendment abolishing slavery, faced the horrible casualty lists and battlefield stalemate of the summer of 1864.

The fortunes of war soon changed the electoral situation. With the fall of Atlanta and Union victories in the Shenandoah valley by early September, Lincoln's prospects rose. Decisive in the election was that eighteen states allowed troops to vote at the front, and Lincoln won an extraordinary 78 percent of the soldier vote. In taking 55 percent of the total popular vote, Lincoln's reelection—a referendum on the war and emancipation—had a devastating impact on southern morale. Without such a political outcome in 1864, a Union military victory, and a redefined nation, may never have been possible.

1864–1865: The Final Test of Wills

During the final year of the war, the Confederates could still have won their version of victory if military stalemate and northern antiwar sentiment had forced a negotiated settlement to end the war. But events and northern determination prevailed as Americans endured the bloodiest nightmare in their history.

The North's long-term diplomatic strategy succeeded in 1864. From the outset, the North had pursued one

NORTHERN DIPLOMATIC STRATEGY

paramount goal: to prevent recognition of the Confederacy by European nations. Foreign recognition would belie Lincoln's claim that the United States was fighting an illegal rebellion and would open the way to the financial and military aid that could ensure Confederate independence. Both England and France stood to benefit from a divided and weakened America. Thus to achieve their goal, Lincoln and Secretary of State Seward needed to avoid both serious military defeats and controversies with the European powers.

Aware that the textile industry employed one-fifth of the British population directly or indirectly, southerners banked on British recognition of the Confederacy. But

The Civil War in Britain

So engaged was the British public with America's disunion and war that an unemployed weaver, John Ward, frequently trekked many miles from Britain's Low Moor to Clitheroe just to read newspapers about the strife.

Because of the direct reliance of the British textile industry on southern cotton (cut off by the war), as well as the many ideological and familial ties between the two nations, the American war was decisive in Britain's economy and domestic politics. The British aristocracy and most cotton mill owners were solidly pro-Confederate and proslavery, while a combination of clergymen, shopkeepers, artisans, and radical politicians worked for the causes of Union and emancipation. Most British workers saw their futures at stake in a war for slave emancipation. "Freedom" to the huge British working class (who could not vote) meant basic political and civil rights, as well as the bread and butter of secure jobs in an industrializing economy, now damaged by a "cotton famine" that threw millhands out of work.

English aristocrats saw Americans as untutored, wayward cousins and took satisfaction in America's troubles. Conservatives believed in the superiority of the British system of government and looked askance at America's leveling tendencies. And some aristocratic British Liberals also saw Americans through their class bias and sympathized with the Confederacy's demand for "order" and independence. English racism also intensified in these years, exemplified by the popularity of minstrelsy and the employment of science in the service of racial theory.

The intensity of the British propaganda war over the American conflict is evident in the methods of their debate: public meetings organized by both sides were huge affairs, with cheering and jeering, competing banners, carts and floats, orators and resolutions. In a press war the British argued over when rebellion is justified, whether secession was right or legal, whether slavery was at the heart of the conflict, and especially over the democratic image of America itself. This bitter debate over America's trial became a test over reform in Britain: those eager for a broadened franchise and increased democracy were pro-Union, and those who preferred to preserve Britain's class-ridden political system favored the Confederacy.

The nature of the internal British debate was no better symbolized than by the dozens of African Americans who served as pro-Union agents. The most popular was William Andrew Jackson, Confederate president Jefferson Davis's former coachman, who had escaped from Richmond in September 1862. Jackson's articulate presence at public meetings countered pro-Confederate arguments that the war was not about slavery.

In the end the British government did not recognize the Confederacy, and by 1864 the English cotton lords had found new sources of the crop in Egypt and India. But in this link between America and its English roots at its time of greatest travail, we can see that the Civil War was a transformation of international significance.

Some southern leaders pronounced that cotton was "king" and would bring Britain to their cause. This British cartoon shows King Cotton brought down in chains by the American eagle, anticipating the cotton famine to follow and the intense debate in Great Britain over the nature and meaning of the American Civil War.   (Granger Collection)

at the beginning of the war, British mills had a 50 percent surplus of cotton on hand, and they later found new sources of supply in India, Egypt, and Brazil. And throughout the war, some southern cotton continued to reach Europe, despite the Confederacy's embargo on cotton production, an ill-fated policy aimed at securing British support. Refusing to be stampeded into recognition of the Confederacy, the British government kept its eye on the battlefield. France, though sympathetic to the South, was unwilling to act independently of Britain. Confederate agents managed to purchase valuable arms and supplies in Europe and obtained loans from European financiers, but they never achieved a diplomatic breakthrough.

■ Both General Grant (*left*) and General Lee (*right*) were West Point graduates and had served in the U.S. Army during the War with Mexico. Their bloody battles against each other in 1864 stirred northern revulsion to the war even as they brought its end in sight. (National Archives)

More than once the Union strategy nearly broke down. An acute crisis occurred in 1861 when the over-zealous commander of an American frigate stopped the British steamer *Trent* and removed two Confederate ambassadors, James Mason and John Slidell, sailing to Britain. When they were imprisoned in Boston, northerners cheered, but the British interpreted the capture as a violation of freedom of the seas and demanded the prisoners' release. Lincoln and Seward waited until northern public opinion cooled and then released the two southerners. Soon forgotten, the incident nevertheless strained U.S.-British relations.

Then the sale to the Confederacy of warships constructed in England sparked vigorous protest from U.S. ambassador Charles Francis Adams. A few English-built ships, notably the *Alabama,* reached open water to serve the South. Over a period of twenty-two months, without entering a southern port (because of the Union blockade), the *Alabama* destroyed or captured more than sixty U.S. ships, leaving a bitter legal legacy to be settled in the postwar period.

On the battlefield, the northern victory was far from won in 1864. General Nathaniel Banks's Red River

BATTLEFIELD STALEMATE AND A UNION STRATEGY FOR VICTORY

campaign, designed to capture more of Louisiana and Texas, quickly fell apart, and the capture of Mobile Bay in August did not cause the fall of Mobile. Union general William Tecumseh Sherman commented that the North had to "keep the war South until they are not only ruined, exhausted, but humbled in pride and spirit." Sherman soon brought total war to the southern heartland. On the eastern front during the winter of 1863–1864, the two armies in Virginia settled into a stalemate awaiting yet another spring offensive by the North.

Military authorities throughout history have agreed that deep invasion is very risky: the farther an army penetrates enemy territory, the more vulnerable are its own communications and supply lines. Moreover, observed the Prussian expert Karl von Clausewitz, if the invader encountered a "truly national" resistance, his troops would be "everywhere exposed to attacks by an insurgent population." The South's vast size and a determined resistance could yet make a northern victory improbable.

General Grant, by now in command of all the federal armies, decided to test these conditions—and southern

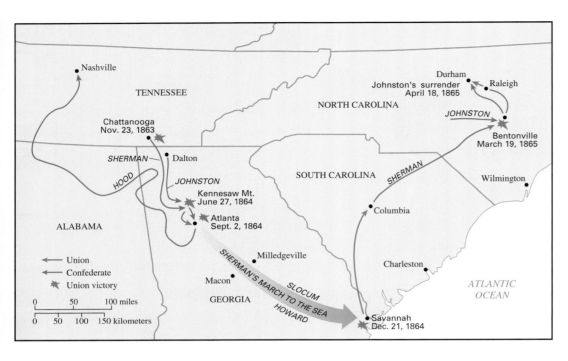

Map 15.4   Sherman's March to the Sea

The West proved a decisive theater at the end of the war. From Chattanooga, Union forces drove into Georgia, capturing Atlanta. Following the fall of Atlanta, General Sherman embarked on his march of destruction through Georgia to the coast and then northward through the Carolinas.

will—with a strategic innovation of his own: raids on a massive scale. Less tied to tradition and by-the-book maneuver than most other Union commanders, Grant proposed to use whole armies to destroy Confederate railroads, thus ruining the enemy's transportation and damaging the South's economy. Abandoning their lines of support, Union troops would live off the land while laying waste all resources useful to the military and to the civilian population of the Confederacy. After General George H. Thomas's troops won the Battle of Chattanooga in November 1863, the heartland of Georgia lay open. Grant entrusted General Sherman with 100,000 men for an invasion deep into the South, toward the rail center of Atlanta.

Jefferson Davis countered by positioning the army of General Joseph E. Johnston in Sherman's path. Davis's entire political strategy for 1864 was based on demonstrating Confederate military strength and successfully defending Atlanta. Davis hoped that southern resolve would lead to the political defeat of Lincoln and the election of a president who would sue for peace. When General Johnston slowly but steadily fell back toward Atlanta, Davis grew anxious and sought assurances that Atlanta would be held. From a purely military point of view, Johnston maneuvered skillfully. But when Johnston fell silent and continued to retreat, Davis replaced him with the one-legged General John Hood, who knew his job was to fight. "Our all depends on that army

FALL OF ATLANTA

at Atlanta," wrote Mary Chesnut. "If that fails us, the game is up."

For southern morale, the game was up. Hood attacked but was beaten, and Sherman's army occupied Atlanta on September 2, 1864. The victory buoyed northern spirits and ensured Lincoln's reelection. A government clerk in Richmond wrote, "Our fondly-cherished visions of peace have vanished like a mirage of the desert." Davis exhorted southerners to fight on and win new victories before the federal elections, but he had to admit that "two-thirds of our men are absent . . . most of them absent without leave." In a desperate diversion, Hood's army marched north to cut Sherman's supply lines and force him to withdraw, but Sherman began to march sixty thousand of his men straight to the sea, planning to live off the land and destroying Confederate resources as he went (see Map 15.4).

Sherman's army was an unusually formidable force, composed almost entirely of battle-tested veterans and officers who had risen through the ranks from the midwestern states. Before the march began, army doctors weeded out any men who were weak or sick. Tanned, bearded, tough, and unkempt, the remaining veterans were determined, as one put it, "to Conquer this Rebelien or Die." They believed "the South are to blame for this war" and were ready to make the South pay. Although many harbored racist attitudes, most had come to support emancipation be-

SHERMAN'S MARCH TO THE SEA

cause, as one said, "Slavery stands in the way of putting down the rebellion." Confederate General Johnston later commented, "There has been no such army since the days of Julius Caesar."

As Sherman's men moved across Georgia, they cut a path 50 to 60 miles wide and more than 200 miles long. The totality of the destruction they caused was awesome. A Georgia woman described the "Burnt Country" this way: "The fields were trampled down and the road was lined with carcasses of horses, hogs, and cattle that the invaders, unable either to consume or to carry with them, had wantonly shot down to starve our people. . . . The stench in some places was unbearable." Such devastation diminished the South's material resources and sapped its will to resist.

After reaching Savannah in December, Sherman marched his armies north into the Carolinas. To his soldiers, South Carolina was "the root of secession." They burned and destroyed as they moved through, encountering little resistance. The opposing army of General Johnston was small, but Sherman's men should have been prime targets for guerrilla raids and harassing attacks by local defense units. The absence of both led South Carolina's James Chesnut Jr. (a politician and the husband of Mary Chesnut) to write that his state "was shamefully and unnecessarily lost. . . . We had time, opportunity and means to destroy him. But there was wholly wanting the energy and ability required by the occasion." Southerners had lost the will to continue the struggle.

Sherman's march drew additional human resources to the Union cause. In Georgia alone as many as nineteen thousand slaves gladly took the opportunity to escape bondage and join the Union troops as they passed through the countryside. Others remained on the plantations to await the end of the war, either from an ingrained wariness of whites or negative experiences with federal soldiers. The destruction of food harmed slaves as well as white rebels, and many blacks lost livestock, clothing, crops, and other valuables to their liberators. In fact, the brutality of Sherman's troops shocked some liberated slaves. "I've seen them cut the hams off of a live pig or ox and go off leavin' the animal groanin'," recalled one man. "The master had 'em kilt then, but it was awful."

It was awful, too, in Virginia, where the path to victory proved protracted and ghastly. Throughout the spring and summer of 1864, intent on capturing Richmond, Grant hurled his troops at Lee's army in Virginia

VIRGINIA'S
BLOODY SOIL

and suffered appalling losses: almost 18,000 casualties in the Battle of the Wilderness, where skeletons poked out of the shallow graves dug one year be-

Map 15.5   The War in Virginia, 1864–1865

At great cost, Grant hammered away at Lee's army until the weakened southern forces finally surrendered at Appomattox Court House.

fore; more than 8,000 at Spotsylvania; and 12,000 in the space of a few hours at Cold Harbor (see Map 15.5).

Before the assault at Cold Harbor (which Grant later admitted was a grave mistake), Union troops pinned scraps of paper bearing their names and addresses to their backs, certain they would be mowed down as they rushed Lee's trenches. In four weeks in May and June, Grant lost as many men as were enrolled in Lee's entire army. From early May until July, when Union forces had marched and fought all the way from forests west of Fredericksburg to Petersburg, south of Richmond, which they besieged, the two armies engaged each other nearly every day. The war had reached a horrible modern scale. Wagon trains carrying thousands of Union wounded crawled back toward Washington. "It was as if war," wrote historian Bruce Catton, "the great clumsy machine for maiming people, had at last been perfected. Instead of turning out its gist spasmodically, with long waits between each delivery, it was at last able to produce every day, without any gaps at all."

Undaunted, Grant kept up the pressure, saying, "I propose to fight it out along this line if it takes all summer." Though costly, and testing northern morale to its limits, these battles prepared the way for eventual victory:

Lee's army shrank until offensive action was no longer possible, while Grant's army kept replenishing its forces with new recruits. The siege of Petersburg, with the armies facing each other in miles of trenches, lasted throughout the winter of 1864–1865.

The end finally came in the spring of 1865. Grant kept battering Lee, who tried but failed to break through the Union line. With the numerical su-

SURRENDER AT APPOMATTOX

periority of Grant's army now greater than two to one, Confederate defeat was inevitable. On April 2 Lee abandoned Richmond and Petersburg. On April 9, hemmed in by Union troops, short of rations, and with fewer than thirty thousand men left, Lee surrendered at Appomattox Court House. Grant treated his rival with respect and paroled the defeated troops, allowing cavalrymen to keep their horses and take them home. The war was over at last. Within weeks, Confederate forces under Johnston surrendered, and Davis, who had fled Richmond but wanted the war to continue, was captured in Georgia. The North rejoiced, and most southerners fell into despair, expecting waves of punishment. In the profound relief and stillness of the surrender field at Appomattox, no one could know the tasks of healing and justice that lay ahead.

With Lee's surrender, Lincoln knew that the Union had been preserved, yet he lived to see but a few days of war's aftermath. On the evening of Good Friday, April 14, he accompanied his wife to Ford's Theatre in Washington to enjoy a popular comedy. There John Wilkes Booth, an embittered southern sympathizer, shot the president in the head at point-blank range. Lincoln died the next day. Twelve days later, troops tracked down and killed Booth. The Union had lost its wartime leader, and millions publicly mourned the martyred chief executive along the route of the funeral train that took his body home to Illinois. Relief at the war's end mingled hauntingly with a renewed sense of loss and anxiety about the future. Millions never forgot where they were and how they felt at the news of Lincoln's assassination.

Property damage and financial costs were enormous, though difficult to tally. U.S. loans and taxes during the conflict totaled almost $3 billion, and

FINANCIAL TALLY

interest on the war debt was $2.8 billion. The Confederacy borrowed over $2 billion but lost far more in the destruction of homes, crops, livestock, and other property. In southern war zones the landscape was desolated. Over wide regions fences and crops were destroyed; houses, barns, and bridges burned; and fields abandoned and left to erode. Union troops had looted factories and put two-thirds of the South's railroad system out of service.

Estimates of the total cost of the war exceed $20 billion—five times the total expenditures of the federal government from its creation to 1861. By 1865, the federal government's spending had soared to twenty times the

■ At the war's end, the U.S. flag flew over the state capitol in Richmond, Virginia, which bore many marks of destruction.   (National Archives)

■ The death of President Lincoln caused a vast outpouring of grief in the North. As this Currier and Ives print shows, on its way to Illinois, his funeral train stopped at several cities to allow local services to be held.   (Anne S. K. Brown Military Collection, John Hay Library, Brown University)

prewar level and accounted for over 26 percent of the gross national product. Many of these changes were more or less permanent, as wartime measures left the government more deeply involved in manufacturing, banking, and transportation. If southerners had hoped to remove government from the economy, the war had now irrepressibly bound them together, a lesson of note for our twenty-first-century debates over the same issues.

The human costs of the Civil War were especially staggering. The total number of military casualties on both sides exceeded 1 million—a frightful toll for a nation of 31 million people. Approximately 360,000 Union soldiers died, 110,000 of them from wounds suffered in battle. Another 275,175 Union soldiers were wounded but survived. On the Confederate side, an estimated 260,000 lost their lives, and almost as many suffered wounds. More men died in the Civil War than in all other American wars combined until Vietnam. Of an estimated 194,743 northerners in southern prisons, 30,218 died; of 214,865 southerners in northern prisons, 25,976 died. The prison story from the war was one in which neither side could claim pride, and it caused embittered debate in war memory for decades.

DEATH TOLL

These unprecedented losses flowed from fundamental strife over the nature of the Union and the liberty of black people. Both sides saw vital interests in the struggle. As Julia Ward Howe wrote in her famous "Battle Hymn," they had heard "the trumpet that shall never call retreat." And so the war took its horrifying course. The first great legacy of the war in the lives of its survivors was, therefore, death itself. Although precise figures on enlistments are impossible to obtain, it appears that 700,000 to 800,000 men served in the Confederate armies. Far more, possibly 2.3 million, served in the Union armies. All these men were taken from home, family, and personal goals; their lives, if they survived at all, were disrupted in ways that were never repaired.

Summary

The Civil War altered American society forever. During the war, in both North and South, women had taken on new roles as they struggled to manage the hardships of the home front, to grieve, and to work for the prosecution of the war. Industrialization and large economic enterprises grew in power. Ordinary citizens found that their futures were increasingly tied to huge organizations. The character and extent of government power changed markedly. Under Republican leadership, the federal government had expanded its power not only to preserve the Union but also to extend freedom. A social revolution and government authority emancipated the slaves, and Lincoln had called for "a new birth of freedom" in America. A republic desperately divided against itself had survived, but in new constitutional forms yet to take shape during Reconstruction.

It was unclear how or whether the nation would use its power to protect the rights of the former slaves. Secession was dead, but whether Americans would continue to embrace a centralized nationalism remained to be seen.

The war ended decisively after tremendous sacrifice, but it left many unanswered questions. How would white southerners, embittered and impoverished, respond to efforts to reconstruct the nation? How would the country care for the maimed, the orphans, the farming women without men to work their land, and all the dead who had to be found and properly buried? What would be the place of black men and women in American life?

In the West, two civil wars raged, one between Union and Confederate forces, and the other resulting in a conquest of southwestern Indians by U.S. troops and land-hungry settlers. On the diplomatic front, the Union government had delicately managed to keep Great Britain and other foreign powers out of the war. Dissent flourished in both North and South, playing a crucial role in the ultimate collapse of the Confederacy, while the Union cause was only marginally affected by sabotage and draft riots.

In the Civil War Americans had undergone an epic of destruction and survival—a transformation like nothing else in their history. White southerners had experienced defeat as few other Americans have ever faced. Blacks were walking proudly but anxiously from slavery to freedom. White northerners were, by and large, self-conscious victors in a massive war for the nation's existence and for new definitions of freedom. The war, including all its drama, sacrifice, and social and political changes, left a compelling memory in American hearts and minds for generations.

LEGACY FOR A PEOPLE AND A NATION
The Confederate Battle Flag

The most widespread and controversial symbol to emerge from the Civil War era is the Confederate flag. Rather than the official flag of the Confederacy, it was a battle flag that soldiers carried to mark the center of a unit's position in the confusion of combat. Over time, this flag has taken on powerful emotional meanings.

At Confederate veterans' reunions and parades from the 1870s well into the twentieth century, the flag was an emblem of the South's Lost Cause. After extended controversy, many captured Confederate flags were returned by the federal government to southern states in 1905 as a gesture of reconciliation. Increasingly, Confederate remembrance merged with white supremacy at the turn of the twentieth century, and African Americans resented the flag.

In the late 1940s the flag became a fixture of popular culture with heightened racial meanings. In 1948 it was a symbol of the States' Rights ("Dixiecrat") Party. By the 1950s waving the Confederate flag became a demonstration of defiance among southern whites against the civil rights revolution. With the spread of American popular culture abroad, the Confederate flag can now be found all over the world, as a symbol of racism and vague demonstrations of defiance against power.

What does this flag mean as a symbol? Some southern whites argue that it is merely a marker of regional pride and identity. Some stress the flag's value as a symbol of rebellion against the establishment, or "political correctness." But to most blacks and to many whites, it expresses racism. The flag is loaded with coded meanings that can be interpreted in opposite ways. Some claim it represents the "nobility" of southern military tradition; others conclude that it stands for the hatred embodied in the history of the Ku Klux Klan.

In recent times, the Confederate flag has been the center of legal and political controversy. Disputes have emanated from city councils, high schools, and universities over public and private uses of the flag. Most visible of all have been the debates in the states of Georgia, South Carolina, Alabama, and Mississippi over whether to cease flying the Confederate flag at official sites, or as part of state flags. The debate over the legacy of the Confederate flag may never end. At issue are important questions: free speech, equal protection under law, perception versus reality, official government endorsement of collective symbols, the significance of race and racism in our national memory, and the meaning of the Civil War itself.

The **history companion** powered by Eduspace®

Your primary source for interactive quizzes, exercises, and more to help you learn efficiently.
http://history.college.hmco.com/students

RECONSTRUCTION: AN UNFINISHED REVOLUTION 1865–1877

The lower half of the city of Charleston, South Carolina, the seedbed of secession, lay in ruin when most of the white population evacuated on February 18, 1865. A prolonged bombardment by Union batteries and gunboats around Charleston harbor had already destroyed many of the lovely town homes of the low-country planters. Then, as the city was abandoned, fires broke out everywhere, ignited in bales of cotton left in huge stockpiles in public squares. To many observers the flames were the funeral pyres of a dying civilization.

Among the first Union troops to enter Charleston was the Twenty-first U.S. Colored Regiment, which received the surrender of the city from its mayor. For black Charlestonians, most of whom were former slaves, this was a time of celebration. In symbolic ceremonies they proclaimed their freedom and announced their rebirth. Whatever the postwar order would bring, the freedpeople of Charleston converted Confederate ruin into a vision of Reconstruction based on Union victory and black liberation.

Still, in Charleston, as elsewhere, death demanded attention. During the final year of the war, the Confederates had converted the planters' Race Course, a horseracing track, and its famed Jockey Club, into a prison. Union soldiers were kept in terrible conditions in the interior of the track, without shelter. The 257 who died of exposure and disease were buried in a mass grave behind the judges' stand. After the fall of the city, Charleston's blacks organized to create a proper burial ground for the Union dead. During April more than twenty black workmen reinterred the dead in marked graves, and built a high fence around the cemetery. They built an archway over the entrance to the gravesite, and painted an inscription, "Martyrs of the Race Course."

◀ "Entrance of the 55th Massachusetts (Colored) Regiment into Charleston, S.C., February 21, 1865." Thomas Nast, pencil, oil, and wash on board, 1865. Black troops celebrated as they marched into the Confederate stronghold, hoisting their caps on their bayonets, and singing "John Brown's Body" as they marched up Meeting Street, Charleston's main thoroughfare.   (Museum of Fine Arts, Boston)

CHRONOLOGY

1865 • Johnson begins rapid and lenient Reconstruction
• Confederate leaders regain power
• White southern governments pass restrictive black codes
• Congress refuses to seat southern representatives
• Thirteenth Amendment ratified, abolishing slavery

1866 • Congress passes Civil Rights Act and renewal of Freedmen's Bureau over Johnson's veto
• Congress approves Fourteenth Amendment
• Most southern states reject Fourteenth Amendment
• In *Ex parte Milligan* the Supreme Court reasserts its influence

1867 • Congress passes First Reconstruction Act and Tenure of Office Act
• Seward arranges purchase of Alaska
• Constitutional conventions called in southern states

1868 • House impeaches Johnson; Senate acquits him
• Most southern states readmitted to the Union under Radical plan
• Fourteenth Amendment ratified
• Grant elected president

1869 • Congress approves Fifteenth Amendment (ratified in 1870)

1871 • Congress passes second Enforcement Act and Ku Klux Klan Act
• Treaty with England settles *Alabama* claims

1872 • Amnesty Act frees almost all remaining Confederates from restrictions on holding office
• Grant reelected

1873 • *Slaughter-House* cases limit power of Fourteenth Amendment
• Panic of 1873 leads to widespread unemployment and labor strife

1874 • Democrats win majority in House of Representatives

1875 • Several Grant appointees indicted for corruption
• Congress passes weak Civil Rights Act
• Democratic Party increases control of southern states with white supremacy campaigns

1876 • *U.S. v. Cruikshank* further weakens Fourteenth Amendment
• Presidential election disputed

1877 • Congress elects Hayes president
• "Home rule" returns to three remaining southern states not yet controlled by Democrats; Reconstruction considered over

And then they planned an extraordinary ceremony. On the morning of May 1, 1865, a procession of ten thousand people marched around the planters' Race Course, led by three thousand children carrying armloads of roses and singing "John Brown's Body." They were followed by black women with baskets of flowers and wreaths, and then by black men. The parade concluded with members of black and white Union regiments and white missionaries and teachers, led by James Redpath, the supervisor of freedmen's schools in the region. All who could fit assembled at the gravesite; five black ministers read from Scripture, and a black children's choir sang "America," "We'll Rally Around the Flag," the "Star-Spangled Banner," and Negro spirituals. When the ceremony ended, the large crowd retired to the Race Course for speeches, picnics, and military festivities.

The war was over in Charleston, and "Decoration Day"—now Memorial Day, the day to remember the war dead and decorate their graves with flowers—had been founded by African Americans. Black people—by their labor, their words, their songs, and their marching feet on the old planters' Race Course—had created an American tradition. In their vision, they were creating the Independence Day of a Second American Revolution.

Reconstruction would bring revolutionary circumstances, but revolutions can go backward. The Civil War and its aftermath wrought unprecedented changes in American society, law, and politics, but the underlying realities of economic power, racism, and judicial conservatism limited Reconstruction's revolutionary potential. As never before, the nation had to determine the nature of federal-state relations, whether confiscated land could be redistributed, how to bring justice to the freedpeople and to aggrieved white folk whose property and lives were devastated. And at the end of the day, Americans faced the harrowing challenge of psychological healing from a bloody and fratricidal war. How they would negotiate this tangled relationship between healing and justice would determine the extent of change during Reconstruction.

Nowhere was the turmoil of Reconstruction more evident than in national politics. Lincoln's successor, Andrew Johnson, fought bitterly with Congress over the shaping of Reconstruction policies. Although a southerner, Johnson had always been a foe of the South's wealthy planters, and his first acts as president suggested that he would be tough on "traitors." Before the end of 1865, however, Johnson's policies changed direction, and he became the protector of southern interests. Jefferson Davis stayed in prison for two years, but Johnson quickly pardoned other rebel leaders and allowed them to occupy high offices. He also ordered the return of plantations to their original owners, including abandoned coastal lands of Georgia and South Carolina on which forty thousand freed men and women had settled by order of General William Tecumseh Sherman early in 1865.

Johnson imagined a lenient and rapid "restoration" of the South to the Union rather than the fundamental "reconstruction" that Republican congressmen favored. Between 1866 and 1868, the president and the Republican leadership in Congress engaged in a bitterly antagonistic power struggle over how to put the United States back together again. Before these struggles were over, Congress had impeached the president, enfranchised the freedmen, and given them a role in reconstructing the South. The nation also adopted the Fourteenth and Fifteenth Amendments, ushering equal protection of the law, a definition of citizenship, and universal manhood suffrage into the Constitution. But little was done to open the doors of economic opportunity to black southerners, and the cause of equal rights for African Americans as the central aim of Reconstruction fell almost as fast as it rose.

By 1869 the Ku Klux Klan employed extensive violence and terror to thwart Reconstruction and undermine black freedom. As white Democrats in the South recaptured state governments, they encountered little opposition from the North. Moreover, as the 1870s advanced, industrial growth accelerated, creating new opportunities and priorities. The West, its seemingly limitless potential and its wars against Indians, drew American resources and consciousness like never before. Political corruption became a nationwide scandal, bribery a way of doing business.

Thus Reconstruction became a revolution eclipsed. The white South's desire to take back control of their states and of race relations overwhelmed the national interest in stopping them. But Reconstruction left enduring legacies the nation has struggled with ever since. ■

Wartime Reconstruction

Civil wars leave immense challenges of healing, justice, and physical rebuilding. Anticipating that process, Reconstruction of the Union was an issue as early as 1863, well before the war ended. Many key questions loomed on the horizon when and if the North succeeded on the battlefield. How would the nation be restored? How would southern states and leaders be treated? As errant brothers, or as traitors? What was the constitutional basis for readmission of states to the Union and where, if anywhere, could American statesmen look for precedence or guidance? More specifically, four vexing problems compelled early thinking and would haunt the Reconstruction era throughout. One, who would rule in the South once it was defeated? Two, who would rule in the federal government, Congress or the president? Three, what were the dimensions of black freedom, and what rights under law would the freedmen enjoy? And four, would Reconstruction be a preservation of the old republic, or a second revolution, a reinvention of a new republic?

Abraham Lincoln had never been antisouthern, though he had grown to become the leader of an antislavery war. He lost three brothers-in-law killed in the war on the Confederate side. His worst fear was that the war would collapse at the end into guerrilla warfare across the South, with surviving bands of Confederates carrying on resistance. Lincoln insisted that his generals give lenient terms to southern soldiers once they surrendered. In his Second Inaugural Address, delivered only a month before his assassination, Lincoln promised "malice toward none; with charity for all," as Americans strove to "bind up the nation's wounds."

LINCOLN'S 10 PERCENT PLAN

Lincoln planned early for a swift and moderate Reconstruction process. In his "Proclamation of Amnesty and Reconstruction," issued in December 1863, he proposed to replace majority rule with "loyal rule" as a means of reconstructing southern state governments before hostilities ended. He proposed pardons to all ex-Confederates except the highest-ranking military and civilian officers. Then, as soon as 10 percent of the voting population in the 1860 general election in a given state had taken an oath to the United States and established a government, the new state would be recognized. Lincoln did not consult Congress in these plans, and "loyal" assemblies (known as "Lincoln governments") were created in Louisiana, Tennessee, and Arkansas in 1864, states largely occupied by Union troops. These governments were weak and dependent on northern armies for survival.

Congress responded with great hostility to Lincoln's moves to readmit southern states in what seemed such a premature manner. Many Radical Republicans, strong proponents of emancipation and aggressive prosecution of the war against the South, considered the 10 percent plan a "mere mockery" of democracy. Led by Thaddeus Stevens of Pennsylvania in the House and Charles Sumner of Massachusetts in the Senate, congressional Republicans locked horns with Lincoln and proposed a longer and harsher approach to Reconstruction. Stevens advocated a "conquered provinces" theory, and Sumner employed an argument of "state suicide." Both contended that southerners had organized as a foreign nation to make war on the United States and, by secession, had destroyed their status as states. They therefore must be treated as "conquered foreign lands" and reverted to the status of "unorganized territories" before any process of readmission could be entertained (by Congress).

CONGRESS AND THE WADE-DAVIS BILL

In July 1864, the Wade-Davis bill, named for its sponsors, Senator Benjamin Wade of Ohio and Congressman Henry W. Davis of Maryland, emerged from Congress with three specific conditions for southern readmission: one, it demanded a "majority" of white male citizens participating in the creation of a new government; two, to vote or be a delegate to constitutional conventions, men had to take an "iron-clad" oath (declaring they had never aided the Confederate war effort); and three, all officers above the rank of lieutenant, and all civil officials in the Confederacy, would be disfranchised and deemed "not a citizen of the United States." The Confederate states were to be defined as "conquered enemies," said Davis, and the process of readmission was to be harsh and slow. Lincoln, ever the adroit politician, pocket-vetoed the bill and issued a conciliatory proclamation of his own announcing that he would not be inflexibly committed to any "one plan" of Reconstruction.

This exchange came during Grant's bloody campaign in Virginia against Lee, when the outcome of the war and Lincoln's reelection were still in doubt. Radical members of his own party, indeed, were organizing a dump-Lincoln campaign for the 1864 election. On August 5, Radical Republicans issued the "Wade-Davis Manifesto" to newspapers; an unprecedented attack on a sitting president by members of his own party, it accused Lincoln of usurpation of presidential powers and disgraceful leniency toward an eventually conquered South.

What emerged in 1864–1865 was a clear-cut debate and a potential constitutional crisis. Lincoln saw Reconstruction as a means of weakening the Confederacy and winning the war; the Radicals saw it as a longer-term transformation of the political and racial order of the country.

In early 1865, Congress and Lincoln joined in two important measures that recognized slavery's centrality to the war. On January 31, with strong administration backing, Congress passed the Thirteenth Amendment, which had two provisions: first, it abolished involuntary servitude everywhere in the United States; second, it declared that Congress shall have power to enforce this outcome by "appropriate legislation." When the measure passed by 119 to 56, a mere two votes more than the necessary two-thirds, rejoicing broke out in Congress. A Republican recorded in his diary: "Members joined in the shouting and kept it up for some minutes. Some embraced one another, others wept like children. I have felt ever since the vote, as if I were in a new country."

THIRTEENTH AMENDMENT

But the Thirteenth Amendment had emerged from a long congressional debate and considerable petitioning and public advocacy. One of the first and most remarkable petitions for a constitutional amendment abolishing slavery was submitted early in 1864 by Elizabeth Cady Stanton, Susan B. Anthony, and the Women's Loyal National League. Women throughout the Union accumulated thousands of signatures, even venturing into staunchly pro-Confederate regions of Kentucky and Missouri to secure supporters. It was a long road from the Emancipation Proclamation to the Thirteenth Amendment—through treacherous constitutional theory, a bedrock of belief that the sacred document ought never be altered, and partisan politics. But the logic of winning the war by crushing slavery, and of securing a new beginning for the nation under law that so many had now died to save, won the day.

Potentially as significant, on March 3, 1865, Congress created the Bureau of Refugees, Freedmen, and Abandoned Lands—the Freedmen's Bureau, an unprecedented agency of social uplift, necessitated by the ravages of the war. Americans had never engaged in federal aid to citizens on such a scale. With thousands of refugees, white and black, displaced in the South, the government continued what private freedmen's aid societies had started as early as 1862. In the mere four years of its existence, the Freedmen's Bureau

FREEDMEN'S BUREAU

supplied food and medical services, built several thousand schools and some colleges, negotiated several hundred thousand employment contracts between freedmen and their former masters, and tried to manage confiscated land.

The Bureau would be a controversial aspect of Reconstruction, within the South, where whites generally hated it, and within the federal government, where politicians divided over its constitutionality. Some Bureau agents were devoted to freedmen's rights, while others were opportunists who exploited the chaos of the postwar South. The war had forced into the open an eternal question of republics: What are the social welfare obligations of the state toward its people, and what do people owe their governments in return? Apart from their conquest and displacement of the eastern Indians, Americans were relatively inexperienced at the Freedmen's Bureau's task—social reform through military occupation.

The Meanings of Freedom

*B*lack southerners entered into life after slavery with hope and circumspection. A Texas man recalled his father telling him, even before the war was over, "Our forever was going to be spent living among the Southerners, after they got licked." Freed men and women tried to gain as much as they could from their new circumstances. Often the changes they valued the most were personal—alterations in location, employer, or living arrangements.

For America's former slaves, Reconstruction had one paramount meaning: a chance to explore freedom. A

**THE FEEL
OF FREEDOM**

southern white woman admitted in her diary that the black people "showed a natural and exultant joy at being free." Former slaves remembered singing far into the night after federal troops, who confirmed rumors of their emancipation, reached their plantations. The slaves on a Texas plantation shouted for joy, their leader proclaiming, "We is free—no more whippings and beatings." A few people gave in to the natural desire to do what had been impossible before. One angry grandmother dropped her hoe and ran to confront her mistress. "I'm free!" she yelled. "Yes, I'm free! Ain't got to work for you no more! You can't put me in your pocket now!" Another man recalled that he and others "started on the move," either to search for family members or just to exercise the human right of mobility.

■ "The Armed Slave," William Sprang, oil on canvas, c. 1865. This remarkable painting depicts an African American veteran soldier, musket with fixed bayonet leaning against the wall, cigar in hand indicating a new life of safety and leisure, reading a book to demonstrate his embrace of education and freedom. The man's visage leaves the impression of satisfaction and dignity.
(The Civil War Library and Museum, Philadelphia)

Many freed men and women reacted more cautiously and shrewdly, taking care to test the boundaries of their new condition. "After the war was over," explained one man, "we was afraid to move. Just like terrapins or turtles after emancipation. Just stick our heads out to see how the land lay." As slaves they had learned to expect hostility from white people, and they did not presume it would instantly disappear. Life in freedom might still be a matter of what was allowed, not what was right. One sign of this shrewd caution was the way freed people evaluated potential employers. "Most all the Negroes that had good owners stayed with 'em, but the others left. Some of 'em come back and some didn't," explained one man. After considerable wandering in search of better circumstances, a majority of blacks eventually settled as agricultural workers back on their former farms or plantations. But they relocated their houses and did their utmost to control the conditions of their labor.

Former slaves concentrated on improving their daily lives. Throughout the South they devoted themselves to

REUNION OF AFRICAN AMERICAN FAMILIES

reuniting their families, separated during slavery by sale or hardship, and during the war by dislocation and the emancipation process. With only shreds of information to guide them, thousands of freed people embarked on odysseys in search of a husband, wife, child, or parent. By relying on the black community for help and information, and placing ads in black newspapers that continued to appear well into the 1880s, some succeeded in their quest, while others trudged through several states and never found loved ones.

Husbands and wives who had belonged to different masters established homes together for the first time, and, as they had tried under slavery, parents asserted the right to raise their own children. A mother bristled when her old master claimed a right to whip her children. She informed him that "he warn't goin' to brush none of her chilluns no more." The freed men and women were too much at risk to act recklessly, but, as one man put it, they were tired of punishment and "sure didn't take no more foolishment off of white folks."

Many black people wanted to minimize contact with whites because, as Reverend Garrison Frazier told General

BLACKS' SEARCH FOR INDEPENDENCE

Sherman in January 1865, "There is a prejudice against us . . . that will take years to get over." To avoid contact with overbearing whites who were used to supervising them, blacks abandoned the slave quarters and fanned out to distant corners of the land they worked. "After the war my stepfather come," recalled Annie Young, "and got my mother and we moved out in the piney woods." Others described moving "across the creek" or building a "saplin house . . . back in the woods." Some rural dwellers established small all-black settlements that still exist today along the back roads of the South.

Even once-privileged slaves desired such independence and social separation. One man turned down the master's offer of the overseer's house and moved instead to a shack in "Freetown." He also declined to let the former owner grind his grain for free because it "make him feel like a free man to pay for things just like anyone else."

In addition to a fair employer, what freed men and women most wanted was the ownership of land. Land

FREEDPEOPLE'S DESIRE FOR LAND

represented self-sufficiency and a chance to gain compensation for generations of bondage. General Sherman's special Field Order Number 15, issued in February 1865, set aside 400,000 acres of land in the Sea Islands region for the exclusive settlement of the freedpeople. Hope swelled among ex-slaves as forty-acre plots, mules, and "possessary titles" were promised to them. But President Johnson ordered them removed in October and returned the land to its original owners under army enforcement. A northern observer noted that slaves freed in the Sea Islands of South Carolina and Georgia made "plain, straight-forward" inquiries as they settled on new land. They wanted to be sure the land "would be theirs after they had improved it." Everywhere, blacks young and old thirsted for homes of their own.

But most members of both political parties opposed genuine land redistribution to the freedmen. Even northern reformers who with Lincoln's encouragement had administered the Sea Islands during the war showed little sympathy for black aspirations. The former Sea Island slaves wanted to establish small, self-sufficient farms. Northern soldiers, officials, and missionaries of both races brought education and aid to the freedmen but also insisted that they grow cotton. They emphasized profit, cash crops, and the values of competitive capitalism.

"The Yankees preach nothing but cotton, cotton!" complained one Sea Island black. "We wants land," wrote another, but tax officials "make the lots too big, and cut we out." Indeed, the U.S. government sold thousands of acres in the Sea Islands, 90 percent of which went to wealthy investors from the North. At a protest against evictions from a contraband camp in Virginia in 1866, freedman Bayley Wyatt made black desires and claims clear: "We has a right to the land where we are located. For why? I tell you. Our wives, our children, our husbands, has been sold over and over again to purchase the lands we now locates upon; for that reason we have a divine right to the land."

Ex-slaves reached out for valuable things in life that had been denied them. One of these was education.

BLACK EMBRACE OF EDUCATION

Blacks of all ages hungered for the knowledge in books that had been permitted only to whites. With freedom, they started schools and filled classrooms both day and night. On log seats and dirt floors, freed men and women studied their letters in old almanacs and discarded dictionaries. Young children brought infants to school with them, and adults attended

■ African Americans of all ages eagerly pursued the opportunity in freedom to gain an education. This young woman in Mt. Meigs, Alabama, is helping her mother learn to read.   (Smithsonian Institute, photo by Rudolf Eickemeyer)

thropy. The Yankee schoolmarm—dedicated, selfless, and religious—became an agent of progress in many southern communities. Thus did African Americans seek a break from their pasts through learning. More than 600,000 were enrolled in elementary school by 1877.

Blacks and their white allies also saw the need for colleges and universities to train teachers, ministers, and professionals for leadership. The American Missionary Association founded seven colleges, including Fisk and Atlanta Universities, between 1866 and 1869. The Freedmen's Bureau helped to establish Howard University in Washington, D.C., and northern religious groups such as the Methodists, Baptists, and Congregationalists supported dozens of seminaries and teachers' colleges.

During Reconstruction, African American leaders often were highly educated individuals; many were from the prewar elite of free people of color. This group had benefited from its association with wealthy whites, many of whom were blood relatives; some planters had given their mulatto children an outstanding education. Francis Cardozo, who held various offices in South Carolina, had attended universities in Scotland and England. P. B. S. Pinchback, who became lieutenant governor of Louisiana, was the son of a planter who had sent him to school in Cincinnati. Both of the two black senators from Mississippi, Blanche K. Bruce and Hiram Revels, possessed privileged educations. Bruce was the son of a planter who had provided tutoring at home; Revels was the son of free North Carolina blacks who had sent him to Knox College in Illinois. These men and many self-educated former slaves brought to political office not only fervor but experience.

Freed from the restrictions and regulations of slavery, blacks could build their own institutions as they saw fit. The secret churches of slavery came into the open; in countless communities throughout the South, ex-slaves "started a brush arbor." A brush arbor was merely "a sort of . . . shelter with leaves for a roof," but the freed men and women worshiped in it enthusiastically. "Preachin' and shouting sometimes lasted all day," they recalled, for the opportunity to worship together freely meant "glorious times."

GROWTH
OF BLACK
CHURCHES

Within a few years independent branches of the Methodist and Baptist denominations had attracted the great majority of black Christians in the South. By 1877, in South Carolina alone, the African Methodist Episcopal (A.M.E.) Church had 1,000 ministers, 44,000 members, and its own school of theology, while the A.M.E.

at night or after "the crops were laid by." Many a teacher had "to make herself heard over three other classes reciting in concert" in a small room. The desire to escape slavery's ignorance was so great that, despite their poverty, many blacks paid tuition, typically $1 or $1.50 a month. These small amounts constituted major portions of a person's agricultural wages and added up to more than $1 million by 1870.

The federal government and northern reformers of both races assisted this pursuit of education. In its brief life the Freedmen's Bureau founded over four thousand schools, and idealistic men and women from the North established others funded by private northern philan-

■ Churches became a center of African American life, both social and political, during and after Reconstruction. Churches, big and small, like this one, Faith Memorial Church, in Hagley Landing, South Carolina, became the first black-owned institutions for the postfreedom generation. (*Aunt Phebe, Uncle Tom and Others: Character Studies Among the Old Slaves of the South Fifty Years After* by Essie Collins Matthews)

Zion Church had 45,000 members. In the rapid growth of churches, some of which became the wealthiest and the most autonomous institutions in black life, the freed-people demonstrated their most secure claim on freedom as they created enduring communities.

The desire to gain as much independence as possible also shaped the former slaves' economic arrangements.

RISE OF THE SHARECROPPING SYSTEM

Since most of them lacked money to buy land, they preferred the next best thing: renting the land they worked. But the South had a cash-poor economy with few sources of credit, and few whites would consider renting land to blacks. Most blacks had no means to get cash before the harvest, and thus other alternatives had to be tried.

Black farmers and white landowners therefore turned to sharecropping, a system in which farmers kept part of their crop and gave the rest to the landowner while living on his property. The landlord or a merchant "furnished" food and supplies, such as draft animals and seed, needed before the harvest, and he received payment from the crop. Although landowners tried to set the laborers' share at a low level, black farmers had some bargaining power, at least at first. Sharecroppers would hold out, or move and try to switch employers from one year to another. As the system matured during the 1870s and 1880s, most sharecroppers worked "on halves"—half for the owner and half for themselves.

The sharecropping system, which materialized as early as 1868 in parts of the South, originated as a desirable compromise. It eased landowners' problems with cash and credit, and provided them a permanent, dependent labor force; blacks accepted it because it gave them more freedom from daily supervision. Instead of working in the hated gangs under a white overseer, as in slavery, they farmed their own plot of land in family groups. But sharecropping later proved to be a disaster. Owners and merchants developed a monopoly of control

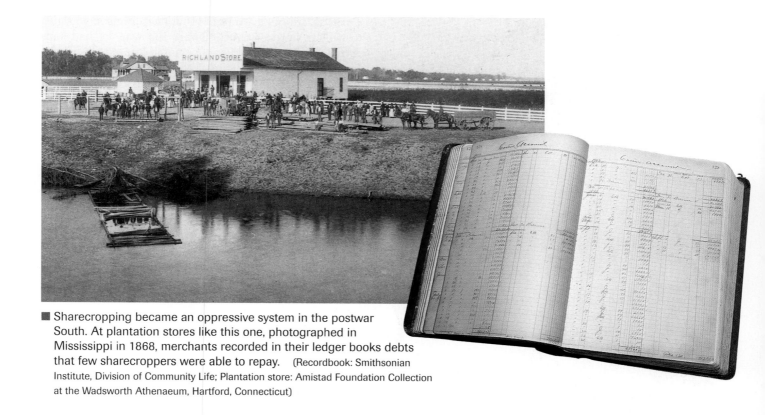

■ Sharecropping became an oppressive system in the postwar South. At plantation stores like this one, photographed in Mississippi in 1868, merchants recorded in their ledger books debts that few sharecroppers were able to repay. (Recordbook: Smithsonian Institute, Division of Community Life; Plantation store: Amistad Foundation Collection at the Wadsworth Athenaeum, Hartford, Connecticut)

over the agricultural economy, as sharecroppers found themselves riveted into ever-increasing debt (see page 554).

The fundamental problem, however, was that southern farmers as a whole still concentrated on cotton, a crop with a bright past and a dim future. In freedom, black women often stayed away from the fields and cotton picking, allowing them to concentrate on domestic chores. Given the diminishing incentives of the system, they placed greater value on independent choices about gender roles and family organization than on reaching higher levels of production. By 1878 the South had recovered its prewar share of British cotton purchases. But even as southerners grew more cotton, their reward diminished. Cotton prices began a long decline, as world demand fell off.

Thus southern agriculture slipped deeper and deeper into depression. Black sharecroppers struggled under a growing burden of debt that reduced their independence and bound them to landowners and to furnishing merchants almost as oppressively as slavery had bound them to their masters. Many white farmers became debtors, too, gradually lost their land, and joined the ranks of

sharecroppers. This economic transformation took place as the nation struggled to put its political house back in order.

Johnson's Reconstruction Plan

When Reconstruction began under President Andrew Johnson, many expected his policies to be harsh. Throughout his career in Tennessee he had criticized the wealthy planters and championed the small farmers. When an assassin's bullet thrust Johnson into the presidency, many former slaveowners shared the dismay of a North Carolina woman who wrote, "Think of Andy Johnson [as] the president! What will become of us—'the aristocrats of the South' as we are termed?" Northern Radicals also had reason to believe that Johnson would deal sternly with the South. When one of them suggested the exile or execution of ten or twelve leading rebels to set an example, Johnson replied, "How are you going to pick out so small a number? . . . Treason is a crime; and crime must be punished."

■ Combative and inflexible, President Andrew Johnson contributed greatly to the failure of his own Reconstruction program. (Library of Congress)

Like his martyred predecessor, Johnson followed a path in antebellum politics from obscurity to power. With

ANDREW
JOHNSON OF
TENNESSEE

no formal education, he became a tailor's apprentice. But from 1829, while in his early twenties, he held nearly every office in Tennessee politics: alderman, state representative, congressman, two terms as governor, and U.S. senator by 1857. Although elected as a southern Democrat, Johnson was the only senator from a seceded state who refused to follow his state out of the Union. Lincoln appointed him war governor of Tennessee in 1862, hence his symbolic place on the ticket in the president's bid for reelection in 1864.

Johnson's political beliefs made him look a little like a Republican, but at heart he was an old Jacksonian Democrat. And as they said in the mountainous region of east Tennessee, where Johnson established a reputation as a stump speaker, "Old Andy never went back on his

'raisin'." Although a staunch Unionist, Johnson was also an ardent states' rightist. Before the war, he had supported tax-funded public schools and homestead legislation, fashioning himself as a champion of the common man. Although he vehemently opposed secession, Johnson advocated limited government. He shared none of the Radicals' expansive conception of federal power. His philosophy toward Reconstruction may be summed up in the slogan he adopted: "The Constitution as it is, and the Union as it was."

Through 1865 Johnson alone controlled Reconstruction policy, for Congress recessed shortly before he became president and did not reconvene until December. In the following eight months, Johnson put into operation his own plan, forming new state governments in the South by using his power to grant pardons. Johnson followed Lincoln's leniency by extending even easier terms to former Confederates.

Johnson had owned house slaves, although he had never been a planter. He accepted emancipation as a result

JOHNSON'S
RACIAL VIEWS

of the war, but he did not favor black civil and political rights. Johnson believed that black suffrage could never be imposed on a southern state by the federal government, and that set him on a collision course with the Radicals. When it came to race, Johnson was a thoroughgoing white supremacist. He held what one politician called "unconquerable prejudices against the African race." In perhaps the most blatantly racist official statement ever delivered by an American president, Johnson declared in his annual message of 1867 that blacks possessed less "capacity for government than any other race of people. No independent government of any form has ever been successful in their hands; . . . wherever they have been left to their own devices they have shown a constant tendency to relapse into barbarism."

Such racial views had an enduring effect on Johnson's policies. Where whites were concerned, however, Johnson seemed to be pursuing changes in class relations. He proposed rules that would keep the wealthy planter class at least temporarily out of power.

White southerners were required to swear an oath of loyalty as a condition of gaining amnesty or pardon, but

JOHNSON'S
PARDON POLICY

Johnson barred several categories of people from taking the oath: former federal officials, high-ranking Confederate officers, and political leaders or graduates of West Point or Annapolis who joined or aided the Confederacy. To this list Johnson added another important group: all ex-Confederates whose taxable property was worth more than $20,000. These individuals had to apply personally to the president for pardon and restoration of their political rights.

Thus it appeared that the leadership class of the Old South would be removed from power, for virtually all the rich and powerful whites of prewar days needed Johnson's special pardon. The president, it seemed, meant to take revenge on the haughty aristocrats and thereby promote a new leadership of deserving yeomen.

Johnson appointed provisional governors, who began the Reconstruction process by calling constitutional conventions. The delegates chosen for these conventions had to draft new constitutions that eliminated slavery and invalidated secession. After ratification of these constitutions, new governments could be elected, and the states would be restored to the Union with full congressional representation. But only those southerners who had taken the oath of amnesty and been eligible to vote on the day the state seceded could participate in this process. Thus unpardoned whites and former slaves were not eligible.

If Johnson intended to strip the old elite of its power, he did not hold to his plan. The old white leadership

PRESIDENTIAL RECONSTRUCTION

proved resilient and influential; prominent Confederates (a few with pardons but many without) won elections and turned up in various appointive offices. Then, surprisingly, Johnson started pardoning aristocrats and leading rebels. He hired additional clerks to write out the necessary documents and then began to issue pardons to large categories of people. By September 1865 hundreds were being issued in a single day. These pardons, plus the rapid return of planters' abandoned lands, restored the old elite to power and quickly gave Johnson the image as the South's champion. He further gained southern loyalty with his hostility to the Freedmen's Bureau.

Why did Johnson allow the planters to regain power? Perhaps vanity betrayed his judgment. Too long an isolated outsider, Johnson may have succumbed to the flattery of the pardon seekers. He was also determined on a rapid Reconstruction in order to deny the Radicals the opportunity for the more thorough racial and political changes they desired in the South. And Johnson needed southern support in the 1866 elections; hence, he declared Reconstruction complete only eight months after Appomattox. Thus in December 1865 many Confederate congressmen traveled to Washington to claim seats in the U.S. Congress. Even Alexander Stephens, vice president of the Confederacy, returned to Capitol Hill as a senator-elect.

The election of such prominent rebels troubled many northerners. So did other results of Johnson's program.

Some of the state conventions were slow to repudiate secession; others admitted only grudgingly that slavery was dead.

Furthermore, to define the status of freed men and women and control their labor, some legislatures merely

BLACK CODES

revised large sections of the slave codes by substituting the word *freedmen* for *slaves*. The new black codes compelled the former slaves to carry passes, observe a curfew, live in housing provided by a landowner, and give up hope of entering many desirable occupations. Stiff vagrancy laws and restrictive labor contracts bound freedpeople to plantations, and "anti-enticement" laws punished anyone who tried to lure these workers to other employment. State-supported schools and orphanages excluded blacks entirely.

It seemed to northerners that the South was intent on returning African Americans to servility and that Johnson's Reconstruction policy held no one responsible for the terrible war. But memories of the war—not yet a year over—were still raw, and would dominate political behavior for several elections to come. Thus the Republican majority in Congress decided to call a halt to the results of Johnson's plan. On reconvening, the House and Senate considered the credentials of the newly elected southern representatives and decided not to admit them. Instead, they bluntly challenged the president's authority and established a joint committee to study and investigate a new direction for Reconstruction.

The Congressional Reconstruction Plan

Northern congressmen were hardly unified, but they did not doubt their right to shape Reconstruction policy. The Constitution mentioned neither secession nor reunion, but it gave Congress the primary role in the admission of states. Moreover, the Constitution declared that the United States shall guarantee to each state a republican form of government. This provision, legislators believed, gave them the authority to devise policies for Reconstruction.

They soon found that other constitutional questions affected their policies. What, for example, had rebellion done to the relationship between southern states and the Union? Lincoln had always insisted that states could not secede—they had engaged in an "insurrection"—and that the Union remained intact. Not even Andrew Johnson, however, accepted the southern position that state governments of the Confederacy could simply reenter the nation. Congressmen who favored vigorous Reconstruction measures argued that the war had broken the Union, and that the South was subject to the victor's will. Moderate congressmen held that the states had forfeited their rights through rebellion and thus had come under congressional supervision.

These theories mirrored the diversity of Congress itself. Northern Democrats, weakened by the war most of them had opposed in its final year, denounced any idea of racial equality and supported Johnson's policies. Conservative Republicans, despite their party loyalty, favored a limited federal role in Reconstruction. The Radical Republicans, led by Thaddeus Stevens, Charles Sumner, and George Julian, wanted to transform the South. Although a minority in their party, they had the advantage of clearly defined goals. They believed it was essential to democratize the South, establish public education, and ensure the rights of the freedpeople. They favored black suffrage, supported some land confiscation and redistribution, and were willing to exclude the South from the

THE RADICALS

Union for several years if necessary to achieve their goals. Born of the war and its outcome, the Radicals brought a new civic vision to American life; they wanted to create an activist federal government and the beginnings of racial equality. A large group of moderate Republicans did not want to go as far as the Radicals but opposed Johnson's leniency.

One overwhelming political reality faced all four groups: the 1866 elections. Having questioned Johnson's program, Congress needed to develop an alternative plan. Ironically, Johnson and the Democrats sabotaged the possibility of a conservative coalition. They refused to cooperate with conservative or moderate Republicans and insisted that Reconstruction was over, that the new state governments were legitimate, and that southern representatives should be admitted to Congress. Among the Republicans, the Radicals' influence grew in proportion to Johnson's intransigence.

Trying to work with Johnson, Republicans believed a compromise had been reached in the spring of 1866. Under its terms Johnson would agree to two modifica-

■ In 1866, as Congress reviewed the progress of Reconstruction, news from the South had a considerable impact. Violence against black people, like the riot in Memphis depicted here, helped convince northern legislators that they had to modify President Johnson's policies. (Library of Congress)

CONGRESS VS. JOHNSON tions of his program: extension of the Freedmen's Bureau for another year and passage of a civil rights bill to counteract the black codes. This bill would force southern courts to practice equality before the law by allowing federal judges to remove from state courts cases in which blacks were treated unfairly. Its provisions applied to public, not private, acts of discrimination. The civil rights bill of 1866 was the first statutory definition of the rights of American citizens.

Johnson destroyed the compromise, however, by vetoing both bills (they later became law when Congress overrode the president's veto). Denouncing any change in his program, the president condemned Congress's action and revealed his own racism. Because the civil rights bill defined U.S. citizens as native-born persons who were taxed, Johnson claimed it discriminated against "large numbers of intelligent, worthy, and patriotic foreigners . . . in favor of the negro." The bill, he said, operated "in favor of the colored and against the white race."

All hope of presidential-congressional cooperation was now dead. In 1866 newspapers reported daily violations of blacks' rights in the South and carried alarming accounts of antiblack violence—notably in Memphis and New Orleans, where police aided brutal mobs in their attacks. In Memphis forty blacks were killed and twelve schools burned by white mobs, and in New Orleans the toll was thirty-four African Americans dead and two hundred wounded. Such violence convinced Republicans, and the northern public, that more needed to be done. A new Republican plan took the form of the Fourteenth Amendment to the Constitution, forged out of a compromise between radical and conservative elements of the party.

Of the four parts of the Fourteenth Amendment, the first would have the greatest legal significance in later

FOURTEENTH AMENDMENT years. It conferred citizenship on the freedmen and prohibited states from abridging their constitutional "privileges and immunities" (see the Appendix for the Constitution and all amendments). It also barred any state from taking a person's life, liberty, or property "without due process of law" and from denying "equal protection of the laws." These resounding phrases became powerful guarantees of African Americans' civil rights—indeed, of the rights of all citizens—in the twentieth century.

Nearly universal agreement emerged among Republicans on the amendment's second and third provisions. The second declared the Confederate debt null and void and guaranteed the war debt of the United States. Northerners rejected the notion of paying taxes to reimburse those who had financed a rebellion, and business groups agreed on the necessity of upholding the credit of the U.S. government. The third provision barred Confederate leaders from holding state and federal office. Only Congress, by a two-thirds vote of each house, could remove the penalty. The amendment thus guaranteed a degree of punishment for the leaders of the Confederacy.

The fourth part of the amendment dealt with representation and embodied the compromises that produced the document. Northerners disagreed about whether black citizens should have the right to vote. As a citizen of Indiana wrote to a southern relative, there was strong feeling in favor of "humane and liberal laws for the government and protection of the colored population." But there was prejudice, too. "Although there is a great deal [of] profession among us for the relief of the darkey yet I think much of it is far from being sincere. I guess we want to compell you to do right by them while we are not willing ourselves to do so." Those arched words are indicative of not only how revolutionary Reconstruction had become, but also how far the public will lagged behind the enactments that became new constitutional cornerstones.

Emancipation made every former slave a full rather than three-fifths of a person, which would increase southern representation. Thus the postwar South stood to gain power in Congress, and if white southerners did not allow blacks to vote, former secessionists would derive the political benefit from emancipation. That was more irony than most northerners could bear. So Republicans determined that if a southern state did not grant black men the vote, their representation would be reduced proportionally. If they did enfranchise black men, their representation would be increased proportionally. This compromise avoided a direct enactment of black suffrage, but would deliver future black voters to the Republican Party.

The Fourteenth Amendment specified for the first time that voters were "male," and ignored female citizens, black and white. For this reason it provoked a strong reaction from the women's rights movement. Advocates of women's equality had worked with abolitionists for decades, often subordinating their cause to that of the slaves. During the drafting of the Fourteenth Amendment, however, female activists demanded to be heard. Prominent leaders such as Elizabeth Cady Stanton and Susan B. Anthony ended their alliance with abolitionists and fought more determinedly for themselves, while others remained committed to the idea that it was "the Negro's hour." Thus the amendment infused new life into the women's rights movement and caused considerable strife among old allies. Many male former abolitionists, white and black, were willing to delay the day of woman suffrage in favor of securing freedmen the right to vote in the South.

In 1866, however, the major question in Reconstruction politics was how the public would respond to the congressional initiative. Johnson did his best to block the Fourteenth Amendment in both North and South. Condemning Congress for its refusal to seat southern representatives, the president urged state legislatures in the South to vote against ratification. Every southern legislature except Tennessee's rejected the amendment by a wide margin.

THE SOUTH'S AND JOHNSON'S DEFIANCE, 1866

To present his case to northerners, Johnson organized a National Union Convention and took to the stump himself. In an age when active personal campaigning was rare for a president, Johnson boarded a special train for a "swing around the circle" that carried his message into the Northeast, the Midwest, and then back to Washington. In city after city, he criticized the Republicans in a ranting, undignified style. Increasingly, audiences rejected his views and hooted and jeered at him. In this whistle-stop tour, Johnson began to hand out American flags with thirty-six rather than twenty-five stars, declaring that the Union was already restored. At many towns he likened himself to a "persecuted" Jesus who might now be martyred "upon the cross" for his magnanimity toward the South. And, repeatedly, he labeled the Radicals "traitors" for their efforts to take over Reconstruction.

The elections of 1866 were a resounding victory for Republicans in Congress. Radicals and moderates whom Johnson had denounced won reelection by large margins, and the Republican majority grew to two-thirds of both houses of Congress. The North had spoken clearly: Johnson's policies were prematurely giving the advan-

Map 16.1   The Reconstruction

This map shows the five military districts established when Congress passed the Reconstruction Act of 1867. As the dates within each state indicate, conservative Democratic forces quickly regained control of government in four southern states. So-called Radical Reconstruction was curtailed in most of the others as factions within the weakened Republican Party began to cooperate with conservative Democrats.

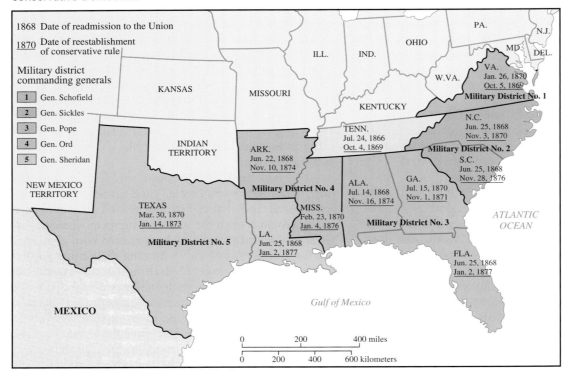

tage to rebels and traitors. Although the Radicals may have been out ahead of public opinion, most northerners feared for "the future peace and safety of the Union" if Johnson's approach to Reconstruction prevailed. Thus Republican congressional leaders won a mandate to pursue their Reconstruction plan.

But, thanks to Johnson and southern intransigence, that plan had reached an impasse. Nothing could be accomplished as long as the "Johnson governments" existed and the southern electorate remained exclusively white. Republicans resolved to form new state governments in the South and enfranchise the freedmen.

After some embittered debate in which Republicans and the remaining Democrats in Congress argued over the meaning and memory of the Civil War itself, the First Reconstruction Act passed in March 1867. This plan, under which the southern states were actually readmitted to the Union, incorporated only a part of the Radical program. Union generals, commanding small garrisons of troops and charged with supervising all elections, assumed control

RECONSTRUCTION ACTS OF 1867–1868

in five military districts in the South (see Map 16.1). Confederate leaders designated in the Fourteenth Amendment were barred from voting until new state constitutions were ratified. The act guaranteed freedmen the right to vote in elections for state constitutional conventions and in subsequent elections. In addition, each southern state was required to ratify the Fourteenth Amendment, to ratify its new constitution by majority vote, and to submit it to Congress for approval (see Table 16.1).

Thus African Americans gained an opportunity to fight for a better life through the political process, and ex-Confederates were given what they interpreted as a bitter pill to swallow in order to return to the Union. The Second, Third, and Fourth Reconstruction Acts, passed between March 1867 and March 1868, provided the details of operation for voter registration boards, the adoption of constitutions, and the administration of "good faith" oaths on the part of white southerners.

In the words of one historian, the Radicals succeeded in "clipping Johnson's wings." But they had hoped Congress could do much more. Thaddeus Stevens, for

---

TABLE 16.1

Plans for Reconstruction Compared

	Johnson's Plan	Radicals' Plan	Fourteenth Amendment	Reconstruction Act of 1867
Voting	Whites only; high-ranking Confederate leaders must seek pardons	Give vote to black males	Southern whites may decide but can lose representation if they deny black suffrage	Black men gain vote; whites barred from office by Fourteenth Amendment cannot vote while new state governments are being formed
Officeholding	Many prominent Confederates regain power	Only loyal white and black males eligible	Confederate leaders barred until Congress votes amnesty	Fourteenth Amendment in effect
Time out of Union	Brief	Several years; until South is thoroughly democratized	Brief	3–5 years after war
Other change in southern society	Little; gain of power by yeomen not realized; emancipation grudgingly accepted, but no black civil or political rights	Expand public education; confiscate land and provide farms for freedmen; expansion of activist federal government	Probably slight, depending on enforcement	Considerable, depending on action of new state governments

FAILURE OF LAND REDISTRIBUTION

example, argued that economic opportunity was essential to the freedmen. "If we do not furnish them with homesteads from forfeited and rebel property," Stevens declared, "and hedge them around with protective laws . . . we had better left them in bondage." Stevens therefore drew up a plan for extensive confiscation and redistribution of land. Only one-tenth of the land affected by his plan was earmarked for freedmen, in forty-acre plots. The rest was to be sold to generate money for Union veterans' pensions, compensation to loyal southerners for damaged property, and payment of the federal debt.

But plans for property redistribution were unpopular measures, and virtually all failed to gain legitimacy. Northerners were accustomed to a limited role for government, and the business community staunchly opposed any interference with private-property rights, even for former Confederates. Thus black farmers were forced to seek work in a hostile environment in which landowners opposed their acquisition of land, even as renters.

Congress's quarrels with Andrew Johnson grew even more bitter. To restrict Johnson's influence and safeguard

CONSTITUTIONAL CRISIS

its plan, Congress passed a number of controversial laws. First, it limited Johnson's power over the army by requiring the president to issue military orders through the General of the Army, Ulysses S. Grant, who could not be dismissed without the Senate's consent. Then Congress passed the Tenure of Office Act, which gave the Senate power to approve changes in the president's cabinet. Designed to protect Secretary of War Stanton, who sympathized with the Radicals, this law violated the tradition that a president controlled appointments to his own cabinet.

All of these measures, as well as each of the Reconstruction Acts, were passed by a two-thirds override of presidential vetoes. The situation led some to believe that the federal government had reached a stage of "congressional tyranny," and others to conclude that Johnson had become an obstacle to the legitimate will of the people in reconstructing the nation on a just and permanent basis.

Johnson took several belligerent steps of his own. He issued orders to military commanders in the South limiting their powers and increasing the powers of the civil governments he had created in 1865. Then he removed military officers who were conscientiously enforcing Congress's new law, preferring commanders who allowed disqualified Confederates to vote. Finally, he tried to remove Secretary of War Stanton. With that attempt the confrontation reached its climax.

Impeachment is a political procedure provided for in the Constitution as a remedy for crimes or serious abuses of power by presidents, federal judges,

IMPEACHMENT OF PRESIDENT JOHNSON

and other high officials in the government. Those who are impeached (judged or politically indicted) in the House are then tried in the Senate. Historically, this power has generally not been used as a means to investigate and judge the private lives of presidents, although in recent times it was used in this manner in the case of President Bill Clinton.

Twice in 1867, the House Judiciary Committee had considered impeachment of Johnson, rejecting the idea

■ Thomas Waterman Wood, who had painted portraits of society figures in Nashville before the war, sensed the importance of Congress's decision in 1867 to enfranchise the freedmen. This oil painting, one of a series on suffrage, emphasizes the significance of the ballot for the black voter.   (Cheekwood Museum of Art, Nashville, Tennessee)

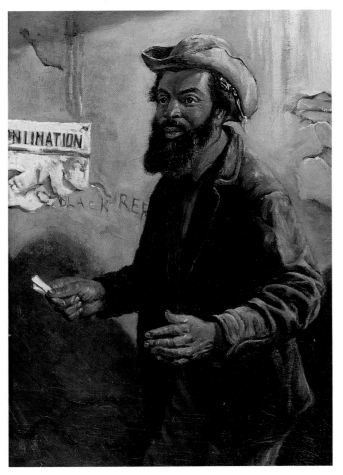

once and then recommending it by only a 5-to-4 vote. That recommendation was decisively defeated by the House. After Johnson tried to remove Stanton, however, a third attempt to impeach the president carried easily in early 1868. The indictment concentrated on his violation of the Tenure of Office Act, though many modern scholars regard his efforts to impede enforcement of the Reconstruction Act of 1867 as a far more serious offense.

Johnson's trial in the Senate lasted more than three months. The prosecution, led by Radicals such as Thaddeus Stevens and Benjamin Butler, attempted to prove that Johnson was guilty of "high crimes and misdemeanors." But they also argued that the trial was a means to judge Johnson's performance, not a judicial determination of guilt or innocence. The Senate ultimately rejected such reasoning, which could have made removal from office a political weapon against any chief executive who disagreed with Congress. Although a majority of senators voted to convict Johnson, the prosecution fell one vote short of the necessary two-thirds majority. Johnson remained in office, politically weakened and with only a few months left in his term. Some Republicans backed away from impeachment because they had their eyes on the 1868 election and did not want to hurt their prospects of regaining the White House.

In the 1868 presidential election Ulysses S. Grant, running as a Republican, defeated Horatio Seymour, a New York Democrat. Grant was not a radical, but his platform supported congressional Reconstruction and endorsed black suffrage in the South. (Significantly, Republicans stopped short of endorsing black suffrage in the North.) The Democrats, meanwhile, vigorously denounced Reconstruction and thus renewed the sectional conflict. Indeed, in the 1868 election, the Democrats conducted the most openly racist campaign to that time in American history. Both sides waved the "bloody

ELECTION OF 1868

■ A Republican Party brass band in action during the 1868 election campaign in Baton Rouge, Louisiana. The Union regimental colors and soldier caps demonstrate the strong federal presence in the South at this pivotal moment in radical Reconstruction. (Andrew D. Lytle Collection, Louisiana and Lower Mississippi Valley Collections, LSU Libraries, Louisiana State University, Baton Rouge, La.)

shirt," accusing each other as the villains of the war's sacrifices. By associating themselves with rebellion and with Johnson's repudiated program, the Democrats went down to defeat in all but eight states, though the popular vote was fairly close. Participating in their first presidential election ever on a wide scale, blacks decisively voted en masse for General Grant.

In office Grant acted as an administrator of Reconstruction but not as its enthusiastic advocate. He vacillated in his dealings with the southern states, sometimes defending Republican regimes and sometimes currying favor with Democrats. On occasion Grant called out federal troops to stop violence or enforce acts of Congress. But he never imposed a true military occupation on the South. Rapid demobilization had reduced a federal army of more than 1 million to 57,000 within a year of the surrender at Appomattox. Thereafter the number of troops in the South continued to fall, until in 1874 there were only 4,000 in the southern states outside Texas. The later legend of "military rule," so important to southern claims of victimization during Reconstruction, was steeped in myth.

In 1869, in an effort to write democratic principles into the Constitution, the Radicals passed the Fifteenth Amendment. This measure forbade states to deny the right to vote "on account of race, color, or previous condition of servitude." Such wording did not guarantee the right to vote. It deliberately left states free to restrict suffrage on other grounds so that northern states could continue to deny suffrage to women and certain groups of men—Chinese immigrants, illiterates, and those too poor to pay poll taxes.

FIFTEENTH AMENDMENT

Although several states outside the South refused to ratify, three-fourths of the states approved the measure, and the Fifteenth Amendment became law in 1870. It too had been a political compromise, and though African Americans rejoiced all across the land at its enactment, it left open the possibility for states to create countless qualification tests to obstruct voting in the future.

With passage of the Fifteenth Amendment, many Americans, especially supportive northerners, considered Reconstruction essentially completed. "Let us have done with Reconstruction," pleaded the *New York Tribune* in April 1870. "The country is tired and sick of it. . . . Let us have Peace!" But some northerners, like radical abolitionist Wendell Phillips, worried. "Our day," he warned, "is fast slipping away. Once let public thought float off from the great issue of the war, and it will take . . . more than a generation to bring it back again."

Reconstruction Politics in the South

From the start, Reconstruction encountered the resistance of white southerners. In the black codes and in private attitudes, many whites stubbornly opposed emancipation, and the former planter class proved especially unbending because of their tremendous financial loss in slaves. In 1866 a Georgia newspaper frankly observed that "most of the white citizens believe that the institution of slavery was right, and . . . they will believe that the condition, which comes nearest to slavery, that can now be established will be the best."

Fearing loss of control over their slaves, some planters attempted to postpone freedom by denying or misrepresenting events. Former slaves reported that their owners "didn't tell them it was freedom" or "wouldn't let [them] go." Agents of the Freedmen's Bureau reported that "the old system of slavery [is] working with even more rigor than formerly at a few miles distant from any point where U.S. troops are stationed." To hold onto their workers, some landowners claimed control over black children and used guardianship and apprentice laws to bind black families to the plantation.

WHITE RESISTANCE

Whites also blocked blacks from acquiring land. A few planters divided up plots among their slaves, but most condemned the idea of making blacks landowners. A Georgia woman whose family was known for its support of religious education for slaves was outraged that two property owners planned to "rent their lands to the Negroes!" Such action was, she declared, "injurious to the best interest of the community."

Adamant resistance by propertied whites soon manifested itself in other ways, including violence. In one North Carolina town a local magistrate clubbed a black man on a public street, and bands of "Regulators" terrorized blacks in parts of that state and in Kentucky. Amidst their defeat, many planters believed, as a South Carolinian put it, that blacks "can't be governed except with the whip." And after President Johnson encouraged the South to resist congressional Reconstruction, some white conservatives worked hard to capture the new state governments, while others boycotted the polls in an attempt to defeat Congress's plans.

Very few black men stayed away from the polls. Enthusiastically and hopefully, they voted Republican. Most agreed with one man who felt he should "stick to the end with the party that freed me." Illiteracy did not

Thanks to a large black turnout and the restrictions on prominent Confederates, a new southern Republican Party came to power in the constitutional conventions of 1868–1870. Republican delegates consisted of a sizable contingent of blacks (265 out of the total of just over 1,000 delegates throughout the South), some northerners who had moved to the South, and native southern whites who favored change. Together these Republicans brought the South into line with progressive reforms adopted earlier in the rest of the nation. The new constitutions were more democratic. They eliminated property qualifications for voting and holding office, and they turned many appointed offices into elective posts. They provided for public schools and institutions to care for the mentally ill, the blind, the deaf, the destitute, and the orphaned.

The conventions broadened women's rights in property holding and divorce. Usually, the goal was not to make women equal with men but to provide relief to thousands of suffering debtors. In families left poverty-stricken by the war and weighed down by debt, it was usually the husband who had contracted the debts. Thus giving women legal control over their own property provided some protection to their families. The goal of some delegates, however, was to elevate women with the right to vote.

■ Thomas Nast, in this 1868 cartoon, pictured the combination of forces that threatened the success of Reconstruction: southern opposition and the greed, partisanship, and racism of northern interests.
(Library of Congress)

BLACK VOTERS AND THE SOUTHERN REPUBLICAN PARTY

prohibit blacks (or uneducated whites) from making intelligent choices. Although Mississippi's William Henry could read only "a little," he testified that he and his friends had no difficulty selecting the Republican ballot. "We stood around and watched," he explained. "We saw D. Sledge vote; he owned half the county. We knowed he voted Democratic so we voted the other ticket so it would be Republican." Women, who could not vote, encouraged their husbands and sons, and preachers exhorted their congregations to use the franchise. With such group spirit, zeal for voting spread through entire black communities.

Under these new constitutions the southern states elected Republican-controlled governments. For the first time, the ranks of state legislators in 1868 included some black southerners. It remained to be seen now how much social change these new governments would bring about. Contrary to what white southerners would later claim, the Republican state governments did not disfranchise ex-Confederates as a group. The vexing questions of land reform and enforcement of racial equality all but overwhelmed the Republican governments.

TRIUMPH OF REPUBLICAN GOVERNMENTS

Land reform largely failed because in most states whites were in the majority and former slaveowners controlled the best land and other sources of economic power. James Lynch, a leading black politician from Mississippi, explained why African Americans shunned the "folly" of disfranchising whites. Unlike northerners who "can leave when it becomes too uncomfortable," landless former slaves "must be in friendly relations with the great body of the whites in the state. Otherwise . . . peace can be maintained only by a standing army." Despised and lacking economic or social power, southern Republicans strove for acceptance and legitimacy.

Far from being vindictive toward the race that had enslaved them, most southern blacks treated leading rebels with generosity and appealed to white southerners to adopt a spirit of fairness and cooperation. In this way the South's Republican Party condemned itself to defeat if white voters would not cooperate. Within a few years Republicans were reduced to the embarrassment of making futile appeals to whites while ignoring the claims of their strongest supporters, blacks. But for a time some propertied whites accepted congressional Reconstruction as a reality and declared themselves willing to compete under the new rules. All sides found an area of agreement in economic policies.

Reflecting northern ideals and southern necessity, the Reconstruction governments enthusiastically promoted

INDUSTRIALIZATION

industry. Confederates had seen how industry aided the North during the war. Accordingly, Reconstruction legislatures encouraged investment with loans, subsidies, and exemptions from taxation for periods up to ten years. The southern railroad system was rebuilt and expanded, and coal and iron mining made possible Birmingham's steel plants. Between 1860 and 1880, the number of manufacturing establishments in the South nearly doubled.

This emphasis on big business, however, produced higher state debts and taxes, drew money away from schools and other programs, and multiplied possibilities for corruption. It also locked Republicans into a conservative strategy. In courting elite whites who never joined the Republican Party, Republicans lost the opportunity of building support among poorer whites.

Policies appealing to African American voters never went beyond equality before the law. In fact, the whites

REPUBLICANS
AND RACIAL
EQUALITY

who controlled the southern Republican Party were reluctant to allow blacks a share of offices proportionate to their electoral strength. Aware of their weakness, black leaders did not push very far for revolutionary economic or social change. In every southern state, they led efforts to establish public schools, although they did not press for integrated facilities. In 1870 South Carolina passed the first comprehensive school law in the South. By 1875, 50 percent of black school-age children in that state were enrolled in school, and approximately one-third of the three thousand teachers were black.

■ One notable success in Reconstruction efforts to stimulate industry was Birmingham, Alabama. Here workers cast molten iron into blocks called pigs. (Birmingham Public Library)

Some African American politicians did fight for civil rights and integration. Many were from cities such as New Orleans or Mobile, where large populations of light-skinned free blacks had existed before the war. Their experience in such communities had made them sensitive to issues of status, and they spoke out for open and equal public accommodations. Laws requiring equal accommodations won passage throughout the Deep South, but they often went unenforced or required expensive legal action.

Economic progress was uppermost in the minds of most freedpeople and black representatives from rural districts. Black southerners needed land, and much land did fall into state hands for nonpayment of taxes and was offered for sale in small lots. But most freedmen had too little cash to bid against investors or speculators. South Carolina established a land commission, but it could help only those with money to buy. Any widespread redistribution of land had to arise from Congress, which never supported such action. The lack of genuine land redistribution remained the significant lost opportunity of Reconstruction.

Within a few years, as centrists in both parties met with failure, white hostility to congressional Reconstruction

MYTH OF
"NEGRO RULE"

began to dominate. Some conservatives had always desired to fight Reconstruction through pressure and racist propaganda. They put economic and social pressure on blacks: one black Republican reported that "my neighbors will not employ me, nor sell me a farthing's worth of anything." Charging that the South had been turned over to ignorant blacks, conservatives deplored "black domination," which became a rallying cry for a return to white supremacy.

Such attacks were inflammatory propaganda, and part of the growing myth of "Negro rule," which would serve as a central theme in battles over the memory of Reconstruction. African Americans participated in politics but hardly dominated or controlled events. They were a majority in only two out of ten state constitutional writing conventions (transplanted northerners were a majority in one). In the state legislatures, only in the lower house in South Carolina did blacks ever constitute a majority; among officeholders, their numbers generally were far fewer than their proportion in the population. Sixteen blacks won seats in Congress before Reconstruction was over, but none was ever elected governor. Only eighteen served in a high state office such as lieutenant governor, treasurer, superintendent of education, or secretary of state. In all, some four hundred blacks served in political office during the Reconstruc-

tion era. Although they never dominated the process, they established a rich tradition of government service and civic activism. Elected officials, such as Robert Smalls in South Carolina, labored tirelessly for cheaper land prices, better healthcare, access to schools, and the enforcement of civil rights for their people. For too long the black politicians of Reconstruction were the forgotten heroes of this seedtime of America's long civil rights movement.

Conservatives also assailed the allies of black Republicans. Their propaganda denounced whites from

CARPETBAGGERS
AND SCALAWAGS

the North as "carpetbaggers," greedy crooks planning to pour stolen tax revenues into their sturdy luggage made of carpet material. Immigrants from the North, who held the largest share of Republican offices, were all tarred with this brush.

In fact, most northerners who settled in the South had come seeking business opportunities as schoolteachers or to find a warmer climate and never entered politics. Those who did enter politics generally wanted to democratize the South and to introduce northern ways, such as industry, public education, and the spirit of enterprise. Carpetbaggers' ideals were tested by hard times and ostracism by white southerners.

In addition to tagging northern interlopers as carpetbaggers, conservatives invented the term *scalawag* to discredit any native white southerner who cooperated with the Republicans. A substantial number of southerners did so, including some wealthy and prominent men. Most scalawags, however, were yeoman farmers, men from mountain areas and nonslaveholding districts who had been restive under the Confederacy. They saw that they could benefit from the education and opportunities promoted by Republicans. Banding together with freedmen, they pursued common class interests and hoped to make headway against the power of long-dominant planters. Cooperation even convinced a few white Republicans that "there is but little if any difference in the talents of the two races," as one observed, and that all should have "an equal start." Yet this black-white coalition was vulnerable to the race issue, and most scalawags did not support racial equality.

Taxation was a major problem for the Reconstruction governments. Republicans wanted to maintain

TAX POLICY AND
CORRUPTION
AS POLITICAL
WEDGES

prewar services, repair the war's destruction, stimulate industry, and support important new ventures such as public schools. But the Civil War had destroyed much of the South's tax base. One category of valuable

■ "Ku Klux Klansman," unidentified photographer, c. 1869. This Klansman posed in full regalia, including flowing cuffs on pants, a complete mask, and a club. The Ku Klux Klan offered some whites the opportunity to enact political terror and express their white supremacy in ritualistic, secret ways. Costumes were essential parts of this violent organization. (Gilman Paper Company, New York, NY)

All these problems hurt the Republicans, whose leaders also allowed factionalism along racial and class lines to undermine party unity. But in many southern states the deathblow came through violence. The Ku Klux Klan (its members altered the Greek word for "circle," *kuklos*), a secret veterans' club that began in Tennessee in 1866, spread through the South, and rapidly evolved into a terrorist organization. Violence against African Americans occurred from the first days of Reconstruction but became far more organized and purposeful after 1867. Klansmen sought to frustrate Reconstruction and keep the freedmen in subjection. Nighttime harassment, whippings, beatings, rapes, and murder became common, and terrorism dominated some counties and regions.

KU KLUX KLAN

Although the Klan persecuted blacks who stood up for their rights as laborers or individuals, its main purpose was political. Lawless nightriders made active Republicans the target of their attacks. Leading white and black Republicans were killed in several states. After freedmen who worked for a South Carolina scalawag started voting, terrorists visited the plantation and, in the words of one victim, "whipped every . . . [black] man they could lay their hands on." Klansmen also attacked Union League clubs—Republican organizations that mobilized the black vote—and schoolteachers who were aiding the freedmen.

Klan violence was not a spontaneous outburst of racism; very specific social forces shaped and directed it. In North Carolina, for example, Alamance and Caswell Counties were the sites of the worst Klan violence. Slim Republican majorities there rested on cooperation between black voters and white yeomen, particularly those whose Unionism or discontent with the Confederacy had turned them against local Democratic officials. Together, these black and white Republicans had ousted officials long entrenched in power. The wealthy and powerful men in Alamance and Caswell who had lost their accustomed political control were the Klan's county officers and local chieftains. They organized a deliberate campaign of terror, recruiting members and planning atrocities. By intimidation and murder, the Klan weakened the Republican coalition and restored a Democratic majority.

Klan violence injured Republicans across the South. One of every ten black leaders who had been delegates to the 1867–1868 state constitutional conventions was attacked, seven fatally. In one judicial district of North Carolina the Ku Klux Klan was responsible for twelve murders, over seven hundred beatings, and other acts of violence, including rape and arson. A single attack on Al-

property—slaves—had disappeared entirely. And hundreds of thousands of citizens had lost much of the rest of their property—money, livestock, fences, and buildings—to the war. Thus an increase in taxes (sales, excise, and on property) was necessary even to maintain traditional services, and new ventures required still-higher taxes. Inevitably, Republican tax policies aroused strong opposition, especially among the yeomen.

Corruption was another serious charge levied against the Republicans. Unfortunately, it often was true. Many carpetbaggers and black politicians engaged in fraudulent schemes, sold their votes, or padded expenses, taking part in what scholars recognize was a nationwide surge of corruption in an age ruled by "spoilsmen" (see pages 545–546). Corruption carried no party label, but the Democrats successfully pinned the blame on unqualified blacks and greedy carpetbaggers among southern Republicans.

abama Republicans in the town of Eutaw left four blacks dead and fifty-four wounded. In South Carolina five hundred masked Klansmen lynched eight black prisoners at the Union County jail, and in nearby York County the Klan committed at least eleven murders and hundreds of whippings. According to historian Eric Foner, the Klan "made it virtually impossible for Republicans to campaign or vote in large parts of Georgia."

Thus a combination of difficult fiscal problems, Republican mistakes, racial hostility, and terror brought

FAILURE OF RECONSTRUCTION

down the Republican regimes. In most southern states, "Radical Reconstruction" lasted only a few years (see Map 16.1). The most enduring failure of Reconstruction, however, was not political; it was social and economic. Reconstruction failed to alter the South's social structure or its distribution of wealth and power. Without land of their own, freed men and women were at the mercy of white landowners. Armed only with the ballot, freedmen in the South had little chance to effect significant changes.

To reform the southern social order, Congress would have had to redistribute land, but most lawmakers opposed an attack on private property. Radical Republicans like Albion Tourgée, a former Union soldier who moved to North Carolina and was elected a judge, condemned Congress's timidity. Turning the freedman out on his own without protection, said Tourgée, constituted "cheap philanthropy." Indeed, many African Americans believed that during Reconstruction, the North "threw all the Negroes on the world without any way of getting along." Moreover, without careful supervision by Congress, the situation of the freed men and women deteriorated. As the North lost interest, Reconstruction collapsed.

Reconstruction Reversed

*N*ortherners had always been more interested in suppressing rebellion than in aiding southern blacks, and by the early 1870s the North's commitment to bringing about change in the South weakened. Criticism of the southern governments grew, new issues captured public attention, and sentiment for national reconciliation gained popularity in politics. In one southern state after another, Democrats regained control, and they threatened to defeat Republicans in the North as well. Whites in the old Confederacy referred to this decline of Reconstruction as "southern redemption," and during the 1870s, "redeemer" Democrats

■ Albion Winegar Tourgée, a former Union soldier severely wounded at the Battle of Bull Run in 1861, became a carpetbagger and was elected a district judge in North Carolina during Reconstruction. In 1879 he published a best-selling novel, *A Fool's Errand,* which told his own story of travail as a Yankee immigrant in the South confronting the Ku Klux Klan and implementing freedmen's rights. (Chautauqua County Historical Society, Westfield, N.Y.)

claimed to be the saviors of the South from alleged "black domination" and "carpetbag rule." And for one of only a few times in American history, violence and terror emerged as a tactic in normal politics.

In 1870 and 1871 the violent campaigns of the Ku Klux Klan forced Congress to pass two Enforcement

POLITICAL IMPLICATIONS OF KLAN TERRORISM

Acts and an anti-Klan law. These laws made actions by individuals against the civil and political rights of others a federal criminal offense for the first time. They also provided for election supervisors and permitted martial law and suspension of the writ of habeas corpus to combat murders, beatings, and threats by the Klan. Federal prosecutors used the laws rather selectively. In 1872 and 1873 Mississippi and the Carolinas saw many prosecutions; but in other states where violence flourished, the laws were virtually ignored. Southern juries sometimes refused to convict Klansmen; out of a total of 3,310 cases, only 1,143 ended in convictions. Though many Klansmen (roughly two thousand in South Carolina alone) fled their states to avoid prosecution, and the Klan officially

The Grants' Tour of the World

On May 17, 1877, two weeks after his presidency ended, Ulysses S. Grant and his wife Julia embarked from Philadelphia on a grand tour of the world that would last twenty-six months. Portrayed as a private vacation, the trip was a very public affair. The taint of corruption in Grant's second term could only be dissipated in the air of foreign lands reached by steamship. The small entourage included John Russell Young, a reporter for the *New York Herald* who recorded the journeys in the two-volume illustrated *Around the World with General Grant.* Their expenses were paid by banker friends and by Grant's personal resources accumulated in gifts.

The Grants spent many months in England attending a bewildering array of banquets, one with Queen Victoria. In Newcastle, thousands of workingmen conducted a massive parade in Grant's honor. He was received as the odd American cousin, simple and great, the conqueror and warrior statesmen. In an age that worshipped great men, Grant was viewed as the savior of the American nation, the liberator of slaves, and as a celebrity—a measure of the American presence on the world stage.

On the European continent the pattern continued as every royal or republican head of state hosted the Grants. In Belgium, France, Switzerland, Italy, Russia, Poland, Austria, and Spain the Grants reveled in princely attentions. In Berlin, Grant met Otto von Bismarck, the chancellor of Germany. The two got along well discussing war, world politics, and the abolition of slavery.

The Grants next went to Egypt, where they rode donkeys into remote villages along the Nile, and then traveled by train to the Indian Ocean, where they embarked for India. They encountered British imperialism in full flower in Bombay, and that of the French in Saigon. Northward in Asia the grand excursion went to China and Japan. In Canton, Grant passed before an assemblage of young men who, according to a reporter, "looked upon the barbarian with . . . contempt in their expression, very much as our young men in New York would regard Sitting Bull or Red Cloud." In Japan the Grants had a rare audience with Emperor Mutsuhito in the imperial palace. Grant found Japan "beautiful beyond description," and the receptions were the most formal of all.

"I am both homesick and dread going home," Grant wrote in April 1879. Sailing across the Pacific, the Grants landed in San Francisco in late June. Why had Grant taken such a prolonged trip? Travel itself had its own rewards, but the tour became an unusual political campaign. Grant sought publicity abroad to convince his countrymen back home that they should reelect him president in 1880. But the strategy failed; Grant had developed no compelling issue or reason why Americans should choose him again. He would spend his final years, however, a war hero and a national symbol. No American president would again establish such personal links to the world until Woodrow Wilson at the end of World War I.

■ On their tour of the world, Ulysses and Julia Grant sat here with companions and guides in front of the Great Yppostyle Hall at the Temple of Amon-Ra in Karnak in Luxor, Egypt, 1878. The Grants' extraordinary tour included many such photo opportunities, often depicting the plebeian American president's presence in exotic places with unusual people. Whether he liked it or not, Grant was a world celebrity. (Library of Congress)

disbanded, the threat of violence did not end. Paramilitary organizations known as Rifle Clubs and Red Shirts often took the Klan's place.

Klan terrorism openly defied Congress, yet even on this issue there were ominous signs that the North's commitment to racial justice was fading. Some conservative but influential Republicans opposed the anti-Klan laws. Rejecting other Republicans' arguments that the Thirteenth, Fourteenth, and Fifteenth Amendments had made the federal government the protector of the rights of citizens, these dissenters echoed an old Democratic charge that Congress was infringing on states' rights. Senator Lyman Trumbull of Illinois declared that the states remained "the depositories of the rights of the individual." If Congress could punish crimes like assault or murder, he asked, "what is the need of the State governments?" For years Democrats had complained of "centralization and consolidation"; now some Republicans seemed to agree with them. This opposition foreshadowed a more general revolt within Republican ranks in 1872.

Disenchanted with Reconstruction, a group calling itself the Liberal Republicans bolted the party in 1872 and nominated Horace Greeley, the well-known editor of the *New York Tribune*, for president. The Liberal Republicans were a varied group, including civil service reformers, foes of corruption, and advocates of a lower tariff. Normally such disparate elements would not cooperate with one another, but two popular and widespread attitudes united them: distaste for federal intervention in the South and an elitist desire to let market forces and the "best men" determine events, both in the South and in Washington.

LIBERAL REPUBLICAN REVOLT

The Democrats also gave their nomination to Greeley in 1872. The combination was not enough to defeat Grant, who won reelection, but it reinforced Grant's desire to avoid confrontation with white southerners. Greeley's campaign for North-South reunion, for "clasping hands across the bloody chasm," was a bit premature to win at the polls, but was a harbinger of the future of American politics. Organized Blue-Gray fraternalism (gatherings of Union and Confederate veterans) began as early as 1874 in some states. Grant continued to use military force sparingly and in 1875 refused a desperate request for troops from the governor of Mississippi to quell racial and political terrorism in that state.

Dissatisfaction with Grant's administration grew during his second term. Strong-willed but politically naive, Grant made a series of poor appointments. His secretary of war, his private secretary, and officials in the Treasury and Navy Departments were involved in bribery or tax-cheating scandals. Instead of exposing the corruption, Grant defended the culprits. In 1874, as Grant's popularity and his party's prestige declined, the Democrats recaptured the House of Representatives, signaling the end of the Radical Republican vision of Reconstruction. The Republican Party faced more unfavorable publicity in 1875, when several of Grant's appointees were indicted for corruption.

The effect of Democratic gains in Congress was to weaken legislative resolve on southern issues. Congress had already lifted the political disabilities of the Fourteenth Amendment from many former Confederates. In 1872 it had adopted a sweeping Amnesty Act, which pardoned most of the remaining rebels and left only five hundred barred from political office holding. In 1875 Congress passed a Civil Rights Act, partly as a tribute to the recently deceased Charles Sumner, purporting to guarantee black people equal accommodations in public places, such as inns and theaters, but the bill was watered down and contained no effective provisions for enforcement. (The Supreme Court later struck down this law; see page 551.)

GENERAL AMNESTY

Democrats regained control of four state governments before 1872 and in a total of eight by January 1876 (see Map 16.1). In the North Democrats successfully stressed the failure and scandals of Reconstruction governments. As opinion shifted, a prominent northern historian published an article condemning the enfranchisement of blacks as "a wholesale creation of the most ignorant mass of voters to be found in the civilized world." Many Republicans sensed that their constituents were tiring of southern issues and the legacies of the war. Sectional reconciliation now seemed crucial for commerce. The nation was expanding westward rapidly, and the South was a new frontier for investment.

Both industrialization and immigration were surging, hastening the pace of change in national life. Within only eight years, postwar industrial production increased by an impressive 75 percent. For the first time, nonagricultural workers outnumbered farmers, and only Britain's industrial output was greater than that of the United States. Government financial policies did much to bring about this rapid growth. Low taxes on investment and high tariffs on manufactured goods aided industrialists. With such help, the northern economy quickly recovered its prewar rate of growth. And between 1865 and 1873, 3 million

RECONCILIATION AND INDUSTRIAL EXPANSION

immigrants entered the country, most settling in the industrial cities of the North and West. As the number of foreigners rose, so did suspicion and hostility among native-born white Americans.

Then the Panic of 1873 ushered in over five years of economic contraction. Three million people lost their jobs, and the clash between labor and capital became the major issue of the day (see Chapter 18). Class attitudes diverged, especially in the large cities. Debtors and the unemployed sought easy-money policies to spur economic expansion (workers and farmers desperately needed cash). Businessmen, disturbed by the widespread strikes and industrial violence that accompanied the panic, fiercely defended property rights and demanded "sound money" policies. The chasm between farmers and workers and wealthy industrialists grew ever wider.

Nowhere did the new complexity and violence of American race relations play out so vividly as in the

THE WEST, RACE, AND RECONSTRUCTION West. As the Fourteenth Amendment and other enactments granted to blacks the beginnings of citizenship, other nonwhite peoples faced continued persecution. Across the West, the federal government pursued a policy of containment against Native Americans. In California, where white farmers and ranchers often forced Indians into captive labor, some civilians practiced a more violent form of "Indian hunting." By 1880, thirty years of such violence left an estimated 4,500 California Indians dead at the hands of white settlers.

In Texas and the Southwest, the rhetoric of national expansion still deemed Mexicans and other mixed race Hispanics to be debased, "lazy," and incapable of self-government. And in California and other states of the Far West, thousands of Chinese immigrants became the victims of brutal violence. Few whites had objected to the Chinese who did the dangerous work of building railroads through the Rocky Mountains. But when the Chinese began to compete for urban, industrial jobs, great conflict emerged. Anticoolie clubs appeared in California in the 1870s, seeking laws against Chinese labor, fanning the flames of racism, and organizing vigilante attacks on Chinese workers and the factories that employed them. Western politicians sought white votes by pandering to prejudice, and in 1879 the new California constitution denied the vote to Chinese.

If we view America from coast to coast, and not merely on the North-South axis, the Civil War and Reconstruction years both dismantled racial slavery and fostered a volatile new racial complexity, especially in the West. During the same age when early anthropologists employed elaborate theories of "scientific" racism to determine a hierarchy of racial types, the West was a vast region of racial mixing and conflict. Some African Americans, despite generations of mixture with Native Americans, asserted that they were more like whites than the nomadic, "uncivilized" Indians, while others, like the Creek freedmen of Indian Territory, sought an Indian identity. In Texas, whites, Indians, blacks, and Hispanics had mixed for decades, and by the 1870s forced reconsideration in law and custom of just who was white and who was not.

During Reconstruction, America was undergoing what one historian has called a "reconstruction" of the very idea of "race" itself. And as it did so, tumbling into some of the darkest years of American race relations, the turbulence of the expanding West reinforced a resurgent white supremacy, a new nationalism, and the reconciliation of North and South.

Following the Civil War, pressure for expansion reemerged (see Chapter 22), and in 1867 Secretary of

■ Anti-Chinese prejudice, intimidation, and violence is depicted in this cartoon of the Native American expressing a sense of solidarity with the Chinese immigrant. Both were the subjects of "banishment" in the face of American expansion. (*Harper's Weekly,* February 8, 1879)

FOREIGN EXPANSION State William H. Seward arranged a vast addition of territory to the national domain through the purchase of Alaska from the Russian government. Opponents ridiculed Seward's $7.2 million venture, calling Alaska Frigidia, the Polar Bear Garden, and Walrussia. But Seward convinced important congressmen of Alaska's economic potential, and other lawmakers favored the dawning of friendship with Russia.

Also in 1867 the United States took control of the Midway Islands, a thousand miles northwest of Hawai'i. And in 1870 President Grant tried unsuccessfully to annex the Dominican Republic. Seward and his successor, Hamilton Fish, also resolved troubling Civil War grievances against Great Britain. Through diplomacy they arranged a financial settlement of claims on Britain for damage done by the *Alabama* and other cruisers built in England and sold to the Confederacy.

Meanwhile, the Supreme Court played its part in the northern retreat from Reconstruction. During the Civil War the Court had been cautious and inactive. Reaction to the *Dred Scott* decision (1857) had been so violent, and the Union's wartime emergency so great, that the Court avoided interference with government actions. The justices breathed a collective sigh of relief, for example, when legal technicalities prevented them from reviewing the case of Clement Vallandigham, a Democratic opponent of Lincoln's war effort, who had been convicted by a military tribunal of aiding the enemy. But in 1866 a similar case, *Ex parte Milligan,* reached the Court through proper channels.

JUDICIAL RETREAT FROM RECONSTRUCTION

Lambdin P. Milligan of Indiana had plotted to free Confederate prisoners of war and overthrow state governments. For these acts a military court sentenced Milligan, a civilian, to death. Milligan challenged the authority of the military tribunal, claiming that he had a right to a civil trial. The Supreme Court declared that military trials were illegal when civil courts were open and functioning, and its language indicated that the Court intended to reassert its authority.

In the 1870s the Court successfully renewed its challenge to Congress's actions when it narrowed the meaning and effectiveness of the Fourteenth Amendment. The *Slaughter-House* cases (1873) began in 1869, when the Louisiana legislature granted one company a monopoly on the slaughtering of livestock in New Orleans. Rival butchers in the city promptly sued. Their attorney, former Supreme Court justice John A. Campbell, argued that Louisiana had violated the rights of some of its citizens in favor of others. The Fourteenth Amendment, Campbell contended, had revolutionized the constitutional system by bringing individual rights under federal protection. Campbell thus articulated an original goal of the Republican Party: to nationalize civil rights and guard them from state interference.

But in the *Slaughter-House* decision, the Supreme Court dealt a stunning blow to the scope and vitality of the Fourteenth Amendment. Refusing to accept Campbell's argument, the Court declared state citizenship and national citizenship separate. National citizenship involved only matters such as the right to travel freely from state to state and to use the navigable waters of the nation, and only these narrow rights, held the Court, were protected by the Fourteenth Amendment.

The Supreme Court also concluded that the butchers who sued had not been deprived of their rights or property in violation of the due-process clause of the amendment. Shrinking from a role as "perpetual censor upon all legislation of the States, on the civil rights of their own citizens," the Court's majority declared that the framers of the recent amendments had not intended to "destroy" the federal system, in which the states exercised "powers for domestic and local government, including the regulation of civil rights." Thus the justices severely limited the amendment's potential for securing and protecting the rights of black citizens—its original intent.

The next day the Court decided *Bradwell v. Illinois,* a case in which Myra Bradwell, a female attorney, had been denied the right to practice law in Illinois on account of her gender. Pointing to the Fourteenth Amendment, Bradwell's attorneys contended that the state had unconstitutionally abridged her "privileges and immunities" as a citizen. The Supreme Court rejected her claim, alluding to women's traditional role in the home.

In 1876 the Court weakened the Reconstruction era amendments even further by emasculating the enforcement clause of the Fourteenth Amendment and revealing deficiencies inherent in the Fifteenth Amendment. In *U.S. v. Cruikshank* the Court overruled the conviction under the 1870 Enforcement Act of Louisiana whites who had attacked a meeting of blacks and conspired to deprive them of their rights. The justices ruled that the Fourteenth Amendment did not give the federal government power to act against these whites. The duty of protecting citizens' equal rights, the Court said, "rests alone with the States." Such judicial conservatism had a profound impact down through the next century, blunting the revolutionary potential in the Civil War amendments.

As the 1876 elections approached, most political observers saw that the nation was increasingly focused on

DISPUTED
ELECTION OF
1876 AND THE
COMPROMISE
OF 1877

economic issues and that the North was no longer willing to pursue the goals of Reconstruction. The results of a disputed presidential election confirmed this fact. Samuel J. Tilden, the Democratic governor of New York, ran strongly in the South and needed only one more electoral vote to triumph over Rutherford B. Hayes, the Republican nominee. Nineteen electoral votes from Louisiana, South Carolina, and Florida (the only southern states not yet under Democratic rule) were disputed; both Democrats and Republicans claimed to have won in those states despite fraud committed by their opponents. One vote from Oregon was undecided because of a technicality (see Map 16.2).

To resolve this unprecedented situation, on which the Constitution gave little guidance, Congress established a fifteen-member electoral commission. In the interest of impartiality, membership on the commission was to be balanced between Democrats and Republicans. Since the Republicans held the majority in Congress, they prevailed, 8 to 7, on every attempt to count the returns, with commission members voting along strict party lines. Hayes would become president if Congress accepted the commission's findings.

Congressional acceptance was not certain. Democrats controlled the House and could filibuster to block action on the vote. Many citizens worried that the nation had entered a major constitutional crisis and would slip once again into civil war, as some southerners vowed, "Tilden or Fight." The crisis was resolved when Democrats acquiesced in the election of Hayes based on a "deal" cut in a Washington hotel between Hayes's supporters and southerners who wanted federal aid to railroads, internal improvements, federal patronage, and removal of troops from southern states. Northern and southern Democrats simply decided they could not win and did not contest the election of a Republican who was not going to continue Reconstruction policies in the South. Thus Hayes became president, inaugurated privately inside the White House to avoid any threat of violence, southerners relished their promises of economic aid, and Reconstruction was unmistakably over.

Southern Democrats rejoiced, but African Americans grieved over the betrayal of their hopes for equality. Tens of thousands considered leaving the South, where real freedom was no longer a possibility. "[We asked] whether it was possible we could stay

BETRAYAL OF
BLACK RIGHTS

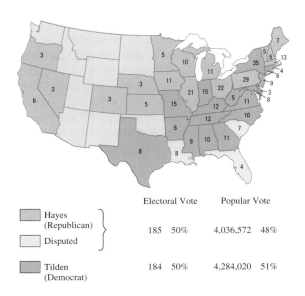

	Electoral Vote		Popular Vote	
Hayes (Republican)	185	50%	4,036,572	48%
Disputed				
Tilden (Democrat)	184	50%	4,284,020	51%

Map 16.2   Presidential Election of 1876 and the Compromise of 1877

In 1876 a combination of solid southern support and Democratic gains in the North gave Samuel Tilden the majority of popular votes, but Rutherford B. Hayes won the disputed election in the electoral college, after a deal satisfied Democratic wishes for an end to Reconstruction.

under a people who had held us in bondage," said Henry Adams. In South Carolina, Louisiana, Mississippi, and other southern states, thousands gathered up their possessions and, like Adams, migrated to Kansas. They were called Exodusters, disappointed people still searching for their share in the American dream. Even in Kansas they met disillusionment, as the welcome extended by the state's governor soon gave way to hostility among much of the white population.

Blacks now had to weigh their options, which were not much wider than they had ever been. The Civil War had brought emancipation, and Reconstruction had guaranteed their rights under law. But events and attitudes in larger white America were foreboding. In a Fourth of July speech in Washington, D.C., in 1875, Frederick Douglass anticipated this predicament. He reflected anxiously on the American centennial to be celebrated the following year. The nation, Douglass feared, would "lift to the sky its million voices in one grand Centennial hosanna of peace and good will to all the white race . . . from gulf to lakes and from sea to sea." Douglass looked back on fifteen years of unparalleled change for his people and worried about the hold of white supremacy on America's historical memory: "If war among the whites brought peace and liberty to the blacks, what will peace among the whites bring?" Douglass's question would echo down through American political culture for decades.

Summary

*R*econstruction left a contradictory record. It was an era of tragic aspirations and failures, but also of unprecedented legal, political, and social change. The Union victory brought about an increase in federal power, stronger nationalism, sweeping federal intervention in the southern states, and landmark amendments to the Constitution. But northern commitment to make these changes endure had eroded, and the revolution remained unfinished. The mystic sense of promise for new lives and liberties among the freedpeople, demonstrated in that first Decoration Day in Charleston, had fallen in a new, if temporary, kind of ruin.

The North embraced emancipation, black suffrage, and constitutional alterations strengthening the central government. But it did so to defeat the rebellion and secure the peace. As the pressure of these crises declined, strong underlying continuities emerged and placed their mark on Reconstruction. The American people and the courts maintained a preference for state authority and a distrust of federal power. The ideology of free labor dictated that property should be respected and that individuals should be self-reliant. Racism endured and transformed into the even more virulent forms of Klan terror and theories of black degeneration. Concern for the human rights of African Americans was strongest when their plight threatened to undermine the interests of whites, and reform frequently had less appeal than moneymaking in an individualistic, enterprising society.

As Reconstruction policies sought for a time to remake the South, industrialization challenged American society and values. How would the country develop its immense resources in an increasingly interconnected national economy? How would farmers, industrial workers, immigrants, and capitalists fit into the new social system? Industrialization not only promised a higher standard of living but wrought increased exploitation of labor. Moreover, industry increased the nation's power and laid the foundation for an enlarged American role in international affairs. The American imagination again turned to the conquest of new frontiers.

In the wake of the Civil War Americans faced two profound tasks—the achievement of healing and the dispensing of justice. Both had to occur, but they never developed in historical balance. Making sectional reunion compatible with black freedom and equality overwhelmed the imagination in American political culture, and the nation still faced much of this dilemma more than a century later.

LEGACY FOR A PEOPLE AND A NATION
The Fourteenth Amendment

Before the Civil War, no definition of civil rights existed in America. Reconstruction legislation, especially the Fourteenth Amendment, changed that forever. Approved by Congress in 1866, and ratified by 1868, the Fourteenth Amendment enshrined in the Constitution the ideas of birthright citizenship and equal rights. The Fourteenth Amendment was designed to secure and protect the rights of the freedpeople. But over time, the "equal protection of the law" clause became one of the most important and malleable provisions in the Constitution. It has been used at times to support the rights of states, cities, corporations, immigrants, women, religious organizations, gays and lesbians, students, and labor unions. It has advanced both tolerance and intolerance, affirmative action and anti-affirmative-action programs. It provides the legal wellspring for the generations-old civil rights movement in the United States.

The amendment as originally written required individuals to pursue grievances through private litigation, alleging state denial of a claimed federal right. At first the Supreme Court interpreted it conservatively, especially on racial matters, and by 1900 the idea of color-blind liberty in America was devastated by segregation laws, disfranchisement, and unpunished mob violence.

But Progressive reformers used the equal-protection clause to advocate government support of health, union organizing, municipal housing, a progressive income tax, and the protection of woman and child laborers. In the 1920s and 1930s, a judicial defense of civil liberties and free speech took hold, especially from Justice Louis Brandeis. The Supreme Court expanded the amendment's guarantee of equality by a series of decisions upholding the rights of immigrant groups to resist "forced Americanization," especially Catholics in their creation of parochial schools.

And, from its inception in 1910, the NAACP waged a long campaign to reveal the inequality of racial segregation in schooling and every other kind of public facility. Led by Charles Houston and Thurgood Marshall, this epic legal battle culminated in the *Brown v. Board of Education* desegregation decision of 1954.

In the multilayered Civil Rights Act of 1964, the equal-protection tradition was reenshrined into American law. Since 1964 Americans have lived in a society where the Fourteenth Amendment's legacy is the engine of expanded liberty for women and all minorities, as well as a political battleground for defining the nature and limits of human equality, and for redistributing justice long denied.

The **history companion** powered by Eduspace®

Your primary source for interactive quizzes, exercises, and more to help you learn efficiently.
http://history.college.hmco.com/students

Appendix

Suggestions for Further Reading

Chapter 1

General

Noble D. Cook, *Born to Die: Disease and New World Conquest, 1492–1650* (1998); Alfred W. Crosby, *The Columbian Exchange: Biological and Cultural Consequences of 1492* (1972); Alfred W. Crosby, *Ecological Imperialism: The Biological Expansion of Europe, 800–1900* (1986); John R. Elliott, *The Old World and the New* (1970); Bernard Lewis, *Cultures in Conflict: Christians, Muslims, and Jews in the Age of Discovery* (1995); D. W. Meinig, *Atlantic America, 1492–1800* (1986); Herman Viola and Carolyn Margolis, eds., *Seeds of Change: Five Hundred Years Since Columbus* (1991); Eric Wolf, *Europe and the People Without History* (1982).

Mesoamerican Civilizations

Inga Clendinnen, *Aztecs: An Interpretation* (1991); Michael Coe, *Mexico from the Olmecs to the Aztecs* (1994); Brian Fagan, *Kingdoms of Gold, Kingdoms of Jade: The Americas Before Columbus* (1991); John S. Henderson, *The World of the Ancient Maya* (1997); Eduardo Matos Moctezuma and David Carrasco, *Moctezuma's Mexico: Visions of the Aztec World* (1992); Linda Schele and David Friedel, *A Forest of Kings* [on the Mayas] (1990).

North American Indians

Kathleen Bragdon, *The Columbia Guide to American Indians of the Northeast* (2002); Kathleen Bragdon, *Native People of Southern New England, 1500–1650* (1996); Sally A. Kitt Chappell, *Cahokia: Mirror of the Cosmos* (2002); Linda S. Cordell, *Ancient Pueblo Peoples* (1994); Brian Fagan, *Ancient North America: The Archaeology of a Continent* (1991); Brian Fagan, *The Great Journey: The Peopling of Ancient America* (1987); Francis Jennings, *The Founders of America: From the Earliest Migrations to the Present* (1993); Alvin Josephy, Jr., ed., *America in 1492* (1992); Theda Perdue and Michael Green, *The Columbia Guide to American Indians of the Southeast* (2001); Elsa Redmond, ed., *Chiefdoms and Chieftaincy in the Americas* (1999); Lynda N. Shaffer, *Native Americans Before 1492: The Moundbuilding Centers of the Eastern Woodlands* (1992); Colin F. Taylor, ed., *The Native Americans: The Indigenous People of North America* (1992); Bruce Trigger and Wilcomb Washburn, eds., *The Cambridge History of the Native Peoples of the Americas*, vol. 1: *North America* (1996); Be-

loine W. Young and Melvin L. Fowler, *Cahokia: The Great Native American Metropolis* (2000).

Africa

Jacob Ade Ajayi and Michael Crowder, *History of West Africa* (1985); Basil Davidson, *Africa in History*, rev. ed. (1991); Philip Curtin et al., eds., *African History: From Earliest Times to Independence*, rev. ed. (1995); John Iliffe, *Africans: The History of a Continent* (1996); Robert July, *A History of the African People* (1992); Paul Lovejoy, *Transformations in Slavery: A History of Slavery in Africa* (1983); Roland Oliver and J. D. Fage, *A Short History of Africa* (1988); John Thornton, *Africa and Africans in the Making of the Atlantic World, 1400–1680* (1992).

Europe in the Age of Discovery

Christopher Allmand, *The Hundred Years' War: England and France at War, ca. 1300–ca. 1450* (1988); Fernand Braudel, *The Mediterranean and the Mediterranean World in the Age of Philip II*, 2 vols., 2d ed. (1977); Roger Chartier, ed., *A History of Private Life, vol. 3: Passions of the Renaissance* (1989); G. R. Elton, ed., *The Reformation* (1990); Anthony Grafton, *New Worlds, Ancient Texts: The Power of Tradition and the Shock of Discovery* (1992); Denys Hay, *Europe in the Fourteenth and Fifteenth Centuries*, 2d ed. (1989); H. G. Koenigsberger et al., *Europe in the Sixteenth Century*, 2d ed. (1989); Robert McGhee, *The Arctic Voyages of Martin Frobisher: An Elizabethan Adventure* (2002); Anthony Pagden, *Lords of All the World: Ideologies of Empire in Spain, Britain and France, 1500–1800* (1995); J. R. S. Phillips, *The Medieval Expansion of Europe* (1988); Philip Ziegler, *The Black Death* (1982).

Exploration and Discovery

Emerson Baker et al., eds., *American Beginnings: Exploration, Culture, and Cartography in the Land of Norumbega* (1994); Fredi Chiappelli et al., eds., *First Images of America: The Impact of the New World on the Old*, 2 vols. (1976); Kathleen Deagan and José María Cruxent, *Columbus's Outpost among the Taínos: Spain and America at La Isabela, 1493–1498* (2002); Felipe Fernández-Armesto, *Before Columbus: Exploration and Colonization from the Mediterranean to the Atlantic, 1229–1492* (1987); Felipe Fernández-Armesto, *Columbus* (1991); Charles Hudson, *Knights of Spain, Warriors of the Sun: Hernando de Soto and the South's Ancient Chiefdoms* (1997);

Jerald T. Milanich, *Florida Indians and the Invasion from Europe* (1995); Jerald T. Milanich and Susan Milbrath, eds., *First Encounters: Spanish Explorations in the Caribbean and the United States, 1492–1570* (1989); Samuel Eliot Morison, *The European Discovery of America: The Northern Voyages, A.D. 1500–1600* (1971); Samuel Eliot Morison, *The European Discovery of America: The Southern Voyages, A.D. 1492–1616* (1974); J. H. Parry, *The Age of Reconnaissance* (1963); J. H. Parry, *The Discovery of the Sea* (1974); William and Carla Phillips, *The Worlds of Christopher Columbus* (1992); David B. Quinn, *North America from Earliest Discovery to First Settlements* (1977); Irving Rouse, *The Tainos: Rise and Decline of the People Who Greeted Columbus* (1992); P. E. Russell, *Portugal, Spain, and the African Atlantic* (1995); P. E. Russell, *Prince Henry "The Navigator": A Life* (2000); Kirsten Seaver, *The Frozen Echo: Greenland and the Exploration of North America, ca. A.D. 1000–1500* (1995); Roger C. Smith, *Vanguard of Empire: Ships of Exploration in the Age of Columbus* (1993).

Early European Conquest and Settlements

Kenneth Andrews, *Trade, Plunder and Settlement: Maritime Enterprise and the Genesis of the British Empire, 1480–1630* (1984); Nancy Farriss, *Maya Society Under Colonial Rule* (1984); Charles Gibson, *Spain in America* (1966); Ross Hassig, *Mexico and the Spanish Conquest* (1994); Paul E. Hoffman, *A New Andalucia and a Way to the Orient: The American Southeast during the Sixteenth Century* (1990); Karen O. Kupperman, *Roanoke, the Abandoned Colony* (1984); Miguel León-Portilla, ed., *The Broken Spears: The Aztec Account of the Conquest of Mexico* (1992); James Lockhart, ed. and trans., *We People Here: Nahuatl Accounts of the Conquest of Mexico* (1993); James Lockhart, *The Nahuas after the Conquest: A Social and Cultural History of the Indians of Central Mexico, Sixteenth Through Eighteenth Centuries* (1992); A. J. R. Russell-Wood, *A World on the Move: The Portuguese in Africa, Asia, and America, 1415–1808* (1993); Hugh Thomas, Conquest: *Montezuma, Cortés, and the Fall of Old Mexico* (1993).

Chapter 2

General

Christine Daniels and Michael Kennedy, eds., *Negotiated Empires: Centers and Peripheries in the Americas, 1500–1820* (2002); David Hackett Fischer, *Albion's Seed: Four British Folkways in America* (1989); Alison Games, *Migration and the Origins of the English Atlantic World* (1999); Karen O. Kupperman, ed., *America in European Consciousness, 1493–1750* (1995); D. W. Meinig, *Atlantic America, 1492–1800* (1986); Gary B. Nash, *Red, White, and Black: The Peoples of Early America*, 4th ed. (2000); Mary Beth Norton, *Founding Mothers & Fathers: Gendered Power and the Forming of American Society* (1996); John E. Pomfret, *Founding the American Colonies, 1583–1660* (1970); Alan Taylor, *American Colonies* (2001); Paula Treckel, *To Comfort the Heart: Women in Seventeenth-Century America* (1996); Alden T. Vaughan, *Roots of American Racism* (1994).

New Spain, New Netherland, New France, and the Caribbean

Karen Anderson, *Chain Her by One Foot: The Subjugation of Native Women in Seventeenth-Century New France* (1991); Charles R. Boxer, *The Dutch Seaborne Empire, 1600–1800* (1965); Denys Delâge, *Bitter Feast: Amerindians and Europeans in Northeastern North America, 1600–64* (1993); Richard S. Dunn, *Sugar and Slaves: The Rise of the Planter Class in the English West Indies, 1624–1713* (1972); William J. Eccles, *France in America*, rev. ed. (1990); Carol Hoffecker et al., eds., *New Sweden in America* (1995); Jonathan Israel, *Dutch Primacy in World Trade, 1585–1740* (1989); Robert Kapitzke, *Religion, Power, and Politics in Colonial St. Augustine* (2001); Karen O. Kupperman, *Providence Island, 1630–1641: The Other Puritan Colony* (1993); Donna Merwick, *Possessing Albany, 1630–1710* (1990); Sidney Mintz, *Sweetness and Power: The Place of Sugar in Modern History* (1985); Peter N. Moogk, *La Nouvelle France: The Making of French Canada, A Cultural History* (2000); Carroll Riley, *The Kachina and the Cross: Indians and Spaniards in the Early Southwest* (2000); Marc Simmons, *The Last Conquistador: Juan de Oñate and the Settling of the Far Southwest* (1991); David J. Weber, *The Spanish Frontier in North America* (1992).

England

Susan Dwyer Amussen, *An Ordered Society: Gender and Class in Early Modern England* (1988); Carl Bridenbaugh, *Vexed and Troubled Englishmen, 1590–1642*, rev. ed. (1976); Patrick Collinson, *The Religion of Protestants: The Church in English Society, 1559–1625* (1982); A. G. Dickens, *The English Reformation*, 2d ed. (1989); Ralph Houlbrooke, *The English Family, 1450–1700* (1984); Peter Laslett, *The World We Have Lost*, 3d ed. (1984); J. P. Sommerville, *Politics and Ideology in England, 1603–1640* (1986); Keith Wrightson, *English Society, 1580–1680* (1982).

Early Contact Between Europeans and Indians

James Axtell, *The Invasion Within: The Contest of Cultures in Colonial North America* (1985); Russell Bourne, *Gods of War, Gods of Peace: How the Meeting of Native and Colonial Religion Shaped Early America* (2002); Alfred Cave, *The Pequot War* (1997); William Cronon, *Changes in the Land: Indians, Colonists, and the Ecology of New England* (1983); Frederic W. Gleach, *Powhatan's World and Colonial Virginia: A Conflict of Cultures* (1997); Francis Jennings, *The Invasion of America: Indians, Colonialism, and the Cant of Conquest* (1975); Karen O. Kupperman, *Indians and English: Facing Off in Early America* (2000); Patrick Malone, *The Skulking Way of War: Technology and Tactics Among the Indians of New England* (1991); Kenneth Morrison, *The Embattled Northeast: The Elusive Ideal of Alliance in Abnaki-Euroamerican Relations* (1984); Daniel Richter, *Facing East from Indian Country: A Native History of Early America* (2001); Daniel Richter, *The Ordeal of the Longhouse: The Peoples of the Iroquois League in the Era of European Colonization* (1992); Helen C. Rountree, *Pocahontas's People: The Powhatan Indians of Virginia Through Four Centuries* (1990); Neal Salisbury, *Manitou and Providence: Indians, Europeans, and the Making of New England, 1500–1643* (1982); Bernard Sheehan, *Savagism and Civility: Indians and Englishmen in Colonial Virginia* (1980); Timothy Silver, *A New Face on the Countryside: Indians, Colonists, and Slaves in South Atlantic Forests, 1500–1800* (1990); Alden T. Vaughan, *The New England Frontier: Puritans and Indians, 1620–1675*, rev. ed. (1979); Peter Wood et al., eds., *Powhatan's Mantle: Indians in the Colonial Southeast* (1989).

Chesapeake Society and Politics

Lois Green Carr et al., *Robert Cole's World: Agriculture and Society in Early Maryland* (1991); David Galenson, *White Servitude in Colonial America: An Economic Analysis* (1981); James Horn, *Adapting to a New World: English Society in the Seventeenth-Century Chesapeake* (1994); Ivor Noel Hume, *The Virginia Adventure: Roanoke to James Towne* (1994); A. J. Leo Lemay, *The American Dream of Captain John Smith* (1991); Gloria L. Main, *Tobacco Colony: Life in Early Maryland, 1650–1720* (1983); Edmund S. Morgan, *American Slavery, American Freedom: The Ordeal of Colonial Virginia* (1975); James Perry, *The Formation of a Society on Virginia's Eastern Shore, 1615–1655* (1990); Darrett Rutman and Anita Rutman, *A Place in Time: Middlesex County, Virginia, 1650–1750* (1984); Alden T. Vaughan, *American Genesis: Captain John Smith and the Founding of Virginia* (1975).

New England Communities, Politics, and Religion

David Grayson Allen, *In English Ways: The Movement of Societies and the Transferral of English Law and Custom to Massachusetts Bay in the 17th Century* (1981); Virginia DeJohn Anderson, *New England's Generation: The Great Migration and the Formation of Society and Culture in the 17th Century* (1991); Richard Archer, *Fissures in the Rock: New England in the Seventeenth Century* (2001); Charles Cohen, *God's Caress: The Psychology of Puritan Religious Experience* (1986); Philip Gura, *A Glimpse of Sion's Glory: Puritan Radicalism in New England, 1620–1660* (1984); David D. Hall, *Worlds of Wonder, Days of Judgment: Popular Religious Belief in Early New England* (1989); Stephen Innes, *Creating the Commonwealth: The Economic Culture of Puritan New England* (1995); Stephen Innes, *Labor in a New Land: Economy and Society in 17th-Century Springfield* (1983); Sydney V. James, *Colonial Rhode Island* (1975); George Langdon, *Pilgrim Colony: A History of New Plymouth, 1620–1691* (1966); Kenneth A. Lockridge, *A New England Town: The First Hundred Years (Dedham, Massachusetts, 1636–1736)* (1970); John Frederick Martin, *Profits in the Wilderness: Entrepreneurship and the Founding of New England Towns in the 17th Century* (1991); Edmund S. Morgan, *The Puritan Dilemma: The Story of John Winthrop* (1958); Darrett Rutman, *Winthrop's Boston* (1965); Roger Thompson, *Divided We Stand: Watertown, Massachusetts, 1630–1680* (2001).

New England Women and Family Life

David Cressy, *Coming Over: Migration and Communication Between England and New England in the Seventeenth Century* (1987); James Deetz and Patricia Deetz, *The Times of Their Lives: Life, Love, and Death in Plymouth Colony* (2000); John P. Demos, *A Little Commonwealth: Family Life in Plymouth Colony* (1970); Lyle Koehler, *A Search for Power: The "Weaker Sex" in Seventeenth-Century New England* (1980); Edmund S. Morgan, *The Puritan Family*, rev. ed. (1966); Amanda Porterfield, *Female Piety in Puritan New England* (1992); Roger Thompson, *Sex in Middlesex: Popular Mores in a Massachusetts County, 1649–1699* (1986); Laurel Thatcher Ulrich, *Good Wives: Image and Reality in the Lives of Women in Northern New England, 1650–1750* (1982).

Chapter 3

General

Colin Calloway, *New Worlds for All: Indians, Europeans, and the Remaking of Early America* (1997); Wesley Frank Craven, *The Colonies in Transition, 1660–1713* (1968); W. J. Eccles, *France in America*, rev. ed. (1990); Jack P. Greene and J. R. Pole, eds., *Colonial British America* (1984); Peter Linebaugh and Marcus Rediker, *The Many-Headed Hydra: Sailors, Slaves, Commoners, and the Hidden History of the Revolutionary Atlantic* (2000); John J. McCusker and Russell R. Menard, *The Economy of British America, 1607–1789* (1985); John J. McCusker and Kenneth Morgan, eds., *The Early Modern Atlantic Economy* (2000).

New Netherland and the Restoration Colonies

Edwin Bronner, *William Penn's "Holy Experiment": The Founding of Pennsylvania, 1681–1701* (1962); Wesley Frank Craven, *New Jersey and the English Colonization of North America* (1964); Joyce Goodfriend, *Before the Melting Pot: Society and Culture in Colonial New York City, 1664–1730* (1992); Donna Merwick, *Death of a Notary: Conquest and Change in Colonial New York* (1999); Donna Merwick, *Possessing Albany, 1630–1710: The Dutch and English Experiences* (1990); Oliver Rink, *Holland on the Hudson: An Economic and Social History of Dutch New York* (1986); Robert C. Ritchie, *The Duke's Province: A Study of Politics and Society in Colonial New York, 1660–1691* (1977); Robert M. Weir, *Colonial South Carolina: A History* (1983).

Imperial Trade and Administration

David Armitage, *The Ideological Origins of the British Empire* (2000); Robert M. Bliss, *Revolution and Empire: English Politics and the American Colonies in the Seventeenth Century* (1991); Lawrence W. Harper, *The English Navigation Laws: A Seventeenth-Century Experiment in Social Engineering* (1939); Marcus Rediker, *Between the Devil and the Deep Blue Sea: Merchant Seamen, Pirates, and the Anglo-American Maritime*

World, 1700–1750 (1987); Robert C. Ritchie, *Captain Kidd and the War Against the Pirates* (1986); I. K. Steele, *Politics of Colonial Policy: The Board of Trade in Colonial Administration* (1968); Stephen Saunders Webb, *Lord Churchill's Coup: The Anglo-American Empire and the Glorious Revolution Reconsidered* (1995); Stephen Saunders Webb, *1676: The End of American Independence* (1984); Stephen Saunders Webb, *The Governors-General: The English Army and the Definition of the Empire, 1569–1681* (1979).

Africa and the Slave Trade

Robin Blackburn, *The Making of New World Slavery: From the Baroque to the Modern, 1492–1800* (1997); Jay Coughtry, *The Notorious Triangle: Rhode Island and the African Slave Trade, 1700–1807* (1981); Philip D. Curtin, *The Atlantic Slave Trade: A Census* (1969); David Eltis, *The Rise of African Slavery in the Americas* (1998); Joseph Inikori and Stanley Engerman, eds., *The Atlantic Slave Trade* (1992); Herbert Klein, *The Middle Passage* (1978); Robin Law, *The Slave Coast of West Africa, 1550–1750: The Impact of the Atlantic Slave Trade on an African Society* (1991); Daniel C. Littlefield, *Rice and Slaves: Ethnicity and the Slave Trade in Colonial South Carolina* (1981); James Rawley, *The Transatlantic Slave Trade: A History* (1981); Barbara Solow, ed., *Slavery and the Rise of the Atlantic System* (1991).

Africans in America

Ira Berlin, *Many Thousands Gone: The First Two Centuries of Slavery in North America* (1998); T. H. Breen and Stephen Innes, *"Myne Owne Ground": Race and Freedom on Virginia's Eastern Shore, 1640–1676* (1980); Judith Carney, *Black Rice: The African Origins of Rice Cultivation in the Americas* (2001); Douglas Deal, *Race and Class in Colonial Virginia: Indians, Englishmen, and Africans on the Eastern Shore During the Seventeenth Century* (1993); Michael A. Gomez, *Exchanging Our Country Marks: The Transformation of African Identities in the Colonial and Antebellum South* (1998); Graham R. Hodges, *Root & Branch: African Americans in New York and East Jersey, 1613–1863* (1999); Allan Kulikoff, *Tobacco and Slaves: The Development of Southern Cultures in the Chesapeake, 1680–1800* (1986); Jane Landers, *Black Society in Spanish Florida* (1999); Edgar J. McManus, *Black Bondage in the North* (1973); Edmund S. Morgan, *American Slavery, American Freedom: The Ordeal of Colonial Virginia* (1975); Lorena S. Walsh, *From Calabar to Carter's Grove: The History of a Virginia Slave Community* (1997); Betty Wood, *The Origins of American Slavery* (1997); Peter H. Wood, *Black Majority: Negroes in Colonial South Carolina from 1670 Through the Stono Rebellion* (1974).

European–Native American Relations in the North

Russell Bourne, *The Red King's Rebellion: Racial Politics in New England, 1675–1678* (1991); John Demos, *The Unredeemed Captive: A Family Story from Early America* (1994);

Matthew Dennis, *Cultivating a Landscape of Peace: Iroquois-European Encounter in Seventeenth-Century America* (1993); James D. Drake, *King Philip's War: Civil War in New England, 1675–1676* (2000); Francis Jennings, *The Ambiguous Iroquois Empire* (1984); Jill Lepore, *The Name of War: King Philip's War and the Origins of American Identity* (1998); Peter Mancall, *Deadly Medicine: Indians and Alcohol in Early America* (1995); Michael Puglisi, *Puritans Beseiged: The Legacies of King Philip's War in the Massachusetts Bay Colony* (1991); Daniel Richter, *Facing East from Indian Country: A Native History of Early America* (2001); Daniel Richter, *The Ordeal of the Longhouse: The Peoples of the Iroquois League in the Era of European Colonization* (1992); Daniel Richter and James Merrell, eds., *Beyond the Covenant Chain: The Iroquois and Their Neighbors in Indian America, 1600–1800* (1987); Richard White, *The Middle Ground: Indians, Empires, and Republics in the Great Lakes Region, 1650–1815* (1991).

European–Native American Relations in the South and West

David H. Corkran, *The Creek Frontier, 1540–1783* (1967); Verner W. Crane, *The Southern Frontier, 1660–1732* (1929); Carl Ekberg, *French Roots in the Illinois Country: The Mississippi Frontier in Colonial Times* (1998); Alan Gallay, *The Indian Slave Trade: The Rise of the English Empire in the American South, 1670–1717* (2002); Ramón Gutiérrez, *When Jesus Came, the Corn Mothers Went Away: Marriage, Sexuality, and Power in New Mexico, 1500–1846* (1991); Elizabeth A. H. John, *Storms Brewed in Other Men's Worlds: The Confrontation of Indians, Spanish, and French in the Southwest, 1540–1795* (1975); Andrew Knaut, *The Pueblo Revolt of 1680* (1995); James Merrell, *The Indians' New World: Catawbas and Their Neighbors from European Contact through the Era of Removal* (1989); Jim Norris, *After the Year Eighty: The Demise of Franciscan Power in Spanish New Mexico* (2000); Daniel H. Usner, Jr., *Indians, Settlers, and Slaves in a Frontier Exchange Economy: The Lower Mississippi Valley before 1783* (1992).

Colonial Politics

Patricia U. Bonomi, *The Lord Cornbury Scandal: The Politics of Reputation in British America* (1998); Lois Green Carr and David W. Jordan, *Maryland's Revolution of Government, 1689–1692* (1974); Richard P. Johnson, *Adjustment to Empire: The New England Colonies, 1675–1715* (1981); David S. Lovejoy, *The Glorious Revolution in America* (1972); Jack M. Sosin, *English America and Imperial Inconstancy: The Rise of Provincial Autonomy, 1696–1715* (1985); Jack M. Sosin, *English America and the Restoration Monarchy of Charles II* (1980); Jack M. Sosin, *English America and the Revolution of 1688* (1982).

New England

Bernard Bailyn, *The New England Merchants in the Seventeenth Century* (1955); Richard Bushman, *From Puritan to Yankee: Character and the Social Order in Connecticut,*

1690–1765 (1967); Christine Heyrman, *Commerce and Culture: The Maritime Communities of Colonial Massachusetts, 1690–1750* (1984); Richard Melvoin, *New England Outpost: War and Society in Colonial Deerfield* (1990); Amanda Porterfield, *Female Piety in Puritan New England* (1991); Laurel Thatcher Ulrich, *Good Wives: Image and Reality in the Lives of Women in Northern New England, 1650–1750* (1982).

New England Witchcraft

Paul Boyer and Stephen Nissenbaum, *Salem Possessed: The Social Origins of Witchcraft* (1974); Elaine Breslaw, *Tituba, Reluctant Witch of Salem: Devilish Indians and Puritan Fantasies* (1996); John Demos, *Entertaining Satan: Witchcraft and the Culture of Early New England* (1982); Richard Godbeer, *The Devil's Dominion: Magic and Religion in Early New England* (1992); Peter Hoffer, *The Devil's Disciples: Makers of the Salem Witchcraft Trials* (1996); Carol Karlsen, *The Devil in the Shape of a Woman: Witchcraft in Early New England* (1987); Mary Beth Norton, *In the Devil's Snare: The Salem Witchcraft Crisis of 1692* (2002); Bernard Rosenthal, *Salem Story: Reading the Witch Trials of 1692* (1993); Richard Weisman, *Witchcraft, Magic, and Religion in 17th-Century Massachusetts* (1984).

Chapter 4

General

Jack P. Greene, *Pursuits of Happiness: The Social Development of the Early Modern British Colonies and the Formation of American Culture* (1988); Richard Hofstadter, *America at 1750: A Social Portrait* (1971); Allan Kullikoff, *From British Peasants to Colonial American Farmers* (2000); D. W. Meinig, *Atlantic America, 1492–1800* (1986); Stephanie G. Wolf, *As Various as Their Land: The Everyday Lives of 18th-Century Americans* (1992).

New France and New Spain

Ramón Gutiérrez, *When Jesus Came, the Corn Mothers Went Away: Marriage, Sexuality, and Power in New Mexico, 1500–1846* (1991); Gwendolyn Midlo Hall, *Africans in Colonial Louisiana: The Development of Afro-Creole Culture in the Eighteenth Century* (1992); Dale Miquelon, *New France, 1701–1744* (1987); G. F. G. Stanley, *New France, 1744–1760* (1968); David J. Weber, *The Spanish Frontier in North America* (1992).

European–Native American Relations

James F. Brooks, *Captives & Cousins: Slavery, Kinship, and Community in the Southwest Borderlands* (2002); Peter C. Mancall, *Deadly Medicine: Indians and Alcohol in Early America* (1995); James H. Merrell, *Into the American Woods: Negotiators on the Pennsylvania Frontier* (1999); Daniel H. Usner, Jr., *Indians, Settlers, and Slaves in a Frontier Exchange Economy: The Lower Mississippi Valley Before 1783* (1992); Richard White, *The Middle Ground: Indians, Empires, and Republics in the Great Lakes Region, 1650–1815* (1991).

Anglo-American Society

T. H. Breen, *Tobacco Culture* (1985); Carl Bridenbaugh, *Cities in Revolt: Urban Life in America, 1743–1776* (1955); Trevor Burnard, *Creole Gentlemen: The Maryland Elite 1691–1776* (2002); Lois Green Carr et al., eds., *Colonial Chesapeake Society* (1988); David Conroy, *In Public Houses: Drink and the Revolution of Authority in Colonial Massachusetts* (1995); Rhys Isaac, *The Transformation of Virginia, 1740–1790* (1982); Christopher Jedrey, *The World of John Cleaveland: Family and Community in Eighteenth-Century New England* (1979); Sung Bok Kim, *Landlord and Tenant in Colonial New York: Manorial Society, 1664–1775* (1978); Peter C. Mancall, *Valley of Opportunity: Economic Culture Along the Upper Susquehanna, 1700–1800* (1991); Gary B. Nash, *The Urban Crucible: Social Change, Political Consciousness, and the Origins of the American Revolution* (1979); Michael Rozbicki, *The Complete Colonial Gentleman: Cultural Legitimacy in Plantation America* (1998); Sharon Salinger, *Taverns and Drinking in Early America* (2002); David S. Shields, *Civil Tongues and Polite Letters in British America* (1997); Peter Thompson, *Rum Punch & Revolution: Taverngoing & Public Life in Eighteenth-Century Philadelphia* (1999).

American Economic Development

Richard Bushman, *The Refinement of America: Persons, Houses, Cities* (1992); Cary Carson et al., eds., *Of Consuming Interests: The Style of Life in the Eighteenth Century* (1994); Marc Egnal, *New World Economies: The Growth of the Thirteen Colonies and Early Canada* (1999); David Hancock, *Citizens of the World: London Merchants and the Integration of the British Atlantic Community, 1735–1785* (1995); Phyllis W. Hunter, *Purchasing Identity in the Atlantic World: Massachusetts Merchants, 1670–1780* (2001); Stephen Innes, ed., *Work and Labor in Early America* (1988); Alice Hanson Jones, *Wealth of a Nation to Be: The American Colonies on the Eve of the Revolution* (1980); Cathy Matson, *Merchants and Empire: Trading in Colonial New York* (1998); John J. McCusker and Russell R. Menard, *The Economy of British America, 1607–1789* (1985); Margaret E. Newell, *From Dependency to Independence: Economic Revolution in Colonial New England* (1998); Gary M. Walton and James F. Shepherd, *The Economic Rise of Early America* (1979).

Anglo-American Politics

Bernard Bailyn, *The Origins of American Politics* (1968); Patricia U. Bonomi, *A Factious People: Politics and Society in Colonial New York* (1971); Richard Bushman, *King and People in Provincial Massachusetts* (1985); Edward M. Cook, Jr., *The Fathers of the Towns: Leadership and Community Structure in Eighteenth-Century New England* (1976); Jack P. Greene, *The Quest for*

Power: The Lower Houses of Assembly in the Southern Royal Colonies, 1689–1776 (1963); Marjoleine Kars, *Breaking Loose Together: The Regulator Rebellion in Pre-Revolutionary North Carolina* (2002); John Gilman Kolp, *Gentleman and Freeholders: Electoral Politics in Colonial Virginia* (1998).

Immigration to British America

Bernard Bailyn, *The Peopling of British North America* (1986); Bernard Bailyn, *Voyagers to the West* (1986); Bernard Bailyn and Philip Morgan, eds., *Strangers Within the Realm* (1991); Marilyn Baseler, *"Asylum for Mankind": America 1607–1800* (1998); Jon Butler, *The Huguenots in America* (1983); R. J. Dickson, *Ulster Immigration to Colonial America, 1718–1775* (1966); David Dobson, *Scottish Immigration to Colonial America, 1607–1785* (1994); A. Roger Ekirch, *Bound for America: The Transportation of British Convicts to the Colonies, 1718–1775* (1987); Aaron Fogleman, *Hopeful Journeys: German Immigration, Settlement, and Political Culture in Colonial America, 1717–1775* (1996); Patrick Griffin, *The People with No Name: Ireland's Ulster Scots, America's Scots Irish, and the Creation of a British Atlantic World, 1689–1764* (2001); Colin Kidd, *British Identities before Nationalism: Ethnicity and Nationhood in the British Atlantic World, 1600–1800* (1999); Ned Landsman, ed., *Nation and Province in the First British Empire: Scotland and the Americas, 1600–1800* (2001); Ned Landsman, *Scotland and Its First American Colony* (1985); A. G. Roeber, *Palatines, Liberty, and Property: German Lutherans in Colonial British America* (1993); Marianne Wokeck, *Trade in Strangers: The Beginnings of Mass Migration to North America* (1999).

African Americans

Ira Berlin, *Many Thousands Gone: The First Two Centuries of Slavery in North America* (1998); Ira Berlin and Philip Morgan, eds., *Cultivation and Culture: Labor and the Shaping of Slave Life in the Americas* (1993); Thomas J. Davis, *A Rumor of Revolt: The "Great Negro Plot" in Colonial New York* (1985); Michael A. Gomez, *Exchanging Our Country Marks: The Transformation of African Identities in the Colonial and Antebellum South* (1998); Graham R. Hodges, *Root & Branch: African Americans in New York and East Jersey, 1613–1863* (1999); Marvin L. Michael Kay and Lorin Lee Cary, *Slavery in North Carolina, 1748–1775* (1995); Allan Kulikoff, *Tobacco and Slaves: The Development of Southern Cultures in the Chesapeake, 1680–1800* (1986); Philip D. Morgan, *Slave Counterpoint: Black Culture in the Eighteenth-Century Chesapeake and Low Country* (1998); Gerald [Michael] Mullin, *Flight and Rebellion: Slave Resistance in Eighteenth-Century Virginia* (1972); Michael Mullin, *Africa in America: Slave Acculturation and Resistance in the American South and the British Caribbean, 1736–1834* (1992); Robert Olwell, *Masters, Slaves, and Subjects: The Culture of Power in the South Carolina Low Country 1740–1790* (1998); William Pierson, *Black Yankees: The Development of an Afro-American Subculture*

in Eighteenth-Century New England (1988); Mechal Sobel, *The World They Made Together: Black and White Values in Eighteenth-Century Virginia* (1987); Betty Wood, *Women's Work, Men's Work: The Informal Slave Economies of Low Country Georgia* (1995); Anne Yentsch, *A Chesapeake Family and Their Slaves* (1994).

American Women, Men, and Families

Carol R. Berkin, *First Generations: Women in Colonial America* (1996); Kathleen M. Brown, *Good Wives, Nasty Wenches, and Anxious Patriarchs: Gender, Race, and Power in Colonial Virginia* (1996); Cornelia Hughes Dayton, *Women Before the Bar: Gender, Law, and Society in Connecticut, 1639–1789* (1995); Kirsten Fischer, *Suspect Relations: Sex, Race, and Resistance in Colonial North Carolina* (2002); Philip J. Greven, *The Protestant Temperament: Patterns of Child-Rearing, Religious Experience, and the Self in Early America* (1977); Joan Gundersen, *To Be Useful to the World: Women in Eighteenth-Century America* (1996); Barry J. Levy, *Quakers and the American Family* (1988); June Namias, *White Captives: Gender and Ethnicity on the American Frontier* (1993); Ann Marie Plane, *Colonial Intimacies: Indian Marriage in Early New England* (2000); Marylynn Salmon, *Women and the Law of Property in Early America* (1986); Daniel Blake Smith, *Inside the Great House: Planter Family Life in Eighteenth-Century Chesapeake Society* (1980); Merril D. Smith, *Breaking the Bonds: Marital Discord in Pennsylvania, 1730–1830* (1992); Linda Sturtz, *Within Her Power: Propertied Women in Colonial Virginia* (2002); Lisa Wilson, *Ye Heart of a Man: The Domestic Life of Men in Colonial New England* (1999).

Anglo-American Education, Science, and the Enlightenment

Patricia Cline Cohen, *A Calculating People: The Spread of Numeracy in Early America* (1982); Lawrence A. Cremin, *American Education: The Colonial Experience, 1607–1783* (1970); Richard Beale Davis, *Intellectual Life in the Colonial South, 1585–1763* (1978); Brooke Hindle, *The Pursuit of Science in Revolutionary America* (1956); J. David Hoeveler, *Creating the American Mind: Intellect and Politics in the Colonial Colleges* (2002); Kenneth Lockridge, *Literacy in Colonial New England* (1974); Henry F. May, *The Enlightenment in America* (1976); Amy R. W. Meyers and Margaret Beck Pritchard, eds., *Nature's Empire: Mark Catesby's New World Vision* (1998); Thomas P. Slaughter, *The Natures of John and William Bartram* (1996); William Sloan and Julie Williams, *The Early American Press, 1690–1783* (1994); Raymond P. Stearns, *Science in the British Colonies of America* (1970).

Religion and the Great Awakening

Robert W. Brockway, *A Wonderful Work of God: Puritanism and the Great Awakening* (2003); Catherine Brekus, *Strangers and Pilgrims: Female Preaching in America, 1740–1845* (1998); Patricia U. Bonomi, *Under the Cope of Heaven: Reli-*

gion, Society, and Politics in Colonial America (1986); J. M. Bumstead and John E. Van de Wetering, What Must I Do to Be Saved? The Great Awakening in Colonial America (1976); Jon Butler, Awash in a Sea of Faith: Christianizing the American People (1990); Michael Crawford, Seasons of Grace: Colonial New England's Revival Tradition in Its British Context (1991); Alan E. Heimert, Religion and the American Mind: From the Great Awakening to the Revolution (1966); Frank Lambert, Inventing the "Great Awakening" (1999); Rebecca Larson, Daughters of Light: Quaker Women Preaching and Prophesying in the Colonies and Abroad, 1700–1775 (1999); David S. Lovejoy, Religious Enthusiasm in the New World (1985); John K. Nelson, A Blessed Company: Parishes, Parsons, and Parishioners in Anglican Virginia, 1690–1776 (2001); Harry S. Stout, The Divine Dramatist: George Whitefield and the Rise of Modern Evangelicalism (1991); Patricia Tracy, Jonathan Edwards, Pastor (1980).

Chapter 5

General

Ian R. Christie and Benjamin W. Labaree, Empire or Independence, 1760–1776: A British-American Dialogue on the Coming of the American Revolution (1976); Barbara DeWolfe, ed., Discoveries of America: Personal Accounts of British Emigrants to North America during the Revolutionary Era (1997); Marc Egnal, A Mighty Empire: The Origins of the American Revolution (1988); Ronald Hoffman et al., eds., The Economy of Early America: The Revolutionary Period, 1763–1790 (1988); Merrill Jensen, The Founding of a Nation: A History of the American Revolution, 1763–1776 (1968); John Phillip Reid, The Constitutional History of the American Revolution (1995); Robert W. Tucker and David C. Hendrickson, The Fall of the First British Empire: Origins of the War of American Independence (1982).

Colonial Warfare and the British Empire

Fred Anderson, Crucible of War: The Seven Years' War and the Fate of Empire in British North America (2000); Fred Anderson, A People's Army: Massachusetts Soldiers and Society in the Seven Years' War (1984); Frank W. Brecher, Losing a Continent: France's North American Policy, 1753–1763 (1998); Stephen Brumwell, Redcoats: The British Soldier and War in the Americas, 1755–1763 (2002); Lawrence Henry Gipson, The British Empire Before the American Revolution (1736–1770); Douglas Leach, Roots of Conflict: British Armed Forces and Colonial Americans, 1677–1763 (1986); William Pencak, War, Politics, and Revolution in Provincial Massachusetts (1981); Geoffrey Plank, An Unsettled Conquest: The British Campaign Against the Peoples of Acadia (2001); Alan Rogers, Empire and Liberty: American Resistance to British Authority, 1755–1763 (1974); John Shy, Toward Lexington: The Role of the British Army in the Coming of the American Revolution

(1965); David C. Skaggs and Larry Nelson, eds., The Sixty Years' War for the Great Lakes, 1754–1814 (2001); Ian K. Steele, Warpaths: Invasions of North America (1994); James Titus, The Old Dominion at War: Society, Politics, and Warfare in Late Colonial Virginia (1991).

British Politics and Policy

Colin Bonwick, English Radicals and the American Revolution (1977); James E. Bradley, Popular Politics and the American Revolution in England (1986); John Brewer, Party Ideology and Popular Politics at the Accession of George III (1976); John Brooke, King George III (1972); John L. Bullion, A Great and Necessary Measure: George Grenville and the Genesis of the Stamp Act, 1763–1765 (1981); Eliga Gould, The Persistence of Empire: British Political Culture in the Age of the American Revolution (2000); Michael Kammen, A Rope of Sand: The Colonial Agents, British Politics, and the American Revolution (1968); Nancy F. Koehn, The Power of Commerce: Economy and Governance in the First British Empire (1994); Colin Nicolson, The "Infamas Governer": Francis Bernard and the Origins of the American Revolution (2000); P. D. G. Thomas, Tea Party to Independence (1991); P. D. G. Thomas, The Townshend Duties Crisis (1987); P. D. G. Thomas, British Politics and the Stamp Act Crisis (1975).

Native Americans and the West

Richard Aquila, The Iroquois Restoration: Iroquois Diplomacy on the Colonial Frontier, 1701–1754 (1983); Andrew Cayton and Fredrika Teute, eds., Contact Points: American Frontiers from the Mohawk Valley to the Mississippi, 1750–1830 (1998); David H. Corkran, The Cherokee Frontier: Conflict and Survival, 1740–1762 (1962); Gregory Dowd, A Spirited Resistance: The North American Indian Struggle for Unity, 1745–1815 (1992); Gregory Dowd, War Under Heaven: Pontiac, the Indian Nation, and the British Empire (2002); Tom Hatley, The Dividing Paths: Cherokees and South Carolinians through the Revolutionary Era (1995); Eric Hinderaker, Elusive Empires: Confronting Colonialism in the Ohio Valley 1673–1800 (1997); Eric Hinderaker and Peter C. Mancall, At the Edge of Empire: The Backcountry in British North America (2003); Francis Jennings, Empire of Fortune: Crowns, Colonies and Tribes in the Seven Years' War in America (1988); James H. Merrell, Into the American Woods: Negotiators on the Pennsylvania Frontier (1999); Howard H. Peckham, Pontiac and the Indian Uprising (1947); Timothy Shannon, Indians and Colonists at the Crossroads of Empire: The Albany Congress of 1754 (1999); Jack M. Sosin, Whitehall and the Wilderness: The Middle West in British Colonial Policy, 1760–1775 (1961); Richard White, The Middle Ground: Indians, Empires and Republics in the Great Lakes Region, 1650–1815 (1991).

Political and Economic Thought

Bernard Bailyn, The Ideological Origins of the American Revolution (1967); J. C. D. Clark, The Language of Liberty,

1660–1832: Political Discourse and Social Dynamics in the Anglo-American World (1994); J. E. Crowley, This Sheba, Self: The Conceptualization of Economic Life in Eighteenth-Century America (1974); Jay Fliegelman, Prodigals and Pilgrims: The American Revolution Against Patriarchal Authority, 1750–1800 (1982).

American Resistance

T. H. Breen, Tobacco Culture: The Mentality of the Great Tidewater Planters on the Eve of the Revolution (1985); Joseph Albert Ernst, Money and Politics in America, 1755–1775: A Study in the Currency Act of 1764 and the Political Economy of Revolution (1973); David Conroy, Drink and the Revolution of Authority in Colonial Massachusetts (1995); Dirk Hoerder, Crowd Action in Revolutionary Massachusetts, 1765–1780 (1977); Woody Holton, Forced Founders: Indians, Debtors, Slaves, and the Making of the American Revolution in Virginia (1999); Benjamin W. Labaree, The Boston Tea Party (1964); Pauline R. Maier, The Old Revolutionaries: Political Lives in the Age of Samuel Adams (1980); Pauline R. Maier, From Resistance to Revolution: Colonial Radicals and the Development of American Opposition to Britain, 1765–1776 (1972); Edmund S. Morgan and Helen M. Morgan, The Stamp Act Crisis: Prologue to Revolution (1953); Gary B. Nash, The Urban Crucible: Social Change, Political Consciousness, and the Origins of the American Revolution (1979); Bruce A. Ragsdale, A Planters' Republic: The Search for Economic Independence in Revolutionary Virginia (1996); Richard Ryerson, The Revolution Has Now Begun: The Radical Committees of Philadelphia, 1765–1776 (1978); Peter Shaw, American Patriots and the Rituals of Revolution (1981); Peter Thompson, Rum Punch & Revolution: Taverngoing & Public Life in Eighteenth-Century Philadelphia (1999); Joseph Tiedemann, Reluctant Revolutionaries: New York City and the Road to Independence, 1763–1776 (1997); John W. Tyler, Smugglers and Patriots: Boston Merchants and the Advent of the American Revolution (1986); Richard Walsh, Charleston's Sons of Liberty: A Study of the Artisans, 1763–1789 (1959); Hiller B. Zobel, The Boston Massacre (1970).

Chapter 6

General

Colin Bonwick, The American Revolution (1991); Edward Countryman, The American Revolution, rev. ed. (2002); Theodore Draper, A Struggle for Power: The American Revolution (1996); John Ferling, A Leap in the Dark: The Struggle to Create the American Republic (2003); Ronald Hoffman and Peter J. Albert, eds., The Transforming Hand of Revolution: Reconsidering the American Revolution as a Social Movement (1995); Robert Middlekauff, The Glorious Cause: The American Revolution, 1763–1783 (1982); Andrew J. O'Shaughnessy, An Empire Divided: The American Revolution and the British Caribbean (2000); Harry M. Ward, The American Revolution: Nationhood Achieved, 1763–1788 (1995); Gordon S. Wood, The American Revolution (2002); Alfred F. Young, ed., Beyond the American Revolution (1993); Alfred F. Young, ed., The American Revolution: Explorations in the History of American Radicalism (1976).

Continental Congress, Committees, and the Declaration of Independence

David Ammerman, In the Common Cause: American Response to the Coercive Acts of 1774 (1974); Richard D. Brown, Revolutionary Politics in Massachusetts: The Boston Committee of Correspondence and the Towns, 1772–1774 (1970); Jay Fliegelman, Declaring Independence: Jefferson, Natural Language, & the Culture of Performance (1993); Pauline Maier, American Scripture: Making the Declaration of Independence (1997); Jerrilyn Marston, King and Congress: The Transfer of Political Legitimacy, 1774–1776 (1987); Garry Wills, Inventing America: Jefferson's Declaration of Independence (1978); Ann Withington, Toward a More Perfect Union: Virtue and the Formation of American Republics (1992).

Military Affairs

Jeremy Black, War for America: The Fight for Independence, 1775–1783 (1991); Wayne Bodle, The Valley Forge Winter: Civilians and Soldiers in War (2002); Richard Buel, In Irons: Britain's Naval Supremacy and the American Revolutionary Economy (1999); E. Wayne Carp, To Starve the Army at Pleasure: Continental Army Administration and American Political Culture, 1775–1783 (1984); Stephen Conway, The War of American Independence, 1775–1783 (1995); Elizabeth Fenn, Pox Americana: The Great Smallpox Epidemic of 1775–82 (2001); Don Higginbotham, The War of American Independence: Military Attitudes, Policies, and Practice, 1763–1789 (1971); Ronald Hoffman and Peter Albert, eds., Arms and Independence: The Military Character of the American Revolution (1984); Richard Ketchum, Saratoga: Turning Point of America's Revolutionary War (1997); Piers Mackesy, The War for America, 1775–1783 (1964); James K. Martin, Benedict Arnold, Revolutionary Hero (1997); James K. Martin and Mark Lender, "A Respectable Army": The Military Origins of the Republic, 1763–1789 (1982); Charles Niemeyer, America Goes to War: A Social History of the Continental Army (1997); Charles Royster, A Revolutionary People at War: The Continental Army and American Character, 1775–1783 (1980); John Shy, A People Numerous and Armed: Reflections on the Military Struggle for American Independence, rev. ed. (1990).

Local and Regional Studies

Michael Bellesiles, Revolutionary Outlaws: Ethan Allen and the Struggle for Independence on the Early American Frontier (1993); Richard Buel, Dear Liberty: Connecticut's Mobilization for the Revolutionary War (1980); Edward Countryman, A People in Revolution: The American Revolution and Political Society in New York, 1760–1790 (1981); Elaine Crane, A

Dependent People: Newport, Rhode Island, in the Revolutionary Era (1985); Jeffrey Crow and Larry Tise, eds., *The Southern Experience in the American Revolution* (1978); Thomas Doerflinger, *A Vigorous Spirit of Enterprise: Merchants and Economic Development in Revolutionary Philadelphia* (1986); John Mack Faragher, *Daniel Boone* (1992); David Hackett Fischer, *Paul Revere's Ride* (1994); Craig T. Friend, ed., *The Buzzel about Kentucky: Settling the Promised Land* (1999); Francis S. Fox, *Sweet Land of Liberty: The Ordeal of the American Revolution in Northampton County, Pennsylvania* (2002); Robert A. Gross, *The Minutemen and Their World* (1976); Eric Hinderaker, *Elusive Empires: Constructing Colonialism in the Ohio Valley, 1673–1800* (1997); Ronald Hoffman, *A Spirit of Dissension: Economics, Politics, and the Revolution in Maryland* (1973); Ronald Hoffman, Thad W. Tate, and Peter Albert, eds., *An Uncivil War: The Southern Backcountry During the American Revolution* (1985); Woody Holton, *Forced Founders: Indians, Debtors, Slaves, and the Making of the American Revolution in Virginia* (1999); Jean B. Lee, *The Price of Nationhood: The American Revolution in Charles County* (1994); Wayne E. Lee, *Crowds of Soldiers in Revolutionary North Carolina: The Culture of Violence in Riot and War* (2001); Stephen Rosswurm, *Arms, Country, and Class: The Philadelphia Militia and the "Lower Sort" During the American Revolution* (1988); John Selby, *The Revolution in Virginia, 1775–1783* (1988).

Indians and African Americans

Colin Calloway, *The American Revolution in Indian Country* (1995); Sylvia Frey, *Water from the Rock: Black Resistance in a Revolutionary Age* (1991); Barbara Graymont, *The Iroquois in the American Revolution* (1972); Isabel T. Kelsey, *Joseph Brant, 1743–1807: Man of Two Worlds* (1984); James H. O'Donnell III, *Southern Indians in the American Revolution* (1973); Anthony F. C. Wallace, *The Death and Rebirth of the Seneca* (1969).

Loyalists

Bernard Bailyn, *The Ordeal of Thomas Hutchinson* (1974); Robert McCluer Calhoon, *The Loyalists in Revolutionary America, 1760–1781* (1973); Mary Beth Norton, *The British-Americans: The Loyalist Exiles in England, 1774–1789* (1972); Janice Potter, *The Liberty We Seek: Loyalist Ideology in Colonial New York and Massachusetts* (1983); Paul H. Smith, *Loyalists and Redcoats: A Study in British Revolutionary Policy* (1964); James W. St. G. Walker, *The Black Loyalists: The Search for a Promised Land in Nova Scotia and Sierra Leone, 1783–1870* (1976).

Women

Richard Buel and Joy Buel, *The Way of Duty: A Woman and Her Family in Revolutionary America* (1984); Patricia Cleary, *Elizabeth Murray: A Woman's Pursuit of Independence in Eighteenth-Century America* (2000); Edith Gelles, *Portia: The World of Abigail Adams* (1992); Ronald Hoffman and Peter J. Albert, eds., *Women in the Age of the American Revolution* (1989); Linda K. Kerber, *Women of the Republic: Intellect and Ideology in Revolutionary America* (1980); Holly Mayer, *Belonging to the Army: Camp Followers and Community during the American Revolution* (1996); Mary Beth Norton, *Liberty's Daughters: The Revolutionary Experience of American Women, 1750–1800* (1980); Rosemary Zagarri, *A Woman's Dilemma: Mercy Otis Warren and the American Revolution* (1995).

Foreign Policy

Jonathan Dull, *A Diplomatic History of the American Revolution* (1985); Ronald Hoffman and Peter Albert, eds., *Peace and the Peacemakers: The Treaty of 1783* (1986); Ronald Hoffman and Peter Albert, eds., *Diplomacy and Revolution: The Franco-American Alliance of 1778* (1981); Lawrence Kaplan, ed., *The American Revolution and a "Candid World"* (1977); Jan Willem Schulte Nordholt, *The Dutch Republic and American Independence* (1982); Richard W. Van Alstyne, *Empire and Independence: The International History of the American Revolution* (1965).

Patriot Leaders

John K. Alexander, *Samuel Adams: America's Revolutionary Politician* (2002); Joyce O. Appleby, *Thomas Jefferson* (2003); Fawn M. Brodie, *Thomas Jefferson: An Intimate History* (1974); Joseph J. Ellis, *American Sphinx: The Character of Thomas Jefferson* (1997); John E. Ferling, *The First of Men: A Life of George Washington* (1988); Eric Foner, *Tom Paine and Revolutionary America* (1976); Don Higginbotham, *George Washington: Uniting a Nation* (2002); Ronald Hoffman, *Princes of Ireland, Planters of Maryland: A Carroll Saga, 1500–1782* (2000); David McCullough, *John Adams* (2001); Edmund S. Morgan, *Benjamin Franklin* (2002); John Rhodehamel, *The Great Experiment: George Washington and the American Republic* (1998); Charles Royster, *Light-Horse Harry Lee and the Legacy of the American Revolution* (1981); Sheila Skemp, *Benjamin and William Franklin: Father and Son, Patriot and Loyalist* (1994); Esmond Wright, *Franklin of Philadelphia* (1986).

Chapter 7

General

Joyce Appleby, *Inheriting the Revolution: The First Generation of Americans* (2000); Richard Beeman et al., eds., *Beyond Confederation: Origins of the Constitution and American National Identity* (1987); Andrew Burstein, *Sentimental Democracy: The Evolution of America's Romantic Self-Image* (1999); John E. Crowley, *The Privileges of Independence: Neomercantilism and the American Revolution* (1993); Francis Jennings, *The Creation of America: From Revolution to Empire* (2000); Mark E. Kann, *A Republic of Men: The American Founders, Gendered Language, and Patriarchal Politics* (1998); Cathy

Matson and Peter S. Onuf, *A Union of Interests: Political and Economic Thought in Revolutionary America* (1990); Forrest McDonald, *Novus Ordo Seclorum: The Intellectual Origins of the Constitution* (1985); Edmund S. Morgan, *Inventing the People: The Rise of Popular Sovereignty in England and America* (1988); W. M. Verhoeven, ed., *Revolutionary Histories: Transatlantic Cultural Nationalism, 1775–1815* (2002); David Waldstreicher, *In the Midst of Perpetual Fetes: The Making of American Nationalism, 1776–1820* (1997); Gordon S. Wood, *The Radicalism of the American Revolution* (1992); Gordon S. Wood, *The Creation of the American Republic, 1776–1787* (1969); Robert E. Wright, *The Origins of Commercial Banking in America, 1750–1800* (2001); Alfred F. Young et al., eds., *We the People: Voices and Images of the New Nation* (1993); Rosemary Zagarri, *The Politics of Size: Representation in the United States, 1776–1850* (1988).

Continental Congress and Articles of Confederation

E. James Ferguson, *The Power of the Purse: A History of American Public Finance, 1776–1790* (1961); H. James Henderson, *Party Politics in the Continental Congress* (1974); Merrill Jensen, *The New Nation: A History of the United States During the Confederation, 1781–1789* (1950); Richard B. Morris, *The Forging of the Union, 1781–1789* (1987); Peter S. Onuf, *Statehood and Union: A History of the Northwest Ordinance* (1987); Jack N. Rakove, *The Beginnings of National Politics: An Interpretive History of the Continental Congress* (1979).

State Politics

Willi Paul Adams, *The First American Constitutions: Republican Ideology and the Making of the State Constitutions in the Revolutionary Era* (1980); Robert Gross, ed., *In Debt to Shays* (1992); Ronald Hoffman and Peter Albert, eds., *Sovereign States in an Age of Uncertainty* (1981); Donald Lutz, *Popular Consent and Popular Control: Whig Political Theory in the Early State Constitutions* (1980); Jackson Turner Main, *Political Parties Before the Constitution* (1973); Jackson Turner Main, *The Sovereign States, 1775–1783* (1973); David P. Szatmary, *Shays' Rebellion: The Making of an Agrarian Insurrection* (1980).

The Constitution

Thornton Anderson, *Creating the Constitution: The Convention of 1787 and the First Congress* (1993); Lance Banning, *The Sacred Fire of Liberty: James Madison and the Founding of the Federal Republic* (1995); Carol Berkin, *A Brilliant Solution: Inventing the American Constitution* (2002); Roger H. Brown, *Redeeming the Republic: Federalists, Taxation, and the Origins of the Constitution* (1993); Saul Cornell, *The Other Founders: Anti-Federalism & the Dissenting Tradition in America, 1788–1828* (1999); Christopher Duncan, *The Anti-Federalists and Early American Political Thought* (1995); Jackson Turner Main, *The Anti-Federalists: Critics of the Constitution, 1781–1788* (1961); Frederick W. Marks III, *Independence on Trial: Foreign Affairs and the Making of the Constitution* (1973); Jack N. Rakove, *Original Meanings: Politics and Ideas in the Making of the Constitution* (1996); Jack N. Rakove, *James Madison and the Creation of the American Republic* (1990); Robert A. Rutland, *The Ordeal of the Constitution: The Antifederalists and the Ratification Struggle of 1787–88* (1966); Abraham Sofaer, *War, Foreign Affairs, and Constitutional Power*, vol. 1: *The Origins* (1976).

Religion, Education, and Culture

Dee Andrews, *The Methodists and Revolutionary America, 1760–1800* (2000); Cathy N. Davidson, *Revolution and the Word: The Rise of the Novel in America* (1987); Joseph M. Ellis, *After the Revolution: Profiles of Early American Culture* (1979); Charles P. Hanson, *Necessary Virtue: The Pragmatic Origins of Religious Liberty in New England* (1998); Ronald Hoffman and Peter J. Albert, eds., *Religion in a Revolutionary Age* (1994); Carl F. Kaestle, *Pillars of the Republic: Common Schools and American Society, 1780–1860* (1983); Mechal Sobel, *Teach Me Dreams: The Search for Self in the Revolutionary Era* (2000); Russel B. Nye, *The Cultural Life of the New Nation, 1776–1803* (1960); Kenneth Silverman, *A Cultural History of the American Revolution* (1976).

Women

Susan Branson, *These Fiery Frenchified Dames: Women and Political Culture in Early National Philadelphia* (2001); Edith Gelles, *Portia: The World of Abigail Adams* (1992); Ronald Hoffman and Peter Albert, eds., *Women in the Age of the American Revolution* (1989); Susan Juster, *Disorderly Women: Sexual Politics and Evangelicalism in Revolutionary New England* (1994); Linda K. Kerber, *Women of the Republic: Intellect and Ideology in Revolutionary America* (1980); Mary Beth Norton, *Liberty's Daughters: The Revolutionary Experience of American Women, 1750–1800* (1980); Sheila Skemp, *Judith Sargent Murray* (1998).

African Americans and Slavery

Ira Berlin, *Many Thousands Gone: The First Two Centuries of Slavery in North America* (1998); Ira Berlin and Ronald Hoffman, eds., *Slavery and Freedom in the Age of the American Revolution* (1983); Patricia Bradley, *Slavery, Propaganda, and the American Revolution* (1998); David Brion Davis, *The Problem of Slavery in the Age of Revolution, 1770–1823* (1975); Paul Finkelman, *Slavery and the Founders: Race and Liberty in the Age of Jefferson* (1996); Carol V. R. George, *Segregated Sabbaths: Richard Allen and the Emergence of Independent Black Churches, 1760–1840* (1973); Michael A. Gomez, *Exchanging Our Country Marks: The Transformation of African Identities in the Colonial and Antebellum South* (1998); Graham R. Hodges, *Root & Branch: African Americans in New York and East Jersey, 1613–1863* (1999); Winthrop Jordan, *White over Black: American Attitudes Toward the Negro, 1550–1812* (1968); Duncan J. Macleod, *Slav-*

ery, *Race, and the American Revolution* (1974); Joanne Pope Melish, *Disowning Slavery: Gradual Emancipation and "Race" in New England, 1780–1860* (1998); Gary Nash, *Forging Freedom: The Formation of Philadelphia's Black Community, 1720–1840* (1988); Donald L. Robinson, *Slavery in the Structure of American Politics, 1765–1820* (1971); Shane White, *Somewhat More Independent: The End of Slavery in New York City, 1770–1810* (1991); T. Stephen Whitman, *The Price of Freedom: Slavery and Manumission in Baltimore and Early National Maryland* (2000); Arthur Zilversmit, *The First Emancipation: The Abolition of Slavery in the North* (1967).

Indians

Harvey L. Carter, *The Life and Times of Little Turtle* (1987); Gregory E. Dowd, *A Spirited Resistance: The North American Indian Struggle for Unity, 1745–1815* (1992); Frederick Hoxie, et al., eds, *Native Americans and the Early Republic* (1999); Dorothy Jones, *License for Empire: Colonialism by Treaty in Early America* (1982); Wiley Sword, *President Washington's Indian War: The Struggle for the Old Northwest, 1790–1795* (1985); Anthony F. C. Wallace, *The Death and Rebirth of the Seneca* (1969); Richard White, *The Middle Ground: Indians, Empires, and Republics in the Great Lakes Region, 1650–1815* (1991).

Chapter 8

National Government and Administration

Charlene Bickford and Kenneth Bowling, *Birth of the Nation: The Federal Congress, 1789–1791* (2002); Kenneth Bowling, *The Creation of Washington, D.C.* (1991); Richard Brookhiser, *Alexander Hamilton, American* (1999); Ralph Adams Brown, *The Presidency of John Adams* (1975); William Casto, *The Supreme Court in the Early Republic: The Chief Justiceships of John Jay and Oliver Ellsworth* (1995); Stanley Elkins and Eric McKitrick, *The Age of Federalism, 1788–1800* (1993); Joseph J. Ellis, *Founding Brothers: The Revolutionary Generation* (2000); Morton Frisch, *Alexander Hamilton and the Political Order* (1991); Ronald Hoffman and Peter J. Albert, eds., *Launching the "Extended Republic": The Federalist Era* (1998); James H. Hutson, ed., *Religion and the New Republic: Faith in the Founding of America* (1999); Richard Kohn, *Eagle and Sword: The Federalists and the Creation of the Military Establishment in America, 1783–1802* (1975); Tadahisa Kuroda, *The Origins of the Twelfth Amendment: The Electoral College in the Early Republic, 1787–1804* (1994); Stuart Leiberger, *Founding Friendship: George Washington, James Madison, and the Creation of the American Republic* (1999); Forrest McDonald, *Alexander Hamilton* (1979); Forrest McDonald, *The Presidency of George Washington* (1974); John R. Nelson, Jr., *Liberty and Property: Political Economy and Policymaking in the New Nation, 1789–1812* (1987); Mark D. Rozell, et al., eds., *George Washington and the Origins of the American Presidency* (2000); James R. Sharp, *American Politics in the Early Republic: The*

New Nation in Crisis (1993); Garry Wills, *Cincinnatus: George Washington and the Enlightenment* (1984).

Partisan Politics

Lance Banning, *The Jeffersonian Persuasion: Evolution of a Party Ideology* (1978); Richard Buel, *Securing the Revolution: Ideology in American Politics, 1789–1815* (1972); Joseph Charles, *The Origins of the American Party System* (1956); Noble E. Cunningham, *The Jeffersonian Republicans: The Formation of Party Organization, 1789–1801* (1957); Manning J. Dauer, *The Adams Federalists* (1953); Richard Hofstadter, *The Idea of a Party System: The Rise of Legitimate Opposition in the United States, 1780–1840* (1970); Thomas Slaughter, *The Whiskey Rebellion* (1986); John Zvesper, *Political Philosophy and Rhetoric: A Study of the Origins of American Party Politics* (1977).

Economics in Thought and Practice

Joyce Appleby, *Capitalism and a New Social Order: The Republican Vision of the 1790s* (1984); Christopher Clark, *The Roots of Rural Capitalism: Western Massachusetts, 1780–1860* (1990); Paul Gilje, ed., *Wages of Independence: Capitalism in the Early American Republic* (1997); James A. Henretta, *The Origins of American Capitalism* (1991); Allan Kulikoff, *The Agrarian Origins of American Capitalism* (1992); Curtis Nettels, *The Emergence of a National Economy, 1775–1815* (1962); Winifred Rothenberg, *From Market-Places to Market Economy: The Transformation of Rural Massachusetts, 1750–1850* (1992).

Foreign Relations

Harry Ammon, *The Genet Mission* (1973); Samuel F. Bemis, *Jay's Treaty* (1962); Samuel F. Bemis, *Pinckney's Treaty* (1960); Jerald A. Combs, *The Jay Treaty* (1970); Alexander DeConde, *The Quasi-War: Politics and Diplomacy of the Undeclared War with France, 1797–1801* (1966); Alexander DeConde, *Entangling Alliance: Politics and Diplomacy Under George Washington* (1958); Felix Gilbert, *To the Farewell Address: Ideas of Early American Foreign Policy* (1961); Reginald Horsman, *The Diplomacy of the New Republic, 1776–1815* (1985); Lawrence Kaplan, *"Entangling Alliances with None": American Foreign Policy in the Age of Jefferson* (1987); Conor Cruise O'Brien, *The Long Affair: Thomas Jefferson and the French Revolution, 1785–1800* (1996); Bradford Perkins, *The First Rapprochement: England and the United States, 1795–1805* (1967); Matthew Spalding and Patrick J. Garrity, *A Sacred Union of Citizens: George Washington's Farewell Address and American Character* (1996); William Stinchcombe, *The XYZ Affair* (1981); William E. Weeks, *Building the Continental Empire: American Expansion from the Revolution to the Civil War* (1996).

Civil Liberties

Ronald Hoffman and Peter Albert, eds., *The Bill of Rights: Government Proscribed* (1997); Leonard W. Levy, *Emergence of a Free Press* (1985); Leonard W. Levy, *Origins of the Fifth Amendment* (1968); Robert A. Rutland, *The Birth of the Bill of Rights, 1776–1791* (1983); James Morton Smith, *Freedom's Fetters: The Alien and Sedition Laws and American Civil Liberties* (1956).

Indians and African Americans

Douglas Egerton, *Gabriel's Rebellion: The Virginia Slave Conspiracies of 1800 and 1802* (1993); Dorothy Jones, *License for Empire: Colonization by Treaty in Early America* (1982); Michael A. Morrison and James B. Stewart, eds., *Race and the Early Republic: Racial Consciousness and Nation-Building in the Early Republic* (2002); Theda Perdue, *Cherokee Women: Gender and Culture Change, 1700–1835* (1998); Theda Perdue, *"Mixed Blood" Indians: Racial Construction in the Early South* (2003); Francis Paul Prucha, *American Indian Policy in the Formative Years: The Indian Trade and Intercourse Acts, 1790–1834* (1962); James Sidbury, *Ploughshares into Swords: Race, Rebellion, and Identity in Gabriel's Virginia, 1730–1810* (1997); Mechal Sobel, *The World They Made Together: Black and White Values in Eighteenth-Century Virginia* (1987); Anthony F. C. Wallace, *The Death and Rebirth of the Seneca* (1969).

Chapter 9

General

Henry Adams, *History of the United States of America During the Administration of Thomas Jefferson and of James Madison*, 9 vols. (1889–1891); Noble E. Cunningham, Jr., *The United States in 1800: Henry Adams Revisited* (1988); Jean V. Matthews, *Toward a New Society: American Thought and Culture, 1800–1830* (1991); John Mayfield, *The New Nation, 1800–1845* (1981); Marshall Smelser, *The Democratic Republic, 1801–1815* (1968).

Political Culture

Catherine Allgor, *Parlor Politics: In Which the Ladies of Washington Help Build a City and a Government* (2000); James M. Banner, *To the Hartford Convention: The Federalists and the Origins of Party Politics in the Early Republic, 1789–1815* (1967); Noble E. Cunningham, Jr., *The Jeffersonian Republicans in Power: Party Operations, 1801–1809* (1963); David Hackett Fischer, *The Revolution of American Conservatism: The Federalist Party in the Era of Jeffersonian Democracy* (1965); Joanne B. Freeman, *Affairs of Honor: National Politics in the New Republic* (2001); Carol Sue Humphrey, *The Press of the Young Republic, 1783–1833* (1994); Roger G. Kennedy, *Burr, Hamilton, and Jefferson: A Study in Character* (1999); Linda K. Kerber, *Federalists in Dissent* (1970); Richard P. McCormick, *The Presidential Game: The Origins of American Presidential Politics* (1982); Drew McCoy, *The Elusive Republic* (1980); Samuel Eliot Morison, *Harrison Gray Otis, 1765–1848: The Urbane Federalist* (1969); David Paul Nord, *Communities of Journalism: A History of American Newspapers and Their Readers* (2001); Peter S. Onuf, *Jefferson's Empire: The Language of American Nationhood* (2000); Jeffrey L. Pasley, *"The Tyranny of Printers": Newspaper Politics in the Early American Republic* (2001); Arnold A. Rogow, *A Fatal Friendship: Alexander Hamilton and Aaron Burr* (1998); James Roger Sharp, *American Politics in the Early Republic: The New Nation in Crisis* (1993); James Sterling Young, *The Washington Community, 1800–1828* (1966).

Jefferson and Madison

Noble E. Cunningham, Jr., *In Pursuit of Reason: The Life of Thomas Jefferson* (1987); Noble E. Cunningham, Jr., *The Process of Government Under Jefferson* (1978); Joseph J. Ellis, *American Sphinx: The Character of Thomas Jefferson* (1996); Annette Gordon-Reed, *Thomas Jefferson and Sally Hemings: An American Controversy* (1997); Ralph Ketcham, *Presidents Above Party: The First American Presidency, 1789–1829* (1984); Drew R. McCoy, *The Last of the Fathers: James Madison and the Republican Legacy* (1989); Peter S. Onuf, ed., *Jeffersonian Legacies* (1993); Merrill D. Peterson, *Thomas Jefferson and the New Nation* (1970); Norman K. Risjord, *Thomas Jefferson* (1994); Robert Allen Rutland, *The Presidency of James Madison* (1990); Robert W. Tucker and David C. Hendrickson, *Empire of Liberty: The Statecraft of Thomas Jefferson* (1990).

The Supreme Court and the Law

Leonard Baker, *John Marshall: A Life in Law* (1974); Robert Lowry Clinton, *Marbury v. Madison and Judicial Review* (1989); Richard E. Ellis, *The Jeffersonian Crisis: Courts and Politics in the Young Republic* (1971); Morton J. Horowitz, *The Transformation of American Law, 1780–1860* (1977); Herbert A. Johnson, *The Chief Justiceship of John Marshall, 1801–1835* (1997); R. Kent Newmyer, *The Supreme Court Under Marshall and Taney* (1968); Thomas C. Shevory, *John Marshall's Law: Interpretation, Ideology, and Interest* (1994); Francis N. Stites, *John Marshall: Defender of the Constitution* (1981).

Louisiana and Lewis and Clark

Stephen E. Ambrose, *Undaunted Courage: Meriwether Lewis, Thomas Jefferson, and the Opening of the American West* (1996); Alexander De Conde, *This Affair of Louisiana* (1976); Albert Furtwangler, *Acts of Discovery: Visions of America in the Lewis and Clark Journals* (1993); Donna J. Kessler, *The Making of Sacagawea: A Euro-American Legend* (1996); James P. Ronda, *Lewis and Clark Among the Indians* (1984); James P. Ronda, ed., *Thomas Jefferson and the Changing West* (1997); James P. Ronda, ed., *Voyage of Discovery: Essays on the Lewis and Clark Expedition* (1998).

Indian Resistance

Gregory Evans Dowd, *A Spiritual Resistance: The North American Indian Struggle for Unity, 1745–1815* (1992); R. David Edmunds, *Tecumseh and the Quest for Indian Leadership* (1984); R. David Edmunds, *The Shawnee Prophet* (1983); John Sugden, *Tecumseh: A Life* (1998); Anthony F. C. Wallace, *Jefferson and the Indians: The Tragic Fate of the First Americans* (1999); James Wilson, *The Earth Shall Weep: A History of Native America* (1998).

Expansionism, the War of 1812, and Foreign Relations

Robert J. Allison, *The Crescent Obscured: The United States and the Muslim World, 1776–1815* (1995); Paul Baepler, ed., *White Slaves, African Masters: An Anthology of American Barbary Captivity Narratives* (1999); Roger H. Brown, *The Republic in Peril* (1964); Clifford L. Egan, *Neither Peace nor War: Franco-American Relations, 1803–1812* (1983); Kenneth J. Hagan, *This People's Navy* (1991); Donald R. Hickey, *The War of 1812: A Short History* (1995); Frank Lawrence Owsley, Jr., and Gene A. Smith, *Filibusters and Expansionists: Jeffersonian Manifest Destiny, 1800–1821* (1997); Bradford Perkins, *The Creation of a Republican Empire, 1776–1865* (1993); Julius W. Pratt, *Expansionists of 1812* (1925); Robert V. Remini, *The Battle of New Orleans: Andrew Jackson and America's First Military Victory* (1999); David Curtis Skaggs and Gerard T. Altoff, *A Signal Victory: The Lake Erie Campaign 1812–1813* (1997); J. C. A. Stagg, *Mr. Madison's War: Politics, Diplomacy, and Warfare in the Early Republic, 1783–1830* (1983); Anders Stephanson, *Manifest Destiny: American Expansionism and the Empire of Right* (1995); Steve Watts, *The Republic Reborn: War and the Making of a Liberal America, 1790–1820* (1987); David J. Weber, *The Spanish Frontier in North America* (1992); J. Leitch Wright, Jr., *Creeks and Seminoles: The Destruction and Regeneration of the Muscogulge People* (1986).

Commerce and Industry

Robert F. Dalzell, Jr., *Enterprising Elite: The Boston Associates and the World They Made* (1987); David A. Hounshell, *From the American System to Mass Production, 1800–1932: The Development of Manufacturing Technology in the United States* (1984); David J. Jeremy, *Transatlantic Industrial Revolution: The Diffusion of Textile Technologies Between Britain and America, 1790s–1830s* (1981): Walter Licht, *Industrializing America: The Nineteenth Century* (1995); Peter Temin (ed.), *Engines of Enterprise: An Economic History of New England* (2000).

Chapter 10

General

Stanley L. Engerman and Robert E. Gallman (eds.), *The Cambridge Economic History of the United States, vol. II, The*

Long Nineteenth Century (2000); Jack Larkin, *The Reshaping of Everyday Life, 1790–1840* (1988); D. W. Meinig, *The Shaping of America: A Geographical Perspective on 500 Years of History*, vol. 2: *Contininental America, 1800–1867* (1993); Charles G. Sellers, Jr., *The Market Revolution: Jacksonian America, 1815–1840* (1991); Melvyn Stokes and Stephen Conway, eds., *The Market Revolution in America: Social, Political, and Religious Expressions, 1800–1860* (1996).

Postwar Nationalism

Harry Ammon, *James Monroe: The Quest for National Identity* (1971); Noble E. Cunningham, *The Presidency of James Monroe* (1996); Mary W. M. Hargreaves, *The Presidency of John Quincy Adams* (1985); Morton J. Horowitz, *The Transformation of American Law, 1780–1860* (1977); Ralph Ketcham, *Presidents Above Party: The First American Presidency, 1789–1829* (1984); Walter LaFeber, ed., *John Quincy Adams and American Continental Empire* (1965); Ernest R. May, *The Making of the Monroe Doctrine* (1976); Paul C. Nagel, *John Quincy Adams: A Public Life, a Private Life* (1997); R. Kent Newmyer, *The Supreme Court Under Marshall and Taney* (1968); Dexter Perkins, *Hands Off: A History of the Monroe Doctrine* (1941); Robert V. Remini, *Henry Clay: Statesman for the Union* (1991); Thomas C. Shevory, *John Marshall's Law: Interpretation, Ideology, and Interest* (1994); William Earl Weeks, *John Quincy Adams and American Global Empire* (1992).

The Market Economy, Manufacturing, and Commerce

Stuart Bruchey, *Enterprise: The Dynamic Economy of a Free People* (1990); Alfred D. Chandler, Jr., *The Visible Hand: Managerial Revolution in American Business* (1977); William Cronon, *Nature's Metropolis: Chicago and the Great West* (1991); Paul A. Gilje, ed., *Wages of Independence: Capitalism in the Early American Republic* (1997); Louis Hartz, *Economic Policy and Democratic Thought: Pennsylvania, 1776–1860* (1954); David A. Hounshell, *From the American System to Mass Production, 1800–1932: The Development of Manufacturing Technology in the United States* (1984); David J. Jeremy, *Transatlantic Industrial Revolution: The Diffusion of Textile Technologies Between Britain and America, 1790s–1830s* (1981); Herbert A. Johnson, *The Chief Justiceship of John Marshall, 1801–1835* (1997); David Klingaman and Richard Vedder, eds., *Essays in Nineteenth-Century History* (1975); Stanley I. Kutler, *Privilege and Creative Destruction: The Charles River Bridge Case* (1971); Walter Licht, *Industrializing America: The Nineteenth Century* (1995); Otto Mayr and Robert C. Post, eds., *Yankee Enterprise: The Rise of the American System of Manufacturers* (1981); Douglass C. North, *Economic Growth of the United States, 1790–1860* (1966); Theodore Steinberg, *Nature Incorporated: Industrialization and the Waters of New England* (1991); Peter Temin (ed.), *Engines of Enterprise: An Economic History of New England* (2000).

Transportation

Albert Fishlow, *American Railroads and the Transformation of the Ante-Bellum Economy* (1965); Carter Goodrich, *Government Promotion of American Canals and Railroads, 1800–1890* (1960); Louis C. Hunter, *Steamboats on the Western Rivers* (1949); Richard R. John, *Spreading the News: The American Postal System from Franklin to Morse* (1995); John Laurite Larson, *Internal Improvement: National Public Works and the Promise of Popular Government in the Early United States* (2001); Harry N. Scheiber, *Ohio Canal Era: A Case Study of Government and the Economy, 1820–1861* (1969); Ronald E. Shaw, *Canals for a Nation: The Canal Era in the United States, 1790–1860* (1990); Carol Sheriff, *The Artificial River: The Erie Canal and the Paradox of Progress, 1817–1862* (1996); George R. Taylor, *The Transportation Revolution, 1815–1860* (1951); James A. Ward, *Railroads and the Character of America, 1820–1887* (1986).

Commercial Farming

"American Agriculture, 1790–1840, A Symposium," *Agricultural History* 46 (January 1972); Jeremy Atack and Fred Bateman, *To Their Own Soil: Agriculture in the Antebellum North* (1987); Allen G. Bogue, *From Prairie to Corn Belt: Farming on the Illinois and Iowa Prairies in the Nineteenth Century* (1963); Christopher Clark, *The Roots of Rural Capitalism: Western Massachusetts, 1780–1860* (1990); Clarence Danhof, *Change in Agriculture: The Northern United States, 1820–1870* (1969); Paul W. Gates, *The Farmer's Age: Agriculture, 1815–1860* (1962); Benjamin H. Hibbard, *A History of Public Land Policies* (1939); Joan M. Jensen, *Loosening the Bonds: Mid-Atlantic Farm Women, 1750–1850* (1986); Robert Leslie Jones, *History of Agriculture in Ohio to 1880* (1983); Peter D. McClelland, *Sowing Modernity: America's First Agricultural Revolution* (1999); Sally McMurry, *Transforming Rural Life: Dairying Families and Agricultural Change, 1820–1885* (1995); Gavin Wright, *The Political Economy of the Cotton South* (1978).

Workers

Mary H. Blewett, *Men, Women, and Work: Class, Gender, and Protest in the New England Shoe Industry, 1780–1910* (1988); Jeanne Boydston, *Home and Work: Housework, Wages, and the Ideology of Labor in the Early Republic* (1990); Thomas Dublin, *Transforming Women's Work: New England Lives in the Industrial Revolution* (1994); Thomas Dublin, *Women at Work: The Transformation of Work and Community in Lowell, Massachusetts, 1826–1860* (1979); Bruce Laurie, *Artisans into Workers: Labor in Nineteenth-Century America* (1989); Howard B. Rock, Paul A. Gilje, and Robert Asher, eds., *American Artisans: Crafting Social Identity, 1750–1850* (1995); Sean Wilentz, *Chants Democratic: New York City and the Rise of the American Working Class, 1788–1850* (1984); David A. Zonderman, *Aspirations and Anxieties: New England Workers and the Mechanized Factory System, 1815–1850* (1992).

Americans on the Move

Joan Cashin, *A Family Venture: Men and Women on the Southern Frontier* (1991); James E. Davis, *Frontier America 1800–1840: A Comparative Demographic Analysis of the Frontier Process* (1977); Stewart Holbrook, *The Yankee Exodus: An Account of Migration from New England* (1950); Julie Roy Jeffrey, *Frontier Women: The Trans-Mississippi West, 1840–1880* (1979); Peter D. McClelland and Richard J. Zeckhauser, eds., *Demographic Dimensions of the New Republic* (1982); Virginia E. and Robert W. McCormick, *New Englanders on the Ohio Frontier* (1998); Gerald McFarland, *A Scattered People: An American Family Moves West* (1985); James Hebron Moore, *The Emergence of the Cotton Kingdom in the Old Southwest: Mississippi, 1770–1860* (1987); James Oakes, *The Ruling Race: A History of American Slaveholders* (1982); Malcom J. Rohrbough, *The Trans-Appalachian Frontier: People, Societies, and Institutions, 1775–1850* (1978); Russell Thornton, *American Indian Holocaust and Survival: A Population History Since 1492* (1987); David J. Weber, *The Spanish Frontier in North America* (1992); Richard White, *"It's Your Misfortune and None of My Own": A History of the American West* (1991).

Native American Resistance and Removal

Linda Barrington (ed.), *The Other Side of the Frontier: Economic Explorations into Native American History* (1999); Robert F. Berkhofer, Jr., *The White Man's Indian* (1978); Paul H. Carlson, *The Plains Indians* (1998); James W. Covington, *The Seminoles of Florida* (1993); Carol Devens, *Countering Colonization: Native American Women and Great Lakes Missions, 1630–1900* (1992); Michael D. Green, *The Politics of Indian Removal: Creek Government and Society in Crisis* (1982); Joseph B. Herring, *The Enduring Indians of Kansas: A Century and a Half of Acculturation* (1990); Stanley W. Hoig, *The Cherokees and Their Chiefs in the Wake of Empire* (1998); William G. McLoughlin, *Cherokee Renascence in the New Republic* (1986); Theda Perdue, *Slavery and the Evolution of Cherokee Society, 1540–1866* (1979); Ronald N. Satz, *American Indian Policy in the Jacksonian Era* (1975); Daniel H. Usner, Jr., *American Indians in the Lower Mississippi Valley* (1998); Anthony F. C. Wallace, *The Long, Bitter Trail: Andrew Jackson and the Indians* (1993); Richard White, *The Roots of Dependency: Subsistence, Environment, and Social Change Among the Choctaws, Pawnees, and Navajos* (1983); James Wilson, *The Earth Shall Weep: A History of Native America* (1998); J. Leitch Wright, Jr., *Creeks and Seminoles: The Destruction and Regeneration of the Muscogulge People* (1986).

Chapter 11

General

George Dangerfield, *The Awakening of American Nationalism, 1815–1828* (1965); Daniel Feller, *The Jacksonian Promise:*

America, 1815–1840 (1995); Isabelle Lehru, *Carnival on the Page: Popular Print Media in Antebellum America* (2000); Jean V. Matthews, *Toward a New Society: American Thought and Culture, 1800–1830* (1991); John Mayfield, *The New Nation, 1800–1845* (1981); Charles Sellers, *The Market Revolution: Jacksonian America, 1815–1846* (1991).

Religion, Revivalism, and Reform

Robert H. Abzug, *Cosmos Crumbling: American Reform and the Religious Imagination* (1994); Michael Barkun, *Crucible of the Millennium: The Burned-over District of New York in the 1840s* (1986); Terry Bilhartz, *Urban Religion and the Second Great Awakening: Church and Society in Early National Baltimore* (1986); Paul K. Conkin, *The Uneasy Center: Reformed Christianity in Antebellum America* (1995); Clifford S. Griffen, *Their Brothers' Keepers: Moral Stewardship in the United States, 1800–1865* (1960); Keith J. Hardman, *Charles Grandison Finney, 1792–1875: Revivalist and Reformer* (1987); Nathan O. Hatch, *The Democratization of American Christianity* (1989); Christine Leigh Heyrman, *Southern Cross: The Beginnings of the Bible Belt* (1997); Winthrop S. Hudson and John Corrigan, *Religion in America*, 6th ed. (1999); Curtis D. Johnson, *Islands of Holiness: Rural Religion in Upstate New York, 1790–1860* (1989); Paul E. Johnson, *A Shopkeeper's Millennium: Society and Revivals in Rochester, New York, 1815–1837* (1978); Steven Mintz, *Moralists and Modernizers: America's Pre-Civil War Reformers* (1995); Timothy L. Smith, *Revivalism and Social Reform in Mid-Nineteenth Century America* (1957); Alice Felt Tyler, *Freedom's Ferment* (1944); Ronald G. Walters, *American Reformers, 1815–1860*, rev. ed. (1997).

Temperance, Asylums, and Antimasonry

Thomas J. Brown, *Dorothea Dix: New England Reformer* (1998); Steven C. Bullock, *Revolutionary Brotherhood: Freemasonry and the Transformation of the American Social Order, 1730–1840* (1996); David Gollaher, *Voice for the Mad: The Life of Dorothea Dix* (1995); Paul Goodman, *Towards a Christian Republic: Antimasonry and the Great Transition in New England, 1826–1836* (1988); Gerald N. Grob, *Mental Institutions in America: Social Policy to 1875* (1973); Kathleen Smith Kutolowski, "Antimasonry Reexamined: Social Bases of the Grass-Roots Party," *Journal of American History* 71 (September 1984): 269–293; W. J. Rorabaugh, *The Alcoholic Republic: An American Tradition* (1979); David J. Rothman, *The Discovery of the Asylum: Social Order and Disorder in the New Republic* (1971); Ian R. Tyrrell, *Sobering Up: From Temperance to Prohibition in Antebellum America, 1800–1860* (1979); William Preston Vaughn, *The Antimasonic Party in the United States, 1826–1843* (1983).

Women and Reform

Barbara J. Berg, *The Remembered Gate: Origins of American Feminism: The Woman and the City, 1800–1860* (1977); Ellen C. Du Bois, *Feminism and Suffrage: The Emergence of an Independent Woman's Movement in America, 1848–1869* (1978); Barbara Leslie Epstein, *The Politics of Domesticity: Women, Evangelism, and Temperance in Nineteenth-Century America* (1981); Lori D. Ginzberg, *Women and the Work of Benevolence: Morality, Politics, and Class in the Nineteenth-Century United States* (1990); Debra Gold Hansen, *Strained Sisterhood: Gender and Class in the Boston Female Anti-Slavery Society* (1993); Nancy A. Hewitt, *Women's Activism and Social Change: Rochester, New York, 1822–1872* (1984); Sylvia D. Hoffert, *When Hens Crow: The Woman's Rights Movement in Antebellum America* (1995); Nancy Isenberg, *Sex and Citizenship in Antebellum America* (1998); Gerda Lerner, *The Grimké Sisters of South Carolina* (1967); Jean V. Matthews, *Women's Struggle for Equality: The First Phase, 1828–1876* (1997); Amanda Porterfield, *Mary Lyon and the Mount Holyoke Missionaries* (1997); Carla L. Peterson, *"Doers of the Word": African-American Women Speakers and Writers in the North, 1830–1880* (1995); Mary P. Ryan, *Cradle of the Middle Class: The Family in Oneida County, New York, 1790–1865* (1981); Mary P. Ryan, *Women in Public: Between Banners and Ballots, 1825–1880* (1990); Jean Fagan Yellin, *Women & Sisters: The Antislavery Feminists in American Culture* (1989).

Antislavery and Abolitionism

James Brewer Stewart, *Holy Warriors: The Abolitionists and American Slavery*, rev. ed. (1996); David Brion Davis, *Slavery and Human Progress* (1984); Frederick Douglass, *Life and Times of Frederick Douglass* (1881); Audrey Fisch, *American Slaves in Victorian England: Aboloitionist Politics in Popular Literature and Culture* (2000); George M. Fredrickson, *The Black Image in the White Mind: The Debate on Afro-American Character and Destiny, 1817–1914* (1971); Paul Goodman, *Of One Blood: Abolitionism and the Origins of Racial Equality* (1998); David Grimsted, *American Mobbing, 1828–1861* (1998); Julie Roy Jeffrey, *The Great Silent Army of Abolitionism: Ordinary Women in the AntiSlavery Movement* (1998); Aileen S. Kraditor, *Means and Ends in American Abolitionism: Garrison and His Critics on Strategy and Tactics* (1967); Henry Mayer, *All on Fire: William Lloyd Garrison and the Abolition of Slavery* (1998); William Lee Miller, *Arguing About Slavery: The Great Battle in the United States Congress* (1995); Richard J. Newman, *The Transformation of American Abolitionism: Fighting Slavery in the Early Republic* (2002); William H. Pease and Jane H. Pease, *They Who Would Be Free: Blacks' Search for Freedom, 1830–1861* (1974); Benjamin Quarles, *Black Abolitionists* (1969); Peter C. Ripley, (ed.), *The Black Abolitionist Papers, vol. I, The British Isles, 1830–1865* (1985); John Stauffer, *The Black Hearts of Men: Radical Abolitionists and the Transformation of Race* (2002); John L. Thomas, *The Liberator: William Lloyd*

Garrison (1963); Ronald G. Walters, *The Antislavery Appeal: American Abolitionism After 1830* (1976); Shirley J. Yee, *Black Women Abolitionists: A Study in Activism, 1828–1860* (1992).

Politics and Diplomacy, 1816–1828

Harry Ammon, *James Monroe: The Quest for National Identity* (1971); Noble E. Cunningham, *The Presidency of James Monroe* (1996); Mary W. M. Hargreaves, *The Presidency of John Quincy Adams* (1985); Morton J. Horowitz, *The Transformation of American Law, 1780–1860* (1977); Ralph Ketcham, *Presidents Above Party: The First American Presidency, 1789–1829* (1984); Walter LaFeber, ed., *John Quincy Adams and American Continental Empire* (1965); Ernest R. May, *The Making of the Monroe Doctrine* (1976); Paul C. Nagel, *John Quincy Adams: A Public Life, a Private Life* (1997); R. Kent Newmyer, *The Supreme Court Under Marshall and Taney* (1968); Dexter Perkins, *Hands Off: A History of the Monroe Doctrine* (1941); Robert V. Remini, *Henry Clay: Statesman for the Union* (1991); Thomas C. Shevory, *John Marshall's Law: Interpretation, Ideology, and Interest* (1994); William Earl Weeks, *John Quincy Adams and American Global Empire* (1992).

Andrew Jackson and the Jacksonians

Donald B. Cole, *Martin Van Buren and the American Political System* (1984); Michael F. Holt, *Political Parties and American Political Development from the Age of Jackson to the Age of Lincoln* (1992); Richard B. Latner, *The Presidency of Andrew Jackson* (1979); John F. Marszalek, *The Petticoat Affair: Manners, Mutiny, and Sex in Andrew Jackson's White House* (1997); Marvin Meyers, *The Jacksonian Persuasion* (1960); John Niven, *Martin Van Buren* (1983); Edward Pessen, *Jacksonian America: Society, Personality, and Politics*, rev. ed. (1979); Robert V. Remini, *The Legacy of Andrew Jackson: Essays on Democracy, Indian Removal, and Slavery* (1988); Robert V. Remini, *The Life of Andrew Jackson* (1988); Harry L. Watson, *Liberty and Power: The Politics of Jacksonian America* (1990).

Democrats and Whigs

William J. Cooper, *The South and the Politics of Slavery, 1828–1856* (1978); Ronald P. Formisano, *The Transformation of Political Culture: Massachusetts Parties, 1790s–1840s* (1983); William W. Freehling, *Prelude to Civil War: The Nullification Controversy in South Carolina* (1966); Michael F. Holt, *The Rise and Fall of the American Whig Party* (1999); Daniel Walker Howe, *The Political Culture of the American Whigs* (1979); Lawrence Frederick Kohl, *The Politics of Individualism: Parties and the American Character in the Jacksonian Era* (1989); Richard P. McCormick, *The Second American Party System: Party Formation in the Jacksonian Era* (1966); Merrill D. Peterson, *The Great Triumvirate: Webster, Clay, and Calhoun* (1987); Norma Lois Peterson, *The Presidencies of William Henry Harrison and John Tyler* (1989); James Roger Sharp, *The Jacksonians Versus the Banks: Politics in the States After the Panic of 1837* (1970).

Manifest Destiny and Foreign Policy

John M. Belohlavek, *Let the Eagle Soar! The Foreign Policy of Andrew Jackson* (1985); T. R. Fehrenbach, *Lone Star: A History of Texas and the Texans* (1968); Norman B. Graebner, ed., *Manifest Destiny* (1968); Thomas R. Hietala, *Manifest Destiny: Anxious Aggrandizement in Late Jacksonian America* (1985); Reginald Horsman, *Race and Manifest Destiny* (1981); Michael Hunt, *Ideology and U.S. Foreign Policy* (1987); Bradford Perkins, *The Creation of a Republican Empire, 1776–1865* (1993); David M. Pletcher, *The Diplomacy of Annexation: Texas, Oregon, and the Mexican War* (1973); Charles G. Sellers, Jr., *James K. Polk: Continentalist, 1843–1846* (1966); Anders Stephanson, *Manifest Destiny: American Expansionism and the Empire of Right* (1995); Paul A. Varg, *United States Foreign Relations, 1820–1860* (1979); David J. Weber, *The Spanish Frontier in North America* (1992); Albert K. Weinberg, *Manifest Destiny* (1935).

The Supreme Court and the Law

Leonard Baker, *John Marshall: A Life in Law* (1974); Francis N. Stites, *John Marshall: Defender of the Constitution* (1981).

Chapter 12

Rural and Utopian Communities

Leonard J. Arrington and Davis Bitton, *The Mormon Experience: A History of the Latterday Saints* (1979); Priscilla J. Brewer, *Shaker Communities, Shaker Lives* (1986); David B. Danbom, *Born in the Country: A History of Rural America* (1995); John Mack Faragher, *Sugar Creek: Life on the Illinois Prairie* (1986); Laurence Foster, *Religion and Sexuality: Three American Communal Experiments of the Nineteenth Century* (1981); Steven Hahn and Jonathan Prude, eds., *The Countryside in the Age of Capitalist Transformation* (1985); Joan M. Jensen, *Loosening the Bonds: Mid-Atlantic Farm Women, 1750–1850* (1986); Sally McMurry, *Families and Farmhouses in Nineteenth Century America: Vernacular Design and Social Change* (1988); Anthony F. C. Wallace, *Rockdale: The Growth of an American Village in the Early Industrial Revolution* (1978); Kenneth H. Winn, *Exiles in a Land of Liberty: Mormons in America, 1830–1846* (1989).

The West

William Benemann (ed.), *A Year of Mud and Gold: San Francisco in Letters and Diaries, 1819–1850* (1999); John Mack Faragher, *Women and Men on the Overland Trail* (1979); Ramón A. Gutiérrez and Richard J. Orsi, eds., *Contested Eden: California Before the Gold Rush* (1998); Julie Roy Jeffrey, *Frontier Women: The Trans-Mississippi West, 1840–1880* (1979); Rudolph M. Lapp, *Blacks in Gold Rush California* (1977); Kenneth N. Owens (ed.), *Riches for All: The California Gold Rush and the World* (2002); Malcolm J. Rohrbough, *Days of Gold: The California Gold Rush and the American Nation* (1997); Quintard Taylor, *In Search of the Racial Fron-*

tier: *African Americans in the American West, 1528–1990* (1998); John D. Unruh, Jr., *The Overland Emigrants and the Trans-Mississippi West, 1840–1860* (1979); David J. Weber, *The Spanish Frontier in North America* (1992); Richard White, *"It's Your Misfortune and None of My Own": A History of the American West* (1991).

Urban Communities

Melvin A. Adelman, *A Sporting Time: New York City and the Rise of Modern Athletics, 1820–1870* (1986); Tyler Anbinder, *Five Points* (2001); Stuart M. Blumin, *The Emergence of the Middle Class: Social Experience in the American City, 1760–1900* (1989); Edwin G. Burrows and Mike Wallace, *Gotham: A History of New York City to 1898* (1999); Susan G. Davis, *Parades and Power: Street Theater in Nineteenth-Century Philadelphia* (1986); Timothy J. E. Gilfoyle, *City of Eros: New York City, Prostitution, and the Commercialization of Sex, 1790–1920* (1992); Karen V. Hansen, *A Very Social Time: Crafting Community in Antebellum New England* (1994); Carl Kaestle, *Pillars of the Republic: Common Schools and American Society, 1780–1860* (1982); Jack Larkin, *The Reshaping of Everyday Life, 1790–1840* (1988); Timothy R. Mahoney, *Provincial Lives: Middle-Class Experience in the Antebellum Middle West* (1999); Edward Pessen, *Riches, Class and Power Before the Civil War* (1973); Christine Stansell, *City of Women: Sex and Class in New York, 1789–1860* (1986); Richard B. Stott, *Workers in the Metropolis: Class, Ethnicity, and Youth in Antebellum New York City* (1990); Alexis de Tocqueville, *Democracy in America*, 2 vols. (1835, 1840).

Family Life

Virginia K. Bartlett, *Keeping House: Women's Lives in Western Pennsylvania, 1790–1850* (1994); Janet Farrell Brodie, *Contraception and Abortion in Nineteenth-Century America* (1994); Lee Virginia Chambers-Schiller, *Liberty, A Better Husband: Single Women in America: The Generations of 1780–1840* (1984); Clifford Edward Clark, Jr., *The American Family Home, 1800–1960* (1986); Nancy F. Cott, *The Bonds of Womanhood: Woman's Sphere in New England, 1780–1835* (1977); Linda Gordon, *Woman's Body, Woman's Rights: A Social History of Birth Control in America* (1976); Joan Hoff, *Law, Gender and Injustice: A Legal History of U.S. Women* (1991); Suzanne Lebsock, *The Free Women of Petersburg: Status and Culture in a Southern Town, 1784–1860* (1984); Glenda Riley, *Divorce: An American Tradition* (1991); Mary P. Ryan, *Cradle of the Middle Class: The Family in Oneida County, New York, 1790–1865* (1981); Kathryn Kish Sklar, *Catharine Beecher: A Study in American Domesticity* (1973); Maris A. Vinovskis, *Fertility in Massachusetts from the Revolution to the Civil War* (1981); Robert V. Wells, *Revolutions in Americans' Lives* (1982); Barbara Welter, "The Cult of True Womanhood, 1820–1860," *American Quarterly* 18 (Summer 1966): 151–174.

Immigrants and Hispanics

Thomás Almaguer, *Racial Fault Lines: The Historical Origins of White Supremacy in California* (1994); Gunther Barth, *Bitter Strength: A History of Chinese in the United States, 1850–1870* (1964); Ronald H. Bayor and Timothy J. Meagher (eds.), *The New York Irish* (1996); Kathleen Neils Conzen, *Immigrant Milwaukee: 1836–1860* (1976); Arnoldo De León, *The Tejano Community, 1836–1900* (1982); Hasia R. Diner, *Erin's Daughters in America: Irish Immigrant Women in the Nineteenth Century* (1983); David A. Gerber, *The Making of an American Pluralism: Buffalo, New York, 1825–60* (1989); David T. Gleeson, *The Irish in the South, 1815–1877* (2001); Victor R. Greene, *American immigrant Leaders 1800–1910* (1987); Noel Ignatiev, *How the Irish Became White* (1995); Matthew Frye Jacobson, *Whiteness of a Different Color: European Immigrants and the Alchemy of Race* (1998); Walter D. Kamphoefner, *The Westfalians: From Germany to Missouri* (1987); Dale T. Knobel, *Paddy and the Republic: Ethnicity and Nationality in Antebellum America* (1986); Sallie A. Marston, "Public rituals and community power: St. Patrick's Day parades in Lowell, Massachusetts, 1841–1874," *Political Geography Quarterly* 8 (July, 1989), 255–269; Timothy M. Matovina, *Tejano Religion and Ethnicity: San Antonio, 1821–1860* (1995); Kerby A. Miller, *Emigrants and Exiles: Ireland and the Irish Exodus to North America* (1985); Brian Mitchell, *The Paddy Camps: The Irish of Lowell, 1821–61* (1988); Stanley Nadel, *Little Germany: Ethnicity, Religion, and Class in New York City, 1845–80* (1990); David Roediger, *The Wages of Whiteness: Race and the Making of the Working Class* (1991); David J. Weber, *The Spanish Frontier in North America* (1992); Mark Wyman, *Immigrants in the Valley: Irish, Germans, and Americans in the Upper Mississippi, 1830–1860* (1984).

Free People of Color and Race

Ira Berlin, *Slaves Without Masters: The Free Negro in the Antebellum South* (1974); Elizabeth Rauh Bethel, *The Roots of African-American Identity: Memory and History in Antebellum Free Communities* (1997); Dale Cockrell, *Demons of Disorder: Early Blackface Minstrels and Their World* (1997); Leonard P. Curry, *The Free Black in Urban America, 1800–1850* (1981); Thomas F. Gossett, *Race: The History of an Idea in America* (1963); James O. Horton and Lois E. Horton, *In Hope of Liberty: Culture, Community and Protest Among Northern Free Blacks, 1700–1860* (1996); Luther Porter Jackson, *Free Negro Labor and Property Holding in Virginia, 1830–1860* (1942); David M. Katzman, *Before the Ghetto: Black Detroit in the Nineteenth Century* (1973); W. T. Lhamon, Jr., *Raising Cain: Blackface Performance from Jim Crow to Hip Hop* (1998); Leon Litwack, *North of Slavery: The Negro in the Free States, 1790–1860* (1961); Eric Lott, *Love and Theft: Blackface Minstrelsy and the American Working Class* (1995); Joanne Pope Melish, *Disowning Slavery: Gradual Emancipation and Race in New England, 1780–1860* (1998); Floyd J. Miller, *The Search for a Black Nationality:*

Black Colonization and Emigration, 1787–1863 (1975); Gary B. Nash, *Forging Freedom: The Formation of Philadelphia's Black Community, 1720–1840* (1988); Benjamin Quarles, *Black Abolitionists* (1969); Patrick Rael, *Black Identity & Black Protest in the Antebellum North* (2002); Quintard Taylor, *In Search of the Racial Frontier: African Americans in the American West, 1528–1990* (1998); Shane White and Graham White, *Stylin': African American Expressive Culture from its Beginnings to the Zoot Suit* (1998); Julie Winch, *A Gentleman of Color: The Life of James Forten* (2002); Arthur Zilversmit, *The First Emancipation: The Abolition of Slavery in the North* (1967).

Chapter 13

The Peculiar South

Wilbur J. Cash, *The Mind of the South* (1939); Carl N. Degler, *Place Over Time* (1977); David Goldfield, *Still Fighting the Civil War: The American South and Southern History* (2002); Drew G. Faust, "The Peculiar South Revisited," in John B. Boles and Evelyn T. Nolen, eds., *Interpreting Southern History* (1987), 78–119; James Oakes, *Slavery and Freedom* (1990); C. Vann Woodward, *The Burden of Southern History* (1960).

Southern Society

Edward L. Ayers, *Vengeance and Justice* (1984); Bradley G. Bond, *Political Culture in the Nineteenth-Century South* (1995); Randolph B. Campbell, "Planters and Plain Folks," in Boles and Nolen, eds., *Interpreting Southern History* (1987); William J. Cooper, *The South and the Politics of Slavery, 1828–1856* (1978); William W. Freehling, *Prelude to Civil War* (1965); Eugene D. Genovese, *The Political Economy of Slavery* (1965); Peter Kolchin, *Unfree Labor: American Slavery and Russian Serfdom* (1987); Donald G. Mathews, *Religion in the Old South* (1977); Christine L. Heyrman, *Southern Cross* (1997); James Hebron Moore, *The Emergence of the Cotton Kingdom in the Old Southwest: Mississippi, 1770–1860* (1987); Frederick Law Olmsted, *The Slave States*, ed. Harvey Wish (1959); Manisha Sinha, *The Counter-Revolution of Slavery* (2000); Charles S. Sydnor, *The Development of Southern Sectionalism, 1819–1848* (1948); Larry E. Tise, *Proslavery* (1987); Ralph A. Wooster, *Politicians, Planters, and Plain Folk* (1975); Gavin Wright, *The Political Economy of the Cotton South* (1978); Bertram Wyatt-Brown, *Southern Honor* (1982).

Slaveholders and Nonslaveholders

Edward L. Ayers and John C. Willis, eds., *The Edge of the South* (1991); Bennet H. Barrow, *Plantation Life in the Florida Parishes of Louisiana*, ed. Edwin Adams Davis (1943); Ira Berlin, *Slaves Without Masters* (1974); Joan E. Cashin, *A Family Venture* (1991); Bill Cecil-Fronsman, *The Common Whites* (1992); Charles B. Dew, *Bond of Iron* (1995); Stanley Engerman, Seymour Drescher, and Robert Paquette, eds., *Slavery* (2001); Paul D. Escott, ed., *North Carolina Yeoman* (1996);

Drew Faust, *James Henry Hammond and the Old South* (1982); Drew Faust, *A Sacred Circle: The Dilemma of the Intellectual in the Old South* (1977); Drew Faust, ed., *The Ideology of Slavery* (1981); J. Wayne Flynt, *Dixie's Forgotten People* (1979); John Hope Franklin, *The Militant South, 1800–1861* (1956); John Inscoe, *Mountain Masters* (1989); Michael P. Johnson and James L. Roark, *Black Masters* (1984); Kenneth S. Greenberg, *Masters and Statesmen* (1985); Stephanie McCurry, *Masters of Small Worlds* (1995); Robert Manson Myers, ed., *The Children of Pride* (1972); James Oakes, *The Ruling Race* (1982); Frank L. Owsley, *Plain Folk of the Old South* (1949); Loren Schweninger, *Black Property Owners in the South, 1790–1915* (1990); J. Mills Thornton III, *Politics and Power in a Slave Society: Alabama, 1800–1860* (1978).

Southern Women

Carol Bleser, *In Joy and in Sorrow* (1990); Carol Bleser, ed., *Tokens of Affection* (1995); Victoria Bynum, *Unruly Women* (1992); Jane Turner Censer, *North Carolina Planters and Their Children, 1800–1860* (1984); Catherine Clinton, *The Plantation Mistress* (1982); Elizabeth Fox-Genovese, *Within the Plantation Household* (1988); Jean E. Friedman, *The Enclosed Garden* (1985); Harriet Jacobs, *Incidents in the Life of a Slave Girl*, ed. Jean Fagan Yellin (1987); Jacqueline Jones, *Labor of Love, Labor of Sorrow* (1985); Frances Anne Kemble, *Journal of a Residence on a Georgia Plantation in 1838–1839* (1863); Suzanne Lebsock, *Free Women of Petersburg* (1984); Ann Patton Malone, *Sweet Chariot: Slave Family and Household Structure in Nineteenth Century Louisiana* (1992); Sally McMillen, *Motherhood in the Old South* (1990); Patricia Morton, ed., *Discovering the Women in Slavery* (1995); Elisabeth Muhlenfeld, *Mary Boykin Chesnut* (1981); Deborah G. White, *Ar'n't I a Woman?* (1985); Virginia Ingraham Burr, ed., *The Secret Eye* (1990).

Conditions of Slavery

Larry E. Hudson, Jr., *To Have and to Hold* (1997); Kenneth F. Kiple and Virginia H. Kiple, "Black Tongue and Black Men," *Journal of Southern History* 43 (August 1977): 411–428; Wilma King, *Stolen Childhood* (1995); Peter Kolchin, *American Slavery, 1619–1877* (1993); Walter Johnson, *Soul by Soul: Life Inside the Antebellum Slave Market* (1999); Randall M. Miller and John David Smith, eds., *Dictionary of Afro-American Slavery* (1997); Randall M. Miller, ed., *The Afro-American Slaves: Community or Chaos* (1981); Orlando Patterson, *Rituals of Blood* (1998); Todd L. Savitt, *Medicine and Slavery* (1978); Mark M. Smith, *Mastered by the Clock* (1997); Kenneth M. Stampp, *The Peculiar Institution* (1956); Robert S. Starobin, *Industrial Slavery in the Old South* (1970); Brenda E. Stevenson, *Life in Black and White: Family and Community in the Slave South* (1996); Michael Tadman, *Speculators and Slaves* (1989).

Slave Culture and Resistance

Herbert Aptheker, *American Negro Slave Revolts* (1943); William F. Allen, Charles P. Ware, and Lucy McKim, *Slave Songs of the United States* (1867); John W. Blassingame, *The Slave Community* (1979); John Blassingame, ed., *Slave Testimony* (1977); Ira Berlin et al., eds., *Remembering Slavery* (1998); Frederick Douglass, *Narrative of the Life of Frederick Douglass*, David W. Blight, ed. (1993); Douglas R. Egerton, *He Shall Go Out Free: The Lives of Denmark Vesey* (1999); Paul D. Escott, *Slavery Remembered: A Record of Twentieth-Century Slave Narratives* (1979); Thomas Wentworth Higginson, "Negro Spirituals," *Atlantic Monthly* 19 (June, 1867); John Hope Franklin and Loren Schweninger, *Runaway Slaves* (1999); Eugene D. Genovese, *From Rebellion to Revolution* (1979); Eugene D. Genovese, *Roll, Jordan, Roll* (1974); Michael A. Gomez, *Exchanging Our Country Marks* (1998); Kenneth Greenberg, ed., *The Confessions of Nat Turner and Related Documents* (1996); Herbert G. Gutman, *The Black Family in Slavery and Freedom, 1750–1925* (1976); Vincent Harding, *There Is a River* (1981); Michael P. Johnson, "Denmark Vesey and His Co-Conspirators," *William and Mary Quarterly* LVIII (October 2001); Charles Joyner, *Down by the Riverside* (1984); Lawrence W. Levine, *Black Culture and Black Consciousness* (1977); Albert J. Raboteau, *Slave Religion* (1978); David Robertson, *Denmark Vesey* (1999); James Sidbury, *Plowshares into Swords: Gabriel's Virginia* (1997); Sterling Stuckey, *Slave Culture* (1987).

Chapter 14

Politics: General

Tyler Anbinder, *Nativism and Slavery* (1992); Maurice G. Baxter, *One and Inseparable: Daniel Webster and the Union* (1984); Paul Bergeron, *The Presidency of James K. Polk* (1987); Frederick J. Blue, *The Free Soilers: Third Party Politics, 1848–1854* (1973); Gabor S. Boritt, ed., *Why the Civil War Came* (1996); Richard J. Carwardine, *Evangelicals and Politics in Antebellum America* (1997); Don E. Fehrenbacher, *The Dred Scott Case* (1978); Don E. Fehrenbacher, *The Slaveholding Republic* (2001); George M. Fredrickson, *The Black Image in the White Mind* (1971); William W. Freehling and Craig M. Simpson, eds., *Secession Debated* (1992); William W. Freehling, *The Road to Disunion* (1990); Holman Hamilton, *Prologue to Conflict: The Crisis and Compromise of 1850* (1964); Michael F. Holt, *Political Parties and American Political Development* (1992); Michael F. Holt, *The Political Crisis of the 1850s* (1978); Daniel Walker Howe, *The Political Culture of the American Whigs* (1979); Stephen E. Maizlish and John J. Kushma, eds., *Essays on American Antebellum Politics, 1840–1860* (1982); William Lee Miller, *Arguing About Slavery* (1996); Chaplain W. Morrison, *Democratic Politics and Sectionalism: The Wilmot Proviso Controversy* (1967); Merrill D. Peterson, *The Great Triumvirate: Webster, Clay, and Calhoun* (1987); David M. Potter, *The Impending Crisis, 1848–1861* (1976); James A. Rawley, *Race and Politics* (1969); Robert V. Remini,

Henry Clay: Statesman for the Union (1991); Richard H. Sewell, *A House Divided: Sectionalism and the Civil War, 1848–1865* (1988); Joel H. Silbey, *The Transformation of American Politics, 1840–1960* (1967); Joel H. Silbey, ed., *The American Party Battle*, 2 vols. (1999); Elbert B. Smith, *The Presidency of James Buchanan* (1975); Kenneth M. Stampp, *America in 1857* (1991); Kenneth M. Stampp, *And the War Came* (1950); Richard White, *"It's Your Misfortune and None of My Own": A History of the American West* (1991); Gerald W. Wolff, *The Kansas-Nebraska Bill* (1977).

The South and Slavery

William L. Barney, *The Secessionist Impulse* (1974); Malcolm Bell, Jr., *Major Butler's Legacy: Five Generations of a Slaveholding Family* (1987); Steven A. Channing, *A Crisis of Fear: Secession in South Carolina* (1970); William J. Cooper, Jr., *The South and the Politics of Slavery, 1828–1856* (1978); Avery O. Craven, *The Growth of Southern Nationalism, 1848–1861* (1953); Daniel W. Crofts, *Reluctant Confederates: Upper South Unionists in the Secession Crisis* (1989); Charles B. Dew, *Apostles of Disunion: Southern Secession Commissioners and the Causes of the Civil War* (2001); Merton L. Dillon, *Slavery Attacked* (1991); Drew G. Faust, *The Ideology of Slavery* (1981); Drew G. Faust, *A Sacred Circle: The Dilemma of the Intellectual in the Old South* (1978); Lacy K. Ford, Jr., *Origins of Southern Radicalism* (1988); Eugene D. Genovese, *The World the Slaveholders Made* (1969); Michael P. Johnson, *Toward a Patriarchal Republic: The Secession of Georgia* (1977); John Niven, *John C. Calhoun and the Price of Union* (1988); James Oakes, *Slavery and Freedom* (1991); David M. Potter, *The South and the Sectional Conflict* (1968); Thomas E. Schott, *Alexander H. Stephens of Georgia* (1988); William R. Stanton, *The Leopard's Spots* (1960); J. Mills Thornton III, *Politics and Power in a Slave Society* (1978); Larry E. Tise, *Proslavery* (1987); Ralph Wooster, *The Secession Conventions of the South* (1962).

The North and Antislavery

Eugene H. Berwanger, *The Frontier Against Slavery* (1967); Gary Collison, *Shadrach Minkins: From Fugitive Slave to Citizen* (1997); David Donald, *Charles Sumner and the Coming of the Civil War* (1960); Paul Finkelman, ed., *His Soul Goes Marching On: Responses to John Brown and the Harpers Ferry Raid* (1995); Eric Foner, *Free Soil, Free Labor, Free Men* (1970); Louis S. Gerteis, *Morality and Utility in American Antislavery Reform* (1987); William E. Gienapp, *The Origins of the Republican Party, 1852–1856* (1986); Joan D. Hedrick, *Harriet Beecher Stowe* (1994); James O. and Lois E. Horton, *In Hope of Liberty* (1997); James O. Horton, *Free People of Color* (1993); Henry V. Jaffa, *Crisis of the House Divided* (1959); Robert W. Johannsen, *Lincoln, the South, and Slavery* (1991); Robert W. Johannsen, *Stephen A. Douglas* (1973); Stephen B. Oates, *To Purge This Land with Blood*, 2d ed. (1984); Lewis Perry and Michael Fellman, eds., *Antislavery Reconsidered* (1979); Benjamin Quarles, *Black Abolitionists*

(1969); Patrick Rael, *Black Identity and Black Protest in the Antebellum North* (2002); Leonard Richards, *The Slave Power: The Free North and Southern Domination, 1780–1860* (2000); C. Peter Ripley, et al., ed., *Witness for Freedom: African American Voices on Race, Slavery and Freedom* (1993); Jeffrey Rossbach, *Ambivalent Conspirators* (1982); Richard Sewell, *Ballots for Freedom: Antislavery Politics in the United States, 1837–1860* (1976); Jason H. Silverman, *Unwelcome Guests: Canada West's Response to American Fugitive Slaves* (1985); Thomas P. Slaughter, *Bloody Dawn: The Cristiana Riot and Racial Violence* (1991); John Stauffer, *The Black Hearts of Men: Radical Abolitionists and the Transformation of Race* (2002); James B. Stewart, *Holy Warriors: The Abolitionists and American Slavery*, 2d ed. (1996); Albert J. Von Frank, *The Trials of Anthony Burns* (1998).

The Mexican War and Foreign Policy

K. Jack Bauer, *Zachary Taylor* (1985); Gene M. Brack, *Mexico Views Manifest Destiny, 1821–1846* (1976); Richard Griswold del Castillo, *The Treaty of Guadalupe Hidalgo* (1990); Neal Harlow, *California Conquered* (1982); Reginald Horsman, *Race and Manifest Destiny* (1981); Robert W. Johannsen, *To the Halls of the Montezumas: The Mexican War and the American Imagination* (1985); Ernest M. Lander, Jr., *Reluctant Imperialists: Calhoun, the South Carolinians, and the Mexican War* (1980); Robert E. May, *The Southern Dream of a Caribbean Empire, 1854–1861* (1973); Frederick Merk, *Manifest Destiny and Mission in American History* (1963); David M. Pletcher, *The Diplomacy of Annexation: Texas, Oregon, and the Mexican War* (1973); Dirk Raat, *Mexico and the United States* (1992); John H. Schroeder, *Mr. Polk's War: American Opposition and Dissent* (1973); Otis A. Singletary, *The Mexican War* (1960); Anders Stephanson, *Manifest Destiny* (1995); David J. Weber, *The Mexican Frontier, 1821–1846* (1982).

Chapter 15

The War and the South

Thomas B. Alexander and Richard E. Beringer, *The Anatomy of the Confederate Congress* (1972); Stephen Ash, *When the Yankees Came* (1995); Edward L. Ayers, *In the Presence of Mine Enemies: War in the Heart of America, 1859–1863* (2002); Richard E. Beringer et al., *Why the South Lost the Civil War* (1986); William A. Blair, *Virginia's Private War: Feeding Body and Soul in the Confederacy* (1998); Gabor S. Boritt, ed., *Why the Confederacy Lost* (1992); Richard N. Current, *Lincoln's Loyalists* (1992); William C. Davis, *Jefferson Davis* (1991); Robert F. Durden, *The Gray and the Black: The Confederate Debate on Emancipation* (1972); Paul D. Escott, *Many Excellent People* (1985); Paul D. Escott, *After Secession: Jefferson Davis and the Failure of Confederate Nationalism* (1978); Eli N. Evans, *Judah P. Benjamin* (1987); Drew Gilpin Faust, *The Creation of Confederate Nationalism* (1988); William

W. Freehling, *The South vs. the South* (2001); Mark Grimsley, *The Hard Hand of War* (1995); J. B. Jones, *A Rebel War Clerk's Diary*, 2 vols., ed. Howard Swiggett (1935); Mary Elizabeth Massey, *Refugee Life in the Confederacy* (1964); Larry E. Nelson, *Bullets, Ballots, and Rhetoric: Confederate Policy for the United States Presidential Contest of 1864* (1980); Alan T. Nolan, *Lee Considered* (1991); James L. Roark, *Masters Without Slaves* (1977); Daniel Sutherland, *Seasons of War* (1995); Emory M. Thomas, *The Confederate Nation* (1979); Emory M. Thomas, *The Confederacy as a Revolutionary Experience* (1971); William A. Tidwell, *April '65* (1995); Bell Irvin Wiley, *The Life of Johnny Reb* (1943); Bell Irvin Wiley, *The Plain People of the Confederacy* (1943).

The War and the North

Ralph Andreano, ed., *The Economic Impact of the American Civil War* (1962); Iver Bernstein, *The New York City Draft Riots* (1990); David Donald, ed., *Why the North Won the Civil War* (1960); J. Matthew Gallman, *The North Fights the Civil War* (1994); James W. Geary, *We Need Men* (1991); Susan-Mary Grant and Peter J. Parish, eds., *Legacy of Disunion: The Enduring Significance of the American Civil War* (2003); Wood Gray, *The Hidden Civil War* (1942); Randall C. Jimerson, *The Private Civil War* (1988); Frank L. Klement, *The Copperheads in the Middle West* (1960); Melinda Lawson, *Patriot Fires: Forging a New American Nationalism in the Civil War North* (2002); James M. McPherson, *Battle Cry of Freedom* (1988); James H. Moorhead, *American Apocalypse* (1978); Mark E. Neely, Jr., *The Union Divided: Party Conflict in the Civil War North* (2002); Phillip S. Paludan, *"A People's Contest": The Union and the Civil War, 1861–1865* (1989); Robert Hunt Rhodes, ed., *All for the Union: The Civil War Diary and Letters of Elisha Hunt Rhodes* (1991); Anne C. Rose, *Victorian America and the Civil War* (1992); George Winston Smith and Charles Burnet Judah, *Life in the North During the Civil War* (1966); George Templeton Strong, *Diary*, 4 vols., ed. Allan Nevins and Milton Hasley Thomas (1952); Maris A. Vinovskis, ed., *Toward a Social History of the American Civil War* (1990); Michael Vorenberg, *Final Freedom: The Civil War, the Abolition of Slavery, and the Thirteenth Amendment* (2001); Bell Irvin Wiley, *The Life of Billy Yank* (1952).

Women

John Q. Anderson, ed., *Brokenburn: The Journal of Kate Stone* (1955); John R. Brumgardt, ed., *Civil War Nurse: The Diary and Letters of Hannah Ropes* (1980); Catherine Clinton and Nina Silber, eds., *Divided Houses: Gender and the Civil War* (1992); Beth Gilbert Crabtree and James W. Patton, eds., *"Journal of a Secesh Lady": The Diary of Catherine Ann Devereux Edmondston, 1860–1866* (1979); Alice Fahs, *The Imagined Civil War: Popular Literature of the North and South* (2001); Drew Gilpin Faust, *Mothers of Invention* (1996); Jacqueline Jones, *Labor of Love, Labor of Sorrow* (1985); George C. Rable, *Civil Wars: Women and the Crisis of South-*

ern Nationalism (1989); Mary D. Robertson, ed., *Lucy Breckinridge of Grove Hill: The Journal of a Virginia Girl, 1862–1864* (1979); Lyde Cullen Sizer, *The Political Work of Northern Women Writers and the Civil War* (2000); Lee Ann Whites, *The Civil War as a Crisis in Gender* (1995); C. Vann Woodward and Elisabeth Muhlenfeld, eds., *Mary Chesnut's Civil War* (1981).

African Americans

Virginia M. Adams, ed., *On the Altar of Freedom: A Black Soldier's Civil War Letters from the Front* (1991); Ira Berlin, ed., *Freedom: A Documentary History of Emancipation, 1861–1867*, Series I, *The Destruction of Slavery* (1979), and Series II, *The Black Military Experience* (1982); Richard M. Blackett, ed., *Thomas Morris Chester: Black Civil War Correspondent* (1989); David W. Blight, *Frederick Douglass' Civil War* (1989); Dudley Cornish, *The Sable Arm* (1956); Barbara Jeanne Fields, *Slavery and Freedom on the Middle Ground* (1985); Joseph T. Glatthaar, *Forged in Battle* (1990); James G. Hollandsworth, *The Louisiana Native Guards* (1995); Leon Litwack, *Been in the Storm So Long* (1979); James M. McPherson, *The Negro's Civil War* (1965); James M. McPherson, *The Struggle for Equality* (1964); Clarence L. Mohr, *On the Threshold of Freedom* (1986); Lynda J. Morgan, *Emancipation in Virginia's Tobacco Belt, 1850–1870* (1992); Benjamin Quarles, *The Negro in the Civil War* (1953); Edwin S. Redkey, ed., *A Grand Army of Black Men* (1992); John David Smith, ed., *Black Soldiers in Blue* (2002).

Military History

Nancy Scott Anderson and Dwight Anderson, *The Generals: Ulysses S. Grant and Robert E. Lee* (1987); David W. Blight, ed., *When This Cruel War Is Over: The Civil War Letters of Charles Harvey Brewster* (1992); Albert Castel, *Decision in the West* (1992); Bruce Catton, *Grant Takes Command* (1969); Bruce Catton, *A Stillness at Appomattox* (1953); Peter Cozzens, *This Terrible Sound* (1992); Michael Fellman, *Citizen Sherman* (1995); Shelby Foote, *The Civil War, a Narrative*, 3 vols. (1958–1974); Douglas Southall Freeman, *Lee's Lieutenants*, 3 vols. (1942–1944); Douglas Southall Freeman, *R. E. Lee*, 4 vols. (1934–1935); Gary W. Gallagher, *The Confederate War* (1997); Gary W. Gallagher, *Lee and His Generals in War and Memory* (1998); Joseph T. Glatthaar, *The March to the Sea and Beyond* (1985); Herman Hattaway and Archer Jones, *How the North Won* (1983); Laurence M. Hauptman, *Between Two Fires: American Indians in the Civil War* (1995); Robert V. Hine and John Mack Faragher, *The American West: A New Interpretive History* (2000); Archer Jones, *Civil War Command and Strategy* (1992); Alvin M. Josephy, Jr., *The Civil War in the American West* (1991); Gerald F. Linderman, *Embattled Courage* (1989); Thomas L. Livermore, *Numbers and Losses in the Civil War in America* (1957); Grady McWhiney and Perry D. Jamieson, *Attack and Die* (1982); Reid Mitchell, *Civil War Soldiers* (1988); Reid Mitchell, *The Vacant Chair* (1993); Roy

Morris, Jr., *Sheridan* (1992); George C. Rable, *Fredericksburg! Fredericksburg!* (2002); Charles Royster, *The Destructive War* (1991); Stephen W. Sears, *To the Gates of Richmond* (1992); Stephen W. Sears, *George B. McClellan* (1988); Emory M. Thomas, *Robert E. Lee* (1995); Emory M. Thomas, *Bold Dragoon: The Life of J. E. B. Stuart* (1987); Noah Andre Trudeau, *The Last Citadel* (1991); Steven E. Woodworth, *Jefferson Davis and His Generals* (1990).

Foreign Relations

Stuart L. Bernath, *Squall Across the Atlantic: American Civil War Prize Cases and Diplomacy* (1970); R. J. M. Blackett, *Divided Hearts: Britain and the American Civil War* (2001); David P. Crook, *The North, the South, and the Powers, 1861–1865* (1974); Charles P. Cullop, *Confederate Propaganda in Europe* (1969); Norman B. Ferris, *The Trent Affair* (1977); Howard Jones, *Union in Peril* (1992); Frank J. Merli, *Great Britain and the Confederate Navy* (1970); Frank L. Owsley and Harriet Owsley, *King Cotton Diplomacy* (1959); Gordon H. Warren, *Fountain of Discontent: The Trent Affair and Freedom of the Seas* (1981).

Abraham Lincoln and the Union Government

Allan G. Bogue, *The Earnest Men: Republicans of the Civil War Senate* (1981); Gabor S. Borit, ed., *The Historian's Lincoln* (1989); Fawn Brodie, *Thaddeus Stevens* (1959); Richard N. Current, *The Lincoln Nobody Knows* (1958); Leonard P. Curry, *Blueprint for Modern America: Non-Military Legislation of the First Civil War Congress* (1968); David Donald, *Charles Sumner and the Rights of Man* (1970); David Donald, *Lincoln* (1995); William E. Gienapp, *Abraham Lincoln and Civil War America* (2002); Allen Guelzo, *Abraham Lincoln: Redeemer President* (1999); Peyton McCrary, *Abraham Lincoln and Reconstruction: The Louisiana Experiment* (1978); James M. McPherson, *Abraham Lincoln and the Second American Revolution* (1990); Mark Neely, *The Fate of Liberty* (1991); Stephen B. Oates, *With Malice Toward None* (1977); Philip S. Paludan, *The Presidency of Abraham Lincoln* (1994); Heather Cox Richardson, *The Greatest Nation of the Earth: Republican Economic Policies During the Civil War* (1997); Joel Silbey, *A Respectable Minority: The Democratic Party in the Civil War Era* (1977); Benjamin P. Thomas, *Abraham Lincoln* (1952); Hans L. Trefousse, *The Radical Republicans* (1969); Glyndon G. Van Deusen, *William Henry Seward* (1967); T. Harry Williams, *Lincoln and His Generals* (1952); T. Harry Williams, *Lincoln and the Radicals* (1941).

Chapter 16

National Policy, Politics, and Constitutional Law

Richard H. Abbott, *The Republican Party and the South, 1855–1877* (1986); Herman Belz, *Emancipation and Equal Rights* (1978); Herman Belz, *A New Birth of Freedom* (1976); Michael Les Benedict, *A Compromise of Principle: Congressional Republicans and Reconstruction, 1863–1869* (1974); Michael Les Benedict, *The Impeachment and Trial of Andrew Johnson* (1973); Charles S. Campbell, *The Transformation of American Foreign Relations, 1865–1900* (1976); Adrian Cook, *The Alabama Claims* (1975); Michael Kent Curtis, *No State Shall Abridge* (1987); David Donald, *Charles Sumner and the Rights of Man* (1970); Harold M. Hyman, *A More Perfect Union* (1973); William S. McFeely, *Grant* (1981); William S. McFeely, *Yankee Stepfather: General O. O. Howard and the Freedmen* (1968); Eric L. McKitrick, *Andrew Johnson and Reconstruction* (1966); James M. McPherson, *The Abolitionist Legacy* (1975); Joel Silbey, *A Respectable Minority: The Democratic Party in the Civil War Era* (1977); Brooks D. Simpson, *Let Us Have Peace* (1991); Brooks D. Simpson, *The Reconstruction Presidents* (1998); Kenneth M. Stampp, *The Era of Reconstruction* (1965); Hans L. Trefousse, *Andrew Johnson* (1989).

The Freed Slaves

Roberta Sue Alexander, *North Carolina Faces the Freedmen* (1985); Ira Berlin, ed., *Freedom: A Documentary History of Emancipation, 1861–1867* (1984); Elizabeth R. Bethel, *Promiseland* (1981); Orville Vernon Burton, *In My Father's House Are Many Mansions* (1985); Edmund L. Drago, *Black Politicians and Reconstruction in Georgia* (1982); Paul D. Escott, *Slavery Remembered* (1979); Eric Foner, "Reconstruction and the Crisis of Free Labor," in *Politics and Ideology in the Age of the Civil War*, ed. Eric Foner (1980); Gerald Jaynes, *Branches Without Roots: The Genesis of the Black Working Class in the American South, 1862–1882* (1986); Leon Litwack, *Been in the Storm So Long* (1979); Edward Magdol, *A Right to the Land* (1977); Robert Morris, *Reading, 'Riting and Reconstruction* (1981); Howard Rabinowitz, ed., *Southern Black Leaders in Reconstruction* (1982); Emma Lou Thornbrough, ed., *Black Reconstructionists* (1972); Clarence Walker, *A Rock in a Weary Land* (1982); Elliot West, "Reconstructing Race," *Western Historical Quarterly* (Spring, 2003).

Politics and Reconstruction in the South

James A. Baggett, *The Scalawags: Southern Dissenters in the Civil War and Reconstruction* (2003); Robert W. Coakley, *The Role of Federal Military Forces in Domestic Disorders, 1789–1878* (1988); Richard N. Current, *Those Terrible Carpetbaggers* (1988); W. E. B. Du Bois, *Black Reconstruction* (1935); Paul D. Escott, *Many Excellent People: Power and Privilege in North Carolina, 1850–1900* (1985); Michael W. Fitzgerald, *The Union League Movement in the Deep South* (1989); Eric Foner, *Reconstruction: America's Unfinished Revolution, 1863–1877* (1988); Eric Foner, *Nothing but Freedom* (1983); Steven Hahn, *A Nation Under Our Feet: Black Political Struggles in the Rural South from Slavery to the Great Migration* (2003); William C. Harris, *The Day of the Carpetbagger* (1979); Thomas Holt, *Black over White: Negro Political Leadership in South Carolina During Reconstruction* (1977); J. Morgan Kousser and James M. McPherson, eds., *Region, Race and Reconstruction* (1982); Elizabeth Studley Nathans, *Losing the Peace* (1968); Michael Perman, *The Road to Redemption* (1984); Michael Perman, *Reunion Without Compromise* (1973); Lawrence N. Powell, *New Masters* (1980); George C. Rable, *But There Was No Peace* (1984); James Roark, *Masters Without Slaves* (1977); James Sefton, *The United States Army and Reconstruction, 1865–1877* (1967); Mark W. Summers, *Railroads, Reconstruction, and the Gospel of Prosperity* (1984); Allen Trelease, *White Terror* (1967); Ted Tunnell, *Carpetbagger from Vermont* (1989); Ted Tunnell, *Crucible of Reconstruction* (1984); Michael Wayne, *The Reshaping of Plantation Society* (1983); Sarah Woolfolk Wiggins, *The Scalawag in Alabama Politics, 1865–1881* (1977).

Women, Family, and Social History

Virginia I. Burr, ed., *The Secret Eye* (1990); Ellen Carol Dubois, *Feminism and Suffrage* (1978); Herbert G. Gutman, *The Black Family in Slavery and Freedom, 1750–1925* (1976); Elizabeth Jacoway, *Yankee Missionaries in the South* (1979); Jacqueline Jones, *Labor of Love, Labor of Sorrow* (1985); Jacqueline Jones, *Soldiers of Light and Love* (1980); Robert C. Kenzer, *Kinship and Neighborhood in a Southern Community* (1987); Mary P. Ryan, *Women in Public* (1990); Rebecca Scott, "The Battle over the Child," *Prologue* 10 (Summer 1978): 101–113.

The End of Reconstruction

Michael Les Benedict, "Southern Democrats in the Crisis of 1876–1877," *Journal of Southern History* 66 (November 1980): 489–524; William Gillette, *Retreat from Reconstruction, 1869–1879* (1980); William Gillette, *The Right to Vote* (1969); Keith Ian Polakoff, *The Politics of Inertia* (1973); Heather Richardson, *The Death of Reconstruction* (2001); John G. Sproat, *"The Best Men": Liberal Reformers in the Gilded Age* (1968); C. Vann Woodward, *Reunion and Reaction* (1951).

Reconstruction's Legacy for the South and the Nation

Robert G. Athearn, *In Search of Canaan* (1978); Edward L. Ayers, *The Promise of the New South* (1992); David W. Blight, *Race and Reunion: The Civil War in American Memory* (2001); Norman L. Crockett, *The Black Towns* (1979); Steven Hahn, *The Roots of Southern Populism* (1983); Leon Litwack, *Trouble in Mind: Black Southerners in the Age of Jim Crow* (1998); Jay R. Mandle, *The Roots of Black Poverty* (1978); Nell Irvin Painter, *Exodusters* (1976); Howard Rabinowitz, *Race Relations in the Urban South, 1865–1890* (1978); Roger L. Ransom and Richard Sutch, *One Kind of Freedom* (1977); Laurence Shore, *Southern Capitalists* (1986); Peter Wallenstein, *From Slave South to New South* (1987); Jonathan M. Wiener, *Social Origins of the New South* (1978); C. Vann Woodward, *Origins of the New South* (1951).

Documents

DECLARATION OF INDEPENDENCE IN CONGRESS, JULY 4, 1776

When, in the course of human events, it becomes necessary for one people to dissolve the political bonds which have connected them with another, and to assume, among the powers of the earth, the separate and equal station to which the laws of nature and of nature's God entitle them, a decent respect to the opinions of mankind requires that they should declare the causes which impel them to the separation.

We hold these truths to be self-evident: That all men are created equal; that they are endowed by their Creator with certain unalienable rights; that among these are life, liberty, and the pursuit of happiness; that, to secure these rights, governments are instituted among men, deriving their just powers from the consent of the governed; that whenever any form of government becomes destructive of these ends, it is the right of the people to alter or to abolish it, and to institute new government, laying its foundation on such principles, and organizing its powers in such form, as to them shall seem most likely to effect their safety and happiness. Prudence, indeed, will dictate that governments long established should not be changed for light and transient causes; and accordingly all experience hath shown that mankind are more disposed to suffer, while evils are sufferable, than to right themselves by abolishing the forms to which they are accustomed. But when a long train of abuses and usurpations, pursuing invariably the same object, evinces a design to reduce them under absolute despotism, it is their right, it is their duty, to throw off such government, and to provide new guards for their future security. Such has been the patient sufferance of these colonies; and such is now the necessity which constrains them to alter their former systems of government. The history of the present King of Great Britain is a history of repeated injuries and usurpations, all having in direct object the establishment of an absolute tyranny over these states. To prove this, let facts be submitted to a candid world.

He has refused his assent to laws, the most wholesome and necessary for the public good.

He has forbidden his governors to pass laws of immediate and pressing importance, unless suspended in their operation till his assent should be obtained; and, when so suspended, he has utterly neglected to attend to them.

He has refused to pass other laws for the accommodation of large districts of people, unless those people would relinquish the right of representation in the legislature, a right inestimable to them, and formidable to tyrants only.

He has called together legislative bodies at places unusual, uncomfortable, and distant from the depository of their public records, for the sole purpose of fatiguing them into compliance with his measures.

He has dissolved representative houses repeatedly, for opposing, with manly firmness, his invasions on the rights of the people.

He has refused for a long time, after such dissolutions, to cause others to be elected; whereby the legislative powers, incapable of annihilation, have returned to the people at large for their exercise; the state remaining, in the mean time, exposed to all the dangers of invasions from without and convulsions within.

He has endeavored to prevent the population of these states; for that purpose obstructing the laws for naturalization of foreigners; refusing to pass others to encourage their migration hither, and raising the conditions of new appropriations of lands.

He has obstructed the administration of justice, by refusing his assent to laws for establishing judiciary powers.

He has made judges dependent on his will alone, for the tenure of their offices, and the amount and payment of their salaries.

He has erected a multitude of new offices, and sent hither swarms of officers to harass our people and eat out their substance.

He has kept among us, in times of peace, standing armies, without the consent of our legislatures.

He has affected to render the military independent of, and superior to, the civil power.

He has combined with others to subject us to a jurisdiction foreign to our constitution, and unacknowledged by our laws, giving his assent to their acts of pretended legislation:

For quartering large bodies of armed troops among us;

For protecting them, by a mock trial, from punishment for any murders which they should commit on the inhabitants of these states;

For cutting off our trade with all parts of the world;

For imposing taxes on us without our consent;

For depriving us, in many cases, of the benefits of trial by jury;

For transporting us beyond seas, to be tried for pretended offenses;

For abolishing the free system of English laws in a neighboring province, establishing therein an arbitrary government, and enlarging its boundaries, so as to render it at once an example and fit instrument for introducing the same absolute rule into these colonies;

For taking away our charters, abolishing our most valuable laws, and altering fundamentally the forms of our governments;

For suspending our own legislatures, and declaring themselves invested with power to legislate for us in all cases whatsoever.

He has abdicated government here, by declaring us out of his protection and waging war against us.

He has plundered our seas, ravaged our coasts, burned our towns, and destroyed the lives of our people.

He is at this time transporting large armies of foreign mercenaries to complete the works of death, desolation, and tyranny already begun with circumstances of cruelty and perfidy scarcely paralleled in the most barbarous ages, and totally unworthy the head of a civilized nation.

He has constrained our fellow-citizens, taken captive on the high seas, to bear arms against their country, to become the executioners of their friends and brethren, or to fall themselves by their hands.

He has excited domestic insurrection among us, and has endeavored to bring on the inhabitants of our frontiers the merciless Indian savages, whose known rule of warfare is an undistinguished destruction of all ages, sexes, and conditions.

In every stage of these oppressions we have petitioned for redress in the most humble terms; our repeated petitions have been answered only by repeated injury. A prince, whose character is thus marked by every act which may define a tyrant, is unfit to be the ruler of a free people.

Nor have we been wanting in our attentions to our British brethren. We have warned them, from time to time, of attempts by their legislature to extend an unwarrantable jurisdiction over us. We have reminded them of the circumstances of our emigration and settlement here. We have appealed to their native justice and magnanimity; and we have conjured them, by the ties of our common kindred, to disavow these usurpations, which would inevitably interrupt our connections and correspondence. They, too, have been deaf to the voice of justice and of consanguinity. We must, therefore, acquiesce in the necessity which denounces our separation, and hold them, as we hold the rest of mankind, enemies in war, in peace friends.

We, therefore, the representatives of the United States of America, in General Congress assembled, appealing to the Supreme Judge of the world for the rectitude of our intentions, do, in the name and by the authority of the good people of these colonies, solemnly publish and declare, that these United Colonies are, and of right ought to be, FREE AND INDEPENDENT STATES; that they are absolved from all allegiance to the British crown, and that all political connection between them and the state of Great Britain is, and ought to be, totally dissolved; and that, as free and independent states, they have full power to levy war, conclude peace, contract alliances, establish commerce, and do all other acts and things which independent states may of right do. And for the support of this declaration, with a firm reliance on the protection of Divine Providence, we mutually pledge to each other our lives, our fortunes, and our sacred honor.

ARTICLES OF CONFEDERATION

Whereas the Delegates of the United States of America in Congress assembled did on the fifteenth day of November in the Year of our Lord One Thousand Seven Hundred and Seventy seven, and in the Second Year of the Independence of America agree to certain articles of Confederation and perpetual Union between the States of Newhampshire, Massachusetts-bay, Rhode-island and Providence Plantations, Connecticut, New-York, New-Jersey, Pennsylvania, Delaware, Maryland, Virginia, North-Carolina, South-Carolina and Georgia in the Words following, viz. "Articles of Confederation and perpetual Union between the states of Newhampshire, Massachusetts-bay, Rhodeisland and Providence Plantations, Connecticut, New-York, New-Jersey, Pennsylvania, Delaware, Maryland, Virginia, North-Carolina, South-Carolina and Georgia.

Article I   The Stile of this confederacy shall be "The United States of America."

Article II   Each state retains its sovereignty, freedom and independence, and every Power, Jurisdiction and right, which is not by this confederation expressly delegated to the United States, in Congress assembled.

Article III   The said states hereby severally enter into a firm league of friendship with each other, for their common defence, the security of their Liberties, and their mutual and general welfare, binding themselves to assist each other, against all force offered to, or attacks made upon them, or any of them, on account of religion, sovereignty, trade, or any other pretence whatever.

Article IV   The better to secure and perpetuate mutual friendship and intercourse among the people of the different states in this union, the free inhabitants of each of these states, paupers, vagabonds and fugitives from Justice excepted, shall be entitled to all privileges and immunities of free citizens in the several states; and the people of each state shall have free ingress and regress to and from any other state, and shall enjoy therein all the privileges of trade and commerce, subject to the same duties, impositions and restrictions as the inhabitants thereof respectively, provided that such restriction shall not extend so far as to prevent the removal of property imported into any state, to any other state of which the Owner is an inhabitant; provided also that no imposition, duties or restriction shall be laid by any state, on the property of the united states, or either of them.

If any Person guilty of, or charged with treason, felony, or other high misdemeanor in any state, shall flee from Justice, and be found in any of the united states, he shall upon demand of the Governor or executive power, of the state from which he fled, be delivered up and removed to the state having jurisdiction of his offence.

Full faith and credit shall be given in each of these states to the records, acts and judicial proceedings of the courts and magistrates of every other state.

Article V For the more convenient management of the general interests of the united states, delegates shall be annually appointed in such manner as the legislature of each state shall direct, to meet in Congress on the first Monday in November, in every year, with a power reserved to each state, to recall its delegates, or any of them, at any time within the year, and to send others in their stead, for the remainder of the Year.

No state shall be represented in Congress by less than two, nor by more than seven Members; and no person shall be capable of being a delegate for more than three years in any term of six years; nor shall any person, being a delegate, be capable of holding any office under the united states, for which he, or another for his benefit receives any salary, fees or emolument of any kind.

Each state shall maintain its own delegates in a meeting of the states, and while they act as members of the committee of the states.

In determining questions in the united states, in Congress assembled, each state shall have one vote.

Freedom of speech and debate in Congress shall not be impeached or questioned in any Court, or place out of Congress, and the members of congress shall be protected in their persons from arrests and imprisonments, during the time of their going to and from, and attendance on congress, except for treason, felony, or breach of the peace.

Article VI No state without the Consent of the united states in congress assembled, shall send any embassy to, or receive any embassy from, or enter into any conference, agreement, or alliance or treaty with any King, prince or state; nor shall any person holding any office of profit or trust under the united states, or any of them, accept of any present, emolument, office or title of any kind whatever from any king, prince or foreign state; nor shall the united states in congress assembled, or any of them, grant any title of nobility.

No two or more states shall enter into any treaty, confederation or alliance whatever between them, without the consent of the united states in congress assembled, specifying accurately the purposes for which the same is to be entered into, and how long it shall continue.

No state shall lay any imposts or duties, which may interfere with any stipulations in treaties, entered into by the united states in congress assembled, with any king, prince or state, in pursuance of any treaties already proposed by congress, to the courts of France and Spain.

No vessels of war shall be kept up in time of peace by any state, except such number only, as shall be deemed necessary by the united states in congress assembled, for the defence of such state, or its trade; nor shall any body of forces be kept up by any state, in time of peace, except such number only, as in the judgment of the united states, in congress assembled, shall be deemed requisite to garrison the forts necessary for the defence of such state; but every state shall always keep up a well regulated and disciplined militia, sufficiently armed and accoutred, and shall provide and constantly have ready for use, in public stores, a due number of field pieces and tents, and a proper quantity of arms, ammunition and camp equipage.

No state shall engage in any war without the consent of the united states in congress assembled, unless such state be actually invaded by enemies, or shall have received certain advice of a resolution being formed by some nation of Indians to invade such state, and the danger is so imminent as not to admit of a delay, till the united states in congress assembled can be consulted: nor shall any state grant commissions to any ships or vessels of war, nor letters of marque or reprisal, except it be after a declaration of war by the united states in congress assembled, and then only against the kingdom or state and the subjects thereof, against which war has been so declared, and under such regulations as shall be established by the united states in congress assembled, unless such state be infested by pirates, in which case vessels of war may be fitted out for that occasion, and kept so long as the danger shall continue, or until the united states in congress assembled shall determine otherwise.

Article VII When land-forces are raised by any state for the common defence, all officers of or under the rank of colonel, shall be appointed by the legislature of each state respectively by whom such forces shall be raised, or in such manner as such state shall direct, and all vacancies shall be filled up by the state which first made the appointment.

Article VIII All charges of war, and all other expences that shall be incurred for the common defence or general welfare, and allowed by the united states in congress assembled, shall be defrayed out of a common treasury, which shall be supplied by the several states, in proportion to the value of all land within each state, granted to or surveyed for any Person, as such land and the buildings and improvements thereon shall be estimated according to such mode as the united states in congress assembled, shall from time to time direct and appoint. The taxes for paying that proportion shall be laid and levied by the authority and direction of the legislatures of the several states within the time agreed upon by the united states in congress assembled.

Article IX The united states in congress assembled, shall have the sole and exclusive right and power of determining on peace and war, except in the cases mentioned in the sixth article—of sending and receiving ambassadors—entering into treaties and alliances, provided that no treaty of commerce shall be made whereby the legislative power of the respective states shall be restrained from imposing such imposts and duties on foreigners, as their own people are subjected to, or from prohibiting the exportation or importation of any species of goods or commodities whatsoever—of establishing rules for deciding in all cases, what captures on land or water shall be legal, and in what manner prizes taken by land or naval forces in the service of the united states shall be divided or appropriated.—of granting letters of marque and reprisal in times of peace—appointing courts for the trial of piracies and felonies committed on the high seas and establishing courts for receiving and determining final appeals in all cases of captures, provided that no member of congress shall be appointed a judge of any of the said courts.

The united states in congress assembled shall also be the last resort on appeal in all disputes and differences now subsisting or that hereafter may arise between two or more states concerning boundary, jurisdiction or any other cause whatever; which authority shall always be exercised in the manner following. Whenever the legislative or executive authority or lawful agent of any state in controversy with another shall present a petition to congress, stating the matter in question and praying for a hearing, notice thereof shall be given by order of congress to the legislative or executive authority of the other state in controversy, and a day assigned for the appearance of the parties by their lawful agents, who shall then be directed to appoint by joint consent, commissioners or judges to constitute a court for hearing and determining the matter in question: but if they cannot agree, congress shall name three persons out of each of the united states, and from the list of such persons each party shall alternately strike out one, the petitioners beginning, until the number shall be reduced to thirteen; and from that number not less than seven, nor more than nine names as congress shall direct, shall in the presence of congress be drawn out by lot, and the persons whose names shall be so drawn or any five of them, shall be commissioners or judges, to hear and finally determine the controversy, so always as a major part of the judges who shall hear the cause shall agree in the determination: and if either party shall neglect to attend at the day appointed, without shewing reasons, which congress shall judge sufficient, or being present shall refuse to strike, the congress shall proceed to nominate three persons out of each state, and the secretary of congress shall strike in behalf of such party absent or refusing; and the judgment and sentence of the court to be appointed, in the manner before prescribed, shall be final and conclusive; and if any of the parties shall refuse to submit to the authority of such court, or to appear to defend their claim or cause, the court shall nevertheless proceed to pronounce sentence, or judgment, which shall in like manner be final and decisive, the judgment or sentence and other proceedings being in either case transmitted to congress, and lodged among the acts of congress for the security of the parties concerned: provided that every commissioner, before he sits in judgment, shall take an oath to be administered by one of the judges of the supreme or superior court of the state, where the cause shall be tried, "well and truly to hear and determine the matter in question, according to the best of his judgment, without favour, affection or hope of reward:" provided also that no state shall be deprived of territory for the benefit of the united states.

All controversies concerning the private right of soil claimed under different grants of two or more states, whose jurisdictions as they may respect such lands, and the states which passed such grants are adjusted, the said grants or either of

them being at the same time claimed to have originated antecedent to such settlement of jurisdiction, shall on the petition of either party to the congress of the united states, be finally determined as near as may be in the same manner as is before prescribed for deciding disputes respecting territorial jurisdiction between different states.

The united states in congress assembled shall also have the sole and exclusive right and power of regulating the alloy and value of coin struck by their own authority, or by that of the respective states—fixing the standard of weights and measures throughout the united states.—regulating the trade and managing all affairs with the Indians, not members of any of the states, provided that the legislative right of any state within its own limits be not infringed or violated—establishing and regulating post-offices from one state to another, throughout all the united states, and exacting such postage on the papers passing thro' the same as may be requisite to defray the expences of the said office—appointing all officers of the land forces, in the service of the united states, excepting regimental officers.—appointing all the officers of the naval forces, and commissioning all officers whatever in the service of the united states—making rules for the government and regulation of the said land and naval forces, and directing their operations.

The united states in congress assembled shall have authority to appoint a committee, to sit in the recess of congress, to be denominated "A Committee of the States," and to consist of one delegate from each state; and to appoint such other committees and civil officers as may be necessary for managing the general affairs of the united states under their direction—to appoint one of their number to preside, provided that no person be allowed to serve in the office of president more than one year in any term of three years; to ascertain the necessary sums of Money to be raised for the service of the united states, and to appropriate and apply the same for defraying the public expences—to borrow money, or emit bills on the credit of the united states, transmitting every half year to the respective states an account of the sums of money so borrowed or emitted,—to build and equip a navy—to agree upon the number of land forces, and to make requisitions from each state for its quota, in proportion to the number of white inhabitants in such state; which requisition shall be binding, and thereupon the legislature of each state shall appoint the regimental officers, raise the men and cloath, arm and equip them in a soldier like manner, at the expence of the united states, and the officers and men so cloathed, armed and equipped shall march to the place appointed, and within the time agreed on by the united states in congress assembled: But if the united states in congress assembled shall, on consideration of circumstances judge proper that any state should not raise men, or should raise a smaller number than its quota, and that any other state should raise a greater number of men than the quota thereof, such extra number shall be raised, officered, cloathed, armed and equipped in the same manner as the quota of such state, unless the legislature of such state shall judge that such extra number cannot be safely spared out of the same, in which case they shall raise, officer, cloath, arm and equip as many of such extra number as they judge can be safely spared. And the officers and men so cloathed, armed and equipped, shall march to the place appointed, and within the time agreed on by the united states in congress assembled.

The united states in congress assembled shall never engage in a war, nor grant letters of marque and reprisal in time of peace, nor enter into any treaties or alliances, nor coin money, nor regulate the value thereof, nor ascertain the sums and expences necessary for the defence and welfare of the united states, or any of them, nor emit bills, nor borrow money on the credit of the united states, nor appropriate money, nor agree upon the number of vessels of war, to be built or purchased, or the number of land or sea forces to be raised, nor appoint a commander in chief of the army or navy, unless nine states assent to the same: nor shall a question on any other point, except for adjourning from day to day be determined, unless by the votes of a majority of the united states in congress assembled.

The congress of the united states shall have power to adjourn to any time within the year, and to any place within the united states, so that no period of adjournment be for a longer duration than the space of six Months, and shall publish the Journal of their proceedings monthly, except such parts thereof relating to treaties, alliances or military operations as in their judgment require secresy; and the yeas and nays of the delegates of each state on any question shall be entered on the Journal, when it is desired by any delegate; and the delegates of a state, or any of them, as his or their request shall be furnished with a transcript of the said Journal, except such parts as are above excepted, to lay before the legislatures of the several states.

Article X   The committee of the states, or any nine of them, shall be authorised to execute, in the recess of congress, such of the powers of congress as the united states in congress assembled, by the consent of nine states, shall from time to time think expedient to vest them with; provided that no power be delegated to the said committee, for the exercise of which, by the articles of confederation, the voice of nine states in the congress of the united states assembled is requisite.

Article XI   Canada acceding to this confederation, and joining in the measures of the united states, shall be admitted into, and entitled to all the advantages of this union: but no other colony shall be admitted into the same, unless such admission be agreed to by nine states.

Article XII   All bills of credit emitted, monies borrowed and debts contracted by, or under the authority of congress, before the assembling of the united states, in pursuance of the present confederation, shall be deemed and considered as a charge against the united states, for payment and satisfaction whereof the said united states, and the public faith are hereby solemnly pledged.

Article XIII   Every state shall abide by the determinations of the united states in congress assembled, on all questions which by this confederation are submitted to them. And the Articles of this confederation shall be inviolably observed by every

state, and the union shall be perpetual; nor shall any alteration at any time hereafter be made in any of them; unless such alteration be agreed to in a congress of the united states, and be afterwards confirmed by the legislatures of every state.

AND WHEREAS it hath pleased the Great Governor of the World to incline the hearts of the legislatures we respectively represent in congress, to approve of, and to authorize us to ratify the said articles of confederation and perpetual union. Know Ye that we the under-signed delegates, by virtue of the power and authority to us given for that purpose, do by these presents, in the name and in behalf of our respective constituents, fully and entirely ratify and confirm each and every of the said articles of confederation and perpetual union, and all and singular the matters and things therein contained: And we do further solemnly plight and engage the faith of our respective constituents, that they shall abide by the determinations of the united states in congress assembled, on all questions, which by the said confederation are submitted to them. And that the articles thereof shall be inviolably observed by the states we respectively represent, and that the union shall be perpetual. In Witness whereof we have hereunto set our hands in Congress. Done at Philadelphia in the state of Pennsylvania the ninth Day of July in the Year of our Lord one Thousand seven Hundred and Seventy-eight, and in the third year of the independence of America.

CONSTITUTION OF THE UNITED STATES OF AMERICA AND AMENDMENTS*

Preamble

We the people of the United States, in order to form a more perfect union, establish justice, insure domestic tranquillity, provide for the common defense, promote the general welfare, and secure the blessings of liberty to ourselves and our posterity, do ordain and establish this Constitution for the United States of America.

Article I

Section 1   All legislative powers herein granted shall be vested in a Congress of the United States, which shall consist of a Senate and a House of Representatives.

Section 2   The House of Representatives shall be composed of members chosen every second year by the people of the several States, and the electors in each State shall have the qualifications requisite for electors of the most numerous branch of the State Legislature.

No person shall be a Representative who shall not have attained to the age of twenty-five years, and been seven years a citizen of the United States, and who shall not, when elected, be an inhabitant of that State in which he shall be chosen.

Representatives and direct taxes shall be apportioned among the several States which may be included within this

*Passages no longer in effect are printed in italic type.

Union, according to their respective numbers, *which shall be determined by adding to the whole number of free persons, including those bound to service for a term of years and excluding Indians not taxed, three-fifths of all other persons.* The actual enumeration shall be made within three years after the first meeting of the Congress of the United States, and within every subsequent term of ten years, in such manner as they shall by law direct. The number of Representatives shall not exceed one for every thirty thousand, but each State shall have at least one Representative; *and until such enumeration shall be made, the State of New Hampshire shall be entitled to choose three, Massachusetts eight, Rhode Island and Providence Plantations one, Connecticut five, New York six, New Jersey four, Pennsylvania eight, Delaware one, Maryland six, Virginia ten, North Carolina five, South Carolina five, and Georgia three.*

When vacancies happen in the representation from any State, the Executive authority thereof shall issue writs of election to fill such vacancies.

The House of Representatives shall choose their Speaker and other officers; and shall have the sole power of impeachment.

Section 3 The Senate of the United States shall be composed of two Senators from each State, *chosen by the legislature thereof,* for six years; and each Senator shall have one vote.

Immediately after they shall be assembled in consequence of the first election, they shall be divided as equally as may be into three classes. The seats of the Senators of the first class shall be vacated at the expiration of the second year, of the second class at the expiration of the fourth year, and of the third class at the expiration of the sixth year, so that one-third may be chosen every second year; *and if vacancies happen by resignation or otherwise, during the recess of the legislature of any State, the Executive thereof may make temporary appointments until the next meeting of the legislature, which shall then fill such vacancies.*

No person shall be a Senator who shall not have attained to the age of thirty years, and been nine years a citizen of the United States, and who shall not, when elected, be an inhabitant of that State for which he shall be chosen.

The Vice-President of the United States shall be President of the Senate, but shall have no vote, unless they be equally divided.

The Senate shall choose their other officers, and also a President *pro tempore,* in the absence of the Vice-President, or when he shall exercise the office of President of the United States.

The Senate shall have the sole power to try all impeachments. When sitting for that purpose, they shall be on oath or affirmation. When the President of the United States is tried, the Chief Justice shall preside: and no person shall be convicted without the concurrence of two-thirds of the members present.

Judgment in cases of impeachment shall not extend further than to removal from the office, and disqualification to hold and enjoy any office of honor, trust or profit under the United States: but the party convicted shall nevertheless be liable and subject to indictment, trial, judgment and punishment, according to law.

Section 4 The times, places and manner of holding elections for Senators and Representatives shall be prescribed in each State by the legislature thereof; but the Congress may at any time by law make or alter such regulations, except as to the places of choosing Senators.

The Congress shall assemble at least once in every year, and such meeting *shall be on the first Monday in December, unless they shall by law appoint a different day.*

Section 5 Each house shall be the judge of the elections, returns and qualifications of its own members, and a majority of each shall constitute a quorum to do business; but a smaller number may adjourn from day to day, and may be authorized to compel the attendance of absent members, in such manner, and under such penalties, as each house may provide.

Each house may determine the rules of its proceedings, punish its members for disorderly behavior, and with the concurrence of two-thirds, expel a member.

Each house shall keep a journal of its proceedings, and from time to time publish the same, excepting such parts as may in their judgment require secrecy; and the yeas and nays of the members of either house on any question shall, at the desire of one-fifth of those present, be entered on the journal.

Neither house, during the session of Congress, shall, without the consent of the other, adjourn for more than three days, nor to any other place than that in which the two houses shall be sitting.

Section 6 The Senators and Representatives shall receive a compensation for their services, to be ascertained by law and paid out of the treasury of the United States. They shall in all cases except treason, felony and breach of the peace, be privileged from arrest during their attendance at the session of their respective houses, and in going to and returning from the same; and for any speech or debate in either house, they shall not be questioned in any other place.

No Senator or Representative shall, during the time for which he was elected, be appointed to any civil office under the authority of the United States, which shall have been created, or the emoluments whereof shall have been increased, during such time; and no person holding any office under the United States shall be a member of either house during his continuance in office.

Section 7 All bills for raising revenue shall originate in the House of Representatives; but the Senate may propose or concur with amendments as on other bills.

Every bill which shall have passed the House of Representatives and the Senate, shall, before it become a law, be presented to the President of the United States; if he approve he shall sign it, but if not he shall return it with objections to that house in which it originated, who shall enter the objections at large on their journal, and proceed to reconsider it. If after such reconsideration two-thirds of that house shall agree to pass the bill, it shall be sent, together with the objections, to the other house, by which it shall likewise be reconsidered, and, if approved by two-thirds of that house, it shall become a law. But in all such cases the votes of both houses shall be determined by yeas and nays, and the names of the persons voting for and against the bill shall be entered on the journal of each house respectively. If any bill shall not be returned by the President within ten days (Sundays excepted) after it shall have been presented to him, the same shall be a law, in like manner as if he had signed it, unless the Congress by their adjournment prevent its return, in which case it shall not be a law.

Every order, resolution, or vote to which the concurrence of the Senate and House of Representatives may be necessary (except on a question of adjournment) shall be presented to the President of the United States; and before the same shall take effect, shall be approved by him, or being disapproved by him, shall be repassed by two-thirds of the Senate and House of Representatives, according to the rules and limitations prescribed in the case of a bill.

Section 8   The Congress shall have power

To lay and collect taxes, duties, imposts, and excises, to pay the debts and provide for the common defense and general welfare of the United States; but all duties, imposts and excises shall be uniform throughout the United States;

To borrow money on the credit of the United States;

To regulate commerce with foreign nations, and among the several States, and with the Indian tribes;

To establish an uniform rule of naturalization, and uniform laws on the subject of bankruptcies throughout the United States;

To coin money, regulate the value thereof, and of foreign coin, and fix the standard of weights and measures;

To provide for the punishment of counterfeiting the securities and current coin of the United States;

To establish post offices and post roads;

To promote the progress of science and useful arts by securing for limited times to authors and inventors the exclusive right to their respective writings and discoveries;

To constitute tribunals inferior to the Supreme Court;

To define and punish piracies and felonies committed on the high seas and offenses against the law of nations;

To declare war, grant letters of marque and reprisal, and make rules concerning captures on land and water;

To raise and support armies, but no appropriation of money to that use shall be for a longer term than two years;

To provide and maintain a navy;

To make rules for the government and regulation of the land and naval forces;

To provide for calling forth the militia to execute the laws of the Union, suppress insurrections, and repel invasions;

To provide for organizing, arming, and disciplining the militia, and for governing such part of them as may be employed in the service of the United States, reserving to the States respectively the appointment of the officers, and the authority of training the militia according to the discipline prescribed by Congress;

To exercise exclusive legislation in all cases whatsoever, over such district (not exceeding ten miles square) as may, by cession of particular States, and the acceptance of Congress, become the seat of government of the United States, and to exercise like authority over all places purchased by the consent of the legislature of the State, in which the same shall be, for erection of forts, magazines, arsenals, dockyards, and other needful buildings; —and

To make all laws which shall be necessary and proper for carrying into execution the foregoing powers, and all other powers vested by this Constitution in the government of the United States, or in any department or officer thereof.

Section 9   *The migration or importation of such persons as any of the States now existing shall think proper to admit shall not be prohibited by the Congress prior to the year 1808; but a tax or duty may be imposed on such importation, not exceeding $10 for each person.*

The privilege of the writ of habeas corpus shall not be suspended, unless when in cases of rebellion or invasion the public safety may require it.

No bill of attainder or ex post facto law shall be passed.

No capitation, or other direct, tax shall be laid, unless in proportion to the census or enumeration herein before directed to be taken.

No tax or duty shall be laid on articles exported from any State.

No preference shall be given by any regulation of commerce or revenue to the ports of one State over those of another; nor shall vessels bound to, or from, one State, be obliged to enter, clear, or pay duties in another.

No money shall be drawn from the treasury, but in consequence of appropriations made by law; and a regular statement and account of the receipts and expenditures of all public money shall be published from time to time.

No title of nobility shall be granted by the United States: and no person holding any office of profit or trust under them, shall, without the consent of the Congress, accept of any present, emolument, office, or title, of any kind whatever, from any king, prince, or foreign state.

Section 10   No State shall enter into any treaty, alliance, or confederation; grant letters of marque and reprisal; coin money; emit bills of credit; make anything but gold and silver coin a tender in payment of debts; pass any bill of attainder, ex post facto law, or law impairing the obligation of contracts, or grant any title of nobility.

No State shall, without the consent of Congress, lay any imposts or duties on imports or exports, except what may be absolutely necessary for executing its inspection laws: and the net produce of all duties and imposts, laid by any State on imports or exports, shall be for the use of the treasury of the United States; and all such laws shall be subject to the revision and control of the Congress.

No State shall, without the consent of Congress, lay any duty of tonnage, keep troops or ships of war in time of peace, enter into any agreement or compact with another State, or with a foreign power, or engage in war, unless actually invaded, or in such imminent danger as will not admit of delay.

Article II

Section 1 The executive power shall be vested in a President of the United States of America. He shall hold his office during the term of four years, and, together with the Vice-President, chosen for the same term, be elected as follows:

Each State shall appoint, in such manner as the legislature thereof may direct, a number of electors, equal to the whole number of Senators and Representatives to which the State may be entitled in the Congress; but no Senator or Representative, or person holding an office of trust or profit under the United States, shall be appointed an elector.

The electors shall meet in their respective States, and vote by ballot for two persons, of whom one at least shall not be an inhabitant of the same State with themselves. And they shall make a list of all the persons voted for, and of the number of votes for each; which list they shall sign and certify, and transmit sealed to the seat of government of the United States, directed to the President of the Senate. The President of the Senate shall, in the presence of the Senate and House of Representatives, open all the certificates, and the votes shall then be counted. The person having the greatest number of votes shall be the President, if such number be a majority of the whole number of electors appointed; and if there be more than one who have such majority, and have an equal number of votes, then the House of Representatives shall immediately choose by ballot one of them for President; and if no person have a majority, then from the five highest on the list said house shall in like manner choose the President. But in choosing the President the votes shall be taken by States, the representation from each State having one vote; a quorum for this purpose shall consist of a member or members from two-thirds of the States, and a majority of all the States shall be necessary to a choice. In every case, after the choice of the President, the person having the greatest number of votes of the electors shall be the Vice-President. But if there should remain two or more who have equal votes, the Senate shall choose from them by ballot the Vice-President.

The Congress may determine the time of choosing the electors and the day on which they shall give their votes; which day shall be the same throughout the United States.

No person except a natural-born citizen, *or a citizen of the United States at the time of the adoption of this Constitution,* shall be eligible to the office of President; neither shall any person be eligible to that office who shall not have attained to the age of thirty-five years, and been fourteen years a resident within the United States.

In cases of the removal of the President from office or of his death, resignation, or inability to discharge the powers and duties of the said office, the same shall devolve on the Vice-President, and the Congress may by law provide for the case of removal, death, resignation, or inability, both of the President and Vice-President, declaring what officer shall then act as President, and such officer shall act accordingly, until the disability be removed, or a President shall be elected.

The President shall, at stated times, receive for his services a compensation, which shall neither be increased nor dimin-

ished during the period for which he shall have been elected, and he shall not receive within that period any other emolument from the United States, or any of them.

Before he enter on the execution of his office, he shall take the following oath or affirmation:—"I do solemnly swear (or affirm) that I will faithfully execute the office of the President of the United States, and will to the best of my ability preserve, protect and defend the Constitution of the United States."

Section 2 The President shall be commander in chief of the army and navy of the United States, and of the militia of the several States, when called into the actual service of the United States; he may require the opinion, in writing, of the principal officer in each of the executive departments, upon any subject relating to the duties of their respective offices, and he shall have power to grant reprieves and pardons for offenses against the United States, except in cases of impeachment.

He shall have power, by and with the advice and consent of the Senate, to make treaties, provided two-thirds of the Senators present concur; and he shall nominate, and by and with the advice and consent of the Senate, shall appoint ambassadors, other public ministers and consuls, judges of the Supreme Court, and all other officers of the United States, whose appointments are not herein otherwise provided for, and which shall be established by law: but Congress may by law vest the appointment of such inferior officers, as they think proper, in the President alone, in the courts of law, or in the heads of departments.

The President shall have power to fill up all vacancies that may happen during the recess of the Senate, by granting commissions which shall expire at the end of their next session.

Section 3 He shall from time to time give to the Congress information of the state of the Union, and recommend to their consideration such measures as he shall judge necessary and expedient; he may, on extraordinary occasions, convene both houses, or either of them, and in case of disagreement between them, with respect to the time of adjournment, he may adjourn them to such time as he shall think proper; he shall receive ambassadors and other public ministers; he shall take care that the laws be faithfully executed, and shall commission all the officers of the United States.

Section 4 The President, Vice-President and all civil officers of the United States shall be removed from office on impeachment for, and on conviction of, treason, bribery, or other high crimes and misdemeanors.

Article III

Section 1 The judicial power of the United States shall be vested in one Supreme Court, and in such inferior courts as the Congress may from time to time ordain and establish. The judges, both of the Supreme and inferior courts, shall hold their offices during good behavior, and shall, at stated times, receive for their services a compensation which shall not be diminished during their continuance in office.

Section 2 The judicial power shall extend to all cases, in law and equity, arising under this Constitution, the laws of the United States, and treaties made, or which shall be made, under their authority;—to all cases affecting ambassadors, other public ministers and consuls;—to all cases of admiralty and maritime jurisdiction;—to controversies to which the United States shall be a party;—to controversies between two or more States;—*between a State and citizens of another State;*—between citizens of different States;—between citizens of the same State claiming lands under grants of different States, and between a State, or the citizens thereof, and foreign states, citizens or subjects.

In all cases affecting ambassadors, other public ministers and consuls, and those in which a State shall be party, the Supreme Court shall have original jurisdiction. In all the other cases before mentioned, the Supreme Court shall have appellate jurisdiction, both as to law and fact, with such exceptions, and under such regulations, as the Congress shall make.

The trial of all crimes, except in cases of impeachment, shall be by jury; and such trial shall be held in the State where said crimes shall have been committed; but when not committed within any State, the trial shall be at such place or places as the Congress may by law have directed.

Section 3 Treason against the United States shall consist only in levying war against them, or in adhering to their enemies, giving them aid and comfort. No person shall be convicted of treason unless on the testimony of two witnesses to the same overt act, or on confession in open court.

The Congress shall have power to declare the punishment of treason, but no attainder of treason shall work corruption of blood, or forfeiture except during the life of the person attainted.

Article IV

Section 1 Full faith and credit shall be given in each State to the public acts, records, and judicial proceedings of every other State. And the Congress may by general laws prescribe the manner in which such acts, records, and proceedings shall be proved, and the effect thereof.

Section 2 The citizens of each State shall be entitled to all privileges and immunities of citizens in the several States.

A person charged in any State with treason, felony, or other crime, who shall flee from justice, and be found in another State, shall on demand of the executive authority of the State from which he fled, be delivered up, to be removed to the State having jurisdiction of the crime.

No person held to service or labor in one State, under the laws thereof, escaping into another, shall, in consequence of any law or regulation therein, be discharged from such service or labor, but shall be delivered up on claim of the party to whom such service or labor may be due.

Section 3 New States may be admitted by the Congress into this Union; but no new State shall be formed or erected within the jurisdiction of any other State; nor any State be formed by the junction of two or more States, or parts of States, without the consent of the legislatures of the States concerned as well as of the Congress.

The Congress shall have power to dispose of and make all needful rules and regulations respecting the territory or other property belonging to the United States; and nothing in this Constitution shall be so construed as to prejudice any claims of the United States, or of any particular State.

Section 4 The United States shall guarantee to every State in this Union a republican form of government, and shall protect each of them against invasion; and on application of the legislature, or of the executive (when the legislature cannot be convened), against domestic violence.

Article V

The Congress, whenever two-thirds of both houses shall deem it necessary, shall propose amendments to this Constitution, or, on the application of the legislatures of two-thirds of the several States, shall call a convention for proposing amendments, which, in either case, shall be valid to all intents and purposes, as part of this Constitution, when ratified by the legislatures of three-fourths of the several States, or by conventions in three-fourths thereof, as the one or the other mode of ratification may be proposed by the Congress; provided *that no amendments which may be made prior to the year one thousand eight hundred and eight shall in any manner affect the first and fourth clauses in the ninth section of the first article;* and that no State, without its consent, shall be deprived of its equal suffrage in the Senate.

Article VI

All debts contracted and engagements entered into, before the adoption of this Constitution, shall be as valid against the United States under this Constitution, as under the Confederation.

This Constitution, and the laws of the United States which shall be made in pursuance thereof; and all treaties made, or which shall be made, under the authority of the United States, shall be the supreme law of the land; and the judges in every State shall be bound thereby, anything in the Constitution or laws of any State to the contrary notwithstanding.

The Senators and Representatives before mentioned, and the members of the several State legislatures, and all executive and judicial officers, both of the United States and of the several States, shall be bound by oath or affirmation to support this Constitution; but no religious test shall ever be required as a qualification to any office or public trust under the United States.

Article VII

The ratification of the conventions of nine States shall be sufficient for the establishment of this Constitution between the States so ratifying the same.

Done in Convention by the unanimous consent of the States present, the seventeenth day of September in the year of our Lord one thousand seven hundred and eighty-seven and of the

Independence of the United States of America the twelfth. In witness whereof we have hereunto subscribed our names.

Amendments to the Constitution*

Amendment I

Congress shall make no law respecting an establishment of religion, or prohibiting the free exercise thereof; or abridging the freedom of speech, or of the press; or the right of the people peaceably to assemble, and to petition the government for a redress of grievances.

Amendment II

A well-regulated militia being necessary to the security of a free State, the right of the people to keep and bear arms shall not be infringed.

Amendment III

No soldier shall, in time of peace, be quartered in any house without the consent of the owner, nor in time of war, but in a manner to be prescribed by law.

Amendment IV

The right of the people to be secure in their persons, houses, papers, and effects, against unreasonable searches and seizures, shall not be violated, and no warrants shall issue but upon probable cause, supported by oath or affirmation, and particularly describing the place to be searched, and the persons or things to be seized.

Amendment V

No person shall be held to answer for a capital, or otherwise infamous crime, unless on a presentment or indictment of a grand jury, except in cases arising in the land or naval forces, or in the militia, when in actual service in time of war or public danger; nor shall any person be subject for the same offense to be twice put in jeopardy of life or limb; nor shall be compelled in any criminal case to be a witness against himself, nor be deprived of life, liberty, or property, without due process of law; nor shall private property be taken for public use without just compensation.

Amendment VI

In all criminal prosecutions, the accused shall enjoy the right to a speedy and public trial, by an impartial jury of the State and district wherein the crime shall have been committed, which district shall have been previously ascertained by law, and to be informed of the nature and cause of the accusation; to be confronted with the witnesses against him; to have compulsory process for obtaining witnesses in his favor, and to have the assistance of counsel for his defense.

*The first ten Amendments (the Bill of Rights) were adopted in 1791.

Amendment VII

In suits at common law, where the value in controversy shall exceed twenty dollars, the right of trial by jury shall be preserved, and no fact tried by a jury shall be otherwise reexamined in any court of the United States, than according to the rules of the common law.

Amendment VIII

Excessive bail shall not be required, nor excessive fines imposed, nor cruel and unusual punishments inflicted.

Amendment IX

The enumeration in the Constitution, of certain rights, shall not be construed to deny or disparage others retained by the people.

Amendment X

The powers not delegated to the United States by the Constitution, nor prohibited by it to the States, are reserved to the States respectively, or to the people.

Amendment XI

[Adopted 1798]
The judicial power of the United States shall not be construed to extend to any suit in law or equity, commenced or prosecuted against one of the United States by citizens of another State, or by citizens or subjects of any foreign state.

Amendment XII

[Adopted 1804]
The electors shall meet in their respective States, and vote by ballot for President and Vice-President, one of whom, at least, shall not be an inhabitant of the same State with themselves; they shall name in their ballots the person voted for as President, and in distinct ballots the person voted for as Vice-President, and they shall make distinct lists of all persons voted for as President, and of all persons voted for as Vice-President, and of the number of votes for each, which lists they shall sign and certify, and transmit sealed to the seat of government of the United States, directed to the President of the Senate;—the President of the Senate shall, in the presence of the Senate and House of Representatives, open all the certificates and the votes shall then be counted;—the person having the greatest number of votes for President shall be the President, if such number be a majority of the whole number of electors appointed; and if no person have such majority, then from the persons having the highest numbers not exceeding three on the list of those voted for as President, the House of Representatives shall choose immediately, by ballot, the President. But in choosing the President, the votes shall be taken by States, the representation from each State having one vote; a quorum for this purpose shall consist of a member or members from two-thirds of the States, and a majority of all the States shall be necessary to a choice. And if the House of Representatives shall not choose a President

whenever the right of choice shall devolve upon them, before *the fourth day of March* next following, then the Vice-President shall act as President, as in the case of the death or other constitutional disability of the President.

The person having the greatest number of votes as Vice-President shall be the Vice-President, if such number be a majority of the whole number of electors appointed; and if no person have a majority, then from the two highest numbers on the list the Senate shall choose the Vice-President; a quorum for the purpose shall consist of two-thirds of the whole number of Senators, and a majority of the whole number shall be necessary to a choice. But no person constitutionally ineligible to the office of President shall be eligible to that of Vice-President of the United States.

Amendment XIII

[Adopted 1865]

Section 1   Neither slavery nor involuntary servitude, except as a punishment for crime whereof the party shall have been duly convicted, shall exist within the United States, or any place subject to their jurisdiction.

Section 2   Congress shall have power to enforce this article by appropriate legislation.

Amendment XIV

[Adopted 1868]

Section 1   All persons born or naturalized in the United States, and subject to the jurisdiction thereof, are citizens of the United States and of the State wherein they reside. No State shall make or enforce any law which shall abridge the privileges or immunities of citizens of the United States; nor shall any State deprive any person of life, liberty, or property, without due process of law; nor deny to any person within its jurisdiction the equal protection of the laws.

Section 2   Representatives shall be apportioned among the several States according to their respective numbers, counting the whole number of persons in each State, excluding Indians not taxed. But when the right to vote at any election for the choice of Electors for President and Vice-President of the United States, Representatives in Congress, the executive and judicial officers of a State, or the members of the legislature thereof, is denied to any of the male inhabitants of such State, being twenty-one years of age and citizens of the United States, or in any way abridged, except for participation in rebellion, or other crime, the basis of representation therein shall be reduced in the proportion which the number of such male citizens shall bear to the whole number of male citizens twenty-one years of age in such State.

Section 3   No person shall be a Senator or Representative in Congress, or Elector of President and Vice-President, or hold any office, civil or military, under the United States, or under any State, who, having previously taken an oath, as a member of Congress, or as an officer of the United States, or as a member of any State legislature, or as an executive or judicial officer of any State, to support the Constitution of the United States, shall have engaged in insurrection or rebellion against the same, or given aid or comfort to the enemies thereof. Congress may, by a vote of two-thirds of each house, remove such disability.

Section 4   The validity of the public debt of the United States, authorized by law, including debts incurred for payment of pensions and bounties for services in suppressing insurrection or rebellion, shall not be questioned. But neither the United States nor any State shall assume or pay any debt or obligation incurred in aid of insurrection or rebellion against the United States, or any claim for the loss of emancipation of any slave; but all such debts, obligations, and claims shall be held illegal and void.

Section 5   The Congress shall have power to enforce, by appropriate legislation, the provisions of this article.

Amendment XV

[Adopted 1870]

Section 1   The right of citizens of the United States to vote shall not be denied or abridged by the United States or by any State on account of race, color, or previous condition of servitude.

Section 2   The Congress shall have power to enforce this article by appropriate legislation.

Amendment XVI

[Adopted 1913]

The Congress shall have power to lay and collect taxes on incomes, from whatever source derived, without apportionment among the several States, and without regard to any census or enumeration.

Amendment XVII

[Adopted 1913]

Section 1   The Senate of the United States shall be composed of two Senators from each State, elected by the people thereof, for six years; and each Senator shall have one vote. The electors in each State shall have the qualifications requisite for electors of [voters for] the most numerous branch of the State legislatures.

Section 2   When vacancies happen in the representation of any State in the Senate, the executive authority of such State shall issue writs of election to fill such vacancies: Provided, that the Legislature of any State may empower the executive thereof to make temporary appointments until the people fill the vacancies by election as the Legislature may direct.

Section 3   This amendment shall not be so construed as to affect the election or term of any Senator chosen before it becomes valid as part of the Constitution.

Amendment XVIII

[Adopted 1919; Repealed 1933]

Section 1   After one year from the ratification of this article the manufacture, sale, or transportation of intoxicating liquors within, the importation thereof into, or the exportation thereof from the United States and all territory subject to the jurisdiction thereof, for beverage purposes, is hereby prohibited.

Section 2   The Congress and the several States shall have concurrent power to enforce this article by appropriate legislation.

Section 3   This article shall be inoperative unless it shall have been ratified as an amendment to the Constitution by the legislatures of the several States, as provided by the Constitution, within seven years from the date of the submission thereof to the States by the Congress.

Amendment XIX

[Adopted 1920]

Section 1   The right of citizens of the United States to vote shall not be denied or abridged by the United States or by any State on account of sex.

Section 2   The Congress shall have power to enforce this article by appropriate legislation.

Amendment XX

[Adopted 1933]

Section 1   The terms of the President and Vice-President shall end at noon on the 20th day of January, and the terms of Senators and Representatives at noon on the 3rd day of January, of the years in which such terms would have ended if this article had not been ratified; and the terms of their successors shall then begin.

Section 2   The Congress shall assemble at least once in every year, and such meeting shall begin at noon on the 3d day of January, unless they shall by law appoint a different day.

Section 3   If, at the time fixed for the beginning of the term of the President, the President-elect shall have died, the Vice-President–elect shall become President. If a President shall not have been chosen before the time fixed for the beginning of his term, or if the President-elect shall have failed to qualify, then the Vice-President–elect shall act as President until a President shall have qualified; and the Congress may by law provide for the case wherein neither a President-elect nor a Vice-President–elect

shall have qualified, declaring who shall then act as President, or the manner in which one who is to act shall be selected, and such persons shall act accordingly until a President or Vice-President shall have qualified.

Section 4   The Congress may by law provide for the case of the death of any of the persons from whom the House of Representatives may choose a President whenever the right of choice shall have devolved upon them, and for the case of the death of any of the persons from whom the Senate may choose a Vice-President whenever the right of choice shall have devolved upon them.

Section 5   Sections 1 and 2 shall take effect on the 15th day of October following the ratification of this article.

Section 6   This article shall be inoperative unless it shall have been ratified as an amendment to the Constitution by the Legislatures of three-fourths of the several States within seven years from the date of its submission.

Amendment XXI

[Adopted 1933]

Section 1   The eighteenth article of amendment to the Constitution of the United States is hereby repealed.

Section 2   The transportation or importation into any State, Territory, or Possession of the United States for delivery or use therein of intoxicating liquors, in violation of the laws thereof, is hereby prohibited.

Section 3   This article shall be inoperative unless it shall have been ratified as an amendment to the Constitution by conventions in the several States, as provided in the Constitution, within seven years from the date of submission thereof to the States by the Congress.

Amendment XXII

[Adopted 1951]

Section 1   No person shall be elected to the office of President more than twice, and no person who has held the office of President, or acted as President, for more than two years of a term to which some other person was elected President shall be elected to the office of President more than once. But this article shall not apply to any person holding the office of President when this article was proposed by the Congress, and shall not prevent any person who may be holding the office of President, or acting as President, during the term within which this article becomes operative from holding the office of President or acting as President during the remainder of such term.

Section 2   This article shall be inoperative unless it shall have been ratified as an amendment to the Constitution by the legislatures of three-fourths of the several States within seven years from the date of its submission to the States by the Congress.

Amendment XXIII

[Adopted 1961]

Section 1   The District constituting the seat of Government of the United States shall appoint in such manner as the Congress may direct:

A number of electors of President and Vice-President equal to the whole number of Senators and Representatives in Congress to which the District would be entitled if it were a State, but in no event more than the least populous State; they shall be in addition to those appointed by the States, but they shall be considered for the purposes of the election of President and Vice-President, to be electors appointed by a State; and they shall meet in the District and perform such duties as provided by the twelfth article of amendment.

Section 2   The Congress shall have the power to enforce this article by appropriate legislation.

Amendment XXIV

[Adopted 1964]

Section 1   The right of citizens of the United States to vote in any primary or other election for President or Vice-President, for electors for President or Vice-President, or for Senator or Representative in Congress, shall not be denied or abridged by the United States or any State by reason of failure to pay any poll tax or other tax.

Section 2   The Congress shall have the power to enforce this article by appropriate legislation.

Amendment XXV

[Adopted 1967]

Section 1   In case of the removal of the President from office or of his death or resignation, the Vice-President shall become President.

Section 2   Whenever there is a vacancy in the office of the Vice-President, the President shall nominate a Vice-President who shall take office upon confirmation by a majority vote of both Houses of Congress.

Section 3   Whenever the President transmits to the President pro tempore of the Senate and the Speaker of the House of Rep-

resentatives his written declaration that he is unable to discharge the powers and duties of his office, and until he transmits to them a written declaration to the contrary, such powers and duties shall be discharged by the Vice-President as Acting President.

Section 4   Whenever the Vice-President and a majority of either the principal officers of the executive departments or of such other body as Congress may by law provide, transmit to the President pro tempore of the Senate and the Speaker of the House of Representatives their written declaration that the President is unable to discharge the powers and duties of his office, the Vice-President shall immediately assume the powers and duties of the office as Acting President.

Thereafter, when the President transmits to the President pro tempore of the Senate and the Speaker of the House of Representatives his written declaration that no inability exists, he shall resume the powers and duties of his office unless the Vice-President and a majority of either the principal officers of the executive department[s] or of such other body as Congress may by law provide, transmit within four days to the President pro tempore of the Senate and the Speaker of the House of Representatives their written declaration that the President is unable to discharge the powers and duties of his office. Thereupon Congress shall decide the issue, assembling within forty-eight hours for that purpose if not in session. If the Congress, within twenty-one days after receipt of the latter written declaration, or, if Congress is not in session, within twenty-one days after Congress is required to assemble, determines by two-thirds vote of both Houses that the President is unable to discharge the powers and duties of his office, the Vice-President shall continue to discharge the same as Acting President; otherwise, the President shall resume the powers and duties of his office.

Amendment XXVI

[Adopted 1971]

Section 1   The right of citizens of the United States, who are eighteen years of age or older, to vote shall not be denied or abridged by the United States or by any State on account of age.

Section 2   The Congress shall have power to enforce this article by appropriate legislation.

Amendment XXVII

[Adopted 1992]

No law, varying the compensation for the services of the Senators and Representatives, shall take effect, until an election of Representatives shall have intervened.

The American People and Nation: A Statistical Profile

Population of the United States

Year	Number of States	Population	Percent Increase	Population Per Square Mile	Percent Urban/ Rural	Percent Male/ Female	Percent White/ Non- white	Persons Per House- hold	Median Age
1790	13	3,929,214		4.5	5.1/94.9	NA/NA	80.7/19.3	5.79	NA
1800	16	5,308,483	35.1	6.1	6.1/93.9	NA/NA	81.1/18.9	NA	NA
1810	17	7,239,881	36.4	4.3	7.3/92.7	NA/NA	81.0/19.0	NA	NA
1820	23	9,638,453	33.1	5.5	7.2/92.8	50.8/49.2	81.6/18.4	NA	16.7
1830	24	12,866,020	33.5	7.4	8.8/91.2	50.8/49.2	81.9/18.1	NA	17.2
1840	26	17,069,453	32.7	9.8	10.8/89.2	50.9/49.1	83.2/16.8	NA	17.8
1850	31	23,191,876	35.9	7.9	15.3/84.7	51.0/49.0	84.3/15.7	5.55	18.9
1860	33	31,443,321	35.6	10.6	19.8/80.2	51.2/48.8	85.6/14.4	5.28	19.4
1870	37	39,818,449	26.6	13.4	25.7/74.3	50.6/49.4	86.2/13.8	5.09	20.2
1880	38	50,155,783	26.0	16.9	28.2/71.8	50.9/49.1	86.5/13.5	5.04	20.9
1890	44	62,947,714	25.5	21.2	35.1/64.9	51.2/48.8	87.5/12.5	4.93	22.0
1900	45	75,994,575	20.7	25.6	39.6/60.4	51.1/48.9	87.9/12.1	4.76	22.9
1910	46	91,972,266	21.0	31.0	45.6/54.4	51.5/48.5	88.9/11.1	4.54	24.1
1920	48	105,710,620	14.9	35.6	51.2/48.8	51.0/49.0	89.7/10.3	4.34	25.3
1930	48	122,775,046	16.1	41.2	56.1/43.9	50.6/49.4	89.8/10.2	4.11	26.4
1940	48	131,669,275	7.2	44.2	56.5/43.5	50.2/49.8	89.8/10.2	3.67	29.0
1950	48	150,697,361	14.5	50.7	64.0/36.0	49.7/50.3	89.5/10.5	3.37	30.2
1960	50	179,323,175	18.5	50.6	69.9/30.1	49.3/50.7	88.6/11.4	3.33	29.5
1970	50	203,302,031	13.4	57.4	73.6/26.4	48.7/51.3	87.6/12.4	3.14	28.0
1980	50	226,542,199	11.4	64.1	73.7/26.3	48.6/51.4	85.9/14.1	2.75	30.0
1990	50	248,718,301	9.8	70.3	75.2/24.8	48.7/51.3	83.9/16.1	2.63	32.8
1998	50	270,299,000	8.0	76.4	NA	48.9/51.1	82.5/17.5	2.62	35.2
2000	50	281,421,906	1.09	74.0	79.0/21.0	49.1/50.9	75.1/24.9	2.59	35.3

NA = Not available.

Vital Statistics

| Year | Birth Rate* | Death Rate* | Life Expectancy in Years | | | | | Marriage Rate | Divorce Rate |
			Total Population	White Females	Nonwhite Females	White Males	Nonwhite Males		
1790	NA	NA	NA	NA	NA	NA	NA	NA	NA
1800	55.0	NA	NA	NA	NA	NA	NA	NA	NA
1810	54.3	NA	NA	NA	NA	NA	NA	NA	NA
1820	55.2	NA	NA	NA	NA	NA	NA	NA	NA
1830	51.4	NA	NA	NA	NA	NA	NA	NA	NA
1840	51.8	NA	NA	NA	NA	NA	NA	NA	NA
1850	43.3	NA	NA	NA	NA	NA	NA	NA	NA
1860	44.3	NA	NA	NA	NA	NA	NA	NA	NA
1870	38.3	NA	NA	NA	NA	NA	NA	NA	NA
1880	39.8	NA	NA	NA	NA	NA	NA	NA	NA
1890	31.5	NA	NA	NA	NA	NA	NA	NA	NA
1900	32.3	17.2	47.3	48.7	33.5	46.6	32.5	NA	NA
1910	30.1	14.7	50.0	52.0	37.5	48.6	33.8	NA	NA
1920	27.7	13.0	54.1	55.6	45.2	54.4	45.5	12.0	1.6
1930	21.3	11.3	59.7	63.5	49.2	59.7	47.3	9.2	1.6
1940	19.4	10.8	62.9	66.6	54.9	62.1	51.5	12.1	2.0
1950	24.1	9.6	68.2	72.2	62.9	66.5	59.1	11.1	2.6
1960	23.7	9.5	69.7	74.1	66.3	67.4	61.1	8.5	2.2
1970	18.4	9.5	70.8	75.6	69.4	68.0	61.3	10.6	3.5
1980	15.9	8.8	73.7	78.1	73.6	70.7	65.3	10.6	5.2
1990	16.6	8.6	75.4	79.4	75.2	72.7	67.0	9.8	4.7
1998	14.4	8.5	76.5†	73.9†	76.1°	74.3†	68.9°	8.9†	4.3
2000	14.7	8.7	76.9	80.0	74.9	74.8	68.2	8.5	4.1

Note: Data per one thousand for Birth, Death, Marriage, and Divorce Rates.

NA = Not available. *Data for 1800, 1810, 1830, 1850, 1870, and 1890 for whites only. †Data for 1997. °Data for 1996.

Immigrants to the United States

| Immigration Totals by Decade | | | |
Years	Number	Years	Number
1820–1830	151,824	1921–1930	4,107,209
1831–1840	599,125	1931–1940	528,431
1841–1850	1,713,251	1941–1950	1,035,039
1851–1860	2,598,214	1951–1960	2,515,479
1861–1870	2,314,824	1961–1970	3,321,677
1871–1880	2,812,191	1971–1980	4,493,314
1881–1890	5,246,613	1981–1990	7,338,062
1891–1900	3,687,546	1991–1997	6,944,591
1901–1910	8,795,386	1991–2000	9,095,417
1911–1920	5,735,811	Total	66,089,431

Major Sources of Immigrants by Country or Region (in thousands)

Period	Asia[a]	Germany	Mexico	Italy	Great Britain (UK)[b]	Ireland	Canada	Austria and Hungary	Soviet Union (Russia)	Caribbean	Central America and South America	Norway and Sweden
1820–1830	–	8	5	–	27	54	2	–	–	4	–	–
1831–1840	–	152	7	2	76	207	14	–	–	12	–	1
1841–1850	–	435	3	2	267	781	42	–	–	14	4	14
1851–1860	42	952	3	9	424	914	59	–	–	11	2	21
1861–1870	65	787	2	12	607	436	154	8	3	9	1	109
1871–1880	124	718	5	56	548	437	384	73	39	14	1	211
1881–1890	70	1,453	2[c]	307	807	655	393	354	213	29	3	568
1891–1900	75	505	1[c]	652	272	388	3	593	505	33	2	321
1901–1910	324	341	50	2,046	526	339	179	2,145	1,597	108	25	440
1911–1920	247	144	219	1,110	341	146	742	896	921	123	59	161
1921–1930	112	412	459	455	340	211	925	64	62	75	58	166
1931–1940	17	114	22	68	32	11	109	11	1	16	14	9
1941–1950	37	227	61	58	139	20	172	28	–	50	43	21
1951–1960	153	478	300	185	203	48	378	104	–	123	136	45
1961–1970	428	191	454	214	214	33	413	26	2	470	359	33
1971–1980	1,588	74	640	129	137	11	170	16	39	741	430	10
1981–1990	2,738	92	2,336	67	160	32	157	25	58	872	930	15
1991–2000	2,796	93	2,249	63	152	57	192	25	463	979	1,067	18
Total	8,816	7,176	6,818	5,435	5,272	4,780	4,488	4,368	3,903	3,683	3,134	2,163

Notes: Numbers for periods are rounded. Dash indicates less than 1,000. [a]Includes Middle East. [b]Since 1925, includes England, Scotland, Wales, and Northern Ireland data. [c]No data available for 1886–1894.

The American Worker

Year	Total Number of Workers	Males as Percent of Total Workers	Females as Percent of Total Workers	Married Women as Percent of Female Workers	Female Workers as Percent of Female Population	Percent of Labor Force Unemployed	Percent of Workers in Labor Unions
1870	12,506,000	85	15	NA	NA	NA	NA
1880	17,392,000	85	15	NA	NA	NA	NA
1890	23,318,000	83	17	14	19	4 (1894 = 18)	NA
1900	29,073,000	82	18	15	21	5	3
1910	38,167,000	79	21	25	25	6	6
1920	41,614,000	79	21	23	24	5 (1921 = 12)	12
1930	48,830,000	78	22	29	25	9 (1933 = 25)	11.6
1940	53,011,000	76	24	36	27	15 (1944 = 1)	26.9
1950	62,208,000	72	28	52	31	5.3	31.5
1960	69,628,000	67	33	55	38	5.5	31.4
1970	82,771,000	62	38	59	43	4.9	27.3
1980	106,940,000	58	42	55	52	7.1	21.9
1990	125,840,000	55	45	54	58	5.6	16.1
2000	138,820,935	54	46	53	57.5	3.7	13.9

NA = Not available.

The American Economy

Year	Gross National Product (GNP) and Gross Domestic Product (GDP)[a] (in $ billions)	Steel Production (in tons)	Corn Production (millions of bushels)	Automobiles Registered	New Housing Starts	Foreign Trade (in $ millions) Exports	Foreign Trade (in $ millions) Imports
1790	NA	NA	NA	NA	NA	20	23
1800	NA	NA	NA	NA	NA	71	91
1810	NA	NA	NA	NA	NA	67	85
1820	NA	NA	NA	NA	NA	70	74
1830	NA	NA	NA	NA	NA	74	71
1840	NA	NA	NA	NA	NA	132	107
1850	NA	NA	592[d]	NA	NA	152	178
1860	NA	13,000	839[e]	NA	NA	400	362
1870	7.4[b]	77,000	1,125	NA	NA	451	462
1880	11.2[c]	1,397,000	1,707	NA	NA	853	761
1890	13.1	4,779,000	1,650	NA	328,000	910	823
1900	18.7	11,227,000	2,662	8,000	189,000	1,499	930
1910	35.3	28,330,000	2,853	458,300	387,000 (1918 = 118,000)	1,919	1,646
1920	91.5	46,183,000	3,071	8,131,500	247,000 (1925 = 937,000)	8,664	5,784
1930	90.7	44,591,000	2,080	23,034,700	330,000 (1933 = 93,000)	4,013	3,500
1940	100.0	66,983,000	2,457	27,465,800	603,000 (1944 = 142,000)	4,030	7,433
1950	286.5	96,836,000	3,075	40,339,000	1,952,000	9,997	8,954
1960	506.5	99,282,000	4,314	61,682,300	1,365,000	19,659	15,093
1970	1,016.0	131,514,000	4,200	89,279,800	1,434,000	42,681	40,356
1980	2,819.5	111,835,000	6,600	121,601,000	1,292,000	220,626	244,871
1990	5,764.9	98,906,000	7,933	143,550,000	1,193,000	394,030	485,453
1998	8,511.0	107,600,000	9,761	129,749,000[f]	1,617,000	682,100	911,900
2000	9,256.1	108,800,000[g]	9,968	131,839,000[g]	1,535,000	695,000	1,025,000

[a]In December 1991 the Bureau of Economic Analysis of the U.S. government began featuring Gross Domestic Product rather than Gross National Product as the primary measure of U.S. production.

[b]Figure is average for 1869–1878.

[c]Figure is average for 1879–1888.

[d]Figure for 1849.

[e]Figure for 1859.

[f]Figure for 1997.

[g]Figure for 1998.

NA = Not available.

Federal Budget Outlays and Debt

Year	Defense[a]	Veterans Benefits[a]	Income Security[a]	Social Security[a]	Health and Medicare[a]	Education[a,d]	Net Interest Payments[a]	Federal Debt (dollars)
1790	14.9	4.1[b]	NA	NA	NA	NA	55.0	75,463,000[c]
1800	55.7	.6	NA	NA	NA	NA	31.3	82,976,000
1810	48.4 (1814: 79.7)	1.0	NA	NA	NA	NA	34.9	53,173,000
1820	38.4	17.6	NA	NA	NA	NA	28.1	91,016,000
1830	52.9	9.0	NA	NA	NA	NA	12.6	48,565,000
1840	54.3 (1847: 80.7)	10.7	NA	NA	NA	NA	.7	3,573,000
1850	43.8	4.7	NA	NA	NA	NA	1.0	63,453,000
1860	44.2 (1865: 88.9)	1.7	NA	NA	NA	NA	5.0	64,844,000
1870	25.7	9.2	NA	NA	NA	NA	41.7	2,436,453,000
1880	19.3	21.2	NA	NA	NA	NA	35.8	2,090,909,000
1890	20.9 (1899: 48.6)	33.6	NA	NA	NA	NA	11.4	1,222,397,000
1900	36.6	27.0	NA	NA	NA	NA	7.7	1,263,417,000
1910	45.1 (1919: 59.5)	23.2	NA	NA	NA	NA	3.1	1,146,940,000
1920	37.1	3.4	NA	NA	NA	NA	16.0	24,299,321,000
1930	25.3	6.6	NA	NA	NA	NA	19.9	16,185,310,000
1940	17.5 (1945: 89.4)	6.0	16.0	.3	.5	20.8	9.4	42,967,531,000
1950	32.2	20.3	9.6	1.8	.6	.6	11.3	256,853,000,000
1960	52.2	5.9	8.0	12.6	.9	1.0	7.5	290,525,000,000
1970	41.8	4.4	8.0	15.5	6.2	4.4	7.3	308,921,000,000
1980	22.7	3.6	14.6	20.1	9.4	5.4	8.9	909,050,000,000
1990	23.9	2.3	11.7	19.8	12.4	3.1	14.7	3,266,073,000,000
1998	16.2	2.5	14.1	22.9	19.6	3.3	14.7	5,555,565,000,000
2000	16.2	2.6	14.0	22.7	19.9	3.5	12.3	5,685,181,000,000

[a]Figures represent percentage of total federal spending for each category. Not included are transportation, commerce, housing, and various other categories.

[b]1789–1791 figure.

[c]1791 figure.

[d]Includes training, employment, and social services.

NA = Not available.

Presidential Elections

Year	Number of States	Candidates	Parties	Popular Vote	% of Popular Vote	Electoral Vote	% Voter Participation[a]
1789	10	**George Washington**	No party			69	
		John Adams	designations			34	
		Other candidates				35	
1792	15	**George Washington**	No party			132	
		John Adams	designations			77	
		George Clinton				50	
		Other candidates				5	
1796	16	**John Adams**	Federalist			71	
		Thomas Jefferson	Democratic-Republican			68	
		Thomas Pinckney	Federalist			59	
		Aaron Burr	Democratic-Republican			30	
		Other candidates				48	
1800	16	**Thomas Jefferson**	Democratic-Republican			73	
		Aaron Burr	Democratic-Republican			73	
		John Adams	Federalist			65	
		Charles C. Pinckney	Federalist			64	
		John Jay	Federalist			1	
1804	17	**Thomas Jefferson**	Democratic-Republican			162	
		Charles C. Pinckney	Federalist			14	
1808	17	**James Madison**	Democratic-Republican			122	
		Charles C. Pinckney	Federalist			47	
		George Clinton	Democratic-Republican			6	
1812	18	**James Madison**	Democratic-Republican			128	
		DeWitt Clinton	Federalist			89	
1816	19	**James Monroe**	Democratic-Republican			183	
		Rufus King	Federalist			34	
1820	24	**James Monroe**	Democratic-Republican			231	
		John Quincy Adams	Independent Republican			1	

Presidential Elections (continued)

Year	Number of States	Candidates	Parties	Popular Vote	% of Popular Vote	Electoral Vote	% Voter Participation[a]
1824	24	**John Quincy Adams**	Democratic-Republican	108,740	30.5	84	26.9
		Andrew Jackson	Democratic-Republican	153,544	43.1	99	
		Henry Clay	Democratic-Republican	47,136	13.2	37	
		William H. Crawford	Democratic-Republican	46,618	13.1	41	
1828	24	**Andrew Jackson**	Democratic	647,286	56.0	178	57.6
		John Quincy Adams	National Republican	508,064	44.0	83	
1832	24	**Andrew Jackson**	Democratic	701,780	54.2	219	55.4
		Henry Clay	National Republican	484,205	37.4	49	
		Other candidates		107,988	8.0	18	
1836	26	**Martin Van Buren**	Democratic	764,176	50.8	170	57.8
		William H. Harrison	Whig	550,816	36.6	73	
		Hugh L. White	Whig	146,107	9.7	26	
1840	26	**William H. Harrison**	Whig	1,274,624	53.1	234	80.2
		Martin Van Buren	Democratic	1,127,781	46.9	60	
1844	26	**James K. Polk**	Democratic	1,338,464	49.6	170	78.9
		Henry Clay	Whig	1,300,097	48.1	105	
		James G. Birney	Liberty	62,300	2.3		
1848	30	**Zachary Taylor**	Whig	1,360,967	47.4	163	72.7
		Lewis Cass	Democratic	1,222,342	42.5	127	
		Martin Van Buren	Free Soil	291,263	10.1		
1852	31	**Franklin Pierce**	Democratic	1,601,117	50.9	254	69.6
		Winfield Scott	Whig	1,385,453	44.1	42	
		John P. Hale	Free Soil	155,825	5.0		
1856	31	**James Buchanan**	Democratic	1,832,955	45.3	174	78.9
		John C. Frémont	Republican	1,339,932	33.1	114	
		Millard Fillmore	American	871,731	21.6	8	
1860	33	**Abraham Lincoln**	Republican	1,865,593	39.8	180	81.2
		Stephen A. Douglas	Democratic	1,382,713	29.5	12	
		John C. Breckinridge	Democratic	848,356	18.1	72	
		John Bell	Constitutional Union	592,906	12.6	39	
1864	36	**Abraham Lincoln**	Republican	2,206,938	55.0	212	73.8
		George B. McClellan	Democratic	1,803,787	45.0	21	
1868	37	**Ulysses S. Grant**	Republican	3,013,421	52.7	214	78.1
		Horatio Seymour	Democratic	2,706,829	47.3	80	

Presidential Elections (continued)

Year	Number of States	Candidates	Parties	Popular Vote	% of Popular Vote	Elec-toral Vote	% Voter Partici-pation[a]
1872	37	**Ulysses S. Grant**	Republican	3,596,745	55.6	286	71.3
		Horace Greeley	Democratic	2,843,446	43.9	[b]	
1876	38	**Rutherford B. Hayes**	Republican	4,036,572	48.0	185	81.8
		Samuel J. Tilden	Democratic	4,284,020	51.0	184	
1880	38	**James A. Garfield**	Republican	4,453,295	48.5	214	79.4
		Winfield S. Hancock	Democratic	4,414,082	48.1	155	
		James B. Weaver	Greenback-Labor	308,578	3.4		
1884	38	**Grover Cleveland**	Democratic	4,879,507	48.5	219	77.5
		James G. Blaine	Republican	4,850,293	48.2	182	
		Benjamin F. Butler	Greenback-Labor	175,370	1.8		
		John P. St. John	Prohibition	150,369	1.5		
1888	38	**Benjamin Harrison**	Republican	5,447,129	47.9	233	79.3
		Grover Cleveland	Democratic	5,537,857	48.6	168	
		Clinton B. Fisk	Prohibition	249,506	2.2		
		Anson J. Streeter	Union Labor	146,935	1.3		
1892	44	**Grover Cleveland**	Democratic	5,555,426	46.1	277	74.7
		Benjamin Harrison	Republican	5,182,690	43.0	145	
		James B. Weaver	People's	1,029,846	8.5	22	
		John Bidwell	Prohibition	264,133	2.2		
1896	45	**William McKinley**	Republican	7,102,246	51.1	271	79.3
		William J. Bryan	Democratic	6,492,559	47.7	176	
1900	45	**William McKinley**	Republican	7,218,491	51.7	292	73.2
		William J. Bryan	Democratic; Populist	6,356,734	45.5	155	
		John C. Wooley	Prohibition	208,914	1.5		
1904	45	**Theodore Roosevelt**	Republican	7,628,461	57.4	336	65.2
		Alton B. Parker	Democratic	5,084,223	37.6	140	
		Eugene V. Debs	Socialist	402,283	3.0		
		Silas C. Swallow	Prohibition	258,536	1.9		
1908	46	**William H. Taft**	Republican	7,675,320	51.6	321	65.4
		William J. Bryan	Democratic	6,412,294	43.1	162	
		Eugene V. Debs	Socialist	420,793	2.8		
		Eugene W. Chafin	Prohibition	253,840	1.7		
1912	48	**Woodrow Wilson**	Democratic	6,296,547	41.9	435	58.8
		Theodore Roosevelt	Progressive	4,118,571	27.4	88	
		William H. Taft	Republican	3,486,720	23.2	8	
		Eugene V. Debs	Socialist	900,672	6.0		
		Eugene W. Chafin	Prohibition	206,275	1.4		
1916	48	**Woodrow Wilson**	Democratic	9,127,695	49.4	277	61.6
		Charles E. Hughes	Republican	8,533,507	46.2	254	

Presidential Elections (continued)

Year	Number of States	Candidates	Parties	Popular Vote	% of Popular Vote	Elec- toral Vote	% Voter Partici- pation[a]
		A. L. Benson	Socialist	585,113	3.2		
		J. Frank Hanly	Prohibition	220,506	1.2		
1920	48	**Warren G. Harding**	Republican	16,143,407	60.4	404	49.2
		James M. Cox	Democratic	9,130,328	34.2	127	
		Eugene V. Debs	Socialist	919,799	3.4		
		P. P. Christensen	Farmer- Labor	265,411	1.0		
1924	48	**Calvin Coolidge**	Republican	15,718,211	54.0	382	48.9
		John W. Davis	Democratic	8,385,283	28.8	136	
		Robert M. La Follette	Progressive	4,831,289	16.6	13	
1928	48	**Herbert C. Hoover**	Republican	21,391,993	58.2	444	56.9
		Alfred E. Smith	Democratic	15,016,169	40.9	87	
1932	48	**Franklin D. Roosevelt**	Democratic	22,809,638	57.4	472	56.9
		Herbert C. Hoover	Republican	15,758,901	39.7	59	
		Norman Thomas	Socialist	881,951	2.2		
1936	48	**Franklin D. Roosevelt**	Democratic	27,752,869	60.8	523	61.0
		Alfred M. Landon	Republican	16,674,665	36.5	8	
		William Lemke	Union	882,479	1.9		
1940	48	**Franklin D. Roosevelt**	Democratic	27,307,819	54.8	449	62.5
		Wendell L. Wilkie	Republican	22,321,018	44.8	82	
1944	48	**Franklin D. Roosevelt**	Democratic	25,606,585	53.5	432	55.9
		Thomas E. Dewey	Republican	22,014,745	46.0	99	
1948	48	**Harry S Truman**	Democratic	24,179,345	49.6	303	53.0
		Thomas E. Dewey	Republican	21,991,291	45.1	189	
		J. Strom Thurmond	States' Rights	1,176,125	2.4	39	
		Henry A. Wallace	Progressive	1,157,326	2.4		
1952	48	**Dwight D. Eisenhower**	Republican	33,936,234	55.1	442	63.3
		Adlai E. Stevenson	Democratic	27,314,992	44.4	89	
1956	48	**Dwight D. Eisenhower**	Republican	35,590,472	57.6	457	60.6
		Adlai E. Stevenson	Democratic	26,022,752	42.1	73	
1960	50	**John F. Kennedy**	Democratic	34,226,731	49.7	303	62.8
		Richard M. Nixon	Republican	34,108,157	49.5	219	
1964	50	**Lyndon B. Johnson**	Democratic	43,129,566	61.1	486	61.7
		Barry M. Goldwater	Republican	27,178,188	38.5	52	
1968	50	**Richard M. Nixon**	Republican	31,785,480	43.4	301	60.6
		Hubert H. Humphrey	Democratic	31,275,166	42.7	191	
		George C. Wallace	American Independent	9,906,473	13.5	46	
1972	50	**Richard M. Nixon**	Republican	47,169,911	60.7	520	55.2

Presidential Elections (continued)

Year	Number of States	Candidates	Parties	Popular Vote	% of Popular Vote	Electoral Vote	% Voter Participation[a]
		George S. McGovern	Democratic	29,170,383	37.5	17	
		John G. Schmitz	American	1,099,482	1.4		
1976	50	**James E. Carter**	Democratic	40,830,763	50.1	297	53.5
		Gerald R. Ford	Republican	39,147,793	48.0	240	
1980	50	**Ronald W. Reagan**	Republican	43,904,153	50.7	489	52.6
		James E. Carter	Democratic	35,483,883	41.0	49	
		John B. Anderson	Independent	5,720,060	6.6	0	
		Ed Clark	Libertarian	921,299	1.1	0	
1984	50	**Ronald W. Reagan**	Republican	54,455,075	58.8	525	53.3
		Walter F. Mondale	Democratic	37,577,185	40.6	13	
1988	50	**George H. W. Bush**	Republican	48,886,097	53.4	426	50.1
		Michael S. Dukakis	Democratic	41,809,074	45.6	111[c]	
1992	50	**William J. Clinton**	Democratic	44,909,326	43.0	370	55.2
		George H. W. Bush	Republican	39,103,882	37.4	168	
		H. Ross Perot	Independent	19,741,048	18.9	0	
1996	50	**William J. Clinton**	Democratic	47,402,357	49.2	379	49.1
		Robert J. Dole	Republican	39,196,755	40.7	159	
		H. Ross Perot	Reform	8,085,402	8.4	0	
		Ralph Nader	Green	684,902	0.7	0	
2000	50	**George W. Bush**	Republican	50,456,002	47.87	271	51.21
		Al Gore	Democrat	50,999,897	48.38	266	
		Ralph Nader	Green	2,882,955	2.74	0	
		Patrick J. Buchanan	Reform/ Independent	448,895	.42	0	

Candidates receiving less than 1 percent of the popular vote have been omitted. Thus the percentage of popular vote given for any election year may not total 100 percent.

Before the passage of the Twelfth Amendment in 1804, the Electoral College voted for two presidential candidates; the runner-up became vice president.

Before 1824, most presidential electors were chosen by state legislatures, not by popular vote.

[a]Percent of voting-age population casting ballots.

[b]Greeley died shortly after the election; the electors supporting him then divided their votes among minor candidates.

[c]One elector from West Virginia cast her Electoral College presidential ballot for Lloyd Bentsen, the Democratic Party's vice-presidential candidate.

Presidents and Vice Presidents

1. President	**George Washington**	1789–1797	
Vice President	John Adams	1789–1797	
2. President	**John Adams**	1797–1801	
Vice President	Thomas Jefferson	1797–1801	
3. President	**Thomas Jefferson**	1801–1809	
Vice President	Aaron Burr	1801–1805	
Vice President	George Clinton	1805–1809	
4. President	**James Madison**	1809–1817	
Vice President	George Clinton	1809–1813	
Vice President	Elbridge Gerry	1813–1817	
5. President	**James Monroe**	1817–1825	
Vice President	Daniel Tompkins	1817–1825	
6. President	**John Quincy Adams**	1825–1829	
Vice President	John C. Calhoun	1825–1829	
7. President	**Andrew Jackson**	1829–1837	
Vice President	John C. Calhoun	1829–1833	
Vice President	Martin Van Buren	1833–1837	
8. President	**Martin Van Buren**	1837–1841	
Vice President	Richard M. Johnson	1837–1841	
9. President	**William H. Harrison**	1841	
Vice President	John Tyler	1841	
10. President	**John Tyler**	1841–1845	
Vice President	None		
11. President	**James K. Polk**	1845–1849	
Vice President	George M. Dallas	1845–1849	
12. President	**Zachary Taylor**	1849–1850	
Vice President	Millard Fillmore	1849–1850	
13. President	**Millard Fillmore**	1850–1853	
Vice President	None		
14. President	**Franklin Pierce**	1853–1857	
Vice President	William R. King	1853–1857	
15. President	**James Buchanan**	1857–1861	
Vice President	John C. Breckinridge	1857–1861	
16. President	**Abraham Lincoln**	1861–1865	
Vice President	Hannibal Hamlin	1861–1865	
Vice President	Andrew Johnson	1865	
17. President	**Andrew Johnson**	1865–1869	
Vice President	None		
18. President	**Ulysses S. Grant**	1869–1877	
Vice President	Schuyler Colfax	1869–1873	
Vice President	Henry Wilson	1873–1877	
19. President	**Rutherford B. Hayes**	1877–1881	
Vice President	William A. Wheeler	1877–1881	
20. President	**James A. Garfield**	1881	
Vice President	Chester A. Arthur	1881	
21. President	**Chester A. Arthur**	1881–1885	
Vice President	None		
22. President	**Grover Cleveland**	1885–1889	
Vice President	Thomas A. Hendricks	1885–1889	
23. President	**Benjamin Harrison**	1889–1893	
Vice President	Levi P. Morton	1889–1893	
24. President	**Grover Cleveland**	1893–1897	
Vice President	Adlai E. Stevenson	1893–1897	
25. President	**William McKinley**	1897–1901	
Vice President	Garret A. Hobart	1897–1901	
Vice President	Theodore Roosevelt	1901	
26. President	**Theodore Roosevelt**	1901–1909	
Vice President	Charles Fairbanks	1905–1909	
27. President	**William H. Taft**	1909–1913	
Vice President	James S. Sherman	1909–1913	
28. President	**Woodrow Wilson**	1913–1921	
Vice President	Thomas R. Marshall	1913–1921	
29. President	**Warren G. Harding**	1921–1923	
Vice President	Calvin Coolidge	1921–1923	
30. President	**Calvin Coolidge**	1923–1929	
Vice President	Charles G. Dawes	1925–1929	
31. President	**Herbert C. Hoover**	1929–1933	
Vice President	Charles Curtis	1929–1933	
32. President	**Franklin D. Roosevelt**	1933–1945	
Vice President	John N. Garner	1933–1941	
Vice President	Henry A. Wallace	1941–1945	
Vice President	Harry S Truman	1945	
33. President	**Harry S Truman**	1945–1953	
Vice President	Alben W. Barkley	1949–1953	
34. President	**Dwight D. Eisenhower**	1953–1961	
Vice President	Richard M. Nixon	1953–1961	
35. President	**John F. Kennedy**	1961–1963	
Vice President	Lyndon B. Johnson	1961–1963	
36. President	**Lyndon B. Johnson**	1963–1969	
Vice President	Hubert H. Humphrey	1965–1969	

Presidents and Vice Presidents (continued)

37. President	**Richard M. Nixon**	1969–1974		Vice President	George H. W. Bush	1981–1989
Vice President	Spiro T. Agnew	1969–1973	41. President	**George H. W. Bush**	1989–1993
Vice President	Gerald R. Ford	1973–1974		Vice President	J. Danforth Quayle	1989–1993
38. President	**Gerald R. Ford**	1974–1977	42. President	**William J. Clinton**	1993–2001
Vice President	Nelson A. Rockefeller	1974–1977		Vice President	Albert Gore	1993–2001
39. President	**James E. Carter**	1977–1981	43. President	**George W. Bush**	2001–2005
Vice President	Walter F. Mondale	1977–1981		Vice President	Richard B. Cheney	2001–2005
40. President	**Ronald W. Reagan**	1981–1989				

For a complete list of Presidents, Vice Presidents, and Cabinet Members, go to http://college.hmco.com.

Party Strength in Congress

Period	Congress	House Majority Party		House Minority Party		House Others	Senate Majority Party		Senate Minority Party		Senate Others	Party of President	
1789–91	1st	Ad	38	Op	26		Ad	17	Op	9		F	Washington
1791–93	2nd	F	37	DR	33		F	16	DR	13		F	Washington
1793–95	3rd	DR	57	F	48		F	17	DR	13		F	Washington
1795–97	4th	F	54	DR	52		F	19	DR	13		F	Washington
1797–99	5th	F	58	DR	48		F	20	DR	12		F	J. Adams
1799–1801	6th	F	64	DR	42		F	19	DR	13		F	J. Adams
1801–03	7th	DR	69	F	36		DR	18	F	13		DR	Jefferson
1803–05	8th	DR	102	F	39		DR	25	F	9		DR	Jefferson
1805–07	9th	DR	116	F	25		DR	27	F	7		DR	Jefferson
1807–09	10th	DR	118	F	24		DR	28	F	6		DR	Jefferson
1809–11	11th	DR	94	F	48		DR	28	F	6		DR	Madison
1811–13	12th	DR	108	F	36		DR	30	F	6		DR	Madison
1813–15	13th	DR	112	F	68		DR	27	F	9		DR	Madison
1815–17	14th	DR	117	F	65		DR	25	F	11		DR	Madison
1817–19	15th	DR	141	F	42		DR	34	F	10		DR	Monroe
1819–21	16th	DR	156	F	27		DR	35	F	7		DR	Monroe
1821–23	17th	DR	158	F	25		DR	44	F	4		DR	Monroe
1823–25	18th	DR	187	F	26		DR	44	F	4		DR	Monroe
1825–27	19th	Ad	105	J	97		Ad	26	J	20		C	J. Q. Adams
1827–29	20th	J	119	Ad	94		J	28	Ad	20		C	J. Q. Adams
1829–31	21st	D	139	NR	74		D	26	NR	22		D	Jackson
1831–33	22nd	D	141	NR	58	14	D	25	NR	21	2	D	Jackson
1833–35	23rd	D	147	AM	53	60	D	20	NR	20	8	D	Jackson
1835–37	24th	D	145	W	98		D	27	W	25		D	Jackson
1837–39	25th	D	108	W	107	24	D	30	W	18	4	D	Van Buren
1839–41	26th	D	124	W	118		D	28	W	22		D	Van Buren
1841–43	27th	W	133	D	102	6	W	28	D	22	2	W	W. Harrison
												W	Tyler
1843–45	28th	D	142	W	79	1	W	28	D	25	1	W	Tyler
1845–47	29th	D	143	W	77	6	D	31	W	25		D	Polk
1847–49	30th	W	115	D	108	4	D	36	W	21	1	D	Polk
1849–51	31st	D	112	W	109	9	D	35	W	25	2	W	Taylor
												W	Fillmore
1851–53	32nd	D	140	W	88	5	D	35	W	24	3	W	Fillmore
1853–55	33rd	D	159	W	71	4	D	38	W	22	2	D	Pierce
1855–57	34th	R	108	D	83	43	D	40	R	15	5	D	Pierce
1857–59	35th	D	118	R	92	26	D	36	R	20	8	D	Buchanan
1859–61	36th	R	114	D	92	31	D	36	R	26	4	D	Buchanan
1861–63	37th	R	105	D	43	30	R	31	D	10	8	R	Lincoln
1863–65	38th	R	102	D	75	9	R	36	D	9	5	R	Lincoln
1865–67	39th	U	149	D	42		U	42	D	10		R	Lincoln
												R	A. Johnson

Party Strength in Congress (continued)

Period	Congress	House Majority Party		House Minority Party		Others	Senate Majority Party		Senate Minority Party		Others	Party of President	
1867–69	40th	R	143	D	49		R	42	D	11		R	A. Johnson
1869–71	41st	R	149	D	63		R	56	D	11		R	Grant
1871–73	42nd	R	134	D	104	5	R	52	D	17	5	R	Grant
1873–75	43rd	R	194	D	92	14	R	49	D	19	5	R	Grant
1875–77	44th	D	169	R	109	14	R	45	D	29	2	R	Grant
1877–79	45th	D	153	R	140		R	39	D	36	1	R	Hayes
1879–81	46th	D	149	R	130	14	D	42	R	33	1	R	Hayes
1881–83	47th	D	147	R	135	11	R	37	D	37	1	R	Garfield
												R	Arthur
1883–85	48th	D	197	R	118	10	R	38	D	36	2	R	Arthur
1885–87	49th	D	183	R	140	2	R	43	D	34		D	Cleveland
1887–89	50th	D	169	R	152	4	R	39	D	37		D	Cleveland
1889–91	51st	R	166	D	159		R	39	D	37		R	B. Harrison
1891–93	52nd	D	235	R	88	9	R	47	D	39	2	R	B. Harrison
1893–95	53rd	D	218	R	127	11	D	44	R	38	3	D	Cleveland
1895–97	54th	R	244	D	105	7	R	43	D	39	6	D	Cleveland
1897–99	55th	R	204	D	113	40	R	47	D	34	7	R	McKinley
1899–1901	56th	R	185	D	163	9	R	53	D	26	8	R	McKinley
1901–03	57th	R	197	D	151	9	R	55	D	31	4	R	McKinley
												R	T. Roosevelt
1903–05	58th	R	208	D	178		R	57	D	33		R	T. Roosevelt
1905–07	59th	R	250	D	136		R	57	D	33		R	T. Roosevelt
1907–09	60th	R	222	D	164		R	61	D	31		R	T. Roosevelt
1909–11	61st	R	219	D	172		R	61	D	32		R	Taft
1911–13	62nd	D	228	R	161	1	R	51	D	41		R	Taft
1913–15	63rd	D	291	R	127	17	D	51	R	44	1	D	Wilson
1915–17	64th	D	230	R	196	9	D	56	R	40		D	Wilson
1917–19	65th	D	216	R	210	6	D	53	R	42		D	Wilson
1919–21	66th	R	240	D	190	3	R	49	D	47		D	Wilson
1921–23	67th	R	301	D	131	1	R	59	D	37		R	Harding
1923–25	68th	R	225	D	205	5	R	51	D	43	2	R	Coolidge
1925–27	69th	R	247	D	183	4	R	56	D	39	1	R	Coolidge
1927–29	70th	R	237	D	195	3	R	49	D	46	1	R	Coolidge
1929–31	71st	R	267	D	167	1	R	56	D	39	1	R	Hoover
1931–33	72nd	D	220	R	214	1	R	48	D	47	1	R	Hoover
1933–35	73rd	D	310	R	117	5	D	60	R	35	1	D	F. Roosevelt
1935–37	74th	D	319	R	103	10	D	69	R	25	2	D	F. Roosevelt
1937–39	75th	D	331	R	89	13	D	76	R	16	4	D	F. Roosevelt
1939–41	76th	D	261	R	164	4	D	69	R	23	4	D	F. Roosevelt
1941–43	77th	D	268	R	162	5	D	66	R	28	2	D	F. Roosevelt
1943–45	78th	D	218	R	208	4	D	58	R	37	1	D	F. Roosevelt
1945–47	79th	D	242	R	190	2	D	56	R	38	1	D	Truman
1947–49	80th	R	245	D	188	1	R	51	D	45		D	Truman
1949–51	81st	D	263	R	171	1	D	54	R	42		D	Truman

Party Strength in Congress (continued)

Period	Congress	House Majority Party	House Minority Party	House Others	Senate Majority Party	Senate Minority Party	Senate Others	Party of President
1951–53	82nd	D 234	R 199	1	D 49	R 47		D Truman
1953–55	83rd	R 221	D 211	1	R 48	D 47	1	R Eisenhower
1955–57	84th	D 232	R 203		D 48	R 47	1	R Eisenhower
1957–59	85th	D 233	R 200		D 49	R 47		R Eisenhower
1959–61	86th	D 284	R 153		D 65	R 35		R Eisenhower
1961–63	87th	D 263	R 174		D 65	R 35		D Kennedy
1963–65	88th	D 258	R 117		D 67	R 33		D Kennedy / D L. Johnson
1965–67	89th	D 295	R 140		D 68	R 32		D L. Johnson
1967–69	90th	D 246	R 187		D 64	R 36		D L. Johnson
1969–71	91st	D 245	R 189		D 57	R 43		R Nixon
1971–73	92nd	D 254	R 180		D 54	R 44	2	R Nixon
1973–75	93rd	D 239	R 192	1	D 56	R 42	2	R Nixon
1975–77	94th	D 291	R 144		D 60	R 37	3	R Ford
1977–79	95th	D 292	R 143		D 61	R 38	1	D Carter
1979–81	96th	D 276	R 157		D 58	R 41	1	D Carter
1981–83	97th	D 243	R 192		R 53	D 46	1	R Reagan
1983–85	98th	D 269	R 166		R 54	D 46		R Reagan
1985–87	99th	D 253	R 182		R 53	D 47		R Reagan
1987–89	100th	D 258	R 177		D 55	R 45		R Reagan
1989–91	101st	D 259	R 174		D 55	R 45		R Bush
1991–93	102nd	D 267	R 167	1	D 56	R 44		R Bush
1993–95	103rd	D 258	R 176	1	D 57	R 43		D Clinton
1995–97	104th	R 230	D 204	1	R 52	D 48		D Clinton
1997–99	105th	R 227	D 207	1	R 55	D 45		D Clinton
1999–2001	106th	R 223	D 211	1	R 55	D 45		D Clinton
2001–03	107th	R 221	D 212	2	D 50*	R 49	1	R G. W. Bush
2003–05	108th	R 229	D 205	1	R 51	D 48	1	R G. W. Bush

AD = Administration; AM = Anti-Masonic; C = Coalition; D = Democratic; DR = Democratic-Republican; F = Federalist; J = Jacksonian; NR = National Republican; Op = Opposition; R = Republican; U = Unionist; W = Whig. Figures are for the beginning of the first session of each Congress, except the 93rd, which are for the beginning of the second session.

*Note: From January 3 to January 20, 2001, with the Senate divided evenly between the two parties, the Democrats held the majority due to the deciding vote of outgoing Democratic Vice President Al Gore. Senator Thomas A. Daschle served as majority leader at that time. Beginning on January 20, 2001, Republican Vice President Richard Cheney held the deciding vote, giving the majority to the Republicans. Senator Trent Lott resumed his position as majority leader on that date. On May 24, 2001, Senator James Jeffords of Vermont announced his switch from Republican to Independent status, effective June 6, 2001. Jeffords announced that he would caucus with the Democrats, giving the Democrats a one-seat advantage, changing control of the Senate from the Republicans back to the Democrats. Senator Thomas A. Daschle again became majority leader on June 6, 2001. Senator Paul D. Wellstone (D-MN) died on October 25, 2002, and Independent Dean Barkley was appointed to fill the vacancy. The November 5, 2002 election brought to office elected Senator James Talent (R-MO), replacing appointed Senator Jean Carnahan (D-MO), shifting balance once again to the Republicans—but no reorganization was completed at that time since the Senate was out of session. (Source: "Party Division in the Senate, 1789–Present" on http://www.senate.gov)

Justices of the Supreme Court

	Term of Service	Years of Service	Life Span		Term of Service	Years of Service	Life Span
John Jay	1789–1795	5	1745–1829	William B. Woods	1880–1887	7	1824–1887
John Rutledge	1789–1791	1	1739–1800	Stanley Mathews	1881–1889	7	1824–1889
William Cushing	1789–1810	20	1732–1810	Horace Gray	1882–1902	20	1828–1902
James Wilson	1789–1798	8	1742–1798	Samuel Blatchford	1882–1893	11	1820–1893
John Blair	1789–1796	6	1732–1800	Lucius Q. C. Lamar	1888–1893	5	1825–1893
Robert H. Harrison	1789–1790	–	1745–1790	Melville W. Fuller	1888–1910	21	1833–1910
James Iredell	1790–1799	9	1951–1799	David J. Brewer	1890–1910	20	1837–1910
Thomas Johnson	1791–1793	1	1732–1819	Henry B. Brown	1890–1906	16	1836–1913
William Paterson	1793–1806	13	1745–1806	George Shiras, Jr.	1892–1903	10	1832–1924
John Rutledge*	1795	–	1739–1800	Howell E. Jackson	1893–1895	2	1832–1895
Samuel Chase	1796–1811	15	1741–1811	dward D. White	1894–1910	16	1845–1921
Oliver Ellsworth	1796–1800	4	1745–1807	Rufus W. Peckham	1895–1909	14	1838–1909
Bushrod Washington	1798–1829	31	1762–1829	Joseph McKenna	1898–1925	26	1843–1926
Alfred Moore	1799–1804	4	1755–1810	Oliver W. Holmes	1902–1932	30	1841–1935
John Marshall	1801–1835	34	1755–1835	William D. Day	1903–1922	19	1849–1923
William Johnson	1804–1834	30	1771–1834	William H. Moody	1906–1910	3	1853–1917
H. Brockholst Livingston	1806–1823	16	1757–1823	Horace H. Lurton	1910–1914	4	1844–1914
Thomas Todd	1807–1826	18	1765–1826	Charles E. Hughes	1910–1916	5	1862–1948
Joseph Story	1811–1845	33	1779–1845	Willis Van Devanter	1911–1937	26	1859–1941
Gabriel Duval	1811–1835	24	1752–1844	Joseph R. Lamar	1911–1916	5	1857–1916
Smith Thompson	1823–1843	20	1768–1843	Edward D. White	1910–1921	11	1845–1921
Robert Trimble	1826–1828	2	1777–1828	Mahlon Pitney	1912–1922	10	1858–1924
John McLean	1829–1861	32	1785–1861	James C. McReynolds	1914–1941	26	1862–1946
Henry Baldwin	1830–1844	14	1780–1844	Louis D. Brandeis	1916–1939	22	1856–1941
James M. Wayne	1835–1867	32	1790–1867	John H. Clarke	1916–1922	6	1857–1945
Roger B. Taney	1836–1864	28	1777–1864	William H. Taft	1921–1930	8	1857–1930
Philip P. Barbour	1836–1841	4	1783–1841	George Sutherland	1922–1938	15	1862–1942
John Catron	1837–1865	28	1786–1865	Pierce Butler	1922–1939	16	1866–1939
John McKinley	1837–1852	15	1780–1852	Edward T. Sanford	1923–1930	7	1865–1930
Peter V. Daniel	1841–1860	19	1784–1860	Harlan F. Stone	1925–1941	16	1872–1946
Samuel Nelson	1845–1872	27	1792–1873	Charles E. Hughes	1930–1941	11	1862–1948
Levi Woodbury	1845–1851	5	1789–1851	Owen J. Roberts	1930–1945	15	1875–1955
Robert C. Grier	1846–1870	23	1794–1870	Benjamin N. Cardozo	1932–1938	6	1870–1938
Benjamin R. Curtis	1851–1857	6	1809–1874	Hugo L. Black	1937–1971	34	1886–1971
John A. Campbell	1853–1861	8	1811–1889	Stanley F. Reed	1938–1957	19	1884–1980
Nathan Clifford	1858–1881	23	1803–1881	Felix Frankfurter	1939–1962	23	1882–1965
Noah H. Swayne	1862–1881	18	1804–1884	William O. Douglas	1939–1975	36	1898–1980
Samuel F. Miller	1862–1890	28	1816–1890	Frank Murphy	1940–1949	9	1890–1949
David Davis	1862–1877	14	1815–1886	Harlan F. Stone	1941–1946	5	1872–1946
Stephen J. Field	1863–1897	34	1816–1899	James F. Byrnes	1941–1942	1	1879–1972
Salmon P. Chase	1864–1873	8	1808–1873	Robert H. Jackson	1941–1954	13	1892–1954
William Strong	1870–1880	10	1808–1895	Wiley B. Rutledge	1943–1949	6	1894–1949
Joseph P. Bradley	1870–1892	22	1813–1892	Harold H. Burton	1945–1958	13	1888–1964
Ward Hunt	1873–1882	9	1810–1886	Fred M. Vinson	1946–1953	7	1890–1953
Morrison R. Waite	1874–1888	14	1816–1888	Tom C. Clark	1949–1967	18	1899–1977
John M. Harlan	1877–1911	34	1833–1911	Sherman Minton	1949–1956	7	1890–1965

Justices of the Supreme Court (continued)

	Term of Service	Years of Service	Life Span		Term of Service	Years of Service	Life Span
Earl Warren	1953–1969	16	1891–1974	Lewis F. Powell, Jr.	1972–1987	15	1907–1998
John Marshall Harlan	1955–1971	16	1899–1971	*William H. Rehnquist*	1972–	—	1924–
William J. Brennan, Jr.	1956–1990	34	1906–1977	John P. Stevens III	1975–	—	1920–
Charles E. Whittaker	1957–1962	5	1901–1973	Sandra Day O'Connor	1981–	—	1930–
Potter Stewart	1958–1981	23	1915–1985	Antonin Scalia	1986–	—	1936–
Byron R. White	1962–1993	31	1917–	Anthony M. Kennedy	1988–	—	1936–
Arthur J. Goldberg	1962–1965	3	1908–1990	David H. Souter	1990–	—	1939–
Abe Fortas	1965–1969	4	1910–1982	Clarence Thomas	1991–	—	1948–
Thurgood Marshall	1967–1991	24	1908–1993	Ruth Bader Ginsburg	1993–	—	1933–
Warren C. Burger	1969–1986	17	1907–1995	Stephen Breyer	1994–	—	1938–
Harry A. Blackmun	1970–1994	24	1908–1998				

Note: Chief justices are in italics.

*Appointed and served one term, but not confirmed by the Senate.

INDEX

Abd al-Rahman (slave), 91
Abenaki Indians, 28, 70, 83
Abolition and abolitionism, 277–281,
    395; northern emancipation and,
    172; in Old Northwest, 180; Quak-
    ers and, 196; women and, 278(illus.),
    280–281, 339; international antislav-
    ery movement and, 279; factions in,
    280; 1844 election and, 294; failures
    of, 322; southern slavery and, 330;
    non-slaveholding westerners on, 349;
    Slave Power and, 359; violence and,
    363; Kansas-Nebraska Act and, 367;
    John Brown and, 370, 374; *Dred
    Scott* decision and, 371–372, 373
Abolition of Negro Slavery (Dew), 330
Abortion and abortion rights, 314
Absalom, Absalom! (Faulkner), 337
Academies: women's education in, 170
Acadia, *see* Nova Scotia (Acadia)
Acadians: as Louisiana Cajuns, 121
Accommodation: by Indians, 264
Acoma pueblo, 35, 35(illus.)
Activism: Townshend Act protests and,
    133; African American, 321
Act of Religious Toleration (Maryland,
    1649), 46
Act of Union (1800, Britain), 297
Adams, Abigail, 159, 170–171, 206
Adams, Charles Francis, 411
Adams, John, 116, 131, 205(illus.);
    Boston Massacre and, 134; on
    Boston Tea Party, 137; at First Conti-
    nental Congress, 143; Continental
    Army and, 152; Declaration of Inde-
    pendence and, 153–154; Treaty of
    Paris and, 162; as vice president,
    196; 1796 election and, 205; political
    dissent and, 206–208, 213; Jefferson
    and, 217; 1800 election and,
    224(map)
Adams, John Quincy, 241, 242(illus.);
    War of 1812 and, 235; Monroe Doc-
    trine and, 243; on gag rule, 280;
    1824 election and, 282–283,
    282(map); U.S. boundaries under,
    293; on Mexican War, 358; on Cuba,
    366
Adams, Samuel, 134–135, 170; Tea Act
    and, 136; at First Continental Con-
    gress, 143; as Antifederalist, 188

Adams-Onís (Transcontinental) Treaty,
    243
Adja kings: slave trade and, 76
Administration: colonial, 81–82, 84,
    108
Adolescence, *see* Youth culture
Advertising: of consumption rituals,
    104(illus.)
Affluence, *see* Prosperity; Wealth and
    wealthy
Africa: human origins in, 5; in 1400,
    11(map); agriculture in, 12; Por-
    tuguese in, 17–18; navigation
    around, 18, 21(illus.); slave origins
    in, 89, 90(map); black emigration to,
    322; cultural influences of, 342. *See
    also* African Americans; Slaves and
    slavery; West Africa
African Americans, 72, 85; task system
    and, 79–80; in North, 81; families of,
    106, 344–345; resistance by, 107; as
    Baptists, 112; in Revolution, 148,
    157, 158(illus.); Sierra Leone and,
    149; redcoats joined by, 160; voting
    by, 171, 321; by end of 18th century,
    208, 211–212, 211(map); at Battle of
    New Orleans, 234(illus.); after War
    of 1812, 236; unions and, 261;
    movement of free people, 263; Semi-
    noles and, 268; at revivals, 273; as
    abolitionists, 279; in California
    gold rush, 304; stereotypes of, 307,
    308(illus.); free, 319–322; popula-
    tion of, 319–322; in middle class,
    321; newspapers of, 321; culture
    of, 321–322; U.S.-born population
    of, 342; citizenship of, 354; *Dred
    Scott* decision and, 371–372, 373;
    in Civil War, 382, 395, 399, 400,
    402–403, 402(illus.); emancipation
    of slaves and, 397; draft riots and,
    408, 408(illus.); Decoration Day
    and, 420; leaders after Civil War,
    425; Fifteenth Amendment and,
    436; southern Republican Party
    and, 436–438; officeholding by,
    437, 439; "Negro Rule" myth and,
    439; Klan and, 440–441; 1876
    election and, 446–447. *See also*
    Abolition and abolitionism; Free
    blacks; Freedpeople (Civil War);

Indentured servants; People of
    color; Race and racism; Slaves and
    slavery
African Methodist Episcopal (AME)
    Church, 173, 320, 320(illus.), 425;
    free blacks in, 335
Africans: in Spanish America, 24; en-
    slavement of, 35, 71–73, 78–80
Agrarianism, 253; Jefferson and, 204,
    217, 327; in North and South, 327
Agriculture: in early Americas, 5; in
    Africa, 12; in Europe, 13; in Canada,
    36; in Chesapeake colonies, 46; in
    New England, 52, 54; bondspeople
    in, 81; manufacturing and, 199–200;
    whiskey tax and, 200–201; Creeks
    and, 210; commercial, 252–254;
    mechanization of, 253, 393; in Cali-
    fornia, 304; in South, 427. *See also*
    Crops; Farms and farming; Planters
    and plantations
Aix-la-Chapelle, Treaty of, 97
Akan States, 12, 76
Alabama: statehood for, 244, 261;
    Creek Indians in, 266; planters in,
    335
Alabama (warship), 411, 445
Alamance, battle at, 110
Alamo, battle at, 291
Alaska, 444–445
Albany: as Fort Orange, 38
Albany Congress (1754), 118
Albany Regency, 288
Alcohol and alcoholism: Indians and,
    104, 225; reduction in, 276. *See also*
    Temperance; Whiskey
Alcott, Louisa May, 314
Alexander VI (Pope), 20
Algiers, 216
Algonquian Indians, 45(illus.); culture
    of, 7; female rulers of, 9; Jamestown
    and, 44; in New England, 53, 54;
    Pequots and, 57; as slaves, 59–60;
    family structure in, 105; Iroquois
    and, 118
Algonquian speakers, 7
Alien Act (1798), 207, 218
Allen, Augustus and Joe Kirby, 316
Allen, Richard, 277–278
Alliance(s): between France and Iro-
    quois, 68; Indian, 123; Franco-